CONFUCIAN PERSONALITIES

STANFORD STUDIES IN THE CIVILIZATIONS
OF EASTERN ASIA

Editors

ARTHUR F. WRIGHT   GEORGE SANSOM   JOHN D. GOHEEN
THOMAS C. SMITH   ROBERT H. BROWER   MARY CLABAUGH WRIGHT

*Earlier volumes published under the auspices
of the Committee on Chinese Thought of
the Association for Asian Studies*

ARTHUR F. WRIGHT, *Editor*
Studies in Chinese Thought
Chicago, 1953

JOHN K. FAIRBANK, *Editor*
Chinese Thought and Institutions
Chicago, 1957

DAVID S. NIVISON AND ARTHUR F. WRIGHT, *Editors*
Confucianism in Action
Stanford, 1959

ARTHUR F. WRIGHT, *Editor*
The Confucian Persuasion
Stanford, 1960

CONFUCIAN PERSONALITIES

Edited by

ARTHUR F. WRIGHT *and* DENIS TWITCHETT

With Contributions by

ALBERT E. DIEN   IGOR DE RACHEWILTZ

HERBERT FRANKE   CONRAD M. SCHIROKAUER

HANS H. FRANKEL   DENIS TWITCHETT

RICHARD C. HOWARD   WANG GUNG-WU

JOSEPH R. LEVENSON   HELLMUT WILHELM

FREDERICK W. MOTE   NELSON I. WU

STANFORD UNIVERSITY PRESS · STANFORD, CALIFORNIA · 1962

Stanford University Press
Stanford, California

© 1962 by the Board of Trustees of the
Leland Stanford Junior University
All rights reserved

Library of Congress Catalog Card Number: 62-16950
Printed in the United States of America

Published with the assistance of the Ford Foundation

Preface

The Committee on Chinese Thought of the Association for Asian Studies presents here its fifth and final symposium volume. This completes a decade of intensive scholarly exploration of Chinese ideas in action. The last five years have been devoted to studies of Confucianism and its role in the development of Chinese civilization. The first of three symposia on this subject was *Confucianism in Action* (1959), which was concerned with Confucianism in its relation to selected institutions and to the political process. The second volume, *The Confucian Persuasion* (1960), dealt with manifestations of Confucianism in diverse facets of Chinese culture, while the present symposium examines the effects of Confucian ideas and prescriptions in the lives of twelve noted Confucians between the sixth and the twentieth centuries.

In the course of the last ten years, the Committee has organized five research conferences, and from each of these a volume has been developed. We have been singularly fortunate in enlisting the cooperation of able and vigorous scholars both in this country and abroad. We have sought, at each step, to foster existing research interests relevant to our inquiries, and the Committee has at no time "commissioned" articles or asked its contributors to write to specifications. The result has been a happy diversity of approach and treatment and, at times, a fruitful clash of interpretive opinion. We believe that this more than compensates for the asymmetry which is as characteristic of this volume as of its predecessors. As we conclude our work, we are acutely conscious of the vast field which we have been able to explore only partially and superficially. It is our hope that others may find in our volumes hypotheses and suggestions that will inspire further and more intensive studies, not only of Confucianism but of the other seminal traditions of Chinese thought. And if, here and there, we have been able to show the relevance of our findings to the study of civilization generally and to comparative studies, we shall feel doubly rewarded.

From its beginnings in 1951 the Committee has been singularly fortunate in its friends and sponsors. The late Robert Redfield gave the Committee wise and generous support in its early years. He and his colleague Professor Milton Singer provided funds from their Program of

Comparative Studies of Cultures and Civilizations to help the Committee through its first two conferences and symposia. Since 1957 the Committee's activities have been generously supported by the Rockefeller Foundation. During those years the Committee has been sponsored and encouraged by the officers and directors of the Association for Asian Studies Incorporated, and Mrs. Victoria Harper, Business Manager of the Association, has handled our business affairs with notable efficiency. First Stanford, then Yale University contributed to the support of the chairman's office. The Stanford University Press, which has published the three volumes on Confucianism, has given expert and sympathetic attention to our problems.

The Committee would also like to thank those who have helped in the preparation of the present volume. Professors Harold D. Lasswell and Mary C. Wright of Yale offered helpful suggestions on methodological and substantive problems. Mr. Jonathan Spence of Cambridge and Yale Universities served as rapporteur of the 1960 conference, out of which this volume developed. Mrs. Alice Durfee has been the Committee's conscientious and able secretary, while Miss Adrienne Suddard has served with skill and devotion as editorial assistant. Mr. Chou Ju-hsi has prepared the Index.

A. F. W.

April 1962

Contents

Contributors

ALBERT E. DIEN received his training in Oriental languages at the University of Chicago and the University of California, Berkeley; he is writing his doctoral thesis on Yen Chih-t'ui. He is now Assistant Professor of Chinese at the University of Hawaii. His research interests are the intellectual and institutional history of medieval China and Central Asian history.

HERBERT FRANKE was a student of law, history, philosophy, and Sinology at the universities of Cologne, Bonn, and Berlin. He received his LL.D. in 1937 and his Ph.D. in 1947 from the University of Cologne and taught there from 1948 to 1951. He was appointed Professor of Far Eastern Studies at the University of Munich in 1952. His chief interest is Chinese political and cultural history. His publications include *Geld und Wirtschaft in China unter der Mongolenherrschaft* (1949) and *Sinologie* (1953).

HANS H. FRANKEL was educated at the Gymnasium of Göttingen, Stanford University, and the University of California, Berkeley, where he received his Ph.D. in 1942. For several years he edited the Chinese Dynastic Histories Translations series at the University of California. He is now Associate Professor of Chinese Literature at Yale, having previously taught at the University of California, National Peking University, and Stanford. His field of interest is Chinese literature, particularly from the second century B.C. to the thirteenth century A.D.

RICHARD C. HOWARD received his B.A. and M.A. from Columbia University in 1948 and 1950. He spent two years in Taiwan and Hong Kong studying Chinese history and language. Since 1959 he has been research associate at the Project on Men and Politics in Modern China, Columbia University. He is engaged on a large-scale study of K'ang Yu-wei.

JOSEPH R. LEVENSON received his B.A. (1941) and Ph.D. degrees from Harvard, where he was a member of the Society of Fellows. He is now Professor of History at the University of California, Berkeley, where he has taught since 1951. He is the author of *Liang Ch'i-ch'ao and the Mind of Modern China* and *Confucian China and Its Modern Fate*.

FREDERICK W. MOTE took his B.A. in Chinese history at the University of Nanking in 1948 and received his Ph.D. from the University of Washington in 1954. He taught Chinese at Leiden on a Fulbright exchange lectureship in 1955–56. He is now Associate Professor of Oriental Studies at Princeton University. His research interests are in late Yüan and early Ming history, and a book on the intellectual history of the fourteenth century is being published by the Princeton University Press.

IGOR DE RACHEWILTZ studied at Rome and Naples, and did postgraduate research at the Australian National University in Canberra, where he received his Ph.D. and is now teaching Far Eastern History. His major interests are the development of Buddhist and Taoist thought and Sino-Mongol culture contacts. He has recently completed a study of Yeh-lü Ch'u-ts'ai, and is at present investigating certain aspects of the Mongol conquest of China.

CONRAD M. SCHIROKAUER received his doctorate from Stanford University in 1960 with a dissertation on the political thought and behavior of Chu Hsi. He is now Assistant Professor of History at the City College of New York. In 1957–58 he studied in Paris under a Fulbright grant, and in 1960–62 he taught at Swarthmore College. His research interests are in the intellectual and political history of the Sung.

DENIS TWITCHETT studied at London and Cambridge Universities and received his doctorate from Cambridge with a thesis on the T'ang financial system. After further study in Tokyo, he became Lecturer in Far Eastern History at London University, and later University Lecturer in Classical Chinese at Cambridge. He is now Professor of Chinese at the University of London. His primary interest is in the economic and institutional history of medieval China. He is the author of a forthcoming book on financial administration under the T'ang dynasty.

WANG GUNG-WU received most of his education in Malaya and also studied at the Central University, Nanking. He obtained his doctorate from London in 1957 and is now Senior Lecturer in history at the University of Malaya in Kuala Lumpur. He has published *The Nanhai Trade, a Study of Early Chinese Trade in the South China Sea*, and *The Structure of Power in North China during the Five Dynasties*.

HELLMUT WILHELM received his Ph.D. in Chinese Studies from the University of Berlin in 1932. He served as Lecturer and Professor at Peking National University and is now Professor of Chinese Studies at the University of Washington, Seattle. His publications include numerous books and articles concerning the intellectual and literary history of China; he is currently at work on a study of intellectual trends in nineteenth-century China.

ARTHUR F. WRIGHT was trained at Stanford, Oxford, and Harvard Universities and studied in Japan and China 1940–47 and 1953–54. He was Chairman of The Committee on Chinese Thought from 1951 to 1962 and contributed, as author and editor, to the Committee's five symposium volumes. His publications include *Buddhism in Chinese History* (1959) and articles on Chinese Buddhism and intellectual history, especially of the period 200–750 A.D. He is now Charles Seymour Professor of History at Yale University.

NELSON IKON WU (WU NO-SUN), Assistant Professor of the History of Art at Yale University, took his B.A. in Language and Literature at the National Southwest Associated University in Kunming in 1942 and his Ph.D. in the History of Art at Yale University in 1954. His doctoral thesis was on Tung Ch'i-ch'ang. His book on Chinese and Indian architecture will be published in 1962.

CONFUCIAN PERSONALITIES

———

INTRODUCTORY ESSAYS

Arthur F. Wright

VALUES, ROLES, AND PERSONALITIES

For more than two millennia the Confucian tradition was an ever-present and pervasive influence. It molded the lives and the thought of the men who created and perpetuated the civilization of China—a civilization that represents one of mankind's great efforts to build, rationalize, and adorn the good society. Approaches to the study of Confucianism are many: the study of the canonical texts which form the corpus of wisdom and prescription; the study of the systems of thought that organized and structured the diverse ideas found in the canon; the study of contemporary communities where one may assess the meaning and force of the Confucian tradition in social life; the study of historic institutions and historic movements where one can see men whose characters had been deeply influenced by the Confucian tradition using and developing its ideas as they grappled with the problems of their time.

The last approach has been attempted in two previous symposia, *Confucianism in Action*, edited by David S. Nivison and Arthur F. Wright, and *The Confucian Persuasion*, edited by Arthur F. Wright. In those volumes were nineteen studies devoted to the examination of Confucian ideas as they operated in Chinese political, social, and cultural life at widely separated points in time; two studies dealt with the transformation and uses of Confucian ideas in modern Japan. Out of these twenty-one studies the editors and contributors attempted to distill certain characterizations of Confucianism as a tradition and to formulate hypotheses that might guide further research. At our 1958 conference it was decided to complete this series of symposia with a collection of biographical studies.

Such a choice commended itself on several grounds. First of all, the close study of individual lives seemed to offer an economical and effective way of testing some of the hypotheses growing out of the earlier studies. Second, what one says in abstractions about "a tradition" finds its ultimate proof or disproof in the lives of men; the study of men's lives guards against the idolization of abstractions and at the same time calls attention to the rich texture of a life in time, the multiple forces that bear in upon it, and the vagaries of chance and choice that give it its final pattern.

We saw other substantial advantages in the biographical approach. In the present rather primitive state of our knowledge of Chinese history, a single biographical study may bring into focus the critical problems and the atmosphere of an age, and thus help to bridge a wide gap in our understanding of the history of Chinese civilization. Further, biography in the sense of a rounded portrait of a personality in the context of his time and milieu is foreign to the Chinese literary tradition, and recent studies have demonstrated that biographies in the modern Western sense may add new dimensions of understanding. They help us to estimate the influence of family and education on the formation of character; they deal explicitly with motivation and growth; they shed light on the network of personal attachments and obligations that stretch between a man and his contemporaries; they can, in some cases, bring into full relief a man's standards of value and his world-view.

The use of traditional sources for the writing of modern biographies is beset by serious problems: the critical evaluation of sources, the relative credibility of one type of evidence in relation to another, the proper weighting of clichés and stereotypes, and many others. Most of these problems have wide implications for the use of Chinese sources in other varieties of historical study. For these reasons, Mr. Twitchett devotes a separate essay (pp. 24–39) to a discussion of historiographical problems in the writing of biography.

Before turning to Confucian creeds and their influence on the lives of our subjects, it may be well to suggest some of the limitations of this symposium. First of all, the years spanned by these biographies are the millennium and a half from the sixth to the twentieth century; thus Chou China, "the classical age," and Han China, the first great age of Empire, are unrepresented. So too are the peasant masses, who appear only as statistical anonymities in our sources, and the merchants, whose lives traditional historians generally disdained to notice. Further, our subjects are not a preselected sample with a rationalized distribution according to periods, roles, and personality types; rather, they are subjects that our contributing scholars had chosen to study, and study in their own various ways. And for each subject the sources have their particular limitations; even if we had wished—contrary to the spirit which has prevailed in the Committee on Chinese Thought—to ask that some common set of subject headings be followed, variations in the available evidence would have made this impossible.

Some further limitations are imposed, not only by the meagerness of our sample but by the predominantly humanistic and historical interests of our contributors. This means that we look for common patterns and recurrent themes in the lives of our subjects, but we do not attempt a profile of "The Confucian Personality" or "The Chinese Elite Personality." We shall attempt, in the following pages, to make general statements about the effects of Confucian creeds in the lives of our subjects, but we shall of necessity stop far short of full systematic formulations. Our search for the individual personality behind the formalism and stereotypes of the traditional sources would have a sad and ironic outcome if we fastened upon these men stereotypes of our own contriving.

It seems unnecessary here to review the various characterizations of Confucianism as an operating creed which have been stated in our earlier volumes. Nor need we recapitulate those mutations and transformations that gave to the Confucian tradition its inner variety and its pattern of growth. But it will facilitate our discussion of the biographies presented in this volume if we note briefly some of the radical continuities in the Confucian tradition, those beliefs and ideals that shaped the creeds and the behavior of the Chinese elite for two millennia. The following summary owes much to earlier studies by my colleagues in the Committee on Chinese Thought.

SOME PERSISTING IDEALS AND VALUES

Confucians of all ages viewed the natural and human worlds as an organism made up of multitudinous interconnected parts. When any one of the parts fell from its place or was disrupted in its functioning, the harmony of the whole was impaired. Heaven, which was neither deity nor blind fate, presided over this organic whole and was a force for harmony and balance. But man was the principal agent which, through ignorance, perversity, or misconduct, could cause serious disruptions and, by the application of knowledge, wisdom, and discipline, could restore harmony. Either man in the mass or an irresponsible elite might disrupt the balance of harmony, but only the learned and the wise could restore it. The wise and the learned were to be found among the Confucian elite, and the wisdom—the keys to harmony—they commanded was found in the Classics and, secondarily, in traditional mores and in the corpus of historical and other writings that contained the past experience of the Chinese.

Learning alone, it was early recognized, did not make a sage—one whose wisdom and power over the minds of men could restore and maintain the desired harmony. A man became a sage only through long study and self-discipline which developed humaneness or love (*jen*) and gave him an almost mystical empathy for his fellow men and an acute sensitivity to all the delicately balanced forces at work in the universe. Such a man, or one approaching him in attainments, might then "govern the state and pacify the world." Indeed, the exercise of power was the goal toward which all his self-cultivation was directed and which represented the final stage of self-fulfillment.

There devolved upon the sage, and, when a sage did not appear, upon men of lesser wisdom, the awesome duty of assuring harmony to the world. Such men had to persuade and coerce their fellow men into behavior conducive to harmony; they had to devise institutions and instrumentalities that would promote such harmony. And they were obliged to do so in the face of appalling obstacles: rulers who governed more often than not by whim and caprice; individuals and groups who persisted in heterodox ways and divisive activities; the disruptions of alien invasions and foreign ideas; the incubus of past events that made their own times unpropitious for the restoration of a harmonious order. What values did the Confucian sage or worthy assert and what institutions did he favor as he persisted, generation after generation, in his Sisyphean labors?

Harmony, universal and unalloyed, was perhaps the highest good, but in a less abstract sense harmony meant the good society. And the good society was seen as a past utopia, the ideally frictionless holistic order that had existed in remote antiquity. That order was a hierarchy —a system in which state and society were fused into a seamless whole and every man knew his place and was content. A hierarchy of roles was thought to be essential to the ideal order, but Confucians insisted that the vital roles of functionary and perpetuator of the cultural heritage should be open to those of moral worth. The monarch who presided over the whole hierarchy had, in the utopia of remote antiquity, been chosen for his merit, but in imperial times Confucians had to resign themselves to the hereditary principle—a source of endless tension and discord. But despite their difficulties Confucians never challenged the idea of a monarch at the summit of the sociopolitical pyramid.

If an ordered and frictionless hierarchy dominated by a benovolent ruler and a wise and worthy elite was an ideal, what means to that end did Confucians advocate? The range is enormous, but we may mention a few of the most fundamental and most persistent. One was the well-ordered family wherein the adults learned how to manage community affairs and direct others for the common good while the young gradually learned to obey and to play their proper roles in the kinship hierarchy. The family was thus seen as a microcosm of the sociopolitical order; the wise father was a model for the wise ruler or minister and dutiful children were the models for properly submissive subjects who knew their place, their role, and their obligations to others.

Transcending the family but including many familistic imperatives were the *li,* the norms of proper social behavior. The ancient sage-kings, it was believed, had prescribed observances, taboos, and rituals that ensured the well-being and happiness of their subjects. Later men had codified these prescriptions, creating a body of norms that provided for all social contingencies. It was the duty of the father to teach the *li* in the household. It was the duty of monarch and officials to make them known to the populace so that one and all might live according to the same time-tested norms.

The *li,* spread by fathers, village elders, and government officials, and supplemented by the discipline of ordered family life, would in turn foster social virtues: filial submission, brotherliness, righteousness, good faith, and loyalty. Further means were advocated and used to spur the development of these cardinal virtues. Public recognition—feasts, monuments, rewards, and many other devices—singled out exemplars of these virtues. Exhortations to virtue were read in the villages, the *Classic of Filial Piety* was drummed into the young, stories of noted exemplars were read by the literate and purveyed to the masses by storytellers and dramatic troupes. The power of example, of models of conduct, had been extolled by Confucius and was a basic principle of child-rearing and education in imperial China.

⌈The prime living exemplars for any age, as the Confucians saw it, were the best of the scholar-officials. Steeped in the Classics and in history, shaped by stern family discipline, tempered by introspection, and sobered by their vast responsibilities, these men were thought to have the power to transform their environment, to turn ordinary folk into the path of virtue. When opportunity offered, they were expected to nurture the same virtues in their official colleagues and in their lord and monarch. They had the obligation to admonish their monarch when in deed or policy he did violence to the *li* and the cardinal virtues. While working this moral transformation, they were to serve as interpreters and transmitters of the heritage and as artists and thinkers who would adorn and enrich it.⌋ If such men prevailed, they would preside over a balanced and homogeneous order; frictions and power struggles could not occur, violence and subversion would wither in the sunshine of the people's content; and a benign nature would smile upon a world where nothing could disturb the delicate balance of all the functioning parts.

Such beliefs and ideals, reiterated in each generation, constituted a set of ultimate values which the subjects of these biographies absorbed as they studied the Classics, the histories, and the literary heritage of the past. Ultimate values imply a set of operating principles and a set of desirable behavior patterns which, if followed, will serve the ideal order and give the individual a sure sense of contributing to its realization. In other words—for the purposes of education and socialization—a society's ideals are translated into a set of approved attitudes and behavior patterns. These in turn affect the choices an individual makes, the roles he assumes or rejects, and the ultimate configurations of his career and his personality. Confucianism's operating principles might be distilled from the whole corpus of the Classics or from didactic writings meant for day-to-day guidance in the conduct of life. I have chosen to look for them in the *Analects* of Confucius, which is both the basic text of the tradition and the cornerstone of Confucian education. This is not to deny that later thinkers elaborated these principles with varying emphases and placed them in diverse philosophic and discursive contexts. But for all the generations covered by our biographies, the authority of the *Analects* was unchallenged and its lessons were sharply etched on the minds of the young. From it, therefore, I have extracted the following list:[1]

Approved Attitudes and Behavior Patterns

(1) Submissiveness to authority—parents, elders, and superiors
(2) Submissiveness to the mores and the norms (*li*)
(3) Reverence for the past and respect for history
(4) Love of traditional learning
(5) Esteem for the force of example
(6) Primacy of broad moral cultivation over specialized competence
(7) Preference for nonviolent moral reform in state and society
(8) Prudence, caution, preference for a middle course
(9) Noncompetitiveness
(10) Courage and sense of responsibility for a great tradition
(11) Self-respect (with some permissible self-pity) in adversity
(12) Exclusiveness and fastidiousness on moral and cultural grounds
(13) Punctiliousness in treatment of others

Some of these attitudes and behavior patterns occur again and again in our biographies. A few of them—reinforced by social conventions and institutions—appear decisive in shaping the lives and characters of many of our subjects. They are so pervasive as to constitute themes or patterns in the lives presented here and to have, perhaps, a wider relevance for understanding the force of Confucian tradition in the lives of the Chinese elite.

THE AUTHORITY OF EXAMPLES AND EXEMPLARS

The Confucian curriculum, designed to instill ultimate ideals and operating principles in the minds of the young, gave relatively little weight to ethical theory, to abstract logically related statements about "the good." Instead it tended to teach by parable and example and, in this process, to make intensive use of minatory and exemplary figures of the past. These figures were not treated simply as bundles of desirable or undesirable character traits. They tended to be viewed in relation to their situations; their dilemmas, their choices, and the circumstances surrounding them were usually known. In this way the youth gradually came to know a variety of character traits operating in concrete situations and labeled with one of the great or notorious names of the Chinese past. The Classical curriculum was supplemented by historical and literary accounts and by popular didactic stories. Thus we find that the young Yüeh Fei, born in a time of crisis, chose the military hero Kuan Yü as his model and, when he himself commanded troops, ordered that stories of the heroic warriors of the past be recounted in his camp to spur his men to emulate them. The youthful Chu Hsi was drawn to the example of Mencius—a sage who, like himself, lived in a time of disorder. More will be said of this in our discussion of roles and role playing.

Living exemplars had an equally important part in the formation of character. Submissiveness of the young to the old, of the unlearned to the learned (1), reinforced the imperative to pattern oneself after an approved exemplar. This might be a father or an uncle, but it was more often a teacher. For example, the artist Tung Ch'i-ch'ang at an early stage of his career took as one of his models the connoisseur Lu Shu-sheng, and three centuries later the young K'ang Yu-wei found his ideal mentor in Chu Tzu-ch'i.

This latter relationship illustrates a further dimension of the authority of exemplars. For, as Mr. Howard shows us, K'ang Yu-wei's teacher, serving as a living model to the young man, persuasively commended to him certain ultimate exemplars—the sages of antiquity. K'ang himself speaks of the deep impression his teacher made upon him and at one point recalls, "I held myself to be above and beyond the rank and file, and took as my companions the sages and heroes of old."

At each stage of his education the youth encountered the minatory figures of the past: the greedy, the self-indulgent, the disloyal, and the rebellious. Such models were meant to be abjured, but as a young man learned more about the Chinese past, the blacks and the whites of his initial impressions became somewhat blurred. He learned, for example, that the third-century military figure Ts'ao Ts'ao was judged to be "a vile bandit in time of peace, a hero in times of disorder." Circumstances, it appeared, were at least as important as moral standards in determining the judgment that history would make of a man. And the reading of history or historical fiction made it plain to the young that the circumstances into which a man might be born were of great variety: times of disunion and strife, times of peace and prosperity, ages of rise or of decline. As a young man became aware of the world about him, as he appraised the circumstances into which he had been born, certain kinds of exemplars seemed more attractive than others—better suited to his own times.

In general, periods of crisis widened the range of models; we see this with particular clarity in Mr. Mote's paper, where the young poet Kao Ch'i and his friends, living in the last days of Mongol rule, had a choice among several models—all formed and validated in earlier periods of disorder. There was the military activist, the loyal-to-the-bitter-end official, the stern moralistic recluse, and, just beyond the confines of Confucianism but still within the culture, another range: the recluse nature-poet, the poetical *bon vivant*, and others.

The molding power of example, held as an article of Confucian faith, favored the establishment of certain fixed roles in life, which the young were exhorted and trained to play. Reinforcing this general tendency were two other attitudes we have noted—submissiveness to authority and to the prevailing norms (1, 2) and reverence for the past and for history (3)—as well as certain constant factors in Chinese social history. The nature and importance of this tendency may best be understood as we see its effects in the lives of our subjects.

ROLE SELECTION AND ROLE PLAYING

Many factors enter into the choice of role that each of our subjects makes: predisposition, training, and family pressures; the range of viable options in his time; the kinds of satisfactions he seeks—power, wealth, affection, moral eminence, high competence in a defined sphere of action, sensuous pleasure, or a detached understanding of the human condition. As we study our subjects' choices, we notice that, even when we discount hagiographical accretions and self-dramatization, the moments of choice are solemn and portentous. We find the reasons for this in certain constant features of the Chinese social order. The men discussed in this volume belonged to a very small elite dispersed over a vast land but bound together by common interests, kinship ties, and political connections. Though scattered in small groups, mainly in county towns and cities, they maintained a sense of elite community by a variety of devices: letter writing, the exchange of poetry and essays, publication and reading of each other's books, visits made for pleasure or as stopovers on the way to a new official post. Surrounding them where they lived and as they traveled were the peasant masses, inarticulate, powerless people whose fate was palpably in the hands of the literate elite. These social facts, with all their psychological overtones, made possible among the elite a large view of the differences one man and one man's choice might make in life and history. Reinforcing such a view was the striking contrast between the boring humdrum life of the peasants, bound by their toilsome work and their legal disabilities, and the islands of affluence and power where an educated man could seek fame and fortune. It is no wonder that the sixth-century moralist Yen Chih-t'ui, discussed here by Mr. Dien, solemnly admonished his young kinsmen to study, work, and serve lest the family suffer the ultimate catastrophe and fall into the faceless, nameless peasant mass.

In such an atmosphere the pressures were great for an early choice of role. Dating back as far as the sixth century was the custom of having a child choose from an assortment of objects, each symbolic of a career, placed in front of him on his first birthday; parents and other relatives noted his choice carefully, regarding the object chosen as a sign of his innate bent and as an augury of his future career.[2] Once his elders, by this and other devices, had appraised the child's talent and proclivities (*ts'ai*), suitable exemplars were brought to his attention, and formal schooling and stern discipline began to shape the child to the desired model. It is not surprising to find in our biographies repeated references to youthful precocity in reading and writing, for the greatest pressure from family and environment was to develop those skills—the skills that brought the greatest rewards in prestige, wealth, and immunities.

As the youth approached puberty and his own aspirations and his own estimate of his talents began to develop, he took the first steps toward choosing his own role in life on the basis of his feelings, what he had learned from others, and what he had observed in the world around him. In Jung's metaphor, this is the process of choosing the persona—the actor's mask that may fit the self well or ill but that signals the adoption of a social role; thereafter society expects of the actor the behavior, attitudes, and gestures associated with that role.

Here we should note two characteristics of the roles a Chinese youth might choose. One was their relative stability as contrasted with those in other mature societies; virtually the same range of roles—each with its variations defined in the careers of historic figures—continued to be *the* options until the collapse of the imperial order. The second was the fullness of their delineation in classical injunctions, in history, and in literature. As one man after another down the centuries played out a role, it accumulated more and more nuances of gesture and attitude. To take the role of poet-recluse, as Kao Ch'i did in the fourteenth century, was to evoke in the minds of one's contemporaries images and recollections of all those who had created and developed that role from Ch'ü Yüan in the fourth century B.C., down through T'ao Ch'ien, Li Po, and many others. Those who live in more fluid societies, where certain roles are created and discarded in a generation, must make a special effort to envision both the historic consistency and the fullness of Chinese social roles.

Yüeh Fei (1103–41), perhaps China's greatest military hero, is said to have begun as a child to play martial games and to have chosen as his model the exemplary warrior of nine centuries earlier, Kuan Yü. Then, as he came of age under a dynasty hard pressed by foreign enemies, he adopted in the public sphere the values, the attitudes, the manners of a warrior. He went on, as Mr. Wilhelm shows, to play out in momentous events the role he had chosen. After his death he was given his place in the official pantheon as the peer of Kuan Yü, his model. Chu Hsi—the great renovator of Confucianism—was, by contrast, a quiet and precocious child absorbed in his books. He tells us that at the age of nine he decided to emulate Mencius and become a sage. His public life, as Mr. Schirokauer describes it, was lived in remarkable accord with the chosen model: there was the same disapproving aloofness from the politics of a decadent age, the same defense—in scholarship and moral argument—of a cherished tradition against the cynical and the corrupt, the same posture of moral superiority, the same resentment at the contumely of the great and the indifference of his peers. As he played out his role, one of the most bitter accusations made by his enemies was that he put on sagely airs. In our checklist of persisting Confucian attitudes and behavior patterns, those manifested in Chu Hsi's career and those in Mencius' are remarkably similar.

Tung Ch'i-ch'ang (1555–1636), the noted artist, critic, and connoisseur discussed in these pages by Mr. Wu, was of humble origin, and there was paternal pressure on the young man to prepare for an official career. He had little taste for his studies but soon developed an interest in calligraphy and gradually became acquainted with painters and connoisseurs. Finally he determined to become a great calligrapher and a gentleman painter. Such a primary role, it should be noted, was of relatively recent origin—a product of the somewhat more fluid society that had been developing from the tenth century onward. Tung was quick to observe that commoners, however great their talent, were under too many social and legal disabilities to become aesthetic eminences. He therefore forced himself through the examination machinery and emerged as an official—for him a secondary role but one instrumental in the fulfillment of the first. Tung rose to be the president of a board, and he seems to have been a reasonably conscientious servant of the decaying Ming house. But his official status was a means to an end—artistic excellence. His villas were stocked with great painting and calligraphy, noted painters and collectors came and went, and his best hours were spent in connoisseurship and painting, in the subtle business of becoming *the* arbiter of taste and style for his time. In his long pursuit of artistic pre-eminence, Tung had always before him the luminous image of Chao Meng-fu (1254–1322), the great master of his own time and model for his successors. In his later years Tung Ch'i-ch'ang came to be acknowledged as the greatest painter and critic of the age. As if this were not enough, the dynasty conferred upon him the same posthumous title that had long before been given to Chao Meng-fu. Tung is one of the few among our subjects who chose his own primary role, worked untiringly to fulfill it, and died in the knowledge that he had.

Lu Chih (754–805), the subject of Mr. Twitchett's study, seems from the surviving record to have chosen his role early and to have followed a set course from youthful precocity to brilliant success in the state examinations to early recognition by his ruler. But at this point, as Mr. Twitchett shows us, circumstances, the personality of his imperial master, and Lu Chih's own temperament brought about an early decline of his fortunes. Having been successful as personal adviser to his prince in perilous times, Lu Chih failed in the political give-and-take of the court. He was outspoken and courageous in trying to check the emperor's follies ((10) in our set of approved Confucian attitudes). Yet the satisfaction he seems to have sought in his career was neither moral eminence nor profound understanding of the human condition. It was rather the satisfaction that comes from high competence in a defined sphere, in this case high state policy especially in the sphere of taxation and fiscal problems. Yet his policies—sound, practical, brilliantly argued though they were—could not win support without political finesse, and this Lu Chih neither had nor cared to cultivate. His active career therefore ended early, and on his second role as recluse and medical antiquarian in an obscure village we have no details.

Feng Tao (882–954), discussed in Mr. Wang's paper, has been roundly condemned by later moralists for his many shifts of loyalty. Yet in Feng Tao's own reflections, written toward the end of his life, he views himself as having played consistently and honorably the role of Confucian minister. The quick opportunistic shifts that time and again saved his life and fortune in a period of political chaos are forgotten in this self-analysis: "I have received the great teachings and opened them to others. I have observed filial piety in the home and shown loyalty to the state. . . . All that I have wished is that I should not deceive earth that is below, man that is with us, and heaven that is above, and I have regarded these 'three no-deceptions' as a rule of be-havior. I have been thus when I was lowly, when I was in high office, when I grew to manhood, and when I was old." When we consider the values invoked by Feng Tao in his self-appraisal, we find there, either stated or implied, literally all the approved Confucian attitudes and behavior patterns listed earlier in this introduction. The serenity of his reflections in old age convinces us that he believed in his own estimate of his life's role and its triumphant fulfillment.

By no means do all our biographies show such decisive choice of role or such consistency in living to a chosen pattern. Chia Ssu-tao, the much maligned minister of the end of the Sung, seems, in Mr. Franke's study, to have been less single-minded, less purposeful than other polit-ical figures; he was not subjected to the examination curriculum, and Confucian ideas and values seem not to have touched him very deeply. We see him as a wily pragmatist, learning the rules as he goes, clawing his way to high office, finding satisfaction there not in moral eminence but in administrative success and in the sensuous and artistic pleasures that came with his growing wealth.

From the various examples we have mentioned, it is clear that the most esteemed of all roles is that of the scholar-statesman—a role that combines literary abilities with integrity of character and a capacity for applying the moral principles of the Classics to affairs of state. As we see in Mr. Frankel's study of one hundred and one T'ang literati, the role of literary man as such is far less honored. It is a secondary role men must fall back to when they lack the capacities for the great role of scholar-statesman. Official biographers make much of the youthful pre-cocity of the literary men, of their prodigious memories and their vir-tuosity with the writing brush. But, as in the secular societies of the modern West, "mere" literary ability tends to be associated with such traits as self-indulgence, egotism, and instability. P'ei Hsing-chien, quoted by Mr. Frankel, sums the matter up: "Whether a gentleman goes far depends primarily on his ability and knowledge, and only secondarily on his literary skill. Although these men possess literary talent, they are unsteady and shallow. Surely they are not made of the stuff required for achieving high rank. . . . " We cannot attribute such discounting of literary talent and the literary role solely to official biographers and their biases, for a high proportion of the poetry and prose of the literary men of all periods is devoted to laments about their failure to succeed in the great role of scholar-statesman.

ROLE SHIFTS

Role shifts in the lives of men everywhere may be brought about by a number of causes. A universal cause is aging, and in Chinese society the transition from an active role to the passive role of "old man" was highly stylized. Other role shifts are brought about by a sharp change in circumstances. In Chinese history the erstwhile bandit who suddenly becomes Son of Heaven is the most dramatic case, dramatic because it was never a simple shift of role, but had the quality of peripeteia, the reversal of roles. Less dramatic but far more common in Chinese history are enforced shifts from active to relatively passive roles. Chinese culture, as it developed, provided a variety of alternatives to those who were driven from the arena of power. One such alternative was the role of "retired scholar," honorable because it combined love of traditional learning (4), self-respect (11), and moral fastidiousness (12). Another was the role of poet-recluse, a role developed down the centuries by men of sensibility who withdrew from the sordid world of politics to sing of their friendships, their moods and feelings, their communion with nature. There are subtle shadings to this role, but it generally meant the renunciation of public life and its rewards, the adoption of a simple mode of life—huts in remote places, coarse clothing, simple food, and only a poor *vin du pays*. In the present collection it is Kao Ch'i, the fourteenth-century poet, who suddenly adopts this role at a moment when all the forces around him make a life of action seem unrewarding and dangerous. This is the time when the young and ambitious Kao Ch'i becomes "The Man of the Green Hill" reveling in his poetry, his freedom, and the natural beauty of his surroundings. Mr. Mote has written in *The Confucian Persuasion* of the varieties of the eremitic role that were open to Confucians in adversity, and he has carefully noted the distinction between these and the roles with a predominantly Taoist character. Kao Ch'i's poet-recluse role, like that of many earlier poets, may have its Confucian overtones but it is strongly

Taoist in its values, conventions, and gestures. It belongs to that sub-ideology which Max Weber so shrewdly termed the "magic garden"—the perennial place of retreat from the ordered hierarchy of the Confucian world.

Kao Ch'i, in his brief life, illustrates yet another role, also characteristic of times of crisis. After his period as a poet-recluse, Kao Ch'i returned to the city to become the leader of a closely knit group of ambitious young men—"the ten friends of the north wall." They were bound together by common tastes in literature and their hopes for a life of heroic action. Aware that their situation was perilous, they studied military strategy, perfected themselves in martial arts, analyzed the heroic models in history, plotted and conspired together, all the while spurring each other on with heroic verse. They were spirited and hopeful, given to large plans and large gestures. The cruel march of events quenched their hopes, aborted all their plans, and scattered them across the land, but not before Kao Ch'i and his fellows had played out their roles as the brave and gifted young men of their generation.

SELF-PROTECTIVENESS

Among the persisting attitudes and behavior patterns of the Confucian tradition we have noted prudence, caution, preference for a middle course (8), and, following it, noncompetitiveness (9). The two are obviously interrelated and we have encountered both in the events and characters of our previous volumes. In *The Confucian Persuasion* I noted a classic characterization of Confucians from the third century B.C.: that their usefulness was not in vigorous action, the seizure of power, but in preserving and consolidating what had been won. Even Kao Ch'i and his young companions, with their high hopes and great plans for a better world, did not attempt a *coup de main*, but waited, as Mr. Mote tells us, for the brave leader, the good prince whom they could serve.

The sixth-century moralist Yen Chih-t'ui, as we see him in Mr. Dien's study, was desperately concerned with the survival of his family and his culture in a period of alien rule. He tries to show his kinsmen how to preserve themselves and maintain their self-respect in a time of adversity (11). The sense of responsibility for a great tradition (10) was heavy upon him, and every page of his volume of injunctions is colored by his reverence for the past, his respect for history, and his love of traditional learning (3, 4). Yet he counsels his family against acts that would dramatize their commitments or involve them in political movements. He enjoins them rather to perpetuate their family traditions of morality and learning, cling to their status as literati, take office but avoid the dangers of political eminence or leadership. He argues that men in exalted positions must have the courage to offer disinterested counsel, and that office of middle rank, with fifty men above and fifty men below, is safer, "adequate to avoid any feeling of shame or disgrace yet not run the risk of getting into dangerous situations." Yen's prudential counsels were quoted again and again in the centuries that followed, and, as Mrs. Hui-chen Wang Liu has shown in *Confucianism in Action,* they became a standard ingredient of the codified clan rules of later times.

Feng Tao, living some two and a half centuries later, showed an astonishing power of survival in a tumultuous age. As Mr. Wang's study shows, Feng ingratiated himself with one ruler after another by the universal expedient of telling the power holders what they wanted to hear; only once, in the last year of his life, did he protest a proposed course of action; his advice was unheeded and the action successful. Feng Tao, unlike Yen Chih-t'ui, was a mediocre scholar. His Confucian utterances are cliché-ridden and thoroughly conventional, yet he stood in his time for the standard Confucian values, prudence and noncompetitiveness perhaps being the dominant ones among those he lived by.

The self-protective strain is strong in the life of Chu Hsi as he successfully played out the role of latter-day sage. Mr. Schirokauer tells us of his repeated refusals of office, his timely illnesses, real, imagined, or psychosomatic, which kept him out of the vortex of power struggles that took their toll of his contemporaries. But there is a further overtone in Chu Hsi's manifestations of this complex of Confucian attitudes and behavior patterns. The sages of antiquity—particularly Confucius and Mencius—who were ever before him as models, coupled moral eminence with political failure. They had taken the moral, and moralizing, posture that unpropitious times and evil princes made it impossible for good men to serve. Chu Hsi, if he had chosen to serve in high office, not only would have been subject to the usual jeopardies but, more importantly, would have sacrificed the moral eminence combined with political noninvolvement that linked him to the prime exemplars of his role. To state the matter differently, and to risk overstatement, political failure was a necessity for Chu Hsi in his role as latter-day sage. In Chu Hsi's case, as in many others we might consider, self-protectiveness is associated with the attitude we shall consider next.

PREFERENCE FOR NONVIOLENT MORAL REFORM IN STATE AND SOCIETY

With few exceptions all our subjects display this attitude, and for many it is asserted as an article of faith. Chu Hsi's memorials, like those of innumerable officials before and after him, often deal with practical policies but always insist that the reform of society begin with the moral reformation of ruler and court, that it will then spread to official-dom, then out to communities and individuals who will be moved to rectitude by the combined forces of example and persuasion.

The young K'ang Yu-wei, living seven hundred years later in the twi-light of the old order, reaffirmed the supremacy of moral power as exercised by the Son of Heaven. His reaffirmation, cast as an idealized retrospect of Chinese history, was particularly fervent because he was aware of the forces that were pressing in upon China from the West. Here, in Mr. Howard's translation, the self-elected sage and savior of his age speaks of the Son of Heaven and of the moral power that is his heritage:

His every frown or smile is as the illumination of the sun or moon; his every expression of joy or anger is as the trembling of thunder. In his folding and unfolding palm, on his opening and closing thighs, the empire is soothed and comforted . . . Living in the present day, he can do so only under conditions such as exist in China alone among all the countries of the globe. This is not because of the vastness of its territory, nor the multitude of its people, nor the abundance of its products; it is because of the reverence for the authority of its sovereign alone. Furthermore, this reverence for his authority is neither extorted by threat of force nor induced by thought of gain: it has been accumulated gradually through the humaneness [jen] of the Two Emperors and the Three Kings, through the public morality [i] of the Han, T'ang, Sung, and Ming dynasties, through the searching efforts, the lofty exhorta-tions, the incitations and encouragements of the former sages, of all the worthies and of hundreds and thousands of people over hundreds and thou-sands of years.

Though none of our Confucian subjects would have denied the prin-ciple that moral force in the sovereign could effect the moral reforma-tion of society, the character of a particular sovereign, the circumstances of a given period influenced the way each man related the principle to his task, while variations in temperament and outlook affected the lines of action each man followed. Idealists like Chu Hsi preached moral reform to rulers who gave few signs of being capable of it. A more realistic statesman like Lu Chih, the T'ang fiscal specialist, lectured his emperor on the necessity for moral reform but concentrated his energies and abilities on practical measures designed to deal with the pressing problems of his time. It is worth noting that Lu Chih's exhortations to moral reform are confined to a period of grave crisis; when the crisis passed, he pressed plans and strategies with few references to moral reformation. Chia Ssu-tao, the late-Sung prime minister, no doubt paid lip service to the principle. But in his frontal attack on the inequitable land system of his time he used all the political pressures and stratagems he could summon. He knew the cupidity of his opponents and the fickleness of his ruler too well to have believed that moral suasion and example could move them or that there could be a sudden conversion to virtue in high places followed by sweeping social reforms.

In times of cataclysm, when the institutions of the state and society were utterly disrupted, a usual attitude was to cling to the primacy of moral reform as a principle but to lie low, stay clear of militant movements, and wait for the day when a ruler appeared who would be amenable to moral pressure. It was natural for Chinese advisers of alien rulers to exhort their princes to virtue. This was, in Confucian thinking, prerequisite to any sound measures of reform; at the same time such exhortations did not bring down upon the minister the wrath of outraged interest groups. Yen Chih-t'ui, living in chaotic times, states this view with particular clarity, and it is echoed by many others who lived in periods of great disorder. This view links the self-protective strain discussed above with the preference for moral reform.

The case of Yeh-lü Ch'u-ts'ai (1189–1243) represents a further variation of this attitude. Prince Igor de Rachewiltz, in his study of Yeh-lü, gives us a vivid picture of North China in the first half of the thirteenth century: the alien Jurchen gradually crushed by the invading Mongols; Chinese institutions in ruins after a century of war and foreign domination; the Chinese, elite and masses alike, at the mercy of Genghis and his ferocious kinsmen, servitors, and successors. Yeh-lü was a Khitan, but he had come up through the Chinese-type examination system established by the Jurchen and was thoroughly Sinicized. Genghis Khan, the dread world conqueror, must have evoked in many Confucians the attitude noted above: lie low and wait for a more malleable object of moral suasion. But Yeh-lü Ch'u-ts'ai combined compassion for the oppressed peoples of North China with extraordinary courage. In 1216 he stated his ambition in this impersonal but pointed way: "The superior man's aim is, 'My prince should be a prince like the sage emperors Yao and Shun, my people should be like the people of Yao and Shun.' . . . Therefore is it not a delight for him to be in power and have sufficient standing to practice the Way of the Sages, and sufficient means to confer extensive benefits upon the people?" Yeh-lü did not transform Genghis and his successor Ögödei into Chinese sage-emperors, nor persuade them to use moral example instead of force. Rather he drew on the traditional Chinese arsenal of political stratagems, administrative measures, institutional devices. Combining these with a subtle understanding of Mongol character, he gained considerable power and went on to use that power with great astuteness to soften and sometimes to abort the barbarous policies the Mongols were disposed to adopt toward the conquered population of North China. Yeh-lü tells us that he was sustained in this difficult and hazardous effort not only by the ideals of Confucianism but also by the ideas and the vision of Buddhism. This brings us to our next theme.

TOLERANCE AND SYNCRETIC TENDENCIES

Neither tolerance nor syncretism is explicitly enjoined in our list of Confucian attitudes gleaned from the *Analects*. But preference for a middle course (8) and noncompetitiveness (9) implied tolerance for other views and adaptation, not holy war, as a reaction to competing systems of ideas. Historically Confucians again and again found their way to new moral-philosophical positions explicable only by reference to ideas and challenges from outside their own tradition. And with the possible exception of the period from about A.D. 1000 to 1300, leading Confucians were often inclined to concede by word and act that their system of ideas was neither self-sufficient nor all-embracing. Taoism and Buddhism were often regarded as complementary traditions to be drawn on for inspiration, for philosophic depth, and occasionally for alternative ways of life. Almost all the subjects of our biographies were in some way involved with one of the rival systems.

Feng Tao played out the role of Confucian worthy in an age when men of passion and purpose were often deeply committed to Buddhism and Taoism. When invited by one of his royal masters to attend lectures on the *Tao-te ching*, Feng responded with a bland statement to the effect that neither the Taoist lecturing on Lao Tzu nor the Buddhist receiving his vows should be taken lightly. And, in instructions regarding his funeral, he made some typically Confucian requests but also enjoined his heirs to omit animal sacrifices in accordance with the Buddhist rule against taking life. Feng Tao's attitude toward other traditions was equivocal, and so was that of innumerable "ordinary" Confucians of all ages.

On a far more intellectual plane the sixth-century moralist Yen Chih-t'ui took a position which is echoed and re-echoed down the centuries. Yen insisted that the authority of Confucianism was supreme in matters concerning the family, the state, and society. At the same time he commended Buddhism to his family for its deeper view of causation-in-time and for its exalted vision of the millennium.

Six hundred years later Yeh-lü Ch'u-ts'ai took a similar position. As de Rachewiltz shows us, he lived in an age of diverse syncretic movements, and even pursued his Confucian studies under a Buddhist monk. We have noted Yeh-lü's courageous efforts to use Confucian statecraft

and concepts of moral reform for the amelioration of intolerable conditions. But he himself believed that this effort could lead to little more
than the restoration of relative peace and order (*hsiao-k'ang*). He drew
Confucian criticism by maintaining that this was all that Confucian
measures could ever attain. When it came to the ultimate utopia which
Yeh-lü, like all Chinese utopian thinkers, called the *ta-t'ung*, that was
to be a world regenerated by the superior ethic of Buddhism. And, if he
agreed with the Confucians that the cultivation of the mind was basic
to the building of a better world, he insisted that Buddhism was far
superior to Confucianism in the depth and subtlety of its prescriptions
for inner cultivation.

The examples we have noted of Confucian tolerance and eclecticism
have all been from the long centuries when the value of Confucian prescriptions for the good society was never seriously challenged and
when a society built to those prescriptions was regarded as the norm to
which China would always return. When, in the nineteenth century,
this certitude was destroyed, eclecticism, tolerance, and the other values
and attitudes we have discussed were deeply changed until, at last, they
became anachronisms in an age of violent and sweeping change.

THE LAST DEFENDERS

Early in this introduction we noted certain stable and persisting
features of Chinese society that survived in the midst of change. We
argued that such things as the monarchical order and the two-class
society dominated by a Confucian elite accounted for the relative stability in the range and character of social roles and in the attitudes and
behavior patterns of the elite. Thus it was possible, across the fifteen
centuries represented by our subjects, for a man to choose a role, to be
identified by his fellows as playing such a role, and to anticipate one of
the several outcomes traditionally connected with the role.

The late nineteenth and early twentieth centuries saw the slow
destruction of the old society. As one after another accepted feature of
the social landscape disappeared, the older roles were gradually emptied
of point and meaning. Long-accepted Confucian attitudes and behavior
patterns came to seem anachronistic and absurd as China strove to
build a new society on the ruins of the old, as new men—professional
soldiers, entrepreneurs, republican politicians, Communist organizers—
created new roles for a new social order in the making.

The lifetimes of K'ang Yu-wei and Liao P'ing span the period that
saw the death throes of the old order and the many-sided struggle for
a new Chinese civilization. Both chose in their youth the long-traveled

road that led from Classical studies through the examination system to positions of power and honor. Liao won the coveted *chin-shih* degree and served in minor official posts in the last days of the empire. K'ang, on the other hand, revolted against the old curriculum and began to see himself in a more exalted role, as savior of his country and his civilization. Both men knew the world where the long-gowned scholar was supreme and lived into a world dominated by Sun Yat-sen in his Japanese-cut Western suits and the war lords in their Western uniforms. Each in his own way became an apologist of the dying Confucianism, while each ransacked it for a message that might inspire and shape a new Chinese order.

K'ang, whatever his unacknowledged debt to Liao's ideas, is the more interesting and influential figure. His early visions, as Mr. Howard shows us, drew heavily upon the Buddhist tradition. K'ang saw himself not only as a Confucian sage who would "pacify the world," but also as a Bodhisattva who would work for the salvation of all living beings. But his early readings in Western books had suggested that even a combination of what was best from Confucianism and Buddhism might prove inadequate for China's survival in the predatory modern world. K'ang then began to work into his eclectic ideology a host of elements from diverse Western traditions: ideas of the equality of the sexes, of a constitutional monarchy, of an eventual union of states and a parliament of man.

In such a mixture, elements of Confucianism tended to be distorted beyond recognition; its integrity as a system with universal application was destroyed. In his later years, K'ang urged that Confucianism be made a state religion, with no more authority than the state churches of Western constitutional monarchies. For all his fatal eclecticism that diluted and then destroyed one Confucian value after another, K'ang did not renounce them all. He clung to the monarchical concept to the last possible moment, sensing through the haze of his ill-digested ideas that monarchy was essential to any Confucian order, however diluted or modernized. Again, he played out his life in the arena of action and persuasion. His bid for great political power in 1898 failed, but he persevered in the role of moralist, critic, preacher. Arguing no longer in audience halls or state offices, but in railway carriages, public auditoriums, and newspapers, he sought to persuade his countrymen to return to the right course.

Liao P'ing, on the other hand, shunned the arena of controversy. As Mr. Levenson presents him, Liao lacked the courage of K'ang Yu-wei and was content to take refuge in the old role of "retired scholar" in the provinces. There he taught a diminishing group of young men who soon moved on to the centers of radical thought. Mr. Levenson draws a sharp contrast between the Confucianism of Hsüeh Fu-ch'eng (1838–94)—an embattled official in a time of great crisis—and the Confucianism of Liao P'ing the retired scholar. For the former the lessons of the Classics and the histories were still relevant, there to be used in the heat of bitter struggles. For Liao the Classics provided esoteric truths, mysterious hints and prefigurings of a never-never world of the future. In Mr. Levenson's words, Liao P'ing "exemplified what he defined, a Confucianism expelled from the world of doers."

After the generation of K'ang and Liao, the Confucian scholar-statesman and scholar-teacher disappear from history. Their roles are now enacted only in the theater, not in life. The traits of character and the patterns of behavior that had evoked respect for two millennia now became the object of savage and satirical attacks from modernizers of all stamps. The lives they led, the values they lived by were denounced as age-old brakes on China's social progress, as perennial barriers to scientific and technological advance. Their legacy was condemned as a collection of habits and attitudes that must be rooted out if a new China was to be built on the rubble of the old.

Yet, if we take a more detached view of the lives unfolded in this volume, we cannot fail to be impressed with the supple strength of the Confucian tradition, its ability to perpetuate its core values and its adaptability to ever-changing circumstances. If it broke some men and condemned others to frustrating lives, it also provided the normative ideas that brought the Chinese order back, again and again, to long periods of stability and creative achievement. For the men represented in the biographies that follow, Confucianism was an ever-present body of wisdom and prescription. It penetrated their thought, shaped their behavior, defined their goals, and deeply affected the choices they made. In these lives we can come to an understanding of how this happened and thus to an appreciation of the force of the Confucian tradition in the development of a distinctive Chinese civilization.

Denis Twitchett

PROBLEMS OF CHINESE BIOGRAPHY

The biographical approach to the study of Chinese history, as Mr. Wright has shown in the foregoing essay, is a particularly rewarding and attractive one. Biographies are an economical means of exploring periods which at our stage of writing Chinese history remain little more than a chronological skeleton. They provide a focus of interest around which the historian writing in the Western biographical tradition is forced to attempt to build up a meaningfully integrated picture of the subject's times. They provide "case histories" of the application of that Confucian ideology with which this series of volumes has been concerned. And last, they help to populate with real personalities the highly impersonal record of the Chinese official historians, and to illustrate for us something of the quality of life in traditional China under the old system of institutions.

In making such studies, the modern Western scholar is almost inevitably driven to the use of biographical writings from traditional Chinese historiography. Official biographies, which constitute one of the irreducible elements of the standard dynastic histories and which in many cases occupy more than half of their chapters, represent only part of the untold wealth of biographical materials in Chinese historical literature. Innumerable additional biographies are contained in the thousands of local histories, privately compiled historical works, special biographical compendia, and works of Buddhist hagiography. Family genealogies and collections of epigraphical materials offer a sometimes dismaying profusion of biographical writings assembled for ancestral cult and commemorative use. These diverse biographical sources, in spite of their having been written for a variety of purposes, share many formal characteristics and form a single tradition. This does not, of course, eliminate the necessity for circumspection. The historian using these materials must understand the tradition as the sum of its parts and be able to judge the relative merits of his sources.

In the following pages I lay special stress upon the problems of interpretation that surround the biographical sections, the *lieh-chuan*, of the dynastic histories, although the *lieh-chuan* in fact constitute a mere fraction of the total corpus of extant biographical writings, and although the papers included in this volume draw upon a far wider and more varied range of source material. There are good reasons for this emphasis. First, the authoritative nature of the dynastic histories makes them the source to which the modern scholar is still likely to turn in the first instance, while—again thanks to official status—the *lieh-chuan* style itself became a literary norm. Second, the form and content of the official biographies are intimately connected with those of the largest group of primary biographical materials, the various categories of commemorative writings—tomb inscriptions, epitaphs, and the formal "accounts of conduct"—and the interpretative problems raised thus have wide relevance. Third, for the modern historian the *lieh-chuan* are doubly attractive in that each biography, in addition to providing a self-contained record of an individual life, forms an integral part of the history as a whole, thereby placing the subject in a broad historical setting and a wide framework of textual reference.

The beginnings of biography in China are obscure. In the first great historical masterpiece, Ssu-ma Ch'ien's *Shih-chi*, completed *circa* 90 B.C., *lieh-chuan*, or "connected traditions," form a large section of their own.[1] We do not know the exact derivation of his biographical form or of the name *chuan*, "tradition"—whether Ssu-ma Ch'ien invented them for himself or whether, as seems more likely, he took them over from some existing form of writing used in ancestral cult worship. The form of the earliest authentic memorial inscriptions (which date from the first century A.D.) is virtually identical, and Mr. Piet van der Loon has adduced what seem irrefutable arguments against their having been influenced by the model of the *Shih-chi*.[2] In view of the dependence of later historians upon just such private memorial inscriptions as source materials for their biographies it seems most likely that Ssu-ma Ch'ien inherited his biographical form from the same source.

Needless to say, the *Shih-chi* biographies themselves do not for the most part derive from actual memorial inscriptions. The *Shih-chi* is in this respect very much a case apart, for it dealt with a very extended period and its source material—in the biographies especially—was notoriously heterogeneous, including much historical romance and tradition whose authenticity was, to say the least, questionable. Such material was in later times channeled into historical fiction or into the semifictional "unofficial histories" which proliferated on the borders between history and fiction.[3]

From the *Shih-chi* onward, the basic, irreducible framework of a dynastic history consisted of the chronological outline of the "annals" together with the illustrative "biographies." By the time that Liu Chih-chi wrote the first systematic critique of historiography early in the eighth century A.D., the two alternative forms in which it was considered that a major history might be cast were the simple "annalistic history" (*pien-nien*) and the "annal-biography" (*chi-chuan*).

The annals and biographies were regarded as standing in a very intimate relationship. This Liu Chih-chi defined by drawing an analogy with the Spring and Autumn Annals (*Ch'un-ch'iu*), the dry court chronicle of the state of Lu traditionally believed to be the work of Confucius, and the "traditions" (*chuan*) which supplemented it, in particular the "Tso tradition" (*Tso-chuan*), a racy narrative history which has been artificially dismembered and appended piecemeal to the dated entries of the Annals. In the later histories the "annals," like the Spring and Autumn Annals, were meant to provide an exactly dated chronological outline of the public acts of the ruler and of events at court. The biographies, like the "Tso tradition," were to supplement and explain the account in the annals and were therefore less concerned with exact chronology, concentrating instead on the acts of ministers and subjects and the events taking place outside the court. The biographies were expected to present an articulated narrative of connected events, a point upon which Liu Chih-chi laid great stress, even coining a special term for this type of record, *pien-shih*, "connected events," as opposed to that commonly used for the purely chronological style, *pien-nien*, literally "connected years."[4]

Now this analogy implied that the biographies were in a sense less authoritative than the annals which provided the public record for each reign, in spite of the fact that the two were designed as a whole and were meant to be read together. It is at least possible that Ssu-ma Ch'ien had already implied this in his choice of the term *chuan*, the same word used for the supplementary "traditions" attached to the Spring and Autumn Annals, as well as for exegetical commentaries to canonical texts.

Liu Chih-chi's advice, referred to above, was directed in the main to individual historians such as Ssu-ma Ch'ien and his immediate successors. But even by Liu's own day the writing of official history had passed from the individual historian to official committees—a development Liu bemoans at some length. Under the T'ang, the compilation of official history, both of past dynasties and of the dynasty in power, had become highly formalized, the bureaucratic function of a special government office, the College of Historians (*shih kuan*), staffed by civil servants and presided over by a high-ranking minister of the government. Established to collect and compile material for the history of their times, this bureaucratic machine was also responsible for the collection and preparation of biographies for the record and for eventual inclusion in the dynastic histories. The *lieh-chuan* designed as drafts for inclusion in some future dynastic history were still being compiled by the republican historiographical office as recently as 1948. In many periods preliminary collections of draft biographies were compiled and even published before the dynastic record itself was completed.

But although the assembling of biographical material was an important aspect of the historiographers' task, a marked difference in method of compilation gave rise to the critical theory that the biographies were less authoritative than the annalistic record. Whereas the basic annals (*pen-chi*) of a history were compiled, after a lengthy process of revision and editing, from day-to-day court records kept for this specific purpose by specially appointed court officers,[5] the biographies were based almost exclusively upon records compiled by private individuals. The most important of these records were the "accounts of conduct" (*hsing-chuang*) submitted to the authorities as drafts for an eventual biography, or as justification for the granting of posthumous titles, or for the erection of memorial *stelae* and the commemorative writings composed for the use of the ancestral cult—in particular, the tomb inscriptions (*mu-chih*) which were buried with the coffin, the epitaphs (*mu-piao* or *shen-tao pei*) which were engraved on stone tablets erected in front of the grave, and the sacrificial speeches (*chi-wen*) addressed to the deceased as part of the funeral ceremonies.[6]

In theory, of course, the official historians could have compiled their biographies from the extensive dossiers on their subjects kept in the Board of Civil Office and in the state archives. But in practice, as I have shown elsewhere, there were considerable difficulties involved, not the least the interdepartmental obstructionism that is always inseparable from bureaucracy. And in any case the contents of the commemorative writings and the "accounts of conduct" were subject to official verification by a department of the Board of Civil Office, and this presumably put a strict check upon any outrageously false statements. Nevertheless, in dealing with the biographies from official histories it is most important to bear in mind that most of them were originally written as private records of the life of their subject by persons intimately connected with him and his family, and also that they were inserted more or less ready-made at a very late stage in the history's compilation, and thus underwent far less thorough editing than did the annals.[7] This raises some important critical problems.

The first is obvious. Where both an official biography and a tomb inscription or other private biography of the same person survive, the private biography is likely to be the fuller and the more reliable. Surprisingly, even in the case of the details of a man's official career, where the official historians could easily have added material available in their files, the private biographies are usually the more informative. In form, the official biography and the first biographical section of the tomb inscription are identical. The beginning gives the man's full names and styles, his place of origin so as to identify his particular family, and some details of his immediate ancestors where these had been in any way notable. Occasionally, where his father had died young and his mother had played an unusually large role in his upbringing, some details are given about her, but normally—as would be expected in a document designed for the clan cult—details are given only of the paternal ancestors.

These particulars are often followed by some formulaic incident or incidents—not necessarily historical—designed to demonstrate how the subject's character had clearly manifested itself even in his childhood. These formulas, which I discuss later, are indications of the character-type to which the historian assigned his subject, and symbolize the life-long consistency of character and conduct which the historian sought to establish.

Next follows the account of the subject's career, from his examination successes, through his *curriculum vitae* as he ascends in the official hierarchy, to his retirement or death and the bestowal of posthumous honors. This account is usually more detailed and more adequately dated in the tomb inscription than in the official biography. It is often followed, in the official history alone, by brief notes upon the subject's sons, if they were themselves noteworthy, and by the historian's summing up and comment, which is clearly marked off from the biography itself, and thus provides no critical problems for the modern reader. Likewise in the tomb inscription or epitaph, the biographical section is followed by a quite separate eulogy (*ming*), which is written in highly formal verse cast in an archaic form.

The framework of the biography is filled out by descriptions of incidents in which the subject figured, by his more notable writings, and by anecdotes about him. It is of course largely upon this matter that the effect of the biography depends, and its quality varies widely. It is perhaps here that the results of private compilation are most apparent. A close relative or friend of the deceased was not, like the official historian, severely restricted as to the length of his biography. It is the extreme concision of the majority of *lieh-chuan* that makes them appear far less lifelike than many of the longer private accounts. In addition, the private writer, composing his biography at the request of the deceased's family and having his literary remains at his disposal, was able to write a vivid narrative with an immediacy and grasp of the subject's individuality such as could never have been achieved by the official historian. It is often claimed, for example, that the conversations included in the biographies of the histories are simply the products of the historians' imaginations. The fact that the original writer of the tomb inscription from which the *lieh-chuan* derived may well have been intimately involved in the same incident throws a new light on such apparently suspect material.[8]

The private biographer wrote from essentially the same Confucian standpoint as the official historian, and shared the official-centered interests common to the whole class of scholar-officials. His great advantage was that he could enliven his account with firsthand knowledge of his subject or with information from the detailed records provided by the subject's family. How did this intimate and personal relationship between author and subject affect the objectivity of the record?

The purpose of biography was essentially commemorative, born from a desire to provide a record of the deceased's achievements and personality for his surviving descendants, relatives, and associates. To a slightly lesser extent, since the epitaph at least was publicly exposed and even the text of the tomb inscription was widely circulated in the case of a well-known figure, the record was also directed at posterity in general. Moreover, from the point of view of the family cult, an epitaph or tomb inscription was an authoritative report made by the members of a clan to their ancestors, announcing the achievements and merits of the deceased man. (Similar records were prepared for the ancestors in ancient Egypt and in Rome, so that the Chinese model is by no means unique.) Last, a biography was not merely a record of fact, but was also—in common with the clan record taken as a whole—designed for a didactic purpose. The biography would serve either as a model to be emulated, suggesting to posterity courses of action likely to lead to success and approbation, or less commonly as a minatory example illustrating errors to be avoided. As Mr. Wright pointed out in the previous essay, examples provided the young with models for their own conduct and with ideals to which they might aspire.

Since "commemorative biographies" were written by persons closely associated with their subjects, it is hardly surprising that they were inclined to be eulogistic and flattering in tone. This does not, however, mean that they are totally unreliable. Although their authors were expected as a matter of course to embellish the account of an ordinary and unremarkable life with incidents taken from tradition, any embellishment that tended to distort the records was condemned. Mr. Nivison, in his recent study of the great historian Chang Hsüeh-cheng as a biographer, tells how Chang refused the request of a family of friends who wished him to incorporate fictional incidents into a tomb inscription for a deceased lady who had led an exemplary and virtuous life.[9] Such intransigence was however rather unusual, and moreover the nature of these embellishments was such that they would be immediately recognizable for what they were. Far from being purely random fictional incidents from the imagination of the author, they were chosen as a subtle and indirect means of indicating the character of the biography's subject, by drawing a parallel with some famous figure of the past who would be well known to the cultured reader.

The slanting of a record could hardly be accomplished by the simple intrusion of fictional incident or by fabrication. The readers for whom it was designed were a small and closely knit circle who were likely to be as well informed on the facts as the author. The chief source of distortion lay in the selection of material for inclusion, and in the exclusion of facts that showed the subject in an unfavorable light or that did not accord with the author's general interpretation of his subject's character as a consistent example of a specific and recognizable type.

When this private record, which in the case of a prominent man would have been written with one eye upon the possibility of its eventual inclusion in the dynastic history, reached the historiographers at the capital, it presented them with a ready-made framework for a biography, already checked and verified in detail by the Board of Civil Office and the Board of Rites. It was, moreover, written in the same context of Confucian social and ethical values as the official histories.

The historians were faced with two problems: first, which persons should have biographies devoted to them, and second, which parts from the available biographical records of those persons should be used. The selection of names for inclusion was an especially difficult problem. As Mr. Frankel has demonstrated,[10] this was a subject upon which the historian was open to a number of violent pressures—from the dynastic house under which he was writing, from the surviving relatives, protégés, and colleagues of the deceased, and from members of his own family. In this connection it is very important to remember that whereas the dynastic history in its final form was not completed until after the fall of the dynasty—often centuries after the events described—the component parts of the history, both the annals and biographies, took shape very shortly after the event, when passions might still run high. Although at least from T'ang times onward constant attempts were made to keep the records of current reigns secret in order to free the historians from political influence, such secrecy was seldom preserved.

As a result of such pressures whole groups of important persons, who happened to be on the losing side in factional struggles, or whose interests clashed with those of the scholar-officials, were either accorded curt references or omitted altogether. The most notable example of this is the very scant treatment given to military leaders. The persistent tension between the civil service and the military, whom the Confucian literati viewed with contempt, led to the complete omission of lives of many able and extremely important military leaders from the *lieh-chuan*, and even those few biographies that were devoted to military heroes tend to be short. Also given scant treatment were the various categories of specialist officials, whose lives did not accord with the Confucian "generalist" ideal, and the eunuchs, the constant rivals of the officials for political influence, who did not pretend to share at all in the Confucian value-system and who are presented almost without exception as minatory figures.

Only the very highest-ranking officials were given a biography as of right. Who else should be included, and on what grounds, were questions which exercised those historians who wrote about their craft throughout the centuries. Biographies in the context of the dynastic histories were, as we have seen, to be illustrative examples of the actions of subjects and ministers. They are thus almost exclusively biographies of the scholar-official class, whose business it was to rule the country and whose training was aimed at a career in public service. In theory, a high official whose life had been routine was to be omitted in favor of an exemplary commoner who had performed meritorious deeds. But the deceased minister's family and friends could exert such pressures that it took a historian with a very strong will to omit his name from the record. Moreover, the exercise of judgment on these matters was made more difficult by the fact that official historiography was a joint enterprise and in any dispute among the compilers the final arbiter was usually a serving chief minister, who would himself often have been personally involved in the deceased's career.

Thus, although the selection of names for inclusion was in theory made on didactic grounds, in practice many biographies, especially in the later histories, appear to us little more than brief *curricula* of conventional official careers. We should remember, however, that the *curriculum* of an official career, even when it was little more than a list of successive appointments, was much more meaningful to a reader with a scholar-official class background than it is to a modern Western reader. Just as the present-day reader of an obituary notice in *The Times* of some prominent civil servant will automatically register the significance of each new appointment, and will know without being explicitly told that appointment to some post of great dignity but little substance means in effect that thereafter the subject was out of the running for high office, the Chinese scholar reading a *lieh-chuan* would automatically register the significance in an official's career of each new post. Until we understand the workings of the administrative machine in this way, we miss a good deal of the insight which the *lieh-chuan* gave to contemporary readers.

In general, the historian did not state explicitly the grounds on which he included biographies. The only clear-cut cases were the "group biographies" of "loyal ministers," "oppressive officials," "recluses," "notable women," "literary men," "filial and righteous persons," etc. Mr. Frankel, in his essay on the group biography of T'ang literati, raises a number of important questions in regard to these sections. Such chapters exemplify the desire of the historian to establish a common pattern for persons filling a given function, which normative pattern—appropriately related to one or more Confucian virtues—was then designed to have a didactic effect upon his readers.

A more subtle judgment and categorization were exercised in the case of men selected for fuller biographical treatment. The successive holders of a single office were not uncommonly grouped together in a single chapter, and by judicious editing and juxtaposition the historian could express an unspoken judgment on each. In such groupings, too, the editor-historian was able to effect an emphasis by bringing together persons sharing a common trait of character.

Once the selection of names had been made, the next stage was the editing of the "accounts of conduct" or commemorative inscriptions. It is very difficult to generalize about this process, since it varied widely. But in general the final text followed the wording of the source biography closely and faithfully, being built up by scissors-and-paste compilation, just as the annals were assembled from court diaries and official documents. The source biography, on the other hand, could present difficulties. The historian sought to establish the subject's basic characterization by categorizing his biography in terms of one of the normalized roles described by Mr. Wright in the foregoing essay. To maintain consistency, the historian often had recourse to the device of recording events that did not fit into this general picture in some other section of the history, often in the annals or in somebody else's biography, so as to leave the picture of the individual intact and at the same time preserve his own professional integrity as a recorder of the true facts.

This raises a further critical problem. The histories were designed to be read as a whole (whether they were often so read is another matter) and as an integrated account of their period. They were not compiled as convenient reference works on their period, as we tend to use them. Their biographies, then, in spite of their having each derived from a separate "account of conduct" or tomb inscription, were to be judged as a corpus of exemplary lives from a given period. By carefully weighting the types of individual whom he considered typical of their times and worthy of note, the historian was able to characterize the period itself. This accounts for the curiously unfinished air that single *lieh-chuan* present in translation. Normally, to collect the data available in a given history on one man it is necessary to read not only his own biography but also those of his contemporaries and, to understand his role fully, the annals and monographs as well.

The individual biographical items were not, then, meant to be read as single documents providing a single focus of interest in their subject, but were part of a larger design, a corpus of official lives providing a cumulative didactic effect. Ssu-ma Ch'ien, it will be remembered, entitled his biographies not simply "traditions" (*chuan*) but "connected traditions" (*lieh-chuan*). Needless to say, this represents a state of theoretical perfection which none of the histories, not even their progenitor, the *Shih-chi*, approaches. But it is worth making the point that the full impact—the full didactic impact—of the biographies can only be felt when they are read in this broader context.

The only part of the *lieh-chuan* the historian himself composed was the "judgment," the note ending the biography, but here he had the opportunity to set forth quite explicitly his view of the subject's career and personality, although he did not always avail himself of this opportunity. Such judgments, always set apart from the record itself and plainly labeled for what they are, thus present the modern scholar with no critical problems but are seldom very useful, being written in extremely formal and stereotyped terms. They do, however, often give the clue to how the historian conceived the individual biography or group of biographies in terms of the grand design of his history.

The above remarks are applicable to the majority of the biographies in the histories, those dealing with persons of whom the historian approved. But the histories also included minatory figures—harsh officials, rebels, brigands. In his paper on Chia Ssu-tao, who was treated as such a minatory example by the historians of his period, Mr. Franke makes the point that for the biographies of their villains the historians did not have the same sort of ready-made source material they used elsewhere. Nobody would have dared to write, much less to submit to the Historiographical Office, an "account of conduct" of a rebel, and the historian had to fall back either on extracting contemporary accounts included in the annals, hence strongly biased on the government's side, or on unofficial histories whose veracity was suspect. A well-known example is the *Chiu T'ang-shu's* biography of the rebel general An Lu-shan, taken from a highly dubious unofficial history, the *An Lu-shan shih-chi.* The biographies of such persons, then, present special critical problems, and need to be used with the greatest care.

One basic critical and interpretative problem is, however, posed by *all* this material. How is the Western writer to use biographies of this conventional type, written for such a highly specialized purpose? How can they be adapted to the very different demands of biography in the modern Western sense?

Western biography in its earliest stages was conceived as serving much the same functions—the commemorative and the didactic—as the Chinese. In its most popular forms, for example, in medieval hagiography, it even produced a comparable stereotyped characterization with a set of conventionalized *topoi.* But in the West there has existed side by side with this early tradition of didactic-commemorative record a stream of biography, beginning at the latest with Plutarch, directed toward giving as full as possible a likeness of the man and preserving the essential individual flavor of his personality. In recent times the tradition of good Western biography has increasingly concentrated upon portraying a man's life in all its aspects, as an integrated whole.

This was not what the Chinese reader expected of a biography. Just as the readers of a medieval saint's life were primarily interested in the record of his sanctity and holy deeds—even if these were portrayed in conventional set forms—so the scholar-bureaucrats for whom the dynastic histories were designed as manuals of precedent were satisfied with the bare account of a subject's performance of his limited role as a member of the bureaucratic apparatus.

Biography of the type that has arisen in Europe since the Renaissance focuses upon subjects whose character and interaction with their circumstances are of interest. In Europe this interest in the individual *per se* is evinced in the hero-epic, a literary form of popular origin which was adapted to the purposes of literary composition and, in its most sharply defined and perfected guise, in the tragedy. It is perhaps symptomatic of a different attitude toward the individual that among the Chinese neither epic heroic poetry nor tragedy has ever taken strong roots. There is a parallel in the kindred art of portraiture, which rarely emerged in China from the functional commemorative role we are accustomed to associate with board rooms and college common rooms.

Olbricht has very rightly pointed out that there is no generic term in Chinese for biography equivalent to our *vita* or *bios* and that the *lieh-chuan* style of biography was essentially an exploration not of a life but of the performance by its subject of some function or role. The whole style of such biographies was directed to producing a model—exemplary or minatory—for the fulfillment of this function. The details of a man's actions, the illustrative episodes characterizing his conduct, the quotations from his writings—all were selected to produce a consistent and integrated picture.

Here the Western historian is faced with one of the least tractable problems in the interpretation of his material. In considering such personalities as those discussed in this volume, what allowance is he to make for the traditional historians' preoccupation with set categories and stereotypes, and how much credence is he to give to *topoi* as these recur in biographies? Again, how far were the roles we find so clearly depicted actually chosen by the subjects and played out in their lives, and how much was ascribed to the life by the Chinese biographer in the search for ideal moral consistency and didactic meaning? The modern historian can go some way to solve these questions in any given case. He knows who compiled a particular history and under what circumstances: he can thus evaluate the compiler's judgments and categorizations. He has, moreover, access to a variety of materials—especially the writings of the subject himself—which will enable him to check, modify, and amplify the standard account.

Last, he can bear in mind that, as Mr. Wright has pointed out in his essay, role playing and self-identification with model exemplars was in the blood of the Chinese scholar class. Individuals commonly made a deliberate choice of the role they were to play, and identified themselves in a highly personal and emotional sense with some model figure in a manner very foreign to modern Western experience. For the Confucian writer, whether he was official historian or biographer writing for the family cult, the chief preoccupation was with the performance by the subject of two set functions, those of the official and of the family member. These two spheres of activity, as Mr. Wright has explained, were viewed as intimately connected, and to them applied a whole system of common moral and ethical attitudes. Within these two broad functions, a range of conventionalized roles was available to the individual. In addition, special categories, such as the "literati" of Mr. Frankel's study, provided acceptable variations upon these norms which were in fact secondary roles. Biographies of such persons often include more personal matter than those of conventional officials, but they should not be taken simply as portraits with an additional perspective. They are exactly the same "functional" type of biography, but written

with reference to another, subtly different set of ideals and conventions
relevant to this secondary role. The same applies to the very numerous
and often lively biographical sketches of famous painters, which portray a wide range and variety of personal eccentricity largely because
eccentric personal behavior was the expected norm for artist-scholars.

This preoccupation with a man's function and career did not mean
that the Chinese were not as curious as we are about the other aspects
of a man's life. Far from it. The notebooks and random jottings (*pi-
chi*, etc.) which form such a vital part of the literary output from T'ang
times onward are full of short notes and anecdotes about individuals,
many of them men with full standard biographies elsewhere. These
notes often throw light on the private aspects of life and upon idiosyn-
crasies of character, and help give a new view of a man's character.
But there is seldom any attempt to develop these notes into an extended
picture of a single life. English readers will be familiar with this sort
of writing from such works as Aubrey's *Brief Lives*. A further shortcoming of these works is that there was no high critical standard applicable to them. Often as not designed to entertain, the *pi-chi* and similar
works include much hearsay and tradition. They are thus unreliable as
sources and merge very easily into the shadowy world of historical romance and fiction.

Compartmentalization of material on various aspects of a man's life
into standardized career records, anecdotal character sketches, etc., undoubtedly contributed to the slow growth in China of a unified biographical style. However, full biographical portraits were not entirely lacking. One such form was the autobiography appended as preface or
introduction to an author's works. Such prefaces were designed to be
self-revealing, to make the author's standpoint and circumstances clear
to his readers. In Mr. Dien's study of Yen Chih-t'ui and in Mr. Wang's
on Feng Tao we can see how such an autobiography can place a man's
life and writings in clear perspective, and incidentally reveal to us the
details of his personal character, in a way all but impossible within a
formal *lieh-chuan*. Autobiography was comparatively unusual before
the Sung, but later became relatively commonplace.

Another form of biography which dealt with the individual as a
unique entity rather than as a representative of a social or hierarchical
group was the "separate biography" (*pieh-chuan*). This form flourished during the period of division and regional autonomy that followed
the fall of the Han, a period in which the traditional ties and relationships became strained and the conventional patterns of behavior broke
down. Moreover, the state-centered Confucian ideology was under
fierce attack from two essentially individual-centered religions, native

Taoism and imported Buddhism. The latter brought in its train a large and highly developed narrative literature in the Jataka stories, produced by a civilization with a long epic tradition. Some of the best extended biographies in Chinese are in fact those of Buddhist notables, and there can be little doubt that Buddhist influence played a large part in the growth of the "separate biography" as well as in the development of narrative prose fiction. The gradual re-emergence under the T'ang of the Confucian tradition as the dominant ideology of the ruling class soon led, however, to the revival of the old restraints.

The bureaucratization of historiography in the same period also helped to establish the *lieh-chuan* form as the standard pattern of biographical record. Unfortunately, the *lieh-chuan*, effective as it was in the context of a bulky history where it formed a part of a whole, was not meaningful as an independent work. To circumvent its shortcomings, a new type of biography, designed to stand alone and known as the *nien-p'u*, was developed under the Sung. An adaptation of the annalistic style of history, the *nien-p'u* was essentially a carefully dated chronological account of a man's life. It could vary from a few pages describing successive official appointments to a book-size treatment of data from a wide variety of sources with not only all the known facts about the subject's life but also the background material necessary to explain his times. Of all the Chinese forms the *nien-p'u* most nearly resembles the Western scholarly biography. But like the annalistic history style upon which it was modeled, the *nien-p'u* is usually a succession of carefully dated discrete facts, with no attempt to connect them in any meaningful causal pattern; it makes no attempt to provide any explicit interpretation of its subject, and is best described as materials for a biography rather than as biography itself.

Under the Ch'ing another type of highly personalized biography emerged, the "unofficial biography" (*pieh-chuan*), which shared the same name as the "separate biography" form in vogue during the post-Han period but represented a completely different genre. *Pieh-chuan* in this new sense were almost always written by a close friend of the deceased man at the request of his relatives. Unlike the impersonal factual record of the tomb inscription or the epitaph, they attempted to give a vivid depiction of the personal character of their subject, and incidentally to commemorate the intimate relationship that had existed between subject and author.[11] This brought into the field of "biography" a type of intimate personal reminiscence that had traditionally been reserved to verse.

It is clear then that in the seventeenth and eighteenth centuries the Chinese were conscious of the deficiencies of the old *lieh-chuan* style,

especially when used for the record of a single life, and were feeling
their way toward more satisfactory biographical conventions. With the
nineteenth century the newly evolving forms and attitudes were applied
to autobiography. On the one hand, it became common practice to
write autobiographical *nien-p'u,* a sort of diary of "life and times," often
in minute detail. On the other, self-revelatory autobiography of an
extremely personal kind became fashionable. Mr. Howard, who has
dealt in detail with these developments elsewhere,[12] has depended to a
large extent upon such autobiographical writings for his especially vivid
account in this volume of K'ang Yu-wei's spiritual development.

But by K'ang Yu-wei's time the Western idea of biography, and,
even more, Western Romantic literature with its almost obsessive emphasis upon the individual personality, had begun to influence the
Chinese. With the turn of the century, a flood of Western biography
at every level of sophistication began to be translated, and the Chinese
tradition was suddenly transformed.[13] At the same time the authority
of the Confucian ideology, which had provided the universal framework of moral reference for the old biographers, was breaking down in
the face of imported ideas, and its old models of conduct and norms of
behavior as exemplified in the traditional biographies were rapidly
becoming anachronistic. However, traditional forms of biography, like
Confucianism itself, did not die without a struggle, and works in the old
styles—*lieh-chuan, nien-p'u,* and traditional autobiography—continued
to appear, while commemorative inscriptions in the old style are still
compiled in some families—at least in Formosa.

The modern scholar attempting to write a life of a historical figure
without question has at his disposal a wealth of biographical material.
Individual biographies, however, must be read in the broad context for
which they were designed, and in the knowledge that, however authoritative the history in which they may be included, they are likely to
have been based upon records compiled for family purposes. They were
also less accurately dated and subjected to far less searching and scru-
pulous editorial criticism than the other sections of the histories. Moreover, they are concerned with only a single aspect—usually the public
aspect—of their subject's life and are almost exclusively concerned with
the members of a single small though influential social group—the class
most heavily indoctrinated with the common Confucian ideology, in
terms of which the historian-biographer too made his judgments.

Within the self-imposed limitations of the historians and those responsible for the family cults, the resulting record was adequate, but
the limitations present a very real problem to the modern scholar, whose

center of interest lies beyond the spectrum of Confucian ethics. The papers in this volume show clearly that to produce a biography acceptable by Western standards it is necessary to go elsewhere for much of one's material, using the works of the official biographers only as a rough outline or guide. With the exception of Mr. Frankel's analysis, which is a special case, not one single contribution draws exclusively or even extensively upon specifically biographical source material. In almost every case the major source has proved to be the subject's own writings.

Although we write from a standpoint far removed from his, Ku Yen-wu's dicta on the biographer's duties—read all the subject's writings, understand his ideas, be thoroughly acquainted with the times in which he lived, and learn everything you can about the state apparatus of which he formed a part—still hold good.[14] To evaluate our subject in terms meaningful to the modern historian, we cannot conscientiously rely for our primary sources upon literal translation of traditional biographies, and indeed unless we adhere carefully to Ku Yen-wu's advice we shall fail fully to interpret even the abbreviated and highly stylized account we shall find there.

CONFUCIAN PERSONALITIES

Albert E. Dien

YEN CHIH-T'UI (531–591+):
A BUDDHO-CONFUCIAN

From the writings of Yen Chih-t'ui (531–91+)[1] emerges a model of behavior for the official that differed from the earlier Confucian ideal. In place of the model Confucian official, distinguishable by his belief in the effectiveness of moral persuasion and his selfless concern for the welfare of the state, Yen idealized the competent and devoted bureaucratic functionary who assumed no responsibility for policy and for whom the greatest political good was preservation of the status quo. Yen's ideas derived to a certain extent from a Buddhist dilution of his Confucianism.[2] But perhaps equal weight should be given to the effect on his attitudes of the extreme social and political instability that characterized the period.

Yen Chih-t'ui was a descendant of Yen Han, a native of Lang-yeh (near modern Lin-i in Shantung) who had come south in the entourage of Ssu-ma Yen and was with him in 317 when, following the loss of the north to the non-Chinese, the prince founded the Eastern Chin dynasty.[3] The émigrés of aristocratic clans were given the positions of power in the southern dynasties; lesser families supplied the minor officials or courtiers of princes, maintaining their status through a tradition of learning. The family Yen Han established in the south belonged to the second category, and Yen Chih-t'ui early joined the staff of a royal prince in Liang state. Liang had, however, been racked by the rebellion of Hou Ching and was all but brought to an end in 554 by the invasion of the Western Wei (later Northern Chou) ruled by the Hsien-pei Yü-wen family. The capital (near modern Chiang-ling in Hupei) was sacked, and thousands of prisoners, Yen Chih-t'ui among them, were taken north to Ch'ang-an.[4] Yen escaped eastward to the Northern Ch'i, hoping eventually to get to the remnant of his state that had survived in the south. But before he could rejoin the Liang court the Ch'en dynasty had replaced the Liang and Ch'en was warring with the Hsien-pei Ch'i state in the northeast. Yen remained at the Northern Ch'i court, rising to relatively high office, until the Northern Chou conquered the Northern Ch'i in 577. Once again Yen was taken to Ch'ang-an but, though mentioned in the Sui period, he held no office there and died some time after 591.[5]

Given the impossibility here of exploring in detail all aspects of Yen Chih-t'ui's life, we shall concentrate on those areas affording the clearest insights into his basic attitudes and values. These, by virtue of his writings, are his thoughts on the upbringing of children, on education, and on the role of the official. His attitude toward the rearing of children, which we shall take up first, sheds much light on his own life and personality. Continuing with his advice to his children concerning education, we shall find candid expressions of his intellectual commitments and his personal Confucianism. For this reason, his writings on education will be considered at length to gain a clearer understanding both of his use of the Confucian canon and of the extent to which his Buddhist faith affected his approach to Confucianism. Finally, we shall look at Yen's ideas on the role of the official, which in a sense represent the end product of his life and intellectual development. Having studied Yen and his beliefs, we shall briefly examine an incident in his life to see how his conduct in the affair is related to the attitudes and values we have discovered in his writings.

An unusual amount and diversity of materials have been preserved to facilitate study of Yen Chih-t'ui, including a long autobiographical poem, "Prose-Poem on Looking at My Life," which with some annotation by Yen was incorporated into his biography in *Pei Ch'i shu.*[6] We shall give particular attention to the *Family Instructions of Mr. Yen (Yen-shih chia-hsün)*, written toward the end of his life for the purpose of transmitting to his family the benefit of his accumulated wisdom. The tradition of writing words of advice to the younger generation went back to China's antiquity—Confucius urging his son to study the *Odes* is an early example[7]—and from the third to the sixth centuries, as clans began emerging as centers of power, this type of writing became an important vehicle for preserving family traditions.[8]

As all other known works of this genre for this period survive only in fragments, the *Instructions of Mr. Yen,* complete, is the earliest example that is fully preserved.[9] Being a practical handbook for the family—to instill certain attitudes and to hold up an ideal pattern of behavior—the work has obvious limitations as a source for the study of Yen's thinking. For our purposes, however, the book has the special advantage of being almost entirely free of the traditional stereotypes one finds in writings intended for the public eye.

A stern attitude toward the rearing of children unfolds in the opening chapters of the *Instructions,* reflecting more than anything else the bitter lessons of Yen Chih-t'ui's own childhood. Yen, who had been brought up by an elder brother after being orphaned at nine, contrasted the careful instruction in proper conduct by his parents to the indulgent, undemanding love of his brother, blaming the latter experience for his poor showing in early life. "Although I read the Rituals and Accounts, I had little love for composition and I tended to be molded and affected by ordinary persons. Self-indulgent and frivolous in speech, I was careless of my person."[10] Bearing out his own assessment is an incident recorded in his biography, which relates that he lost an official post after being found intoxicated at a time he should have been on duty.[11] Yen says that he realized the faults of his character and strove to improve himself, but that this was extremely difficult. "After I was thirty, great faults were rare in me, but my mind was ever at odds with what I said and my inmost nature at war with my emotions. In the evening I realize the mistakes of the morning, and today I regret the errors of yesterday; I pity myself that I was without instruction in childhood and have come to this."[12] One reason for writing the *Instructions* was to warn against the pitfall of indulgence in child-rearing. Behind this lies the assumption that one's natural tendencies are toward evil and must be firmly controlled.

Yen was clear about the necessary discipline. Swift and immediate punishment must be meted out for any infraction of the rules. Only when the child had grown a little and his personality had been sternly shaped could the beatings and punishments be slackened.[13] If anyone were to dispense with them, the faults inherent in the child would become ingrained.[14] Parents who claimed that they could not bear to punish their child were actually doing it more harm, for just as illness called for unpleasant remedies, so the faults in a child required stern measures.[15] He said, "As I have observed the world of men, love without instruction has invariably been unsuccessful."[16]

Yen held up several examples of undisciplined children who had brought on discord and calamities. Chief among these was Kao Yen, a prince of Northern Ch'i who was indulged by his parents, and who came to expect treatment equal to that of his elder brother, the heir apparent and later emperor. In the end, Kao Yen, still a child, obtained by ruse authorization to kill a chancellor whom he disliked, and was himself put to death after coming near open rebellion.[17] Later historians criticized Kao Yen's presumptuous behavior, but seem to have given tacit approval to his insubordination, for the chancellor, Ho Shih-k'ai, was portrayed as a standard Confucian villain.[18] Yen, who lived through these events, condemned the young prince, for he had brought disorder into the state, whatever the vices of his victim. The moral Yen drew from this was that the indulgence of children endangered the family, corrupted society, and weakened the state.

In speaking of the necessity of training and controlling children, Yen made use of the metaphor of polishing and grinding, a significant choice in his case.[19] He says that when he was eighteen or nineteen, he was but little acquainted with the "smooth and coarse whetstones" that should have polished and refined his character; rather, he behaved like an unpolished stone.[20] Elsewhere he says that study is like dressing a rough gem[21] and that solitary study is inadequate since it does not permit one to cut and polish oneself against others, and thus make one more precise.[22] That this is more than a metaphor is to be seen in the variety of terms used. The process of polishing implies also control of oneself, a hard precision that is the enemy of indulgence. We will see later how this admiration of the polished, acquired patterns of behavior brought Yen to condemn inspiration, and also affected his attitudes toward life in general.

Much can be learned about Yen's world view from the attitudes toward education expressed in the *Instructions*. To Yen, the purpose of education appeared twofold: self-improvement as sanctioned in the Confucian tradition, and preservation of the family tradition of learning to ensure family prestige and security. Yen's concern for family security was heightened by his own experiences in a turbulent period in history.

Discussing education as self-improvement, Yen wrote, "The reason for reading books and acquiring learning is basically a desire to enlarge the mind and make perceptive the eye, and to improve one's conduct."[23] There followed an elaboration of the ways in which study of the ancients could teach children their duty toward their parents, and teach the cruel to be humble, the miserly to be charitable, the proud to be respectful. In each case the person learns to subordinate himself to the good of others and to place restraints on his own will. Yen Yen-chih, a collateral ancestor of Yen Chih-t'ui, had said study of the ancients gave one perspective and made one's sorrows seem superficial.[24] Yen Chih-t'ui would use the past not to make the present more tolerable but to guide men toward improvement.

To illustrate the evils of a lack of education, Yen pointed to the dissolute aristocrats.

I often see the gentle-grandees, shamefully involving themselves in the affairs of farmers or merchants, or ignominiously employing themselves in the work of artisans and artists. If one of them shoots, he is unable to pierce an armor plate, and if he picks up a brush, he can barely write his name. Eating his fill and getting drunk on wine, he is indifferent and idle. Thus he fritters away his days and thus he ends his years. He may perhaps be a remnant of a family with hereditary office, and if he gets a half grade of the first official rank, he is satisfied with himself and is utterly oblivious to self-cultivation and study. When there are great issues involving success or calamity, when there are debates and discussions on the relative advantages or disadvantages of policy, then purblindly he lets his mouth sag and sits as in a cloud of fog. At banquet gatherings both public and private, when the guests talk of antiquity and write poetry, he bows his head; struck dumb, he can only yawn and stretch. An acquaintance watching him from the side would bury himself in shame for him. How can one begrudge a few years of assiduous study if without it one grows up to a lifetime of shame and disgrace?[25]

Being unlettered and uncouth was fault enough but the gentle-grandees were also guilty of opportunism. Yen contrasted the scholars of antiquity who studied to benefit others and to correct any deficiencies in their own conduct with the men of his day who studied only for self-advancement.[26] Yen's disgust with such opportunism is illustrated by his disapproving account of the gentleman grandee at the Ch'i court who wished his son to study the Hsien-pei language and the mandolin so that he could ingratiate himself with the alien ruling house and further his career.[27]

Men of principle, in Yen's view, could find in family traditions of learning the basis of right conduct; further, such traditions provided the knowledge necessary for official careers and thus helped ensure the survival of the family in the favored class of Chinese society. After the conquest of Northern Ch'i in 577, Yen was brought to Ch'ang-an, where he lived in comparative poverty. His eldest son, Ssu-lu, complained that there seemed to be no hope of reward in study and that his obligations to his parents compelled him to seek some way of supporting them. Yen replied that more important than the son's filial duties were the responsibilities of the father to provide his children with a good education.

If I were to cause you to abandon studies to seek for wealth, so as to give me richer clothing and food, when I ate such food, could it taste sweet? When I wore such clothes, could they feel warm? If we devote ourselves to the Way of the former kings and hand on the family's traditional apportioned task [*yeh*], though there be pigweed broth or hempen quilts and coarse woolens, it would be what I personally would desire.[28]

At another place Yen urges his children to maintain their studies lest they slip down into the category of the uncouth and rude.[29] This was not just rhetoric, for the family tradition of learning gave security and a favored social status to the family and ensured against a catastrophic fall to the level of the peasantry.

Though obviously opposed to study for personal gain or profit, Yen was too practical to repudiate this motive entirely. The situation in his time gave him an argument much more convincing than simple responsibility for a family tradition. As long as society had been relatively stable, one could rely on family connections and hereditary claims for entry into and advancement in the bureaucracy. But even in fairly normal times, Wang Seng-ch'ien (426–85) could warn his family that they must consider the eventuality of his not being able to provide "shadow," that is, influence in getting office, and that education might make the difference between success and failure.[30]

Yen Chih-t'ui, on the other hand, knew that he was living in an age of disorder and insecurity. He knew from personal experience that those who held office purely through nepotism proved in times of crisis to have "no more worth than a swaybacked nag."[31] One sees here clearly Yen's disdain for such people, and his pride in his own survival. Of those taken prisoner in the wars he observed,

Although for a hundred generations their predecessors had been persons of no consequence, those who knew how to read the *Analects* and the *Classic of Filial Piety* were elevated to be teachers of men; but of those who did not understand writings and records, though for a thousand years their families had worn caps of officials, there were none who did not plow the fields or raise horses.[32]

Yen goes on to argue that study, even if not used to improve one's character, still has the advantage of providing one with security. Actually, he admits, this security could be provided by many skills and accomplishments, but "for an accomplishment easily practiced and still honorable, none exceeds the reading of books."[33] Such utilitarianism is surprising and would seem to resemble the very opportunism he condemned, but Yen avoids this by stressing the quality he expected in learning and the application of that learning in a worthy official career.

Deploring the tendency to memorize by rote without the saving grace of intelligence, Yen complained that modern students but "vapidly preserve the letter of the text and simply intone the words of their master. When it comes to applying these to worldly affairs, there are almost none who can do so."[34] Their studies no longer meaningful to them, these men were ill-equipped even for the regulating of a subprefecture or the deciding of a case at law; nor did they know the parts of a house or the seasons for crops.

They moan and sigh, chat and ridicule, chant and intone, and make phrases and write compositions; in their affairs they are excessively leisurely, in their materials increasingly vague and beside the point. The principles of military and state affairs are almost never applied by such men. The ridicule and opprobrium heaped upon them by the military and common officials are largely because of this.[35]

Clearly Yen saw study and learning as a practical preparation for an official career. The contents of the Classics were not to be hummed or droned, or weighed down with masses of commentary, but applied to real situations, especially in official life. Learning was valuable because it improved one's character, and also because it supplied one with the precedents and knowledge to act as a wise and effective official.

If in pre-industrial England "the term gentleman marked the exact point where the traditional social system divided up the population into two extremely unequal sections,"[36] the term *shih* provided an analogous division in China between the small class of "gentles" or *shih* and the great masses of commoners, *shu jen* or *min*. Although there were many gradations within the upper stratum,[37] all shared certain common values in a common tradition, and a member of the gentle class could be distinguished by his fulfillment of certain patterns of behavior enjoined by the tradition. Yen Chih-t'ui, in writing his *Instructions*, was assuming that his descendants would be members of this gentle class, and was supplying them with what he believed was the valid, and traditional, code of behavior of the gentle. The source of his code was the Classics and tradition. Only by learning the lessons and examples of the past, Yen insisted, could one properly aspire to be a gentleman, and only the Classics gave coherence and authority to the gentleman's code. This reliance on the Classics attested to Yen's Confucianism.

But Yen was not only a Confucian; he was also a Buddhist. He lived during a period when Buddhism was extremely widespread and an integral part of the culture. In the last chapter of the *Instructions*, while giving directions to his children for his own funeral and rites after death, he mentions as a matter of course that the Ullambana (the Buddhist mass for the dead) was to be performed, and asks for no other offerings or services.[38] Yen does not discuss his belief in Buddhism as such, nor does he explicitly point out its effects on his life. This was a personal matter not bearing on the patterns of behavior with which he was concerned. But the *Instructions* included a chapter answering certain criticisms made against Buddhism, and in this apology were some cursory equations between elements in Confucianism and Buddhism.[39] On this basis Yen has been termed a syncretist,[40] but this term is misleading, and we need to examine at greater length the relationship between Buddhism and Confucianism in Yen's writings.

Some understanding of how Yen interpreted the Confucian canon may be gained by contrasting Yen with Yang Hsiung, against whom Yen directed his sharpest criticism on the matter of spontaneity. In a section on literary composition, Yen Chih-t'ui discussed various aspects of what we might call the technical craft of writing: the elements of style, the proper use of terms, and the necessity for being exact in one's facts. In all of these he emphasized conscious control of one's material. To Yen, intuition and inspiration were poor substitutes for maturity and control, and this extended to the writing of literature. Yen quoted Yang Hsiung, who contended that a child might write excellent poetry by reason of his inborn naturalness or spontaneity. Yen disagreed and offered as evidence the poetry in the *Book of Odes* written by the Duke of Chou and others in their mature years.[41] Further, Yen says, Confucius said that unless one knew the *Odes,* one had not the means to speak. This would obviously make it impossible for a child who had not yet mastered the *Odes* to write anything of worth or importance. Finally, Confucius used the *Odes* in proving his points in the *Classic of Filial Piety.* "How could Yang Hsiung dare to disregard this?" Yen asks. This long excursus seems overdone, but this is not the end of Yen's criticism of Yang Hsiung. He goes on to say,

I moreover have never known what Hsiung himself considered a mature person to be. Having written "The Virulent Ch'in and the Admirable Hsin" [to bolster Wang Mang], he recklessly threw himself from a tower [to escape what he thought was impending execution by Wang Mang]; he looked about in fear, not understanding his heaven-bestowed fate. These are the acts of a child.[42]

This seems to be rather gratuitous criticism, for it does not bear directly on Yang Hsiung's statement. Most probably we come to the basis of Yen's aversion for Yang Hsiung when he touches on the latter's *T'ai-hsüan ching.*

The Confucian canon, as a whole, is a rather homogeneous body of material with the exception of the *Book of Changes.* This Classic, filled with mystical and cryptic references, stands apart from the other works, which directly or indirectly bear on the social and moral life of man. Its mysticism gave the *Book of Changes* an important place in the Confucian tradition, as a bridge between the human and divine worlds and as a beginning toward understanding the seeming unreasonableness of nature. The later accretions to the *Changes* phrased themselves in Confucian terminology, but its fundamental mysticism had to remain, or it would have been useless for its purpose. Those within the Confucian fold who were attracted by the problems of man's place in the universe gravitated to the study of the *Changes.* In the Han, Yang Hsiung had taken the concepts of the *Changes* as his basis in writing the *T'ai-hsüan ching.* In it he formulated a cosmological system, one which also borrowed heavily from the *Tao-te ching. T'ai-hsüan* itself refers to the Tao. We find that the *T'ai-hsüan* is the cause of all things, within and yet without, and at the basis of all change. He who harmonizes with this *hsüan* is noble, he who does not is ordinary. Because this force, or spirit, permeates, creates, and controls the world, there is a unity that can then be described and understood. Basically, comprehension of the system remained mystical and in this respect had close affinities with Taoism.[43] An essential difference between Yen Chih-t'ui and Yang Hsiung is discernible in their uses of the *Book of Changes*. Yang elicited a basis for a unified cosmological world view and, especially as interpreted by later followers such as Wang Pi and Sung Chung, tried to dismiss the divinatory aspects. Yen used the *Book of Changes* as an oracle book—its traditional guise—rejecting the work as a metaphysical treatise.[44] Yen, while staying within the Confucian tradition, reserved to Buddhism all systematic speculation on ultimate values and the nature of the universe.

Taoism was another matter. The Taoists themselves came in for rather dispassionate criticism from Yen, who claimed the subject bored him. What validity had a philosophy whose adherents were unable to live up to their ideals? Their only contribution, in his opinion, was in the field of medicine and the care of the body. It was particularly galling to have Yang Hsiung, an opponent within the Confucian tradition, seriously embrace certain Taoist concepts, and Yen became vitriolic. Liu Hsin had once remarked to Yang that later men would be unable to understand his work and would probably use the *T'ai-hsüan ching* to cover their sauce pots.[45] Yen commented that "this man, simply to expound some mathematical calculations and to explain the *yin* and *yang*, wrote the *T'ai-hsüan ching*, and it has deluded the several philosophers . . . The *T'ai-hsüan ching*—after all, what use has it, even to cover a sauce pot."[46]

In his approach to the Classics, Yen was not seeking in them, or in their implications, an answer to his higher needs, nor was he trying, except in rare instances, to correlate them with Buddhist doctrines. The chapter in the *Instructions* dealing with Buddhism is essentially an answer to various criticisms, with little evidence of any attempt at an eclectic synthesis. Aside from the pairing of certain Confucian and Buddhist precepts, mentioned above, it also includes several incidents illustrating retribution coming to those who acted against the Buddhist commandments.[47] Most important, this chapter contains Yen's vision of the perfect world. He is answering criticisms of Buddhism and its clergy: "If one will be able to lead and convert the black-headed [i.e., the people] so that all enter the Bodhimandala [place of enlightenment], it will be as the world of Abhirati or the state of Saṅkha; then there will be natural paddy rice and inexhaustible stores of treasures."[48] It is in this vision of a Buddhist millennium that he parts company with

the traditional Confucian classicist and with those influenced by Neo-
Taoism, and it is this which underlies his essentially different approach
to the Classics.

For Yen, therefore, the Buddhist vision and the classical tradition
were both valid, each in its own sphere. The classical tradition to Yen
served the same function as it did to any Confucian: it encompassed the
perfect code of behavior and the values of the past sages, a way of life
which had the sanction of tradition. Yen was not a literalist, and he
was willing to consider different patterns which might have developed
in the absence of any specific pronouncement in the Classics. What Yen
did insist on, however, was that the Classics constituted the repository
of examples of the highest morality of the past. He was a relativist then
in a limited sense, and rejected out of hand the absolute relativism of
the Neo-Taoist.

There is one point on which Yen and the followers of Yang Hsiung
did agree, and this was in their rejection of the classical scholarship
usually associated with the north. During the period of disunion, it was
recognized that there was a difference between the traditions of classical scholarship in the north and south, but precisely what this difference was is not clear. There were of course the differences of interpretation of specific passages and textual variants,[49] but aside from this
natural product of time and distance there was a more fundamental contrast. As early as the fifth century, in the *Shih-shuo hsin-yü*, it is said
that "the learning of the northerners profoundly interweaves the broad
and wide" while "the learning of the southerners lucidly penetrates the
fundamentals and essentials." There Chih Tun adds that northerners
in their learning are like one who looks at the moon from a brightly
illuminated place, while the southerners are like one who views the sun
through a lattice window.[50] This impressionistic description was repeated centuries later, in a T'ang appraisal of the period, when the
southerners were said to have been "brief and concise, obtaining the
blossoms and flowers" while the northerners were "greatly overgrown,
exhausting the branches and leaves."[51] It would seem that in the commentaries drawn up for the Classics, the northerners spent themselves
in voluminous collections, examining the text in its minutiae, whereas
the southerners were interested in the purport of the text and had little
interest in exhaustive discussions of all possibilities of interpretation.

Yen Chih-t'ui, if there is anything in this contrast, was very much a
southerner. He had little patience with lengthy discussions of minor
points in the Classics, considering them mere displays of pedantic
virtuosity.

The writings of the sages provide the means for giving instruction, but to understand and practice the texts of the Classics, it is enough to go roughly over the commentary and meaning. This would ordinarily benefit one in word and deed, and this is enough for anyone. Why is it necessary for the phrase "Chung-ni dwells" to require two pages of clarifying explanation, whether it was in his own rooms or the Lecture Hall, or wherever?[52]

In general, the difference between north and south is ascribed to the spread in the south of *hsüan-hsüeh,* the interest in cosmology and metaphysics influenced by Neo-Taoist ideas. This movement was manifested by the popularity of Yang Hsiung's *T'ai-hsüan ching,* and by the writing of commentaries for certain Classics, chiefly the *Book of Changes* and the *Analects,* which served as vehicles of Neo-Taoist theories.[53] Opposed to such theorizing, the dedicated classicist saw the Classics as repositories of all truth and all relevant wisdom for the conduct of life; for him the most detailed and exhaustive exegesis of the Classics was therefore justified. Yen Chih-t'ui shared with the *hsüan-hsüeh* thinkers a commitment to ultimate truths—in his case Buddhist truths—that lay outside and beyond the Confucian system. For this reason he was impatient with the northern exegetes and their attention to every minute detail of Confucian classical texts. It followed that Yen was intolerant of those literalists who strained to "reconcile" the dicta of the sages with new knowledge and new facts of life in an epoch the sages could hardly have envisioned.[54]

We see this intolerance in two incidents recorded in the *Instructions.*

The common classicist gentles [*ju-shih*] have not waded through the mass of books. Aside from the Classics and apocrypha, they have seen only the explanations and clarifications. When I first entered Yeh [the capital of Northern Ch'i], I exchanged visits with Ts'ui Wen-yen of Po-ling. We once spoke of "Raising Difficulties on Matters Pertaining to Cheng Hsüan's Commentary on the *Shang shu*" in Wang Ts'an's collection.[55] Ts'ui in turn spoke of it with some classicists. Before he had opened his mouth they rudely pushed and jostled him saying, "The literary collections should contain only poetry, prose-poems, epitaphs, and eulogies. Is it proper for one to discuss classical questions in them? Moreover we have also not heard of Wang Ts'an being included among the classicists of yore." Ts'ui laughed and in the end did not show them Ts'an's collection.

The second incident is similar:

When Wei Shou served on a Discussion Commission, once in discussing the problem of the Ancestral Temple with some Erudites [*po-shih*], he cited the *Han shu* as evidence. The Erudites laughed and said, "We have not heard that the *Han shu* has become admissible as evidence in matters of the classical art." Shou then became angry and did not again speak. He pulled out the biography of Wei Hsüan-ch'eng, pitched it at them, and went out. The Erudites the whole night together unrolled it and looked into it. When they had penetrated and understood it, they came and expressed regret saying, "We would not have thought that Hsüan-ch'eng was so learned as this."[56]

While we may be inclined to sympathize with Yen's criticism of the narrowness displayed by these scholars, they might well have answered that as the canon contained the words of the sages, the rest of literature was hardly relevant to the great questions of man and society, and from their viewpoint this was true.

The body of the Confucian canon formed for Yen the basis of learning, but it was to be taken at face value, and its place in his intellectual pursuits was limited by the commitments we have mentioned above. At the same time he had a major interest in philology and lexicography. This interest found expression in the philological exegesis of the Classics, which allowed Yen to involve himself in classical studies in a way which was meaningful to him. The tradition of philological scholarship appeared early in the Confucian tradition, for the *Erh-ya*, a part of the canon, is a philological work.[57] Yen criticized those who were interested only in practical glossaries or pragmatic handbooks of pronunciation for the Classics and who rejected the less immediately useful philological and etymological dictionaries. He himself was the author of several dictionaries, of which only fragments remain, and he is mentioned as one who cooperated in compiling the *Ch'ieh-yün*, the famous dictionary of 601.[58] Throughout the *Instructions*, Yen points out errors of graphs, allusions, and meanings in the Classics and general literature, and constantly emphasizes the necessity for care and precision in one's studies. In his own home, no one gave the pronunciation for a graph without first consulting a dictionary. This could not fail to make a strong impression on his children and helps to explain the similar interests they were to show in their careers.

Yen's criticism of the Classics and reliance on the dictionaries, most notably the *Shuo-wen*, did not pass unnoticed.

A guest challenged the host [Yen] saying, "The Classics and canon of the present, you, sir, consider to be false, but what the *Shuo-wen* says, you, sir, in every case say is correct; thus then, Hsü Shen [author of the *Shou-wen*] surpasses Confucius, does he not?" The host clapped his hands, laughing heartily, and answered, "The Classics and canon of today, are they all the traces of Confucius' own hand?" The guest said, "Is the *Shuo-wen* of today all the traces of Hsü Shen's hand?" I [Yen] replied saying, "Hsü Shen investigated, using the six types of graphs, joining them in groups and divisions, so that there could be no mistake. If there is a mistake, then one is aware of it. For Confucius, the meaning is preserved, but he did not discuss his script.

Previous classicists were able to alter the script to accord with their opinions. How much more has this happened as the books and writings have come down and been transmitted to us."⁵⁹

To prove his lack of prejudice he went on to adduce examples of error in the *Shuo-wen,* but one feels that the guest had put his finger on an important point: that, for Yen, the wording of the canon had no sanctity.

As discussed above, Yen considered the Classics the repository of tradition, a venerable source book as it were of proper behavior and moral conduct. But Yen denied any sharp line of division between canonical and profane literature. In the passages quoted above, Yen made specific reference to worth-while knowledge to be found in later literature, especially the histories, which he cited constantly in the *Instructions.* If the Classics, particularly those relating to *li,* were the repository of codes of conduct, then the histories, beginning with the canonical ones but continuing with later ones also, were the best source of actual examples of the traditional code in operation. In this sense, the Classics and profane history could be said to merge into one, a literature of edification and instruction. This attitude probably under-lay Yen's criticism of Pan Ku: "The Excellent Scribe in his writings in general selects trifles of certain individuals' 'ardent and yet cautious nature' [personal defects], merely discussing success and failure in government, not what was accomplished by the masterly scions [*chün-tzu*] among the gentles who protected the laws and regulations."⁶⁰ The focus of history should not be the state, but rather the patterns of behavior exhibited by men in the past.

With this view of the histories, it is natural that they are used throughout the *Instructions* to supply pertinent examples, and are commended as worthy of close study. Whether Yen himself wrote history is still uncertain, but he seems to have passed on to his descendants this same high regard for it.⁶¹ Thus we find that his own son, Yen Min-ch'u, wrote a commentary on the *Han shu,* some of which was incorporated into the more famous one by Yen's grandson, Ssu-lu's son, Yen Shih-ku. Their interest in history may well be traceable to Yen's exhortations in the *Instructions.* At one place, after conceding that "those who are born and know, these need no further study," Yen pointed out to his children that they were most probably not geniuses, and "so for you not to be instructed by the traces of the past would be like your lying covered over with a quilt."⁶²

To summarize, Yen's commitment to the Confucian canon was limited, since he saw the perfect society of the future achieved through Buddhism rather than through the words of Confucius. Intellectually, the canon was able to absorb Yen's interest as an object of philological study, but as the Classics lost their sacred status for Yen, histories became their extension in time. This diluted Confucianism affected Yen's view of the individual's role as official, to which we now turn.

Some one hundred years before, Yen Chih-t'ui's ancestor, Yen Yen-chih, had also prepared a volume of advice and counsel for his descendants, the *Kao-t'ing* (Announcement to the Courtyard), which in many ways provides an interesting contrast to the writings of Yen Chih-t'ui.[63] In it, Yen Yen-chih had classified the gentles into three groups. The highest lived in solitary retirement, disdaining to have anything to do with the world. The second held office, but did not seek it. The third, and lowest, actively sought office and fame.[64] Yen Chih-t'ui would have recognized only the last two categories, for to him the first was unacceptable. Everyone must have an apportioned task (*yeh*), and for the gentle, this was holding office. Yen Chih-t'ui felt that for a man to ignore the world and his responsibilities was ignoble, and for "the masterly scions [*chün-tzu*] among the gentles who have a place in the world of men, their worth and ability should have a beneficial effect on things, not merely high talk and empty discussions—to the left a lute and to the right a book—wasting the emolument of a ruler of men."[65]

In this case, the difference between Yen Chih-t'ui and his earlier, illustrious relative may have been largely the result of living under different conditions. Yen Yen-chih lived in an era of relative stability, in which retirement to one's estate was possible if it seemed proper or appealing, and with the financial security of landed property, the most prudent policy for safeguarding the family may well have been to refrain from active participation in dangerous court politics. Eremitism was sanctioned in the Confucian system as a form of individual protest, but it was not the ideal pattern.[66] One suspects the influence of the Neo-Taoist tradition in Yen Yen-chih's threefold classification. By the time of Yen Chih-t'ui, the older world had collapsed, and Yen had seen how rapidly one could sink to the level of the lowest peasant. In a period of great instability, when estates were confiscated and the family uprooted, the security of the family depended on the individual, and employment in the bureaucracy was the only course for survival as a gentle. It was dangerous to associate with the military and shameful to have any connection with the other occupations.

If holding office was "praiseworthy and honorable,"[67] there were still many admonitions about how one should conduct oneself in office and obtain advancement, and Yen defines two extreme types. On the one hand there is the incompetent official. This may be the man of letters who is refined in his conduct but who has no practical sense,[68] or the decadent wastrels of the southern courts.[69] On the other extreme there are those who brawl and clamor for a place and who obtain advancement by pointing out the faults of their superiors. The bystander, Yen continues, will believe that only by such activities can one succeed, and that those who remain passive deprive themselves of future benefits. Not so, for all is controlled by fate, and the masterly scion "ought to protect the Way and venerate Virtue, store his valuable gifts and bide his time."[70] Here again there is no question of withdrawal, but rather a passive reliance upon one's worth for eventual recognition and promotion. Related to this acceptance of fate was the question of one's innate quality, which determined one's eventual success or failure.[71]

For the pattern of behavior expected of the official, Yen again turns to antiquity.

For those who do not yet know how to serve their lord, I would desire they contemplate the ancients' attending to their duties without any aggressiveness and, on encountering danger, giving up their lives. They did not neglect sincere remonstrance if in this way they might benefit the state altars of grain and soil. Then, grieved at any selfish consideration for themselves, in their thoughts they desired to fulfill their duty.[72]

The state made use of men in a variety of categories, according to Yen, and one might serve in any capacity, for all are equally good.[73] But aside from their specialized duties, officials are under the moral duty to offer their advice and criticism to the court. Yen traced the origin of such functions to the Warring States period, and classified them as remonstrations with the emperor, accusations against officials, proposals for the best interests of the state, and general advice.[74] The masterly scion would be ashamed if unable to offer constructive advice to the state, and the literary gentle should rejoice in offering his services.[75] Unfortunately, those who have something to contribute often hold back, while those who do come forward with plans and petitions offer but the "chaff and husks of minor affairs."[76]

Many of these observations are rather stereotyped Confucian views. But at certain points in his discussion Yen's own attitudes clearly emerge. Yen had served in high office, and the dangers to which this had exposed him convinced him of the soundness of the admonition of his ancestor Yen Han: that no one of the family, when in office, should rise to an emolument of more than 2,000 measures of grain. Yen Chih-t'ui himself said that an office of middle rank, with fifty men above and fifty below (thus taking literally the expression "hundred officials"), was "adequate to avoid any feeling of shame or disgrace and to avoid the risk of getting into dangerous situations."[77]

In speaking of the individual's role as official and of personal responsibility, Yen Chih-t'ui offers important prescriptions. The conflict between the individual and society is a universal one, and one which must be resolved by everyone. Yen, as might be expected, decided in favor of duty to the state, rather than to one's personal beliefs. In his de-emphasis of individual identity in relation to the state, he had reservations about the principle of loyalty to any one house or ruler that would prevent one from serving another. In the past, he said, the sages were able to exhibit such highly moral attitudes, but the modern world does not allow this luxury, for the categories of ruler and ruled are no longer stable, and service in more than one state is not to be seen as iniquitous. Further, the official follows his orders, despite the dictates of his own conscience. "When one is under the commands of a prince and cannot exercise one's own responsibility, this is a great calamity for the cultivated man, but it is his duty to go along with it."[78] Not to do so would give rein to displays of individual feeling, which Yen sought to avoid.

What then could provide a check on the despotic potentialities of the ruler? For Yen the check would come from one of the four official functions quoted above, that of remonstrance. Here too, interestingly enough, Yen makes certain restrictions, and he reinforces these with canonical authority. The function of remonstrance and advising the ruler is to correct the errors of the ruler. The official who may do this

must be in a place where his words will be effective, and he ought to fulfill to the fullest extent the conventions for assisting his ruler, and not allow himself to shirk or steal his ease, nor may he hang his head and close his ears to what he considers improper. If his thoughts do not arise from the duties of his office or if he intervenes where it is not his responsibility to do so, then he is a criminal. Therefore the *Piao chi* says, "In serving the ruler, if distant and admonishing, then one is flattering; if close and not admonishing, then one is profiting from a sinecure." The *Analects* say, "If one has not yet the confidence of one's prince and admonishes, then the prince will consider that one is vilifying him."[79]

This then suffices as a guide for one's behavior when such a situation arises. One is to act forthrightly and bravely, if it is one's place to do so; otherwise one is guilty of overstepping the proper bounds. The citation of two authorities is rather unusual, and indicates the importance Yen assigned to this principle.

Over a hundred years before, Yen Yen-chih in his *Kao-t'ing* spoke of the depths of depression into which he was thrown when he was not given special consideration at court. "To have one's advice ignored and to be treated as an ordinary courtier though a close friend of those in high position make one confused, as if one has missed the road and lost one's companions; one is in a black mist, as if in deep night one has snuffed out the candle; stilling one's voice, one eats at one's spirit [i.e., hidden hatred]; abashed and silent one returns home."[80]

In distinct contrast was Yen Chih-t'ui's reaction to the effects of his friendship with the chancellor Tsu T'ing. In his autobiographical poem, Yen says:

Inserting the sable tails and cicada wings I went into the ranks,
Holding the umbrella and standard, I entered the echelons of functionaries.
Detained as a guest by the one chancellor who was an old friend,
I was congratulated as one whom the ruler of a myriad chariots knew.
I would only that the boon of an evening's talk not be thought of,
And rather that the treasuring of a hair brush be considered adequate presumption.[81]

In his commentary to these lines, Yen mentions that he was appointed Constant Attendant of the Cavaliers with Direct Access (*T'ung-chih san-chi ch'ang-shih*), from which position he was later transferred to the post of Attendant-worthy of the Secretariat (*Chung-shu shih-lang*), and he identifies his friend as Tsu T'ing, who will be discussed further below. The last lines refer to *Han-fei tzu*, which says that a man whom a chancellor detains in conversation will become wealthy, while even one whose comb is carried by the ruler is considered to be especially favored and becomes an important person.[82] Evidently Yen felt he was being honored too highly, and thus was too vulnerable, for, as he continued, "I was pierced by slanderous words more damaging than spears and battle-axes."

It is clear from the writings of the two men that they had quite different personalities. Yen Yen-chih seems to have been a volatile, brilliant, unconventional person, while Yen Chih-t'ui was sober and strongly self-disciplined. But further than this, we may see perhaps a difference in the two courts at which they served. The earlier Yen lived during the Southern Sung, as a distinguished scion of an eminent family. In the political scramble he suffered occasional eclipses, but his was a struggle among equals. Yen Chih-t'ui held office by virtue of his ability as an individual, in a court where the capriciousness of the Hsien-pei ruler was the norm, and instant execution the penalty of attracting too much unfavorable notice. Yen Yen-chih might storm at the slights of uncertain fortune, but Yen Chih-t'ui had to live with the constant possibility of eradication of his whole family. These conditions must have done much to shape Yen Chih-t'ui's attitudes.

Demonstrably, then, the norms for official conduct presented in the *Instructions* are derived from Confucian political thought, with certain interesting reservations. It is one's duty not only to serve as an official, but to do so capably and efficiently. One of the chief values of education was to provide the knowledge that enabled one to be such an official. The reader of the *Instructions* is urged to be sincere, loyal, and worthy, and to aid his ruler in any way he can. But at the same time, Yen places certain restrictions on official activity. One tries to hold a worthy office, but one's interests are confined to one's duties. As a functionary, one serves in the administration without bonds of loyalty to any one ruler or house that would prevent one from serving another, for this would be to place the principles of the individual above his duty to serve. Remonstrance is for the few officials close to the emperor, and Yen urged his descendants not to hold these high posts. Even a friend in high office can cause one much grief. We turn to an incident from Yen's life, in which we may see how these principles affected his behavior.

In November 573, a tense atmosphere prevailed in Yeh, the capital of the Northern Ch'i state, for the Ch'en state to the south had launched a campaign against the Northern Ch'i. Some twenty years before, when Hou Ching had rebelled against the Liang, troops of the Eastern Wei (the predecessor of the Northern Ch'i) had moved south and occupied the territory west from the coast and south of the Huai River, almost to the Yangtze itself. During some ten years of strife, Northern Ch'i had managed to maintain its grip on this area, and from 563 to 573 had enjoyed uncontested control. Now, however, the Ch'en armies were moving northward and thus far had been successful. The troops of Northern Ch'i had been dispatched to bring aid to Shou-yang, a key city on the northern bank of the Huai, and the issue had yet to be decided.[83] It was at this moment of crisis that the emperor, Kao Wei, decided to leave for Chin-yang, the alternate capital farther west, as was his annual custom. Some of the courtiers, understandably enough, felt this was an inappropriate moment to leave, since the people might assume the departure had been provoked by a military setback in the south and interpret the emperor's leaving as flight. A group at the court, acting apparently as responsible officials, petitioned the emperor to remain in the capital until the crisis passed. While the problem was being debated at the court, a Hsien-pei official, Han Feng, suggested to the emperor that the remonstrance was basely motivated and that the Chinese officials were planning to rebel. With little further investigation, those who had signed the petition were summoned, and six of the principals were decapitated, their families enslaved, and their estates confiscated. Two days later, the emperor left for Chin-yang.[84]

There are many aspects of this incident that remain unclear, not the least being the violence and cruelty of the reprisal, which does not seem at all consonant with the remonstration itself. Behind the whole affair we may glimpse the friction between the Chinese and the Hsien-pei at the court, and in consideration of this question, the figure of Tsu T'ing comes to the fore. Tsu T'ing[85] was a brilliant and versatile Chinese who, despite his blindness, had maneuvered himself by 572 into a controlling position in the government. But in trying to entrench himself, he had antagonized some of the Hsien-pei favorites of the emperor. Earlier in the year 573 he had been sent away in disgrace, and Han Feng, who is said to have despised the Chinese, sought to exterminate Tsu's clique. It was to this end, it is claimed, that he made his allegation of the Chinese officials' intention to rebel. In fact, of the six who were executed, only three can be connected to Tsu, and regarding two there is no information. The remaining one of the six was actually an opponent of Tsu.[86] Thus the reasons underlying the execution of this group were probably more complex than merely an attempt to purge Tsu's clique.[87]

Yen Chih-t'ui was a close friend of Tsu T'ing, and this relationship put him in a dangerous position, as it made him conspicuous at court. About the incident, his biography says:

Ts'ui Chi-shu and others were going to remonstrate, but Chih-t'ui became apprehensive and returned to his dwelling, thereby not joining in signing his name to the petition. When they summoned the remonstrators together Chih-t'ui was also brought in, but in the inquiry his name did not come up; thus he was able to avoid disaster.[88]

In his poem, Yen did not speak directly about his decision concerning the remonstrance, but he did say:

I heeded the advice of doubling one's furs to overcome cold,
And used the proverb about taking out the firewood so that the boiling would cease.

These are conventional phrases which signify that unwelcome attentions and criticisms can best be avoided by cautious and unprovocative behavior.[89] To these lines he added a note:

At the time the military officers [i.e., the Hsien-pei] detested the civilians [i.e., the Chinese]. Each time Chih-t'ui received some ceremonial treatment, it brought with it affliction. Thus, when the Attendant on the Center Ts'ui Chi-shu and others, six in all, were executed, Chih-t'ui on that day was implicated in the disaster, but he managed to avoid being included in this group.[90]

Plausible reasons for Yen's decision to avoid identification with the remonstrance are easy to find. The atmosphere at the court was rife with suspicion and resentment—particularly between the Hsien-pei and the Chinese—and instability was punctuated by violence. The dangers attendant on Yen's friendship with Tsu T'ing, now fallen from favor, were magnified by these conditions. It would seem obvious that caution lay behind Yen's decision, but to judge that his action stemmed solely from concern for his own person is an oversimplification. The incident of 573 was one of the experiences that had a part in molding his thinking and defining his attitudes.[91] We would suggest that, viewed in a larger context, Yen's behavior appears to have been consistent with the pattern advocated in the *Instructions,* and that equally important as determinants of his action were his intellectual commitments and his views on political responsibility.

Yen had emphasized that remonstrance was the duty of those very close to the emperor, who were in a position to influence policy. Yen was in relatively high office, but he was charged only with preparing the drafts of imperial orders, a duty described in some detail in his biography and his own notes to his poem.[92] The functionary, as Yen preferred to see himself, followed orders, for expression of one's own will leads to disorder within the state. Someone convinced of the value of his suggestions in formulating state policy, and holding in mind the traditional Confucian picture of the relations that should exist between the ruler and his ministers, might still be moved to action. But Yen's emphasis was on doing one's assigned duty, and he does not give much weight to the traditional view that one may change society by the example of one's own conduct.[93]

Finally, Yen was capable of fearless and forthright action. Only four years later, when Northern Ch'i was being overrun by the Chou armies, Yen stood forth to offer a plan to the emperor, and to assist in carrying it out when the other high ministers were surrendering or in flight. At least two factors were now different. Yen was now Attendant-worthy of the Yellow Portal (*Huang-men shih-lang*), one who was a "remonstrating and advising official . . . who was not to allow himself to shirk or steal ease." Second, the state was in serious danger. Thus, although the situation was extremely perilous, for Yen had to oppose the close cronies of the emperor and risk punishment from the Chou for continuing to resist, he took as his model the ancients who were willing to give their lives to preserve the state altars of grain and soil.

Yen Chih-t'ui's compartmental approach to the definition of official duty reflects the basic conflict in his attitude toward high office. Grounded in traditional Confucian theory, Yen averred that one was to remonstrate and to offer advice for the benefit of the state. But his own life

experiences—through the fall of his native Liang state and in the dangerous and uncertain politics of the Northern Ch'i court—led him to temper
this ideal with a proviso that in practice this duty applied to those very
close to the emperor. The result, as we have seen, was the glorification
of the bureaucratic functionary, effective and conscientious regarding
his assigned responsibilities but dissociated from policy making.

To achieve this balance between involvement and passivity required
self-discipline, a virtue highly valued by Yen Chih-t'ui. His own indulgent upbringing had induced his conviction that the fundamental
cause of his own faults in early life and of the tragic careers of the historic villains was failure to train the child in self-discipline.

In his *Instructions*, written for his own family, Yen had in mind the
education of the younger members of a family with a tradition of
learning and official service, belonging to the upper or "gentle" class.
To maintain this status he urged education also for the security it offered.
For the ideal pattern of behavior he looked to the Confucian canon,
but did not see in it the solution to society's ills. His view of the Classics
was strongly influenced by his faith in Buddhism and his belief in the
eventual perfection of society through that religion. For this reason,
he had little understanding of the traditional scholar who saw this perfection of society made possible by the Confucian canonical literature,
and little patience with their long commentaries on various aspects of
that message. To Yen, the Classics contained a distillation of the knowledge handed down by paragons and sages of the past. As such they
were of immense importance for training the young, both as "gentles"
and as officials. In the same way, the histories and other literature continued this past record of society, and were also worthy of attention.
Yen's own scholarly activities were devoted mainly to philology and
lexicography—to borrow his own metaphor, they were an attempt to
polish and perfect the rough spots of the literature.

Yen urged his descendants to be effective and conscientious as officials, and not to make sinecures of their posts. At the same time, he
advised them not to aspire to the highest posts, for these were sources
of danger to oneself and one's family. This had been the traditional
advice in the Yen family, handed down from the time of its founder,
Yen Han, in the early fourth century, but must have seemed even more
sensible in the dangerous and uncertain conditions of the Northern
Ch'i court.

Yen's idealization of the role of the bureaucrat must have been especially attractive to the large number of gentles whose fortunes were
dependent on their own talents and who would find little support elsewhere. There was the reinforcing argument that if the millennium were

to be a Buddhist one, rather than a Confucian one, what value was there in exposing oneself unnecessarily to the dangers inherent in attempting to create a perfect Confucian society by individual criticism of the emperor and state policies?

This attempt by a pluralistic approach to resolve the conflict produced in men who had a higher loyalty to Buddhism and yet had of necessity to be officials in a Confucian state involved a reordering of traditional values and attitudes. Whether Yen Chih-t'ui himself lived according to his teachings is difficult to determine, but the popularity of his *Instructions* would indicate that the compromise he developed proved relevant and appealing to many.

Hans H. Frankel

T'ANG LITERATI:
A COMPOSITE BIOGRAPHY

The T'ang period, 618–907, was one of the great ages of
Chinese literature. The volume of writing, both poetry and prose, was
unprecedented in a culture where the elite had long prided themselves
on their literary accomplishments. Poetry was written, chanted, and
appreciated by all literate classes of T'ang society, down to the lowliest
monks and courtesans, and an elegant prose style was deemed essential for all serious communications, public or private. Emperors, princes,
and high officials surrounded themselves with distinguished men of letters, and even hard-bitten generals employed literati to write their proclamations, reports to the throne, and other documents. Great writers
emerged who remain among the giants of Chinese literary history.
They wrought significant changes in the form and content of prose and
poetry. Literary skills were required for passing the examinations which
fed personnel into the vastly expanded bureaucracy. For all these reasons, the man of letters looms large in T'ang society and culture. Hence
it is only natural that a long section in the official history of the period
is devoted to the lives of one hundred and one selected writers.

It is with these biographies that my paper deals. In deviating from
the pattern of the other essays in this volume, each of which takes up
a single life, I conform to the conception of my Chinese sources, where
the literati are viewed not as individuals but as a group. I propose to
examine first of all the scope of this section of the official history, to
discuss the historians' criteria of inclusion and exclusion, their scale of
values, and related questions. Second, I shall take up the content of
these biographies under three headings, corresponding to the three
aspects of the lives in which the historiographers are interested: official careers, literary achievements, and character. In trying to discern
how the literary man lived and worked in T'ang times, we shall have
to slice through many layers of historiographical conventions. The resulting composite biography is bound to be fragmentary and distorted,
but it may nevertheless shed some light on the attitudes and behavior

patterns of the T'ang man of letters, and his role in the society of his time.

The section of the *Old History of the T'ang Dynasty* (completed in 945) that comprises the biographies of one hundred and one literati is entitled "Garden of Letters."[1] This "Garden of Letters" is one of the special biographical categories (sometimes called "classified biographies") that appear, in varying numbers, in all the Chinese dynastic histories. These special categories seem to be reserved for those who fall short of the Confucian ideal of a well-rounded gentleman—the biographies of the greatest men of the dynasty are always unclassified. Furthermore, the classifications follow each other on a descending scale which roughly reflects the value system of the historiographers. On this scale, the literati rank rather low in the *Old History of the T'ang Dynasty*: the only categories below them are technicians, recluses, exemplary women, barbarians, and rebels.

Thus the selection of writers included in the "Garden of Letters" is not based on literary criteria alone. To be sure, some of the best-known poets and prose writers are included—men like Ch'en Tzu-ang, Li Hua, Wang Wei, Li Po, Tu Fu, Li Shang-yin, Wen T'ing-yün, and Ssu-k'ung T'u. But one misses others of equal stature, such as Chang Yüeh, Han Yü, Po Chü-i, and Li Te-yü. The explanation has already been suggested above: the latter were prominent statesmen, whereas the "Garden of Letters" is reserved for those who were famous *only* as literati, and this, in the view of the Confucian historiographer, is a shortcoming. Though brilliant and successful as writers, they all failed to win top positions in government service. Nearly all of them, however, did serve in the bureaucracy.

With this restriction in mind, it might be supposed that the one hundred and one biographies give us a fairly representative sampling of bureaucrats who were active in literature from all parts of China throughout the three hundred years of T'ang rule. But this is not the case. The selection is uneven in both time and space. If we divide the T'ang epoch into six periods of approximately fifty years each, and assign each of the one hundred and one literati to the period in which all or most of his political and literary activities occurred, we get the following distribution:

Period I	(618–649):	13	Period IV	(756–805):	6
Period II	(649–705):	38	Period V	(805–859):	6
Period III	(705–756):	33	Period VI	(859–907):	5

That is to say, seventy-one of the one hundred and one literati were active between the mid-seventh and the mid-eighth century, during the reigns of Kao-tsung, the Empress Wu, Hsüan-tsung, and some brief interregna; only thirteen belong to the first two reigns (Kao-tsu and T'ai-tsung); and a mere seventeen are registered for the entire second half of T'ang, beginning with the An Lu-shan insurrection, which marks indeed a turning point in many respects. The irregular distribution in time is partly due to the fact that many literati are assigned by the historiographers to categories other than the "Garden of Letters."

The distribution in space is also uneven. If we list the home regions of the literati in terms of modern provinces and arrange them in the order of frequency, the regional picture looks like this:

Honan:	23	Shantung:	5
Hopei:	14	Hupeh:	5
Kiangsu:	12	Szechwan:	5
Chekiang:	12	Kansu:	2
Shensi:	11	Anhwei:	1
Shansi:	10	Home unknown:	1

Many parts of China are not represented at all—regions in which the cultural level was still low in T'ang times.

By rearranging the above table to form larger regional units, we obtain the following:

Northeast (Honan-Hopei-Shantung):	42
Southeast (Kiangsu-Chekiang-Anhwei):	25
Northwest (Shansi-Shensi-Kansu):	23
West-central (Hupeh-Szechwan):	10

I have found no correlation between temporal and spatial distribution, that is, the regional distribution does not change significantly in the course of the T'ang dynasty.

I will now consider the official careers of the literati. The first point of interest in a man's career is how it started. This is usually but not always indicated in our biographies. The most-traveled route to office was the examination system, especially after the system was revamped and strengthened in the reigns of Kao-tsung and the Empress Wu. (For the two preceding reigns, 618–49, our record contains not a single instance of an examination leading to a career.) Of the eighty-eight literati who flourished from the mid-seventh century to the end of T'ang, all except three had official careers. One half of these eighty-five men—namely, forty-three—entered their career through an examination, usually the *chin-shih* examination (thirty-two instances).

Another important aid in getting an appointment was recommendation by an influential patron. This is reported in twenty-one of the

ninety-six biographies that register an official T'ang career. Eight of
these twenty-one record both an examination (the *chin-shih* in seven
cases) and a patron. There were numerous other possible starts for a
career. Some of these are of sufficient interest to be cited here.

K'ung Shao-an, the first of the one hundred and one literati, had the
good fortune and foresight to befriend Li Yüan, the future founder of
T'ang, when the latter was a military commander under the preceding
dynasty, Sui, "punishing rebels" for the last Sui emperor. K'ung was
then a Provincial Censor (*chien-ch'a yü-shih*), and his assignment was
to check on the activities of Li Yüan. As soon as Li Yüan openly rebelled
against the Sui and set up his own dynasty, K'ung hastened to the
newly established T'ang court to demonstrate his loyalty to the new
regime. He was rewarded with the job of Director of Decrees in the
Imperial Secretariat (*nei-shih she-jen*) and with gifts of a house, two
fine horses, money, rice, silk, and cotton. (We may note in passing that
K'ung Shao-an was following a family tradition: his ancestors were
nearly always on the winning side in one power struggle after another
through four hundred of the most turbulent years in China's history.[2])
However, K'ung was surpassed by another man, Hsia-hou Tuan, who
had also formerly been a Provincial Censor "supervising" Li Yüan's
army. This man got to the T'ang court ahead of K'ung, and therefore
received a better job, Director of the Imperial Library (*mi-shu chien*).
K'ung expressed his chagrin in a manner befitting a man of letters: he
improvised a poem at an imperial banquet, when the emperor called
for poems on the theme "pomegranate." K'ung's contribution contained
the couplet:

> A late comer am I,
> My blossoms don't open in time for spring.[3]

(The pomegranate blooms later than other flowering trees in China.)

Not every man of letters had the opportunity to cultivate the friendship of a future emperor, but obviously many successful careers depended on knowing the right people. Recommendation and patronage have
already been mentioned. An interesting case of recommendation which
did not come off is that of Hsiao Ying-shih (717–68). When he received
the *chin-shih* degree in 735, he was familiar with the leading literati of
his time. That was why, according to his biography, Chief Minister Li
Lin-fu wanted to appoint him to a government office, and summoned
him to his official residence. At the interview Hsiao appeared dressed
in coarse hempen clothing (he was mourning his mother). Li was offended, and severely reprimanded him. Result: no recommendation,
no appointment, and enmity between the two men. Hsiao then wrote a

fu ridiculing Li, entitled "Fa ying-t'ao fu," parts of which are quoted in the biography.[4]

Just as French intellectuals gravitate to Paris, so the T'ang literati were for the most part anxious to be stationed at or near the imperial court. But it was usual for them to begin their official careers with a humble position in a provincial administration. As many as forty-five of our biographies mention a provincial post in the early part of the career. This seems to have been an established procedure. When Hsüeh Feng was recommended for the office of Director of Decrees in the second half of the ninth century, his enemy Liu Chuan objected, stating in a memorial that according to the system established in previous T'ang reigns, no one could become Director of Decrees in the Imperial Secretariat or the Imperial Chancellery who had not previously served in a provincial post. Hsüeh was consequently given a provincial appointment.[5]

But the initial provincial appointment did not necessarily cut the young writer off from the mainstream of cultural life. He often managed to be placed in a district near one of the imperial capitals or other metropolitan centers. In fact, our record does not contain a single case of the apprenticeship being served in a really remote province. Assignment to outlying areas does occur, as we shall see, as a punishment.

Some literati commenced their careers by serving in the court of an imperial prince as tutors, clerks, readers, librarians, or drafters of official documents. Fifteen such initial assignments are recorded in our biographies. They are a holdover from pre-T'ang times. Hence they are most common in the early period of T'ang rule, then gradually decrease, and cease altogether in the middle of the dynasty. Here are the details: In Period I (618–49), out of eleven literati who became T'ang officials, six started in a princely court; in Period II (649–705), seven out of thirty-seven; in Period III (707–56), two out of thirty-one; but none of the seventeen literati who lived in Periods IV–VI (756–907) began their careers that way.

An instructive example of a man of letters who got started on his career through princely patronage is Yüan Ch'eng-hsü. I quote from his biography:

During the Wu-te era (618–27), his reputation came to the notice of Li Yüan-chi, Prince of Ch'i, who summoned him to become a scholar in his court. Later the Prince's court was abolished. . . . When Kao-tsung was a prince and Emperor T'ai-tsung was selecting men of learning and character to be in his entourage, the emperor asked the Vice-President of the Imperial Secretariat, Ts'en Wen-pen: "Who among the renowned ministers of Liang and Ch'en may be cited as outstanding? And furthermore, are there any junior members of their families who may be summoned?" Wen-pen replied:

"When the Sui army invaded Ch'en, all the officials fled and scattered; none remained except Yüan Hsien, who stayed at his lord's side. When Wang Shih-ch'ung attempted to usurp the throne from the Sui, the regional officials petitioned him to proclaim himself emperor. But Yüan Hsien's son, the Director of Decrees of the Imperial Chancellery, Yüan Ch'eng-chia, pleaded illness and was the only one not to sign. These men, father and son, may well be called loyal and upright, and Yüan Ch'eng-chia's younger brother, Yüan Ch'eng-hsü, is a man of integrity and refinement. He is truly carrying on the family tradition." Consequently the emperor summoned him to become a Companion to the Prince of Chin and to be his Tutor, and also appointed him Scholar in the Academy for the Advancement of Letters.[6]

In the second half of the T'ang dynasty, and to a lesser extent before, the princes were replaced as patrons of the literati by powerful officials, civil and military. These officials surrounded themselves with scholars and writers for practical reasons as well as for prestige. For a talented young man, association with an influential person was often the only way to get ahead. But it always involved the risk of a sudden downfall if the patron should die or lose his position of power. "Guilt by association," an uncomfortably familiar concept in present-day America, was a common offense in T'ang China. It was the most frequent reason for inflicting demotion, exile, imprisonment, death, or some other form of punishment on the literati. Out of forty-two literati for whom punishment is recorded, twenty-six were charged with "having formerly befriended" some powerful personage who had suddenly become a criminal. Six of them fell when Chang I-chih and his brother Chang Ch'angtsung, former favorites of the Empress Wu, were executed in 705; the two brothers had brought many literati into the government. Fourteen were found guilty of some personal crime other than association (including two who were charged with association in addition to a crime of their own), and four were punished for unspecified crimes.

Wang Wu-ching was one of those who were disgraced and exiled (in his case to Ling-piao, in the extreme south) when Chang I-chih and his clique were executed, "because of his former association" with that group.[7] But in this and many other instances, it is difficult to determine whether the former association was the real reason for the man's downfall or merely a welcome excuse. Wang had been in trouble before. Once, when serving as Palace Censor, he had pointed out in open court that two Chief Ministers were violating court etiquette by leaving their places and chatting. The two Ministers did not take kindly to this criticism, and arranged for his speedy transfer from the Imperial Palace to the Palace of the Heir Apparent.[8]

"Association" is a cardinal feature in the biographies—not only as a criminal offense. We read much about who was associated with whom, and in what pursuit. Patronage, friendship, collaboration, and political cliques were very real phenomena in the lives of the literati. To seek out these associations was also an important concern of the historiographers. One of their tasks, as they saw it, was to fit each man into the proper groups, affiliations, classifications, and categories. They did this on a large scale when they made their selections for the "Garden of Letters." This category is in turn broken down into a number of special groups, some of which overlap. The subtle process of grouping within the chapter becomes partly visible in the peculiar phenomenon of the "attached" biographies. To be sure, in many cases this means simply grouping together various members of one family, a well-established practice in the dynastic histories. (An example of this use of the device is the first biography in the "Garden of Letters," the biography of K'ung Shao-an: attached to his life are brief notices of his father Huan, his elder brother Shao-hsin, his son Chen, Chen's son Chi-hsü, and another grandson of Shao-an, named Jo-ssu; only one of these—brother Shao-hsin—is presented as a man of letters in his own right.) But "attachment" was also used traditionally for grouping together men who were felt to belong together for reasons other than family ties.

Thus to the biography of Yüan Wan-ch'ing are attached those of four of his colleagues. The five were brought together by the Empress Wu in the late seventh century, and became known in their own time as "The Scholars of the Northern Gate" (*Pei-men hsüeh-shih*).[9] This appellation shows that the grouping was already an accomplished fact when the biographers went to work. Another group with a fixed name were "The Three Eminent Men of the Northern Capital" (*Pei-ching san chieh*). Two of these, Fu Chia-mo and Wu Shao-wei, were friends and colleagues. The third one, Ku I, is linked to them simply because he served in the same region (T'ai-yüan, the Northern Capital) at the same time (around 700), and because he was equally famous as a writer.[10]

The same lack of homogeneity is evident in the group of six contemporary writers attached to Ho Chih-chang (659–744). Five of them were, like Ho, from the area of modern Chekiang, but the sixth one, Li Ch'eng-chih, was from what is now Honan, and I have discovered no reason for his inclusion in the group.[11]

Another rather incongruous series of lives is appended to the biography of Li Hua: first, there is his friend and classmate Hsiao Ying-shih (both took the *chin-shih* degree in 735); then comes Li Hua's nephew Li Han, who was himself a writer of some note; next, there is Li Hua's friend Lu Chü; next, there are three other writers of the same period— Ts'ui Hao, Wang Ch'ang-ling, and Meng Hao-jan—who "acquired fame but no high official rank." The last biography in the group is that of Yüan Te-hsiu, another friend of Li Hua's.[12]

Association, then, is a cardinal but loosely used concept in the structuring of the biographies. Another key concept is "precedent." The biographer takes pains to record actions and events that started new procedures or served as models for later generations. He is interested in such precedents regardless of whether they affect the life of the individual. For example, the highest state examinations were held only in one place, the Western Capital (Ch'ang-an), down to 764. In that year, one of our literati, Chia Chih, proposed that they be held in the Eastern Capital (Lo-yang) as well, and his proposal was adopted. "This practice," says the biographer, "was initiated at that time."[13] He does not comment on this institutional change, which strengthened and expanded the examination system and made possible a greater influx of literati, particularly from northeastern China, into the bureaucracy. It is significant that Chia Chih, who proposed this innovation, was himself one of the northeastern literati; his family home was in Lo-yang.

In the biography of Kuo Cheng-i it is stated that when he was appointed Honorary Vice-President of the Imperial Secretariat in 681, he thereby became Minister Ranking with the Chief Officers of the Imperial Secretariat and the Imperial Chancellery (*t'ung chung-shu menhsia p'ing-chang-shih*, often abbreviated *p'ing-chang-shih*), and that "the title *p'ing-chang-shih* as an appellation for Chief Ministers [*tsaihsiang*] was first applied to Cheng-i and his colleagues."[14] Here it is clear that the historiographer is more interested in the change in bureaucratic nomenclature than in the man who was graced with a new title.

In the case of Chang Yün-ku, the manner of the subject's death leads to the establishment of a precedent. Chang was one of Emperor T'ai-tsung's favorites, but he was accused of mishandling a judicial case and executed by T'ai-tsung's order in 631. Then the emperor regretted his hasty decision and instituted a new procedure, providing that every death sentence was to be reviewed five times before it could be carried out. "This procedure," states the historian, "originated with the case of Chang Yün-ku."[15]

We turn now from the official careers of the literati to their literary activities. The biographies reveal a stereotyped image which the tenth-century historiographers had formed of the art of letters and of those who practiced it. The man of letters, as seen by them, was likely to be precocious, profoundly learned, endowed with a prodigious memory, and able to write at incredible speed. He tended to be haughty, and hence to offend his colleagues and superiors.

Precociousness will be discussed below in a different context. The association of book learning with literary excellence is entirely in keeping with the Confucian tradition. The stereotyped feature of a photo-

graphic memory—a natural corollary of the erudition prerequisite to
literary composition—is repeatedly illustrated by graphic detail, which
arouses our suspicions.[16]

Of Chang Yün-ku, for example, it is said that "he was able to recite
stone inscriptions from memory, and to reconstitute the arrangement of
a chessboard."[17] The same *topos* of memorizing stone inscriptions occurs also in the biography of Hsiao Ying-shih (717–68): "Once he went
on an excursion to the Dragon Gate, south of Lo-yang, together with
Li Hua and Lu Chü. The three of them read old stone inscriptions by
the roadside. Hsiao Ying-shih could recite each one after reading it
once; Li Hua had to read them twice before he could remember them;
and Lu Chü thrice. Critics ranked the three men's intellectual stature
in the same order."[18] This ranking of literati according to their intellectual and artistic abilities is one of the biographers' preoccupations.

Speed of literary composition is another *topos*. It crops up in eleven
of the biographies, and also in the Introduction to the "Garden of Letters." It reflects, on the one hand, an actual phenomenon of literary
craftsmanship in T'ang times. There were many occasions in the lives
of the literati that called for improvisation and swiftness in writing:
literary games and contests, public and private parties and celebrations,
imperial commands and state examinations. The stock phrase *hsia pi
ch'eng chang* ("as soon as the brush touches the paper, a composition is
finished"), already common in earlier dynastic histories, occurs frequently in our biographies. It even became institutionalized in T'ang
times as the name of a state examination.

On the other hand, the *topos* of speedy composition reflects a blurred
concept of the art of writing in the layman's mind. The work of a
creative genius appears to the outsider to be accomplished effortlessly
and instantaneously.

The historiographer reveals himself to be an outsider when faced
with the phenomenon of purely literary composition. One may even
detect a trace of hostility in his attitude toward the man of letters. This
is reflected in the frequent references to literary pride—another *topos*.

A typical anecdote brings together two poets of the early seventh
century, Cheng Shih-i and Ts'ui Hsin-ming. I quote from the biography
of Cheng Shih-i (whom the historian labels "frivolous"):

At that time, Ts'ui Hsin-ming considered his own writings to be nonpareil.
. . . Cheng Shih-i once met him traveling on a river and said to him: "I have
heard of your line, 'Maple leaves fall on the Wu River, cold.'" Ts'ui Hsin-
ming, delighted, showed him more than a hundred of his poems. Cheng
Shih-i looked at them, and without finishing his perusal, he said: "What I
have seen is not as good as what I had heard." With these words he tossed
them into the river. Ts'ui Hsin-ming was speechless, and rowed away.[19]

The haughtiness of the T'ang poets may have been exaggerated by their unsympathetic biographers, but it was certainly a real phenomenon, and not restricted to T'ang China. One of our contemporary English poets has said:

It is evident that a faith in their vocation, mystical in intensity, sustains poets. . . . Although it is true that poets are vain and ambitious, their vanity and ambition is of the purest kind attainable in this world, for the saint renounces ambition. They are ambitious to be accepted for what they ultimately are as revealed by their inmost experiences, their finest perceptions, their deepest feelings, their uttermost sense of truth, in their poetry.[20]

Hart Crane used to hand a sheet or two fresh off the typewriter to his friends at Sunday afternoon parties, and he would say: "Read that! Isn't that the grrreatest poem ever written!"[21]

The biographies are concerned not only with literary men's attitudes toward creativity but also with the sources of their inspiration. Hu Ch'u-pin (fl. second half of seventh century, died before 689) is stated to have needed alcohol in order to write,[22] and the drinking of wine is also mentioned in four other biographies.[23] The association of wine with literary creation was a well-established tradition in the T'ang period. It can be traced back to the time when the literati as a class achieved their prominent position in Chinese society, namely, the end of Later Han.[24] But the compilers of the *Old History of the T'ang Dynasty* were actually less interested in wine as inspiration for writers than in its effect on a man's official career. In the biography of Hu Ch'u-pin, they note that his intoxication never caused him to betray state secrets. And leaking official secrets, as we shall see, is an offense charged to several other literati. Of Ts'ui Hsien (*chin-shih* of 807, d. 834), they report that as a provincial administrator, he drank with his friends all day, then did excellent work on official documents all night, which caused his subordinates to admire him as a "divine being" (*shen jen*).[25]

Another source of inspiration for writing—music—is mentioned in the biography of Li Han: "During the T'ien-pao era [742–56] he lived in Yang-ti. He perfected his writings with the utmost care, and his ideas formed slowly. He often requested musicians from the magistrate of Yang-ti district, Huang-fu Tseng. Whenever the flow of his ideas dried up, he had music played until his mind was at ease; then he proceeded to write."[26]

Finally, the specific occasion that led to the writing of a work of poetry or prose is frequently told, and in some cases, the work itself is quoted wholly or in part—a well-established feature in the biographies of the dynastic histories. But the compilers of the *Old History of the T'ang Dynasty* depart from earlier tradition by quoting only works they consider "useful," never those that are merely "beautiful." They thus carry out a policy credited to Emperor T'ai-tsung, under whose personal direction historiography was thoroughly reorganized and systematized as a state institution. The *Chen-kuan cheng-yao* by Wu Ching (670–749) sets forth T'ai-tsung's viewpoint as follows:

In the early part of the Chen-kuan era [627–50], T'ai-tsung said to Fang Hsüan-ling, who was in charge of compiling the history of the reigning dynasty: "Reading the Histories of Former and Later Han, We find that they quote Yang Hsiung's 'Fu on the Sacrifice to Heaven at the Palace of the Sweet Springs' and his 'Fu on the Emperor's Hunt with the Yü-lin Guards'; Ssu-ma Hsiang-ju's 'Fu of Tzu-hsü' and his 'Fu on the Imperial Hunting Park'; and Pan Ku's 'Fu on the Two Capitals.' Since these works are written in frothy and flowery style, they are of no use as exhortations and admonitions; why should they be incorporated in books of history? But memorials to the throne and discussions of affairs with trenchant and straight wording and ideas, capable of benefiting the art of government—all such works should be included in the history of this dynasty, regardless of whether We have followed them or not."[27]

In accordance with this policy, we find a total of twenty-four works quoted in whole or in part in twenty-two of the one hundred and one biographies. The reasons for quoting these works are in some cases quite obvious, in others less so. As I see it, every quotation meets one or more of three qualifications: (1) it develops a concept dear to the historiographer's heart; (2) it criticizes a person or group disliked by the historiographer; (3) it illustrates the talent or character of the subject of the biography.

The first qualification is met by most of the quoted memorials and other communications addressed to emperors and heirs apparent. Though they are usually concerned with a specific problem which was acute at the moment, the historiographer must have felt that they all possessed a "timeless" value which warranted their inclusion in the dynastic history, for the indoctrination and edification of future generations.

Four of these quoted documents follow an established Confucian tradition in setting before incoming and future emperors the image of a perfect ruler. In one of these, Liu Hsien (d. 711 or 712) urges the Heir Apparent—later the Emperor Hsüan-tsung—to cultivate Confucian virtues rather than gratify sensual desires; he emphasizes the value of the Confucian Classics as models of style, and warns against flowery elegance. The biographer adds that Hsüan-tsung was pleased with the memorial and rewarded its author.[28]

Another memorial to the same Hsüan-tsung as Heir Apparent deals with a more specific situation: Chia Tseng (d. 727) opposes the employment of singing girls in the Heir Apparent's palace. (Hsüan-tsung's interest in music and musicians is a historic fact.) The Prince's reply, acceding to Chia Tseng's request, is also quoted.[29] It is noteworthy that, T'ai-tsung's opinion notwithstanding, the requests embodied in the quoted memorials were in most cases granted. In other words, the historiographer preferably cites documents that positively affected decisions and thus made history.

Some of the memorials in the "Garden of Letters" deal with state ceremonies and Confucian ritual. Ho Chih-chang outlines the procedure to be followed in the imperial sacrifice at Mount T'ai in 725.[30] Yang Chiung during the I-feng era (676–79) argued at length—and successfully—against a proposed change in the official robe patterns.[31] When Emperor Kao-tsung died in Lo-yang, the Eastern Capital, in 683, Ch'en Tzu-ang presented convincing arguments for proceeding with his burial right there, rather than at the Western Capital.[32] This is historically important in connection with the Empress Wu's shift of the capital from Ch'ang-an to Lo-yang, and the concomitant loss of power of the northwestern aristocracy centered around Ch'ang-an. In the early part of the K'ai-yüan era (713–42), a memorial by Hsü Ching-hsien succeeded in reducing the lavish awards to officials who did well in archery contests.[33]

The three last-mentioned memorials all stress the Confucian idea of economy in government expenditures. Others concern filial piety and ancestor worship: Sun T'i complained in 736 that his father was merely a District Magistrate (*hsien ling*), while he himself was already a Director of Decrees in the Imperial Secretariat (*chung-shu she-jen*). This demonstration of filiality got his father a promotion.[34] Hsü Ch'i-tan (630–72) pointed out in a memorial that it was unfair to degrade a man's ancestral shrine to atone for crimes committed by his descendants. He, too, carried his point.[35]

In the category of criticism of persons and groups disliked by the historiographers, there is Hsiao Ying-shih's *fu* satirizing Li Lin-fu (see above), and a long diatribe against the eunuchs, written by Liu Fen in 828 in response to an examination question set by the emperor himself.[36]

The third criterion for quoting from a man's works is mentioned specifically in several instances, and is perhaps applicable to other quotations as well: the passages are stated to represent the man's "special talent" (*ts'ai*), or some trait of his character, good or bad. For example, a statement presented to the throne by Kuo Cheng-i in 678, during a Tibetan invasion, advocating a more defensive military policy vis-à-vis Tibet, is quoted with evident approval and asserted to be typical of Kuo Cheng-i's "talent" (*ts'ai*).[37] On the other hand, Ssu-k'ung

T'u's (837–908) "Essay on the Hsiu-hsiu Pavilion" is quoted as "typical of his perverseness and swaggering pride."[38]

As far as references to literary style in the biographies are concerned, the historiographers show interest in matters of priority, imitation, innovation, and precedents. (We noted above a similar interest in precedents in connection with official careers.) The just-mentioned essay by Ssu-k'ung T'u is stated to be an imitation of Po Chü-i's "Tsui-yin chuan." Stylistic innovations are credited to Fu Chia-mo and his friend and colleague Wu Shao-wei (both fl. around 700). They created a new style, says their biographer, for stele inscriptions and eulogies. Based on the Confucian Classics, it became known as the "Fu-Wu style."[39] (A modern literary historian agrees that Fu's and Wu's prose writings mark a significant step in the development of the *ku-wen* movement.[40]) Li Shang-yin (812?–58?) began to write in "modern style" under the influence of his patron Ling-hu Ch'u.[41]

While the historiographers make occasional references of this sort to literary styles, they pay more attention to the *practical* aspects of literature. They tell us how the literati made use of their literary abilities in their workaday lives. Many of them found employment as tutors, secretaries, clerks, editors, librarians, propagandists, and the like, in government bureaus and private establishments. Some became ghost writers for highly placed officials: under the reign of the Empress Wu, Yen Chao-yin and Sung Chih-wen "secretly" wrote many of the pieces published under the names of the empress's favorite Chang I-chih and his associates.[42]

Li Shang-yin was in charge of composing documents at the headquarters of General Wang Mao-yüan. The General "admired his talent and married off his daughter to him." "Wang Mao-yüan," the biography goes on to explain, "though literate and trained in Confucian learning, came from a family of military men."[43]

Li Yung (678?–747) managed to amass a fortune by writing on commission. He ground out hundreds of obituaries, eulogies, and other prose pieces for private individuals, and for Buddhist and Taoist temples. The historiographer does not approve of such commercialism. He cites the opinion of "critics at the time" who held that "from antiquity down, no one had ever gone as far as Li Yung in selling his writings to acquire wealth."[44] In the style of these biographies, the historian often bestows praise and condemnation indirectly, through unnamed "critics at the time," and occasionally by citing the opinion of a prominent individual.

An understanding of the subtleties of literature was frequently a practical asset. For instance, during the campaign against Koguryö in

667, the commander of the Chinese garrison at Pyongyang wished to inform his commander in chief, Li Chi, that he was short of men and supplies. To keep this information from the enemy, he coded the message in the form of a *li-ho shih*—a poem in which one has to split the characters and recombine the elements in order to get the hidden meaning. When General Li Chi received the poem, he exclaimed: "What's the use of writing poetry in a military emergency like this? That man should be beheaded!" The situation was saved by one of our literati, Yüan Wan-ch'ing, who was on Li Chi's staff. He deciphered the code message, and reinforcements and supplies were dispatched at once to the Chinese garrison.[45] Though the historiographer does not say so explicitly, he is obviously delighted to expose the dullness of the military mind. (Compare the remark about General Wang Mao-yüan above.)

But during the same Korean campaign, Yüan Wan-ch'ing got into trouble through an indiscretion in the application of his literary skills. Li Chi ordered him to write the official proclamation of war. In the proclamation, Yüan included the phrase: "Koguryö does not know how to defend the strategic Yalu." This tipped off the enemy commander: he promptly stationed troops at the Yalu River fords, and the Chinese forces were unable to cross. For this mistake, Yüan was exiled to the extreme south—but he was amnestied soon thereafter.[46]

A critical situation which arose at a solemn court function in the last decade of the seventh century was retrieved through the literary skill of Wang Chü. Five imperial princes were being installed in their fiefs, and when the ceremony was already under way it was discovered, to everyone's dismay, that the documents of investiture had not been brought along. Then Wang Chü improvised the five complicated documents on the spot, dictating them to five scribes simultaneously, and the ceremony went on as planned.[47] (Again the *topos* of instantaneous composition.)

Another writer whose literary skills impressed the historiographers was Li Chü-ch'uan (d. 898). "Since the empire was then very unsettled, with people wandering hither and thither, eager for salary and position, he served various highly placed men as a writer in different parts of the country. . . . Li Chü-ch'uan's style and ideas were clever and swift, his brush sped as if it were flying, it spread to the far borders and left nothing unmoved." When he served on the staff of the warlord Wang Ch'ung-jung, "it was due to Li Chü-ch'uan's assistance that Wang Ch'ung-jung repeatedly acquired merit." Later Wang Ch'ung-jung was killed by his subordinates, and Li "was found guilty by the court councillors of having served" Wang. Consequently he was sent to an obscure provincial post. There he met another warlord and former acquaintance,

Yang Shou-liang, who exclaimed: " 'Heaven has bequeathed Secretary Li to me!' " In Yang's service, Li together with his master was captured by an opposing military commander, Han Chien. But while Yang was killed by his captor, Li wrote a poem which so moved Han Chien that he released him and later put him on his own staff. On another occasion, when the emperor took up his temporary abode in the region governed by Han Chien, the latter found the local resources insufficient to support this added burden.

He therefore commissioned Li Chü-ch'uan to write an urgent appeal which was sent to all parts of the empire, asking for help in supplying provisions for the royal household and setting up the imperial residence. The appeal went out in all four directions, and in response supplies poured in. When Li Chü-ch'uan put ink on paper and set forth his arguments, both form and reasoning were perfect. Emperor Chao-tsung esteemed him profoundly. At that time Li Chü-ch'uan's fame spread all over the empire. When Chao-tsung returned to the capital, he gave him a special appointment as Imperial Adviser. He concurrently continued in his post as assistant to Han Chien.

As Li Chü-ch'uan had lived by the power of his brush, so he died by it, according to the biography. When the mighty warlord Chu Ch'üan-chung was preparing to make himself independent (he did overthrow the T'ang dynasty nine years later), he consulted Li about his plans. Li presented him with a statement, setting forth both the advantages and the disadvantages of Chu's plan. Chu Ch'üan-chung was displeased. On top of this, another man of letters in Chu's service was jealous of Li and pointed out to Chu: " 'Imperial Adviser Li's statement is sincerely and beautifully written, but it does not redound to my master's advantage.' On that day," concludes the biography, "Li Chü-ch'uan was killed by order of Chu Ch'üan-chung."⁴⁸

As we turn now to the third aspect of the biographies—character and personality—we find several key concepts emerging. One of these is the orthodox Confucian association of intellectual and moral qualities. For example, we saw above that Yüan Ch'eng-hsü was selected by Emperor T'ai-tsung as one of several "men of learning and character" to serve in the entourage of the Heir Apparent, and that he was said to have inherited these sterling qualities from his ancestors. The theory of inherited qualities accounts in part for the habit of listing ancestors, with official titles, near the beginning of many biographies. Another reason is the need to establish a man's family background and his aristocratic lineage, if any. An interesting case of inherited characteristics is described in the biography of Sung Ling-wen (fl. second half of seventh century): he was a strong man, a fine calligrapher, and a good writer; and each of his three sons inherited one of his three distinctions.[49]

Another key phenomenon is the biographers' failure to conceive a human life in dynamic terms of growth and development. Rather, they think of personality, career, and the capacity to achieve (in literature or any other field) as more or less fixed from the very beginning. This view is evident, for example, in the biography of Ts'ui Hsin-ming (b. in 580's, d. after 632):

Ts'ui Hsin-ming was born exactly at noon on the fifth day of the fifth month. At that time, several unusual birds with extremely small, five-colored bodies gathered on a tree in the courtyard, drummed their wings in unison, and chirped beautifully. The Director of the Imperial Observatory of Sui, Shih Liang-shih, had just come to Ch'ing Prefecture and happened to be present. He interpreted the omens as follows: "The fifth month is fire; fire is brightness; brightness is literary splendor. The exact hour of noon means the acme of literary perfection. Then there are birds of five colors, beating their wings and chirping. This boy will surely become a brilliant writer whose fame will spread over the entire world. Since the birds are small, his salary and rank will probably not be high." As he grew up, his learning was broad, and his memory keen. As soon as his brush touched paper, a composition was finished [hsia pi ch'eng chang]. Kao Hsiao-chi, who lived in the same rural area, had a knack for appraising character. He often told people: "Ts'ui Hsin-ming's talent and learning are rich and vigorous. Though his fame will be unsurpassed in his time, his rank will unfortunately not be exalted."[50]

A brilliant writer with low official rank—this formula fits practically all the literati in this chapter. We note in this passage four of the *topoi* encountered previously: spreading fame, broad learning, keen memory, and instantaneous creation.

This is the only reference to birth in the biographies. And it is mentioned here, not because the historian is interested in the event itself (he does not even state the year of birth) but because it reveals the pattern for the whole life. The pattern is not visible to ordinary mortals, but open to interpretation by experts. There are altogether nine predictions that were later fulfilled in the "Garden of Letters."

The concept of the fixed pattern also accounts, I believe, for the frequent references to youth. A man's early life is viewed not as a stage in his development but as the period when his personality type first becomes apparent. Thirty-three of the biographies mention traits manifested in youth, often in stereotyped terms. The statement that a man early in his life "was good at writing" (*shan shu wen*) occurs eight times in these same words, and ten more times in different words. In three biographies we are told that the boy could write well at a specified young age (six, eight, and nine *sui* respectively). The phrase "broadly learned" (*po hsüeh*) is applied to four young literati, and of three others it is said in different words that they studied hard in their youth. Five men of letters are asserted to have won early fame through writing, and five others through unspecified achievements (which are also likely to be literary in the context of the "Garden of Letters").

Should some of these allegations of precocious literary ability be discounted as exaggerations? This is hard to determine. We should note the historic fact that two of our literati, Yang Chiung (b. 650, d. between 692 and 705) and Wu T'ung-hsüan (fl. 779–94), actually passed the state examination for "divine youths" (*shen-t'ung*).[51]

Besides literary skill and book learning, there are other traits—good and bad—which may be manifested in a man's early life. Of Yüan Te-hsiu (696–754) it is said that "in his youth he was renowned for his filial piety,"[52] and the same formula is applied to Wang Chung-shu (762–823).[53] The biography of Wang Han (fl. first half of eighth century) states that "in his youth he was unconventional and unrestrained." In the course of the same biography, we learn that he was fond of horses, singing girls, hunting, drinking, and wild parties.[54] All these are vices charged to many other literati. It is apparent that the historiographer is not interested in a man's early life as such but in bringing to light early manifestations of his innate character.

The concept of the fixed pattern does not rule out the possibility of changes of character. In the biography of T'ang Fu (*chin-shih* of 810, d. 839 or 840) it is pointed out that in the first part of his life he was a good official and an upright man, but in the last years of his life, when he held powerful and lucrative positions on the southeastern coast (modern Fukien), he became greedy and corrupt. This came to light, notes the biographer, after his death, when his servants and concubines fought over his property, which was found to amount to 100,000 strings of cash.[55]

Ch'i Huan (d. between 746 and 756) is portrayed as a strange mixture of good and bad qualities. As Provincial Censor (*chien-ch'a yü-shih*) "he prosecuted those who had committed wrongs, but first tried to sway them from their evil ways. His contemporaries considered this to be a praiseworthy way of discharging the duties of that office." (Indirect praise, attributed to "contemporaries," as noted above.) Again, as prefect of Pien prefecture, "he governed with integrity and strictness; the people and his subordinates sang his praises." In another of his many provincial assignments, he improved transportation and increased revenue by altering river courses. In further attempts to repair waterways he failed. Once he was demoted for a mistake committed by many literati: he indiscreetly reported a private conversation with the emperor to another official. Later he was found guilty of embezzling goods, in collusion with eunuchs. He also maltreated one of his concubines. Yet such affairs are never mentioned unless it be to demonstrate a trait in the man's character, or to furnish the clue to an event in his career.

So far, Ch'i Huan looks like T'ang Fu: an inconstant type who changed from good to bad. But the end of the biography presents him in a different light: in the 740's Ch'i Huan was punished repeatedly, having incurred the enmity of Li Lin-fu, the dictatorial Chief Minister who got a bad press in the official histories. After Ch'i Huan died, "when Su-tsung ascended the throne, he was rehabilitated as one of those who had been entrapped by Li Lin-fu, and posthumously honored."[56] This concludes the biography. The historiographer apparently concurs in the final and official rehabilitation, which may or may not be intended to cancel the previously noted defects in the man's character.

Several other biographies are less ambiguous. They clearly depict their subjects as mixtures of good and evil. Ts'ui Hao (d. 754), for instance, "had superior talents but lacked the behavior of a gentleman. He was addicted to gambling and drinking. When he was in the capital, he would marry a girl for her beauty, and then abandon her as soon as he was even slightly displeased with her. Altogether he was married four times."[57]

Li Yung (678?–747) is praised repeatedly in his biography as a literary genius of early and steadily increasing fame. Some of his writings, says the biographer, "are highly esteemed by men of letters." He got his first (?) official appointment—as Imperial Adviser of the Left —through the recommendation of two high functionaries, Li Ch'iao and Chang T'ing-kuei. Their recommendation stated that "his writings are lofty and his behavior straight: he is fit to become an admonishing and warning official." One of his memorials, successfully opposing the appointment of a heterodox wizard, Cheng P'u-ssu, as Director of the Imperial Library, is quoted at length—a sign of approval. The same biography characterizes him as "boastful" and "gay and extravagant," and notes that "he freely engaged in wild hunting." He is furthermore criticized, as already mentioned, for amassing wealth by writing on commission.[58]

The rationale behind the mixture of good and evil is, if I am not mistaken, a key concept in the historiographers' over-all view of the literati: they are imperfect because they fail to achieve the dual Confucian ideal of self-cultivation and distinguished public service. Had they been equally successful in both pursuits, they would not have been relegated to the "Garden of Letters."

In one of the biographies, this view is neatly summed up by P'ei

Hsing-chien, who is credited, like Ts'ui Hsin-ming's neighbor, with "a knack for appraising character." Speaking of the four famous literati Wang P'o, Yang Chiung, Lu Chao-lin, and Lo Pin-wang (they flourished in the second half of the seventh century), P'ei said: "Whether a gentleman goes far depends primarily on his ability and knowledge, and only secondarily on his literary skill. Although P'o and the other three possess literary talent, they are unsteady and shallow. Surely they are not made of the stuff required for achieving high rank. . . . "[59]

In epitome, what is the composite picture of the T'ang literary man emerging from these one hundred and one biographies? He was usually a bureaucrat, but rarely rose to the top. He entered his career through the civil service examination system, or through the recommendation of a patron, or both. Much of his life and work was influenced by his associations with relatives, friends, colleagues, superiors, and subordinates. His fate was closely linked to the rise and fall of his present or former patrons. His innate talent as a writer became manifest early in his life. He was precocious, bookish, learned, and endowed with a prodigious memory. He could produce poetry and prose at fantastic speed when the occasion demanded it. He was inordinately proud of his literary achievements. He tended to seek inspiration for his work in wine, music, horses, singing girls, and other pursuits unworthy of a Confucian gentleman. He was often indiscreet in divulging confidential information. Nevertheless, imperial and princely courts, high officials, and military commanders sought his company and found his services indispensable.

This was fortunate for posterity, for it made possible the creation of literary masterpieces that have endured to this day.

Denis Twitchett

LU CHIH (754–805):
IMPERIAL ADVISER AND
COURT OFFICIAL

Lu Chih is comparatively little known in the West. Although some of his writings were translated in Du Halde's *Description de la Chine* in 1735,[1] the only extensive translation from his voluminous writings is that by Balázs of his longest and most famous memorial on finance.[2] More recently Pulleyblank has dealt briefly with him in a discussion of the intellectual scene at the end of the eighth century.[3] In China he came to be highly esteemed by historians as a stylist and as a Confucian worthy, and under the Manchus was eventually included in the rites in the state Confucian temple, but very little has been written about him in recent times. Most scholars would probably agree with Balázs that "his work was more important than his life."

I find it difficult to accept this judgment, especially in view of the fact that the entire corpus of his surviving work consists of state documents and memorials written in the course of his duties as an official. Ssu-ma Kuang, in dealing with the decade 784–94 in his *Tzu-chih t'ung-chien,* quoted from no fewer than thirty documents by Lu Chih, which alone would seem to prove that during this period Lu Chih was at the center of affairs and exercised considerable power.

Lu Chih has also been tentatively put forward as representative of the more conservative type of Confucian scholar, in contrast with such men as Tu Yu and Liu Tsung-yüan, who were involved in the contemporary ferment of new political and intellectual developments.[4] There is a certain amount of truth in this view. But Lu Chih was not—as far as we know, and we shall see the sources are very defective—primarily an intellectual concerned with abstract ideas and principles. That he was a lucid thinker and a sound and widely read classical scholar is proved by his writings. His extant writings are, however, all official documents, an unlikely place for the expression of any really original thought.

In the following study I treat Lu Chih in the terms in which he was seen by his contemporaries, the professional civil servant par excellence and the practical statesman called upon to give and formulate orders on specific problems. Lu Chih's memorials were, of necessity, couched in conventional Confucian terms with a profusion of classical precedent drawn from a wide range of authors. But where for many T'ang officials such quotations became little more than conventional embellishment, Lu Chih applied his learning with remarkable appositeness, and, although his memorials are often long and complex, very little in them is simply verbiage. The policies advocated were always practical and to the point.

By no means a routine figure in his civil role, Lu Chih is of major historical interest as the first of the personal advisers to the emperor from the Han-lin Academy—a group which came in late T'ang times to rival the influence of the Chief Ministers of the Outer Court. This development of a sort of unofficial "inner cabinet" was the first of a series of changes that gradually robbed the Chief Ministers—and by extension the bureaucratic body—of their influence and led to the growth of imperial autocratic power under the Sung. By the time Lu Chih was thirty he wielded such influence with the emperor that he was already spoken of as the latter's "unofficial Chief Minister" and as a future Chief Minister. At forty he held the highest office and was at the peak of a notably precocious career. But the more formal atmosphere of politics in open court dictated more conventional procedures, and personal friction arose between himself and the emperor. The following year he was driven into banishment, and he remained there for the rest of his life.

His career was notable not only for his spectacular rise and fall but also for his strategic importance in a critical period. During the ten years he was a power in politics at the capital, the T'ang faced a very serious domestic crisis. Lu Chih wrote voluminously about all the major issues of his time: finance, defense, provincial separatism, the recruitment of officials. Although it is impossible to agree completely with Su Shih (1036–1101), who in an oversimplified picture sees all Lu Chih's good schemes opposed and frustrated by his imperial master Te-tsung,[5] there can be no doubt that the personal friction that developed between them robbed the T'ang court of its most able and articulate statesman at a crucial point in the history of the dynasty, and for the time being made the revival of the dynasty's power unlikely.

The sources for Lu Chih's life are the biographies included in the *Shun-tsung shih-lu*[6] and the *Chiu T'ang-shu*,[7] together with the preface to his collected works prepared by Ch'üan Te-yü (759–818).[8] These all derive from a common source, almost certainly an Account of Conduct (*hsing-chuang*) prepared for inclusion in the *Shih-lu*. The *Chiu T'ang-shu* biography is filled out with quoted documents, taken either from the Veritable Record of Te-tsung's reign or straight from the collected works. These documents are quoted verbatim, though in summary form. The long biography in *Hsin T'ang-shu* consists almost entirely of résumés of Lu Chih's memorials, reworded and paraphrased, and is of little value.[9]

All of these sources derive from material prepared for and processed by the official historiographers. The only independent material remaining for the modern scholar is that included in Lu Chih's own collected works. Even the independence of these may be illusory, since there is some evidence that the compiler of the collection as we have it[10]—the collection to which Ch'üan Te-yü's preface belongs—was the same person who compiled the Veritable Record (*Te-tsung shih-lu*) of the period covering his official career. Moreover, there is a strong possibility that this man was a maternal relative of Lu Chih.[11]

The edition of the collected works that survives represents only a part of Lu Chih's writings. Ch'üan Te-yü tells us that there was also a *Pieh-chi* comprising fifteen chapters of miscellaneous literary works; in addition we know that during his enforced retirement Lu Chih composed extensive works on medicine.[12] He also compiled an encyclopedia entitled *Pei-chü wen-yen*, classed in various early bibliographies with Tu Yu's *T'ung-tien*,[13] and is said to have written a number of minor historical works, including an account of the reign of Hsüan-tsung.[14]

The loss of his encyclopedia, which might well have given us a valuable insight into his views on political theory, as does Tu Yu's *T'ung-tien*, and even more the complete disappearance of his personal writings, which must have contained some clues to his very elusive personal relationships and would have enabled us to form some picture of the man in the round, present a serious problem to anyone attempting his biography. Moreover there is a curious lack of reference to him both in the writings of his contemporaries and in the unofficial histories and collections of historical anecdotes, which are very rich for his period. I have been able to trace only a single poem addressed to him,[15] and he seems to have stood somewhat aloof from the lively social life of the capital, a solitary figure engrossed in his official duties.

The limitations imposed by the source material are obvious: the modern biographer is forced to discuss Lu Chih in relation to the role assigned him by his contemporary biographer and all later scholars as the exemplary yet depersonalized political figure. Ch'üan Te-yü's preface makes it clear that to him the state documents were the important thing, and the private writings, however we may regret their loss, comparatively trivial.[16] But even the official writings are incomplete. The memorials included in all editions of his works were written during two brief periods, the first from the eighth month of 783 to the sixth month of 784 when he was acting as personal adviser to Te-tsung during his exile in Feng-t'ien, the second from the eighth month of 792 to the eleventh month of 794 when he served as Chief Minister. These two groups of documents form separate sections of his collected works, selected, as the preface informs us, to exemplify his actions in two different relationships with the emperor. Lu Chih must have presented many other memorials on a variety of subjects—indeed fragments are quoted elsewhere—for during the intervening years, apart from a period of mourning, he remained in highly responsible posts close to the throne and was engaged in a number of important matters upon which it would be enlightening to know his views.

We thus have first a summary outline of his official career in the biographies, and second the details of his policy recommendations made in two brief but crucial phases of his career. This limitation of sources more or less determines the shape of the account that follows.

Lu Chih was born in 754, son of Lu K'an,[17] a minor official of Li-yang county near modern Nanking. Lu K'an, although himself of comparatively low rank, was a member of the important and influential Lu family of Su-chou. Already firmly established in the south during the Nan-pei ch'ao period, as various ancestors had held high ministerial office under the Liang and Ch'en dynasties,[18] the Lu family ranked as one of the four clans of Wu-chün in the list of "notable clans" (*wang-shih*) promulgated in 634.[19] (In the late tenth century Lu was still classified as one of the "four surnames" of Wu-tu.[20]) A clan genealogy compiled in the late seventh century by Lu Ching-hsien[21] showed the clan divided into several branches with extensive local ramifications. Shortly after Lu Chih's death Hsien-tsung issued an edict officially recognizing the various branch families.[22]

Although the clan remained very influential up to recent times, there appears to have been a brief period of decline during Lu Chih's childhood. In the early ninth century we hear that the clan properties and residence in Su-chou city had been for the most part sold off, only a tenth of their old site remaining in their hands. This decline is said to have dated back to the beginning of the eighth century.[23] We know that Lu Chih himself no longer resided in the city of Su-chou, but in the country to the north of the walls.[24] This fits well enough with what we otherwise know of his immediate ancestors, whose official ranks had declined steadily. Under Kao-tsung his great-grandfather Lu Tun-hsin had been acting President of the Chancellery and was ennobled as Viscount of Chia-hsing. Lu Chih's grandfather Lu Ch'i-wang rose to be Deputy-Director of the Palace Library, a rank just high enough to entitle his son Lu K'an to enter official employment through hereditary privilege. He in his turn rose no higher than magistrate (*ling*) of Li-yang county.[25]

The Lu family did, however, retain their social position as a gentry clan of high rank, and Lu K'an was married to a member of the extremely powerful Wei family, one of the greatest of the aristocratic clans of Kuan-chung, whose members intermarried with the imperial family and produced a constant stream of officials of the highest rank. Lu K'an died while Lu Chih was still a small child, and Lu Chih, brought up by his mother,[26] developed ties with his maternal clan that were stronger than would normally have been the case. His connection with the Wei family proved to be an important factor in his later career.[27]

As a child Lu Chih showed precocious talent in conventional Confucian learning and in 773 at the comparatively early age of twenty (Chinese style) was a candidate for the *chin-shih* doctoral examination at Ch'ang-an. Lu Chih passed sixth out of thirty-four successful candidates[28] and returned home to the congratulations of his friends. The *chin-shih* doctorate, entitling its holder to take the placement examinations and thus enter an official career, was normally the last examination for which candidates sat. There were, however, two advanced doctorates: the *Po-hsüeh hung-tz'u*, sometimes taken in the same year as the *chin-shih* but more commonly one or two years later; and the *Shu-p'an pa-ts'ui*, which was very infrequently taken. Both were reserved for candidates of outstanding literary and scholarly distinction, and together constituted the highest possible examination qualification, giving the successful candidate a place in an elite of the elite.

Lu Chih took both of these examinations, but it is not clear at what dates. It is possible that he took the *Po-hsüeh hung-tz'u* with his *chin-shih* in 773, but more likely that he took it in a later year.[29] He was successful and given an appointment as Chief of Employees (*wei*) at Cheng-hsien in Hua-chou close to the capital. But he resigned and returned to Su-chou.[30] On his way he stopped to visit Chang I, then prefect of Shou-chou in Honan. Chang I was a famous scholar in his time and a member of another Su-chou clan of even greater distinction than the Lu clan.[31] Lu Chih made a very favorable impression on Chang I, and it is possible that the latter, who held high office early in Te-tsung's reign, had some influence on Lu Chih's rapid rise to favor.[32]

Later Lu Chih took the second advanced doctorate, *Shu-p'an pa-ts'ui*, which was designed to test a candidate's ability to write official decisions. As a result of his success, he was appointed Registrar (*chu-pu*) of Wei-nan county, a part of the administrative district of the capital.[33] This was probably in 777 or 778. Shortly afterward he became an Examining Censor.[34] These were normal first steps in the career of a promising young man after entering the bureaucracy through the examination system.

Lu Chih's career began to take shape with his appointment by Emperor Te-tsung in 779 as a scholar of the Han-lin Academy.[35] The relation of the academy to the emperor had been changing in a kind of parallel development to the general deterioration of the central government after the An Lu-shan rebellion.[36] The Academy of Hsüan-tsung's reign had consisted of experts in the various arts whose primary function seems to have been to make the emperor's life more agreeable. During Tai-tsung's reign (762–79) the academy scholars came to resemble a personal secretariat attached to the emperor. By the time Te-tsung succeeded Tai-tsung, the Han-lin group had grown accustomed to constant access to the emperor and were exerting a personal influence much as the eunuchs had done.

Given these conditions, the immediate flourishing of a close personal relationship between Te-tsung, then a comparatively young man of thirty-seven, and Lu Chih is not surprising. Lu Chih became the emperor's intimate companion and not only discussed current problems and politics with him but also sang, recited poetry, and pursued frivolous pleasures in his company.[37] It must have been a complex relationship. Te-tsung was one of the most intelligent and toughest members of the T'ang royal family, with a marked streak of pigheadedness, while Lu Chih, for all his Confucian virtues of loyalty and faithfulness, was outspoken and severe in his judgments and as stubborn as his emperor. In later life, after the disappointments of his early years on the throne, Te-tsung became more and more autocratic and obsessed with the minutiae of administration, and Lu's biographers ascribed his fall to the ensuing clash of wills. But it would seem that until 791 Te-tsung remained amenable to reason, and indeed some of Lu Chih's memorials would seem to have pressed the Confucian ideal of blunt directness to the very limit. The causes of his eventual fall certainly lay in part at least in his own unbending character.

Lu Chih first caused some public notice with a memorial submitted to the throne early in 780 on the dispatch of Commissioners for Advancement and Disgrace throughout the empire.[38] These Commissioners (*Ch'u-chih shih*) had been an established feature of T'ang administrative practice, employed at infrequent intervals to inspect the local administration in the provinces and to make recommendations for its improvement.[39] But in this instance they had been revived with a very specific object in view, the imposition of the new tax system known as the *liang-shui*—a matter to which I shall revert later. Lu Chih's memorial, which is not preserved in full, suggested a schematic formula by which the Commissioners might treat the local situation in their reports. It is interesting to see that this formula assumes that the Commissioners were being employed in their normal function, with no mention of the specific purpose of their appointment. It is unlikely, however, that this implies criticism of the new tax system. Taxation was one of the many matters into which the Commissioners were normally required to inquire, and it is duly listed as such by Lu Chih. It seems to me that Lu's memorial was a discreet reminder that more needed attention in the provinces than the collection of taxes, and that the Commissioners should, in addition to fulfilling all their traditional functions, make a very wide-ranging inspection. There is evidence that at this time Lu Chih was a supporter of Yang Yen, the originator of the *liang-shui* scheme,[40] giving us no reason to suppose that he had already formulated the opposition to the measure that he was to express at length some fourteen years later.[41] In fact it is most unlikely that he should have done so, since his later opposition was based upon the consequences of its imposition, which could not have been foreseen in 780.

Although Lu Chih was already in close contact with the emperor in 780, he was by no means the only personal aide of this kind. In 780–81 a more important personal assistant was P'ei Yen-ling, a mature scholar at least twenty years older than Lu Chih. A member of one of the branches of the very influential P'ei clan of Ho-tung,[42] he had already held minor office during the first days of the An Lu-shan rising, but had then become one of the large number of scholars who migrated at this time to southern China.[43] P'ei Yen-ling settled at O-chou on the middle Yangtze, where he devoted himself to historical scholarship, continuing and completing the famous commentary to the *Shih-chi* of Pei Yin, and acquiring some reputation as a scholar.[44] Later, Tung Chin (724–99), a scholar from the same region as P'ei who had turned military man and was defense commissioner for the T'ung-kuan pass, gave him a post on his provincial staff.[45] Here the Commissioners for Advancement and Disgrace heard about him,[46] and upon their recommendation he was given a sinecure post in the Board of Rites and a concurrent appointment as Assistant Scholar in the Chi-hsien College.[47] This college of scholars, though outwardly resembling the Han-lin Academy, was not attached to the emperor's person, forming instead part of the Secretariat of State (*Chung-shu sheng*).[48] Nevertheless Te-tsung employed P'ei for a long time as his personal secretary.[49] Their relationship must have been a close one. P'ei was a protégé of Lu Ch'i, the second Chief Minister, who was engaged in a bitter personal feud with Yang Yen. It seems probable that only a close link with Te-tsung himself enabled P'ei to survive the fall of Lu Ch'i in 783 and to retain his post in the Chi-hsien College until 786 or 787.

Lu Chih, too, was involved in these factional disputes, if only indirectly. In 781 Lu Ch'i drove Yang Yen from office and his place as Chief Minister was filled by Lu Chih's old patron Chang I.[50] The latter did not last long at the capital, however, for early in the next year he was, at Lu Ch'i's instigation, appointed Military Governor of the vitally important strategic area of Feng-hsiang—the only barrier between Ch'ang-an and the Tibetans, who had overrun the northwestern province of Lung-yu (modern Kansu) in 763–64.[51] Chang I's period as Chief Minister seems to have had no material effect on Lu Chih's career, but the part played by Lu Ch'i in Chang's downfall certainly intensified Lu Chih's opposition to Lu and his faction.[52] It is interesting to see then that Lu Chih and P'ei Yen-ling were already committed to opposite sides in factional politics, for it was the bitter animosity between them that later became the immediate cause of Lu Chih's downfall.

However, in 780–81 the maneuverings and intrigues at court were completely overshadowed by events in the provinces, which had built up into the most serious crisis since 763. The final suppression of the An Lu-shan and Ssu Shih-ming risings had been effected only with the establishment throughout China of the very type of semi-autonomous, combined civil and military provincial administration that had provided An Lu-shan with the means to power. These administrations had, hitherto, been confined to the northern and western frontier zones. The new provinces, over forty in number, varied greatly among themselves in power and in their relation to the throne. In the south and in central China the governors were mostly civil officials appointed directly by the emperor, as were their subordinate prefects and magistrates. In the north, however, the picture was very different. During the 760's the Tibetans had overrun most of China's Central Asian dominions and the whole of the modern province of Kansu, leaving their forces within constant striking distance of the capital, Ch'ang-an. As a result the northwestern border provinces had to be very heavily garrisoned and maintained in a continual state of preparedness—a heavy drain upon the empire's resources in money, grain, and manpower. The governors of these provinces, chosen by the emperor with great care and kept under constant supervision, for the most part remained loyal, but they wielded great personal power.

Even more powerful were the governors of Hopei and modern

Shantung. Hopei had been a center of separatist feeling even in the seventh century,[53] and after the An Lu-shan rebellion the area became completely dominated by its military governors. During Tai-tsung's reign these provinces not only had openly defied the central government, but had fought among themselves and supported risings in other provinces with impunity.[54] Finally in 778 the governors of P'ing-lu (modern Shantung), Ch'eng-te, and Wei-po (southern Hopei), together with the powerful governor of Hsiang-yang in the Han valley, made a solemn agreement claiming hereditary succession to their provinces and pledging mutual support against the imperial government should the latter attempt to impose a nominee upon any of their provinces.[55] When in 779 T'ien Ch'eng-ssu, governor of Wei-po and one of the parties to the agreement, died, the succession passed to his son T'ien Yüeh, and at the request of the other governors concerned in the agreement this appointment was confirmed by the emperor.[56] Hopei and Shantung, apart from the province centering on modern Peking, which remained loyal, were virtually independent. The governors rendered no taxes, maintained large standing armies of professional troops, appointed their own subordinates, and refused to attend court. The only way in which they acknowledged loyalty was by regularly sending to Ch'ang-an large tribute gifts, which became a part of the emperor's personal revenue rather than of the public funds.[57]

To contain the potential military threat posed by these provinces, the central government maintained very powerful imperial armies under governors and generals of proved loyalty in Ho-tung and Ho-chung (Shansi) and in northern Honan. The latter region was of crucial importance, since not only was there no natural frontier to defend, but here the Pien canal system, upon which the capital region depended for the transport of grain from the south, lay within easy striking distance of the armies of P'ing-lu province.[58]

From the beginning there was no doubt of Te-tsung's determination to restore the authority of the court and bring the mutinous northeastern provinces under control. The dispatch, within a few months of his accession, of the Commissioners for Advancement and Disgrace with their wide investigative authority certainly alerted the northeastern governors to his intentions, especially when the Commissioners demanded that the size of their armies be slashed and the disbanded troops settled on vacant lands as taxpaying peasants.[59] The governors made some gestures of compliance, but their suspicions were confirmed with the imposition of the *liang-shui* tax scheme, under which (as we shall see below) each province was assigned a quota of taxes to be collected according to a new and simplified system and sent to the capital. To the northeastern provinces, which had retained their own revenues and even managed to stay independent of the salt monopoly administration,[60] this scheme posed a double threat—first, the loss of a substantial portion of their revenues and, second, the possibility that increased imperial revenues would put the central government in a position to reassert its authority over them.

The attitude of the emperor was made quite clear later in 780. Under Tai-tsung the provinces had been accustomed to sending in regular tribute gifts to ensure the imperial favor. On the emperor's birthday in 780, the provincial governors sent in their offerings as usual. T'ien Yüeh of Ch'eng-te and Li Cheng-i of P'ing-lu made particularly lavish gifts to serve both as a "gesture of loyalty" and as a demonstration of their wealth and power. The emperor, however, refused to accept any of this tribute for himself, ostentatiously transferring all tribute to the regular treasuries as though it were an installment of the provincial taxes which had remained unpaid for many years.[61]

Matters came to a head at the beginning of 781 with the death of Li Pao-ch'en, governor of Ch'eng-te. Li Pao-ch'en had designated his son Li Wei-yüeh to succeed him as governor and had before his death taken the precaution of eliminating all likely opponents to this plan within his own province. T'ien Yüeh of Wei-po, whose own succession Li Pao-ch'en had strongly supported in 779, now repaid his obligation by urging the court to confirm Li Wei-yüeh as governor. The emperor refused, at the same time making clear that in his view all the provincial governors, like lesser local officials, held their appointments subject to his will.[62]

This sparked a rebellion of the provinces of Wei-po, Ch'eng-te, and P'ing-lu, supported by Liang Ch'ung-i at Hsiang-yang, whose rising cut the Han valley route from the capital to the middle Yangtze. Powerful forces were at once sent to deal with the risings, and there were some initial successes:[63] T'ien Yüeh suffered a crushing defeat at the hands of Chu T'ao, the loyal governor of Lung-lu province (the area around modern Peking);[64] and late in 781 Li Wei-yüeh was murdered by one of his subordinate commanders, Wang Wu-chün, who submitted to the T'ang court.[65] However, Te-tsung failed to reward either Chu T'ao or Wang Wu-chün as lavishly as they had expected, and in 782 they too rebelled.[66] The whole of Hopei and Shantung and the north of Hupeh were now in rebellion, and the rebel governors each in turn assumed the title of King.[67]

At this point Te-tsung's prestige received yet another blow. Li Hsi-lieh, the governor of the strategically vital province of Huai-hsi, had succeeded in suppressing Liang Ch'ung-i's rebellion in the Han valley, and as a result controlled a tract of territory to the north of the Yangtze stretching from Hupeh to southern Honan.[68] Ordered to proceed north and attack Li Na, the new governor of P'ing-lu province, Li Hsi-lieh instead made common cause with the rebels Li Na and Chu T'ao, styled himself Grand Generalissimo of the Empire, and himself took the title of King.[69] His defection was extremely grave, for not only did it transform overnight one of the dynasty's most powerful supporters into its most dangerous enemy, but it meant also that both routes by which Ch'ang-an could be supplied from the south, the Han valley and the Pien canal in Honan, were cut. The emperor was now confined to Shansi and Shensi, with access only to Szechwan. His sole hope for alleviation of the situation came from growing tension between the rebel leaders Chu T'ao and Wang Wu-chün in Hopei.[70]

In the fourth month of 783 the emperor signed a treaty with the Tibetans, agreeing on a frontier line to the west of the capital,[71] which temporarily removed the threat from that quarter. It also tempted the emperor to redeploy against the rebels the frontier troops and palace armies previously engaged in the defense of the western borders of Kuan-chung. Although militarily desirable, this placed an extremely heavy burden on the finances of the capital, for the provincial armies from the frontier, self-supporting in their home province, had to be paid out of central funds if employed on campaign elsewhere, the provincial government remaining responsible only for the support of dependents. The additional expense—estimated at 1,300,000 strings of cash per month —was far beyond what could be met from the normal tax income.[72] Moreover, the emperor was without the immense reserves of accumulated tax revenue that had been available during the first years of the An Lu-shan rebellion. Te-tsung had inherited a depleted treasury, and the income from the new *liang-shui* taxes had hardly begun to come in. The fact that all supplies from the Yangtze valley, the principal source of revenue, had been cut off by the rebels only added to the central government's already desperate position. Chao Tsan, Lu Ch'i's chief financial expert, attempted to meet the crisis by introducing a number of measures designed to raise short-term revenue from the immensely wealthy merchant class of the capital. His predecessor, Tu Yu, had exacted loans from merchants[73] and Chao Tsan made further exactions. In addition, taxes were imposed on a great variety of commodities (tea, lumber, and bamboo among them), the monopoly tax on salt was doubled, monopoly taxes were imposed on all sales of liquor and iron, and a percentage levy was taken on all mercantile transactions. Besides these taxes, which resulted in greatly increased commodity prices, the government attempted to impose a tax on all buildings according to their size, and even suggested a reallocation of lands.[74] The last straw was a 20 percent increase in the tax under the *liang-shui* system. Widespread unrest developed among the hard-pressed population of the capital.[75]

From this critical period date the earliest of Lu Chih's surviving memorials, two extremely long and remarkably shrewd appraisals of the situation in the rebellious provinces[76] and in the region of Kuan-chung surrounding the capital.[77] The emperor's advisers—Lu Ch'i, although his name is not specifically mentioned, is obviously implied—were blamed for having underestimated the strength of the rebels in the early stages of the rising and for letting the situation deteriorate to a point where conscription, labor levies, and increased taxation had bred disaffection among the people.[78] Lu Chih also pointed out the grave dangers of overextending the imperial forces and of employing the frontier forces in campaigns in Hopei and Huai-hsi. He suggested that the imperial forces concentrate on defeating Li Hsi-lieh, who posed a real threat to the dynasty, rather than on the Hopei rebels, who were merely the heirs of a long-standing local situation and who were not themselves such formidable enemies.[79] He further advocated that the emperor withdraw the palace armies—the crack troops under direct imperial command—to Kuan-chung to protect the heart of the empire and retain the frontier garrisons at their posts to guard against the possibility of a Tibetan invasion.[80] Lu Chih had drafted some of the state correspondence with the Tibetans during the treaty negotiations,[81] and to all appearances he felt that despite the treaty they might try to take advantage of the emperor's weak position. He also urged the abolition of the emergency taxes imposed by Chao Tsan, so as to regain the support of the populace in the capital.[82]

Even had Te-tsung been inclined to adopt Lu Chih's proposals, he was in no position to do so, for his armies were committed in the field. In the fifth month of 783 his general Li Sheng had been heavily defeated in northern Hopei and forced to retreat,[83] while the southern campaign against Li Hsi-lieh in the Han valley was going very badly and by the end of the year seemed likely to end in complete disaster. Li Hsi-lieh surrounded the main imperial army, and routed the detachments of the palace armies which had been sent to relieve them.[84] The only battle-ready troops available were the frontier garrison armies in Kuan-chung. So, late in the ninth month, a supreme commander was appointed to coordinate the campaign against Li Hsi-lieh, and a force of crack troops from the frontier province of Ching-yüan was ordered to march south and to reopen the Han valley route.[85] Early in the next month these troops arrived at Ch'ang-an in a pitiful condition after a

long march through severe winter weather, expecting the customary
lavish gifts and feasting. When their treatment failed to come up to
their expectations, they became mutinous. Last-minute attempts to pla-
cate them failed, and they broke into the treasuries and overran the
capital, inciting the populace to rebel in support of them. The result
was a new and formidable rebellion in the capital itself, led by Chu
Tz'u, a relative of the rebel Chu T'ao who was living in retirement in
Ch'ang-an. The emperor and a small retinue fled the city and took refuge in Feng-t'ien to the west.[86] The new rebellion had cut him off from
contact with his most powerful armies in Hopei and Ho-tung, and it is
difficult to imagine how the future of the dynasty could have looked
blacker than it did at the end of 783.

It was during this desperate period that Lu Chih emerged as one
of the most powerful figures at the T'ang court. He was one of the
small group of officials who fled with the emperor, first to Hsien-yang
and then to Feng-t'ien, and he became the emperor's personal secretary
and drafter of state papers. As his biographer says:[87]

The whole empire was in turmoil and beset with difficulties. Affairs of state
piled up, mobilization and exactions had to be carried out near and far. The
policies of state had to follow up innumerable lines of action. Each day several tens of edicts had to be promulgated. All these came from Lu Chih's
hand. Wielding the brush and holding the paper he completed his drafts in
an instant, and yet he never needed to rewrite anything. Although it appeared
that he had given no thought to the matter in hand, when it was completed
there was never any detail of the affair which had not been covered, and it
was exactly what was needed for the circumstances. The clerks making copies
of these documents had no rest, while his colleagues just sat and sighed with
folded arms, unable to assist in any way . . .

This has the familiar ring of one of the historians' favorite *topoi*, but
there can be no doubt that Lu Chih had phenomenal facility in composition and in the handling of documents. The streams of precedents
in some of his longer memorials, with examples not only from the distant classical past but also from his own dynasty, seem to pour forth
spontaneously, and many of his documents have a rhetorical quality
suggesting eloquent (though of course highly formal) speech. Even if
the "several tens of edicts a day" are an exaggeration, the extant collected works contain more than eighty documents from the period 783–
85, ranging from Acts of Grace of the highest importance to brevets,[88]
and including the numerous memorials in which he presented his own
views to the emperor. Moreover, these documents were not simply
formulations by Lu Chih of policy devised by Te-tsung and his chief

ministers. It is quite clear that he himself was closely involved in the making of policy, and his contemporaries began to refer to him as the "Inner Chief Minister" (*Nei-hsiang*).[89]

The military situation continued to deteriorate. At the end of 783 Chu Tz'u's troops were harrying Feng-t'ien and the imperial forces were hard-pressed. The emperor considered retiring to Feng-hsiang, whose governor, Chang I, was the former Chief Minister and Lu Chih's old patron. But one of his subordinate officers murdered Chang and went over to Chu Tz'u, who now proclaimed himself emperor of a new Ch'in dynasty.[90]

Fortunately, Chu Tz'u failed to press home his attacks upon Feng-t'ien, giving the emperor time to get reinforcements from loyal frontier provinces in Kuan-chung, and to levy troops in Feng-t'ien itself. At the same time, too, news of the events in Ch'ang-an reached the imperial armies on campaign in Hopei. Their commanders withdrew into Ho-tung, leaving small forces to pin down the Hopei rebels, while Li Huai-kuang led his main army westward to relieve Feng-t'ien.[91] The emperor also made approaches to Li Na, Wang Wu-chün, and T'ien Yüeh, offering them a free pardon and additional titles of nobility if they would submit to the throne.[92] The object of this attempt at conciliation was clearly to enable the imperial forces to concentrate on the more immediate dangers posed by Li Hsi-lieh and Chu Tz'u. However, although the three governors were willing to accept, Chu T'ao, who was not included in the offer, presumably owing to his relationship with Chu Tz'u, remained adamant and proposed to lead his armies and Uighur mercenaries to the aid of Chu Tz'u, urging T'ien Yüeh to make a diversionary attack in Honan to draw off the imperial armies in Ho-tung while he did so.[93]

This temporary respite in the military situation allowed a resumption of political life at court. Chief Minister Lu Ch'i, who had guaranteed that Chu Tz'u would remain loyal despite Chu T'ao's rebellion, was disgraced and three new Chief Ministers appointed.[94] The ground for his dismissal was prepared by a memorial drafted by Lu Chih,[95] which put new courage into Te-tsung by suggesting, with a wealth of historical parallels, that the situation was not the result of having lost the Mandate of Heaven, but was entirely the fault of his advisers, chief of whom was Lu Ch'i.

In further memorials Lu Chih urged the emperor to make it easier for his officers to make their opinions known to him, since "unless emperor and subjects wish for the same ends, the emperor cannot gain his subjects' loyalty."[96] A similar request had recently been made by the veteran statesman-ritualist Yen Chen-ch'ing,[97] and it is clear that these memorials were part of a general movement to restore to all officials the freedom of access to the imperial presence they had had during the early years of the dynasty. The object of this was not so much to keep the emperor in touch with the views of his subjects as to prevent small pressure groups among the highly placed ministers from ensuring that the emperor heard only their version of events. The intimate relationship between the emperor and his Chief Ministers, who held an informal meeting with him daily after the end of the formal court session, made this a real danger, and it was felt that Lu Ch'i had abused his position in this respect.

On Lu Ch'i's disgrace, Lu Chih and his fellow Han-lin scholar Wu T'ung-wei were promoted, Lu Chih becoming Chief Secretary of the Department of Merit Assessments, a part of the Board of Civil Office.[98] He at first declined this promotion on the grounds that personal advisers such as himself should be the last to be rewarded.[99] We may perhaps see emerging here his opposition to another type of pressure group, the "inner" advisers such as the Han-lin academicians, who were rapidly gaining influence at the expense of the normal organs of the bureaucracy. This opposition was later expressed quite specifically in a memorial of 787 which requested that the Han-lin scholars no longer be employed in drafting state documents, this being properly the responsibility of the State Secretariat.[100]

During the last days of 783, Lu Chih presented three further memorials which reveal his shrewd grasp of the temper of the times and of the very delicate relationship between the throne and the loyal provinces of the south. The first of these[101] discussed the terms in which edicts should be couched, and insisted that Te-tsung should follow the classical precedents of rulers in similar desperate situations, and take upon himself all responsibility for the troubles that had affected his dynasty. This stress upon humility and self-criticism runs through all the memorials of this period. Te-tsung, however, was not yet convinced, clinging instead to his plan to bolster his prestige by adopting a new and resplendent title, "Divinely Spiritual Civil and Military." Lu Chih dissuaded him by pointing out that not only were such titles unknown in antiquity, but the adoption of a pretentious title in such precarious times would undoubtedly cost him the sympathy of the people.[102] Te-tsung thereupon decided that he would merely change his reign-title to *Hsing-yüan* (with the comparatively modest implications of a dynastic revival). The change of a reign-title was always the occasion for the promulgation of a general Act of Grace (*ta-she*) and amnesty, and Lu Chih was entrusted with its composition. He suspected that his previous memorials had been favorably received only because the emperor was in such difficult straits, and that once the situation improved the emperor would again become arrogant (events proved him correct), and therefore Lu Chih took the opportunity to harangue Te-tsung yet again, pointing out the perilous situation of the dynasty, with four false kings and two pseudo-emperors vying for power, while all the other provinces waited on the outcome before finally committing themselves. At this critical juncture it was imperative, he insisted, that the emperor show he sincerely held the people's interests at heart and offer them some tangible respite.[103]

The Act of Grace drafted by Lu Chih was long and complicated but very well designed to meet the situation.[104] Its frequent quotation in later times was a tribute to both its soundness and its rhetoric.[105] There was a humble beginning in which the emperor took upon his own shoulders the responsibility for the terrible sufferings of the empire, the result of his lack of virtue and his ignorance of government, engendered by his education in the seclusion of the Palace. The emperor then offered amnesty to Li Na, T'ien Yüeh, Wang Wu-chün, and Li Hsi-lieh, with confirmation of their positions as provincial governors. Their rebellions, the emperor explained, might all be attributed to his having "lost the Way of government": "Since I have not acted as a proper ruler, what crimes can the people have committed?" The amnesty was extended to all subordinates of the governors, and to Chu T'ao, despite his support of Chu Tz'u, provided he would withdraw his forces and reaffirm his allegiance. Chu Tz'u could not himself be pardoned, for he was guilty of heinous treason (*ta pu-tao*) and desecration of the imperial tombs, but any of his followers who surrendered were to be freed from punishment. Next came the catalogue of criminal pardons and reductions of sentences and the list of promotions for soldiers and officials that always accompanied such an Act of Grace. The last part of the document dealt with financial concessions. All the taxes on the sale of commodities, on commercial transactions, and on buildings, as well as the monopoly imposed upon sales of iron, were abolished. A half of the summer tax was remitted for the population of the capital region, and five years of all taxation for Feng-t'ien—which must have been entirely ruined by the descent upon it of the imperial retinue and armies. Moreover, all provincial tribute was suspended, and all superfluous official appointments and unnecessary administrative expenses were pruned.

The terms of this Act of Grace show that Lu Chih, in addition to being responsible for drafting the document, helped determine its content. The offer of amnesty to the rebel leaders indicates that, faced with the far more serious rising of Chu Tz'u, the emperor was abandoning

his attempt to reimpose central authority over the northeastern provinces. Acceptance of the status quo in Hopei had been advocated by
Lu Chih some months previously in connection with Li Hsi-lieh's defection.[106] As Lu Chih had then pointed out: "The Court placed the
Ho-shuo region [i.e., the northeast] outside the scope of its policies,
and this situation has persisted for about thirty years. It is not an urgent
crisis which has arisen in a single day." The financial concessions had
all been suggested in an earlier memorial too,[107] as a means of regaining
the allegiance of the people of the capital.[108]

The effect of this Act of Grace upon the rebels was negative, although it undoubtedly prepared the ground for the eventual settlement.
The two pseudo-emperors merely assumed new and more pretentious
dynastic titles.[109] But upon the uncommitted loyal provinces the Act of
Grace and the edicts that had preceded it produced a powerful effect.
The histories again resort to clichés, with a picture of the hardened
troops weeping openly when they heard the edicts read aloud, but all
contemporary accounts agree that they helped greatly to restore confidence in the emperor. This was especially true among the waverers in
the south, where the provincial governors had been building up trained
forces and accumulating stores of money and grain, but had remained
reluctant to throw their resources into battle until they could foresee an
imperial victory.[110]

Having achieved some measure of financial reform, Lu Chih now
turned his attention to another financial abuse, which closely affected
the emperor himself. The financial concessions of the Act of Grace
applied for the most part to the capital, which was in fact still in enemy
hands. The income the emperor still received consisted entirely of
tribute and taxes from the provinces. Te-tsung, avaricious by nature,
attempted to have all of this income paid into his own personal treasuries, the Ta-ying k'u and the Ch'iung-lin k'u. Such misappropriation of
public funds had been common practice under Tai-tsung, and was one
of the abuses against which Yang Yen's financial reforms of 780 had
been aimed.[111] Lu Chih reprimanded the emperor for his offense in an
extremely outspoken memorial, chiding him for setting an example of
avarice and self-interest to the people, who were forced to share in the
emperor's misfortunes but were thus denied any share of his "profits,"
and once again stressed the necessity of avoiding the creation of a difference of interests between the throne and the people. He further
urged that the personal treasuries be entirely abolished and their contents employed to reward the army and meritorious subjects, thus laying
the foundation for the recovery of the capital.[112]

A further abuse which Yang Yen had sought to curb was the growing power of the eunuchs. This question now again caused a clash at
court. At this time eunuchs were for the first time being appointed as
commanders in the palace armies, and this development was sharply
criticized by the new Chief Minister, Hsiao Fu.[113] The emperor was displeased, since he supported the new policy, and when Hsiao Fu presented a further memorial blaming the troubles of the empire on the
policies of the new reign, attacking Yang Yen and Lu Ch'i without distinction, Te-tsung removed him from court by appointing him to a high-
sounding post as Commissioner for the Pacification of the Southern
Provinces.[114] Hsiao Fu was not only, like Lu Chih, a member of the
anti–Lu Ch'i faction, but also Lu Chih's immediate superior in the
Board of Civil Office.[115] Lu Chih protested strongly his new appointment[116] but to no avail.

The arrival in Kuan-chung, early in 784, of the palace armies under
Li Sheng, and of the provincial armies from Ho-chung—recently withdrawn from the Hopei front—under Li Huai-kuang, ended the immediate
threat to Feng-t'ien from Chu Tz'u, who was forced to raise the siege
and withdraw his forces to Ch'ang-an. But the emperor soon faced a
new problem, which began with the development of a tense rivalry between Li Huai-kuang and Li Sheng. Li Huai-kuang claimed the palace
armies were being better treated than his provincial armies. Li Sheng
defended any preferential treatment by pointing out the difference in
behavior between his own highly disciplined forces and Li Huai-kuang's
troops, who had been plundering the countryside. It soon became apparent that Li Huai-kuang was turning from his losing fight with Li
Sheng to thoughts of rebellion. Disturbed by the possibility of mutiny,
Te-tsung sent Lu Chih to the encampment at Hsien-yang to assess the
situation. Lu Chih reported that Li Huai-kuang was, in fact, on the
verge of rebellion, and that precautions should immediately be taken.[117]
The palace troops were moved and quartered a short distance from Li
Huai-kuang's provincial army, while Li Sheng detached some of his
best officers and crack troops to garrison the emperor's line of retreat
into Szechwan. At the same time it was announced that the court was
to be transferred to Hsien-yang, where Li Huai-kuang would be directly under the emperor's eye. Li Huai-kuang, who had already begun
secret negotiations with Chu Tz'u, now openly rebelled. The emperor
withdrew with his court from Feng-t'ien to Liang-chou, on the border
between Szechwan and the Wei valley.[118]

The emperor's exile in Liang-chou (later renamed Hsing-yüan fu
after the new reign-title) was not, however, a period of desperate crisis

like the early days at Feng-t'ien. The imperial armies under Li Sheng, and forces from the south, gradually regained the initiative and put down first Chu Tz'u then Li Huai-kuang.[119]

By the seventh month of 784 the emperor was able to return in triumph to Ch'ang-an.[120] Moreover the urgency of the situation in Hopei was lessened as fighting had broken out between the rebellious governors.[121] Only Li Hsi-lieh's rebellion lingered on in Huai-hsi and Honan until, after a series of heavy defeats, he was poisoned early in 786[122] by one of his subordinates.

At Liang-chou Lu Chih retained his favored position as personal adviser to the emperor. As the tide of events turned he continued to present memorials advising lenient treatment for surrendered rebel troops,[123] commenting on various official appointments, or advocating caution regarding the undependable Tibetans.[124] He also continued to draft large numbers of official documents, from brevets to edicts allowing tax relief to areas that had suffered severely during the hostilities.[125] But a change had come over the advice which he now gave. At Feng-t'ien, Lu Chih had been above all a moral preceptor on the classical Confucian model, exhorting his ruler to exercise power by a display of virtue and humility. After the move to Liang-chou the fervent advocacy of Confucian rule through personal example and moral suasion is no longer so strong, and by the time the emperor returned to Ch'ang-an Lu Chih seems to have reverted to the more normal role of personal secretary to the emperor and compiler of routine documents.

He also now began to emerge from the purely personal employment of a Han-lin scholar into a normal official career. In the sixth month of 784 he was given the post of Grand Councillor (*Chien-i ta-fu*) as a reward for his services.[126] At the end of the year he was further promoted to Chief Secretary of the State Secretariat,[127] a very important and responsible post. He had now arrived. He continued to hold his post as Han-lin scholar, which meant that his intimate relationship with the emperor remained unbroken. But he now also held a high position in the regular executive machine as well. Unfortunately, none of his memorials dating from the period after the return to the capital have survived, and it would seem that when Lu Chih[128] came to compile his collected writings he felt that with the return of the court from exile in Liang-chou one distinct phase of his career—that of sage adviser to the emperor—had come to an end.

Very little is known of Lu Chih's life during the next few years. There can be no doubt that he was busily occupied with his official duties, for a great number of edicts drafted by him during these years

are included in his collected works. The most important of these documents were the three long Acts of Grace issued on the emperor's return
to Ch'ang-an in 784, at the inauguration of a new reign-title in 785, and
at the great winter ceremony of the same year.[129] These Acts of Grace,
together with a series of edicts granting pardon to those who had
served under the rebel leaders (also Lu Chih's work), marked the settlement of the rebellion. There can be no doubt, here again, that Lu Chih
had a large hand in their contents, for the settlement followed closely
the line he had advocated in 783. It amounted, in effect, to the acceptance of the semi-autonomous status of the provinces in Hopei and
Shantung which had started the whole struggle. The only risings actually crushed by imperial troops were the secondary risings of Chu Tz'u
and Li Huai-kuang (Li Hsi-lieh was also defeated eventually, but at the
time of the Acts of Grace was still active in Huai-hsi). Chu T'ao had
been first defeated by his fellow rebel Wang Wu-chün, and then had submitted. Almost immediately he fell sick and died.[130] T'ien Yüeh was
murdered by his half-brother T'ien Hsü, who then submitted.[131] The
governors of the rebellious provinces were confirmed in their posts,
granted exalted nominal ranks, and in the case of T'ien Hsü even given
a royal princess in marriage.[132] Among Lu Chih's works is a document
which he had to draft appointing Li Na as nominal Chief Minister and
Vice-President of the Department of State, written in terms of the most
fulsome flattery and more suited to some loyal elder statesman than to
a man who had for three years been in open rebellion against imperial
authority.[133]

The empire settled down to an uneasy calm broken only by border
troubles with the Tibetans and minor disorders in the provinces. At
court, a complex factional struggle continued, but Lu Chih seems to
have remained aloof. He was still essentially the emperor's man rather
than a member of any faction, and it seems possible that he was related
through his mother to the emperor's new favorite consort, née Wei, who
may have been a factor in his continuing intimacy with Te-tsung.[134]

In 787 Lu Chih's mother died, shortly after the emperor had specially
sent a eunuch envoy to bring her to the capital, where she had been
received with great honors.[135] Lu Chih wished to have his father's
coffin removed from Su-chou, where it had been first buried, to Lo-yang,
so that his parents might be buried together. The emperor again sent
a eunuch envoy to perform this duty, a singular mark of respect.[136]

Lu Chih spent the three years' mourning period in the Feng-lo ssu,
a Buddhist temple on Sung-shan in the outskirts of Lo-yang, refusing
the condolences and gifts offered him by provincial officials. The only
person whom he allowed to share his grief was Wei Kao, the rapidly

rising young provincial officer who had recently been appointed Governor of western Szechwan.[137] Their relationship is nowhere specifically stated, but it would be reasonable to assume that Wei Kao was a maternal relative. Otherwise we know nothing whatever of Lu Chih's activities during these years of retirement.

In 790, at the end of the three-year period, he returned to Ch'ang-an and was appointed temporary acting Vice-President of the Board of War, and again given his old post in the Han-lin Academy.[138] By this time factional disputes had reached such a pitch that it was no longer possible to stand aside. Lu Chih almost at once fell foul of Tou Shen, who had become Chief Minister in 789. He openly criticized Shen, and denounced him for corruption—a charge amply justified.[139] The emperor, who had received him on his return to court with a great show of affection, still supported him, and in 791 he was confirmed in his acting post at the Board of War, and at last relieved of his duties in the Han-lin Academy, being given instead the very responsible duty of administering the state examinations for the year.[140] He was at this time only thirty-seven years old, and at court he was confidently expected to become Chief Minister.

The series of examinations held under Lu Chih in 792 was one of the most successful in the whole of the T'ang dynasty.[141] He was assisted in his task of selection by two fine scholars, Liang Su and Ts'ui Yüan-han. The latter was a more or less orthodox Confucian scholar, but Liang Su had studied widely in Buddhism and Taoism as well as in the more conventional classical fields. He had come to the capital as a protégé of the Taoist Chief Minister Li Pi, to whose son he had been tutor,[142] and had become a major figure in the early *ku-wen* movement. It is perhaps worth noting that both Lu Chih and Te-tsung dabbled in medicine, a field that was based almost entirely upon Taoist theory, and Lu's orthodoxy was quite possibly confined to his formal political and ethical writings.[143]

Between them these examiners managed to select an astonishing crop of graduates, of whom a dozen or so became important political figures during the next decades, including such persons as Han Yü, Li Chiang, Li Kuan, Ou-yang Chan, Ts'ui Ch'ün, P'ei Tu, and Wang Ya.[144] The list was so impressive that the year's graduates were later referred to as the "dragon and tiger list" (*lung-hu pang*).[145]

Although so notably successful as an examiner, Lu Chih, in common with many of his contemporaries, seems to have mistrusted examinations as a means of selecting candidates for official employment. Even during his examining he is said to have placed heavy reliance upon the recommendations of his assistants, and he seems to have believed in personal recommendation as the most reliable grounds for selection. Such recommendation was an established practice, and inevitably involved the canvassing of examiners by candidates.[146] This may be what lay behind the accusation made by Lu Chih's former colleague in the Han-lin Academy, Wu T'ung-hsüan, that he had accepted bribes as an examiner, though the charge itself was clearly put up by Wu and Lu Chih's enemy Tou Shen.[147]

In the fourth month of 792, Tou Shen was dismissed, and Lu Chih was appointed Chief Minister in his place.[148] Almost his first act was to reform the machinery for appointing successful candidates. Since the An Lu-shan rising, it had become customary to assemble candidates for appointment to office once every three years. So many candidates presented themselves on these occasions that it was impossible to check their records and credentials thoroughly, and a great deal of graft and inefficiency had resulted. Lu Chih made this assembly annual, which reduced its size and the attendant disadvantages while also eliminating the scandal of posts remaining long unfilled although qualified candidates were waiting for appointment.[149]

Another memorial requested that the heads of certain of the more important government offices be permitted to recommend persons for subordinate posts within their departments—a long-established practice in provincial government.[150] Again in an Act of Grace issued in the eleventh month of 793 and drafted by Lu Chih, the provincial governors were urged to recommend to the throne talented and virtuous retired scholars.[151] Lu Chih was clearly of the opinion that personal knowledge of the deeper springs of a man's character and experience of his work were better grounds for selection than the elegant exercises written in the examination hall. This was not a personal attitude, but was common among Confucian scholars of his period, who were frequently opposed to the whole system—which we tend to imagine as a stronghold of Confucian orthodoxy—on the same grounds.

With Lu Chih's appointment as Chief Minister we are once again adequately informed about his actions and policies. There is, however, a great difference between the documents surviving from this period and those written in 783–85 when he was the emperor's personal adviser. In contrast to the highly personal moral exhortations and homilies of the earlier years, the writings dating from 792–94 are almost entirely confined to discussions of state policy.

There is also evidence that relations between Lu Chih and Te-tsung had begun to be strained. Lu Chih had already protested against the autocratic Te-tsung's attempts to abrogate powers normally exercised by the central bureaucracy. For example, he had memorialized the throne that the special status of the Han-lin Academy was irregular, a development of the period of emergency following the An Lu-shan rebellion, and that it was high time the responsibility for the drafting of documents was returned to the Secretariat of State—that is, to the normal court officers.[152] Since Lu Chih was himself serving in the Secretariat at the time this memorial was written,[153] his advice may not have been purely disinterested. But after his career in the Han-lin Academy he was in a better position than almost any of his contemporaries to estimate the power to influence held by such irregular offices attached to the imperial person.

When Lu Chih became Chief Minister, he was no longer able to exercise his influence upon the emperor in private. Although T'ang Chief Ministers were on far more intimate terms with their emperor than were the highest officials of later dynasties, and there was an informal meeting to discuss policy after each court session, the bulk of their mutual business had to be done in open court. Here Lu Chih was no longer the personal, confidential adviser, but had to act as spokesman for the officials of the central administration. Blunt outspokenness in accordance with the Confucian tradition may have been possible when Lu Chih and Te-tsung were working together in private. It was a very different matter when, for example, he denounced the emperor's avarice and plans for personal enrichment before all the ministers. Most of Lu Chih's policies as Chief Minister were well thought out, show considerable foresight, and were highly praised in later times. But he actually achieved very little, and for this the blame must be laid upon the failure of both Lu Chih and the emperor to adjust to the new relationship.

The two major problems facing the court during his brief tenure as Chief Minister were defense and finance. Lu Chih was not, of course, called upon to control or to conduct military operations. But with the end of the provincial rebellions and the abandonment by Te-tsung of his attempt to reimpose central authority, the court had become much engaged in devising a military system that would allow the maintenance of forces strong enough to repel any further incursions by the Tibetans and at the same time relieve the pressure of a huge standing army upon the empire's economy.[154] In 786–87, for example, Li Pi had suggested the revival of the militia system of the early years of the dynasty, modified so that the peasants forming the new militias would live in the area where their military units would be permanently stationed. These peasants were to be supplied with draft animals, seed, and equipment and promised guaranteed prices above market value for their surplus agricultural produce.[155]

Lu Chih's proposals were of a similar nature, and it is clear that the idea of colonizing the frontier zones with the families of soldiers was much in the air. Yang Yen had formulated such a scheme in 781,[156] and in 789–90 two attempts had been made to carry out this type of colonization in the northwest.[157] Lu Chih's first proposal for reducing the expense of the frontier forces, contained in a very detailed and closely reasoned memorial presented late in 792,[158] suggested that the bulk transportation of grain from southern China and Honan be greatly reduced and the frontier troops supplied instead by "Harmonious Purchase" (*ho-ti*)—that is, compulsory purchase by the government at high prices—from farmers in the Kuan-chung area. By grading prices so that the highest were paid to settlers closest to the frontier, the government would, it was hoped, also encourage exploitation of the lands along the border. This was followed in 793 by a more general disquisition on the requirements for frontier defense,[159] in which Lu Chih advocated suspension of the system by which provincial forces were detached, at great expense, for service on the frontiers. In its place Lu Chih advocated the settlement of frontier troops with their families on their own lands, so that they would be largely self-supporting.[160] The whole document follows the same general line as Li Pi's earlier proposals, but is worked out in far greater detail. The emperor was favorably disposed to the scheme, which also earned widespread support among the officials,[161] but it proved impossible to put into effect. It is very interesting to note that Tu Yu, whose basic political attitudes were the antithesis of those of Lu Chih,[162] put forward a similar plan in the early years of the ninth century.[163] In presenting his plan, Tu Yu relied on parallels between such a scheme and the legalist organization of the Ch'in state, where the peasantry combined the roles of basic producers and trained fighting units.

These memorials on military matters were essentially administrative, designed to reduce the cost of maintaining the armies. But Lu also gave considerable thought to the military aspect of army organization, in particular to the cumbersome and ineffective chain of command. At this period the frontier generals had to refer to the capital for approval of their plans, and for specific orders in an emergency. They were thus prevented from making on-the-spot decisions, and usually by the time the Board of War approved their plans and sent reinforcements, the highly mobile Tibetan raiding columns had long withdrawn. Lu Chih advocated some measure of freedom for the frontier generals to take independent action, but stressed that in granting such freedom care would have to be used to avoid encouraging the generals to assume autonomous powers.[164]

Curiously Lu Chih never mentions what was perhaps the most significant military development of his time—the emergence of the eunuchs as commanders of the palace armies, in particular the crack Shen-ts'e armies, the most powerful and best trained force at the emperor's immediate disposal.[165] The eunuchs had of course long exercised supervisory powers over the armies, through eunuch "commissars" (*chien-chün*) attached to the staffs of commanders in the field as representatives of the emperor (there had been many cases since An Lu-shan's time of friction caused by the overbearing conduct of these supervisors). However, it was not until 784 that the first eunuchs were themselves given command of palace armies. As we have seen above, Hsiao Fu and others had protested strongly against this, and since Lu Chih remonstrated with the emperor over Hsiao Fu's subsequent removal from court, we may assume that he shared the latter's views.[166]

This growth of eunuch power was very significant. On the one hand, the greatly strengthened palace armies under eunuch generals provided the means for Hsien-tsung (805–20) to conquer the provincial magnates and revive the dynasty's authority. On the other, their control of great military forces made the eunuchs a powerful and baneful influence in ninth-century court politics, and did much to undermine the power of later emperors. Lu Chih may well have foreseen the outcome of this change. While serving as a Han-lin scholar in close association with Te-tsung, he must have been in continual contact with the eunuchs of the imperial household and must have been familiar with the other center of their power, the eunuch-staffed Palace Secretariat (*Shu-mi yüan*), which duplicated some of the functions of the Han-lin Academy.[167] However, Te-tsung's reign was not a period of great eunuch influence, as his predecessor's had been, and the problem may not have presented itself in such urgent terms to Lu Chih and his contemporaries.

At this time, moreover, there was a general improvement in the strategic situation. The Tibetans, who had resumed hostilities immediately after 785, were now defeated by their northwestern neighbors, the Uighurs,[168] while in the southwest the Chinese position was greatly strengthened by Lu Chih's relative, Wei Kao, who not only built up very powerful forces to defend Szechwan, but also induced Nan-chao, the independent kingdom in Yunnan, to break its alliance with the Tibetans and renew its allegiance to the T'ang court.[169] The later years of Te-tsung's reign saw a slow but steady improvement in the frontier situation as well.

An even more urgent problem for the court after 786 was the reorganization of finance. Lu Chih devoted much of his attention to this problem, the culmination being his great six-part memorial of 794. To understand his contribution fully, however, it is necessary to go back even before the beginning of Te-tsung's reign.[170]

During the long years of the An Lu-shan and Ssu Shih-ming risings (755–63) the whole of the former administrative and fiscal structure of the empire had been disrupted. The old tax system (*tsu-yung-tiao*), a complex of head taxes and labor obligations imposed at a uniform rate upon all registered males of taxable age and status, could no longer function when the local authorities ceased to have either the power or the opportunity to register the population carefully. Already in 736 tax quotas had been imposed by locality for administrative convenience and to save assessing every area's liability afresh each year.[171] Now, with the complete collapse of the mechanism for reregistration, collection of all taxes was being attempted in accordance with these old quotas. But the rebellions had brought about large-scale movements of population and this led to a very inequitable distribution of the tax load; even in areas where the actual population had suddenly multiplied several times over, the whole of the old quota for the *tsu-yung-tiao* continued to be levied upon the small proportion of officially registered native families, the bulk of the new immigrant settlers escaping scot-free.[172] Moreover, the more independent of the new provincial administrations, in particular those of the north and northeast, paid no taxes to the central administration, and thus demands upon the remaining loyal areas were proportionately heavier. In these areas there was much hardship, and a large variety of supplementary taxes, upon the acreage of land in cultivation or upon property assessments, were imposed.

In spite of such supplementary taxation, the revenues of the central government from direct taxation—which until 755 had provided almost the whole of their annual income—fell off sharply, much of what was actually collected being expended by the local authorities. To replace this lost revenue, the government under Tai-tsung had entrusted the chief financial expert, Liu Yen, with the reimposition of the salt monopoly devised under the Han dynasty. This scheme, which put all salt production under the control of the authorities, who sold salt to the distributor merchants with a very heavy surcharge, was essentially an indirect tax upon retail trade.[173] Since the government controlled most, though not all,[174] of the regions where salt was produced, the scheme enabled the central government to collect revenue through retail merchants from the population of those provinces where its control was insecure.

By the end of Tai-tsung's reign the salt revenue amounted to more than half of the total state revenues.[175] But these funds were administered by a new semi-independent department, the Salt and Iron Commission (*Yen-t'ieh shih*), which was directly responsible to the central executive and independent of the established Board of Finance. Moreover, its income, instead of being paid into the regular treasury departments, or disposed of through the established Department of Public Revenues (*Tu-chih*), was used to finance the reconstruction and maintenance of the canal network. The canals made it possible for the overpopulated and comparatively unproductive region around Ch'ang-an to draw grain supplies from the Yangtze valley, the richest and most productive region in China. The Salt Commission also invested in a variety of other enterprises and became a semi-autonomous organization, based not in the capital but in Yang-chou, with virtual control of the finances of southern China.[176]

As a result of these developments, the old-established central finance offices under the Board of Finance (*Hu-pu*) declined rapidly in power, and by 779 had become sinecures. The disposition of the comparatively meager revenues available to the authorities in Ch'ang-an passed in large measure into the hands of the eunuch managers of the emperor's household treasuries.[177] The established financial organization of the first half of the dynasty thus lost ground in every direction— to the eunuchs at the capital and to the governors and the salt administration in the provinces.

When Te-tsung ascended the throne in 779 he was, as we have seen, ambitious to restore imperial authority. Central to his plan was the creation of a new financial structure that would enable him to build up and maintain a powerful regime without a critical dependence on the Salt Commission, which threatened at any time to become a semi-autonomous regional organization even more powerful than any of the provincial governments. The formulation and implementation of this policy was entrusted to Yang Yen, a former partisan of Tai-tsung's favorite Yüan Tsai. Yang had been banished to a provincial post when Yüan Tsai fell from power in 777 and was a bitter personal enemy of Liu Yen.

Yang Yen's reform, the *liang-shui fa*, swept away the chaotic tax structure of the preceding decades, replacing the old *tsu-yung-tiao* and its numerous supplementary taxes with a new tax levied upon acreage of cultivated land and upon the assessed property of all households. Although quotas of adult males were maintained as the basis for emergency levies of labor services (*tsa-yao*), the male adult (*ting*) ceased to be the basic unit of taxation. The new system contained no innovations in taxation, but merely rationalized and reorganized the previous system,

the old *tsu-yung-tiao* being submerged in what had formerly been supplementary systems of taxation based on property and land. All the new
taxes were to be collected in two annual installments, one in summer
and one in autumn (hence the name *liang-shui*, literally "two tax").[178]
The land tax was to be paid in grain and the household property tax
either in cash or in goods paid in lieu of a cash assessment.[179] It is almost impossible to say whether the measure increased or reduced the
fiscal burden of the average taxpayer, but it must have seemed a great
advantage to be liable only to two annual contributions at a known and
regular rate instead of the endless petty levies and impositions under the
old system. Moreover, the abandonment by the government of the
theoretically equally endowed male adult (a fiction rooted in the *chün-
t'ien* land-allotment scheme which had long since fallen into desuetude)
as the basic unit of taxation, and his replacement by the more solid
realities of land and property, were also clearly a step toward a more
equitable distribution of the fiscal burden. Last, the old distinction
between native (*chu*) and settler (*k'o*) families was abolished, ending
yet another source of unfair treatment.[180]

But important as these features are—and the new system remained
the basis of the direct tax system of China until the sixteenth century—
it is likely that Yang Yen's contemporaries thought of the measure as
essentially an *administrative* rather than a fiscal reform. The memorial
in which Yang Yen suggested his program makes this clear. As I mentioned above, the new system was designed to effect a compromise between the central authorities and the individual provinces, by which
each of the latter agreed to pay annually to the capital a fixed quota of
taxes. The exact proportions of the provincial revenues to be devoted
to prefectural, provincial, and central expenditures were also fixed.[181]
In return, the provinces were allowed wide latitude to collect taxes as
they found it convenient within the general framework of the *liang-shui*
system, and were given authority to dispose freely of a fixed proportion
of their total tax quota for local expenditure. This meant too that actual
tax rates varied widely from province to province and from one prefecture to another within the same province. This was the first general tax
system that did not incorporate the principle of a uniform tax rate for
the whole empire, and that combined a wide variety of local tax rates
with the general principle of progressive taxation based upon a property
assessment. By the quota system the central power abandoned its claim
to a detailed control of local finances (even auditing was delegated
to the provincial authorities) in return for the promise of a fixed revenue.

Like the changes in the methods of taxation, these administrative

changes were also more of a stabilization of the status quo than a radical
change in practice, and represent the last stage in a process of administrative simplification that went back almost half a century. A quota
system had been introduced as early as 736 in Li Lin-fu's Permanently
Applicable Orders (*Ch'ang-hsing chih-fu*), although the purpose then
had been merely to avoid the excessively complicated bookkeeping
under the old system whereby the expected income and expenditure
of every prefecture and county had to be calculated afresh each year.
The central authorities, however, did not relinquish their right to control the last detail of prefectural finance, and the quotas were subject
to reassessment by the central government. Furthermore, they contained no element of compromise between central and regional interests.

The new reform transferred the quotas to the provinces (though
these quotas were broken down into specific quotas for each area down
to the county level), making the provinces now the largest unit of local
government in place of the smaller prefectures, and all quotas were
reassessed. The provincial governments had become the effective tax-
collecting authority long before 780, and had been auditing their own
accounts since 777, and here again the reform only formalized existing
practices. But, whereas Li Lin-fu's quotas were a temporary expedient
and their periodic revision could be expected, the quotas negotiated
with the provincial governors by the Commissioners for Advancement
and Disgrace in 780 were expected to be more or less permanent.[182]

This reform, by assuring regular revenues from each province, led
to the revival of direct taxation as the major source of revenue. In its
first year of operation the *liang-shui* produced more than the total state
revenues of preceding years, including the revenue from salt.[183] Yang
Yen was able to abolish the Salt Commission as an independent authority, and to attempt restoration of financial power to the old, regularly
established offices at the capital. This was no easy task, for many of
these offices had completely ceased to function. But the treasuries were
restored, and control of the state's reserves of money, grain, and commodities was taken from the hands of the eunuchs, who had for many
years been deeply involved in financial matters.[184]

There can thus be no doubt that Yang Yen's reforms were essentially
well conceived. They led to increased central revenues, a more assured
annual income, simplification of administrative practice, the abolition
of the semi-independent Salt Commission, and the return to the regular
bureaucratic organs of financial authority; at the same time they made
tax collection more regular and spread the fiscal load more equitably
among the population. The system certainly laid the foundation for the

dynastic revival of Hsien-tsung's reign, and no serious attempt to change it radically was made during T'ang times.

Nevertheless, it was put into operation at a doubly unfortunate time. As we noted earlier, Te-tsung's determination to revive central power at the expense of the provincial authorities, and his emphasis on financial reforms to accomplish this, had led to prolonged rebellions and, finally, to his acceptance of the status quo, at least in the case of the northeastern provinces. At the same time these rebellions had placed the government under such a financial strain that a spate of supplementary taxes had had to be temporarily imposed. Although these minor taxes were speedily abolished in the face of a fresh rebellion, the government was also forced to make all-round increases in the provincial quotas for the *liang-shui* tax,[185] and to revert to its old dependence upon the income from salt, the Salt Commission being once again allowed to become a powerful organ of government.[186] These developments, which meant a considerable increase in the burden of both direct and indirect taxes, assessed mainly in cash, remained in force even after the end of the rebellions in 786.

The year 780 was not only an unfortunate time to attempt the reassertion of central authority but also a particularly unfortunate time, from the economic point of view, to attempt a reassessment of taxes. China was then at the end of a period of rapidly growing inflation, which had persisted unchecked since the An Lu-shan rising. The *liang-shui* quotas and the local tax rates were thus fixed in terms of a seriously inflated currency.[187] After 786, however, the situation was reversed, and a period of progressive deflation set in, which lasted until the 820's. The result of this was that the tax load, assessed at the very inflated prices of 780 and subsequently increased by 20 percent during the rebellion, became more and more onerous as the value of goods, in which almost all taxes were actually paid, fell. The financial officials of Hsien-tsung's reign (805–20) estimated that the tax load as paid in terms of commodities, in particular in silk cloth, had risen between 300 and 500 percent since 780.[188]

What then were the reactions of Lu Chih to this serious situation, which by 792 had reached a critical point? We noted that he had opposed the imposition of heavy irregular taxation during 783, and that he had been instrumental in drafting the series of Acts of Grace in 784–85 which reduced these impositions, granted extensive remissions of taxation, and canceled arrears so as to permit a speedy return to normal. We know that Lu Chih had supported Yang Yen against Lu Ch'i, and it is interesting to see, from the Act of Grace promulgated in the first month of 785, that he accepted the fact that the *liang-shui* system had represented an improvement in fiscal administration: [189]

Formerly taxes were both onerous and multifarious, so that the people were unaware of the true state of the law. When the *liang-shui* was fixed, quotas were established which were easy to follow.

However, when the rising of the armies ensued, the original assessments were overstepped, and the letter of the law was not adhered to. Petty officials became increasingly corrupt and caused trouble to our people. These should now be allowed some respite. All levies and labor services beyond the *liang-shui* that have been instituted on an emergency basis must be abolished. All arrears due the common people in the environs of the capital in respect of "harmonious procurements" [i.e., compulsory purchase by the state] are to be paid up by the Public Revenue Department. . . .

At approximately this time[190] Lu Chih also drafted an edict ordering the officials concerned to give counsel on the reduction of salt prices, which is of interest, since Yang Yen's program of 780 had deliberately attempted to reduce the role of salt revenue.

Under the system established by the Three Dynasties of antiquity, the mountains and marshes were not closed to the common people, and the materials and benefits of Heaven and Earth were shared with the people. But the Kingly Way gradually declined, and the powerful Hegemon Kings strove to gain leadership. Then there was established protection by the "overseers of the seas" [*chi-wang*], and the system of monopolies began to flourish to supplement the taxes to pay for the armies and to relax the impositions on the land. Nevertheless, they still spoke of "sharing the marshes between the state and the people," and this principle was respected for generation after generation, and so eventually became a fixed rule.

Recently, however, for the past thirty years invasions have brought widespread disorders. Among the subjugated population of the borders, agriculture has been completely disrupted; in the villages shuttle and loom lie empty and idle. The war chariots grow more numerous, and the demand for army rations constantly increases. Many of the people have fled, and their farmlands have reverted to waste and weeds. As a result the state has taken complete control of the profits from refining salt from the sea as a source of revenue. If we estimate the income therefrom, it is double the land revenue [*t'ien-tsu*] in any one year.

Lately the expenses of the armies have increased day by day, and the price of salt has risen daily until now one *tou* of rice exchanges for one *sheng* of salt. The basic and secondary occupations [i.e., agriculture and trade] have changed places, and the maintenance of the laws is rendered precarious. We are anxious lest the poor and needy shall lose the means of nourishing themselves. For, if the five flavors lose their correct balance, the hundred sicknesses will begin to breed and the people will thus be grievously afflicted by premature death.

Alas, we have not continued the policies of the former Sage-Kings, and have merely regarded from afar the laws of the former rulers. Already unable to pacify the country and thus relieve our financial needs, we have been unable to rescind the prohibition [i.e., the salt monopoly] and thus benefit the common people. Our striving for profit in competition with the people has become an increasingly grave abuse; their barren and exhausted condition causes us distress. If we ourselves do not show them pity, who will be able to alleviate their sufferings?

Regarding the salt monopoly in Chiang-Huai and Shan-nei [i.e., Szechwan] we order that the Chancellery and Secretariat together with the Department of Public Revenue discuss it and give us counsel, so as to arrange a reduction in price while at the same time radically reforming the abuses. They shall speedily draft detailed proposals and submit them to the throne. They shall do away with harsh impositions and put an end to dishonest cheating. They shall devote their energies to benefiting the people, and must certainly accord with our will.

It is clear from this that although Lu Chih, as an orthodox Confucian, disapproved of the salt monopoly as offending against the physiocratic view of the primacy of agriculture as the basis for a state's economy, and saw it as a degenerate departure from the ideal financial methods of antiquity to be blamed upon the Hegemon Huan of Ch'i (as is implied by the silent quotation from the *Tso-chuan* referring to the office of *"chi-wang"*) and thus associated with the Legalists, he nevertheless realized that the state would be unable to exist without it. He therefore suggested that the system be reformed and made less of a burden on the people, not that it be abandoned.

In the years that followed, it became more and more obvious that no drastic and radical change could be made in the financial system which had grown up during the rebellion. In 786 Ts'ui Tsao attempted to reunify all financial administration under the Board of Finance, as Yang Yen had done for a brief period in 780. But this move was frustrated by Han Huang, the extremely powerful governor of the Yangtze delta region and also transportation commissioner, whose exertions had to a large extent financed the central government during the later stages of the rebellion. By 792, when Lu Chih took office, a rancorous tension existed between the Public Revenue Department, which had become the chief effective organ in the Board of Finance and controlled northern China, and the Salt Commission, which was theoretically subordinated to the Board of Finance but effectively independent and in control of the south. This tension, aggravated by the personal enmity between the heads of the two departments, led to a crisis when in 792 the two flatly refused to cooperate.[192]

Almost the first act of Lu Chih as Chief Minister was to formalize this division. Control of all the empire's finances, including both monopoly income and direct taxation, was divided geographically between the Public Revenue Department, which became the dominant financial authority at the capital and in the north, and the Salt Commission, which gained complete control of southern China, by far the richer of the two regions. This division of authority on a regional basis was a reversion to the state of affairs in Tai-tsung's reign, and an open admission of the central government's failure to impose its control over the empire's finances. The settlement seems to have been made by the emperor in person,[193] but Lu Chih must have concurred. Some such arrangement was in the circumstances unavoidable. Unfortunately Lu Chih's surviving works contain nothing bearing on the incident. But if he had disagreed with such a radical change of policy, he would almost certainly have memorialized against it, and his memorials for this period seem rather fully preserved. One factor that may have influenced him, quite apart from considerations of expediency, was that the new Salt Commissioner who gained financial control of the south, Chang P'ang, was one of his personal supporters.[194] Moreover, the danger of the Salt Commissioners' becoming completely autonomous provincial magnates had been temporarily reduced after the death of Han Huang by splitting the vital Yangtze delta region into a number of smaller provinces, and by forbidding the Salt Commissioners from concurrently holding office as provincial governors.[195]

Under Lu Chih's administration, both the Salt Commission and the Public Revenue Department began to develop multifarious new interests, for the most part unrelated to centralized policy. When Lu Chih took office, the whole of the Honan-Hopei plain and much of the Yangtze valley had been ravaged by disastrous floods,[196] which curtailed all financial developments in 793 and made relief of the victims a matter of extreme urgency. The charitable granaries (i-ts'ang), maintained for relief purposes during the early days of the T'ang dynasty, had fallen into disuse, and to replace them Lu Chih deputed Chang P'ang to devise a system for the taxation of tea, now a very important item in internal trade. The income was to be used for relief purposes, but, like the income from the old charitable granaries, was soon transformed into a source of ordinary revenue.[197] The tea tax was Lu Chih's only permanent contribution to the financial system, which is somewhat ironical when one considers his basic opposition to the taxation of property and trade.

Lu Chih's most important single act in the financial field was, however, the submission in 794 of his great six-part memorial, "On making taxation equitable and thus showing pity for the common people," a searching criticism of the liang-shui system and the many abuses that had grown up since its imposition.[198] Lu Chih, who as we have seen had supported Yang Yen during his ministry and accepted the benefits

of his reform as late as 785, had now not only come round to reintroduc-
ing the system of regional finance established under Yang Yen's enemy
Liu Yen but also developed a violent opposition to Yang's basic policy.

The memorial begins with an attack upon the *liang-shui* system
from the standpoint of conventional Confucian (and for that matter
Legalist) physiocratic economic theory. All the precedents of antiquity
supported taxation levied upon the peasant-producer at a uniform fixed
rate, and by somewhat forced analogies the *tsu-yung-tiao* system was
equated with the practice of the ancient sage-kings. These "did not demand from any man more than the just amount, but also did not allow
him to escape by paying less. A man's taxes were not increased if he
labored hard at his crops, nor lightened if he abandoned farming. Thus
the people were encouraged to sow as much as possible . . . Only in
such ways could the people be caused to live contentedly in their abodes,
and labor to the best of their powers." In such a system it was possible
to follow the dictum of the Confucian *Analects* that "he who rules a
state or household is to be concerned not with poverty but with inequity,
not with lack of numbers but with lack of harmony."

Lu Chih held that the financial chaos of Tai-tsung's reign had been
the result not of the shortcomings of the laws, but of the deterioration of
the political situation. The new system had not taken this into account,
and "if the times are at fault, one must restore the times to order." This
was perhaps an unfair criticism, since Te-tsung and Yang Yen had, in
their own way, been determined to put the times in order, and had only
lacked the power to do so. Far more relevant was Lu Chih's contention
that the new system had been put into force before it had been worked
out in detail, that no adequate policy direction had been given to the
commissioners who had worked out the quotas, and that the consequences of its imposition had not been foreseen.

The whole *liang-shui* system is dismissed as a permanent system
constructed out of a variety of expedients, which perpetuated the abuses
of Tai-tsung's times rather than rectifying them. In particular it perpetuated the inequalities between various districts resulting from population shifts, and by doing so encouraged further migration from regions
of high tax rates, leaving still fewer taxpayers to meet the local quotas.
The quotas fixed in 780 robbed the whole financial structure of flexibility
in the face of local emergencies.

The analysis of the abuses under the new system is lucid and thought-
ful. For example, in his treatment of the abandonment of the "adult
male" (*ting-fu*) basis for taxation in the classical systems, and its replacement by a property assessment, he does not merely denounce the
new system for neglecting the "basic form of livelihood" (i.e., agricul-

ture). He goes on to a very pertinent discussion of the inequalities that
arose from a simple property assessment (the *liang-shui* assessment appears to have included movable and immovable assets, accumulations
of currency and goods, etc.). He points out that different types of
property brought in very different rates of return, and that to levy a tax
on a flat valuation of possessions led to gross inequality in actual taxation. He also points out a number of anomalies, e.g., that land was
included in property assessments and thus subject to double taxation
since the owner also had to pay the separate tax on cultivated land.
It is perhaps missing the point to describe Lu Chih's arguments as
essentially conservative. Certainly he compared the situation and the
institutions of his time unfavorably with those of the early T'ang. But
he was undoubtedly correct in blaming the financial position upon the
emergence of a new political situation, and any of his contemporaries
would have agreed that the dynasty was in decline—witness their constant comparisons between their own times and the Ch'un-ch'iu period,
or between the early T'ang and the early Chou, and the preoccupation of
scholars with the "feudalism" of the Ch'un-ch'iu and Warring States
periods. Lu Chih certainly looked to the past for examples—but this
again was a universal attitude of mind. Tu Yu, who differed from Lu
Chih in approving the *liang-shui* reform, represented a far more radical
outlook on most political questions, and believed in continuous progress,
also believed that "the Way of the ancients" was an inexhaustible source
of models for present circumstances,[199] though his point of comparison
is often the Ch'in state rather than the hazy utopia of the Three
Dynasties.

Lu Chih's theoretical misgivings as an orthodox Confucian were
however secondary in importance to the demands of the actual situation that as a practical statesman he had to face. It is here, in the analysis and presentation of complex practical problems, that his great memorial far surpasses anything written on finance by any other T'ang
statesman. His solutions moreover are in no way reactionary. He
clearly accepted the fact that Yang Yen's reform could not be reversed,
whatever its failings, and he nowhere suggests that the whole scheme
be scrapped and the old land-allotment and tax system revived. He
advocates quite concrete measures for eliminating the worst inequalities of the *liang-shui* system and for preventing its further deterioration.
These suggestions were practical, and it would seem proof of their
soundness that, although Te-tsung was much too preoccupied with
raising short-term revenues to do anything about Lu Chih's suggestions,
the reforms actually carried out later in the dynasty under Hsien-tsung
and his successors are all mentioned implicitly or explicitly in this
document.

This great tour de force yielded no immediate results, however. The main reason for its negative reception lay in Lu Chih's own increasingly difficult political situation. Over the years Te-tsung had become more and more avaricious, and a situation now occurred similar to that which had arisen at Feng-t'ien, when Lu Chih had castigated him for attempting to take the state revenues into his own hands. In 792 Lu Chih had been instrumental in the fall of the corrupt Chief Minister Tou Shen. In the next year he was also involved when Tou was ordered to commit suicide. Even before the order to commit suicide had been issued, Te-tsung ordered an inventory taken of all Tou Shen's property, so that it could be confiscated for his private treasury, such confiscated properties, particularly lands, being administered as part of the emperor's personal estate by the eunuch Household Commissioners for Estates (*Nei chuang-chai-shih*).[200] Lu Chih presented a very succinct memorial pointing out that there were only two legal grounds for such confiscation of property, rebellion and the recovery of the profits of criminal acts, neither of which was operative in Tou Shen's case. If the emperor were to go on with his proposed action, Lu Chih said, "I fear that he will compromise his own righteousness through his desire for possessions."[201] Te-tsung seemed to have been dissuaded, but as soon as Tou Shen had committed suicide, the eunuchs took possession of all his valuables and his slaves and brought them back to the capital.[202]

A further incident involving the emperor's personal income and the eunuchs had occurred at the end of 792, when it had been proposed to establish a Household Commissioner for Foreign Shipping (*Shih-po chung-shih*) in Annam in addition to the Commissioner (*Shih-po-shih*) at Canton. The duties of these commissioners were to control and tax all goods—mostly luxury products—coming from abroad. Hanoi had become an important port, rivaling Canton, but, as Lu Chih was quick to point out, the proposal was not to appoint a regular career official, as was done at Canton, but to send a eunuch. This, he said, would "display a covetous disposition to the world, openly invite the use of bribery at court, befoul the pure atmosphere of the times, and corrupt the divine imperial task of transformation through virtue."[203] One can hardly be surprised that Te-tsung viewed advice expressed in such blunt terms with disfavor.

Lu Chih's attempts to frustrate the emperor in his efforts to enrich himself were of no avail, since he was saddled with a bitter opponent in control of the Public Revenue Department. This was P'ei Yen-ling, who as we have seen above had, like Lu Chih, been a personal aide to the emperor during the early years of his reign. Since the ministry of Ts'ui Tsao in 786, P'ei had served in a succession of financial posts, advancing rapidly while his old patron Tung Chin was Chief Minister from 789 to

792.[204] When, shortly after Lu Chih came to power, Pan Hung, the con-
tentious and none-too-honest head of the Public Revenue Department,
died, Lu proposed the appointment of his own protégé Li Sun. Li Sun
was a very talented young man, who later came under the patronage of
Tu Yu and became a power in finance under Hsien-tsung, producing a
crop of excellent young subordinates who dominated the financial administration until about 830,[205] and there can be no doubt that this
would have been an excellent appointment. The emperor, however, insisted upon the appointment of P'ei Yen-ling, who was not only an older
and far more experienced administrator, but also a person on whom
he could depend for help in his schemes for personal enrichment. Lu
Chih opposed this appointment in a memorial outspoken even for him.[206]
After first tracing the history of the Public Revenue Department's development into a key organization in the administration of finance, he
argued that appointments to it should be made with the greatest care,
and then went on to attack P'ei Yen-ling's personal reputation in the
most specific terms. The emperor, however, took no heed, and the
appointment went through.

The appointment of P'ei Yen-ling might be said to mark the beginning of Lu Chih's downfall. There had been continual conflict between
them: P'ei Yen-ling took every opportunity to slander Lu Chih to the
emperor; and Lu continually petitioned for P'ei's dismissal. Tension
between them mounted through 793 and 794. P'ei Yen-ling immediately
set about imposing a variety of irregular supplementary taxes, and
established a whole series of irregular treasuries into which these taxes
and regular tax arrears were to be paid. He also greatly expanded the
personnel of his department.[207]

A crisis arose over the supply of fodder for the cavalry of the palace
armies, which were by now firmly in the control of the eunuchs. P'ei
Yen-ling wished to have all the taxes of the metropolitan district around
Ch'ang-an paid in terms of hay and fodder rather than grain, and to
take possession of vacant lands in the region as summer pastures for the
cavalry horses. This was in fact a very urgent problem, since the Tibetan
invasion of Kansu had robbed the Chinese of all the great pasturages
maintained by the state before the An Lu-shan rebellion, and efforts to
replace them had been unsuccessful. But P'ei's plan, which would
have not only led to a deficiency in tax income in the capital, but also
paralyzed the complicated labor-procurement system, was ill-conceived,
and Lu Chih counseled the emperor strongly against it.[208]

The emperor was now clearly veering toward the support of P'ei
Yen-ling. In the sixth month of 794 one of the vice-presidents of the

Censorate had impeached P'ei on charges of corruption, but P'ei had slandered him to the emperor, and succeeded in having him banished to a petty post in the provinces.[209] Moreover, one of the emperor's advisers in the Han-lin Academy, Wu T'ung-hsüan, Lu Chih's former colleague, also bore Lu a grudge, and slandered him to the emperor, accusing him of taking bribes.[210] Last, Lu Chih had serious differences of opinion with his fellow Chief Minister, Chao Ching.[211]

Lu Chih must have realized that his dismissal was now only a matter of time. In the eleventh month of 794 he therefore presented a massive and circumstantial indictment of P'ei Yen-ling, particularizing all his offenses and attacking his character on every point. After this document had been received, Te-tsung was forced to choose between the two men, and as was almost inevitable chose P'ei Yen-ling.[212] Lu Chih was demoted to a minor post in the household of the Heir Apparent.[213] Early in 795 P'ei accused Lu Chih of slandering him and by implication the emperor as well, and as a result Lu and his principal supporters were banished to distant posts in southern China.[214]

It was generally expected that the emperor would now have Lu Chih executed, but the Heir Apparent, Yang Ch'eng, the President of the Censorate, and many other high-ranking officials interceded for him at court.[215] At the same time Wei Kao, the extremely powerful provincial governor in Szechwan who was Lu's maternal relation, several times offered to resign command of his province to Lu Chih.[216] The emperor could afford to take no chances with Wei Kao, who had been largely responsible for the great improvement in the strategic situation on the Tibetan frontier, and Lu Chih was allowed to live in obscure retirement.

In his provincial post Lu Chih is said to have lived behind closed doors in his yamen, so that the local populace never even knew what he looked like.[217] He wrote nothing further of a controversial or political nature, and devoted himself to the study of medicine, compiling an extensive collection of prescriptions in fifteen chapters entitled *Lu-shih chi-chien fang*, which was still extant in Ming times but has since disappeared.[218] This was an interest which Lu Chih shared with the emperor. In his youth Te-tsung had for a while been tutored by the Taoist Li Pi, who later became his Chief Minister while Lu Chih was serving as his personal aide. Te-tsung himself had compiled a short *materia medica*.[219] It is just possible that Lu Chih hoped by this new line of work to recommend himself to the emperor while at the same time underlining his withdrawal from active politics. When Te-tsung died in 805 the new ministers wished to recall Lu Chih to office, but it was found that he had died shortly before.

Lu Chih's career illuminates for us the all-important relationship between an emperor and his personal advisers. Rising to power as he did through the Han-lin Academy, Lu Chih was placed from the beginning in an exceptionally intimate relationship with Te-tsung, a relationship strengthened by the extraordinary circumstances of the emperor's exile from the capital. This relationship certainly accelerated Lu Chih's career. He had none of the frustrating periods in minor provincial offices that were the usual lot of officials, even the most successful. But it appears that although Lu Chih was a very good confidential adviser, as a minister his uncompromising and outspoken attitudes helped to make controversies centering upon him particularly fierce in tone. With his extremely critical judgments of other ministers, and his habit of expressing his criticisms in very sharp language, it was inevitable that sooner or later he would fall foul of his royal master. When this finally happened, Lu Chih could not fall back upon the support of a powerful party of his own. As a palace adviser he had been isolated from the politics of the court, and when he lost the imperial favor, although he had many sympathizers among the ministers, their protest was in vain. Te-tsung's taste for autocratic power, which had led him to favor such irregular institutions as the Han-lin Academy and thus permit Lu Chih to rise so quickly to the highest office, now ensured that he would override the opinions of his courtiers and sacrifice Lu Chih for a more pliant favorite. Lu Chih's career is above all an example of the hazards attendant on a career as a personal servant of an autocratic emperor.

Wang Gung-wu

FENG TAO:
AN ESSAY ON CONFUCIAN LOYALTY

During the eighteenth century, the editors of the *Hsü T'ung-chih* classified disloyal ministers and officers into ten groups. In the category reserved for the worst examples were only two men, the soldier Hou I (886–965) and the minister Feng Tao (882–954), both of the period of the Five Dynasties (907–59) and both accused of having "confounded the great relationships and not known shame."[1]

The *Hsü T'ung-chih*, which consists largely of biographies of the T'ang, Five Dynasties, Sung, and Yüan periods, was compiled by imperial order in the years 1767–85, during the Ch'ing dynasty. Under the circumstances,[2] the Chinese editors, as one would expect, placed a great deal of emphasis on the question of dynastic loyalty and expressed themselves strongly about those who had disgraced the profession of "official." It is not surprising that they should consider Feng Tao reprehensible, for no other man had served as a chief minister to five different imperial houses and ten emperors. Hou I could be taken less seriously as he was by origin a mere soldier and, unlike Feng Tao, a devout Buddhist who had never pretended to be a Confucian.[3] But the editors were, in a sense, not responsible for heaping so much odium on Feng Tao. They were merely carrying to a logical conclusion the judgment of two famous Sung historians, Ou-yang Hsiu (1007–72) and Ssu-ma Kuang (1019–89), who had in the eleventh century made a new and vigorous Confucianism the basis of their historiography.

Ou-yang Hsiu, rewriting the history of the Five Dynasties, singled out Feng Tao as the symbol of the period's degeneracy. It was in his preface to Feng Tao's biography that he made his pronouncements on honor and loyalty and bemoaned the fact that the prominent Confucians of the time lacked both.[4] Ssu-ma Kuang enlarged upon this in the *Tzu-chih t'ung-chien* and argued that whatever good Feng Tao might have done by remaining in office was as nothing since he had lived without honor. "The Superior Man [*ta-jen*] will achieve humanity through sacrifice but not prolong his life if it would destroy that humanity."[5]

These were very strong words to use about a man who had been respected in his lifetime. Feng Tao was highly regarded among many of his contemporaries as a conscientious Confucian, a temperate man, and even a model Chief Minister. For nearly a hundred years after his death this reputation survived in some circles, although it was acknowledged that he had done little to justify the faith placed in him by the various emperors. Among those who thought well of him were Fan Chih (911–64), the first historian of the Five Dynasties,[6] Hsüeh Chü-cheng (912–81) and the other compilers of the *Chiu wu-tai shih*,[7] and later, Wu Ch'u-hou (fl. 1060–86), a contemporary of Ou-yang Hsiu and Ssu-ma Kuang.[8] But the adverse judgment of the two great Sung historians prevailed, and from then onward Feng Tao was the example of how not to serve a dynasty and the butt of many jokes about loyalty. His name even went into the Chinese idiom in somewhat the same way as "the Vicar of Bray" went into the English.

What was Feng Tao really like? Was he really unworthy of the respect his contemporaries had for him? Or did his contemporaries really regard him as highly as has been made out? Also, did he deserve to be "revalued" in the annals of China or was he merely a victim of a great change in social, political, and philosophical values? This paper proposes to consider some of the possible answers to these questions.

The period in which Feng Tao lived has been given little attention by Western historians. Even among Chinese historians the Five Dynasties have always been treated either as an extension of the T'ang or as the prelude to the Sung. Only recently has a more systematic approach begun to reveal the significance of the period as a time of great social and political change,[9] lending a new dimension to its usual characterization as a time of anarchy and confusion. So unstable were the conditions that the T'ang empire was divided intermittently among six to eight "kingdoms," and North China saw a succession of five dynasties, the longest of which lasted sixteen years and the shortest only four.

North China was especially unstable. The rebellion of An Lu-shan in the middle of the eighth century resulted in the loss to central control of much of North China, and throughout the ninth century the region of Ho-pei (roughly the present province of Hopei) proceeded to develop independently of the rest of the empire. The descendants of An Lu-shan's officers, including many non-Chinese (Khitan, Hsi, Koreans, and Uighur Turks), commanded the three major armies that came to dominate the affairs of the area, and in the third decade of the ninth century, after a series of abortive attempts to appoint its own governors, the imperial court gave up trying to control internal affairs there. In line with its policy of tolerance, the imperial government resigned itself to accepting tribute in lieu of regular taxes from the arrogant military governors of the three "provinces" of Lu-lung, Ch'eng-te, and Wei-po in the Ho-pei region.[10]

Feng Tao was a man of Ho-pei. According to him, his family was originally from Chi-chou in Ch'eng-te province, but, as far as we know, his immediate ancestors had lived for a long while in Ying-chou.[11] Although not far from Chi-chou, Ying-chou came eventually under the jurisdiction of the military governor of Lu-lung (capital at Yu-chou, the modern Peking). Ying-chou was one of the frontier prefectures of this extensive province and one that was often fought over by rival governors from the east, west, and south. The situation there was especially unstable during the last decade of the ninth century, and if Feng Tao did spend his early years in his home town, it is possible to imagine him growing up under conditions that would have well prepared him for the troubled era of the Five Dynasties. The province of Lu-lung was notorious for its powerful army, whose organization of guards chose the governor or unseated him virtually at will. From 821 to 894, for example, the province had nineteen governors, one of whom governed for twenty-two years. The eighteen remaining governors averaged less than three years each. In fact, of the nineteen governors, only four died in office (two of them within a year of taking office) and one retired (also within a year). Of the rest, six were killed and eight were driven out, in most cases by the very guards organization that had put them in.[12]

This frequent change of governors would have made administration virtually impossible had it not been for officials recruited locally from the gentry families of the province. These families provided the literate assistants to the governor and to his aides and some of the accountants and clerks who handled the routine business of provincial government. This local "civil service" was not entirely independent of the central government at Ch'ang-an. It was possible for the senior officials to acquire honorific titles and to have a minor court rank while holding a local provincial office. Eventually, if some of them decided that it was to their advantage to leave for the capital, their titles and qualifications would give them a fair chance of getting a regular official appointment. If, on the other hand, their intention was to follow their careers within Lu-lung province, they had to develop a high degree of resilience. In order to survive the quick succession of governors, the wise official avoided too close an identification with any particular governor and cultivated a reputation for discretion and trustworthiness. By contrast, young men of gentry families elsewhere in the empire, being without an autonomous provincial service in which to build their careers, were dependent ultimately on the favor of the central government for advancement. Feng Tao, having grown up on the border of the province, would have been well aware that in Lu-lung he could rise to high provincial office with only local competition. There is no evidence that he ever left the province in his youth, nor is there evidence that experience elsewhere would have qualified him better for his local career.

Regionalism had by this time so undermined the T'ang empire that all that was needed to destroy the empire altogether was another sizable rebellion, and this Wang Hsien-chih and Huang Ch'ao provided from 875 on. The rebellion burned its way through most of China, leaving in its trail a greatly intensified regional growth. What land remained in the hands of the T'ang imperial court was then bitterly fought over until Chu Wen, one of Huang Ch'ao's generals who had surrendered to the T'ang, thought himself ready to found a new dynasty. Without waiting to crush the regional governments which had partitioned the old T'ang empire, he established himself as emperor of Liang. The problem of regionalism persisted and troubled the empire for the years that formed the period of the Five Dynasties. The dynasties were:

LIANG (907–23)

T'ai-tsu (Chu Wen), 907–12
Prince of Ying (Chu Yu-kuei), 912–13
Prince of Chün (Chu Yu-chen),
   913–23

T'ANG (923–36)

Chuang-tsung (Prince of Chin, Li
   Ts'un-hsü), 923–26
Ming-tsung (Li Ssu-yüan), 926–33
Prince of Sung (Li Ts'ung-hou),
   933–34
Prince of Lu (Li Ts'ung-k'o), 934–36

CHIN (936–46)

Kao-tsu (Shih Ching-t'ang), 936–42
Shao-ti (Shih Ch'ung-kuei), 942–46

Interlude 947

Liao (Khitan) emperor T'ai-tsung
  (Yeh-lü Te-kuang), 927–47

HAN (947–50)

Kao-tsu (Liu Chih-yüan), 947–48
Yin-ti (Liu Ch'eng-yu), 948–50

CHOU (951–59)

T'ai-tsu (Kuo Wei), 951–54
Shih-tsung (Ch'ai Jung), 954–59
Prince of Liang (Ch'ai Tsung-hsün),
  959

These dynasties, when not fighting for survival, were struggling against the deep-rooted regionalism that had grown up during the ninth century.

Feng Tao was born just after the peak of the Huang Ch'ao rebellion in 882 in the county of Ching-ch'eng in Ying prefecture. Feng Tao's family had at this time every reason to be grateful for the regionalism that was to destroy the T'ang dynasty, for it was this very regionalism that protected the Ho-pei region from the Huang Ch'ao rebels, the only region, except Szechwan, to enjoy this freedom. After the rebellion, the region became one of the major battlegrounds in the long struggle for supremacy among the military governors of North China. Before Feng Tao was ten, there had been a mutiny of the prefectural garrison, which the county magistrate had been able to put down only by rounding up some thousand citizens in the area. This magistrate, Liu Jen-kung (d. 914), later governor of Lu-lung province, was the father of the man who gave Feng Tao his first provincial post.[13]

Feng Tao's autobiography claims that his family was descended from the aristocratic Feng clan of the old commandery of Ch'ang-lo (also called Hsin-tu, later Chi-chou, the present Chi-hsien).[14] His immediate ancestors, however, appear to have been content to be gentleman farmers professing themselves Confucians. None of them was known to have held any office, and Feng Tao seems to have been proud of his humble but once eminent family. Liu Jen-kung must have known the Feng family, a prominent one in his county, and possibly it was through Liu Jen-kung that Feng Tao was able to get a post at the provincial capital.

We first find him mentioned in our records only after he was twenty-five, that is, after 907. A great mystery surrounds his youth. He himself says nothing about it except that he had lost his parents during the troubled times when he was young and thus did not know the exact date of his birth.[15] In the eulogistic biography preserved in the *Chiu wu-tai shih*, based probably on his Account of Conduct (*hsing-chuang*),[16] it is said that "when he was young, he was sincere, fond of learning, and talented in writing. He was not ashamed to have poor clothes and poor food. Apart from carrying rice to offer to his parents, he worked only on his reading and reciting. Although his house might be covered by a heavy fall of snow or his whole mat by thick dust, he remained undisturbed."[17]

It is difficult to determine how much truth there is in these stock phrases about the filial son and earnest scholar. They do, however, match the account of the deep effect on him of his father's death and they agree with his later frugality and stoicism. Although the greater part of what we know of Feng Tao seems to have come from Feng Tao himself or from his sons and friends, there is no reason to doubt that this general picture of him as a simple man with the conventional virtues is a correct one.

Certainly his youth was filled with vivid experiences. In 894, when he was twelve, the governor of his province was driven out of the capital and, while passing through the county of Ching-ch'eng, was murdered by the neighboring governor from the province to the east.[18] Six years later, Ching-ch'eng was the battleground between Chu Wen, fighting in the name of the T'ang emperor, and the new governor of Lu-lung province. The prefecture was captured by Chu Wen's forces and Feng Tao probably experienced a little of Chu Wen's administration.[19] Feng Tao was eighteen at the time, old enough to have been conscious of the military and political struggles taking place.

His early career at Yu-chou, the provincial capital, was precarious, and it is claimed in his biography that he counseled the brash young governor Liu Shou-kuang (d. 914) to be cautious and was jailed for his pains. After his release in 911 he escaped to T'ai-yüan to join the leader of the Sha-t'o Turks, at that time the main opponent of Chu Wen's Liang dynasty and the professed leaders of the movement to "restore the T'ang." There Feng Tao, who was then twenty-nine, entered the service of the old eunuch Chang Ch'eng-yeh (846–922) in the Office of Army Supervision,[20] serving in this office for eight years. His service was without distinction and there is no record of what he did. As he was known only for his literary talents, it is supposed that he acted as one of the eunuch's secretaries. He was no longer young at the time (twenty-nine to thirty-seven years old) and had no special skill to justify rapid promotion. What he learned, however, must have been very important to him and may even explain many features of his later life. Chang had served off and on for more than forty years at the T'ang court and could have taught his aide many things about court practice, the role of a civilian in a military organization, and the pitfalls awaiting an official in such unstable times. Feng Tao apparently absorbed much useful information from the successful eunuch, for soon after the Sha-t'o leader, the Prince of Chin, had lost his chief secretary during a battle in 918, Feng Tao was promoted to this post over the head of an ex-T'ang official from a distinguished family.[21] As chief secretary to the prince most likely to succeed to the throne at a time when most of the Prince's earlier supporters were either dead or very old, Feng Tao was virtually assured of a successful career.

Almost immediately after his appointment, he made a show of courage by standing up to the Prince during one of the Prince's childish bursts of anger.[22] It is important to note the prominence given the accounts of Feng Tao's courage in front of Liu Shou-kuang in 911 and before the Prince of Chin in 919 in Feng Tao's biography. Never again until the last year of his life did he disagree with his emperor. His sons and his friends must have been conscious of this and after his death carefully inserted the accounts of these incidents in his biography. The fact is that when Feng Tao admonished the Prince of Chin, he was still under the patronage of Chang Ch'eng-yeh and was to remain under his influence until Chang's death at the end of 922. His so-called act of courage before the Prince in 919 was thus made while still a protégé of Chang's and reflected not the moralistic protests of a Confucian literatus but the tactful advice of an intimate counselor.

The theme of intimacy and highly personal relationship between ruler and minister which derived from the old provincial organization runs through the Five Dynasties. Such relationships were evident at the very first court Feng Tao served, the court of the Prince of Chin himself, better known as the Emperor Chuang-tsung (923–26). This was the court of the T'ang "restoration," and Chuang-tsung set about restoring the T'ang court organization with the eunuchs and their entourage as well as filling most of the posts in the imperial central government. But at the same time, like the Liang emperors before him, he retained most of his provincial officers by giving them posts as commissioners around him, and made his commanders generals in the imperial army. Chuang-tsung was, moreover, unusually fond of acting and kept his own troupe of actors and musicians, who were allowed to advise him on affairs of state. In the ensuing struggle for power among the various groups, the bureaucrats and the generals who were remote from the emperor lost. Of the remaining three groups—eunuchs, actors, and ex-provincial officers—the most influential was the favored acting troupe, which came from the lowest class of society. Against the actors, even Kuo Ch'ung-t'ao (d. 926), Chuang-tsung's most intimate adviser, who had served since 917 in his provincial government, was powerless. And in 926, the actors and the eunuchs were to cause the death of Kuo, thus touching off the mutiny that brought Chuang-tsung to his death and the "restoration" to an end.[23]

This was the last time the eunuchs played a prominent part in politics for many centuries and the last time actors had a chance to do so. The period 923–26 was not a time for the bureaucrats, and it was just as well that Feng Tao was in mourning for about half that time. But he could not have missed the significance of the power struggle in Chuang-tsung's court. It was not between the eunuchs and the bureaucrats as in the past but between imperial favorites, including eunuchs, and the new class of former provincial officers. The bureaucrats, utterly discredited by their weak leadership in the last years of the T'ang,[24] could not regain their power and authority without aligning themselves with one side or the other. Feng Tao and his colleagues were forced to act as old members of the provincial organization rather than simply as traditionally aloof Confucian bureaucrats.

Feng Tao played no part in any of the maneuvers for power. Under Chuang-tsung's successor, Ming-tsung (926–33), his literary ability was further recognized and he rose quickly to the post of Chief Minister. Just before this appointment, there was more evidence that the bureaucrat was at a disadvantage against the officer from the provincial cadre. While Jen Huan, the Chief Minister, tried to appoint a literatus of known ability to assist him, An Ch'ung-hui and his supporters of the provincial cadre supported a man who was pliant and nearly illiterate. Emperor Ming-tsung suggested, as a compromise, Feng Tao, who was acceptable largely because "he had no quarrel with any living thing" (yü-wu wu-ching).[25] Soon after his appointment, he became a trusted friend of Ming-tsung. He knew how to flatter, he had a good sense of humor, and at the same time he had an air of earnestness and a readiness to quote the Confucian classics to support any advice he gave.

This was the key to his success with the nine other emperors he served in the twenty years after Ming-tsung's death. With the tolerant Ming-tsung, he first perfected the art of good-natured advice and gentle flattery and was recognized by his contemporaries as a man skilled in the intimate and personal approach to emperors. The emperors liked him, above all, because "he had no quarrel with any living thing" and never failed to have pleasing, comforting words.

From 927 to his death in 954, there were only two breaks in Feng Tao's career as prime minister and fond intimate of emperors. In the middle of 934 he was sent out to be governor of a minor province for more than a year. This was directly connected with his failure to act with propriety when Ming-tsung's adopted son, the Prince of Lu, claimed the throne from Ming-tsung's young son, the Prince of Sung. The act of usurpation early in 934, just four months after Ming-tsung's death, had taken Feng Tao by surprise. Feng became unduly agitated and, while waiting for the Prince of Lu's entry into the capital of Lo-yang, Feng ordered his secretary to call upon the Prince to ascend the throne. When the secretary refused, Feng himself exhorted the Prince to do so.[26] His efforts did not save him entirely and soon afterward he was asked to leave for the provincial appointment. On his return from the provinces in the middle of 935, he was unemployed for about six months, the only time he was unemployed in his whole career. But he seems to have been indispensable, and by early 936 he was back at the court as Ssu-k'ung, one of the highest offices of the empire.[27]

The incident of Feng Tao's intervention at the gates of Lo-yang is omitted in his official biography. In fact, while Feng Tao was alive, no attempt was made to compile the Veritable Records (Shih-lu) of the two brief reigns of the Prince of Sung and the Prince of Lu, and it was not until 957, three years after Feng Tao's death, that the first official record of his part in the accession of the Prince of Lu appeared. Before that, his part was probably well known among his contemporaries, but no one, except possibly the compilers of the Account of Conduct of Lu Tao (866–941), the secretary who refused to comply with his orders, placed it on record.[28] It is also an interesting reflection on Chinese biographical compilations that a dishonorable incident like this should not appear in Feng Tao's own biography in the *Chiu wu-tai shih* but only as a story in the career of Lu Tao.

Feng Tao's loss of court office in 934–35 was short and his discomfiture virtually ignored by his friends. But his loss of office in the middle of 944, during the reign of Shao-ti (942–46) of Chin, was more serious. Once again Feng Tao was sent out to a minor province for a year and a half, and after that to another until the Khitan conquest of North China in early 947. This time he was away for two and a half years, very important years in Chinese history. The Khitan victory, which finally cut off the sixteen northern prefectures from Chinese control for 420 years,[29] could not in any way be attributed to Feng Tao. In fact, he was probably appointed to the provinces because he opposed the war policy of the emperor's chief advisers. Whether or not this was so, it is clear that he was of little use to the Chin court. It was apparently the consensus that "Tao is a good prime minister only for normal times, for he can do nothing to rescue the empire in a period of difficulties, rather like a Ch'an priest with no skill in falconry."[30]

Loss of court office in this case proved no embarrassment to Feng Tao. When the Khitans entered the Chin capital, K'ai-feng, Feng Tao left his province to pay his respects to their emperor and found himself welcomed as someone who did not have the taint of having defied them. He promptly exercised his tact on the emperor and, by fortuitous circumstances, soon afterward found himself in a position to save many Chin officials' lives.[31]

Feng Tao's long career also had its more positive side. In 932, under the Emperor Ming-tsung, he and two of his colleagues ordered the editing and first printing of the Nine Classics, one of the best-known events of the Five Dynasties period and one that was to revolutionize education and civil service recruitment in the centuries following.[32] Under Chin Kao-tsu (936–42), Feng Tao was the head of the important mission to the Khitans in 938, which preceded the official handing-over of the sixteen northern prefectures of the Ho-pei and Ho-tung regions (present northern Hopei and Shansi provinces). Feng Tao was present when all the prefectural and county records, including those of his own prefecture of Ying-chou and county of Ching-ch'eng, were delivered to the Khitans. At this memorable ceremony, Feng Tao saw his county being made into the southernmost county of the Khitan empire. He handled the mission so well that on his return Kao-tsu entrusted him with the difficult task of maintaining the peace. At Kao-tsu's deathbed, he was asked to see that Kao-tsu's baby son succeeded to the throne. But Feng Tao did not think this was wise and, after Kao-tsu's death, helped in making his nephew, aged twenty-eight, the new emperor (Shao-ti, 942–46).[33]

Under the Han dynasty (947–50), he lived very quietly and wrote the unusual autobiography, the *Ch'ang-lo lao tzu-hsü*, that was to turn the weight of historical opinion against him during the Sung (see discussion below of Feng Tao's biographers). But his active career really came to an end in the first weeks of 951, when Kuo Wei (Chou T'ai-tsu, 951–54) sent him as emissary to welcome a member of the Liu clan who aspired to the Han throne. Feng Tao's reputation as a sincere and honest man was the reason for his choice, and he may have suspected that he was being used as a decoy to bring a claimant to the throne into Kuo Wei's hands. Feng Tao was entirely successful: Kuo Wei killed the prince and seized the empire. For his part in Kuo Wei's smooth accession, Feng Tao was further rewarded with the highest court titles. He was already an old man of sixty-nine, old enough to be Kuo Wei's father, and so respected that Kuo Wei never called him by name.[34]

It has been noted that Feng Tao never openly opposed the wishes of the emperors he served. He criticized the Lu-lung governor Liu Shou-kuang in 911, and stood up to the Prince of Chin in 919, but thereafter always accepted his emperor's decisions, right or wrong, without question or protest. In his last year of life, almost as if he had suddenly become conscious of this defect in his record, Feng Tao reversed himself and made a spirited protest against Emperor Shih-tsung's (954–59) proposal personally to lead his armies into battle. The protest angered Shih-tsung and was ignored. Two weeks later Shih-tsung won a great victory, and less than a month after that Feng Tao was dead following a very short illness. In his third and final venture into criticizing an emperor Feng Tao had blundered dramatically.[35]

There is no doubt that Feng Tao himself and most of his contemporaries thought that he lived a Confucian life and acted as a Confucian in his public career. Few men of his distinction in the T'ang and the Five Dynasties periods could claim comparable aloofness from Taoism and Buddhism. The insistently Confucian and conventional tone that permeates all his writings and reported conversations was so obvious that his contemporaries delighted in telling stories attributing to him some of the Confucian absurdities of the time. These stories, though probably apocryphal, convey a vivid impression of prevailing attitudes.

Feng Tao's punctiliousness regarding the taboo on personal names in conversation produced this story using a pun on his own name. Feng Tao, commenting on a young scholar, Li Tao, pointed out that the young man's name sounded like his own, but added, in an unlikely joke at his own expense, that Li Tao's *tao* had the character for "inch" under the phonogram that was Feng Tao's personal name. In the Chinese idiom, a man without "inch" was one without a proper sense of values.[36]

Another story concerns Feng Tao's failure while governor of a province in Honan to repair a temple to Confucius after a dozen or so "liquor households" had petitioned to be allowed to do so. Someone then appended a poem to the petition mocking Confucian scholars who reached high office but waited for such lowly people to repair Confucian temples.[37]

These stories reflect an age renowned neither for its Confucians nor for the prevailing view of Confucianism, and it is important, I think, to see Feng Tao clearly in this context. The cultural history of the Five Dynasties period has been notable for its anarchy and for hermits and great poets in the *tz'u* form. The prose of the time was later regarded as exceptionally bad and the thought and the thinkers undistinguished. It was under such circumstances that Feng Tao became famous in his time as a prose writer and Confucian. Among the emperors he served, two could be said to have been ardent believers in the supernatural (the Prince of Lu and Chin Kao-tsu). All the rest were also practicing Taoists and Buddhists.[38] Feng Tao was an intimate friend to at least eight of the eleven emperors and had opportunity enough to increase that intimacy by sharing in their religious practices if not in their faith. But he seems to have been able to remain on intimate terms without reference to religion. In all the literature there is on Feng Tao's relations with his emperors, he is only once said to have been consulted on anything not pertaining to the Confucian state. This was when the Emperor Chin Kao-tsu asked him about the value of the *Tao-te ching* and invited him to attend the classes given by a prominent Taoist at the palace. It is not known whether Feng Tao ever went, but his answer to the emperor was entirely consistent with his way of mixing flattery and a ponderous earnestness. He gave the tolerant but equivocal reply that neither the Taoist lecturing on Lao Tzu nor the Buddhist receiving his vows should be taken lightly.[39]

In fact, Feng Tao's firm adherence to Confucianism was unusual for his time. Most of his successful contemporaries were inconsistent in their beliefs: for example, the two men Chao Feng (885–935) and Liu

Hsü (888–947), both of whom were also from Lu-lung province in Ho-pei and had served as Chief Ministers together with him. Chao Feng became violently anti-Buddhist in later life but had been a Buddhist priest as a youth. Liu Hsü (who was related to Feng Tao by marriage) was closely associated with both Buddhist priests and Taoist hermits. Again, Ma Yin-sun (d. 953), Chief Minister in 936 when Feng Tao was out of favor, had started life as a great admirer of Han Yü (786–824) and then turned to Buddhism with enthusiasm.[40]

Perhaps it would be more accurate to say that the majority of men at the court were either indifferent or lukewarm toward religion and Confucianism. This was in keeping with the traditions of the ninth-century T'ang court—traditions of artistic virtuosity and sophistication which, from the Confucian point of view, were very superficial. Feng Tao seems to have scorned these traditions and is known to have played his part in suppressing "the frivolous and unstable" (fou-tsao) men descended from distinguished T'ang families while helping impoverished scholars of promise.[41] In the well-known anecdote of Feng Tao's encounter with two snobbish court officials who laughed at his use of a popular reference book of Confucian quotations—the T'u-yüan ts'e (a sort of "selections from the classics")—Feng Tao is said to have retorted that the old quotations were surely more worthy of reading than the pretty phrases of the examination hall plagiarized from the successful candidates.[42]

Yet it is clear that Feng Tao was not an impressive Confucian in any way. His professed Confucianism was supported by a limited knowledge of the classics, and even his understanding of the Confucian state seems to have been vague. It is, of course, easy to be unfair to him since his collected works have not survived. Apart from a few congratulatory messages and a number of formal addresses to the throne which had little to do with either Confucian institutions or state policy, we cannot identify any surviving state papers as having been written by Feng Tao.[43]

Feng Tao undeniably had a part in the memorials from the Imperial Secretariat (chung-shu) and the Chancellery (men-hsia), particularly during the reigns of T'ang Ming-tsung and Chin Kao-tsu when he was the senior minister. But we have evidence that he avoided all difficult policy decisions, especially if they involved finance or the army. These were the two realms where there was always potential conflict with more ambitious and specialized officers, and he was probably prudent to stay away from them and leave them to the military secretaries and finance commissioners. On the other hand, he was not active in the strictly Confucian spheres of government either. There is no evidence that he contributed anything to the fields of rites, law, music and ceremonies, examination, and recruitment. Here again, he preferred to leave the work to specialists. If this is taken together with the anecdote about Feng Tao's dependence on a Confucian phrase book, it sustains the picture of Feng Tao as a very superficial Confucian.

There remains the historic printing of the Nine Classics in 932, which nearly every history ascribes to Feng Tao. But it is by no means clear that Feng Tao himself initiated the project. The other Chief Minister in 932, Li Yü (d. 935), who was a great admirer of Han Yü, is also named, and since the knowledge of the advantages of printing had come from Szechwan after the conquest of the kingdom of Shu in 926 and Li Yü had been the senior executive secretary in the Szechwan campaign, it is more likely that he or one of his colleagues during the campaign was responsible for proposing the official enterprise.[44] The work of re-editing the classics for printing was left largely in the hands of T'ien Min (880–971) and his assistants, and Feng Tao is not known to have contributed any scholarship. His Sung biographer Ou-yang Hsiu went so far as to give him no credit at all for the printing of the classics. Feng Tao's main connection with the publication seems to have been that he was the senior Chief Minister in 932 and still the highest official in the empire when the completed work was presented to the throne in 953.[45]

What then have we left to help us to define, if possible, Feng Tao's Confucianism? We have extracts from a few memorials, we have his many reported conversations, and finally we have two informal but important documents written in 950 when he was sixty-eight.

The extracts from memorials do not reveal much. Several of them exhorted the Emperor Ming-tsung (926–33) to be careful and to learn the lessons of his predecessor's downfall. Others assured Ming-tsung that the empire, primarily because of the emperor's sagacity, was at peace.[46] We also have one that dealt with the order of precedence at the audiences of the Emperor Chin Kao-tsu (936–42).[47] Perhaps the best example of Feng Tao's Confucianism can be found in his memorial of the second month of 933 concerning the education of Ming-tsung's heir apparent. Here he argued that the empire's foundations lay with having virtuous men around the throne and showed how Chuang-tsung's (923–26) failure to rule by virtue (*te*) was the main reason for his downfall. He then argued,

The strength of the empire is found in its men. The men at present important to the empire are just the military governors, the prefects, the magistrates, and the county secretaries. If the men are rightly chosen, there is good government. If the men are poorly selected, there will be confusion. One cannot but choose carefully. As the *Book of History* says, "It is like treading on a tiger's tail or walking on spring ice." Each day there is need for greater caution. I merely ask Your Imperial Majesty not to forget dangers in times of peace and not to forget anarchy in periods of good government.[48]

His reported conversations are more interesting. He was the only man in the Five Dynasties period to have snatches of his conversation preserved in the official records. The *Chiu wu-tai shih* quotes these conversations both in the Basic Annals and in his biography, while scattered throughout the *Ts'e-fu yüan-kuei* are several more not preserved in the official History. Since these two compilations are known to have followed closely the Veritable Records (*shih-lu*), there is no reason to doubt that the conversations were taken from those sources. The Veritable Records were themselves compiled from the Imperial Diary (*ch'i-chü chu*), the Court Diary (*shih-cheng chi*), the Daily Record (*jih-li*), and the Account of Conduct (*hsing-chuang*) of each prominent official. At each stage of compilation, the Chief Minister had a great deal to say about what was to be included. This was particularly true with regard to the Court Diary, which was compiled by one of the Chief Ministers himself. It is, of course, often noted that Confucians dominated the business of history writing in all dynasties and there is nothing unusual in the inclusion of Feng Tao's Confucian sayings for their own sake.[49]

But it is interesting to note that almost all of Feng Tao's sayings (as well as most of his memorials) were recorded for the reigns of T'ang Ming-tsung and Chin Kao-tsu. These are two of the longer reigns in the period (seven and six years respectively), and Feng Tao got on very well with both emperors. But a problem does arise when it is noted that their Veritable Records are only two of the four compiled in Feng Tao's lifetime, the other two being those of Chin Shao-ti (942–46) and Han Kao-tsu (947–48).[50] Excluding the Khitan emperor in 947 and T'ang Chuang-tsung, whom Feng Tao did not serve as Chief Minister, there were five other emperors whose Records were not compiled until three to six years after their death. For the Records of Chin Shao-ti compiled in 950–51 the various Diaries were probably incomplete because of the Khitan wars. Feng Tao, who was away from the court during the later half of the reign, might not in any case have cared to be associated with an emperor who had failed disastrously. As for the Records of Han Kao-tsu compiled in 949, although the reign was so short, we have a full account of Feng Tao's role in saving the Chinese from the Khitans by the way he spoke to the Khitan emperor. There is, I believe, sufficient evidence to suspect that Feng Tao had a prominent part, if not in the compilation of the Veritable Records, at least in preparing the Imperial and Court Diaries. This does not necessarily mean that Feng Tao tampered with the archives. Feng Tao did have the right to include or exclude material, and it would be in keeping with his concept of Confucian duty to include as much Confucian wisdom as possible, even his own. I have already shown that the one great embarrassment in his career, occurring when the Prince of Lu usurped the throne in 934, was never recorded in his lifetime. When the Records of the two Chin emperors were being compiled in 950–51, it would not have been out of place to consider filling the gap in the official records between 934 and 936, but this was not done. Feng Tao could not have prevented this gap from being filled, but if he was as embarrassed as he appears to have been, he might easily have discouraged it.[51]

Feng Tao's reported conversations must therefore be examined in the light of his own involvement in history compilation. Considering how some of his admirers, who noted that he died at the same age as Confucius,[52] were ready to compare him to Confucius himself, these conversations take on the coloration of the "sayings of a sage." He himself was not averse to making the same comparison, and in a conversation with a colleague about his supporters and detractors, he said, "All men who agree with you will approve of you, all who do not will defame you and nine out of ten perhaps defame me [at the court]. In ancient times, Confucius was a sage and yet he was slandered by Shu-sun Wu-shu. How much more would people slander someone as empty and mean as me!"[53] This smacks of false modesty; it mentions Confucius and himself in the same passage while following the convention of comparing oneself unfavorably with the ancient sages.

In fact, the most striking thing about the many sayings of this articulate sage is their conventionality and their complete lack of originality. A typical conversation ran as follows:

The Emperor Ming-tsung asked, "How are the affairs of state?" Feng Tao replied, "The crop seasons are regular and the people at peace." The emperor asked again, "Apart from this, what is there to note?" Tao replied, "Your Majesty is pure and virtuous and truly in accord with the wishes of heaven. I have heard that rulers like Yao and Shun have been admired by all and masters like Chieh and Chou have been hated by all. This is the difference between those with principles and those without. Now Your Majesty carefully observes self-restraint and pays full attention to the art of government. The people are not weighed down by taxes and services and tell one another that this is like the years of Yao and the days of Shun. This is merely because the people are satisfied and everyday things are abundant. After the tenth year of Chen-kuan [636], the Minister Wei Cheng memorialized T'ang T'ai-tsung, asking that all should be like the beginning of the Chen-kuan period. Now I also wish Your Majesty to think of the good things you did at the beginning of your reign. If Your Majesty would do so, then the empire would be fortunate indeed."[54]

Even the pattern of the conversations changed but little. There was the profound Baconian theme followed by the exposition and then the admonition. This was the formula of the sages and, no doubt, Feng

Tao's pretensions stem from the noblest of motives—to reaffirm tradition and order in an age of troubles. The consistent, almost dreary, reiteration of Confucian tenets that characterized his conversations reflected a deep conviction that a return to traditional ways, rather than startling innovation, was the solution to the problems besetting the state and the people. Young Confucians of the time, used to the widespread neglect of their creed, must have been heartened by the sight of so successful an official espousing Confucianism. The mediocrity of his life and thought, if noted at all by his young admirers, would have detracted little from his singular importance as proof of the flexibility possible in applying the old Confucian principles.

There are, finally, the preface to his poems for a deceased friend and his famous autobiography, the *Ch'ang-lo lao tzu-hsü*, both written in 950 when he was an old man. The preface, completed in the second month of 950 soon after the death of his fellow provincial and early associate, Liu Shen-chiao (877–950), revealed an intense, in some ways romantic belief in the superiority of Confucian duty. After eulogizing Liu Shen-chiao as a good man who had done harm to no one, Feng Tao took note of his undistinguished public record but asked: Why then was he so loved by the people in the prefecture he administered?

It is really because he did not use whippings and beatings and was not oppressive. He did not take advantage of his office for private ends nor did he harm others to profit himself. He certainly worked in a way becoming a high official. He lightened punishment and forgave wrong; he was careful in his conduct and economical in his expenditure. It was enough for him to be content with his emoluments and live with decorum.

Of all those who served in this capacity, who could not achieve what he did? But the prefects before him were not like that. That is why the people sigh with admiration for him. In these days when the empire has suffered from war and everywhere there can still be seen the consequences of banditry, when the looms are empty while the taxes are burdensome, when the people are scattered and the granaries depleted, it is not easy to say that there is well-being and peace. If the nobles and provincial officials felt concern for this situation, they would not amass private fortunes, or kill the innocent. If they had realized that people form the base of the country and good government is the life of the people and all acted with benevolence and moderation, what then would there be to praise in the work of Mr. Liu? And why need they fear they will not reach great fame?[55]

Feng Tao used the occasion to make a general comment on the prevailing standards of public office. He was obviously aware that when rapacious officials were everywhere, the selfless official, even an undistinguished one, gained stature. Whether he realized it or not, his comments could have been applied to himself. He stood out in his generation not because of his own excellence, but because he withheld himself from the decadence around him. It is hard to believe that he was insensitive to his own inadequacies. More likely he was gratified by his own incorruptibility.

The death of his friend moved him deeply, and I think it was reflection upon his friend's life and small achievements that brought him to think of his own and, about two months afterward, to write his autobiography.[56] This was a curious piece of writing, quite unprecedented in its form, and more like a skeleton of an autobiography. It carried all his ranks and titles and all the formal information about his family. Only at the end did he set forth what he thought were the minimum requirements of a Confucian life.

I quietly think of what is important and what is not and what blessings extend to life and death. Through imperial favors and by strictly following our clan traditions, I have received the great teachings and opened them to others. I have observed filial piety in the home and shown loyalty to the state. Also, my mouth has not spoken what is improper and my gates have not been open to things I should not have. All that I have wished is that I should not deceive earth that is below, man that is with us, and heaven that is above, and have regarded these "three no-deceptions" as a rule of behavior. I have been thus when I was lowly, when I was in high office, when I grew to manhood, and when I was old. In the service of my relatives, my emperor, and my elders, and in my relations with my fellow men, I have been favored by the mercy of heaven. Several times when I encountered trouble and escaped with fortune and when I was in the hands of the barbarians and returned safely to the Central Plain [China], it was not due to the devices of man but to the protection of heaven.[57]

He was a great believer in the good man being protected by heaven and never failed to say so in both prose and poetry on appropriate occasions. As this was obviously an article of faith with him, he must have been sincere in the modesty of the following passage:

Thus in the world there is one who is fortunate, one who will have a decent grave when he dies. As he is inferior to the ancients, he does not deserve to be buried with jade or pearl in his mouth, but should have his body prepared in his ordinary clothes and buried simply on a coarse bamboo mat at a place selected because it did not yield crops. There should not be the sacrifice of male goats, for one should abstain from taking life. There should instead only be the sacrifice of things without life.[58] As there have not been inscriptions for the graves of three generations of his ancestors, there should also not be an inscription. And as he has no virtue to speak of, there should not be a request for posthumous titles.[59]

It was probably the death of Liu Shen-chiao that turned Feng Tao's mind to thoughts of death. And having written about the inconsequential life of his friend, he must have wondered how posterity would consider him. He knew well the power of history in Chinese civilization.

Was his conscience disturbed by the thought of his negative virtues? Or did he believe that he should present his life for the betterment of all the Confucians to come? From all that we know of him, I feel that the latter belief would be consistent with his idea of Confucian duty.

Feng Tao was certainly no scholar of the classics, nor did he give unbending loyalty to any emperor, but in his adherence to the prevailing brand of Confucianism he was honest and firm. Few of his contemporaries would have denied that he was a genuine Confucian. Yet in the age of Confucian revival which followed a century later, he was denounced as despicable, and the new biography written from that vantage point soon became the accepted story of his life.

The first to condemn Feng Tao was Ou-yang Hsiu, followed soon after by Ssu-ma Kuang. Both contrasted Feng Tao's Confucian pretensions with his disloyalty and self-satisfaction. Ssu-ma Kuang carefully reinforced his predecessor's argument to meet the objections to their judgment that had been raised by other historians of the time. Men like Wu Ch'u-hou had pointed to Feng Tao's many good acts.[60] Others had expressed the opinion that Feng Tao was being made the scapegoat for all the ills of the Five Dynasties period. The defense of Feng Tao ran thus: Thousands of officials had been disloyal. Why pick on Feng Tao? And even if he did act disloyally at least five times, was it so much more hateful to be disloyal more than once? Wasn't once enough?

Ssu-ma Kuang angrily answered,

Feng Tao was Chief Minister to five dynasties and eight surnames, like an inn to many travelers. Enemies at the break of dawn would become emperor and minister by evening. He changed his face and transformed his words and never once was he ashamed. Such having been his attitude toward loyalty, what is there to praise if he did do a little good? . . . While the emperors followed one another closely in their rise and fall, Feng Tao prospered as before. He is the worst of treacherous officials. How can he deserve to be compared with other men?[61]

This has been the main theme of all of Feng Tao's later critics—the number of times he had been disloyal. It must have appeared absurd to have a man serve eleven emperors in a row. There was no emperor Feng Tao could have served whom he did not serve. This was unprecedented. And even more extraordinary was that he should have held the highest ranks in all but one of these reigns. Certainly no civilian official in the whole history of China had ever had a comparable career. How was he to be classified? How could he be classified? The majority opinion was that he was the worst of the worst and a little ridiculous as well.

But there were a few who spoke up in Feng Tao's favor. For example, Wu Ch'u-hou in defending him quoted the famous minister Fu Pi (1004–83), who had compared him to Mencius' Superior Man (*ta-jen*). And Wu Tseng (fl. 1150–60) said that Feng Tao was highly regarded by Su Shih (1036–1101) and Wang An-shih (1021–86) and argued that Ou-yang Hsiu was probably very young when he condemned Feng Tao. But Wu Ch'u-hou and Wu Tseng were associated with Ts'ai Ching (1046–1125) and Ch'in Kuei (1090–1155) respectively, both condemned in Chinese history as "evil officials" (*chien-ch'en*). Their opinions were therefore not taken very seriously.[62]

After the twelfth century, when Ou-yang Hsiu's and Ssu-ma Kuang's views prevailed, there were very few voices raised in Feng Tao's defense. There were Wang Shih-chen (1528–93) and Li Chih (1527–1602), but both were regarded as literary men trying to be "different." On the other hand, the praise of the Ming martyr Wen Huang (1585–1645) was more difficult to dismiss. His main argument was that Feng Tao was a good man with honest intentions who had been cruelly dealt with by historians. It is indeed true that the only historian of distinction to try to understand Feng Tao was Chao I (1727–1814), who argued that loyalty was simply not a problem during that period; but even he maintained that Feng Tao was without shame. On the whole, the few voices raised on behalf of Feng Tao have been regarded as either eccentricity or special pleading.[63]

The fact is that the Five Dynasties period was an extraordinary one. The conditions at the end of the T'ang and throughout those dynasties were unprecedented and the actions of a whole generation were peculiar to the times. Never before had the empire been divided into seven or eight states, and there was no way to fit the scheme of things into the orthodox view of imperial succession (*cheng-t'ung*). Was there in fact an empire? After all, none of the so-called emperors controlled more than a third of the T'ang empire at any one time. And there was no reason why the *cheng-t'ung* should have remained in the north. In Szechwan to the west, in the Yangtze provinces, even in Kwangtung and later in Fukien, claims to be the only true emperor were made by various people from time to time. The claims of the rulers of Nan T'ang on the Yangtze were no less valid than those of the northern dynasties.

Then after fifty-three years of uncertainty the Sung dynasty succeeded the last of the Five Dynasties and, eighteen years later, conquered all the other states. It was this that the Confucian historians seized upon to help explain what could not be reconciled within the orthodox framework. The Sung emperors inherited the empire, and that could only be so because the emperors of the Five Dynasties had each inherited the empire before them. Therefore, those Five Dynasties were obviously bearers of the Mandate of Heaven and all the standards of the Confucian state could fairly be applied to them.[64] By these standards, it was clear that the emperors were inferior, the regimes consequently short-lived, the ministers un-Confucian, and, most of all, men like Feng Tao appallingly disloyal.

I think it is necessary to see the period as it was and to see how it differs from the Confucian distortion so essential to justify the Sung empire. If we return to the beginning of the struggle to replace the T'ang, that is, to the years after 884, we see the struggle developing until Chu Wen, who held the whole stretch of the Yellow and the Wei rivers, was pitted against the northern alliance of the Sha-t'o Turks and the Ho-pei armies. As neither side could win decisively, Chu Wen was rushed into killing the last T'ang emperor and founding his dynasty of the Liang. The struggle continued for sixteen years into the next generation. Then in 923 the other side won and, under the dynastic names of (later) T'ang, Chin, Han, Chou, and Sung, the Sha-t'o and Ho-pei alliance controlled North China. And, conforming to the traditions of the Turks and the unstable pattern of gubernatorial succession in the Ho-pei provinces, twelve emperors succeeded one another between 926 and 960. All twelve were from the original alliance, whose continuity was remarkable and which through the years had become identified as one progression (hsi-t'ung), even one organization. Of the twelve, three were sons, two were adopted sons, one was a nephew, and one a son-in-law of emperors.[65] Of the remaining five, the first Emperor Chuang-tsung was the son of the original leader of the alliance and the other four were either previous commanders in chief or chiefs of staff who usurped power in the best traditions of the Ho-pei provinces.[66]

Since all the successions had taken place within the same allied grouping, it is obvious that the concept of loyalty in the eyes of Feng Tao and his contemporaries was different from that of the Sung historians a hundred years later. Feng Tao served ten of these emperors, the first Emperor Chuang-tsung, two sons, two adopted sons, one nephew, and one son-in-law of emperors in addition to three others. Of the three others, Ming-tsung in 926 was an able and popular general who had not set out to usurp the throne, Han Kao-tsu in 947 had merely recovered Chin territory from the Khitans, and Chou T'ai-tsu in 951 was a victim of court intrigue who became emperor in order to save his own life.[67] All three men had been friends and colleagues of Feng Tao and respected him for his sagacity. In fact, had Feng Tao lived another six years, he would have seen the foundation of the Sung by yet another Ho-pei Chinese who was born into the organization, and no doubt

Sung T'ai-tsu (960–76) would also have employed him.[68] Thus ten of the eleven emperors whom Feng Tao served were members of the same Sha-t'o and Ho-pei organization. The question of disloyalty did not occur to him, or to his contemporaries, or even to the emperors, who were happy to employ him.

The only emperor who came from outside the group was the emperor of the Khitans, whom Feng Tao served for four months in 947 till the Khitan's death. Yet even in this relationship, there were the links of the Sha-t'o tradition. The Khitan emperor had been Chin Kao-tsu's "Imperial Father" (*fu huang-ti*) since 938, and Feng Tao had led one of the missions sent to arrange for this.[69] And if the links are traced further back, the Khitan founder, A-pao-chi (872–926), and the founder of the Sha-t'o and Ho-pei alliance, Li K'o-yung (856–908), were sworn brothers in 905.[70] Anyway, the wars of 944–46, which ended in Khitan victory, had arisen partly because Chin Shao-ti was only willing to be a "grandson" (*sun*) but not a "minister" or "subject" (*ch'en*) of the Khitan ruler.[71] The Khitans themselves regarded the war as partly a war to chastise a disrespectful member of the family. Since to Feng Tao the Khitan emperor did have a claim to North China, it would not have been disloyal to serve him.[72]

It is easy to see how such a series of imperial successions in North China baffled Confucian historians and how the problem of Feng Tao's loyalty defied classification. But, once it was decided to treat the self-professed dynasties in the orthodox way, Feng Tao naturally came to be judged by the orthodox definition of loyalty to emperor or at least loyalty to dynasty. By this definition, he was undoubtedly disloyal. But when the Confucian distortion is removed and Feng Tao and his contemporaries are seen as the officials of a rather unstable organization that had seized control of a part of China, then the concept of loyalty in a Confucian state would not apply. Such a concept should have been limited to those T'ang officials who had abetted Chu Wen in the downfall of the T'ang or to those Liang officials who were glad to serve Chuang-tsung after 923. These were clear examples of disloyalty by any definition, and Ou-yang Hsiu's collection of "six T'ang ministers" who turned from the T'ang to the Liang certainly represents the most culpable kind of disloyalty of the whole period.[73] At worst, Feng Tao could have been regarded as a man who kept himself aloof from the internal intrigues and quarrels of his leaders and who saw no reason to abandon high office at every change in their fortunes.

The Sung biographers of Feng Tao applied *their* Confucian dynastic view to the history of the Five Dynasties. His exceptional career could not be taken lightly. It had to be evaluated and classified, and in the context of the new Confucianism of Sung it was obviously unforgivable, even disgusting. Thereafter, this remained the only possible view of Feng Tao.

Yet his biographers were not entirely to blame for judging him by eleventh-century standards. After all, Feng Tao claimed to have lived a Confucian life and followed a Confucian career. He was even compared with Confucius, and his "sayings" were prominent in the official records. Not only that; he wrote an account of his own life which showed clearly how pleased he was with his Confucian achievements. This was the crucial point. In every discussion of Feng Tao, there is reference to this unusual piece of writing, his autobiography. In a sense, Feng Tao had invited comparison with the best, and this to men like Ou-yang Hsiu and Ssu-ma Kuang was intolerable conceit.

Autobiography has tended to be self-justification and Chinese autobiographies are no exceptions. But most of the examples we still have from before the Sung were written in order to explain a lack of interest in high office. Beginning with the poet Yang Hsiung's (53 B.C.–A.D. 18) *Chieh-ch'ao* and the historian Pan Ku's (A.D. 32–92) *Pin-hsi chu-jen*, autobiographical writing gradually evolved toward essays justifying the life of a recluse, such as those written by Huang-fu Mi (215–82, *Hsüan-shou lun*), T'ao Ch'ien (365–427, *Wu-liu hsien-sheng chuan*), and Liu Chün (462–521, *Tzu-hsü*).[74] A slightly different tradition was that of the Han humorist Tung-fang So (b. 160 B.C.), who wrote his *Ta-k'o nan* to show his political views.[75] Somewhat similar to this tradition was the *Tzu-hsü* of Yüan Chen (779–831), the T'ang poet, but Yüan Chen's was much more of an autobiography with short comments on his own career.[76] Another example of autobiographical writing, Wang Ch'ung's (A.D. 27–97) account of his philosophical development, stood alone until the Sung dynasty.[77] Except for Yüan Chen's *Tzu-hsü*, there was nothing in Chinese tradition to justify a proud account of one's official career. But Yüan Chen had been content merely to mention some of the problems he had dealt with. There was certainly no precedent for Feng Tao's detailed list of all the emperors he had served, all his ranks, offices, and titles, and all the honors conferred upon his ancestors as well as all the ranks and offices held by his sons. The tradition in autobiography had clearly been to disparage high office, but Feng Tao did not follow this tendency toward what might be described as inverted snobbery. Instead, he preferred to record his connection with an eminent family and give a full account of how he had done his Confucian duty to his ancestors (the posthumous honors), to his family (his children's achievements), and to his sovereign (his own titles as evidence of his emperors' gratitude). As he said,

I have been a son, a brother, a minister of the emperor, a teacher, a husband, and a father, and I have sons, nephews, and grandchildren. What I have given to my times has been inadequate. Where I have been inadequate is that I have not helped my emperor to unify the empire and bring order to the country. I am truly ashamed to have held all my various offices and ranks without success and wonder how I can repay the gifts of heaven and earth.[78]

He had clearly broken with tradition, and this Ou-yang Hsiu and Ssu-ma Kuang must have noted with disapproval. Even his modesty in the passage quoted above could not have absolved him from the terrible heresy of pride in high office. And to have done it with reference to Confucian principles was in very bad taste indeed. Furthermore, Feng Tao had spoken of his loyalty to the state and of the "three no-deceptions" and, even worse, attributed to heaven's protection his success in outliving all his emperors (as quoted above). He mentioned the possibility of official burial, of eulogistic inscriptions, of ritual sacrifice and posthumous titles for himself. Although he had asked all this to be denied to him, it was vulgar conceit to have even thought about these subjects. Finally, he was contented and self-satisfied. With obvious complacence he wrote, "I sometimes open a book and sometimes drink a cup of wine. Is there not food to be tasted, music to be heard, and colors to wear till I grow old and contented in these times? When one is happy with oneself when old, what happiness can compare with that?"[79]

Feng Tao could not have known that a higher Confucianism was to develop a century after his death. He could not have known that he was living in an age of transition and that important changes in social, political, and philosophical values were about to take place. He asked to be considered as a Confucian, not realizing that the Confucianism of his time would prove ineffectual and shallow and be replaced by a more severe and vigorous creed. He saw himself as loyal and true and did not anticipate the judgment of a later orthodoxy. His contribution to his times was too slight to matter in later ages. Men of the eleventh century, bent on revitalizing the Confucian tradition, showed little tolerance for the rather flaccid Confucianism of Feng Tao. Generally overlooked was his contribution as a "Confucian" in his own time who had helped keep alive in adversity the rudiments of the tradition, giving those who followed a foundation on which to build the vigorous new Confucian system.

Hellmut Wilhelm

FROM MYTH TO MYTH:
THE CASE OF YÜEH FEI'S BIOGRAPHY

There is no dearth in Chinese history of personalities whose lives have become the object of mythologization. Emperors and commoners, poets and bandits, officials and warriors—all have had their words and deeds transfigured. Few, however, have been so intensively mythologized as the heroic warrior, patriot, and tragically frustrated savior of his country, Yüeh Fei (1103–41), who became the first warrior to have his mythologized life exhaustively and exclusively treated in a great Chinese novel.[1] Even in the generation after his death the number of temples dedicated to him seems to have been considerable. Only one other warrior shares with Yüeh Fei the honor of a place in the official pantheon.[2]

Taken together, the "historical" facts of Yüeh's life quickly yield the germination point of this process. To be sure, for reasons to be discussed later, biographical data on Yüeh Fei are scanty and unusually unreliable. But even those facts definitely or at least very probably historical produce a picture of Yüeh Fei's life rich in the substance of myth. His life story resembles strangely the myths of St. George, Siegfried, or other sun-heroes in a Chinese variation: the forceful youth of almost unknown family background, as proud as he is naïve, who overnight gains entrance into his chosen vocation; the loyal attachment to those who guide him in his activities; his somewhat ostentatious display of all the shining virtues the tradition demands; his always successful battles against the enemy which is devastating his country; his sudden retreat at the peak of his success; and his end at the hands of a villain of blackest hue, Ch'in Kuei. We even find the evil woman who urges the villain on to commit the fatal deed. These and other elements of the Yüeh Fei biography were highly conducive to the creation of the Yüeh Fei image of later popular and official lore, but I shall resist the temptation to analyze more closely this superb example of the myth-making process. To keep these elements in mind might, however, contribute to an understanding of Yüeh Fei's attitudes, words, and deeds. As will be shown, he constantly and consciously worked toward producing an image of himself as a hero of mythological proportions, rigidly patterning himself after the myths of the past. This "impersonation" of a myth was to dictate the events of his life and, finally, his fate.

We are singularly unfortunate with regard to the sources on Yüeh Fei's life. The circumstances of his death precluded the tomb inscription or other obituary matter on which biographies in the *Sung shih* to a large extent depend. Instead, his official biography is based on a rewritten version of a biography by his grandson Yüeh K'o, written sixty years after Yüeh Fei's death.[3] This biography was incorporated by Yüeh K'o into a collection compiled with the avowed purposes of re-establishing the prestige and stature of his grandfather.[4] In addition to the natural bias of filial piety, and the promotion of family interests which it shares with the biographies based on obituaries, it is open to doubt on account of this propagandistic purpose. Furthermore, in sixty years, knowledge about the facts of Yüeh Fei's life had already become blurred. This is reflected in a number of verifiable errors.[5] How many other, unverified errors it contains will probably remain forever unknown.[6]

We are not much better off with regard to the official documentation of Yüeh Fei's public activities. The contemporary official records, of course, do not survive. They were used, however, at the time of the compilation of some sections of the *Sung shih* pertinent to Yüeh Fei's life, particularly the Annals of Emperor Kao. They were also available to Sung historians like Hsiung K'o,[7] Liu Cheng,[8] and Li Hsin-ch'uan.[9] From the indirect quotation of the official records concerning Yüeh Fei in these compilations it becomes abundantly clear—and this seems to be the present consensus—that these records were doctored during the decade and a half Ch'in Kuei remained in power after Yüeh Fei's death. We have thus to cope not only with the poor quality of the *Sung shih* in general but also with the fact that Yüeh Fei's official record has been falsified.[10]

Parts of these records have survived outside the official archives. Yüeh K'o incorporated in his compilations a number of memorials and reports addressed to the throne by Yüeh Fei as well as various imperial rescripts and decrees addressed to Yüeh Fei. This appears to be the most reliable body of documentary material available, as there is no reason to suspect tampering. It is, however, highly improbable that this collection of documents is complete. The tenor of the imperial rescripts is almost uniformly appreciative of Yüeh Fei's character and his actions, with next to nothing in the way of criticism or reprimand.[11]

It is inconceivable that an emperor who constantly expressed this degree of indebtedness and even tender personal care would have condoned the course of action that led to Yüeh Fei's death. Either Yüeh Fei himself failed to keep those documents critical of him and his actions or Yüeh K'o's compilation was highly selective.

Yüeh Fei's own writings have come down to us in very sad condition.[12] Except for memorials and official reports (seven out of eight *chüan*), there are only a few stray items. There is evidence that Ch'in Kuei had Yüeh Fei's home raided and his writings destroyed.[13] Equally scanty are references to Yüeh Fei in the writings of his contemporaries and independent biographical sources.[14] It is from this brittle material, then, that we have to build our image of Yüeh Fei, the man.

I do not propose to present here an integrated biography of Yüeh.[15] I would like, rather, to discuss Yüeh Fei as a historic figure seen in the context of his time and, second, to see how the historic character is related to the heroic tradition of which he was self-consciously a part.[16]

Yüeh Fei's family background is not well explored. It is not only recent Communist descriptions which stress that he came from a farming family. His father, Yüeh Ho, appears to have been a man of modest affluence, in a position at least to earmark some of his income for welfare projects. He is specifically reported to have drawn income from a field of rushes, although this was swept away, and his financial status in consequence seriously curtailed, by a flood that occurred when Yüeh Fei was still a baby. Yüeh Fei's miraculous escape from this flood together with his mother (née Yao) in a big water jar was an event that contributed to the myth of his life. A similarly prophetic incident was the flight of a large bird over the house at the time of his birth. This was responsible for his name Fei as well as his *tzu* P'eng-chü, without doubt a reference to the roc, which had been made famous by Chuang-tzu and remained the symbol of a superior and imaginative personality.

That Yüeh Ho chose this *tzu* for his son indicates the sophisticated level of his education, especially for a man of his rural surroundings. He is reported to have tutored his son personally, and some of the Confucian virtues Yüeh Fei exhibited with such consistent devotion must have been instilled in him by his father. There is no evidence, however, that Yüeh Ho ever endeavored to pursue an examination career.

Without question, the extent of Yüeh Fei's own learning and his general love of scholarship were very considerable. In his youth he was particularly attracted by the *Tso-chuan* and the military classics of Chou. A sustained effort was, however, necessary to achieve the intensity of historical knowledge and the subtlety of historical interpretation that Yüeh Fei displayed in his surviving writings. Moreover, he wrote a smooth, almost elegant style and his calligraphy has become a model for later artists in this field.[17] But, like his father, he never pursued an examination career.

Yüeh Fei seems to have been a serious-minded and taciturn child, at the same time endowed with unusual physical strength. In addition to his literary studies he took up archery, swordsmanship, and lance-play, apparently under the tutelage of a certain Chou T'ung. When Chou T'ung died, Yüeh Fei paid him unusual posthumous honors. This overdramatized behavior testifies to an important trait in Yüeh Fei's character: a penchant for giving symbolic expression to genuinely felt emotions. There are too many incidents in Yüeh Fei's biography to leave any doubt that his reverence for his tutors and guides was genuine, representing more than mere compliance with a Confucian imperative. This is shown by his relationship to Chang So, who had launched him on his military career.[18] When about a decade later Yüeh Fei received by imperial grace the privilege of promoting his own son, he substituted Chang So's son. The closeness of Yüeh Fei's relationship in later life to his colleagues and more particularly to his subordinates is universally attested to. His paternal care for them and his liberal rewards have become almost proverbial. But always dramatic expression was given to a genuinely felt and also consciously cultivated human emotion. His somewhat ostentatious sacrifice at the tomb of Chou T'ung sets the pattern for this kind of attitude: the reticent youth makes a considered display of himself, and the pattern of the hero he knows he is and wants to be is established in the public eye.

The sacrifice at the tomb of Chou T'ung was the occasion for one of those anticipatory remarks that are part and parcel of almost every biography, the remark that presages the future fate of the hero. His father took him to task for his action, saying: "When you are employed to cope with the affairs of the time, will you then not have to sacrifice yourself for the empire and die for your duty?" The only logical meaning of this remark is that once Yüeh Fei had aimed for a high public position, he would have to live up to the image he had created of himself, even to the point of sacrificing his life. Yüeh Fei did live up to this image and eventually paid the ultimate price. The remark also made it possible for posterity to interpret his death as a sacrifice to the empire and to his duty and to brand the one who had brought about this death as an enemy of the empire and a villain. Myth in the making!

To play the role he had assumed for himself, however, Yüeh Fei had to find an appropriate route to prominence. His family was apparently not well enough established or affluent enough to permit his rise "the easy way" through inheritance or sponsorship. One incident in his life might indicate that for a time he strove to establish relations with influential persons who might sponsor his entry into officialdom. He became a tenant-retainer of the Han family, a gentry-official family of high standing in the neighboring district of An-yang. His functions there included the exercise of strong-arm methods to prevent the depredations of marauding bands on the Han property.[19] But he soon abandoned this approach.

This left only two ways open to him, development of his literary skills and development of his martial skills. He chose the second. This fateful choice seems strange. There is no doubt that Yüeh Fei would have qualified for a literary career. The literary career undoubtedly offered much more security and, particularly at the time when Yüeh Fei's decision was taken, much higher prestige. This was the year 1122, the last period of Hui-tsung's reign. The power of the Chin was already in the ascendant; it was the year in which they conquered the Southern capital of the Liao, Peking. Their future onslaught against the Sung was, however, by no means anticipated. Thus there was not yet an urgent need to strengthen the military in order to save the country.

Furthermore, military prestige at the end of Northern Sung was particularly low, considerably lower than could be explained by the traditional ideological precedence of the civilian over the military. All through Northern Sung times, the performance of the military had been mediocre. There had not been any glorious campaigns or any feats of personal military prowess like those for which earlier dynasties had been justly famous. This was at least in part due to conscious government policy. The founder of Sung, even though, or possibly because, he had come to power through the military, was particularly aware of the double-edgedness of his own profession; and ever since then it had remained an unshaken principle of the government to keep the military in check rather than to make positive use of it. To be sure, in the later part of Northern Sung the military had proliferated again, but even then the military career was despised. Why should an ambitious youth planning his career have thrown in his lot with a profession that counted for so little?

One reason might be that government civil service had not been a tradition in the Yüeh family; what was a compelling reason for some youngsters to go through the examination drudgery—to maintain and raise the family position by emulating or surpassing their elders—was of no account for Yüeh Fei. It might also be noted that the high degree of centralization of civilian government in Northern Sung times left very little beyond routine activities for even the high official, with the consequence that excess energy found an outlet in clique struggles, which were ideologically and personally repulsive and reduced individual security to a very low level. The same degree of control over the military had not yet been achieved. Although the government had succeeded in keeping the military conspicuously inactive, there remained, within the military establishment, appreciably greater opportunity for the exercise of personal initiative.

Finally, we must remember that Yüeh Fei was not yet twenty when he made this decision. A youth of his age and temperament might well have been acting under the inspiration of great heroes of the past, but Yüeh Fei's decision is likely to have stemmed also from a conviction that this was in accord with his appointed destiny. He felt within himself the potential of the submerged dragon.

Having made his decision, Yüeh Fei now had to establish a reputation for military skills and define a personal goal. The occasion offered itself in 1122, when Liu Chia, staff officer of T'ung Kuan, recruited daredevils (*kan chan shih*).[20] Yüeh Fei enlisted and participated in the attempt by the Sung army to capture Peking from the Liao. History records the tumultuous retreat of T'ung Kuan's army, Peking was left to the Chin, but Yüeh Fei had glimpsed with his own eyes the awesome walls of this great and long-lost northern metropolis, in his myth-oriented terminology the City of the Yellow Dragon, which from that time on figured so largely in his strategic reasoning.

When T'ung Kuan returned to Kaifeng, Yüeh stayed with Liu Chia, then stationed at Chen-ting. Liu employed him mainly in the suppression of "local bandits." Colorful descriptions exist of his first military encounters. He was portrayed not only as a powerful wielder of the sword and bow, endowed with an almost superhuman courage, but also —his study of the military classics had not been in vain—as a sharp strategist and clever tactician who knew how to use tricks and ruses.

This first experience of organized military life lasted less than a year. Toward the end of that year his father died, and Yüeh Fei, true to the imperatives of an established behavior pattern, immediately returned home. This unquestioning self-denial was genuine but at the same time exemplary. Although it meant reverting to obscurity for four long years, the young dragon had made his appearance in the field.

By the time Yüeh Fei returned to military life, in response to a recruitment drive late in 1126, the political situation had changed considerably: the Northern Sung dynasty was at an end. In the ensuing turmoil circumstances had arisen whose configuration suggested a potential "restoration" of the dynasty.[21] To bring this potential to fruition required among other things: an image of the empire which was persuasive enough to command not just routine loyalty but personal commitment to the cause of restoration; a head of government who would in his person symbolize the common cause and be ingenious enough to marshal and coordinate the necessary forces; a number of imaginative restoration leaders who would have the drive as well as the freedom of action to gather up, organize, and lead the shattered parts of the empire; and finally an entirely new pre-eminence of the military. Yüeh Fei saw his opportunity.

On rejoining the military Yüeh had at first enjoyed the sponsorship of Chang So. Following Chang's dismissal, Yüeh joined an at best semi-independent commander, Wang Yen. Incompatibility of personal ambitions led Yüeh to leave Wang, and for a time Yüeh became the entirely independent commander of an independent army unit, officially speaking a "bandit" or at best a petty warlord. Then he rejoined the official army under the command of Tsung Tse,[22] whom he highly respected, and after Tsung's death he served under his successor, Tu Ch'ung,[23] who eventually surrendered to the Chin. In this period Yüeh fought his colleagues rather than the common enemy, gradually assembling an army of great potential striking power and immaculate prestige, his own army, the Yüeh-chia-chün.

Episodes abound that show how Yüeh forged this tool for action and maintained its sharp edge ever after. Very strict discipline prevailed in his army, and heavy punishment was meted out even for inadvertent mistakes. Recognition, rewards, and grants of responsibility and initiative came to those who lived up to Yüeh's expectations. And as Yüeh's military genius guaranteed that no military action undertaken ever ended in defeat, he succeeded in creating unique cohesion and spirit in his army.

The prestige of his army was also increased by its irreproachable behavior. Again episodes abound to illustrate this point. Its repute, and that of its commander, surpassed all others. Wise rehabilitation measures, by which reconquered territory was restored to productivity and the roaming population resettled in a new kind of security, contributed to this effect. His army was made to carry out these rehabilitation measures in addition to performing its martial functions.

His grandson Yüeh K'o summarized his technique for welding an army together as follows:

Among the methods by which Yüeh Fei managed his army, there were six great ones. The first was: careful selection. He stressed quality and did not stress quantity. From those selected, one counted as much as a hundred. Once the emperor had transferred to his army the troops of Han Ching and Wu Hsi; not all of them were used to battle, and many of them were old and weak. After he had selected those who could be used, he had not got even a thousand men; the rest were all dismissed and sent home. After a few months of training he had in consequence an army unit of high quality.

The second was: careful training. When the troops were stationed at garrison quarters, he had them instructed in all the pertinent arts. This instruction became increasingly strict until they would not enter for a visit when they passed their own gate, and until they would regard days of leave like days of action. For instance, they had to crawl through moats and jump over walls, and all that in full armor. When they had completed their training, people would regard them as saints.

The third was: justice in rewards and punishments. He treated all his people alike. A private named Kuo Chin from the unit of Chang Hsien had earned merits at Mo-yeh-kuan.[24] Yüeh unhooked his golden belt and gave it to him as a reward together with silverware for his personal use, and in addition he promoted him. His son Yüeh Yün once was practicing jumping a moat in heavy armor when his horse stumbled and fell. Yüeh Fei, angry on account of his lack of training, said: "Would you also act this way when facing the great enemy?" And then he ordered him to be decapitated. All his generals knelt before him and begged that his son be spared. Thereupon he had him bastinadoed a hundred times and let him go. Other examples are Fu Ch'ing, who was executed because he had boasted of his merits; Hsin T'ai, who was dismissed because he had not followed orders; and Jen Shih-an, who was bastinadoed because he had followed an order too slowly. All failures, irrespective of their seriousness, were heavily punished. When Chang Chün[25] once asked him about the art of using soldiers, he replied: "Humaneness, reliability, wisdom, courage, and strictness [*jen, hsin, chih, yung, yen*]; of these five not one may be missing." And when Chang asked about strictness, he replied: "Those who have merits are heavily rewarded; those who have no merits are stiffly punished."

The fourth was: clear orders. He gave his soldiers clear delineations and his commissions were always clear and simple, so that they could be easily followed. Whoever went against them was invariably punished.

The fifth was: strict discipline. Even when his army was on the march, there was never the slightest misdemeanor such as the trampling of the people's fields, damaging of agricultural labor, or inadequate payment for purchases. This he would never condone. A soldier once had taken a hempen rope from a man in order to tie his hay. He questioned him as to where he had got it and had him immediately decapitated.

The sixth was: community of pleasure and toil. He treated his men with grace [*en*]. He always ate the same things as the lowest of his soldiers. When there was wine or meat he shared it equally with all his subordinates. When there was not enough wine to go around, he had it diluted with water until everybody got a mouthful. When the army was on the march, he camped in the open together with his officers and soldiers; even when quarters had been prepared for him, he would not enter them alone.

To be sure, these rules and episodes have been compiled by a pious grandson. There is no reason, however, to doubt their authenticity. They all fit into the character of a man who genuinely endeavored to live up to his ideal of a warrior-hero.

The prestige of Yüeh Fei's army and the stature of his personality soon attracted a large number of civilian hangers-on. In this respect, Yüeh Fei's army was not unique; the great armies of Liu Kuang-shih,[26]

Han Shih-chung,[27] and others also welcomed and employed civilian degree-holders, who were used for administrative tasks or just kept around to lend color to the camp and wit to the feasts. They were called "serving personnel" (*hsiao-yung shih-ch'en*). Their exact functions have to my knowledge not yet been properly explored, but they seem to have been the forerunners of the *mu-yu* of later times.[28] Scholars were welcome at Yüeh Fei's camp at all periods of his career. Yüeh Fei had genuine respect for scholarship, and he also used the scholars to enliven the spirit of his soldiery by having them recount the great deeds of the heroic warriors of the past. These deeds were no doubt told in the legendarized versions already current in Yüeh Fei's time. Thus Yüeh kept before his soldiers the models on which his own life was patterned. He did not even hide his desire to go down in history as the peer of these past heroes and may have hoped that among the scholars were some who would help to establish his future position as a mythological hero. He specifically mentioned that he wanted to be likened to the great men of the period of the Three Kingdoms, Kuan Yü in particular. Later official mythology has actually put him on a par with his great model.[29]

Yüeh Fei's respect for scholars is referred to repeatedly and it is also recorded that he discussed current affairs with them and listened to their advice. It was in one of these conversations that Yüeh Fei, who was always quick to coin a winged phrase, was asked when the empire would have peace again and replied: "When the civilian officials do not love money, and when the military officials are not afraid to die, the world will get peace all by itself."[30] How could he help growing into a myth when he could answer the burning human question of his time with such a highly quotable phrase? He also said, however, that his great care always to exhibit "virtuous" conduct was motivated by the fear that the Confucianists in his camp might otherwise record personal behavior for which later generations would condemn him. Thus he built up an image of his personality not only for his time but for posterity.

Parenthetically, his relationship to women might be mentioned here, as it brings out the contours of his character. His extreme filial piety toward his mother is of course widely praised. However, when his position in the north became untenable and he had to retreat southward with his army, he left her behind in the care of his wife. Circumstances dictated this rather unfilial behavior, unfilial in particular because he must have known that his wife was not one to endure adversity. Actually his wife left him (and his mother) and remarried. His mother subsequently experienced some real hardships. Eventually rescuing his mother, he settled her adequately but not luxuriously in the Lushan Mountains near Kiukiang. At her death in 1136, Yüeh Fei immediately left camp for the prescribed mourning, even though the military situation made his personal conduct of affairs imperative. A number of imperial messages to recall him to active duty went unheeded; and only repeated pressure from his officers "to substitute loyalty for piety" brought him back to the front.

His relationship to his second wife was more intimate. He even discussed affairs with her. But she always had to take second place to his mother, whose care, under pain of severe reprimands, was her responsibility. He did not tolerate her interference with his plans, even if this concerned her own safety and that of his mother.

He did not permit his sons to have concubines. Once a colleague, who had been entertained at his camp and apparently found his hospitality somewhat dull because of the absence of girls, sent him a girl as a present. Before he had set eyes on her he asked her through a screen whether she would be willing to share the hardships of camp life. When she giggled in reply, he took this as a sign that she was frivolous and sent her back. Had she possessed the presence of mind to give him a heroic reply, he would have kept her. One is reminded of the role the girl plays in the life of the hero in Western films.[31]

He did drink rather heavily during his earlier career, apparently believing this fitted the image of a martial hero. Only the emperor's personal intervention, after Yüeh had almost killed a colleague in drunken anger, exacted from him a promise not to touch wine again until the Chin had been defeated.

Yüeh Fei's conception of the empire was far from petty. What he wanted restored was not only the original frontier of Northern Sung, but all Chinese lands north of it, including Peking and Tatung, and beyond that the territory up to the passes. Early in his career, when he was still serving under Chang So, he argued this conception in a colorful and symbol-ridden exposition, which reveals the strength of his emotional commitment to his goal as well as the soundness of his strategic reasoning. The conception remained his own, however, and not the court's.

When he discussed restoration in his memorials to the emperor, the great Han model loomed large in his argument. The element he took from this model was the inspired leadership of the Kuang-wu emperor. But the role of the general Kuo Tzu-i, who had restored the tottering T'ang empire, also figures conspicuously in his reasoning. The task of restoration had been carried out by a great military leader and Yüeh Fei was seeking the analogous role.

But again it has to be stressed that Yüeh Fei's commitment to this empire—his patriotism—was as much an emotional commitment as a reflection of conscious or even studied attitudes. This is revealed in the few remaining fragments of his nonofficial prose, a handful of poems and three songs. No one who was not genuinely committed to the point of obsession would have been able to produce as powerful a patriotic song as his *Man-chiang-hung.* It needed a Yüeh Fei to garb this emotion with words that have remained symbols of patriotism ever since:[32]

> My hair bristles in my helmet
> I lean against the railing, the pattering rain has ceased.
> I raise my eyes, and toward the sky I utter a long-drawn shout.
> My breast is filled with violence.
> At the age of thirty fame and merits are but earth and dust,
> Eight thousand miles of land are like the moon covered with clouds.
> Do not tarry! The hair of youth grows white.
> Oh, vain sorrows.
> The shame of the year Ching-k'ang [1126] not yet wiped away,
> When will the hate of the subject come to an end?
> Oh, let us drive endless chariots through the Ho-lan Pass.
> My fierce ambition is to feed upon the flesh of the Huns,
> And, laughing, I thirst for the blood of the Barbarians.
> Oh, let everything begin afresh.
> Let all the rivers and mountains be recovered,
> Before we pay our respect once more to the Emperor.

The last two verses of this song speak his dream of recovering the north, the old mountains and rivers, and his dream of entering the palace gate for his final and triumphant audience. His conception of and commitment to the empire included its symbolic actual head, the emperor. The special flavor of Yüeh Fei's loyalty and subservience reveals his character structure more clearly than anything else. Again there is no doubt that Yüeh Fei felt genuinely loyal to the emperor and that he genuinely felt himself to be a servant in the cause of which the emperor was the highest exponent. But again his image of the emperor was idealized. What he revered was the model emperor, composite image of all the model emperors of the past, the saint of immaculate virtues— an image that had been built up by successive generations of Chinese political philosophers. This emperor image coincided with the actual Emperor Kao only accidentally. In the case of Yüeh Fei this incongruity meant, however, more than the implicit tension between the ideal and its actual representative. He himself strove to be a model and exemplar, and his loyalty was attached to the emperor only in so far as he was, in the eyes of Yüeh Fei, a model and exemplar. To those manifestations of the emperor's character and the emperor's will that could not be thus designated he owed nothing. Loyal to his own ideals and goals, and confident of the power of his army, Yüeh in his responses to imperial commands frequently came close to insubordination. It is little wonder that an autocratic emperor like Kao-tsung had little use for Yüeh Fei's kind of loyalty.

There are accounts of Yüeh Fei's efforts to persuade the emperor to act more in accord with the ideal. Yüeh had been received in audience by the future Emperor Kao-tsung, at that time still the Prince of K'ang, in 1127, and apparently made a brilliant impression. But immediately after Kao-tsung had ascended the throne, Yüeh Fei, then barely in his mid-twenties, submitted with touching naïveté—or was it naïveté?—a memorial urging the emperor to provide the inspired leadership Yüeh Fei felt was needed. Yüeh could hardly have been surprised that his newly gained first official title was taken away from him for this presumption. On another occasion Yüeh Fei attempted to influence an imperial decision regarding the heir apparent. Again he was rebuffed with the rebuke that a military official should not interfere in civilian affairs.[33]

This does not mean that Yüeh did not show satisfaction and pride whenever imperial grace came his way. When he was made Regional Commandant (*chieh-tu-shih*) in 1134, that is, in his early thirties, he had even the *hybris* to liken himself to the founder of the dynasty, the only person coming readily to his mind who at an equally early age had achieved such a high position. He responded to imperial grace always with the utmost formality. Going beyond the dictates of propriety, he declined the honor of the *chieh-tu-shih* four times; his appointment to the position of a Lesser Protector (*shao-pao*) he even declined five times. Such excesses of modesty were interpreted as arrogance.

In the foregoing discussion the information on Yüeh Fei's character has been telescoped. Incidents and reactions from different parts of his life have been used to illustrate a certain trait or a certain attitude. It is not by chance that our sources induce this kind of treatment. They already present a highly typified Yüeh Fei, a man who from cradle to grave was consistent and uniform. A closer scrutiny of the verifiable and datable material reveals, however, that there was an unusual consistency in his character structure. There is very little evidence of a developing and maturing process. He appears to have entered the stage with a set of ready-made attitudes to which he stuck unflinchingly until his final hours. It is the force of the Chinese tradition, more specifically the Confucian tradition—generalized to be sure and congealed into a myth—that imposed this consistency on him and that makes him look like a bronze monument rather than a living human being, more immovable than a mountain, as the Chin said of him. It was natural for Chu Hsi to praise Yüeh Fei as the unsurpassed hero of his time.

What did change, however, were the circumstances of his life, which led him with clocklike precision to penultimate triumph and ultimate disaster. The main stations along this fatal road are quickly recounted. When, after the capitulation of Tu Ch'ing in 1129, the position of Yüeh's army in the north became untenable, he withdrew, as did the other army leaders, to the south of the Yangtze. He stationed his army at I-hsing, immediately west of the T'ai-hu lake. This was not an assigned garrison but a place of his own choice, and again for a time he and his army led an almost entirely independent existence. In the general military debacle, his army was, however, too strong a force for the court to neglect. Thus he was gradually raised in rank and responded to imperial calls for assistance. Several skirmishes with Chin troops are recorded after they had crossed the Yangtze, and in 1130 Yüeh was mainly responsible for raising the siege of Chien-k'ang (Nangking). He was then stationed at T'ai-chou (north of the Yangtze, east of Yangchow) to guard the frontier, then shifted to Hung-chou (west of Lake Poyang), Chiang-chou (present-day Kiukiang), and eventually in 1132 to O-chou (present-day Wuchang).

During this period he was mainly active in suppressing "bandits." The banditry he had to cope with was of two entirely different types. The first was represented by military leaders who, like Yüeh himself, had succeeded in extricating themselves and their armies from the military debacle in the north and had attempted to carve out for themselves independent spheres of activity south of the river. Formally, their position differed very little from Yüeh's during his I-hsing period. Unlike Yüeh, however, they had failed to recognize and acknowledge the gradual reassertion of imperial power and organized government.

The second type of banditry was local uprisings, unconnected with the development in the north. One of these was the revolt led by Li Tun-jen in Kiangsi, in which gentry influence seems to have been strong. The most interesting among these movements is the one founded by Chung Hsiang and later led by Yang Yao (original name T'ai). This rebellion seems to have had a secret-society type of ideology with certain egalitarian slogans. What Chung vowed to eradicate by his movement were: officials, scholars, monks, shamanistic medicine men, and sorcerers. The power of his organization must have been quite formidable, as he could boast of a navy that included paddle-wheel ships "swift like birds."[34] Contemporaries pointed out that this movement was an expression of genuine popular feelings, quite different in nature from the roaming army bandits, and that it should be utilized rather than suppressed. As it stood in the way of his cause, Yüeh Fei suppressed it as swiftly and as skillfully as he had suppressed the others.

It is interesting to note that later in his career Yüeh Fei did not hesitate to recognize, and cooperate with, local independent movements. His successes during his northern campaigns are at least in part explained by the fact that he could rely on these "rebellions." They paved the way for his army and acted as his intelligence.

Beginning in 1134, Yüeh Fei's army was active in a number of major campaigns against "the great enemy," the Chin and the puppet state of Ch'i, which the Chin had established as a buffer between themselves and the Sung. These campaigns were conceived within the framework of an empire-wide strategic plan and had to be coordinated with the movements of other major bodies of troops. Several of these campaigns were designed to secure the Huai-hsi region, others led deep into central and western North China. In 1134 his army went up to Kuo-chou and Ch'ang-shui on the one hand and to Ts'ai-chou on the other; and in his final and most penetrating campaign of 1140, Yüeh proceeded up to Ying-ch'ang and from there sent pincers to Lo-yang and Ch'en-chou.[35] In these campaigns Yüeh scored major successes against the army of Ch'i and finally also against the armies of Chin. It might be true that the Chin felt so hard pressed that they contemplated withdrawing beyond the Yellow River, as Yüeh stated in one of his memorials.

This last major campaign of Yüeh's army coincided, however, with the endeavors of the Sung court to come to an understanding with the Chin by surrendering Sung claims to the territory north of the Huai and submitting to a series of other conditions made by the Chin. In the last phase of this campaign, the understanding had actually been concluded. The Sung court had therefore a vital interest in having the advance armies withdrawn in accordance with the conditions of the treaty. This included Yüeh Fei's army. The emperor is reported (possibly spuriously) to have sent twelve urgent messages within one day ordering Yüeh Fei to withdraw. Yüeh did withdraw, not simply in obedience to an imperial command, but in response to the pressure of his officers, who pointed out that after the other armies had withdrawn, their position was strategically untenable. He had to withdraw or lose his army. Yüeh was aware that this was the end of his dreams. He is reported to have said: "The merits of ten years are wiped out in one morning; all the recovered territory is completely lost in one day. The altars of the empire, its rivers and mountains, will hardly be restored again. The universal world [*ch'ien-k'un shih-chieh*] can no longer be recovered."

What had happened here? Why is it that the Sung court conceded defeat in the face of a very real chance of victory?

After the debacle of 1126, the Sung court had a choice of two policies—restoration or retrenchment. A restoration policy would, as mentioned, have involved a pre-eminence of the military and a great amount of freedom of action for the military leaders. As long as the Chin or Ch'i were on the attack, the court could not but give the military free play. As soon as the Chin showed signs that they wanted to come to terms, the Sung court chose the second way, that of retrenchment. The military leaders could not be left under the impression that they were indispensable. Strict civilian control was more important than lost territory.

In the late thirties, Ch'in Kuei was responsible for the implementation of this policy. He therefore was made the villain in the piece, and was actually the one primarily responsible for the dirty work involved. It was, however, Emperor Kao-tsung's policy, and many besides Ch'in Kuei had argued for it. To break the license of the generals was a task of greater importance than to beat the Chin. This is most dramatically expressed in a remark of Emperor Kao-tsung, after one of the attacks of Ch'i had been turned back: "What makes me happy is not that Ch'i has been defeated, but that the generals have obeyed orders." In the end there was no such thing as a Sung restoration.

After Yüeh Fei had withdrawn his army, he was used once more in a minor campaign designed to ward off a supposed threat to the region south of the Huai; then he was called to the capital for an audience. On this occasion the policy of retrenchment was finally consummated: the three principal generals, Han Shih-chung, Chang Chün, and Yüeh Fei—Liu Kuang-shih had already been eliminated—were stripped of their commands, given high civilian titles, and appointed to a vaguely defined supervisory committee. Central control over the army was thus established; despotism had triumphed.

Deprived of their leaders, the armies were, however, not yet deprived of their spirit. This called for more drastic action. The first army to experience this was Han Shih-chung's. Next was Yüeh Fei's. One of the chief subcommanders of the Yüeh army, Chang Hsien, and Yüeh's son were accused of plotting to revolt, and Yüeh Fei himself was said to have been involved in this plot and imprisoned. The court could with impunity publicly execute Chang Hsien and Yüeh Yün on the strength of this trumped-up charge and have Yüeh Fei himself murdered in prison.

It is inconsequential whether or not the death of Yüeh Fei was one of the secret conditions laid down by the Chin in treaty negotiations. It is also inconsequential whether Ch'in Kuei had Yüeh Fei murdered on his own initiative or in collusion with the emperor. How the emperor felt about Yüeh Fei's death is indicated by the fact that Ch'in's position was in no way impaired by this deed.

Thus ended Yüeh Fei's life, but not his role in Chinese history and in the Chinese tradition. By creating a myth of himself, his army, and his cause, he was not able to save himself or his country, but he was able to establish a persuasive symbol for later generations. Being the hero in a dawning new age, he shared, to borrow a phrase from Campbell, "the supreme ordeal, not in the bright moments of his tribe's great victories, but in the silences of his personal despair."[36]

Conrad M. Schirokauer

CHU HSI'S POLITICAL CAREER:
A STUDY IN AMBIVALENCE

At the time of Chu Hsi's birth in October 1130, the Sung dynasty was fighting for survival. Earlier that year, Emperor Kao-tsung (r. 1127–62), fleeing from the forces of the Chin (Jurchen) armies, had been forced to take to his ships off the south China coast, and the dynasty had reached a new low. During 1130, however, the fortunes of war began to turn in favor of the Sung armies, which were gradually able to regain possession of the south. After the south was secure, a group of generals and statesmen, led by the famous Yüeh Fei (1103–41), began arguing passionately for continuation of the war and an attempt at reconquest of the north. In opposition to this view Ch'in Kuei (1090–1155) and his followers counseled prudence and advocated a peace settlement with the enemy. After a bitter political struggle, Ch'in Kuei won out over the war faction, clearing the way for the peace of 1142. The Sung ceded the territory north of the Huai River and agreed on an annual payment of 250,000 ounces of silver plus an equal number of rolls of silk. Furthermore, the Sung was forced to acknowledge the suzerainty of the Chin.

The treaty of 1142 marked the beginning of a period of military stalemate and uneasy coexistence between the Sung and the Chin. Military action by the Chin in 1161 and by the Sung in 1206 failed to alter the balance of power, which was disrupted only by the emergence of the Mongols, who were to put an end to both the Chin (1234) and the Sung (1278).

The Sung was left in control of the rich rice lands of the south as well as the centers of commerce of the southeast, which flourished as never before. Most splendid was the new capital, Hangchow, the cosmopolitan city that was to delight the Venetian Marco Polo. Here ambitious merchants made fortunes in trade while shopkeepers, artisans, and entertainers of every sort catered to a lively and varied clientele. Fine restaurants, exciting cabarets, and beautiful scenery offered a measure of personal solace to officials mindful of the loss of the Central Plain, the ancient homeland of Chinese culture. Yet neither the prosperity of the south nor the amenities of life in Hangchow could hide the fact that Chinese prestige and self-respect had been dealt a severe blow. The loss of the north preyed on men's minds, served as a constant reproach to those in power, and lent a sense of urgency to proposals for military and civil reform. It was a disgrace to the dynasty, irrefutable proof that something was drastically wrong.

Southern Sung emperors and their ministers never officially relinquished the idea of ultimate reconquest of the north and until the end kept up the pretense that Hangchow was merely the temporary residence of the court. The emperors, however, were for the most part weak rulers incapable of carrying out any consistent long-range policy. It is significant that all three changes of throne during Chu Hsi's lifetime were effected by the abdication of the emperor, an unusual practice in China. In the bureaucracy, factional conflicts were intense. Officials spent a great deal of energy in political battles, intrigues, and attempts to win imperial favor. Political controversy ranged from carefully reasoned policy discussions to personal slander and vilification.

Confucian scholars found ample cause for dissatisfaction with this state of affairs but differed in their personal commitments to political action and in their doctrinal positions. The range of ideas in the new Confucianism was wide and made for a lively intellectual life. In books, letters, and conversations scholars debated the interpretation of their common heritage. While Lu Chiu-yüan (1139–92) formulated his philosophy of self-cultivation, more politically minded thinkers sought for ways to solve the problems besetting the dynasty. Yeh Shih (1150–1223) rejected Neo-Confucian metaphysics as tainted with Buddhism and Taoism and as lacking in practical application. Instead he interested himself in statecraft and tried to find solutions for such pressing problems as agrarian reform, monetary policy, taxation, and military policy.[1] These interests were shared by Ch'en Fu-liang (1141–1207), author of the first military history of China,[2] who together with Yeh Shih provided the leadership for the Yung-chia school, named after the capital of Wen-chou in Chekiang, where both men were born. Another leading representative of the tendency exemplified by the Yung-chia school was Ch'en Liang (1141–91), who vainly hoped for official adoption of his political and military proposals.[3]

Chu Hsi was thoroughly familiar with the intellectual currents of his time and in a voluminous correspondence discussed a wide range of issues. His most lasting contribution to Chinese thought was the elaboration of the ideas of the great Northern Sung philosophers, especially

Ch'eng I and Ch'eng Hao, continuing their work of providing Confucianism with strong metaphysical foundations. In this Chu Hsi was so successful that he came to be regarded as the greatest of all the Sung philosophers. His writings exercised a profound influence over Chinese thought for some seven centuries and became the official orthodoxy of the Chinese state.

Hitherto scholars have been largely concerned with Chu Hsi's philosophic doctrines, but the political importance of his theories and the homage paid to Chu Hsi the man suggests that an examination of his political career and his attitude toward government is long overdue.

Chu Hsi's family can be traced back to the tenth century, when an ancestor of his commanded a force of three thousand men under General T'ao Ya of the state of Wu (902–29).[4] The family established itself in Wu-yüan, modern Anhwei, but Chu Hsi himself was born in Fukien. His father, Chu Sung (1097–1143), was the first man in the family in at least three generations to hold an official post; he served as Correcting Editor of the Imperial Library and also as a Division Chief in the Ministry of Personnel.[5] Chu Sung's opposition to the peace policies of Ch'in Kuei cost him these positions and led to his retirement from official life in 1140.[6]

From his father Chu Hsi acquired a strong aversion to Ch'in Kuei and a love of learning. Chu Sung had a reputation as a poet and scholar and had studied under Lo Ts'ung-yen (1072–1135), a disciple of Yang Shih (1035–1135), who in turn was a student of the Ch'eng brothers. This combination of adherence to the teachings of the Ch'eng brothers and opposition to Ch'in Kuei was not unusual in the years following the restoration of the Sung in the south. In 1131 the emperor bestowed posthumous honors on Ch'eng I, but six years later, when the peace party was in control, Kao-tsung complied with a request that the theories of the Ch'eng brothers be proscribed. Ch'eng I's doctrines were denounced as "wild words and strange sayings, immoral talk and vile discourse" and his behavior was stigmatized as haughty.[7] Chu Hsi always considered himself a disciple of the Ch'eng brothers, an allegiance that involved him in doctrinal conflicts and political controversy.

Chu Hsi was a bright child and at an early age received instruction in the Confucian classics.[8] In 1134 he entered elementary school and is said to have written in his copy of the *Classic of Filial Piety* that "not to be like this is not to be a man."[9] The influence of this work was no doubt reinforced by accounts of the exceptional filial piety of Chu Hsi's maternal grandfather.[10] Chu Hsi's biographers also tell various stories supposed to illustrate his precocity. For example, it is said that at the age of seven he was found tracing the diagrams of the *I-ching* in the sand while his companions were at play.[11] Of greater interest is Chu Hsi's own statement that when he was nine, he decided to emulate Mencius and become a sage.[12]

In 1140 Chu Sung, out of office, personally undertook the education of his son, drilling him carefully in the *Great Learning* and the *Doctrine of the Mean*. At his death in 1143, Chu Sung entrusted his son to three friends, one of whom was later to become Chu Hsi's father-in-law.[13] For our purpose, it is noteworthy that these three men shared Chu Sung's opposition to Ch'in Kuei and his policies. The following years were spent in study, and in 1148 Chu Hsi obtained his *chin-shih* degree, no mean feat for a young man of eighteen.[14] He received his first official appointment as Subprefectural Registrar in T'ung-an, Fukien, and assumed his duties in 1153.

The duties of a subprefectural registrar in Sung China were many, and Chu Hsi performed them conscientiously, supervising the registers, promoting education, reporting on public morality, and even assisting in measures of bandit defense.[15] Especially successful was Chu Hsi's rehabilitation of the local school where later a shrine to him was erected by a disciple of Yeh Shih.[16] Chu Hsi completed his term in 1156 but, because his replacement died, had to remain in T'ung-an until 1158. During the next twenty years Chu Hsi held a number of temple guardianships which amounted to sinecures and did not again assume a substantive office until 1179. This period saw the emergence of Chu Hsi as a noted scholar and philosopher. During this time he became a national figure and began to attract a following of students and disciples. His political views took shape. His way of life became set.

According to the eulogistic account of Chu Hsi's life composed by his disciple and son-in-law Huang Kan (1152–1221), Chu Hsi lived the frugal and disciplined life of a sage.[17] His demeanor was grave; his movements relaxed but respectful. He sat up straight and when tired rested by closing his eyes without changing his posture. We are told that he arose before daylight, put on his long robe, hat, and square shoes, and began the day by worshiping his ancestors. He went to bed at midnight, and if he awoke in the night sat up in bed until dawn. His physical wants were few: enough clothes to cover his body, enough food to still his hunger, a house to keep out wind and rain. He is said to have been content in surroundings that other people could not have borne.

According to Huang Kan, Chu Hsi showed the right measure of respect, courtesy, and warmth to visitors, neighbors, and relatives. He never lost his composure, and it goes without saying that he is presented as a model of filial piety. Punctilious in his attention to the details of ritual observances, whether in offering sacrifices or in celebrating a birthday or wedding, Chu Hsi carried concern for precise order into the routine of his daily life. Huang tells us that his desk was always arranged in an orderly fashion and that Chu Hsi was very fussy about the way his dining table was set. It is reported that the last act of the dying Chu Hsi was to motion to a disciple to adjust his kerchief.[18]

The value of this type of eulogy is, of course, limited. Nor is it of much help to be told in a poem by Ch'en Liang that Chu Hsi had "a mild harmony in the countenance, a rich fullness in the back," a description used by Mencius to characterize the "superior man."[19] We need not believe that Chu Hsi never lost his temper or slumped at his desk. Yet this account of Chu Hsi by a disciple who knew him well does tell us that in his private life Chu Hsi strove to live according to what he conceived of as the rigorous standards of a sage. In doing so, Chu Hsi won the respect, and even affection, not only of disciples but of men like Ch'en Liang and Lu Chiu-yüan, who vigorously disagreed with his philosophic views.

The years out of office gave Chu Hsi welcome time for the pursuit of his scholarly and philosophical interests, but he was never entirely removed from political cares. In 1159, only a year after he left T'ung-an, Chu Hsi along with three other men was summoned to court by Emperor Kao-tsung. He had been recommended by a minister known for his courage and patriotism, but another minister saw to it that the audience never took place.[20] At this time Chu also sent poems to two men who had recently received appointments: Hu Hsien, one of his three guardians, and Liu Kung, a man who had opposed the policies of Ch'in Kuei.[21] Although Chu Hsi in these two poems contrasted the position of Hu and Liu with his own retirement, there is no indication that he was unhappy with his sinecure. In any case, it was not until Kao-tsung abdicated and was succeeded by Hsiao-tsung in 1162 that Chu Hsi played a part in national affairs.

One of the new emperor's first acts was to invite memorials from scholars and officials. Chu Hsi responded by submitting a sealed memorial and in 1163 was granted an audience in which he presented three further memorials.[22] In these Chu Hsi admonished the emperor to study the principles of government and morality and perform the duties of his high calling, advocated a strong foreign policy, and appealed for enlightened personnel policies. The last two topics were controversial. With the collapse of the Chin attack in 1161 and the withdrawal of enemy forces a year later, war and peace advocates once again disputed at the Sung court. Chu Hsi roundly condemned the peace advocates as inferior persons who considered only their own selfish interests and disregarded the moral duty of reconquering the Central Plain. Their policy, he maintained, would lead to the destruction of moral bonds and to ruin.[23] While this attitude antagonized the members of the peace faction, remarks concerning the undue influence of sycophants and favorites offended a number of powerful men—including Ts'eng Ti and Lung Ta-yüan, who had won Hsiao-tsung's confidence while he was still crown prince and who held powerful positions in the Palace Postern.[24] Hsiao-tsung himself accepted Chu Hsi's general admonishments graciously but was not pleased with the advice on foreign and personnel policies.[25] As a result of his audience, Chu Hsi was appointed Professor Designate in the Military Academy.[26]

Emperor Hsiao-tsung was persuaded to adopt a war policy, but the Sung forces, after initial success, were defeated. This led to the ascendancy of the peace party and the treaty of 1165, similar to the settlement of 1142. In the same year Chu Hsi was urged to assume his duties in the Military Academy, but declined to serve in a government controlled by the peace advocates he had so bitterly denounced. He resigned and was reappointed to a temple guardianship. Although a professorship in the Military Academy would seem a highly desirable position for a man bent on the reconquest of the north, Chu Hsi's resignation of 1165 was the logical outcome of his opposition to the policies of the men in power. More subtle reasons prompted him to decline a number of other positions until he finally accepted office in 1179.

Two years after he declined the position in the Military Academy, Chu Hsi was appointed Compiler Designate in the Bureau of Military Affairs. He was recommended for this position by Liu Kung, now Co-administrator in the Bureau of Military Affairs, and by Ch'en Chün-ch'ing, a statesman who had opposed the peace advocates, criticized the emperor's personnel policy, and shared Chu Hsi's hostility toward Ts'eng Ti. Chu Hsi held Ch'en in high esteem and was later to write a record of his life.[27] By the time Chu Hsi was called on to assume his post in 1169, Liu Kung had been dismissed but Ch'en Chün-ch'ing was at the height of his power.[28] Pleading a foot ailment, Chu Hsi asked to be excused. He pointed out that his family was poor and his mother old and requested to be continued in his temple guardianship.[29] There was, however, considerable pressure for Chu Hsi to accept the post, and it became increasingly difficult for him to persist in his refusal on personal grounds alone, even though his concern for his mother was eminently respectable. Chu Hsi was about to give in when in the seventh month of 1169 he learned that a friend, Wei Shan-chih, had been dismissed from his position in the National University because he had criticized Ts'eng Ti. This event provided Chu Hsi with political justification for refusing the office.

Chu Hsi, explaining his refusal in a letter to one of Ch'en Chünch'ing's colleagues, complained that high officials, such as councillors of state and censors, had failed in their duty of remonstrance and that in consequence lower officials had felt called upon to perform this duty, thereby going beyond what was proper to their station. Then, according to Chu Hsi, these officials instead of being treated graciously were dismissed from office and even denied the usual privilege of "requesting punishment." Chu Hsi maintained that the issue at stake was not the dismissal of Wei Shan-chih but the treatment of scholars in general. "What does concern me," wrote Chu Hsi, "is to note how you gentlemen treat the scholars of the realm and conduct myself accordingly."[30] These were strong words for a man who had held only minor office and enjoyed a sinecure for ten years. Moreover, since Ts'eng Ti was demoted to a provincial post in the very month this letter was written, it would probably have been very difficult for Chu Hsi to persist in his declination.[31] The death of Chu Hsi's mother in the ninth month of 1169 resolved a situation that threatened to develop into a crisis.

Chu Hsi's declination of 1169 shows a typical mixture of personal and political reasons. The need he felt to justify his withdrawal on political grounds reflects his feeling of obligation to serve as an official, a traditional Confucian sense of social duty reinforced by the critical situation of a dynasty that had lost the north. It also reflects the Chinese practice of using personal reasons as pretexts for politically motivated declinations of office, so that the men in power were in any case inclined to interpret a declination as a political act. By bringing in political reasons for his declination Chu Hsi could justify his conduct to himself and also hope to convince the men in power of his sincere determination to refuse the appointment. This brings out one of the prime difficulties confronting the student of the career of a scholar-official. Personal reasons, especially pleas of ill health, could serve as pretexts for withholding political support from a regime; likewise, a declination on grounds of political principle might serve to reinforce, if not to hide, personal reasons for refusing an appointment. In 1169 Chu Hsi's personal reasons were more convincing than the political criticism he voiced in his personal letter to a high official, and he was finally enabled to avoid office by the death of his mother.

When in 1170 Chu Hsi was summoned to court on the recommendation of another former opponent of Ch'in Kuei, he excused himself on the unassailable ground that he was in mourning.[32] In 1172 he gave the same reason for declining another summons to court and reinforced it with the plea that he was short of funds and suffering from an abscess.[33] The famous historian Li Hsin-ch'uan (1166–1243), an admirer of Chu Hsi, believed that this declination originated out of a difference between Chu Hsi and Yü Yün-wen, who was then in power.[34] Li, however, remained silent on the substance of this disagreement. This declination was followed by four others, the last of which Chu Hsi submitted in 1173. From these documents, written in the customary stilted style, it is difficult to discern Chu Hsi's motives.[35]

Out of office, Chu Hsi had ample time for his scholarly pursuits. He completed his first book in 1159 and by the end of 1173 had finished a total of thirteen works, which established him as a scholar and a leading interpreter of the great Northern Sung philosophers. Among his works were commentaries on the writings of Chou Tun-i (1017–73) and Chang Tsai (1020–77) as well as a compilation of the works of the Ch'eng brothers and a collection of notes taken by disciples of the Ch'eng brothers. Now that he was a prominent man of learning, Chu Hsi's political conduct was of special concern to the men in power. It became increasingly difficult for them to disregard him. Furthermore, Chu Hsi's apparent unwillingness to accept office left him open to attack, and in 1173 an official, whose name is not known, cast aspersions on his scholarship and claimed that Chu Hsi was bogged down in dogma.[36] This attack is of interest mainly as a sign of things to come and did not harm Chu Hsi, who was defended by an important minister. The emperor commended Chu Hsi, raised his rank, and appointed him to another sinecure. Chu Hsi sought to decline this sinecure in a series of official communications expressing his lack of merit and his uneasiness in being advanced when seeking to withdraw.[37] A hostile observer might have construed his refusal to accept office as a stratagem to obtain another sinecure, and Chu Hsi tried to avoid this impression. He assumed the new sinecure in 1174.

The next attempt to bring Chu Hsi to the capital occurred in 1176 when he was appointed Librarian of the Imperial Library on the recommendation of Kung Mao-liang. Once again, he declined. This aroused considerable criticism, directed both at Chu Hsi himself and at Kung. The emperor was displeased, and after a second declination Chi Hsi received another sinecure, the guardianship of a monastery.[38]

Chu Hsi explained the reasons for his declination in a letter to a man who had supported his appointment.[39] After stating that all he wanted was to devote himself to scholarship, Chu Hsi discusses his embarrassment at being given positions for which he maintained, in a subtle mixture of humility and criticism, he was unfit. He then proceeds to the subject at hand, his present declination:

If I now do not decline office but blindly accept it, there would surely still be cases of differences in judgment between myself and my superiors. This would do no good to the government and would provide an occasion for my being jeered at by the petty crowd. Whatever I may hope to accomplish would remain incomplete and be destroyed. If when I die, by good luck, I have accomplished something, people will merely consider what I have written to be untested and will not read it.[40]

Chu Hsi is saying that acceptance of office under existing political conditions would run counter to the doctrines to which he has devoted his life and vitiate what he has accomplished as a philosopher and teacher. Acceptance would not give him an opportunity to apply his ideas, but, on the contrary, would entail the abandonment of his standard of conduct and thus expose him to ridicule and undermine his teachings. Chu Hsi goes on, in the next sentence, to make it quite clear that accepting the appointment would be inconsistent with his pattern of political behavior and the principles on which it is based: "Even more to the point, if I now all at once come forth and take office, my carefully considered reasons for hesitating to take office on previous occasions will fail to be clear to people."

Continuing the letter, Chu Hsi states that acceptance of office is not merely a matter of personal predilection but depends on the general political situation. Complaining of the corruption and rapacity of officials, Chu Hsi protests that he does not want to be forced to join this unscrupulous band: "Although I am unworthy, I cannot bear such an insult to my person, which will cause those who discuss it in later times to revile and despise me."[41] Chu Hsi maintained that his acceptance of office would demoralize his students and asserted the need for consistency between words and deeds.

In this letter Chu Hsi developed the idea suggested in his letter of 1169 that the government was unworthy of the support of a truly moral man. The issue at stake was not specific government policy but the ethos of political life. Chu Hsi affirmed the right of the Confucian scholar-official not only to criticize the government but to set ideal terms for his own participation in it, to demand such high standards of political conduct that he would, in effect, always be justified in declining office. Chu Hsi preferred to guard his moral prestige by withholding support from the government rather than make an attempt to work for reform from within, even if this weakened men like Ch'en Chün-ch'ing and Kung Mao-liang, who had recommended him in an attempt to raise the standard of government. Moreover, Chu Hsi's position implied a strong sense of moral superiority over those men who did accept office and undoubtedly fostered resentment against him in official circles.

It is not known whether resentment against Chu Hsi contributed to the attack, early in 1178, by the General Censor Hsieh K'uo-jan on the doctrines of both Ch'eng I and Wang An-shih. Another attack on the teachings of the Ch'eng brothers followed.[42] Although Chu Hsi was not the object of direct attack, he must have felt the force of criticism directed at his philosophic mentors. These attacks apparently did not have an immediate effect on his career except to put his political behavior more than ever into the limelight. It was in 1178 that events occurred leading to Chu Hsi's acceptance of office in the following year.

In the third month of 1178 Shih Hao, who had held high office in 1163, became Right Grand Councillor, a position he was to hold until the eleventh month of that year, when he was succeeded by Chao Hsiung. Shih Hao was eager to have Chu Hsi assume an official post, since this would strengthen the moral standing of the government. At first Shih Hao wished to bring Chu Hsi to the capital but was dissuaded by Chao Hsiung, who proposed that for the present Chu Hsi should be given a provincial assignment. Chao Hsiung pointed out to Shih Hao that in this way they could avoid taking a definite stand for or against Chu Hsi should he proffer unwelcome criticism and advice.[43] Chao's plan was, in effect, to associate Chu Hsi with the government without really endorsing his views. Chao convinced Shih, and Chu Hsi was appointed prefect of Nan-k'ang in modern Kiangsi.

True to form, Chu Hsi declined the appointment, pleading illness and lack of experience. Shih Hao, however, insisted that he take office, and friends likewise urged him to accept. Chu Hsi's friend Chang Shih wrote a letter warning that refusal to accept office would lead to the charge that scholars were unwilling to serve the state and would thus harm the doctrines for which Chu Hsi stood.[44] This was a reversal of Chu Hsi's earlier argument that it would harm his doctrines if he were to assume office. The fact that both arguments were convincing reflects the dilemma of the Confucian scholar committed both to a set of ideal moral principles and to an obligation to serve a government that, although far from ideal, was not so completely vicious as to warrant unqualified opposition. Yielding to mounting pressure, Chu Hsi accepted the post and assumed his duties in 1179. Chu Hsi was assigned to Nan-k'ang because the men in power believed it would involve them in only a limited commitment to support Chu Hsi; perhaps Chu Hsi himself felt that a position as prefect entailed a looser association with the government than did the posts at the capital he had previously declined.

Chu Hsi's administration of Nan-k'ang is known mainly for his restoration of the White Deer Grotto Academy, which flourished under his direction and attracted many students. The Academy offered students a heavy mixture of ethics and scholarship as well as occasional lectures by visiting scholars. Among these was Lu Chiu-yüan, who chose as his text a passage from the *Analects*: "The superior man is conversant with righteousness; the inferior person is conversant with gain."[45] Chu Hsi did not let the Academy distract him from his other duties. When the area was struck by drought, he was very busy providing relief. He had some experience in this, since in 1167–68 he had participated in emergency famine relief in Fukien and in 1171 had established a communal loan granary as a measure of famine insurance.[46] In Nan-k'ang, Chu Hsi submitted numerous official requests for relief of various kinds.[47] He pursued his duties energetically and gained a considerable reputation as a relief administrator. At the same time, Chu Hsi was not happy with his position and made a number of unsuccessful requests for leave.[48]

In the fourth month of 1180, just prior to another request for leave, Chu Hsi responded to an imperial proclamation by submitting a sealed memorial admonishing the emperor and denouncing the men in whom he put his trust. Chu Hsi went so far as to say that the emperor was in the hands of an unscrupulous clique of favorites and sycophants. He told the emperor that while good men despair and criticism is stifled, these vicious men confuse the imperial mind, control appointments, steal the emperor's wealth, and usurp his authority:

As the power of these people waxes and as their prestige becomes established, throughout the land everyone bends before them like grass before the wind, with the result that Your Majesty's edicts, promotions, and demotions no longer issue from the court, but from the private houses of these one or two favorites. Ostensibly these acts are Your Majesty's individual decisions, but in fact it is this handful of men who secretly exercise Your power of control.[49]

The emperor was enraged by this memorial but was persuaded by Chao Hsiung not to punish Chu Hsi and to reassign him to his previous post. Chao is said to have warned the emperor: "The more Your Majesty shows your hatred of fame-seekers like this, the more numerous will their admirers be. If you do anything, will it not just serve to enhance his prestige?"[50]

Chao Hsiung, aware of the workings of opinion, here demonstrated considerable finesse in handling a prominent and righteous critic of the government. It was not only the Confucian scholar who was faced with a dilemma vis-à-vis the government; the government was faced with an equally vexing problem in dealing with a man whose prestige it sought but whose advice was frequently unpalatable. Chu Hsi's appointment to Nan-k'ang and his continuation in that post marked a temporary resolution of the dilemmas confronting both himself and the government.

Chu Hsi's term in Nan-k'ang expired in the fourth month of 1181. In the previous month, the emperor, after turning down a suggestion that Chu Hsi be sent to Szechwan, appointed him as an intendant designate for Chiang-nan West.[51] Four months later this appointment was changed to Auxiliary Official in the Imperial Archives. Chu Hsi declined this office three times, protesting that the government had failed to reimburse four men who had made substantial contributions to famine relief in Nan-k'ang.[52] Thereupon, in the eighth month, the appointment was changed once again. On the advice of the Chief Councillor of State, Wang Huai, Chu Hsi was appointed Intendant for Ever-normal Granaries, Tea, and Salt for Eastern Liang-che (modern Chekiang), an area suffering from famine.[53] The urgency of the situation, in one of the richest provinces, made refusal well nigh impossible. Chu Hsi accepted the position. In January 1182 he was granted an imperial audience, in which he again vigorously criticized the government and in a discussion of agrarian problems recommended the establishment of communal granaries.[54] Following the audience, Chu Hsi left to assume his duties as an intendant, a post entailing great responsibilities as well as considerable political danger.

Chu Hsi took his duties as intendant very seriously and worked hard to bring relief to the stricken population and ease their tax burden. One of his duties was to inspect the conduct of local officials, and Chu Hsi soon discovered and indicted a number of remiss and corrupt officials.[55] This was all very well as long as the men indicted did not have powerful political connections. But when he indicted the prefect of T'ai-chou, T'ang Chung-yu, a man related by marriage to Wang Huai, Chu Hsi suddenly found the most powerful men in the government aligned against him.

Chu Hsi's six reports on T'ang Chung-yu contain particulars concerning a wide range of improper activities, among them various instances of misappropriation of official funds and supplies, illegal activities involving the clothing, book, and fish shops owned by the T'ang family, the forging of paper money, and other examples of the misuse of power.[56] Since T'ang was a scholar whose interests and opinions were quite different from those of Chu Hsi, it has been suggested that Chu Hsi was biased against T'ang.[57] This, however, is unlikely in view of the nature of the indictments themselves and the fact that Chu Hsi was on excellent terms with philosophers whose views he disputed.[58] A particularly damaging version of the affair which may well have been fabricated by Chu Hsi's enemies is recounted by Chou Mi (1232–99). According to this account, Chu Hsi's friend Ch'en Liang had a grudge against T'ang involving a singing girl. When Chu Hsi asked him, "What does little T'ang have to say these days?" Ch'en allegedly answered, "T'ang says that you still cannot make out characters; how can you be an intendant?" When Chu Hsi went to T'ai-chou and T'ang was late in coming out to greet him, Chu Hsi's bad impression was confirmed.[59]

The view that the issue in the T'ang Chung-yu case was simply a doctrinal or personal dispute between scholars was fostered by T'ang's supporters, and Wang Huai succeeded in persuading the emperor that this was indeed the case.[60] Other officials not only supported T'ang but attacked Chu Hsi. This attack took the form of a wholesale denunciation of the entire school of philosophy with which Chu Hsi was associated. This time the object of attack was not only the doctrine of the Ch'eng brothers but the "Doctrine of the True Way," Tao-hsüeh, a term derived from Han Yü's account of the orthodox transmission of the "Way" through the early sages to Confucius and Mencius.[61] It was an elastic term, which could be applied to any of the participants in the Sung Confucian revival. In his attack on Tao-hsüeh, the Minister of Personnel Cheng Ping accused the proponents of this doctrine of "swindling the world and stealing fame." The Censor Ch'en Chia, a protégé of Wang Huai, told the emperor that the followers of Tao-hsüeh were pretentious and insincere. Ch'en asked Hsiao-tsung to remove these men so as to display true discrimination between right and wrong. Ch'en Chia's statement was couched in general terms, but the immediate object of his attack was Chu Hsi.[62]

The "Doctrine of the True Way" was not without its defenders. One official, for example, repeated the claim of Han Yü and assured the emperor that this was the teaching of Yao and Shun, Yü, T'ang, Wen and Wu, Chou Kung, Confucius, and Mencius, and denounced the attack as an attempt to slander superior men.[63] Emperor Hsiao-tsung wavered. He was not prepared to take decisive action one way or the other. The outcome of the case was that T'ang lost his position in T'ai-chou as well as a post as Judicial Intendant, which he was to have assumed after completing his term as prefect. Chu Hsi was appointed to the intendancy thus vacated, but refused to accept a position that might cast doubt on his motives for bringing up the T'ang Chung-yu case. In declining the post, Chu Hsi complained bitterly that supporters of T'ang occupied important positions in the government, that "they were spread about like men on a chessboard or like stars" and had misled the court. He also told Hsiao-tsung that any favor the emperor might show him would only serve to intensify the animosity of his enemies.[64] After Chu Hsi had declined the appointment three times, Hsiao-tsung in 1183 once again appointed him to a sinecure.

The T'ang Chung-yu case and the resulting controversy marked something of a turning point in Chu Hsi's political career. After 1182 Tao-hsüeh was a controversial term and Chu Hsi a controversial figure. A precedent had been set and a way devised to discredit Chu Hsi should he again prove troublesome to the men in power. Chu Hsi himself, on the other hand, was confirmed in his diagnosis that political life was totally corrupt, and strengthened in his belief that a truly virtuous man should have as little as possible to do with an unworthy government. This attitude, however, was to furnish ammunition to Chu Hsi's enemies and embarrass his friends.

In permitting Chu Hsi's self-righteous withdrawal in 1183, Emperor Hsiao-tsung may have envisioned a return to the situation earlier in his reign when open conflict between Chu Hsi and the government had been avoided. In any case, Chu Hsi enjoyed a four-year respite from politics. His sinecure expired in 1185, only to be followed by another. In 1187 the emperor again appointed Chu Hsi guardian of a temple. But in the seventh month of that year he was once more drawn into political life. He was recommended for substantive appointment by Yang Wan-li, a statesman seriously concerned with strengthening the dynasty.[65] Chou Pi-ta, a prominent minister who had withstood Ts'eng Ti and Lung Ta-yüan, suggested that Chu Hsi be appointed Fiscal Intendant. When it was objected that taxation was not Chu Hsi's strong point, the appointment was changed to a judicial intendancy.[66]

Chu Hsi declined on the grounds of illness: "My spirit is confused, my ears are heavy, and my eyes are dim. I can hardly support flesh and bones; there is a pain in my waist, and my feet are weak."[67] After three declinations had been rejected, Chu Hsi set out for his post in 1188 but became ill on the way and submitted a fourth declination.[68] Two months later he had recovered sufficiently to proceed to the capital for an audience. The political atmosphere was now quite favorable to Chu Hsi. Ts'eng Ti was dead. Wang Pien, another notorious palace favorite, had been exiled. Wang Huai was dismissed from the government early in 1188. Yang Wan-li and Chou Pi-ta were men whom Chu Hsi could respect.

On his way to audience Chu Hsi was warned that "talk about rectifying the mind and making the thoughts sincere is what the emperor detests hearing."[69] He answered that these were the subjects of his life's study and not to speak of them would be to deceive his prince. The audience itself went well. The emperor commended Chu Hsi for his work in famine relief and treated him graciously.[70] As a result of the audience Chu Hsi was appointed to a post in the Ministry of War but he declined, pleading a foot ailment.

This provided an opportunity for a new attack on Chu Hsi. Lin Li, an official in the Ministry of War, had disputed with Chu Hsi concerning the *Book of Changes* and a work by Chang Tsai. Lin now denounced Chu Hsi, accusing him of plagiarizing Chang Tsai and Ch'eng I, making false claims for himself as a scholar, and honoring himself by calling what he did Tao-hsüeh. He went on to denounce Chu Hsi for propagating a self-righteous attitude toward government:

The disciples whom he has undertaken to lead number several dozen[71] and all have an attitude taken from the Ch'un-ch'iu and Warring States Period. They falsely strive for the reputation of a Confucius or a Mencius going from one place to another waiting for an invitation.

Specifically, Lin charged that Chu was unwilling to accept the Ministry of War post because it failed to satisfy his ambition, that "he haughtily looked askance for many days and was unwilling to assume his duties."[72] Here Lin struck at Chu Hsi where he was most vulnerable.

Hsiao-tsung felt that Lin's attack had gone too far. Chou Pi-ta assured the emperor that Chu Hsi had not feigned illness, and the emperor himself noted Chu Hsi had limped when he came to audience.[73] The most vigorous defense of Chu Hsi was made by Yeh Shih, the tough-minded political thinker from Yung-chia. Yeh Shih traced Lin's charges back to the attack on Chu Hsi by Cheng Ping and Ch'en Chia following the T'ang Chung-yu case and interpreted the attempt to discredit Chu and the Tao-hsüeh as a maneuver by corrupt officials to block any attempt at reform. Yeh Shih charged that Wang Huai and Lin Li wished to destroy upright men by slander. Furthermore, according to Yeh Shih, far more was involved than the treatment of Chu Hsi: the underlying issue was the status of the upright scholar in government. If the unscrupulous attack on Chu Hsi were to succeed, other scholars would feel threatened.[74]

The indecisive emperor did not accept Yeh Shih's arguments but did demote Lin Li. Chu Hsi was reassigned to a judicial intendancy, but after declining this appointment received yet another sinecure. He now had both powerful friends and enemies at court but was able to keep out of political controversy and declined a further summons to court in the autumn of 1188. Instead of going to court, he sent in an important and lengthy sealed memorial.[75] At the beginning of this memorial, he explained his conduct by telling Hsiao-tsung that it was difficult for him to determine the reasons for the summons: it could not be that the emperor wanted to hear his views since he was familiar with them and had rejected them; it also could not be to show him grace since any addition to the grace he had already been shown was inconceivable. Furthermore, Chu Hsi told the emperor that if his advice were rejected and he were nevertheless assigned a post, he would be in a most difficult position. Finally, Chu Hsi maintained that going to court would expose him to the machinations of men close to the throne who resented criticism. After thus explaining his own position, Chu Hsi devoted the bulk of the memorial to an exposition of his ideas on government and to criticism of the present government. A brief analysis of the most important of his ideas will serve to clarify Chu Hsi's attitude toward government service, for his ambivalence toward power was not without theoretical foundations.

The key concept of this memorial is that good government can be achieved only through the "rectification" of the emperor. This theme was stressed by Chu Hsi on many occasions and accounts, in great part, for the strongly moralizing tone of his pronouncements on government. Following in the tradition of Mencius and the *Great Learning,* as well as Tung Chung-shu and the Ch'eng brothers,[76] Chu Hsi held that the rectification of the emperor would set off a chain reaction of moral regeneration leading from the emperor to his family, the court attendants, the bureaucracy, and ultimately all mankind. Chu Hsi did not go to the extreme of postponing all considerations of policy until the emperor should have achieved perfect virtue, but he did assign priority to imperial rectification. This, he maintained, was fundamental. For better or worse, the welfare of the realm depended on the moral state of the imperial mind.

It follows from this theory that moral turpitude in the palace, abuse of power by attendants, and corruption in the bureaucracy are indications of the emperor's failure to achieve rectitude. Following the schematic stages by which the transcending power of the imperial virtue was thought to progress, Chu Hsi in this memorial proceeds to condemn the whole government and the entire reign of Hsiao-tsung. He draws a devastating picture of universal corruption and oppression permeating the entire government. In turn he denounces shady dealings and vicious gossip in the palace, usurpation of power by palace attendants, the nefarious influence of eunuchs, the passive acquiescence of high officials, and the greed of generals who fatten themselves at the expense of their soldiers. The evidence is overwhelming—it is all too clear that the emperor has failed in his self-cultivation.

The crucial political problem is thus the rectification of the emperor. Chu Hsi, like all Confucians, insisted that the emperor could not achieve rectitude by himself, that he needed the guidance of wise and righteous ministers. In effect, the emperor was held responsible for his choice of ministers, but the ministers were in turn held responsible for the moral development of the emperor. The character of the emperor and the characters of his associates were mutually dependent. Both were to blame for an unsatisfactory state of affairs, and Chu Hsi bitterly criticized the men around the throne who, far from assisting the emperor in cultivating his virtue, actually corrupted the imperial mind.

The theory of moral rectification was thus an effective weapon against both the emperor himself and those men in the palace and in the high bureaucracy who had access to him. It was less satisfactory as a basis for political action. The double assertion that the emperor could attain rectitude only if he were surrounded by worthy men and that he would surround himself with worthy men only if he had, in fact, attained rectitude leads to the paradox that only an emperor who had already achieved rectification could achieve rectification. The theory failed to provide a clear solution to the vexing problem of initiating the process of moral regeneration.

As long as the channels of communication remained open to him, Chu Hsi could hope to persuade the emperor to cultivate the goodness he believed inherent in every man. This Chu Hsi tried to do, using the standard Confucian arguments ranging from moral exhortation backed by references to the classics and history to warnings that the emperor's misconduct would lead to disaster. Chu Hsi also appealed to the emperor's desire to exercise his authority, warning him that vicious men were usurping that authority.

The key position of the emperor in the actual power structure gave political import to the emphasis on persuading the emperor to mend his ways. At the same time, the emperor needed the bureaucracy, and the view that imperial rectification depended on the character of the men around the throne both justified and intensified factional conflict within the bureaucracy. Chu Hsi, like most Confucians, considered factionalism an evil per se, a symptom that something was drastically wrong with the government. Yet, to condemn all factionalism would have meant relinquishing any hope for effective change through the bureaucracy and placing total reliance on the self-cultivation of an emperor whose mind was on other things. Under the Northern Sung, Fan Chung-yen and Ou-yang Hsiu had resolved this problem by making a qualitative difference between factions of "superior men" motivated by principle and factions of "inferior persons" motivated by gain.[77] In a note in his memorial of 1188 Chu Hsi told the emperor:

Know those who are worthy and employ them. Then in giving them office fear only lest they do not have sole authority; in gathering them fear only lest they are not many; and do not fear lest they become a faction. Know those who are unworthy and remove them. Then in removing them, fear only that this may not be done rapidly; in eliminating them, fear only that this may not be done thoroughly; and do not be anxious lest there be partiality.[78]

Here Chu Hsi retreats from the total condemnation of factionalism and encourages the emperor to ally himself with a faction of "worthy" men. The initiative lies with the emperor, but it would seem to follow that the genuine Confucian should also align himself with a group of like-minded men.

The paradox of the theory of moral rectification intensified the dilemma of Confucian officials such as Chu Hsi. The emphasis on the rectification of the imperial mind implied that the scholar, the potential teacher of the emperor, must first rectify himself, cultivate his scholarship and his moral character, and take care not to soil his reputation by engaging in politics. On the other hand, the role of ministers in rectifying the emperor implied that the scholar should exert himself to further the elevation of "worthy" men, and this could be done only through factional politics.

Chu Hsi himself remained very reluctant to become involved in politics. Emperor Hsiao-tsung got up from bed to read the memorial by candlelight but decided that he could not make use of Chu Hsi's advice.[79] Following the memorial Chu Hsi declined several positions and was reinstated in his current sinecure. In this way Hsiao-tsung once again solved the problem of what to do about Chu Hsi. Perhaps the emperor now felt that a similar solution for his own personal problems was in order. In any case, in the second month of 1189, Hsiao-tsung, weary of his political cares, abdicated in favor of his son, who became Emperor Kuang-tsung.

Three months after the accession of Kuang-tsung, Chu Hsi received a new title and was favored with the purple cloth and fish-pouch decoration. Then, on the recommendation of the councillors Wang Lin and Liu Cheng,[80] he was appointed Fiscal Intendant but succeeded in declining this post. The presence of a new emperor on the throne made it difficult for Chu Hsi to persist in refusing office, and he was finally prevailed upon to accept the post of prefect of Chang-chou in Fukien. He took up his duties in the fourth month of 1190.

In Chang-chou, Chu Hsi once again showed himself to be an excellent local administrator, deeply concerned with the economic as well as moral welfare of the population. His most noteworthy action in Chang-chou was an attempt to carry out a land-survey program in this and two neighboring prefectures.[81] By conducting such a survey, Chu Hsi hoped to force rich and powerful families to pay their proper share of taxes and ensure a uniform and equitable system of taxation which would benefit both the poor and the government. He worked out detailed plans for the drawing up of maps and cadastre rolls and gave careful attention to the employment of personnel and the financing of the survey. This type of program represented no new solution to the agrarian problem. It was essentially similar to a measure undertaken by Wang An-shih and more recently, in 1142–50, by Li Ch'un-nien. Chu Hsi himself interpreted his program as a continuation of Li's measures, which had never been implemented in Chang-chou and the other two prefectures.[82] He showed no desire to alter the system of landholding itself, but his land survey was an effort to remedy some of the worst abuses of a system under which those least able to pay had to bear the brunt of taxation. Chu Hsi's efforts ran into strong opposition.

In the tenth month of 1190 Chu Hsi asked to be relieved of his duties. He reported that since the previous month there had been earthquakes in the area, that he was afraid he had been remiss in not reporting this before, and that suddenly his old pains had reappeared.[83] He described the ailment as "chiao-ch'i," usually translated "beri-beri," and complained of fever. The disease, according to Chu Hsi, had spread to both feet and also to his right arm and had forced him to miss official functions. He reported that although he was now better, the medicines had produced a great deal of perspiration and left him completely exhausted.[84] His request for leave was not granted.

It is exceedingly difficult to determine the extent to which ill health was a determining factor in this or other attempts by Chu Hsi to avoid government service. It will be recalled that he pleaded illness on numerous previous occasions. In 1188 he had even limped when he came to audience, and yet his biographer Wang Mou-hung has pointed out that there were also political reasons for his declination of office in that year. In 1190 political conditions were not much better: as Wang expressed it, "the virtuous" and "the vicious" were being employed indiscriminately.[85] Also, Chu Hsi did not have the full backing of the Grand Councillor Liu Cheng for the land-survey program.[86] In turning down Chu Hsi's request for leave, his superiors evidently did not think he was seriously ill. In the light of Chu Hsi's circumstantial statement of his symptoms, it is impossible to rule out health as an important factor in his behavior, even though pleas of illness were a standard means for avoiding office. The timing of his attacks suggests that an investigation along psychosomatic lines might be fruitful, but more research is needed before definite conclusions can be reached.

Early in 1191 Chu Hsi's eldest son died, and he requested leave to mourn him. For this purpose Chu retired to Chien-yang in Fukien. It was in the same year that Chu Hsi wrote a remarkable letter to Liu Cheng dealing with the highly controversial problem of factionalism.[87] Subscribing to the belief that factionalism was an evil, Chu Hsi nevertheless pointed out that an attempt to eliminate this evil could easily lead to a disregard of the true criteria of personnel selection, a man's virtue and ability. Chu Hsi told Liu Cheng that "superior men" by virtue of their contrast to "inferior persons" easily took on the appearance of a faction. Membership in such a faction was not an indication that a man was unworthy. Chu Hsi went on to encourage Liu Cheng to associate himself with a faction of "superior men," saying that this was the Grand Councillor's duty. Chu Hsi went a step further and maintained that Liu Cheng not only should be concerned with the advancement of worthy men but should himself take the lead in organizing a faction of worthy men: "Not only do not fear to place yourself in a faction, but also lead superior men to form a faction, and do not be afraid."[88]

In this letter Chu Hsi showed a willingness to face the facts of political life and encourage the only form of activity that might lead to reform, for the new emperor showed even less inclination to cultivate his virtue than his father had. This, however, did not mean that Chu Hsi himself was prepared to take a more active part in affairs. Until January 1194 he declined a number of positions for which he had been recommended by Liu Cheng.[89] Clinging to his old pattern of behavior, Chu Hsi complained of his health, the failure of the land survey, and the general state of the government.

In January 1194 Chu Hsi was appointed prefect of T'an-chou, modern Changsha, and Pacification Official for the province in which T'an-chou was located. According to one account, his reputation had, by this time, spread even to the Chin, who made inquiries about him to members of a Sung embassy.[90] The Tutor of the Heir Apparent and a lecturer in the princely household had suggested that Chu Hsi be given a more important post, but Liu Cheng had become exasperated by Chu's conduct and considered him too inflexible.[91] Chu Hsi's declinations of the prefectural post were not accepted.

Chu Hsi had been in T'an-chou for only a month when he resigned, in the sixth month of 1194. This time Chu Hsi's resignation was an expression of indignation against a scandalous situation at court that had aroused widespread anger throughout the bureaucracy.[92] Emperor Kuang-tsung had been ill when he inherited the throne, and as his reign progressed he came increasingly under the domination of his empress. The situation was especially serious because the empress hated her father-in-law, the abdicated Emperor Hsiao-tsung. After a quarrel with Hsiao-tsung over the succession, she forced Kuang-tsung to break completely with his father. A reconciliation was not effected despite the efforts of officials, including those of the Administrator of the Bureau of Military Affairs, Chao Ju-yü, an associate of Liu Cheng and member of a minor branch of the imperial family. When Hsiao-tsung became ill in 1194, the heir apparent was allowed to visit his grandfather, but there was still no reconciliation. Then, in the sixth month of 1194, Hsiao-tsung died. Kuang-tsung did not perform the mourning rites, pleading illness. This flagrant violation of the duties of filial piety caused widespread indignation among officials and precipitated a crisis in the government culminating in the abdication of Kuang-tsung and the accession of Ning-tsung in the seventh month of 1194.

The transfer of the throne from Kuang-tsung to Ning-tsung was accomplished through a series of clever maneuvers involving the widows of Hsiao-tsung and Kao-tsung. Heading those trying to effect a change of emperor was Chao Ju-yü, who enjoyed the support of many officials who were shocked by the emperor's behavior. In addition, Chao Ju-yü also benefited from the active collaboration of the Administrator of the Palace Postern, Han T'o-chou, a descendant of the distinguished Northern Sung statesman Han Ch'i (1008–75). Han's connections within the palace were instrumental in effecting the transfer of the throne. Han himself could expect to profit from the situation since his niece was Ning-tsung's empress. When Chao Ju-yü failed to satisfy Han's political ambitions, the stage was set for a bitter political battle in which Chu Hsi was directly involved.

Upon the accession of Ning-tsung, Chao Ju-yü at first had the upper hand over his rival, who, however, used his palace connections to strengthen his own political position. One of Chao's first acts was to recommend two men to the emperor: Chu Hsi and Ch'en Fu-liang of Yung-chia. Through the influence of his tutors Ning-tsung had, while still crown prince, formed a very high opinion of Chu Hsi. Chu first declined the summons to court but was soon persuaded to proceed to the capital, where he was appointed Auxiliary Academician in the Huang-chang Pavilion and concurrently Lecturer. In one of his decli-

nations of this appointment, Chu Hsi warned the emperor against letting favorites gain a foothold in the palace. Under the circumstances,
this amounted to an attack on Han T'o-chou. Chu Hsi arrived in the
capital on October 17, 1194.

Two days after his arrival Chu Hsi presented five memorials, in
which he admonished Ning-tsung to act in accordance with the true
principles of government, tried to convince him of the need for true
learning, and reported on conditions in T'an-chou.[93] After another unsuccessful attempt to decline his appointment, Chu Hsi officially assumed his duties as Academician and Lecturer on October 25. His
period at court was very short. He was granted leave on December 5
and left the capital on the 25th.

At court Chu Hsi frequently lectured to the emperor, employing
such texts as the *Great Learning*. He also submitted a number of memorials and delivered discourses on affairs of state. Along with the
usual moral exhortations, Chu Hsi discussed various practical matters,
e.g., the need for the prompt burial of Hsiao-tsung, irregularities in the
weather, and a proposed remodeling of the Eastern Palace, to which
Chu Hsi objected. Of greater immediate political consequence was
Chu Hsi's criticism of palace favorites. Once again he warned Ning-
tsung, as he had warned Hsiao-tsung, that unscrupulous men were
usurping the imperial authority.[94] Chu Hsi soon became known as a
strong opponent of Han T'o-chou. It is said that Han himself gave
priority to the removal of Chu Hsi, after which he thought it would be
easy to dispose of his other enemies.[95]

In the struggle for political power, Han T'o-chou worked behind the
scenes both to remove Chu Hsi and to discredit other associates of Chao
Ju-yü. He used his access to the palace to good advantage. Once, for
example, he is said to have staged a play in the palace in which an
actor, dressed in a high hat and wide sleeves, presented a clever cari-
cature of Chu Hsi.[96] Chu's departure from court thus marked a significant victory for Han. Chu Hsi himself declined further appointments
and retired to Chien-yang in Fukien.

Han T'o-chou was quick to exploit his success in obtaining Chu Hsi's
dismissal. Men who supported Chu Hsi soon found themselves out of
office, and in 1195 Chao Ju-yü was exiled and murdered. A purge of
all sympathizers of Chao Ju-yü followed, accompanied by an attack on
Tao-hsüeh. Vehement denunciations were aimed at Chu Hsi. The old
charges against him were revived and new ones fabricated.

A censor who had once visited Chu Hsi and felt that he had not
been properly received now asked for Chu's death.[97] The most intense
denunciation was made by one Shen Chi-tsu. Like Lin Li before him,

Shen charged Chu Hsi with plagiarism and improper behavior toward the government. Other, more sensational, charges ranged from involvement in Manichaean magical practices to the seduction of two Buddhist nuns who allegedly became Chu's concubines. Shen stated that Chu had organized a pack of scoundrels and that his students were cattle thieves. Shen placed particular emphasis on what he termed the six great crimes of Chu Hsi: lack of filial piety, disrespect for the emperor, disloyalty, trifling with the court, paying no heed to morality, and harming customs and religion. To substantiate each charge Shen gave particulars. For example, to prove that Chu Hsi was unfilial, Shen asserted that Chu had given his mother only low-quality rice and begrudged her good white rice.[98] Chu Hsi's opponents not only attacked his political behavior but took pains to undermine his reputation as a scholar and a man of virtue, for it was this reputation that had lent weight to his political views.

With the attack on Chu Hsi, the denunciation of Tao-hsüeh gained momentum. Proponents were charged with falsely trading on their reputations, causing factionalism, and usurping the emperor's authority. The emperor was warned that these men were ruining the state and should be branded a rebel clique. Some memorialists sounded a moral note asking Ning-tsung to rid himself of these depraved falsifiers and return to the teachings of Confucius and Mencius. Tao-hsüeh was equated with Wei-hsüeh, false or bogus learning, and after some initial hesitation the emperor proscribed Tao-hsüeh in 1196.[99]

The attack culminated in 1198 with the drawing up of a list of fifty-nine men guilty of belonging to the "rebel clique of false learning."[100] Included were four men who had held the highest office in the state—Chao Ju-yü, Liu Cheng, Chou Pi-ta, and Wang Lin. Chu Hsi was named along with such supporters of his as his good friend and disciple Ts'ai Yüan-ting. Yeh Shih and Ch'en Fu-liang were listed as well as six other men from Yung-chia. The presence of these men on the list is of special interest, since on his way to court in 1194 Chu Hsi himself had a premonition that the activities of members of the Yung-chia school would involve him in disaster.[101] Over half the men on the list were intellectuals of some prominence, representing the whole range of Southern Sung thought.[102] Thus, the chief disciple of Lu Chiu-yüan was included, and one man belonged to a school of learning founded by Ssu-ma Kuang.

An analysis of the controversy is beyond the scope of this paper, but anti-intellectualism seems to have been an important element. Although a few men of learning supported Han T'o-chou, the majority were apparently associated with Chao Ju-yü.[103] After Chu Hsi's death, Han T'o-chou was to attack the Chin in a war that ended in defeat and the delivery of Han's head to the enemy. However, foreign policy does not appear to have been an important issue in the battle between the followers of Han and Chao. The issues have been greatly obscured by the bias of Chinese historians, whose reverence for Chu Hsi reinforced their loathing for a man who rose to power through his relationship with the empress and who led the Sung forces to defeat. Only an occasional scholar has pointed out that the Tao-hsüeh group included career-minded opportunists as well as high-minded Confucians.[104]

After his departure from court, Chu Hsi himself took no part in affairs. In the middle of 1195 he did draft a memorial attacking Han and his followers. At first Chu Hsi rejected the advice of disciples and friends who urged him not to submit the memorial. In the end, however, he was persuaded to leave the decision to divination. After the verdict of the milfoil, Chu Hsi burned the draft and contented himself with declining all rank and office.[105]

The last five years of his life were devoted exclusively to study and teaching, although in 1199 he was partially reinstated as a "retired official." Chu Hsi died on April 23, 1200. His funeral was widely attended and was described as a gathering to mourn the "teacher of rebellious falsehood."[106] After Han's death and the disgrace of his followers, opinion became more favorable to Chu Hsi. In 1241 he was accorded accessory sacrifices in the Confucian temple, and his doctrines were on their way to becoming the state orthodoxy.[107] Chu Hsi himself became an object of reverence and even began to acquire some of the legendary characteristics of a sage. Perhaps the most extraordinary of these legends is that just as a unicorn appeared when Confucius completed the six classics, a dragon-horse was born when Chu Hsi finished his commentaries on the four books. This miraculous animal with the head of a dragon and the body of a horse is said to have been similar to the dragon-horse whose markings suggested the eight diagrams to the legendary culture hero Fu-hsi.[108]

Confucianism traditionally demanded that a scholar occupy himself not only with self-cultivation but with improvement of society as well. Chu Hsi accepted this double demand, but the record of his political career suggests that he failed to translate his feeling of social responsibility into effective political action.

Chu Hsi fulfilled his Confucian obligation to society to his own satisfaction not only by propagating the "true teachings" of the sages but by criticizing the government in memorials and conscientiously performing his duties when in office. He did not, however, take the further step of actively fighting for his ideas. Whenever possible Chu Hsi avoided office and shunned politics. It is probably no coincidence that most of the appointments he did accept were on the local level and that prior to 1194 he repeatedly declined posts that would have brought him to the capital. His political career shows a consistent, although ultimately unsuccessful, attempt to avoid involvement in factional controversy and political intrigue.

In refusing various posts Chu Hsi frequently gave personal reasons such as ill health, but he also felt a need to justify his declinations on grounds of political morality. At times there were indeed compelling political reasons for him to reject office. For example, the outcome of the T'ang Chung-yu case implied that the government lacked confidence in Chu's indictments, and he could hardly have accepted a post previously reserved for T'ang. Or again, when he left court in December 1194, it was not to be expected that he would accept another post. Most of his appointments, however, were made on the recommendation of men who did expect him to accept, and in declining these appointments Chu Hsi did not object to specific political acts but protested against the general character of the government.

As a form of protest, Chu Hsi's declinations were an expression of nonsupport for a government he deemed unworthy. More than that, the declinations were also meant by Chu Hsi to protect his moral stature and reputation from contamination by participation in factional politics. As a political argument, this implied that his standing had importance not only for himself but for society as a whole. The theory of imperial rectification gave some substance to this position, since it saw the Confucian scholar as the emperor's teacher and guide. A scholar's self-cultivation and personal righteousness, when combined with forthright criticism of the emperor and the bureaucracy, were thought to have definite importance for society. In practice this was true only in so far as Chu's prestige lent weight to his memorials.

As a child Chu Hsi expressed the desire to became a sage like Mencius; later he was attacked for pretending to behave like a Mencius or a Confucius. Chu Hsi's political behavior suggests that he did indeed seek to become known as a latter-day sage, a man above politics, whose counsel would be universally respected and whose advice would be followed by those in power. If the emperor and his ministers were so misguided as to disregard the advice of the sage, the fault was theirs, not his. Even Confucius did not see his advice adopted. A sage must guard the purity of his doctrine and of his conduct. He does not compromise.

A sage is the guardian of the Truth, and Chu Hsi believed that he knew the Truth and proceeded to reinterpret the classics in the light of this truth even when it meant forcing the text.[109] He knew he was right and drew strength from this certainty. And yet, Chu Hsi also knew that the age of the sages was past. It was all too obvious that the real world of Sung politics had little in common with an idealized antiquity.

Like the majority of Confucians, Chu Hsi looked back to an idealized antiquity as a model for all government. He rejected the view put forward by Ch'en Liang that the difference between the Three Dynasties and later ages was merely one of degree. Yet Chu Hsi realized that a return to antiquity was impossible and argued against those who wished to restore institutions long dead. In grappling with such perplexing problems as the agrarian situation, Chu Hsi showed himself willing to work for limited, feasible measures of reform and rejected any attempt to return to the well-field system. Moreover, the vision of a perfect society ruled by virtue did not lead him to deny the legitimacy of less ideal means of government such as punitive law. In fact, Chu Hsi thought punishments too lenient.[110] He not only was well aware that he was not living in ideal antiquity but understood that in his day the perfection of antiquity could not be recaptured. He was less clear on the implications this view held for political behavior.

The realization that the age of the sages was past probably served to undermine Chu Hsi's desire to model himself on the sages. When the pressure was on, he was unable to maintain his stance of righteous aloofness and accepted office even though the government had not markedly improved. Persistent refusal to serve the government could endanger his reputation. Perhaps he also came to realize that complete reliance on influence through prestige was as unrealistic as total dependence on government by virtue. As he grew older, Chu Hsi even came to see positive value in factionalism—and then refused appointments for which he had been recommended by the very man he had advised to create a "faction of superior men." Chu Hsi could not be a sage, but his attachment to this ideal prevented him from becoming an effective politician. In the end, Chu Hsi was denounced as a false sage and accused of belonging to a clique, i.e., behaving like a politician.

Chu Hsi's moral aloofness and his wholesale condemnation of political life created a great deal of resentment and left him open to attack. When he finally did become involved in political controversy, his enemies exploited his reluctance to assume office and his attitude of moral superiority. When the T'ang Chung-yu case broke and the attack on Tao-hsüeh began, Chu Hsi at fifty-two had little to show in the way of political service. His political behavior provided ammunition for his enemies and the enemies of the men who supported him. In his attack on Tao-hsüeh, Han T'o-chou showed little concern for matters of doctrine but exploited a convenient slogan, using it to condemn all his enemies. This was effective not only because emperors naturally became weary of constant moral admonition but also because it pointed to a pattern of behavior that many men resented as pretentious and self-righteous. In attacking Chu Hsi, Han not only rid himself of a sharp critic but struck at the opposition where it was peculiarly vulnerable. As a courageous critic Chu Hsi was a thorn in the flesh of his enemies, but as an aloof moralizer he was a liability to his friends and associates.

Chu Hsi's behavior ultimately requires psychological interpretation. His persistent efforts to avoid political entanglements suggest that this may have been a defensive reaction of an insecure individual. The need for acceptance as a sage, for approval by disciples, and the tone of moral righteousness with which he confronted the world tend to reinforce this view. An evaluation of his character, however, must take into consideration his private life, his appreciation of the beauties of nature, his capacity for friendship, and the wide range of his intellectual interests. An examination of his poetry and correspondence with intimate friends may reveal more about Chu Hsi the man; until this is done all conclusions regarding his personality remain speculative.

Whatever the psychological make-up of Chu Hsi's personality, his political behavior did not detract from the wide admiration accorded him in later times. His reputation rested, of course, on his work as a scholar and philosopher; he was not known as a great statesman. Nevertheless, Confucian scholar-officials could find much to admire in his outspoken memorials and to praise in a political career that ended with a touch of martyrdom. They could agree with Li Hsin-ch'uan that Chu Hsi was "not one who spent his life in retirement. He wanted to put the Way into operation but did not find the means to do so."[111] They could look to his life as an attempt to reconcile the demands of sagehood and politics, a compromise between withdrawal and participation in political life, and a mean between self-cultivation and activism. His career offered an example of how one might serve both the "Way" and the state without losing either one's self-respect or one's life.

Igor de Rachewiltz

YEH-LÜ CH'U-TS'AI (1189–1243):
BUDDHIST IDEALIST AND
CONFUCIAN STATESMAN

The present paper is a biographical study of Yeh-lü Ch'u-ts'ai (1189–1243), secretary-astrologer to Cinggis Qan and later Chief of the Secretariat under his son Ögödei Qaghan. Although a famous figure in the history of China, Yeh-lü Ch'u-ts'ai has not been the subject of a thorough investigation: his life, career, and thought are therefore only imperfectly known. The only biography worth mentioning in a Western language is the essay published by the French Sinologue J.-P. Abel-Rémusat in 1829.[1] Sixty years later, E. Bretschneider published in his *Mediaeval Researches from East Asiatic Sources* a translation of a fragmentary text of Yeh-lü Ch'u-ts'ai's *Hsi-yu lu* ("Record of a Journey to the West"), a complete manuscript copy of which has since been discovered in Japan.[2] In recent years various aspects of Yeh-lü Ch'u-ts'ai's administrative activity have been discussed by H. Franke and H. F. Schurmann in their works on Yüan economic history.[3] Several studies on Yeh-lü Ch'u-ts'ai, mostly short articles of uneven value, have appeared in China and Japan in the last decades.[4] By far the most important of these is the *Nien-p'u* by Wang Kuo-wei.

Yeh-lü Ch'u-ts'ai's fame rests chiefly on the administrative reforms that were carried out under his leadership during the reign of Ögödei (T'ai-tsung, r. 1229–41), and on his constant endeavor to mitigate the harsh Mongol rule in North China. It is mainly for these activities that he has been praised as one of the greatest political figures in the history of Asia.[5] His achievements, however, are known to us only through Chinese sources; no mention of him is found in the works of the Persian historians or in the so-called *Secret History of the Mongols*. This fact led the great Turkologist W. Barthold to suggest that Yeh-lü Ch'u-ts'ai's political role may have been exaggerated by the Chinese historians;[6] while E. Blochet, pressing the argument further in an article published in 1926, made a daring but vain attempt to identify him with a well-known Muslim official of the time.[7] Until very recently the extent of his authority at the Mongol court has been open to question.[8]

Moreover, the biographies of Yeh-lü Ch'u-ts'ai written by Confucian scholars give us a one-sided view of his personality, seeing him as an exemplar of the humane and wise Confucian statesman. It is only from his literary works that we learn about his deep Buddhist faith. To what extent then was Yeh-lü Ch'u-ts'ai the genuine Confucian that the historians claim him to be, and were his actions truly motivated by orthodox thought?

Sometimes, general statements are also made about his "civilizing influence" on the Mongols and its indirect effect on the policies later pursued by Qubilai. One wonders how far these statements are true.

In the present paper I shall attempt to throw some light on these problems by reviewing Yeh-lü Ch'u-ts'ai's actions in relation (a) to his milieu and the historical context, and (b) to his political ideology and religious beliefs, so far, at least, as they can be discerned from his extant writings.

Yeh-lü Ch'u-ts'ai's lineage, as given in his funerary inscription, begins with T'u-yü, eldest son of the founder of the Liao dynasty, A-pao-chi.[9] T'u-yü, whose personal name was Pei, is well known to history. A fervent admirer of Chinese culture, he was himself a scholar in both Khitan and Chinese, as well as a skilled painter. He ruled over Tung-tan, i.e., the old kingdom of Po-hai, from 926 to 930 (whence his title of Prince of Tung-tan), and shortly afterward had to flee Liao for fear of being assassinated by his brother Te-kuang (T'ai-tsung, r. 927–47), in whose favor he had been forced to abdicate the throne. He met a violent death in exile in 937.[10]

Next in line comes T'u-yü's second son, Lou-kuo, younger brother of Emperor Shih-tsung (r. 947–51). He became governor of Yen-ching, the southern capital of Liao, and Chief of the Political Council. In 952 he plotted rebellion against Emperor Mu-tsung (r. 951–69) in order to assert the claims of the senior branch of the clan to the imperial succession (Mu-tsung was a member of the junior line). He was discovered and arrested, and subsequently committed suicide.[11] Of Lou-kuo's descendants for the next four generations we know only the names and official titles. Among them figure two Grand Preceptors.

T'u-yü's sixth-generation descendant, Te-yüan, took service under the Chin dynasty and rose to be Commanding Prefect of the Hsing-p'ing Commandery (near modern Lu-lung hsien, Hopei). Having no sons of his own he adopted the son of a younger cousin and made him his heir. Te-yüan's adopted son, called Lü, was the father of Yeh-lü Ch'u-ts'ai.[12]

Born in 1131, Yeh-lü Lü entered the civil service through the *yin* privilege and rapidly gained renown as a translator from Chinese into Khitan and Jurchen. He held various posts in the Department of National Historiography, the Imperial Academy, the Ministry of Rites, and the provincial administration. He attracted the attention of Emperor Shih-tsung (r. 1161–89), who, during his last illness, made him his personal attendant. After the emperor's death, Yeh-lü Lü "gained merit" in connection with the enthronement of Chang-tsung (r. 1190–1208). Thereupon he rose to be President of the Ministry of Rites and Assistant of the Right in the Presidential Council. He died in office in 1191.[13] His biographies portray him as a capable and thoroughly Sinicized official. His funerary inscription relates several anecdotes illustrating his Confucian outlook. For example, when Chang-tsung was still Heir Apparent, Yeh-lü Lü dissuaded him from studying the *Tso chuan* because, although a classic, "it is on the whole full of intrigues and lacking purity." Instead he recommended he concentrate on the *Shang-shu* and *Meng-tzu*, for these works "contain the pure Way of the Sages."[14] Also, at the time when Yeh-lü Lü was serving in the Ministry of Rites, the question arose whether Shih-tsung's late mother should be buried separately, as stated in her will (she had become a Buddhist nun on her husband's death), or together with him, in the way proper to an Imperial Consort. Yeh-lü Lü memorialized that her will should not be taken into account, on the ground that the "regular statutes" have precedence over the Buddhist precepts, and the status of Queen Mother over that of devotee. This advice was followed.[15]

During his long and successful career, Yeh-lü Lü accumulated a considerable fortune, and instances of his munificence are recorded in his biography.[16] The family also enjoyed the income derived from a hereditary appanage in Tung-p'ing, Shantung, the origin of which is unknown.[17] Yeh-lü Lü married three times. By his first two wives he had two sons. The third son, born to his third wife (a lady née Yang), was Yeh-lü Ch'u-ts'ai.

Yeh-lü Ch'u-ts'ai was born on August 3, 1189,[18] in the Chin capital, Chung-tu. (This corresponds to Peking and will hereafter be referred to by that name.)

His father died when he was only two years old. His mother, a scholarly woman who later became tutoress at the palace, brought him up and personally took care of his formal education.[19] At the age of twelve he was busy studying the *Shih* and the *Shu*.[20] At seventeen he had the opportunity to enter the Chin civil service on the strength of the *yin* privilege, to which he was entitled as the son of a Chief Minister. He declined, however, in order to compete for the *chin-shih*. Shortly afterward he was granted special permission to compete in the "decree examination" conducted by Chang-tsung and came out first on the list. We have no information regarding his first appointment, but we know that upon conclusion of the "examination of merits" he was promoted to Vice-Prefect of K'ai-chou (modern Pu-yang *hsien*, Hopei).[21] From references contained in one of his poems, it appears that he held this post in 1213.[22]

Meanwhile, the Mongols had begun their invasion of Chin. It may be recalled that since 1211 the Mongol army had been carrying out a series of attacks against the Jurchen fortresses in northern Shansi and Hopei, and in Jehol. In the autumn of 1213, Cinggis Qan, taking advantage of the confusion following the murder of the Chin ruler Wei-shao Wang in a palace revolution, launched a three-pronged offensive which took his armies deep into Shansi, Hopei, and Shantung. They eventually converged on Peking, but failed to take it owing to the city's exceptional defenses. A peace treaty was then concluded between the newly elected Emperor Hsüan-tsung (r. 1213–24) and the Mongol emperor. No sooner had Cinggis Qan retired than Hsüan-tsung, feeling unsafe in Peking, decided to move the capital south. At the end of June 1214 he transferred the court to Pien-liang (K'ai-feng), leaving Wan-yen Ch'eng-hui in charge of Peking under the orders of the Heir Apparent. Yeh-lü Ch'u-ts'ai, who had in the meantime been recalled from K'ai-chou, was appointed on Wan-yen Ch'eng-hui's recommendation Auxiliary Secretary of the Boards of Right and Left in the old capital.[23]

Cinggis Qan, enraged at the news of the emperor's flight to Pien-liang, resumed hostilities, and in August his army again invested Peking. The siege lasted ten months. Of Yeh-lü Ch'u-ts'ai's activity in this period we know nothing, except that even in the two months of serious famine before the fall of the city "he attended to his official duties as usual."[24]

Peking was captured at the end of May 1215. One month of looting followed, in the course of which thousands of people were killed and a great part of the city was burned down. The suffering experienced by Yeh-lü Ch'u-ts'ai during the siege affected him deeply, precipitating a mental crisis.

Up to this time Yeh-lü Ch'u-ts'ai had shown a certain interest in Buddhism, but his knowledge of it was superficial. In the preface to one of his poems he says: "In my youth I had a liking for Buddhism, as that was my natural inclination. When I reached manhood I had read superficially many Buddhist texts and although I gained a certain knowledge from these, I rather exaggerated my achievement."[25] He was particularly attracted by Ch'an Buddhism, which was predominant at the time, and before the fall of Peking he often visited the monk Ch'eng of the Sheng-an Temple, discussing with him the "sayings" (*yü-lu*) of the old masters. However, as this was a favorite pastime among the literati, the monk Ch'eng had never taken Yeh-lü Ch'u-ts'ai's interest seriously.

After the fall of Peking, Yeh-lü Ch'u-ts'ai decided "to seek the Patriarch's doctrine more earnestly," and with this in mind he once more went to see his friend at the Sheng-an Temple. Ch'eng immediately realized that this time Yeh-lü Ch'u-ts'ai's desire for enlightenment was genuine, not a merely intellectual pursuit as in the past. But Ch'eng, pleading old age and inadequate knowledge of Confucianism, declined to instruct the young man. Instead Ch'eng directed him to Wan-sung, the abbot of the great Pao-en Temple, as one "well versed in both Confucianism and Buddhism and very thorough in doctrine and expression," in other words, an outstanding teacher.[26] Yeh-lü Ch'u-ts'ai could not have been given better advice, as Wan-sung was indeed one of the leading Ch'an masters of the time.[27] Besides being a learned Buddhist scholar he was equally versed in Confucianism and Taoism. Although officially belonging to the Ts'ao-tung school[28] Wan-sung was in reality a syncretist who combined in his teaching the views on enlightenment peculiar to other schools of Ch'an (Yün-men and Lin-chi in particular), and maintained the theory, very popular in this period, of the common origin of the Three Religions.[29]

Yeh-lü Ch'u-ts'ai began his training as a lay disciple under Wan-sung sometime in 1215, and pursued it relentlessly for three years. During this period of rigorous instruction he cut himself off from family and friends, devoting himself single-mindedly to his quest for the realization of truth. He finally attained enlightenment, and his master recognized the achievement by conferring on him "the seal of discipleship," and the Buddhist style of Chan-jan Chü-shih Ts'ung-yüan.[30]

On April 12, 1218, Yeh-lü Ch'u-ts'ai was summoned by Cinggis Qan to Mongolia.[31] The Mongol conqueror had in the past rallied many Khitan hereditary leaders, including several descendants of the imperial house of Liao (such as Yeh-lü Liu-ko and the two brothers Yeh-lü A-hai and T'u-hua), who had proved faithful allies in the struggle against Chin. Besides racial affinity, Khitans and Mongols were united by common hatred for the Jurchen. This is shown in the well-known words pronounced by Cinggis when he met Yeh-lü Ch'u-ts'ai for the first time at his *ordo* in the Sāri Steppe: "Liao and Chin have been enemies for generations; I have taken revenge for you." To which Yeh-lü Ch'u-ts'ai replied: "My father and grandfather have both served it [i.e., Chin] respectfully. How can I, as a subject and a son, be so insincere at heart as to consider my sovereign and my father as enemies?" The Mongol is said to have been impressed by this frank reply, as well as by Yeh-lü

Ch'u-ts'ai's looks (he was a very tall man with a magnificent beard) and sonorous voice. He gave him the nickname *Urtu Saqal* (Long Beard) and placed him in his retinue.[32]

In the spring of the following year, Cinggis Qan set out on his punitive expedition against the Khwārezmian empire. Yeh-lü Ch'u-ts'ai accompanied him to Central Asia and remained there till 1226. His duties in this period were varied. He combined the office of *bicigeci* (scribe-secretary) in charge of official documents in Chinese, with that of court astrologer-astronomer. Concerning the latter activity, several anecdotes are related in his funerary inscription. Cinggis Qan, like all the Mongols, had a superstitious fear of unusual natural phenomena, and used to consult him whenever these occurred. Yeh-lü Ch'u-ts'ai on such occasions would take the omens in the Chinese fashion, while the emperor, as an additional safety measure, took them in the traditional Mongol way by burning the thigh-bone of a sheep. According to our source, Yeh-lü Ch'u-ts'ai correctly predicted the successful outcome of the war against Khwārezm, the death of its ruler Muhammad, and that of the Chin emperor Hsüan-tsung.[33] It was through his remarkable skill as an astrologer that he acquired renown, and gradually established his authority at the Mongol court.[34]

One episode related in the funerary inscription is of particular interest. I refer to the famous story of the apparition of the unicorn ("la farce de la Licorne," as Wieger calls it[35]), whose interpretation by Yeh-lü Ch'u-ts'ai is said to have caused the withdrawal of the Mongol army from India. The inscription states that when Cinggis was encamped at the Iron Gate Pass (present Buzgala Pass in Uzbekistan) his bodyguard saw a green-colored animal with a deer's body, a horse's tail, and a single horn. Addressing the bodyguard in human speech, it said: "Your Lord should return home immediately." When Cinggis Qan questioned him on the incident, Yeh-lü Ch'u-ts'ai explained that this prodigious animal, called *chüeh-tuan,* could travel eighteen thousand *li* a day and speak all languages. Being a symbol of hatred for bloodshed, it had been sent by heaven to warn the emperor against further killing. On the same day, the inscription says, the emperor issued the order to withdraw the army.[36]

This story, which is also related by several other contemporary authors, has up till now been interpreted as a clever means devised by Yeh-lü Ch'u-ts'ai to prevent the Mongol conqueror from engaging in further warfare by playing upon his superstitious nature. I doubt the truth of this. In the account of the same event by Yeh-lü Liu-ch'i, a grandson of Yeh-lü Ch'u-ts'ai, the *chüeh-tuan* is described as having "two eyes like torches, a scaly five-colored body, a single horn on top of its head, and empowered with speech." According to him, Yeh-lü Ch'u-ts'ai advised the emperor to prepare offerings and to sacrifice to it in the place where it had appeared.[37] It seems to me that we are dealing here with a real incident. It is very likely that some Mongol soldiers saw a rhinoceros.[38] This may well have happened during the raid into the Punjab in the summer of 1222. Although on its way to extinction, the rhinoceros was still to be found in the Punjab and Sind in the fourteenth century, and in the region of Peshāwar as late as the fifteenth century.[39] The report of such a sight could have easily been distorted and exaggerated by the witnesses themselves, to whom the animal was totally unknown.

Yeh-lü Ch'u-ts'ai's identification of the animal and interpretation of the incident are, of course, based on Chinese literary sources. The *chüeh-tuan,* a legendary animal closely related to the *ch'i-lin,* is already mentioned by Ssu-ma Hsiang-ju (second century B.C.) as one of the marvelous creatures that lived in the Imperial Park of Ch'ang-an.[40] Yeh-lü Ch'u-ts'ai had no hesitation in identifying the animal seen by the Mongols with the *chüeh-tuan* rather than with the *ch'i-lin,* because the former is traditionally believed to possess the gift of languages and the ability to cover large distances.[41] His interpretation of the sight was also orthodox, in that the *chüeh-tuan,* like the *ch'i-lin,* is a symbol of all goodness and benevolence.

We know from the Persian historians that in 1222 Cinggis Qan had considered returning to Mongolia via India, the Himalayas, and Tibet. One of the reasons that dissuaded him from putting his plan into effect was, according to Jūzjānī, the advice of the soothsayers not to go to India.[42] Yeh-lü Ch'u-ts'ai's oracle probably had something to do with it, although it was by no means the only determining factor.[43]

Of Yeh-lü Ch'u-ts'ai's secretarial activity we have evidence in letters inviting the celebrated Taoist master Ch'iu Ch'u-chi (1148–1227), better known as Ch'ang-ch'un, to join the Mongol conqueror in Central Asia. Cinggis Qan summoned Ch'ang-ch'un on the advice of Liu Wen, a Chinese physician and arrow maker in his service.[44] We know, however, that Yeh-lü Ch'u-ts'ai had also recommended him to the emperor. Liu Wen's aim was to introduce to Cinggis Qan an adept in possession of the elixir of life; Yeh-lü Ch'u-ts'ai expected, on the other hand, that Ch'ang-ch'un would acquaint the emperor not only with the Taoist tenets, but also with the doctrines of Confucius and Buddha. His assumption was based on the fact that the Ch'üan-chen sect, of which Ch'ang-ch'un was the leader, professed a syncretist philosophy based on the *Tao-te ching,* the *Hsin ching* (*Prajñāpāramitāhridayasūtra*), and the *Hsiao ching.* Yeh-lü Ch'u-ts'ai, under Wan-sung's influence, had also become an advocate of syncretism. As Ch'ang-ch'un enjoyed a high reputation in China, it is not surprising that Yeh-lü Ch'u-ts'ai thought of him as the right person to teach Cinggis Qan the Way of the Three Sages. In the *Hsi-yu lu* he states:

As I saw it, at the time of the foundation of the National [Mongol] Dynasty, since government affairs were very numerous and war was going on in the Western Regions, there was then no leisure to cultivate civil virtues and to exalt goodness. Now the teachings of the Three Sages are all of benefit to mankind. When I read the two books on the Way and the Virtue [i.e., the *Tao-te ching*], my admiration was deeply roused. I wished to make Our Sovereign [Cinggis Qan] tread loftily in the footsteps of the ancient worthies. This is the reason why I supported [Ch'ang-ch'un], whom, of course, I also intended to be an advocate of Confucianism and Buddhism.[45]

In the letter that Liu Wen personally took to Ch'ang-ch'un in 1219 (which, I believe, was written by Yeh-lü Ch'u-ts'ai himself), the Taoist adept is invited to join the emperor in order to advise him on matters of government and the means of prolonging life.[46] Ch'ang-ch'un set out under Mongol escort, but when he arrived in Te-hsing (present Cho-lu *hsien* in Chahar), distressed at the thought of the distance he still had to cover, he sent the emperor a message requesting permission to end his journey there on the grounds of his great age and incompetence in administrative affairs.[47] Upon receipt of Ch'ang-ch'un's message, Cinggis, who was anxious to meet the adept, ordered Yeh-lü Ch'u-ts'ai to draft another letter urging him to continue his journey.[48] Yeh-lü Ch'u-ts'ai in very polite phraseology makes clear the emperor's wish and, in answer to Ch'ang-ch'un's objections, states that political advice is not at all what the emperor expects from him, but only moral advice. To emphasize further the importance of Ch'ang-ch'un's mission to Cinggis, he quotes the cases of Bodhidharma, who traveled to the east in order to transmit the Mind, and of Lao Tzu, who went west to convert the barbarians and attain enlightenment, i.e., to become Buddha.[49]

I think that Yeh-lü Ch'u-ts'ai used the latter illustration to suggest a parallel between the civilizing work of Lao Tzu and that of Ch'ang-ch'un, both engaged in the conversion (*hua*) of the barbarians (*hu*). The parallel is particularly apt, as the barbarians supposedly converted by Lao Tzu were in the west and so were Cinggis Qan and his Mongols at this time. However, in drawing this comparison, Yeh-lü Ch'u-ts'ai implied that he accepted the thesis propounded by the apocryphal *Book of the Conversion of the Barbarians* (*Hua-hu ching*). True, he inserted as a safeguard a hypothetical *huo* in his statement ("when Lao Tzu went to the west, it was, so it seems, to convert the barbarians . . . "). Nevertheless, this must have laid him open to attack from Buddhists when, a few years later, the followers of Ch'ang-ch'un began propagating on a large scale the idea that Buddha was merely one of Lao Tzu's incarnations.

Ch'ang-ch'un did continue his journey, and his meeting with Cinggis Qan and subsequent deeds are well known through his disciple's account, the *Hsi-yu chi*. Significantly, there is no mention of Yeh-lü Ch'u-ts'ai in this work; for information on the relationship between him and Ch'ang-ch'un, as also for references to those of Ch'ang-ch'un's doings that are not recorded in the *Hsi-yu chi*, we must turn to the *Hsi-yu lu*. There, Yeh-lü Ch'u-ts'ai admits that his relations with Ch'ang-ch'un were at first very friendly; he was, naturally enough, looking for congenial company after four years spent in alien surroundings and among most unenlightened people. The two men exchanged poems (which we still possess),[50] drank tea together, made trips to the famous gardens around Samarqand, and conversed late into the night.[51] Ch'ang-ch'un, however, was not particularly eager to exert his civilizing influence on the Mongol conqueror in the way desired by Yeh-lü Ch'u-ts'ai. On the contrary, he used all his skill to convert the emperor to "alchemical" or esoteric Taoism, relating the mystical feats of Lin Ling-su and Emperor Hui-tsung of Sung, and extolling the ecstasies and trances dear to the followers of the Ch'üan-chen sect.[52] But it was in his attitude toward Buddhism that, according to Yeh-lü Ch'u-ts'ai, Ch'ang-ch'un finally revealed his true self. Not only did he show contempt for the members of the Ch'an sect, but through a casual remark he betrayed his utter ignorance of Buddhist doctrine. "Thereafter," says Yeh-lü Ch'u-ts'ai, "in his presence I behaved politely, but in my mind I thought little of him."[53] To add insult to injury, Ch'ang-ch'un's disciples suggested that Yeh-lü Ch'u-ts'ai should become a lay disciple of their master. Yeh-lü Ch'u-ts'ai brushed them off, saying: "In my youth I practiced Confucianism; when I grew older I embraced Buddhism. Why should I 'descend from lofty trees to enter into a dark valley'?"[54]

Yeh-lü Ch'u-ts'ai's hopes of enlightening the emperor were thus frustrated. Although his disappointment was intense, particularly as Cinggis showed a genuine liking for Ch'ang-ch'un, he refrained from criticizing him openly. "As our faiths were different," he says in the *Hsi-yu lu*, "had I attacked him it would have created a dispute. This is why I disapproved of him in my mind and laughed at him in private."[55]

Ch'ang-ch'un's subsequent actions were to turn disappointment into bitter resentment. In his sermons delivered to the emperor, Ch'ang-ch'un had touched upon the subject of practical administration and suggested that the people of North China, harassed by many years of war, be relieved of taxation for three years.[56] Cinggis did not follow this advice but, shortly before Ch'ang-ch'un and his party left for China, gave orders that the Taoist leader be granted an edict exempting the clergy from taxes and corvée.[57] According to the *Hsi-yu chi*, the exemption was granted only to Ch'ang-ch'un and his disciples.[58] Yeh-lü Ch'u-ts'ai, on the other hand, states in the *Hsi-yu lu* that Ch'ang-ch'un had requested Cinggis Qan to exempt from taxation all persons who had entered monastic life, and that Cinggis had acceded to the request on condition that there be no further ordinations. However, as the man in charge of drafting imperial decrees (presumably Yeh-lü Ch'u-ts'ai himself) was away at the time, the Taoists were given permission to draft the edict themselves. Instead of making clear that taxation was remitted for both Buddhist and Taoist monks, Ch'ang-ch'un phrased the edict in such a way as to make it valid only for the "monks" subject to him.[59] The term for monks used in the edict was *ch'u-chia*, literally "those who have left home," a term originally applied to Buddhist monks. The text of the edict thus opened the way to a double interpretation of which the Taoists soon took advantage in order to gain control over the Buddhist clergy.[60] Armed with the "forged" edict and a warrant that authorized them to make free use of the postal relay service, the Taoist party returned to China. Once back, they immediately began appropriating Buddhist and Confucian temples. The possession of the powerful warrant enabled them to move freely from place to place for this purpose.[61] In Peking, where Ch'ang-ch'un had established his headquarters, the Taoist clergy enjoyed, moreover, the protection of Shih-mo Hsien-te-pu, the local military commander, a great admirer of Ch'ang-ch'un.[62] Within a few years the Ch'üan-chen sect reached the apex of its power, and by the time Ch'ang-ch'un died (1227), many of the Buddhist clergy had passed under its control.

Meanwhile Yeh-lü Ch'u-ts'ai was busy in Central Asia and, although acquainted with events at home, could do little to remedy a state of affairs for which, no doubt, he felt partly responsible. In the *Hsi-yu lu* he says that when he heard of the abuses that Ch'ang-ch'un was perpetrating in China, he wanted to condemn his evil-doings frankly to his face but was prevented by official duties from meeting him.[63] This may be true, but it is not the whole truth. Until the year of his death the conqueror continued to show friendship for Ch'ang-ch'un and to bestow favors on him.[64] Thus, it is very doubtful whether Yeh-lü Ch'u-ts'ai would have taken a definite stand against Ch'ang-ch'un with the emperor still alive. In 1226 he wrote an attack against the Dhūta (Ch. T'ou-t'o), a Buddhist heretic sect which had quite a number of followers in China but of which almost nothing is known. In the preface, the only surviving part of the work, Yeh-lü Ch'u-ts'ai refers to Yang Chu and Mo Ti as the "evil of Confucianism," and to the Dhūtaists as the "evil of Buddhism."[65] He does not mention, however, the followers of the Ch'üan-chen sect as being the evil of Taoism, as he does in the preface to the *Hsi-yu lu,* written three years later.⁶⁶ His anti-Ch'üan-chen feelings during the years in Central Asia are only expressed in a few poems satirizing some of his friends in Peking, who, during his absence, had turned philo-Taoists, and on the whole these are in the form of mild reprimands.⁶⁷

When Yeh-lü Ch'u-ts'ai returned to Peking in the winter of 1227 "to search for some literary texts,"⁶⁸ the situation had changed considerably. Cinggis Qan was dead, and so was Ch'ang-ch'un. If he still had any doubts as to the truth of the reports he had received about the misdeeds of the Taoists, they were dispelled by the sight that confronted him.

Former Buddhist temples, now turned Taoist, were crowded with "converts" whose only aim was to avoid the heavy taxes imposed by the Mongols.⁶⁹ The Buddhist clergy were reluctant to defend their rights for fear of incurring the wrath of the authorities who, impressed by the marks of favor accorded by the emperor to Ch'ang-ch'un, supported and protected the Ch'üan-chen sect.⁷⁰

Banditry had assumed alarming proportions in the city owing to the bad administration of Shih-mo Hsien-te-pu, a corrupt and cruel official. Robbers had become so daring that they operated in broad daylight, and even took carts with them when making their forays.⁷¹ The local intelligentsia blamed Yeh-lü Ch'u-ts'ai for having initially supported Ch'ang-ch'un, and held him indirectly responsible for the abuses of the Taoists.⁷² To clarify his position he immediately set to writing the *Hsi-yu lu,* a kind of apologia in the form of a dialogue with an imaginary guest, in which he answers the main criticism raised against him. On his return to Mongolia shortly afterward, he received an order from Tolui (Jui-tsung, r. 1227–29), then Regent of the Empire—no doubt at his own prompting—to go back to Peking to deal with the local banditry. He and his Mongol colleague, Tācar, arrested and executed the ringleaders, who proved to be either relatives of Shih-mo Hsien-te-pu or members of powerful families.⁷³

On September 13 (or 11), 1229, Ögödei was elected qaghan by a Mongol assembly convoked at Köde'e-aral, on the Kerülen. Yeh-lü Ch'u-ts'ai's role on this occasion is not very clear. We know from the Chinese sources that there was disagreement in the assembly, a section of which supported Tolui's candidature against Ögödei's. According to the *Yüan shih,* Tolui wished to postpone the election on account of this disagreement. Yeh-lü Ch'u-ts'ai as court astrologer insisted that the day fixed was auspicious and no deferment should be made. Moreover, he persuaded Caghatai (the eldest surviving son of Cinggis) that he should himself lead the imperial clan and court officials, and that they all pay obeisance to Ögödei in the order assigned by their rank.[74] Yeh-lü Ch'u-ts'ai has therefore been credited not only with bringing about the enthronement of Ögödei, the successor designated by Cinggis Qan, but also with the introduction of two new elements in the Mongol inauguration ritual, i.e., the obeisance of the clan elders to the new qaghan and the assignment of proper places to the princes of the blood, members of the imperial clan, and Mongol notables, according to their dignity. These innovations suggest a Chinese model. Similarly, Yeh-lü Ch'u-ts'ai's stand in support of the legal succession has a strong Confucian tinge. To what extent the Chinese sources are reliable on this issue it is difficult to determine. No doubt Yeh-lü Ch'u-ts'ai may have exerted a certain influence on the assembly as court astrologer, and he may well have been responsible for the fixing of the inauguration day. However, his direct intervention in the affairs of the assembly could have been justified only if he had been personally entrusted with Cinggis Qan's testament. Although a passage from one of his biographies seems to support this view,[75] the question can hardly be settled, since it is not certain that Cinggis ever left a written will.

As for Ögödei's investiture, we learn from the Persian sources that it was carried out in the Mongolian traditional form, and no reference is made to a hierarchical placing *more Sinico*.[76] Moreover, if such procedure was in fact introduced, it remained an isolated case and it was not followed by the Mongols at their subsequent assemblies until 1271, the year in which the Chinese court ceremonial was officially adopted by Qubilai. In the biography of the Academician Wang P'an (1202–91) it is stated that at the beginning of the Chih-yüan period (1264) there were as yet neither audience halls nor a fixed court ceremonial, and that "whenever they were to greet [the emperor], the court officials and the commoners, without distinction of rank, all gathered in front of the imperial pavilion."[77] It is possible that here, as in the case of Cinggis Qan's "withdrawal" from India, Yeh-lü Ch'u-ts'ai's role may have been somewhat exaggerated by his biographer.

After his enthronement, Ögödei was faced with a double task in North China: first, to annihilate Chin; second, to consolidate the Mongol rule and devise effective means of exploitation in the conquered territory. The campaign against Chin presented tactical problems which Ögödei and his generals could easily manage; the second task was beset, however, by serious difficulties. In the course of the long war against Chin, the Mongols had enforced in the newly conquered territories their customary law and the modes of exploitation peculiar to their nomadic society. Large groups of people in the occupied areas were given as slaves to victorious generals and nobles by the court, and were often removed from their homes. The heavy exactions and harsh rules imposed by the Mongol officials in the territories under their jurisdiction had also caused many "to flee and disperse," thus adding to the already considerable number of civilians uprooted by the war with Chin. The monasteries gradually became populated with escaped prisoners, army deserters, displaced civilians, and frightened peasants. The land suffered, particularly as the Mongols, like their Jurchen predecessors, requisitioned large tracts of it for grazing.[78] A "conservative" section of the Mongol court, led by Begder, was in favor of the complete annihilation of the native population, and insisted that the entire occupied territory should be turned into pasture land. Yeh-lü Ch'u-ts'ai opposed this radical suggestion and with figures illustrated the material advantages to be gained by a more rational exploitation of the country. He won his argument and in 1229 was put in charge of the taxation program for North China.[79] Knowledge of conditions in China as well as of the Mongolian point of view made him admirably suited for this task.

His first step was to obtain from Ögödei a decree to the effect that crimes committed prior to the first month of 1229 should not be dealt with. This was an important measure as the Chinese were not yet acquainted with the conquerors' code and were constantly infringing the Mongol prohibitions. It was also the first time an amnesty was granted by the Mongols, a practice so far unknown to them.[80] He then addressed to the emperor an eighteen-point plan designed to obviate the state of chaos in North China. Only the principal measures proposed by Yeh-lü Ch'u-ts'ai in his memorial are known.[81] His chief concern was to restore order and to create a strong, centralized government, a prerequisite for the systematic and effective exploitation of the country. This was impossible, however, unless a strict division was to be made between military and civil authority. At the time there was no separation between the two, and the conquered areas were under the control of military leaders (called in Chinese *hsing-sheng*), virtually independent of the court.[82] Yeh-lü Ch'u-ts'ai divided the country into ten principal administrative units or districts (*lu*) and established in the center of each a tax collection bureau administered by two civil officials. These were drawn from the former personnel of Chin, who had rallied to the Mongols.[83] The appointment of such officials, who were directly responsible to the court (at this time synonymous with the government), was especially designed to stop the arbitrary collection of taxes by the local military officials. This served a dual purpose. On the one hand, it asserted the authority of the court versus local rule; on the other, it tended to reduce the fiscal burden on the subject people. Before Yeh-lü Ch'u-ts'ai was put in charge of the fiscal program, there had been no regular system of taxation in North China. The Chinese populace was irrationally exploited, the levies imposed by their masters consisting of periodical and irregular exactions of goods and labor (*ch'ai-fa*).[84] Yeh-lü Ch'u-ts'ai's fiscal reforms of the years 1229–30 represented the first step toward transforming these confused fiscal practices into a rational system on Chinese lines. He introduced a land tax on a household basis, as well as a poll tax on all adults, but with different rates for town dwellers and peasants. The taxes were to be paid in silk (usually commuted to silver) and grain. He also introduced a tax on commerce and the traditional Chinese duties on liquor and vinegar, salt, iron smelters, and mining products.[85]

The clergy had so far been exempted from levies of any kind, thanks to the edict issued by Cinggis Qan. Consequently, the monasteries had grown in number and power, the monks now possessing land and engaging in commerce. Immediately after his election, Ögödei, no doubt on Yeh-lü Ch'u-ts'ai's recommendation, issued an edict to the effect that Buddhist and Taoist monks below the age of fifty should pass an examination on their respective scriptures in order to qualify for the priesthood and be allowed to reside in monasteries. Furthermore, the edict warned monks of both faiths against the unlawful appropriation of temples and the destruction of religious images. Finally, it imposed fiscal obligations on monks who cultivated land and engaged in commerce.[86]

These measures are clear evidence of Yeh-lü Ch'u-ts'ai's intention to curb the power of the clergy, one of the traditional enemies of the Chinese government. But mere fiscal reforms were doomed to failure as no supporting network of civil officials capable of enforcing their application existed. The appointment of tax collectors was the initial step toward the establishment of a local bureaucracy. However, the appointment of Chinese nationals to positions of responsibility was regarded with disfavor by the ruling Mongols. Like all the other alien rulers before them, they had an evident distrust of a politically independent Chinese leadership. Yeh-lü Ch'u-ts'ai's civil background and outlook had already been subject to criticism at court. During Cinggis Qan's lifetime some had pointed out the incongruity of a man of letters holding office in a military society.[87] The dispute with Begder must certainly have brought him more enemies. His establishment of the tax collection bureaus dealt a serious blow to the authority of the powerful military leaders. One of the most prominent among them, the aforementioned Shih-mo Hsien-te-pu, with the support of Ögödei's uncle Temüge-otcigin, accused Yeh-lü Ch'u-ts'ai of harboring a "treacherous mind," because of his appointment of former Chin personnel and the fact that members of his family were still serving Chin. Yeh-lü Ch'u-ts'ai was able to clear himself, but it is significant that no action was taken against the slanderer.[88]

In September 1231, Yeh-lü Ch'u-ts'ai's fiscal reforms bore their first fruit. In Yün-chung (modern Ta-t'ung *hsien* in Shansi), the tax collectors of the ten districts submitted to Ögödei the granary inventories and the revenue (in silver and silk) collected for the treasury. The amount raised tallied with the figure originally stated by Yeh-lü Ch'u-ts'ai. The emperor was so pleased that he appointed Yeh-lü Ch'u-ts'ai Chief of the Secretariat (*chung-shu-ling*) on the spot.[89] The Secretariat (*chung-shu-sheng*) was nothing more than the Sino-Uighur chancellery established under Cinggis Qan, in which Yeh-lü Ch'u-ts'ai had worked since the beginning of his career with the Mongols. Hence, what Ögödei did while in Yün-chung was not to create a new administrative body, but rather to ratify the establishment of his former chancellery as a supreme administrative bureau planned on Chinese lines, and to place at its head Yeh-lü Ch'u-ts'ai, the man chiefly responsible for its organization and efficiency. It was also on this occasion that Chinese titles conferred on government officials (although they had been in use before this date) were first formally sanctioned by the emperor.[90]

Such concessions on the part of Ögödei might be interpreted as a victory for the more enlightened element within the court and as a sign of progressive acculturation. To a certain extent this is, no doubt, true. We must not forget, however, that these changes were purely formal and did not really affect the basic attitude of the Mongols toward their subjects. The adoption of certain traditional elements of Chinese culture was only designed to ensure a better and more efficient system of exploitation.

The number of civil officials in charge of tax collecting was small at first. Yeh-lü Ch'u-ts'ai fully realized that in spite of his initial success it was not wise to antagonize the conservative Mongols. Moreover, while the war with Chin dragged on, it made the full enforcement of his administrative program increasingly difficult. The Mongol armies in China were in constant need of goods and revenue, and continued to exact these from the local population over and above what the latter—under the new regulations—had to pay to the court. As the administrative machinery was still rudimentary, the revenue exacted by the court was collected in the form of annual quotas, fixed by Yeh-lü Ch'u-ts'ai in 1230 at 10,000 ingots of silver (equal to 500,000 taels).[91] The displacement of population, in addition to the famines and epidemics that characterized the early period of Ögödei's reign, seriously reduced the number of taxpayers at a time when the government's need of revenue was increasing. Yeh-lü Ch'u-ts'ai tried in vain to impose on the privileged non-Chinese residents of North China (Mongols, Central Asians, and so on) the same fiscal obligations as those to which the Chinese were subject.[92] Contrary to what is stated by Sung Tzu-chen, his proposal was not carried into effect. Instead, we know that by 1232–33 the land tax (for the Chinese!), which was originally two bushels, had been raised to four bushels. With the conquest of Honan in 1233–34, the annual quota of silver was also doubled.[93]

Although the reforms of 1229–30 represented a step toward the resurrection of the Chinese administrative tradition and state power, in practice they had the effect of rendering even more intricate the already confused fiscal system and of aggravating the tax burden on the individual. Before tax categories could be redefined it was necessary to carry out a general census, which was not possible until after the annihilation of Chin. By this time (1234), the floating population had reached enormous proportions: according to Sung Tzu-chen, the number of slaves owned by the Mongol princes, dignitaries, and army leaders constituted half the population of North China.[94] The Mongol high officials, dissatisfied with Yeh-lü Ch'u-ts'ai's rearrangement of the fiscal program along Chinese traditional lines and anxious to increase revenue above the limit imposed by him, insisted that the basic unit for taxation purposes should be the individual adult male (instead of the household). They pointed out that this was the practice followed by the Mongols as well as being the one enforced in the Western Regions, whereas the system introduced by Yeh-lü Ch'u-ts'ai was based on the administrative rules of a defeated country. Yeh-lü Ch'u-ts'ai opposed the redefinition and won his point by stating that if it were introduced, the population would pay taxes for one year, but would then flee and disperse.[95]

The national census ordered by Ögödei in 1234 upon Yeh-lü Ch'u-ts'ai's recommendation was completed in 1236.[96] While Yeh-lü Ch'u-ts'ai was in favor of the census for administrative reasons, the incentive for it, on the Mongol side, was a very different one. For Yeh-lü Ch'u-ts'ai the registration of the population was indispensable to fix the social status and obligations of those registered, so as to do away eventually with the Mongol system of arbitrary tributes and levies. For the Mongol rulers the census not only marked the definite taking possession of the new territory, but also enabled them to grant equitable shares of land (and the people attached to it) to members of the imperial family and the nobility. The Mongols had by now realized the impracticability of displacing large sections of conquered people and had started granting land to the aristocracy as hereditary fiefs. Upon the completion of the census, Ögödei, in spite of Yeh-lü Ch'u-ts'ai's remonstrances, divided

North China into a series of appanages and distributed them among the princes and the meritorious officials. This measure brought about a further decentralization, as the court had no effective control over the newly created domains. Yeh-lü Ch'u-ts'ai then proposed the appointment of government officials entrusted with the collection of revenue from the appanages, which was to be handed over to the treasury and redistributed to the appanage holders.[97] Although the proposal was adopted in theory by Ögödei, it was not until the reign of Qubilai that the central government actually gained financial control over the appanages. The parceling of the country into a series of independent administrative units was a serious obstacle to Yeh-lü Ch'u-ts'ai's policy of building up a strong centralized administration. This did not prevent him, however, from carrying out the proposed program of fiscal reforms.

The land tax that Yeh-lü Ch'u-ts'ai had introduced in 1229–30 on a household basis was now (1236–37) reassessed according to the quality and quantity of the land owned, thus fully conforming to the traditional Chinese system. The poll tax was continued but at reduced rates; and a new silk tax, assessed on the basis of the household, was created to replace the loose system of specifically Mongolian tributes. Labor service and duties on commerce, salt, liquor, etc., were of course retained. All in all, the new rates represented about one-tenth of those previously exacted.[98]

Yeh-lü Ch'u-ts'ai then proceeded to reorganize the civil service. With the fall of Pien-liang and the subsequent annexation of Chin, the administrative machinery of the Jurchen state had fallen into the hands of the Mongols. Immediately after the capitulation of Pien-liang, Yeh-lü Ch'u-ts'ai, in response to a moving appeal by the great Chin literatus Yüan Hao-wen (1190–1257), had rescued from captivity a few scores of former leading Chin scholars and grandees, including the fifty-first lineal descendant of Confucius, K'ung Yüan-ts'u. On Yeh-lü Ch'u-ts'ai's recommendation K'ung was restored by imperial edict to the title of Duke Yen-sheng and to his traditional privileges.[99] With the assistance of K'ung Yüan-ts'u and other Chinese officials in the Mongol service more scholars were gathered in the following years. Yeh-lü Ch'u-ts'ai was now faced with the difficult task of finding suitable appointments for them. While some found employment in the Mongol administration, others were absorbed in newly created institutions, such as the Bureau of Compilation (*Pien-hsiu-so*) in Peking and the Bureau of Literature (*Ching-chi-so*) in P'ing-yang (modern Lin-fen *hsien*, Shansi), both established by Yeh-lü Ch'u-ts'ai in 1236 to edit and publish books under official sponsorship.[100] Private academies (*shu-yüan*) were also set up in Peking, to which a number of scholars were appointed to lecture on

the Chinese classics to the Mongol princes and to the sons of the great
dignitaries.[101] The appointment of Confucians as tutors to the Mongol
aristocracy is of particular significance, for, as far as we know, the very
limited literary education of the nobles had till then rested primarily
with the Taoists.[102] Later in the dynasty this task was to be shared by
Buddhists and Confucians, although instances of Taoist preceptors are
not unknown.[103]

The scholars thus recruited by Yeh-lü Ch'u-ts'ai and his colleagues
were the surviving elite of the former Chin administration, and their
assignment to various offices had been made possible, as in the case of
the earlier tax collectors, through the personal recommendation of
Yeh-lü Ch'u-ts'ai or of other high dignitaries. Not only were the great
majority of former Chin officials still unemployed, but a considerable
number of them, after the collapse of the dynasty, had been attached
to the households of Mongol leaders and subsequently registered as
slaves (ch'ü-k'ou) in the census lists. In order to redeem them from
bondage and at the same time promote the creation of a Chinese bureaucracy vis-à-vis the Mongol and Central Asian officialdom, Yeh-lü
Ch'u-ts'ai memorialized in 1237, advising the selection of Chinese for
office through competitive examinations. Ögödei gave his consent. Examinations were then held in the various districts, the required subjects
being classical exegesis, poetry, and essays. The rules set up by Yeh-lü
Ch'u-ts'ai were such as to enable the largest possible number of candidates to participate. Severe penalties (our text speaks of capital
punishment) were decreed for all owners of enslaved scholars who
prevented them from attending. The examinations resulted in 4,030
successful candidates, about a thousand of whom, formerly slaves, "were
sent back to their homes," i.e., gained their freedom.[104] Regarding their
employment, the Yüan shih informs us that they were allowed to take
part in the administration of their native places as "councillors" (i-shih-
kuan).[105] In the case of most of them, this simply meant that they were
used in an advisory capacity on local administrative matters by their
Mongol or Central Asian superiors, who naturally continued to hold all
the senior posts. They were, however, exempted from taxes and corvée.

According to Sung Tzu-chen, at the same time that he introduced
government examinations for Confucian scholars, Yeh-lü Ch'u-ts'ai prescribed special examinations on the canonical texts for Buddhist and
Taoist monks.[106] We have seen that a decree to this effect had already
been issued in 1229; it appears, however, that it was never actually enforced, probably because of resistance on the part of the clergy. At the
time of the great census another attempt was made to enforce the holding of the examination; this failed, we know, because of the opposition

of the famous Ch'an master Hai-yün, who argued that Buddhist monks should be concerned not with the knowledge of books but with the cultivation of virtue. Hai-yün obtained the support of the powerful judge Šigi-Qutuqu, and as a result the examination was reduced to a mere formality, with no candidate failing and admission to the monasteries continuing virtually as before.[107] In 1237 the question of the examination for the priesthood was probably discussed again in connection with the civil service examination, and a new attempt was made to carry it out. However, no practical results ensued and the question did not arise again until the end of Qubilai's reign, when an edict was issued to the effect that only persons versed in the canons were allowed to take up monastic life.[108] It is doubtful whether this condition alone ever constituted a serious obstacle for those wishing to enter a monastery. The civil service examination also proved short-lived: no examination was held after 1238.

Yeh-lü Ch'u-ts'ai's failure effectively to introduce the traditional examination system coincides with, and is partly to be explained by, the decline of his power at the Mongol court. Several factors contributed to this decline. After 1235 Ögödei withdrew more and more from active participation in government affairs. The anti-Chinese element at court, opposed from the beginning to Yeh-lü Ch'u-ts'ai's policy, had been further aroused by the reforms of 1236. These had imposed a limit on the fiscal exploitation of Chinese subjects at a time when the lavish use of revenues by the emperor and his entourage necessitated drawing an increasing amount of silver from the conquered territories. The Central Asian merchants who had followed in the wake of the Mongol invasion and now monopolized the money-lending business in North China, came forward with the alluring offer of multiplying the income of the Mongol court by the well-known system of tax-farming. Yeh-lü Ch'u-ts'ai, aware that such a measure, if adopted, would weaken the authority of the government and bring about a still greater decentralization, vigorously opposed it. He declared that the annual quota (which in 1238 was 22,000 ingots) could be doubled, but only through the enforcement of stern laws, and that the people would become destitute and inevitably take to robbery. His words were of no avail: the emperor, influenced by the opinion prevailing at court, in 1239 conferred the privilege of farming the taxes in North China on the Muslim businessman 'Abd ar-Rahmān. The annual quota was then raised to 44,000 ingots.[109]

Yeh-lü Ch'u-ts'ai's authority had also been undermined in this period by personal conflict with his nearest colleagues in the Secretariat. It seems that there had already been some dissension with Left Prime Minister Cinqai before these events.[110] Cinqai, who later showed

marked hostility toward the Muslims, at this stage supported them, perhaps to antagonize Yeh-lü Ch'u-ts'ai.[111] Charges of embezzlement and
corruption brought against the latter and some of the Chinese tax collecting officials (in the case of these, apparently not unfounded) had
worsened Yeh-lü Ch'u-ts'ai's position. Serious doubts grew even in the
emperor's mind as to the true worth of the principles proposed by him,
and as to the honesty of the Confucians.[112]

The struggle between the various factions and cliques at the Mongol
court during the latter part of Ögödei's reign helped to weaken the
already precarious administrative structure established by Yeh-lü Ch'u-
ts'ai. The pro-Chinese party that he headed was replaced in power by
the pro-Muslim section of the court. In 1240 all tax bureaus of North
China were placed under 'Abd ar-Rahmān's direction. Soon after, another Muslim from Central Asia, the famous Mahmūd Yalawac, was
given a key administrative post in Peking.[113] Yeh-lü Ch'u-ts'ai retained
his title of Chief of the Secretariat and continued to perform his astro-
logical duties; however, he no longer had a part in government affairs.

After the death of Ögödei (December 1241) his widow Töregene
assumed the regency of the empire. The question of succession was
debated at court, and Yeh-lü Ch'u-ts'ai once more raised his voice
against suggestions violating the will of the deceased emperor.[114] Although our sources are cautious here and mention no names, it appears
that Yeh-lü Ch'u-ts'ai spoke in favor of the election of Širemün, the successor designated by Ögödei, whereas Töregene favored the candidature of Ögödei's son Güyüg, who was eventually elected in 1246.

Yeh-lü Ch'u-ts'ai's protests no longer carried any weight. Töregene
resented his opposition, but, according to Sung Tzu-chen, "she still endeavored to treat him with respect and deference, in consideration of
his long and distinguished service during the previous reigns."[115] This
might have changed to active hostility, involving a violent death for
Yeh-lü Ch'u-ts'ai, had he not died (some say of a broken heart) in 1243.
As it was, his death was openly regretted by many. The Mongol capital
went into mourning, and his wish to be buried with his wife at the foot
of Weng-shan, one of the Western Hills near Peking, was honored.[116]

Yeh-lü Ch'u-ts'ai believed that the Mongol dynasty possessed the
Heavenly Mandate and clearly stated this in his works. For him the
success that accompanied Cinggis Qan's expedition against the state
of Chin was granted by heaven. The emperor's "pacification" of the
country in less than five years (sic) was a feat "that human power
[alone] could not have achieved."[117] In other words, Cinggis Qan had
proved his right by victory, and Yeh-lü Ch'u-ts'ai considered himself free

from allegiance to Chin when he took up service with him. Having been an eyewitness of the Mongols' conquest of Central Asia and North China, Yeh-lü Ch'u-ts'ai no doubt believed that the whole of China would eventually be unified under their rule. The following words addressed to Hsü T'ing—Sung envoy to North China in 1235–36—seem to confirm this view: "You [Southern Sung] only rely on the Great River [Yangtze, for protection], but our horses' hoofs can reach any place, be it heaven or sea!"[118] Yeh-lü Ch'u-ts'ai's conviction that the Mongols were in possession of the mandate to rule "all-under-heaven" may have also been reinforced by his rulers' dogmatic faith in the heaven-ordained submission of the world to Mongol sovereignty.

But legitimacy of the new imperial house was not sufficient in itself to ensure good government. Yeh-lü Ch'u-ts'ai realized that it was imperative to make the emperor appreciate and adopt those principles that would guide him in organizing a stable and efficient rule, once the destruction that inevitably accompanies a period of transition was over. He plainly stated in the *Hsi-yu lu* that he wished to make Cinggis Qan "tread in the footsteps of the ancient worthies," and this, we know, he hoped to achieve by acquainting him with the doctrines of the Three Sages. Yeh-lü Ch'u-ts'ai, as has been mentioned, held the view that Confucius, Buddha, and Lao Tzu had taught the same truth. In that age of philosophical syncretism the old theory of the fundamental identity of the Three Religions was very popular. Indeed it was a characteristic feature of the intellectual history of the Chin period. Wan-sung, Yeh-lü Ch'u-ts'ai's teacher, maintained that the three doctrines had a common origin in the Storing Center of Ideation (*ālaya-vijñāna*),[119] a view influenced no doubt by the monistic Hua-yen philosophy in which he was particularly well versed, and which had by now been fully assimilated by Ch'an Buddhism.

Under Wan-sung's influence, Li Ch'un-fu (1185–1231) and Yeh-lü Ch'u-ts'ai, his most prominent lay disciples, developed syncretic tendencies.[120] While Li Ch'un-fu's attempt to combine Confucianism and Taoism with Buddhism in a grandiose synthesis embracing and fusing diverse and complex teachings shows preeminently philosophical preoccupations, Yeh-lü Ch'u-ts'ai's synthesis was animated by a practical spirit.

His premise was of course the same, namely, that the doctrines of the Three Sages had a common origin, and that the different traditions of their schools (*tsung-feng*) had developed only to meet the exigencies of the times. Although essentially identical—only the fool, said Yeh-lü Ch'u-ts'ai, would deny this truth—the three doctrines in relation to man and society had thus acquired individual characteristics and

fulfilled different purposes. Taoism and Confucianism were the repository of ancient wisdom and as such illustrated the teachings of the Sage-
Kings of the past; the doctrine of Buddha and the Patriarchs, on the
other hand, penetrated in its temporal and real aspect both the realms
of the absolute and the relative-phenomenal.[121] With regard to their
specific functions, he stated that the aim of Taoism was to foster man's
nature (*yang-hsing*); Confucianism, with its emphasis on man's proper
duties and well-defined obligations, provided the key to social order;
while Buddhism constituted the ideal means of self-cultivation.[122]

Although Yeh-lü Ch'u-ts'ai emphasized the need for the teachings
of the Three Sages to "stand firmly in the world like the three legs of
a tripod,"[123] it is quite clear that he did not attribute equal value to each
of the three doctrines. His syncretism was, in fact, strongly biased in
favor of Confucianism and Buddhism. His practical formula for social
and mental transformation was twofold, not threefold: "To rule the
state with Confucianism and the mind with Buddhism."[124] In giving
advice to his son Chu on his fifteenth birthday, he exhorted him not to
neglect the Confucian doctrine, and to cherish that of the Ch'an Patriarchs, but he made no mention of Taoism.[125] To a friend who warned
him against forgetting Confucius' tenets, Yeh-lü Ch'u-ts'ai replied: "To
grasp fully the universal principle and get to the bottom of one's nature,
nothing is better than the *Buddhadharma*; to help society and pacify
the people, nothing is better than the teachings of Confucius. In office,
I follow the constant Way of Hsüan-ni [Confucius]; in private, I enjoy
the Absolute Truth of Buddhism. Surely this is not wrong?"[126]

Yeh-lü Ch'u-ts'ai's urge to convert Cinggis Qan to the Way of the
Sages shows the statesman's concern with the ideals of education and
transformation (*chiao-hua*) so strongly advocated by Confucianism.
Even before his encounter with the Mongol emperor he cherished the
ambition of attaining enough power to put these ideals into practice.
In 1216, at the time when he had just started his training under Wan-
sung, he wrote:

Now, the reason why a superior man pursues his study is not a selfish one.
His aim is: "My prince should be a prince like Yao and Shun; my people
should be like the people of Yao and Shun." And, even if there were only one
man or woman who did not enjoy the benefits of Yao and Shun, would not the
superior man feel ashamed? Therefore, is it not a delight for him to be in
power and have sufficient standing to practice the Way of the Sages, and sufficient means to confer extensive benefits upon the people?[127]

The task he had set himself was fraught with immense difficulties.
No real "transformation" could in fact be carried out without first edu-
cating the ruler and bringing him to an understanding of the social
situation he had to deal with in his newly conquered empire. The Mon-

gols were not interested in the mores of the Chinese, but merely in the exploitation of their territory and resources. Nor did they consider Chinese culture to be superior to their own; on the contrary, they despised it. It would have been vain to exalt the rules of civilized life unless their adoption offered hopes of greater material gain. Yeh-lü Ch'u-ts'ai's plans for social and administrative reform therefore did not stress the moral so much as the practical aspect. Yeh-lü Ch'u-ts'ai has passed into history for his humanitarian acts; these, however, could not have been carried out except by appealing to the Mongols' cupidity. When he pleaded with the emperor to spare the people of Honan, he pointedly remarked that "they could be used as a source of troops and revenue as the occasion may demand."[128] He is also said to have prevented the wholesale massacre of the inhabitants of Pien-liang in 1233 by showing that the destruction of the population, which included skilled artisans, would have meant a loss of valuable services for the Mongols.[129] In order to obtain Ögödei's endorsement of his proposal for the reinstitution of civil service examinations, he again referred to the "skilled artisans," drawing a parallel between their useful role and that of the Confucian officials.[130] Similarly, when he opposed a bad scheme put forward by some of the other court dignitaries, he carefully pointed out the material loss that would eventually ensue if it were enforced. The gain-and-loss argument, however, was not always successful, owing to the Mongols' insatiable cupidity and their unwillingness to modify substantially their traditional law and customs.

In addition to strong factional opposition within the court, Yeh-lü Ch'u-ts'ai had furthermore to contend with the hostility of the clergy. Following his bitter struggle with the Taoists he faced the antagonism of the Buddhist authorities when he tried to reintroduce the special examination for monks. We have already seen that his attempt was foiled by the direct intervention of the Buddhist leader Hai-yün. In these circumstances it is not surprising that many of his proposals met with failure. According to Sung Tzu-chen, of all his plans only "two or three out of ten" were actually put into effect.[131]

Yeh-lü Ch'u-ts'ai's Confucian attitude is also clearly present in his emphasis on "rectification" and orthodoxy. He used the age-old argument of the "rectification of names" to repudiate what he considered heterodox teachings. Speaking of the *Hsi-yu lu*, he wrote:

In it, I have been rather concerned with the distinction between orthodoxy and heterodoxy in the teachings of the Three Sages. Some people have criticized my love of making distinctions. My reply to them is: "The *Lun-yü* says: 'What is necessary is to rectify names,' and it also says: 'Have no depraved thoughts.'" This means that to discriminate between orthodoxy and heterodoxy should not be neglected.

After this introduction he listed the theories that he regarded as heterodox. Among them were the philosophies of Yang Chu, Mo Ti, and T'ien P'ien; the teachings of the Chen-yen, Dhūta, and White Lotus; and the doctrines preached by the Ch'üan-chen, Ta-tao, Hun-yüan, and T'ai-i sects. He dismissed the "alchemical" practices of the Taoists as the corruption of the "techniques" (*fang-chi*), and noted with regret that "the tolerance and benevolence advocated while the State was in the making" had resulted in a growth of falsehood. He concluded by stating that Han Yü's repudiation of Buddhism and Taoism represented "the wrong way of discriminating," while Mencius' repudiation of Yang Chu and Mo Ti as well as his own rejection of the Dhūta and of Ch'ang-ch'un represented the correct one.[132]

Yeh-lü Ch'u-ts'ai's conception of "evil" (or "heterodox") was basically Confucian. His violent denunciation of sects like the Dhūta and the Ch'üan-chen arose from the actions, harmful to other religious groups or to the whole community, carried out by their followers. He accused the Dhūtaists of destroying Buddhist images, oppressing the Buddhist monks, failing to help people in distress, and corrupting filial custom.[133] Similarly, his criticism of the Ch'üan-chen sect was aimed mainly against the behavior of its members, not against their doctrine. He was obviously more concerned with Ch'ang-ch'un's appropriation of temples and illegal use of travel credentials than with his religious tenets. He considered Lin Ling-su an archcriminal for having gained his position at the Sung court through "prodigies and artful powers," but maintained that he was not as bad as the followers of the Ch'üan-chen sect, for "he did not dare to rename Buddhist temples as Taoist temples or change Buddhist images into Taoist ones."[134]

This clearly illustrates the emphasis Yeh-lü Ch'u-ts'ai placed on the moral duties of the individual toward society. But if adherence to the Confucian norm was the best way to achieve social stability, according to his twofold formula the cultivation of the self, or mind transformation, was best carried out by following the Buddhist doctrine. It was in Buddhism, not in Confucianism, that Yeh-lü Ch'u-ts'ai found his source of moral strength. In the preface to the *Hsi-yu lu* he wrote:

When in the past superior men went beyond the great mountain ranges in the south or the Yang Pass in the west, however strong and determined they were, they could not help feeling sad and discouraged. When, by imperial decree, I undertook a trip of several tens of thousands of *li* to the west, it was by virtue of my training in the vast expanse of the Law [*dharma*], and not of other methods, that I remained steady and unperturbed.[135]

Does this mean that he regarded the Confucian teachings as inadequate for self-cultivation and the principles of Buddhism as unsuitable for the practical affairs of the state? The answer to this important question is given by Yeh-lü Ch'u-ts'ai himself. Wan-sung once wrote to him on the subject of the formula quoted above and warned him against the danger of furthering Confucianism at the expense of Buddhism. The text of Wan-sung's letter is lost, but we possess Yeh-lü Ch'u-ts'ai's reply. This can be summarized as follows: Man's most important undertaking was the cultivation of the mind, for, as stated in the *Ta-hsüeh,* it was only when the mind was rectified that the state could be properly ruled. In so far as mind cultivation was concerned, however, the teachings of Confucius could not match Buddhism, for they lacked the latter's depth. According to Yeh-lü Ch'u-ts'ai, the Confucian doctrine of the Five Constant Virtues (*wu-ch'ang chih tao*) corresponded to the more superficial teaching of Buddha. As Buddhism alone provided the ideal means of self-cultivation, it followed that it was also the doctrine best suited for government. He would then dispense with the Confucian tenets altogether, but, in order not to displease the "petty Confucian scholars" (*yung-ju*), he had adopted—as a mere "expedient"—his conciliatory formula. Even so, the petty scholars are vexed and dissatisfied; they "gnash their teeth" and accuse him of "violating the doctrine and forgetting the fundamentals." Such being the case, exclaimed Yeh-lü Ch'u-ts'ai, "it is certainly not worth speaking of the Great Doctrine!"[136] From these statements it would seem that Yeh-lü Ch'u-ts'ai conceived as the ultimate goal the realization of a society that transcended Confucianism. He envisaged, as we can infer from his reference to the Great Doctrine (*ta-tao*), the utopian order of the Great Unity (*ta-t'ung*)—a world morally regenerated by the superior ethic of Buddhism. However, because of the disruption of contemporary society, all Yeh-lü Ch'u-ts'ai could hope to attain in his own lifetime were conditions of relative social and administrative stability. His Confucian-inspired reforms were therefore directed toward the restoration of the Small Tranquillity (*hsiao-k'ang*), a task for which he still required the traditional services of the "petty Confucian scholar." For all his leanings toward syncretism and his personal devotion to Buddhist ideals he was yet forced as a practical statesman to admit the immediate superiority of Confucianist realism.[137]

His decline and death marked the end of Chinese influence at the Mongol court and a return to the state of administrative confusion similar to that existing before the accession of Ögödei. 'Abd ar-Rahmān held administrative control over North China from 1243 to 1246 and continued his policy of reckless exploitation, as a result of which "the people did not know how to move hand or foot."[138]

The Secretariat nominally remained in existence (with Yeh-lü Ch'u-ts'ai's son Chu heading it), but we know that at the end of Ögödei's reign it had actually ceased to function as the central administrative bureau. The *Yüan shih* laconically states: "From the year *jen-yin* [1242] onward, the law was no longer one; there was dissension inside and outside the court, and the good government of T'ai-tsung declined."[139]

The election of Möngke in 1251 and the transfer of rule from the line of Ögödei to that of Tolui saw the beginning of the reconstruction of state power. The fiscal reforms carried out under Möngke by Mahmūd Yalawac were directed toward a further rationalization of tributes and levies (the aim pursued by Yeh-lü Ch'u-ts'ai) and paved the way to the centralizing fiscal reforms of Qubilai (Shih-tsu, r. 1260–94).[140] Möngke reaffirmed, however, the conquerors' preference for a non-Chinese officialdom and, although he also exempted the Confucians from taxation and corvée, he did not conceal his contempt for them as a class having, he considered, no practical use.[141]

It was with the advent of Qubilai and the removal of the capital from remote Qara-Qorum to Peking that complete centralization was achieved. The administrative reforms of the early part of Qubilai's reign represented the outcome of the slow process of acculturation or Sinicization that had started during the reign of Ögödei. The re-establishment of the Secretariat as the supreme administrative body in 1260, and the subsequent creation of a bureaucratic structure modeled on the Chinese, the adoption of the *nien-hao* and of the Chinese court ceremonial, the unification and systematization of the tax structure, the separation of civil from military authority, the subordination of the appanages to the fiscal control of the central government, the promotion of agriculture, the restriction of privileges of the *ortaq* merchants and the clergy, the promotion of learning through the founding of schools and academies for Mongols, Muslims, and Chinese, all showed the progress made from the time that Yeh-lü Ch'u-ts'ai drew up the blueprint for the Mongol administrative organization. The pattern of civilian, as opposed to military, control that he had restored under Ögödei was carried on under Qubilai by an elite group of Chinese counselors, among whom was the famous Buddho-Confucian statesman Liu Ping-chung (1216–74). Like Yeh-lü Ch'u-ts'ai, he maintained—in terms used by Confucians since the founding of the Han—that "although the empire had been conquered on horseback, it could not be administered on horseback."[142]

It would be incorrect, however, to think that the reforms in the civil administration, carried out on the recommendation of Qubilai's Chinese advisers, were inspired by similar reforms previously introduced or ad-

vocated by Yeh-lü Ch'u-ts'ai. Owing to the particular *forma mentis* of
the Chinese, who recognize no culture other than their own, and the
irreconcilable character of the Chinese and Mongol societies, the conquerors had to choose: they must either annihilate Chinese civilization
or adapt themselves to it. Since they had rejected the former course,
thanks to Yeh-lü Ch'u-ts'ai's momentous intervention, a change in their
original policy became unavoidable.

The scholar-officials, who in their capacity as experts on local conditions helped to elaborate the new policy, were, apart from the clergy,
the principal link between the Mongol and Chinese cultures.

It is for his role of mediator between two ways of life that Yeh-lü
Ch'u-ts'ai commands our special interest. As a Sinicized Khitan, he was
particularly well fitted to undertake this task. His racial origin made it
possible for him to become a trusted adviser, first of Cinggis, then of
Ögödei, neither of whom would have entertained as readily the advice
he proffered had it come from a Chinese. On the other hand, Yeh-lü
Ch'u-ts'ai, though trained in Chinese ways and thoroughly familiar with
the Confucian tradition, gave to neither his unqualified allegiance. His
intellectual horizon, as witness his acceptance of Buddhism as the higher
ethic, refused to be bounded by Confucianism alone. His racial origin,
and subsequent political experience, gave him "a foot in both camps";
and his syncretic turn of mind seems, at least to some degree, to have
been a reflection of this.

He was unrivaled in his understanding of the Mongols, and, above
all, of their motivation. He recognized the Mongol power, which in
China he sought to bridle and restrain, for what it was: a predatory
nomadic feudalism. He was fully conscious that his arguments, if these
were to influence Mongol policy, would have to be directed to the cupidity of the conquerors. Hence his choice of weapons. The appeal to
Buddhist idealism would have to be deferred to less troubled times,
while for the moment policies based on hard-headed Confucian prac-
ticality offered the better chances of success. It is almost as if Yeh-lü
Ch'u-ts'ai had taken as his guide an early version of the nineteenth-
century *t'i-yung* formula, which we might express as: *Fo-hsüeh wei t'i,
Ju-hsüeh wei yung* ("Buddhism for the substance, Confucianism for the
functions"). For him, however, this reflected a personal, much more
than a cultural, dilemma.

The success he achieved, of preventing the devastation of North
China and its reduction to pastures for the horses of the nomads, was
a real one. His tragedy was that, this once achieved, he found himself
discarded in favor of Muslim advisers whose willingness to appeal to
the rapacity of their Mongol employers was uninhibited by even the

"lower" social ethic by which Yeh-lü Ch'u-ts'ai had been constantly guided.

Historians have increasingly turned their attention to periods of Chinese history marked by the contact, and conflict, of cultures. Perhaps a closer study of such "mediating figures" as Yeh-lü Ch'u-ts'ai will throw a clearer light on the dynamics of the acculturation process.

Herbert Franke

CHIA SSU-TAO (1213–1275) :
A "BAD LAST MINISTER"?

Incompetence, treason, cowardice, laziness, arrogance—all have been attributed to Chia Ssu-tao at one time or another by Western historians. Chia Ssu-tao, the leading figure in Southern Sung politics toward the end of the dynasty,[1] is almost universally blamed for the eventual decline and fall of Southern Sung. The accuracy of this historical judgment, which is derived from Chinese historiography, becomes less certain, however, on closer study of the factual record of Chia's career. Eberhard[2] has suggested that the condemnation of Chia Ssu-tao was a direct consequence of his agrarian reforms, which inevitably antagonized the landlord class that produced most of China's historians.

Chia's biography in the *Sung shih* is found in the section reserved for "treacherous officials," a fact of considerable interest. The biographies in the dynastic histories, whether drawn from official writings or from family records and private biographies, customarily contained only the information the compilers deemed relevant to their larger purposes.[3] The mere fact that a person had a separate biography (unless it was in one of the sections devoted to "treacherous officials," "rebellious subjects," etc.) was to be taken as laudatory. This led sometimes to a deliberate suppression of those facts and episodes that would mar the picture of a model state servant. One example from early Ming times: Li Ch'ang-ch'i (1376–1452), scholar-official and writer, had a biography in the *Ming shih* based on an epitaph by his friend and Han-lin colleague Ch'ien Hsi-li. This epitaph did not mention the degradation and punishment of Li which occurred about 1419.[4]

The reverse of this favorable bias is seen in the treatment of officials who died in disgrace or were executed. It would be unthinkable for biographies of persons like Chia Ssu-tao, who were *expressis verbis* ranked as treacherous officials, to be based on sources of the family-record kind. Disgrace or execution almost invariably affected the family as a whole, and no learned friend or colleague would dare write an epitaph or necrology. The Accounts of Conduct in the personnel departments of the government were rewritten if preserved or used at all, the only exceptions to this rule being in cases where a person owed his condemnation to flagrant abuse of power or short-lived political movements directed against him or his faction. Yüeh Fei, the famous general and patriot of the twelfth century, is in this latter category.

But in the case of officials who were active toward the end of a dynasty, such change of opinion is less frequent and less probable. This leads us to ask just which sources were consulted in compiling the biographies of "treacherous officials" like Chia Ssu-tao. One glance at most of those biographies shows a striking difference between them and "normal," i.e., favorably biased, biographies. Age and date of birth are very seldom given, with the irritating consequence that often not even these basic data on a person's life can be made out with any certainty. For Chia, even the most recent biographical handbook gives only the year of death (1275), and the fact that he was born in 1213 can be found only in a source where one would not expect it.[5] As for the factual data given in the *lieh-chuan* of a person like Chia, no integral source such as a *vita* with negative bias seems to have existed. Biographies of Yüan dynasty "villains" seem to me usually nothing but superficial patchworks of data tendentiously culled from Veritable Records or Basic Annals.[6] The same seems to be true for Chia's *lieh-chuan,* but even so not all the data recorded in the Basic Annals of the *Sung shih* have been used. On the other hand, semi-official sources like the *Sung-chi san-ch'ao cheng-yao*[7] seem to have been used. But they were compiled by Sung loyalists, former officials of the dynasty who shared the common bias against Chia. When the *Sung shih* was compiled in the 1340's, only these strongly biased sources were available, and the compilers of the *Sung shih,* working as it seems in a great hurry, did not bother to find out to what extent the more or less emotional bias against Chia after the fall of the Sung was based on fact.

There exists, at present, no detailed study of Chia's career and activity in any Western language,[8] and to supply such a study is beyond the scope of this article. But perhaps a more objective appreciation of his major achievements and failures can be given here by reviewing the sources available to his biographers to determine if the data support the accusations made against Chia or if, on the contrary, the data would admit of a different interpretation.

Accusations against Chia Ssu-tao seem to fall into three major categories: (1) his general incompetence or, put another way, his complete dependence on his sister's position as a harem favorite for his rise to power; (2) his advocacy, and enforcement, of radical agrarian and economic policies; and (3) his treachery in negotiation with the Mongols as well as his culpability for a disastrous foreign policy. The incident repeatedly mentioned in the sources as indicative of his treachery concerns the withdrawal of the Mongol armies in 1259. Chia Ssu-tao is accused of having bought the withdrawal by promising tribute and the cession of all territory north of the Yangtze River and, further, of having confined the Mongol peace envoy Hao Ching in 1260 in an effort to keep his secret agreement from coming to light.

Other accusations relate to his alleged avarice, covetousness, cruelty, and debauchery, but as such references occur mostly in sources of an unofficial and even gossipy nature they will be dealt with separately.

Chia Ssu-tao came from a family of medium-grade military officials which does not seem to have had any close connections with influential persons. It is true that, like every other high-ranking official of his time, he had in his later years a clique of followers, but the significant fact remains that he did not enjoy the protection of elder statesmen or famous scholars.[9] His grandfather, Chia Wei, came from a T'ien-t'ai family and was for some time prefect of K'ai-chiang, Szechwan. He also held minor military offices.[10] Chia Wei's son, Chia She (d. 1223), is described in his biography as a man of good education, wide reading, and outstanding abilities, who served primarily in military positions and took part in the frontier defense against the Chin in the Shantung and Huai areas. He was instrumental in securing the cooperation of Li Ch'üan during the 1219 campaigns and was made commander in the newly conquered territories of Huai-tung province. At the same time he was appointed commander of the infantry and cavalry forces in the Ching-tung and Hopei areas. Chia She was apparently a man of uncompromising character; he once had the commanding officer in a town executed as a warning when the town was lost to the Jurchen. His military record was a very successful one, and his abilities were rewarded by posthumous ranks and titles.[11] In 1254 he was even awarded the posthumous designation of *Chung-su* (Loyal and Stern), certainly following action taken by his son Ssu-tao, who already held high office in 1254.[12]

Chia Ssu-tao was born August 25, 1213.[13] As a young man in Hang-chou, he frequented the gay quarters, gambled, and in general lived the life of a *jeunesse dorée*. His conduct was a disappointment to his mother, née Hu, as we know from an anecdote in a *pi-chi* work.[14] Chia would have been eighteen when his elder sister joined the imperial harem in 1231 with the title *Wen-an chün fu-jen*. Her status as a favorite was immediately apparent: within a month Emperor Li-tsung had promoted her to *Ts'ai-jen* (Talented Person)[15] and within a year to *Kuei-fei* (Precious Consort), the highest rank attainable by a concubine.[16] But any direct influence his sister may have possessed came to an end with her death in the second month of 1247. This date is important and must be taken into account in considering the historiographers' claim that Chia Ssu-tao owed his rise to prominence solely to the influence of his sister.[17] A look at Chia's official career[18] all but refutes the claim out of hand. In 1247 Chia Ssu-tao held high but by no means exceptional offices and his real rise to power took place in the 1250's. His appointment as Chancellor of the Empire (*Ch'eng-hsiang*) came in 1259, a full twelve years after his sister's death.

Chia was only one among a great number of male relatives of the harem, and any early favors from Emperor Li-tsung are more likely to be explained on the basis of a reported incident in 1236. The emperor had fallen ill during the hot season and a certain Wang Chih-tao, about whom nothing else is known, conspired to bring about the emperor's withdrawal by having him "pensioned" as *T'ai-shang huang* (Supreme Emperor). Chia, learning of the plot, informed his sister, who in turn warned the emperor.[19]

At the time of his appointment in 1259 as a leading minister of state, Chia had at least twenty years of experience in various metropolitan and provincial offices. The allegation by Western historians that he lacked even the ability to fill a minor post must be regarded as a gross misrepresentation of facts—unless we assume that it was possible for a Sung official to spend twenty years of his career in absolute incompetence. Although his first metropolitan appointment, in 1234, may have been due to his sister's influence, this was merely a ritual office—certainly nothing but a sinecure.

Left out of account are those early offices of his mentioned in his *lieh-chuan* without a date. This applies to the office of Executive Assistant of the Court of Imperial Sacrifices (*T'ai-ch'ang ch'eng*, grade 7a), apparently obtained after his sister had become Li-tsung's concubine, i.e., shortly after 1231. Before 1234 he must also, again according to his biography in the *Sung shih*, have held for some time the office of prefect of Li-chou (Hunan province). One thing is, in any case, certain: if we read of the same stations of career in somebody else's biography we would not hesitate to speak of a "long and distinguished official career." Chia's career was, moreover, continuous. Unlike many of his contemporaries, he was never out of office for any considerable period. In short, I think that the alleged incompetence of Chia is nothing but a myth, particularly because, to my knowledge, no substantiated accusations were raised against his official conduct during the first twenty years of his career.

One more observation on his rise to power and prominence: Chia spent a considerable part of his early career in financial positions connected with the state granaries, the imperial treasury, tax bureaus, and military colonies. His experience was, therefore, chiefly of the economic and, to a lesser degree, military kind. It is true that he is said to have passed his examination by fraud, but as orphan son of a distinguished military official he could claim the privilege of entering the official service on account of his father's undisputed merits. His activity and competence in financial and economic matters culminated in his later agrarian reforms.

Finally, one striking fact in Chia Ssu-tao's career must be mentioned. After he inaugurated the agrarian reform laws in 1261–64 he is extremely seldom mentioned in the Basic Annals of the *Sung shih*. He seems to have taken little part in the affairs of government, and it is only after 1273 that he became active again. This semi-retirement undoubtedly explains the *hao* he adopted in those years: *pan-hsien lao-jen* ("The Old Man Who Is Half Idle"). An unofficial source attributes Chia's lack of interest in these years to the generally favorable situation: rich harvests kept state income high; there was no widespread discontent in the Sung empire, and even the military situation was in some ways stabilized.[20] This short period of internal stability and comparative prosperity made Chia careless and arrogant and, our author suggests, led to a serious underrating of the increased threat to the Sung empire from the Mongol side after the fall of the city of Hsiang-yang in 1273.

The biography of Chia in the *Sung shih* repeatedly speaks of signs of imperial favor, obviously in order to indicate that such favors bestowed on Chia were excessive. But one glance into the Basic Annals will suffice to show that these honors and distinctions (such as exemption from court attendance during the morning audiences) were accorded to practically every minister of state. They were by no means exceptional in Chia's case. The same is true for Chia's repeated applications to withdraw from office, all of which were rejected by the emperor. It may be said that these moves were not meant sincerely, but we must not forget that the Chinese code of behavior demanded this in certain cases, for example, after the death of an emperor. It is perhaps unfair to blame Chia for something regarded as part of the normal ritual conduct of state servants. To sum up: a comparison of Chia's career with that of other high-ranking officials in Southern Sung times shows that there are very few if any uncommon characteristics peculiar to Chia and that his rise to the highest office was as slow and gradual as that of other statesmen in his day. Nor can it be conclusively proved that he was an incompetent official.

Before we attempt a closer investigation of Chia's military and foreign policy, particularly of his alleged treacherous negotiations with the Mongols in 1259 and the affair of Hao Ching in 1260, a few words should be said regarding his actions in domestic and court politics. The first time we hear of a political movement by Chia is the year 1238.[21] In the second month of that year he memorialized that action should be taken against corrupt sub-officials (*li*), his argument being that their removal from office would result in substantial improvement of state finances. Curiously enough, this passage in the Basic Annals concerns, again, financial matters.

It has been noted that Chia's family was not influential, belonging rather to what one could term the medium-grade military bureaucracy. It is no wonder that he had to try to establish his power by creating a clique of his own and by eliminating other ministers when he himself reached high office. During the first three years of his chancellorship (1260–62) numerous trials were held of members of the cliques of Wu Ch'ien and Ting Ta-ch'üan, both former chancellors. Ting Ta-ch'üan, who held the *chin-shih* degree, has been included in the category of *chien-ch'en* ("treacherous officials"); his biography in the *Sung shih* seems to show that he was indeed no great figure, and no actions allowing a favorable interpretation, as in Chia's case, are recorded. Wu Ch'ien, however, is regarded as a meritorious official and one of the innocent victims of Chia Ssu-tao, by whom he was ousted from his office, and even brought to his death in 1262.[22] Immediately after Chia's fall in 1275 Wu Ch'ien was posthumously reinstated to his former offices and even raised in rank.[23] It is perhaps significant that Chia's intrigues were directed at the same time against members of different factions. He may have had to fear opposition from both sides.

We need not go into the details of the repeated accusations against Chia as chancellor. In every case he succeeded in either eliminating his adversaries or having them transferred to minor provincial posts. In his choice of advisers and in his general personnel policy Chia seems to have favored persons who had previously held only lesser offices, such as prefect of an outlying district—a clever move because these were neither members of court cliques nor, given their complete dependence upon his benevolence, likely future organizers of cliques against him. Our sources agree in blaming Chia for not employing "able people" and for not letting them participate in important policy decisions. In this connection the names of Yeh Meng-t'ing, Ma T'ing-luan, and Chiang Wan-li are mentioned, all three of whom held ministerial posts concurrently with Chia Ssu-tao.[24] (One must not forget that during the fifteen years of his chancellorship Chia was never the only chancellor, so that any blame laid upon the Sung government as such during those years would more or less involve these "blameless" officials too.)

In short, Chia Ssu-tao does not seem to have followed a consistent policy in his conduct of internal affairs. The "small people" whom he favored apparently very seldom rose to really influential positions. Side by side with him there served scholar-officials in whose conduct not even the most orthodox Confucian historians could detect a flaw. Chia also maintained in some cases a friendly attitude toward his political opponents. Hsieh Fang-te, who was to enjoy the highest praise from historians as a Sung loyalist, received friendly overtures from Chia even during his banishment for his part in Chia's impeachment in 1264. Chia's shrewd attempt to win Hsieh to his side failed, however, and Hsieh stayed out of office until he was amnestied.[25]

Among Chia's moves in court politics there are a few that even the scholar-officials who wrote the historical sources grudgingly concede to have had some merit: he eliminated the influence of eunuchs, curbed the political ambitions of imperial clan members and of the empresses' families, and generally tried to keep protectionism at a minimum. He secured a decree forbidding imperial clan members to hold executive ranks.[26] This struggle against the currents, in particular against Tung Sung-ch'en, whom historians condemn for his frequent interference with the legal authorities, would have won unmitigated praise from Chinese historians were it not for the fact that it was Chia who took these steps.

Several very interesting administrative measures marked his early chancellorship. In 1260 he installed public letter boxes where people could place complaints or denunciations. The fact that this minor incident is recorded in an annalistic source shows that it was considered irregular.[27] To invite complaints from outsiders was incompatible with the theory that only the officials themselves, chiefly in the censorate, should draw the emperor's or ministries' attention to shortcomings in the state machinery. Obviously such a system could be used, if necessary, against enemies within the bureaucratic apparatus, for "complaints" could be fabricated easily. Shortly afterward Chia reformed the regulations for the seven bureaus of the Ministry of Officials (*li-pu ch'i-ssu*), which meant presumably a change in handling promotions and appointments.[28] A similar measure established conduct assessment lists which had to be submitted each year;[29] supervision and control by higher authorities were to be strengthened by this measure, which is perhaps identical with the creation of "population registers of scholars" (*shih-chi*), mentioned for 1270 by another source.[30]

Chia Ssu-tao's activity in foreign and military affairs has always been most strongly criticized, and he is even blamed for the final collapse of the Sung empire. I cannot say to what extent his choice of generals in the field or his purely military actions were to be commended, as practically no source contains details on what actually happened during the fighting. We learn about his treatment of generals and of dissensions on the general staff level, but even there the wording of the sources is laconic. The first time we hear about Chia's interest or activity in the field of foreign policy is in 1238, when he memorialized that if envoys from the north, i.e., the Mongols, came it would be better to set up formal rules—in modern language, arrange the details of diplomatic recognition.[31] In later years Chia is repeatedly mentioned in the Basic Annals but never in a way that would make his conduct of affairs appear exceptional. In 1254 he had the town of Tung-hai (Shantung) walled, in 1255 Kuang-ling. In the same year Chia is credited with the defeat of Li Sung-shou, son of Li Chüan, a member of a family that had for more than half a century held power in Shantung and, as circumstances dictated, transferred their loyalty from Sung to Chin to the Mongols.[32] When Tung-hai was lost to the Mongols in 1258, Chia forwarded a self-accusation to the throne and obtained pardon because of his former merits (he was permitted to buy himself free in lieu of actual punishment).[33]

His relations with the generals at the front ranged from warm and patient to suspicious and demanding. To his credit, Chia, whenever he memorialized a victory, generously praised those in command, even where personal or political antagonism existed. A good example is the case of Kao Ta, who bitterly resented an attempt Chia had once made to denounce him to the emperor. There are vivid descriptions of Kao's treatment of Chia in the field when Chia came to inspect troops. Kao would order his soldiers to shout abuses at Chia's quarters and would himself pass remarks such as, "What use is that man with the high hat? When there is a battle he must be given a reward beforehand or he will not move at all." Nevertheless in 1260 Chia recommended Kao Ta to the emperor for his brave defense of O-chou, and Kao received a gift of money as an imperial reward.[34] Chia's chief generals seem to have been Kao Ta, Lü Wen-te, Li T'ing-chih, Fan Wen-hu, and Hsia Kuei. Lü and Fan were criticized by a contemporary writer—Lü is described as an illiterate and rustic person, Fan as a whoremonger and drunkard.[35] Fan surrendered to the Mongols in 1275, whereas the others stayed loyal to the Sung.

On the other hand, Chia behaved rather ungratefully toward some distinguished military leaders. After the campaigns of 1259 he ordered a general audit and started an investigation of some commanders who were accused of wasteful expenditure of public money.[36] It is equally possible to interpret this as a move to eliminate military leaders whom he disliked or to regard this as evidence for Chia's fiscal probity, or both. The persons involved (not more than half a dozen are mentioned) lost their offices and had to pay back to the treasury the amounts spent without authorization—obviously ruinous to the families concerned. But much earlier, in 1250, Chia had memorialized the throne that the commanding officer in Chiang-ling had oppressed the population while building fortifications in that town.[37] Shall we say that Chia wished to damage the officer's reputation or that he was really opposed to misconduct by military leaders out of consideration for the civilian population? Again both interpretations or their combination are possible. In any case, such actions could not fail to foster dissension among military leaders and to increase their discontent with the civil authorities. No wonder then that after the fall of Hang-chou in 1276 Sung generals who had been made prisoner by the Mongols said to the victorious Qubilai, "Chia preferred the civil officials and hated the military"[38] —an excuse, however, that is common among defeated generals everywhere after a lost war. We might, if we give Chia the benefit of the doubt, describe him as a political figure who followed narrow financial and economic policies to the detriment of national defense, although, as we shall see later, he tried the most unorthodox methods to increase the state income for defense purposes.

The bitterest condemnation, however, is voiced against Chia's behavior regarding the general situation at the front. Western and Chinese historians alike maintain that he deliberately kept the emperor uninformed and "bathed himself in the limelight of fictitious heroic exploits."[39] Within the scope of this short study we cannot investigate one by one the cases where Chia (or the commanders at the front) announced successes when there were perhaps none. Exaggeration of successes is rather common in the military history of all nations, and the Mongols too, as we can see from the *Yüan shih*, sometimes claimed victories that were, to say the least, infinitesimal.

But in one case it can be shown that Sung historians writing after the fall of the Sung empire were guilty of gross exaggeration. According to these historians, in 1270 the emperor asked what had become of Hsiang-yang, then beleaguered for three years. Chia answered, "Who has told you that? The Northern armies have already withdrawn." He found out that an imperial concubine had told the emperor that Hsiang-yang was not yet free; he accused her, wrongly, and forced her to commit suicide. "After that nobody dared to speak to the emperor of the military situation."[40] This anecdote fits well into the general picture that the historians wished to give of Chia Ssu-tao. But for that same year, repeated rewards and gifts for the troops garrisoned in Hsiang-yang and elsewhere are recorded in the Basic Annals of the *Sung shih,* and an imperial decree rewarded with promotion and gifts of money several brave officers who had smuggled official letters into the besieged town of Hsiang-yang.[41] Even if we assume that a decree need not necessarily have issued from the emperor in person, it is simply not true—and, considering the amount of paper work in Chinese government, not even credible—that the court and the central government in Hang-chou could have been deliberately kept in "blindness and ignorance of the real situation" by Chia. The entries in the Basic Annals show that the court was well aware of the situation at Hsiang-yang.

Chia's dealings with the Mongols, in particular his actions in 1259 and later, have been denounced as foolish and treacherous. Chia is supposed to have concluded a secret agreement with the Mongols in 1259, promising the Yangtze frontier and annual tribute.[42] But when Qubilai, after his enthronement in 1260, sent Hao Ching as his envoy, Chia did not let this diplomatic official proceed to the Sung capital but kept him in confinement in Chen-chou. This he did, so all our sources say, in order to keep his agreement of 1259 from becoming known, which would have been detrimental to his claim of having won a military victory over the Mongols in that year. This action would obviously have been exceedingly dangerous to Chia because it meant an attempt to cheat both the Mongols and his own government. A closer investigation of the texts concerned shows, however, that no such treaty was ever concluded. Chia undoubtedly tried to enter into negotiations with the Mongols, offering cession of land and tribute. This is attested by Sung and Mongol sources alike. But even the *Yüan shih* nowhere mentions that this offer by Chia was ever *accepted.* Chia Ssu-tao sent as envoy his general Sung Ching asking for peace. Chao Pi, a Chinese officer of Qubilai, answered for the latter: "Your intentions may be good because you are in favor of peace for the sake of living beings. But I have received orders to fight in the south—how could I stop halfway? If you really have the intention to serve [as a smaller state serves] the big state, you should ask our court."[43] A more detailed account is given in Chao Pi's biography:

When Chao Pi besieged O-chou, Chia Ssu-tao of the Sung sent an envoy, who asked for safe conduct in order to make peace. Pi wanted to meet him but Qubilai said, "When you have mounted the city wall, you must carefully look out for my flag—if I move the flag you have to come back quickly." After Pi had mounted the wall, the Sung general Sung Ching said, "If the Northern [the Mongol] army withdraws, we shall make the Yangtze our frontier, and in addition pay annual tribute of 200,000 each of silver and textiles." Pi answered, "We received a similar proposal after our Great Army had reached

P'u-chou [Honan]; then we could perhaps have consented. But now, after we have already crossed the Yangtze, what use are these words? Where is Commander Chia standing now?" Pi happened to look out and noticed that Shih-tsu's [Qubilai's] flag moved, so he said, "We have to wait for a later day to negotiate," and returned.[44]

It is clear from these two accounts that Sung Ching offered negotiations, but that no offer was accepted by the Mongol leader. The withdrawal of the Mongol armies led by Qubilai was caused primarily by the necessity to take part in the assembly (*quriltai*) for the election of the new Grand Qan; Möngke Qan had died in August 1259. It was by no means prompted by the Sung peace offer, which seems, rather, to have been taken by the Yüan historians as an additional, secondary reason. The *Yüan shih*[45] records that Qubilai told his generals on the *hsin-wei* day of the eleventh month (December 17, 1259) that they had to withdraw from O-chou within six days. Sung Ching's mission is recorded *after* Qubilai's order. But also from a purely military point of view the siege of O-chou was by no means a military success for the Mongols. This is even admitted by the *Yüan shih*, which relates under October 5 that the Sung general Lü Wen-te with his reinforcements managed to enter O-chou at night so that "the defense became increasingly strong."[46] The stubborn resistance of O-chou and the obviously vital necessity for Qubilai to assert his claims at the forthcoming *quriltai* were sufficient reasons to give up for the moment the continuation of his campaign. It is unthinkable that Chia Ssu-tao and the other Sung leaders *did not know* this state of affairs, and it is perhaps possible to interpret Chia's peace offer not as a serious invitation to negotiate but as a sort of stratagem, possibly designed to gain time. This interpretation can be supported by a passage in Hao Ching's biography in the *Yüan shih*,[47] which summarizes the long discourse by which Hao persuaded the Mongol generals that the campaign against the Sung should be stopped and the emperor enabled to return quickly to take part in the *quriltai*. The text continues: "It happened that the Sung commander Chia Ssu-tao also sent an envoy in order to sow dissension [*chien-shih*], who asked for peace. Therefore our armies returned." The fact that no agreement was concluded invalidates also the allegation that Chia kept the Mongol envoy Hao Ching in confinement in order to keep this agreement from becoming known. It is fortunate that Yüan sources allow us to check this statement. When Hao Ching, then Han-lin reader, Ho Yüan, Han-lin redactor, and Liu Jen-chieh, a Ministry of Rites official, were appointed, on May 21, 1260, as envoys to the Sung (*kuo-hsin shih*),[48] they had been given a letter of Qubilai's addressed to the Sung emperor dated May 18. This letter has been preserved in an absolutely reliable source (but not in the *Yüan shih*).[49] It contains no word referring to any sort of agreement or treaty and does not even mention the word "tribute." Qubilai in his letter warned the Sung emperor of military actions and asked for proof of sincerity on the Sung side. In modern diplomatic language this document would be judged to indicate the desire to establish normal diplomatic relations, nothing more. It is true that there may be an indirect reference to the Yangtze River as a frontier, because the Sung emperor is regarded as "ruling over the territory between Annam and Canton province in the south, Shu and Pa in the west, the Yangtze in the north, and the sea in the east," but this may as well be a mere figure of speech. In other words, Qubilai asked for a diplomatic agreement, but did not refer to a previous one. Also the letter that the Mongol government addressed to the Sung government in June 1261, when it had become known that the Sung had held back Hao Ching and his embassy,[50] does not speak of the frontier problem, the alleged recognition of Mongol suzerainty (which is mentioned only in Chia Ssu-tao's *lieh-chuan* in the *Sung shih*, not in other contemporary sources), or tribute. Peking warns Hang-chou not to engage in military actions or the Mongol emperor would wage a full-scale war against the Sung empire.

The real reason for Hao Ching's confinement must, therefore, remain in the dark. Perhaps he was considered to be a valuable hostage who could be made use of in case of future negotiations.[51] Hao tried repeatedly to obtain permission to enter the Sung empire, but his letters to the court in Hang-chou were not answered. He wrote not only to Chia Ssu-tao, but also to the commanding officer of the Huai region, Li T'ing-chih. The latter answered, but in his letter doubted Hao Ching's good faith,[52] a suspicion certainly unwarranted as we know the contents of the letter from Qubilai that Hao was to present to the Sung emperor.

The policy adopted in the case of Hao Ching was surely mistaken. In 1259 and for some years thereafter it would have been possible for the Sung to have concluded an agreement with the Mongols that could have guaranteed peace for a certain time, similar to the agreements that had been concluded previously with the Liao and Chin. An interesting entry in the Basic Annals of the *Sung shih* illuminates the attitude of Chia Ssu-tao. In 1260 Emperor Li-tsung asked Chia what to do if the Mongols sent envoys. Chia answered that one had to be careful and that envoys should be admitted only if they came as good and peaceful neighbors.[53] Although it was perhaps known at the Sung court that Hao Ching had drawn up plans for a campaign against Sung prior to 1259,[54] it was certainly oversuspicious to deny the Mongol envoys access to the Sung empire and to frustrate their mission, which could have resulted in peaceful relations between the two powers, who were at that time sharing the rule over China. The diplomatic decisions taken by the Sung were perhaps mistaken, but there is nothing in the sequence of events to support the charges of treachery and deceit leveled against Chia Ssu-tao.

Chia Ssu-tao's economic policy has been condemned by Chinese historians almost as strongly as his foreign and military policy, a perhaps predictable result of the antagonism Chia drew from the ruling classes by his ruthlessness in fiscal matters. As financial commissioner in various provinces he seems to have done everything in his power to fill the public treasuries and granaries, even to collecting taxes overdue ten to twenty years.[55] In 1261 he advocated strong measures to prevent hoarding of grain by the rich.[56] His revolutionary "public field laws" displayed a singular disregard for established rights, as did the measure taken in 1274, shortly before his fall, to make the lands of Buddhist and Taoist monasteries taxable in order to meet military expenditures.[57] Other financial and fiscal decrees issued during his chancellorship must be regarded as normal (gifts of grain to the army or famine areas, remission of taxes in case of drought or floods). But his public field legislation is unique in the economic history of the Sung dynasty. We may be brief here because it has been studied recently in detail.[58]

The concentration of land in the hands of big landowners, who were usually also officials and therefore exempt from taxes and corvée duties, had for more than a century been a critical problem for the Southern Sung. But opposition by high-ranking officials to any change in their privileged status doomed to failure all attempts at reform. Chia Ssu-tao, intent on increasing state revenues and unimpressed by the traditional arguments, was the first to take effective measures toward a solution. In March 1263 a group of minor officials presented to the throne a plan to remedy the most glaring defects in the fiscal system. In order to maintain the huge Sung armies, the state authorities had resorted to a scheme called the "harmonious purchase of grain" (*ho-ti*), i.e., obligatory sales to the state. But as more and more grain was bought up by the public granaries, more and more paper money had to be issued, causing a corresponding decrease in the value of paper money. The proposed plan contained measures for abolishing the obligatory sales, securing the army supplies, diminishing the circulation of paper money, and stabilizing the general price level. A certain limit was to be set on the size of landed properties, gradated according to the rank held by the owner. One-third of the land exceeding the limit was to be bought up by the state and converted into public fields, the income from which

would meet the requirements of the army. At first this plan applied
only to landowning officials, but it was soon extended to cover private
landowners as well. The maximum area exempted from obligatory
cession was 500 *mou*. The purchase price was paid by the state not only
in money but also in rank patents and tax remission certificates. The
greater the amount of land offered for sale, the more attractive the
means of payment was made. A landowner who sold more than 5,000
mou was paid for his land in the following way: 50 percent in rank
patents, 20 percent in tax remission certificates, 5 percent in silver, and
25 percent in paper bills. The price for sales of land between 300 and
500 *mou* was paid entirely in paper money. A list giving the value of
various ranks was drawn up (wives of landowners could also obtain
court ranks). The tax remission certificates (*tu-tieh*, originally certificates of ordination for the clergy) also had their fixed price.

Quite naturally this plan met with fierce resistance from the big
landowners, and that meant, in effect, from the overwhelming majority
of officials. Chia Ssu-tao, however, who was at the height of his power
in those years, not only backed these reforms, but enforced them ruth-
lessly. The fiscal effect was by no means small. The revenues from the
state lands—which by the end of the dynasty amounted to about 20
percent of the arable land in Che-hsi province—were alone sufficient to
guarantee the food supply for the army (about six million hundred-
weight per annum).

The public field laws were effective for twelve years, from 1263 to
1275. When Chia was dismissed from his offices on March 26, 1275, the
very first action taken by his adversaries was to abolish the public field
system. Only four days after Chia's fall, his successor, Ch'en I-chung,
suggested handing the public fields back to their former owners—which
shows how keenly Chia's opponents had been waiting for an opportunity to abolish the agrarian laws. But the imminent military danger
from the approaching Mongol armies prevented the actual return of
the expropriated land to the former landlords. When the Mongols occupied the Che provinces a few months later, they found vast state
lands which they either gave as appanages to their own princes and
generals or used for their intended purpose, i.e., for provisioning their
own garrisons.

There can be no doubt that Chia's agrarian policy had a deep effect
on the last years of the Sung empire. Having become accustomed to
more or less open tax evasion, the gentry class and *ipso facto* the majority of government officials felt affronted by the new policy, and, with
their loyalty to the Sung weakened, they became more receptive to the
blandishments of the Mongols, surrendering in great numbers. This is

less surprising than it seems. No other statesman under the Sung, not even Wang An-shih, who has been termed in the West a state socialist, could match Chia's achievement in daring to expropriate in order to increase the state revenues. A contemporary critic of the public field laws even said that the purpose of these laws had been "to subdue the mighty and to impoverish the rich."[59] And the writer Chou Mi wrote openly after the fall of the dynasty: "When in our days the Sung seized the land of the people they lost the affection of the people."[60] "People," *min*, in this context can only mean "the landlords," of course. The "toiling masses" were neither better nor worse off when exploitation by the landlords was replaced by exploitation by the state. Chia's reforms resulted in what one might term bureaucratic agrarian capitalism, but also in his defamation by the class whose interests he had damaged. He alone had had the energy to put into effect what had been asked for in dozens of memorials during the Southern Sung dynasty: limitation of land ownership. An interesting question in historiography is whether the Communist Chinese historians will one day praise Chia as a sort of precursor of state socialism or will continue to condemn him for his failures in foreign and military affairs.[61]

So much for the concrete allegations made against Chia by the official historians. There remain the more personal attacks upon his reputation which are to be found in early Yüan and Ming sources. These, mostly written after his disgrace and the fall of the Sung empire, must of course be used with great caution, but they do throw light upon the popular picture of him which grew up side by side with the historians' picture of an incompetent and dishonest minister.

Many anecdotes concern prophecies of his career. It appears that Chia himself did not from the beginning regard himself as a successful state servant or even a careerist. In his young gay days he once met a Taoist who predicted an excellent career and said that Chia would later become a minister of state. Chia was very much surprised, believing that the Taoist had made fun of him, and continued to amuse himself in the brothel quarters of Hang-chou. At a subsequent meeting the Taoist declared that Chia had ruined his fate and that he would come to a bad end.[62] This anecdote is typical of a great number of stories with a prophecy of his fame and eventual disgrace. These stories are all, however, clearly of later origin. A more sober appraisal is again given by Chou Mi when he judges Chia as able and competent but vain and eager to win power. His crimes were, according to Chou, that he had learned nothing (which cannot be quite true, considering his long official career) yet reached high rank, and that he tried to do everything alone (which may be true) and discouraged free discussion (which again is exaggerated; witness the many memorials criticizing his public field laws which he had to counter somehow).[63]

There must have been countless epigrams and songs criticizing Chia when he was still in office. Not a few of them have been preserved, mostly in works that were written during the first decades of the Yüan dynasty.[64] Some of them were popular, because the sedan chair bearers who transported Chia to his banishment in the south in 1275 sang such Hang-chou songs on the instigation of Cheng Hu-ch'en, the commander of his guard.[65] It was Cheng who later killed Chia near Chang-chou (Fukien). Chia's death is the subject of a late Ming short story in the vernacular, "The Revenge of Cheng Hu-ch'en in the Mu-mien Temple."[66] But there also were earlier stories which gave more or less romantic versions of his last months.[67] In Ming and Ch'ing times Chia Ssu-tao became the prototype of a "bad minister." He figures as inmate of the deepest hell in an early Ming story, along with Ch'in Kuei, Han T'o-chou, and Ting Ta-ch'üan,[68] and in a Ch'ing story he appears as a bad incarnation in a Buddhist context.[69] His ghost turns up at a literary ghost party in K'ang-hsi's days, contributes a poem which however is not his own, and is finally changed into a tiger.[70]

From references to his personal conduct there emerges the picture of a man known for his drinking, gambling, and, according to his *lieh-chuan*, sexual depravity. Chia is said to have taken into his harem court ladies, singing girls, and even Buddhist nuns provided they were pretty. An early Ming story also depicts him as cruel and jealous.[71] But Chia was wealthy—the memory of the splendor of his parks and villas on the Ko-ling hills lingered for centuries—and the question is whether his conduct differed much from that of the average rich man in thirteenth-century Hang-chou.

Chia certainly had other than sensual pleasures. He was, for instance, a keen connoisseur and collector of antiques.[72] His closest friend and confidant was Liao Ying-chung, a scholar of high reputation whose surviving works include commentaries on Han Yü's and Liu Tsung-yüan's works[73] as well as a collection of T'ang and Sung anecdotes.[74] Liao is best known, however, for his editorial activities, and his prints were considered flawless. As friend and chief literary and artistic adviser, Liao assisted Chia in his manifold literary enterprises, such as the preparation of critical editions of the classics and other texts (*Chan-kuo ts'e, Wen-hsüan,* Poems of Su Tung-p'o).[75] It was probably at Liao's suggestion that Chia, who owned a copy of the *Lan-t'ing hsü* written by Wang Hsi-chih, had this most famous example of Chinese calligraphy reproduced in facsimile and had reprinted in small editions the autographs in his collection of Sung authors like Chiang K'uei and Jen Hsi-i.[76] Liao, whose eulogy on Chia's successes at the Yangtze front in 1260 brought him the label of sycophant,[77] remained faithful to his friend even after his fall from power, finally committing suicide in order to avoid disgrace.[78]

An interesting sidelight on Chia's life is his fascination with cricket fighting, which resulted in his treatise *Ts'u-chih ching*, a systematic handbook on the raising and training of cricket champions.[79] Less informative is another work, of which we have only a fragmentary version, the *Yüeh-sheng sui-ch'ao* ("Random Excerpts of the Hall Where One Enjoys Life"). This studio name of Chia's is significant, just as the pseudonym with which he signs the preface: "Old Man Who Is Half Idle."[80] The surviving fragments contain gleanings from earlier works, mostly anecdotes of the Five Dynasties and the Sung period.

Whereas the *Ts'u-chih ching* reflects a hobby for which he had become famous, no inferences can be made from the other work because it shows no personal bias in its selection of texts. The anecdotes are partly humorous, partly moral, partly antiquarian. The long dissertation on parks and their beauties included in the work may, but does not necessarily, reflect Chia's particular interests. We also know of a poem by Chia which he composed for the Cold Meal Feast of 1275. It runs:

> For the Cold Meal Feast willow branches are put up in every house,
> One would like to retain the spring but they last not many hours.
> As long as a man is alive and has wine, he should get drunk.
> How many sons or grandsons will weep at his green grave?[81]

The *carpe diem* mentality of these verses is not incompatible with what we know of Chia's personality.

To summarize, it was perhaps Chia Ssu-tao's ill luck to have lived so late and so long. Had he died around 1265 there would have been every chance that historians would have ranked him with other agrarian reformers like Wang An-shih. But he continued in office until the Sung dynasty began to collapse. The fall of the dynasty made him a "last minister" (although he was not actually the last one), and the unpopularity of his agrarian legislation among the scholar-official and landlord class led to an overemphasis in the Chinese sources on the less successful sides of his career and the unengaging sides of his character. He was, from a Confucian point of view, a highly unorthodox person. Apparently he did not care for Neo-Confucian philosophy or for abstract discussions.[82] He was a pragmatist, preoccupied with fiscal policy, energetic,[83] at times ruthless, overconfident of his own abilities, and at the same time a man who enjoyed life and had a refined taste. The nearest comparison I can find is some politicians of the Italian Renaissance with their ruthlessness verging on amorality, their sensuality, their unscrupulousness in politics, and their artistic connoisseurship.[84] This is, however, perhaps already too much generalization, for we have seen some of the difficulties in reconstructing a man's life and character from sources that are incomplete, laconic, and often tendentious.

Frederick W. Mote

A FOURTEENTH-CENTURY POET:
KAO CH'I

The poetry of Kao Ch'i, like the best and most characteristic poetry of traditional China, tended to be lyrical and reflective,
brief, richly allusive, archaistic in form and mood. His poems represented art of a highly stylized kind, and yet achieved an extremely intense, highly personal character, being at once a typical expression of
his cultural tradition and the unique achievement of a gifted individual.

A great quantity of Kao Ch'i's poetry survives[1]—by no means all that
he wrote or even all that he chose to save, but more than we might expect from a man whose works were not published until a generation
after his death and whose name was under a cloud. Kao Ch'i was executed by the state on suspicion of sedition, for a technical impropriety
that seemed to have treacherous implications, and in the political and
social world of Ming China such a death jeopardized the preservation
of a man's name and works. But Kao Ch'i's poetry had been greatly
admired even during his own lifetime, and in China the poetry of a
recognized master of the art was perhaps a more enduring monument
to the individual than any other. So, luckily, we still have many hundreds of his poems and a few dozen essays, which together with the
writings of his contemporaries can be made to yield a remarkable image
of Kao Ch'i, both as a poet and as a historical figure.

The reconstruction of his life in the almost complete absence of the
usual kind of biographical materials serves to illustrate a problem in
biography, a method in the study of Chinese history. But beyond that,
Kao Ch'i's life is intrinsically very interesting, particularly in regard
to his role as a sensitive and intelligent participant in historical events
of great importance to our understanding of early modern Chinese history, more specifically in the recovery of Chinese cultural forms after
the destructive Mongol invasion and rule and the establishment of the
native Ming dynasty which succeeded the alien Mongols. Kao Ch'i was
on the scene at one of the most critical points in Chinese history; this
makes his life and his poetry valuable to the historian.

A further aspect is that Kao Ch'i, like most Chinese poets, was in his own eyes and those of his contemporaries only secondarily a poet. In this subjective view, Kao Ch'i is the accomplished scholar and expectant statesman, seeking and in some measure finding an active career of participation in the great events of his time, in the role of the man of affairs. That we know him today as a poet, and know about him almost exclusively through the direct study of his poetry, is a fact that should convey to us the frustration of his life, not the fulfillment of it. Here again the consideration of Kao Ch'i's life reveals something of the nature of the civilization in which he lived.

Implicit in all the foregoing are warnings against easy analogies with the lives of poets in our own cultural tradition. The similarities, and especially dissimilarities, are instructive. Perhaps when the artistic achievement is totally abstracted from all elements of the environment and the tradition, some analogies between the Chinese poet and the Western poet can be established. But the more we relate artistic achievements to their cultural and social milieu and analyze the poets' lives socially and functionally, subjectively (from the point of view of their own culture) and historically, the less meaningful become the superficial parallels between the poet there and the poet here.

One further point should be mentioned. The poet's art is surely one of the most difficult for the scholar to deal with, for poetry cannot be subjected to disassembling, translation, or partial citation *and remain poetry*. A poem can be re-created in another tongue or for another age by another poet, but it cannot be directly translated as poetry. The translated poem (as opposed to the rare poetic re-creation of a poem) is a much paler shadow of the original work of art than is the black-and-white photograph of a painting or the piano transcription of a symphony. This is true when French or German or even early English poetry is translated into modern English; it is far more strikingly apparent when the poetic art of a distant and unrelated civilization like the Chinese is translated into English. Yet the historian using poetry as a source for history has to translate it (selecting one of its multiple levels of meaning, usually the most literal one), disassemble it, and make use of the resultant bits and pieces. Kao Ch'i's poems are under consideration here as documents for the historian. His greatness as a poet must be appreciated directly from reading of the originals, or taken on faith. In this respect Chinese poetry is no different from that of any other civilization.

With this as introduction, let us look first at the bare outlines of his biography, as history has preserved it.

Kao Ch'i's biography is included in the official *Ming History* (*Ming shih*, ch. 285) in its section of biographies of men of letters. An almost identical biography appears in an analogous place in the *Draft Ming History* (*Ming shih kao*) and in the *Ming shu,* and in the other historical compilations dealing with the whole dynasty. In all cases, he is ranked with the poets and writers, and his life is briefly recounted, in about one page—no more than two hundred characters in the *Ming History,* for example. These accounts say that he displayed poetic genius as a youth and attracted the attention of members of the rebel government of Chang Shih-ch'eng, which controlled (1356–67) the Soochow area in which Kao lived, but that he refused to have anything to do with the rebel regime, and withdrew to a place called the Green Hill (*Ch'ing-ch'iu*) to write poetry. Subsequently he was called to the capital at Nanking to serve on the *Yüan History* commission in the second year (1369) of the new Ming dynasty, then (1370) was offered and declined high office at the Ming court, and finally returned to Soochow to live in retirement. There he became involved in the affairs of the prefectural governor Wei Kuan and was executed with him in the seventh year of the dynasty (1374) on charges of sedition. Elsewhere we learn that the charges against the governor were posthumously withdrawn, so by implication Kao Ch'i's name also was cleared. In any event, his seditious deed was the composition of a poem (perhaps also an essay) congratulating the governor on an apparently harmless official act—an act regarded by the emperor's spies as treacherous. None of this is discussed in Kao Ch'i's biographies. There it simply states that he was executed in 1374 at the age of 39 *sui*; it closes in conventional fashion by listing the titles of his poetry and prose collections, all published posthumously.

This is the Kao Ch'i of history. His is a life obviously marked by the workings of bad fortune. When we fill in the background from our general knowledge of Chinese history, we note first of all that Kao Ch'i had the bad luck to have been born in 1336, in the disorderly period of the late Yüan. At that time, the usual careers for bright young men were out of the question, so certainly he experienced the sense of frustration characteristic of his age. Also we note that he lived in the richest and most fortunate region of China at that time, the lower Yangtze delta, in the great city of Soochow. But this was a mixed blessing. We can readily understand the unfortunate circumstance of his having lived in the region controlled by Chang Shih-ch'eng, the hated rival of the Ming founder. This complicated the lives of many persons in the early Ming period, for many of the talented and educated men of the mid-fourteenth century were concentrated in the region held by Chang Shih-ch'eng, and most of these men suffered something from having been associated, at least superficially, with an unsuccessful claimant for the Mandate of Heaven at a moment of political transition. And we can further sympathize with Kao Ch'i's difficulties as a literary figure at the court of that unpredictable tyrant, the Ming founder. That he should choose to return to Soochow and lead the obscure poet's life, as his biographies suggest, rather than to endure the constant threat that hung over the heads of all the emperor's officials, particularly his high civil officials at court, is readily understandable. Then the tragic end of the poet's life caps a career through which bad luck had run like a thread. He had declined high office, fame, and fortune, because, as we can easily guess, the court atmosphere of the early Ming repelled him. However, he still fell victim to the tyrant emperor, his poetry and his literary life being again the things that involved him in the political world and that brought about his death. This link between the literary and the political spheres, quite usual in Chinese history, is evident throughout his life—from his youthful efforts to escape involvement in the rebel regime of Chang Shih-ch'eng, to his invitation to serve on the *Yüan History* commission, to his rejection of a career at the Ming court, and finally, inexorably if unexpectedly, to his curious death as the consequence of an act that any literary figure might have performed a hundred times—the composition of a congratulatory piece of purely formal and perfunctory character. But the history of the Ming founder's reign is all too full of references to the sudden deaths of hapless literary figures who ran afoul of their suspicious emperor.

Thus the facts given in the brief historical account about Kao Ch'i, taken together with the background any person slightly familiar with the history of the age would immediately supply, combine to make a coherent whole. The story fits our general impressions of fourteenth-century history. The historian concerned with this period might well go no further, feeling that he had looked intelligently at the biography of Kao Ch'i and had fitted it meaningfully into history.

But it is possible to go beyond the vague shadow cast by the historical figure of Kao Ch'i to apprehend much more of his life. Something like a full biography can be reconstructed,[2] and from it one comes to comprehend much more of the history of his age. As an exercise in biography it demonstrates something about the link between history and literature; as an exercise in historiography it provides valuable information about the events of an epoch and about the workings of a civilization. And it brings us into an encounter with a great poet, a personality which rewards our effort to understand it. A fuller life of Kao Ch'i, so recovered from informal historical materials, contemporary records, belletristic writings of his circle of associates, and, above all, from the man's own poetry, has been made the subject of a book by the present writer.[3] Without attempting to duplicate the effort toward which that book is directed, I shall discuss here some aspects of Kao Ch'i's life that seem to be most relevant to the concern with Confucian lives to which the present volume is devoted.

Why did Kao Ch'i become a poet? To say that he became a poet for the same reason that Keats became a poet—or Shakespeare a dramatist, Rembrandt a painter, Mozart a musician—is to limit our observation to recognition of the universal need of artistic genius to find expression. It is to disregard the special cultural, economic, social, and political influences on an artist in Kao Ch'i's day, a complex without an easy analogue elsewhere. Artistic self-expression, the goal of the talented few in the West, was for the educated Chinese a cultural and political requisite, an integral part of the cultivated life. This was particularly true in regard to the ability to think in poetic terms and to create poetry. But, having demonstrated a degree of skill or even genius in poetry, the Chinese was under far less cultural, social, or psychological influence than his counterpart in the West to pursue the life of a poet or man of letters as an end in itself. The rewards for literary success were by no means insignificant, enduring fame being as certain for the poet of genius as for the military or political hero, but the gifted individual in China did not, characteristically, see his own role as primarily that of poet or artist. True, Kao Ch'i is only one of many great literary figures historians would have difficulty classifying under any other heading, but failure to achieve any other claim to fame was interpreted as a personal failure, in their own eyes as well as in the view of their civilization. Particularly from T'ang times onward, with the expanded reliance upon and regularization of the examination system as the means of recruiting men of talent for careers in the civil service, the life of public service was that which beckoned talent, giving the individual his opportunity to achieve greatness and win enduring fame, while also providing the greatest material rewards and the greatest returns in prestige and public acclaim. A man's responsibilities to family and society, responsibilities his cultural background made all-important to him, could best be met by public service. There were no competing avenues to success, or other equally attractive ways of life (except for the eccentric). There was no career in the church, no birthright of aristocratic privilege with its fixed pattern of activities and duties, no materially rewarding life in high finance or large-scale business enterprise. There was no knighthood, and even the military career was a subsidiary avenue of the civilian public service. The ambitious and talented had only one way to exercise their talent and to secure for themselves and their families the good things of their civilization.

Artists in the graphic arts, in sculpture, in music, in architecture—all were mere craftsmen, competing with cultivated men (that is, civil servants actual or potential) who perfected themselves in the arts as an avocation. Among cultivated men, calligraphy carried the greatest prestige, with painting second. All of the calligraphers and, from the Sung period (tenth to thirteenth centuries) onward, most of the great painters were men who regarded their artistic activities as secondary to their roles as educated men, eligible for and anxious to pursue careers in the public world.

Kao Ch'i, the poet, was no exception. Poetry was even more obviously an activity that combined naturally with, while remaining subsidiary to, the public life. The Chinese language has in traditional China lent itself so perfectly to poetic expression that a man of the fourteenth century was the heir to an incredibly rich heritage, one that had developed in an unbroken continuum for over two thousand years. Discussions of this could take us into questions about the nature of language and poetry that go beyond the scope of this essay. Here it suffices to note that from very early times the importance granted to poetry demanded that men of education be capable of creating (or producing) it, and brought great rewards of fame and advancement to those most gifted in the art. Government service traditionally demanded evidence of skill in literary expression as the primary test for entrance, and in many periods the formal examination in poetry was part of the test. The interest in poetry never slackened, and the intimacy of its connection with human greatness was never questioned.

All of the foregoing is a commonplace of Chinese history, yet it warrants reiteration here, for only by considering these things can we understand the life of Kao Ch'i. He was a great poet—perhaps the most gifted poet of his time, though his life was cut short before his art had fully matured. He won wide recognition in his own time for his achievement and for his promise. Yet poetry was not the chief concern of his life; ideally it was an activity which was to accompany the larger life.

But for us it is both the mirror in which his life and times are reflected and the thread of continuity running through all of the pieces of his biography that we succeed in establishing. Hence several meanings are intended when we speak of Kao Ch'i's "life in poetry."

Kao Ch'i claimed descent from the martial Kao clan which had ruled North China under the Northern Ch'i dynasty (550–77). Such lineage, virtually meaningless in any material or social way in imperial Chinese society, had nonetheless its own importance to Kao Ch'i, who made several direct references to it in his poetry, and who sometimes signed his essays "Kao Ch'i of Po-hai" (Po-hai being the place from which the Northern Ch'i founder had come). We know that Kao Ch'i's family had emigrated, coming south at the end of the Northern Sung dynasty (1126) when the North was overrun by invaders. Again, it is from references in his poetry that we know that the family had lived in the Northern Sung capital (modern K'ai-feng) until the early twelfth century, but that Kao Ch'i's first knowledge of the continued existence of relatives there came from a chance encounter with a member of the K'ai-feng branch of the clan. Thus the Kao family into which he was born was, like many families of the Yangtze basin, a displaced Northern family of proud traditions that had found roots in the South,[4] and had come to regard that region as home.

The family is said to have been well-to-do but not prominent; no member of the clan since the Northern Ch'i emperors seems to have merited a biography in any dynastic history. But they owned land near Soochow, and presumably had produced members of the lower officialdom. In the two or three generations immediately before Kao Ch'i they appear to have been cultured people of substance in their community. That Kao Ch'i received the best education—where or under whom we do not know—is evident in the fact that by his late teens he had mastered the Classical learning, was widely read in literature, and had already earned a reputation as a poet.

From his poems—some dated, some with brief prefaces explaining their origin, some roughly datable from less direct evidence—we can follow the growing circle of his acquaintances and discover something of his interests, his family circumstances, and his activities. We also learn that he was marked out as a great talent, a youthful genius who might flower into a great poet. The family was not as well-to-do as it had been in his grandfather's time, but his own growing reputation as a poet could make up for that. For example, he had been affianced to the daughter of a wealthy neighbor family, presumably when still a child. Subsequently orphaned, without close family except an older brother away from home, he could not afford to carry out the wedding preparations. But a poem written at the request of his future father-in-law served to make up for the awkwardness caused by lack of wealth matching that of his bride's family. It made possible the wedding, and made acceptable the socially unconventional manner of its arrangement. His father-in-law was happy to have such a talented son-in-law; his excellent relations with his wife's father and brothers all turned on their common interest in and high evaluation of poetry.

It was at this time that Soochow was captured by the rebel Chang Shih-ch'eng. Chang was as typical of Chinese civilization, in his way, as was Kao Ch'i. A man of bold action, a rebel leader in a time of trouble, he came from the lower strata of society and owed his position entirely to his unlettered capacity for daring action and his ability to command desperate men. As his ambitions grew, the only patterns for greatness in his world, beyond banditry, were those drawn from the great tradition; thus his future depended on his ability to draw men of Kao Ch'i's kind into collaboration with him. In these years when Soochow was his base and his "capital," we see him falling naturally into the only formula for political leadership that the Chinese mind knew. He controlled an area the size of a province, and he arrogated to himself the title "Prince of Wu," Wu being an old designation for Soochow and for the larger area of southern Kiangsu and northern Chekiang. He set up a court and a government on imperial lines, proclaimed a calendar, established his officialdom. To become an emperor, which clearly was his ambition, as it was also the ambition of a dozen rivals in this period of transition, he had to cease being a ruffian and mere gangleader. He had to honor the civil virtues, foreign though they were to his nature. He had to call upon civilian administrators to staff his government and to acquire the character and demeanor of a refined sponsor of literature and learning. Thus Chang became a patron of the arts, and prominent literary figures were all pressed to serve his regime.

This brought Kao Ch'i face to face with a difficult decision. As a young man of twenty-one, a recognized talent among the younger poets and men of promise in the region, he was put under pressure to associate himself with Chang's regime. Should he do so? It was not a decision to be made lightly. According to Confucian morality, Chang was a bandit defying the legitimate bearers of the Mandate of Heaven. That these were the hated Mongols, who no longer had the military power to maintain firm grasp on their imperial position, only complicated the moral and political issues. If Chang were to win out and become the founder of a new dynasty, now was the time to ally oneself with the new bearer of the Mandate. But if he were to prove to be merely an unsuccessful rebel contender, one's future might well be ruined by association with him. What should the young Kao do? A less prominent literary talent could have evaded the issue more easily.

Kao Ch'i adopted a course devised to free himself from involvement for a time and thus defer judgment on Chang's chances. It was a response determined by his life in poetry: he moved away from Soochow, away from the closely knit life of the metropolis, to a place about thirty miles from the city, called the Green Hill, near his father-in-law's estate and his own family property. In becoming a "rustic" in the classical, formalized manner, he declared that only the writing of poetry could interest him and that he had come to scorn all mundane ambitions.

As poetry had provided his justification for withdrawal at a moment of crisis and indecision, so it was in a poem that he announced to the

world his new role. To maintain dignity and honor in the role of
"rustic" demanded a certain flamboyant brilliance; Kao Ch'i's poem
"Song of the Man of the Green Hill," written in 1358, enhanced his reputation, and the name "Green Hill" (*Ch'ing-ch'iu*) became his literary
cognomen, fixed for all time. Though impressive enough to gain for
him the right to indulge in such eccentric behavior, the poem appears
to us today to be evidence more of promise than of greatness, for it
still indulged in immature display. Moreover, in all likelihood it derived much of its meaning from allusions to contemporary affairs, allusions that are no longer comprehensible. Thus in reading it today one
is forced to take it rather literally, whereas other levels of meaning
probably made it more interesting to Kao's contemporaries. But it
still is valuable for its evidence of the young poet's spirit, his conception
of himself as poet, and his lively imagination. He himself supplied the
introductory preface, in which he shifts from the first to the third person, in setting the mood for his fanciful poem about himself.

THE SONG OF THE MAN OF THE GREEN HILL

AUTHOR'S PREFACE: *By the Yangtze's edge there is the Green Hill. I've moved
my home to the south of it, and so have adopted the cognomen "the man of
Ch'ing-ch'iu." This man lives there in idleness, with nothing to do. All day
long he works earnestly at writing poems, and while there he happened to
write this "Song of the Man of Ch'ing-ch'iu" in which he speaks his mind, in
the hope of dispelling the ridicule he has suffered for his addiction to poetry.*

The man of Ch'ing-ch'iu, he is thin and unsullied—
Originally he was a genie-courtier at the Pavilion of Five-colored Clouds.
What year was he banished to this lower world?
He tells no one his real name.
He wears rope sandals, but he has wearied of distant roaming.
He shoulders a hoe, but he is too lazy to till his own fields.
He has a sword, but he lets it gather rust.
He has books, but he leaves them piled in disorder.
He is unwilling to bend his back for five catties of rice.
He is unwilling to loosen his tongue to bring about the fall of seventy cities.
But he is addicted to the search for poetic lines.
He hums them to himself, he sings them for his own pleasure.
He wanders through the fields, dragging his cane, wearing a rope-belt.
Bystanders, not understanding him, laugh and ridicule,
Calling him a "muddleheaded scholar of Lu," a veritable "madman of Ch'u."
The man of Ch'ing-ch'iu hears it but cares not at all—
Still the sound of poetry-chanting comes in unbroken gurgle from his lips.
He chants poetry in the morning till he forgets to eat;
He chants poetry in the evening till he has dispersed all ill-feelings.
When intent on his poetizing
He groans like a man sick from too much drinking;
He finds no time to comb his hair,
And has no time to attend to family affairs.

His children cry, and he knows not to pity them.
Guests call, and he shows them no hospitality.
He is not concerned that shortly he will be destitute;
He envies not at all the way Mr. Yi prospered.
It grieves him not that he wears rough uncut homespun;
He longs not at all for the colored tassels of an official's hat.
He pays no attention to the bitterly fought duel of dragon and tiger,
Nor gives he notice to the frightened scurryings of the golden crow and the
    jade rabbit.
Instead, he sits alone, facing the shore.
He walks alone, in the grove.
He sharpens his native powers, he conserves his native energies.
None of creation's myriad creatures can conceal their nature from him.
Through the vast, misty realm of the eight farthest limits he wanders in his
    imagination.
Sitting there, he makes the formless become real.
He has acquired the sensitivity of the one who could shoot an arrow through
    a suspended flea,
The strength of one who could behead a great whale.
He becomes pure as one who drinks the nourishing dew,
Lofty as the ranks of soaring crags and cliffs.
Towering above, the bright clouds open to him.
Luxuriantly the frozen plants again grow.
He ascends to clutch at the roots of Heaven, seeking out the caves of the
    moon.
With rhinoceros horn magic lens he scans the Oxen Ford, seeing the myriad
    wonders in its depths—
Wonderful, suddenly, to be in the company of gods and spirits,
Grand spectacle, vaster than the expanse of rivers and mountains.
The stars and the rainbows lend him their radiance;
The mists and the dews nourish his heroic spirit.
The sounds he hears are divine harmonies,
The tastes, the flavors of the unearthly broth.
"In this world below there is no object which delights me;
Even instruments of bronze and jade emit harsh clanking sounds.
In my thatched hut, by the river's edge, the storm clears;
Behind my barred gate, now I've slept out my sleep, and I've just finished a
    poem.
So I strum the wine pot and sing a joyous song,
Giving no thought to startled mundane ears.
I want to call to the old man of Mount Chün, to bring out the long flute of
    magic powers
And accompany this song of mine, under the bright moon.
But then I think sadly how the waves would suddenly rise,
Birds and beasts would shriek in fright, the very hills shake and crumble.
The Lord of Heaven would hear it and be angered,
Would send a white heron to fetch me back.
He would let me go on no longer with these tricks of this world;
I would don again my jeweled waist pendants, and go back to the City of
    Jade."[5]

Kao Ch'i wrote this poem in the form of a song, with long and short lines, a strong rhythm, and a recurring rhyme on the syllable *ing* in alternate lines. His many classical and literary allusions defy adequate explanation in Western equivalents, but the Western reader can readily discern Kao Ch'i's attitude toward the surrounding world of day-to-day affairs and can sense the scope of the poetic imagination that lifted Kao Ch'i from that world into a vast and unlimited realm of excitement and delight.

And yet, we also see a reluctance to forgo the day-to-day world, though he claims to scorn the things it can offer him. He will not "bend his waist" for the sake of the trifling emolument of office (ever, or just in times like these?); he will not use his superior talents of mind and of skillful speech "to bring about the fall of seventy cities" (in the service of any ruler, or merely those on the scene at this time?). But he does implicitly affirm his confidence in his own powers and abilities by the comparisons these allusions bring to himself—that is, he *could* do so, but he scorns to do so. He ignores the "duel of dragon and tiger," meaning the struggle for the mastery of the world, in which Chang Shih-ch'eng and his chief rival, Chu Yüang-chang, and the Yüan court were embroiled. He gives no notice to the "scurryings of the golden crow and the jade rabbit," which mean the sun and the moon—that is, the passage of time—but which in this context might also have been intended to refer to the scurryings of the lesser animals, the hangers-on at the courts of the powerful. He states that he will withdraw from the ways of the world and refine his senses, improve his powers, and conserve his strength. This is all stated in traditional metaphor, mostly Taoist in flavor, and with exuberant imaginative force, but it also clearly could refer to his decision to withdraw from the contemporary struggle merely until the air had cleared and the future was more certain. In the meantime, he proclaims, the poet's life brings him the only rewards he desires, and it is a life of freedom and of independence from the world about him. People may ridicule him for eccentricity, but he doesn't care; he will not be moved by such ridicule to abandon these ideals.

Kao Ch'i could, as this poem declares, occupy himself completely with poetry when circumstances demanded, but those who knew him best knew that this implied no surrender of the larger ideal. His exuberant youthful poetry, however much it denied other ambitions, in reality displayed a great spirit and a vast talent only temporarily deflected from the larger course of action. Kao Ch'i's other poetry from this period frequently testifies to his interest in the world, to his envy and admiration of friends who were able to follow more active careers, and yet satisfaction in the rewards that poetry brought during the period of withdrawal and waiting.

Again it is only in his poetry that we find evidence bearing on important events of his life in the years immediately thereafter. At this juncture, the evidence is not as full as we would like, for the poems in question exist only in the form in which Kao Ch'i thought it safe to preserve them when, six or seven years later, he edited and somewhat rewrote them. Kao Ch'i lived in an age when the expression of certain sympathies or the admission of having been involved in certain kinds of activity was regarded as evidence of hostility toward the new Ming dynasty, and of potential threat to it. In the first year of the dynasty he edited his poetry, and the assumption is that he removed whatever might have been incriminating. After he was executed, in consequence of allegations of that kind, his heirs and editors tried further to rehabilitate him, and shield themselves, by again removing questionable poems and lines. This editing is in itself revealing, but it also of course often succeeds in concealing specific information. In the case of Kao Ch'i's poems about his travels in the years 1358–60 it very evidently has succeeded in removing information that might help us understand his actions in these years. But from the fact that they have been edited (Kao Ch'i tells us in his preface that he has edited them, but supplies a conventional reason for having done so) we probably are safe in assuming that something about these two years of travel would have incriminated him in the eyes of the new Ming government. Hence we know that he was not just idly sightseeing as he traveled through southern Kiangsu and northern Chekiang in these years. The route of his travels and his thoughts as a traveler can be reconstructed in rough outline from the poems he wrote as he journeyed. There is a fascinating set of travel poems which, when read in light of the history of the region in that period, reveal much to us. We can conclude that Kao Ch'i left the Green Hill, his wife and family, and the embarrassing presence of Chang Shih-ch'eng's rebel government, to travel for two years in search of a more active way of life than his self-proclaimed career as a genie of poetry. We know from his travel poems that he often felt driven to go on with this quest, that he was often homesick and wished to be back in Soochow, but that he also was deeply stirred by current events and by historical associations in the regions through which he passed. We can safely conclude also that he returned to Soochow having failed to accomplish whatever mission he had been about. Here is an important period in his life that defies fuller reconstruction. But without the evidence in his poetry we would know nothing whatsoever about it.

When Kao Ch'i returned to Soochow in 1360, he was older (twenty-four) and wiser. He had failed to find satisfying employment of his talents away from Soochow. Whether for these personal reasons, or because the Soochow scene had in the meantime acquired a new appearance, he was ready now to put aside the negative role he had proclaimed for himself when he wrote the "Song of the Man of the Green Hill." Once again, the editing of his poems may have reduced the amount of explicit evidence, but the general outline of his actions and his attitudes becomes very clear when we read with care his poetry and that of his enlarging circle of intimate associates.

The circle of associates and friends in which a man was active often assumes great importance in our understanding of its separate members. In the case of Kao Ch'i, and characteristically for scholar-official literary figures of early modern China, the circle enables us to know and understand the man. Kao Ch'i became, in the years between 1360 and 1366—that is, between his twenty-fourth and thirtieth years—the leading spirit in an unusual circle of young men. After that their lives were interrupted by the defeat of Chang Shih-ch'eng's rebel movement at the hands of the Ming founder. Their city of Soochow was besieged and taken, and they were scattered as the new dynasty forced new ways of life upon all of them. But this circle of friends remained the most important of the poet's associates, and he never developed another set of friends who were so close in spirit and understanding.

Any group of high-spirited, somewhat idealistic young men may look upon themselves as unusual, and the historian, who frequently can be guided by his subjects' judgments, here must be more objective. In the case of Kao Ch'i's circle, however, the weight of historical evidence convinces us that Kao Ch'i and his friends were indeed as remarkable a collection of able and talented young men as could have been found in China at that time. The normally heavy concentration of talent and learning in Soochow had been further increased by the particular political and social conditions of the late Yüan. More than half of Kao Ch'i's friends were from families only temporarily resident there, drawn by the region's comparative prosperity and stability in an age of general breakdown. In addition to that, the young men of Kao Ch'i's generation were denied the usual outlets for their energies and ambitions. If we look upon Kao Ch'i's circle as the cream of a very big crop of idle talent, it becomes less surprising that it contained so many unusual persons.

Kao Ch'i's circle has been known in history variously as the "Ten Talented Ones" (or the "Ten Literary Geniuses") and as the "Ten

Friends of the North Wall" (quarter of Soochow). Kao Ch'i himself wrote a cycle of ten poems recalling and characterizing each of his "ten friends" of this period. The various lists in the secondary sources and that of Kao Ch'i's set of poems do not entirely coincide, and a study of all the poetry of Kao Ch'i and the others makes it possible to build up a circle of fifteen or more names, all men roughly Kao Ch'i's own age, who held ideas, attitudes, and interests in common with him. From their occasional poems, written when they gathered together, visited one another, saw off departing friends, or celebrated events together, we can build up a clear picture of their mode of life and their activities. From their more personal and reflective poems, we can learn a great deal about their thought, their attitudes toward contemporary persons and events, and their ambitions. From their prefaces to these poems, we can fill in much important data about their actions, their participation in government, and the like. The problem of historical reconstruction is made the more interesting by the literary charm of the materials involved.

There are two keys to the relationships existing within this circle. The one is poetry. It is a very common link in groupings of this kind, the one we would expect to find. All of the group were practicing poets, students of poetry, and critics of it.[6] Three of the others traditionally have been grouped with Kao Ch'i as the "Four Outstanding Ones" (*ssu chieh*) of early Ming poetry, and their works exist in extensive collections.[7] These three others also were among the most intimate of Kao Ch'i's friends; hence their poetry collections give us important information about Kao Ch'i and his circle.

The second important key to their relationship is something rather unexpected, and indeed it might well escape the careful student of any one figure of the group, but it emerges very clearly when they are studied jointly, as a group of fellow spirits. It provides the most important insights on our understanding of Kao Ch'i's own life at that time, for it clarifies their common attitude toward the world of affairs and their ideas concerning their roles in that world. To state it most briefly, all of them shared a concept of the heroic life and strove to prepare themselves for heroic action. Their concept of the heroic life was not in itself unusual, being drawn directly from their Confucian tradition and the innumerable examples provided by history. But the manner of their preparation for heroic deeds was unexpected, for despite their backgrounds and the civilian and literary orientation of their lives, it included an unusual stress on military knowledge and skills. Understanding this stress on heroism and the manner of its intended accomplishment as they apparently conceived of it, we are then able to explain the real significance of Kao Ch'i's life in these years, to interpret his actions, and even to suggest the probable solution to the mystery of his death.[8]

That a man is judged by his associates is a universal maxim. In China, particularly in studying historical figures of the more recent centuries, for which much fuller documentation exists,[9] the possibilities for studying the individual through his group and the group through the individuals who composed it are very great. A biographical study undertaken without regard for the writings and the careers of a man's associates, without an attempt to formulate a characterization of their corporate existence, may in many cases produce defective results. Kao Ch'i's case illustrates this very well. Here, the character of the group emerges clearly, and tells us much.

The statement made earlier that they were an unusual group can be verified by reference to their individual achievements. In addition to the four leading poets of the age, the group included two of the foremost painters of the time[10] and a leading calligrapher.[11] As in Kao Ch'i's case, all were men whose achievements in the arts were incidental to their major preoccupation with and preparation for the world of public life. Many others had careers, even distinguished careers, in public life, though most suffered from the early Ming prejudice against men from rival rebel areas. One at least was spectacularly successful; Kao Ch'i's intimate friend, the monk Tao-yen, is better known to history as Yao Kuang-hsiao. Under the son of the Ming founder, the Yung-lo emperor, he served for many years as confidential adviser and virtual prime minister. There is full evidence that a number of the others possessed unusual abilities, but circumstances prevented their utilization.

Thus, when this group saw themselves as men possessing the abilities that could transform their chaotic age and set the world aright, as unusual men awaiting opportunities to perform heroic deeds and win lasting fame, they were not indulging in pure fantasy. Nor did they leave detailed, analytical, or vulgarly explicit statements advertising their heroic caliber. How do we know then that they were impelled by this concept of heroism, and that it set the tone of their lives in these portentous years? The history of Chinese literary criticism informs us that poetry was regarded as a subtle but infallible reflection of a man's true character. Kao Ch'i and his friends all felt that a man's qualities and capacities could best be seen through his poetry, if one were himself sensitive enough to character to be able to read it there. From their poetry we know that Kao Ch'i and his circle agreed on what constituted the heroic life and that they recognized the potential opportunities for heroic action that lay before them in the political and military situation of their times. Undeniably idealistic, they were not, however, mere bookish romantics, idly daydreaming about dashing careers. Instead, we have evidence that they were serious students of the special skills they thought they might be called upon to display. We learn, quite indirectly in most cases, that their number included several accomplished students of military history, military geography, tactics, weapons, and military-political strategy. We learn that they studied methods of personal combat, swordsmanship, horsemanship, Taoist military lore, and other practical matters. They analyzed and discussed historical examples; they knew all the battles and campaigns of history, and the shortcomings of heroes of the past who had failed to achieve their goals. The extent of their concern with military affairs is stressed here precisely because it is the unexpected aspect of their interests and activities, and because it lends substance to their concept of the heroic life.

In the civilian world of traditional China, for the military hero to aspire to and at least to imitate civil and literary values is the pattern. But for aspiring men of the civilian world—for a man who is marked from early youth for greatness in the literary world—to be so deeply concerned with military accomplishments is a striking oddity. For if there is a recognized *topos* of Chinese biographical writing on the military hero, piously pictured as ever intent on the thoughts of the classical philosophers, reading ancient works by torchlight in his tent throughout his campaigns, even writing poetry at the front, there is an unexpected quality in the image that here emerges of Kao Ch'i and his friends—genuine literati—being proud of their swordsmanship or possessing obscure knowledge about the design of siege machinery. For Kao Ch'i especially had the assurance of literary fame and had in his early youth begun to enjoy some of the foretaste of such fame. Yet the truth about his real and practical accomplishments in the military arts is strongly indicated, and it is undeniably a feature of the character of his circle, despite the evidence that Kao Ch'i and his posthumous editors wished to conceal it.

How is this unusual aspect of Kao Ch'i's life to be explained? Does it mean that times so disorderly and so frustrating to the man of civilian mentality as the late years of the Yüan forced the heroic-minded idealist to be more realistic than he might have been in times of peace? Does it indicate that the ruder Yüan period had begun to impress on the civil-minded Chinese literati class a new recognition of the primacy of force, and had given object lessons in the importance of military skills to the man of ambition? Or is it possible that the venerated image of a man like Wen T'ien-hsiang, literatus par excellence, who brilliantly led Sung resistance in the field against the Mongol invaders in the 1270's, had created, at least temporarily, for high-spirited Confucian youth, a new ideal of the scholar-warrior? Perhaps all of these things contributed in some measure to the atmosphere in which Kao Ch'i and his friends developed their concept of heroism. In any event, though these men might not have qualified as Spartan officers in their physical training or as members of the German general staff in their over-all military competence, the group clearly emerges as one that, for traditional China, possessed a quite distinctive character.[12] The age had a special quality, and Kao Ch'i and his circle displayed an unusual emphasis and intensity in this respect. Of course they had Confucian precedents, in an ideal sense, but we can find few similar groups of poet-activists in other centuries of later imperial history.

In the years from 1360 to 1366, Kao Ch'i and these friends looked at the world expectantly, knowing that a great change was about to take place as the decrepit Yüan dynasty fell to pieces about them, and that a new world order would be created in the dust of its collapse. They felt confident that they would find heroic roles to play in that great transformation. Poetry was the key to their understanding of each other, and they communicated among themselves in poetry of heroic scope and tone. They were ready to attempt great deeds. But if they had no opportunity to perform the deeds of which they were sure they were capable—that is, if *fate* did not grant them the chance to win immortality as actors on the great stage of human events—their poetry would still preserve the evidence of their greatness of spirit and of their heroic capacities. Poetry in its own right could be a guarantor of immortality. At best, the creation of such poetry could in itself assume the proportions of a heroic act, different in form but not perhaps in value from the heroic deed. So to the intensity of the devotion to poetry evidenced in the "Song of the Man of the Green Hill" was now added a vastness of scope. The life in poetry had a broader horizon, for it reflected the vast possibilities for human achievement that they all felt now lay at hand.

But for this group, those possibilities depended on one man—Chang Shih-ch'eng, the rebel chieftain whose regime was centered in their city of Soochow. Chang may well have come to appear to them to be the best hope for China among all the rebel claimants for the Mandate of Heaven. The Mongols clearly were losing it. China had already broken up into a patchwork of rebel regimes. Most of them were loosely allied to a superstitious peasant movement, an outgrowth of vulgarized Buddhistic secret societies, known variously as the Red

Turbans, as the Incense-burning Armies, or as the followers of Maitreya. Most of these declared themselves to be directed by Heaven to restore the Sung dynasty. These were, however, rabble movements. Although their nominal adherence to the Sung seems to evidence a concern for traditional Chinese values, in the eyes of the educated (and in fact) they were as destructive of the cultural values of Chinese civilization as the Mongols themselves. Educated Chinese could not pin any hopes on association with them. Chu Yüan-chang, ultimately to become (in 1368) the founder of the new Ming dynasty, himself emerged from this background, and in the early 1360's was still identified with it in the eyes of the Soochow gentry. Chu Yüan-chang, in his base at Nanking, was both the greatest threat to Chang Shih-ch'eng and his nearest potent enemy. Other rebel movements on the horizon were even less appealing. Chang Shih-ch'eng, to be sure, was far from being an ideal emperor. But for the time being, his regime defended the Soochow region against the incursions of others, and even was granted legitimacy by the Mongol court, which pardoned him and conferred regional rule on him in return for his support. No one could have misunderstood Chang's ambitious motives or the Yüan court's desperation in this move, but perhaps it showed that Chang was susceptible to the right kind of influences. Some very respectable literati, men of position and government experience, now associated themselves with Chang's regime. No one could ignore the possibility that out of this might come a properly directed and motivated political-military movement that would lead to the restoration of order in the world and the foundation of a glorious new dynasty. In 1360 this might have seemed possible, particularly to the circle of young enthusiasts of which Kao Ch'i was a leader. Some members of the circle took up positions in Chang's regime; all of them formed close personal relations with some members of it.

But in the following half-decade, it gradually became apparent that Chang was not a vessel of sufficient capacity for the great undertaking. His government deteriorated, and he himself was corrupted by princely living. Kao Ch'i wrote earnest essays on military administration and on statecraft, undoubtedly in the hope of reforming Chang's movement. At the same time, he and his friends tended to pull back from too close association with it, to grow disillusioned, and to wait for further developments. Study of the rebellions in medieval and early modern Chinese history shows that it is characteristic that no man of Kao Ch'i's class, however heroic-minded or military-oriented, tried to seize the reins of power from a Chang Shih-ch'eng and supplant him as the leader of a rebellious movement. The rebel leaders were not men of the Confucian great tradition. Kao Ch'i and his circle waited for an invincible leader that they could serve heroically, but they did not cast themselves in the rebel leader's role.

By the late 1360's (Chang's movement collapsed in defeat in 1366–67) the mood of disillusionment was strong in their poetry. One poem, on internal evidence probably written in 1366, is "Addressed to My Friends of the North City Wall," that is, to his circle of intimate associates in Soochow:

> As youths we rushed off to famous cities;
> How earnestly we desired to be noble men.
> These foolish sentiments were at odds with the times;
> The more actively pursued, the more regret there followed.
> Rest from your travels, return to your humble homes!
> Don't set yourselves again upon the highways.
> Though living in poverty, will you be without companions?
> You will find three or four whose spirits match your own.
> We have gathered often under the tall pines,
> Sitting and drinking in total informality.
> After passing the goblets back and forth
> The talking and joking sometimes have been a bit too free.
> Although that could be called excessively open and direct,
> Still, it has never involved matters of great importance.
> We let ourselves go in the woods and the wilds;
> Why not, for the time, free our spirits in this way?[13]

Here Kao Ch'i urges his friends to let themselves enjoy life even though in ordinary times this might be considered frivolous. For they are now in the camp of the loser. Chang's region is encircled by Chu Yüan-chang's armies and there is nothing for them to do except wait out the storm. He acknowledges the "foolish sentiments" that had impelled them to seek action; they were "at odds with the times." However, their group spirit must continue to bolster them, until the times should take a turn for the better. Why not drink wine, and talk, in gatherings of great informality? But if this poem makes the acceptance of bitter fate seem an easy thing, other poems from these same years attest to the deep concern and burning frustration that also were bitterly felt.

The outcome of the struggle among the contending rebels could scarcely have been worse for the literati-gentry of Soochow. Soochow was encircled for almost a year and its population suffered greatly. Chu Yüan-chang, the hated and feared enemy to the west, besieged and defeated Chang Shih-ch'eng. The gentry of Soochow, who had supported him or at least accepted him for ten years, were further punished by the vengeful conqueror. The rich were banished. Punitive taxation was imposed on the region. Harsh governors were sent to watch over the area. Peace and order did come into the world, as the new Ming dynasty succeeded in 1368–69 in bringing China under its unified rule. But Soochow was identified as the seat of a stubborn enemy. Kao Ch'i and his friends were suspect; they would have no opportunity for heroic action in the service of this new world conqueror. The circle was scattered, many of its members being among the banished rich landlords. Kao Ch'i escaped direct punishment and withdrew to the country, this time neither a genie of poetry as at the age of twenty-one or twenty-two nor the confident hero-in-waiting as in the early 1360's. But again he turned to poetry, now for reflection on the cosmic process, for deeper understanding of the lessons of history, and for philosophic solace. His poems at this time were often pessimistic and resigned, but they often show as well a deep interest in local history and the fates of men of the past who had associations with Soochow. If his poetry now was characterized less by the intensity of youth, and lacked the expansive spirit of the heroic years, it gained in depth and richness.

But the fate on which he mused in these years (1367–68) took an unexpected turn. Early in 1369 he was called to the capital at Nanking to serve with fifteen other scholars as members of the imperial commission for the compilation of the official history of the Yüan dynasty. He was one of the youngest members of the group, and the great honor came to him in recognition of his reputation as a literary figure and man of learning. It was his poetry, thus, which was to involve him inevitably in public life, and since public life had always been his goal, he of course went eagerly to take up the appointment. It was obvious to everyone that the historical commission was intended to serve as a steppingstone to high office. Kao Ch'i spent the year 1369 at the capital, and after the completion of his tasks later that year was retained as a courtier without specific assignment, awaiting appointment to a ministry or a post in the provinces.

From the first poems written after his appointment, we can see how easily he slipped into the role of the man of public life, like one putting on comfortable shoes of perfect fit that he had long been prepared to wear. And indeed, in view of the whole focus of his education and the prevailing values of his civilization, what could have been more natural to the long-expectant official than to become the actual official? Immediately he began to write the occasional poems appropriate to a public figure, formal and elegant, proper in their allusions, dignified in tone. At Nanking he wrote masterly examples of the type, often on imperial command, to commemorate some event of the court or ceremony of state. All of the richness of his learning and his mastery of classical language is displayed. If these poems are dull and unrewarding reading today, it is not because they do not measure up to a very high standard for works of their type.

But these are not the only poems from the two years at court. He also wrote many very personal poems, often quite different in spirit, showing that his preoccupation with the affairs of official life was not complete. In fact, we have much evidence that the long-expectant poet-official was disturbed to discover that, no matter how naturally and how skillfully he could function as a courtier, it was not really the career for him after all. He began to complain, in some of these very personal poems, about the rigors of court life, and to idealize a rustic life as a simple man of Soochow. When at last, in the early autumn of 1370, he was summoned before the emperor and offered an assistant ministry, he protested elaborately that he was too lacking in experience and begged to be allowed to return to private life.

Why? Undoubtedly the reasons for this lie less in any personal distaste for official life than in the particular conditions of the early Ming court. To sum them up, Kao Ch'i probably resented the atmosphere of the Ming court and may well have been afraid for his life also. The Ming court proved to be an extremely dangerous place for courtier-officials, especially for literary figures of suspect background like Kao Ch'i. We must hypothetically reconstruct the reasons for Kao Ch'i's distaste for court life, drawing on the records of the first years of the new dynasty and on the hints in Kao Ch'i's poetry. Some of his reasons are easy to guess. Although the infamous literary inquisition of the founder's reign had not yet started, already this awesome emperor was showing signs of becoming the pathologically suspicious yet shrewd tyrant of later notoriety. Kao Ch'i witnessed some frightening and distressing events, some of them victimizing men he knew and respected. And there may also have been more specific and more personal causes for his fear of the court. It would not have been inaccurate to characterize him as a former leader among a group of would-be heroes, a man possessing military knowledge, and a conspirator-opportunist under the regime of Chang Shih-ch'eng. The Ming emperor was much interested in such characterizations of his officials, particularly when there was a suggestion of latent loyalty to the hated Chang Shih-ch'eng. There is, of course, no explicit evidence to support this hypothesis, but it is not unreasonable. And it is an equally reasonable assumption that Kao Ch'i quickly came to fear and scorn the Ming founder and also, because of the special nature of his own background, had powerful reasons to wish to stay clear of the emperor.

So, having made the distressing decision to forgo an official career, and having successfully extricated himself (no easy task), Kao Ch'i was faced with the necessity of justifying these steps. He was voluntarily rejecting the way of life that he had always wanted, for which he had prepared, and which his family and his society must have held to be the best and the most natural for him. It meant forgoing most of the rewards which his society could give to a man of talent. Whether he made the decision simply on grounds of taste and temperament or, as seems likely, for more serious reasons, it was in any case one that could not be made lightly. It demanded much thought, much readjustment of his values and goals, and serious justification. But little of this could be openly stated even in his most personal poems.

Upon his return to Soochow, he at first took up the role and attitudes of a simple rustic, a man of no ambition and no special skills. He presented himself as a man happy just to be alive to breathe the beneficent sage-emperor's air, and grateful for the inordinate honors that the court had bestowed upon him. These again are formal attitudes, suspiciously like protective coloring, consistent with the decision not to be a courtier, and appropriate to the innocent image of himself that he wished to project. It is, of course, through his poetry that he projects it, as in this poem:

> Who says I've been too long of humble status?
> In a glorious age I've known official emolument.
> Who says I'm suffering in lowly poverty?
> My empty bins still hold a bit of grain.
> I took leave of the court in order to go into this retirement;
> Returning to one's home certainly is not banishment!
> The old house has my shelf of books,
> The unkempt garden still a few clumps of chrysanthemums.
> My worldly affairs are the concern of my wife,
> My household tasks are borne by a servant or two.
> By nature indolent, it is natural that I early seek leisure—
> What need is there to rush about on into one's later years?
> I still wear my court scholar's hat
> But I've newly had made for myself this rustic's robe.
> Deep my cup, and deep am I in wine by afternoon;
> Warm my blankets, and sound is my morning sleep.
> Others laugh at my lonely uneventful existence,
> But a lonely uneventfulness is precisely my desire.
> To the end of my days, what further might I seek?
> I fear only to lose this present good fortune.
> Fame and glory are like a delicious flavor
> In which to dip your finger once and taste is forever enough.
> Why seek a surfeit of it
> When it can only cause a poison in one's bowels?
> Remember if you will that Marquis Liu retired from court
> And was far better off than the whole clan of Chu-fu.
> I therefore follow Lao Tzu's dictum:
> "Know satisfaction with what you have, and feel no shame in humble
>   status."[14]

The last lines are an allusion to an overly ambitious official of the Han dynasty who at last overstepped, incurred the emperor's anger, and was put to death along with all his clan. Has Kao Ch'i revealed here the fears that caused him to choose to return to retirement rather than to enjoy the rewards of high office? He made this allusion, and other similarly ominous ones, in several poems written shortly after leaving office.

In the last four years of his life (1370-74), his thirty-fifth to thirty-eighth years, Kao Ch'i devoted himself assiduously to poetry. It now seems to have become a way of life in itself, as he came to accept the fate that had determined it for him. From these last years came his best poems, and many of them convey a deep philosophic contentment. The following poem, the last of a set of five written about his ancestral home in the countryside near Soochow, expresses this mood:

> After sitting a long time my body is cramped;
> I close my book away and wander out my garden gate.
> Coming to the stream, I unconsciously look to the west.
> Suddenly, squarely before me, I see the Ch'in-yü mountain.
> The wilds are stilled, the bare trees stand sparsely;
> The stream flows far on, and the birds of dusk return.
> Instantly a poem forms itself in my mind—
> In a wave of good feelings my cares all disappear.
> Then I go along home with the woodcutters and herdsmen
> And we sing and laugh, as the evening sun goes down.[15]

Part of the glowing contentment must have come from the discovery that even in his chosen obscurity there were important and gratifying things for a scholar of diminished worldly ambitions to do. This discovery was made gradually as Soochow began to recover its normal intellectual life in the first years of peace and stability under the new dynasty. Kao Ch'i, eminent in reputation now as a poet and a retired official (at the age of thirty-five!), inevitably was drawn into this reviving intellectual life.

In 1372 a new governor was sent to Soochow, a senior statesman of distinguished reputation, by the name of Wei Kuan. Kao Ch'i had known Wei at Nanking, where Wei had held an important post in the Ministry of Rites. Wei was the kind of man Kao Ch'i could admire; he was a poet and a scholar, and he was also a vigorous administrator who quickly gained the good will of the people of Soochow. He cultivated the friendship of distinguished local figures like Kao Ch'i, to gain their help in informal ways in the tasks of governing. He was a most successful governor, and Kao Ch'i was his close associate and friend throughout his tenure of office. They exchanged poems and discussed poetry. Poetry, as always in Kao Ch'i's life, lay at the center of their relationship. Neither man could have conceived of poetry divorced from the ethical and social ideals of their civilization. That a poem (and perhaps an essay) written for Wei Kuan should bring about Kao Ch'i's death was no less tragic and no less unjust in their eyes than in ours, but less bizarre. They were accustomed to attaching significance to the expression of a man's thought in poetry, and to a man's being judged by it.

Yet the particular significance that the Ming emperor chose to attach to Kao Ch'i's poem written for Wei Kuan, and to the significance of their friendship, to which it attested, led to a great injustice. The emperor's spies accused Wei Kuan and Kao Ch'i and another Soochow poet-scholar-official of having shared a seditious intent. The whole event is so improbable that historians and gossips have often looked for a deeper explanation. Superficially the histories say that Wei chose to rebuild the prefectural government offices on their traditional site, ignoring the fact that the site had also been that of Chang Shih-ch'eng's main government building, which had been razed when the Ming armies took Soochow in 1367. Wei Kuan was accused of "raising again a base that had been righteously leveled to the ground." Did this not possess sinister implications in the suspicious atmosphere of early Ming? Kao Ch'i had written a congratulatory poem and perhaps also an essay (if so, it no longer exists). The poem is the most perfunctory and harmless kind of formal writing. Nonetheless it implicated Kao Ch'i as a cohort who rejoiced with Wei Kuan in his misdeed. For this, both were executed within a month of their denunciation. The emperor, in an act unusual for him, later admitted his error in Wei's case, and restored his good name. Kao Ch'i was not mentioned again officially, and he remained in limbo, one of the first of the countless thousands of innocent victims of the Ming founder's wrath.

But the Ming founder was shrewd as well as cruel. Is there some further explanation for Kao Ch'i's involvement and punishment? Legend has it that a poem Kao Ch'i had written while at court in Nanking had made slyly veiled references of a most unflattering kind to the emperor himself, and that the emperor now took his revenge. There are no good reasons for believing this story, but it may convey a hint that Kao Ch'i's death demands fuller explanation. Was Kao Ch'i killed because the emperor knew of his past ambitions and interests and felt that such a man, unwilling to serve his government in the proffered high office, might harbor dangerous thoughts? The fact that Kao Ch'i himself, in editing the manuscripts of his lifelong accumulation of poems, seems to have removed *almost* all of the direct references to this side of his past suggests that it was potentially incriminating. Kao

Ch'i's death assumes more significance and seems more consistent with his whole history if indeed we can conclude that he was executed by the emperor in full knowledge of his true capacity, to rid the dynasty of a potentially dangerous enemy and to intimidate others of his kind. In any event, the inexorable link between the life of action and the life in poetry both spurred him on and harassed him, from his late teens until it finally brought about his early death. The life in poetry had come to a logically consistent, if tragic, end.

Nelson I. Wu

TUNG CH'I-CH'ANG (1555–1636): APATHY IN GOVERNMENT AND FERVOR IN ART

There is a tendency among writers on the late Ming period to invest all aspects of the Chinese scene from about the middle of the sixteenth century to the fall of the dynasty in 1644 with what may be called a post-1644 significance. Preoccupied with their knowledge of what happened after the year 1644, historians are apt to examine the thought and conduct of the late Ming exclusively against the final debacle. Thus the stories of the three most observable troubles of the times—the intrigues at court, the military alarms on the borders, and the roaming hungry masses everywhere else—are perennially retold as background and all events of the period are made to yield a relationship, real or contrived, to the political failure.

The post-1644 attitude of the historians had a counterpart in the search for causes that obsessed the intellectuals in the tumultuous years after the fall of Ming. The debacle had a tremendous emotional impact and many scholars and artists contritely reviewed their private lives for evidence of their own guilt. Ch'en Hung-shou (1599–1652), painter, poet, and illustrator, who adopted a new name, "calling himself Hui-ch'ih [Repenting Belatedly], after the year 1644,"[1] was but one of many examples among the artists. Literary figures detailed their repentance in a more elaborate manner. We do not have to look far to find in Ch'en's friend Chang Tai (1597–1684?), the noted author and historian, a good case. Typical of people of his means, Chang Tai, in the years before the dynasty fell, indulged in extravagance and luxury, and earned early fame for his taste in exquisite houses, beautiful women, and art, as well as for being a connoisseur of spring water for tea. But he was more respectfully remembered for his austerity and continued productivity in his later life as a hermit writer in the mountains of Chekiang after that province was overrun by the Manchus. In his somewhat exaggerated account, which nevertheless was studded with touches of vivid authenticity, Chang Tai, obviously for political reasons under the Manchu rule, veiled but thinly his bitter disappointment beneath the camouflage of Buddhist idioms of retribution and repentance when he wrote:

Now I am a man without a country and without a family. I have no place to go but into the wilderness of the mountains with my hair unbraided, looking as terrible as a wild man. . . . Thinking in repentance of the luxurious days in my noble family, I am going to wear a bamboo helmet over my head and put bamboo buckets on my feet instead of hairpin and shoes. I shall do this in repentance of my past extravagance. There will be quilted cotton clothing instead of fur, and hemp instead of fine weave, wild vegetables instead of meat, coarse grain instead of the usual rice, to repay for the light and warm garments that I wore and the sweet delicacies that I have consumed. A straw mat will be my bed, and a stone my pillow; I shall enjoy no warmth or softness. . . . When I travel, I shall go on foot and shoulder my own bags; there will be no more servants. I shall record every episode of my past life as it comes to mind and present it to Buddha as my confession.[2]

Today, the tangible details in Chang Tai's account and in similar writings by his contemporaries serve as significant underpainting for any portrayal of late Ming life. Such post-1644 confessions throw into high relief the surprising lack of awareness among people of the late Ming period that the end was near for their weary and weakened government and society.

Few recognized at the time that among the forces threatening the continuation of Ming rule, the barbarous Manchus would be the founders of the next dynasty, marching in the course of one year from Peking to Nanking. Even when the Manchu army was near Nanking, the court of Southern Ming still felt that there should be no difficulty in talking terms with the barbarians as in the past; the opposing factions within the government were deemed the greater threat.[3] The annoying symptoms of disorder were attributed to evil influences and deviant ideologies whose fortuitous removal would in due time restore harmony. The essential soundness of the traditional systems was beyond question.

It is easy to imagine the frustration of the few who sensed the dangers in the deteriorating situation. Reading through various pre-1644 *pi-chi*, one searches in vain for the kind of general awareness that must precede adequate action. In one such book, we read about massacres of the defenseless people in Yangtze valley and coastal towns by Japanese pirates, sometimes with the aid of Chinese elements, next to an item on an eclipse of the sun which tells us that the frogs, believing it was night, all started to sing. A rumor of an enemy raid, again we read, caused a stampede to the city and many lost their lives when a ferryboat capsized. These disasters, echoes of an ugly and persistent reality, received perfunctory attention; the soft life of fragile sentiments and indulgence in sophisticated tastes continued to absorb the majority of those with wealth and leisure.[4]

In the darkness of history lie the facts about the life of the masses, for contemporary writings contained few references to their lot. Perhaps the masses would have indulged the same luxurious tastes, given the opportunity, but their choices in life were severely limited. Imagine their dilemma, say, in a battle between government forces and the rebel troops of Li Tzu-ch'eng (1605?–45). As the revolt had been provoked by the notorious oppression of the officials, it naturally had the sympathy of the oppressed. But to join the rebels without benefit of a special skill or some other specific usefulness brought the almost certain fate of being assigned to fill the "fourth wall" in Li's famous "three-wall battle formation"; Li's crack troops made up the inner circles.[5]

Late Ming China presents a picture of a society so heterogeneous as to make the term relatively meaningless outside the chronological frame. The diversity of political and intellectual movements and the wide range of individual attitudes toward life and the court, set in a landscape rich in regional differences, produce a complex composition whose divergent elements all may be called typically late Ming. As illuminated by the writings and traced by the travels of late Ming intellectuals, this world emerges as a dumbbell-shaped area superimposed on the map of China. The northern end, having as its center the national capital of Peking, was the political arena for all, where prizes in fame, riches, and posthumous titles were given as frequently as severe punishment was meted out. Punitive measures included everything from the immediate clubbing to death of the individual to the stripping from one's family of all accumulated honors and privileges, a punishment sometimes more painful than death to the traditionally trained Confucian gentry,[6] followed by the thorough liquidation of all members of the family. Connected to this political nerve center by a narrow passageway roughly paralleling the Grand Canal was the cultured land of the lower Yangtze valley, with such illustrious towns as Soochow, Ch'angchow, Sungkiang, Kashing, Hangchow, and the southern capital of Nanking. This area nurtured Ming developments in Chinese painting and most of the important movements in the intellectual history of the period.

Straying into this dumbbell-shaped land of relative stability from the surrounding darkness were the tribesmen of the north, the Japanese along the coast, visitors and representatives from foreign lands, plus a prince or two chased by bandits.[7] Coming in more regularly, however, were the provincial scholars, armed with learning, ambition, and skill in writing the eight-legged essay, to compete at the examinations, to serve in the government, to advance their interests, to become initiated into the esoteric fashions of the cultured life, and generally to be caught by the currents of the turbulent time.

Outside of this area, events echoed what was happening in these centers. Toward the end of the dynasty, the separation of the two parts became more serious, with the secure inner area shrinking steadily. Beginning in the 1620's, from the northwestern border of Yen-sui, reports of local unrest began to come in. The oppressed hungry masses, renegades, and border invaders formed groups of roaming bandits, extending the area of lawlessness to the south and to the east, engulfing the provinces of Hupeh, Honan, Szechwan, Kiangsu, and Anhwei.[8]

The continuously shrinking world of the late Ming was rapidly reduced to the southern end of the dumbbell shortly after 1644, to be united with the rest of the land only by an alien conquest.

While the existence of this isolated island of culture was reassuring, people throughout China already breathed uneasily with its irregular pulse. Spells of efficient government, lower and fairer taxes, and reliable national defense alternated with discouraging turns of events usually involving tragedies for men whose integrity and ability had been the empire's last real hope.[9] The fitful events and the leading personalities in this small arena—not the larger swells of the political current which few understood—form the background of our study of Tung Ch'i-ch'ang. Here we shall find the various specific problems Tung encountered in his official and artistic careers and see his solutions in relation to the special combination of opportunities and pitfalls presented by late Ming society.

Tung Ch'i-ch'ang, looking back on his life before his death at eighty-two,[10] must have recalled with satisfaction his long record of official service and felt pride in his recognition as the greatest painter and calligrapher of his time, admired even as far away as Japan and the Ryukyu Islands.[11] There may have been a little self-congratulation for having survived some half-century of treacherous political currents,[12] but what would his reaction have been had he been told that eight years after his death the dynasty he had served would collapse from internal weaknesses? Certainly Tung would have recalled his voluminous studies of the deteriorating political situation, written with great earnestness in the twilight of his life and with his personal funds, which had received only routine commendation at court before being consigned to the Bureau of History to gather dust.[13] This mute moment of sober reflection would have been succeeded by elation had he also been told that, after the fall of Peking, the short-lived court in Nanking managed in that difficult year of its existence to honor him, most thoughtfully indeed, with the posthumous name of *Wen-min*.[14] No other laudatory title could have pleased him more, for *Wen-min*, transmitting a luminous image of literary refinement and personal brilliance, had also been the posthumous name given to the grand old master of calligraphy and painting, Chao Meng-fu (1254–1322) of the Yüan dynasty. Tung Ch'i-ch'ang had always imagined Chao Meng-fu as his rival in history, frequently comparing his own career with the Yüan master's.[15]

There had been, as in most lives, scenes he would not have cared to recall, and in his youthful years there had been experiences that he rather wanted the world to forget. What would have been the consequences, should these have been rediscovered?[16]

We are not interested in attempting a moral judgment on Tung Ch'i-ch'ang's character and career. We are, however, fascinated by the intricate pattern of his life and experiences, in which the lessons from others' lives are quite discernible, particularly because, after what almost amounts to a well-meant censorship, the traditional account of his life in the Ming History provides only a stereotyped image of "by far one of the best scholar-official-artists."

Tung Ch'i-ch'ang was one of those rare people who in their lifetime are allowed an exciting awareness of a place in history. He was sophisticated enough not to think of himself as the best artist of all times, but he openly claimed to be the most important man in three hundred years of Chinese art. We certainly can see his point and can understand why he specified three hundred years, i.e., since Chao Meng-fu.[17] But we are even more willing to grant that for three hundred years more his influence was to have a significant effect on Chinese art. His theories, whether later critics agreed with them or not, would force them into heated discussions, and, indeed, were to be cited by fundamentally different schools in support of their positions.[18] After Tung Ch'i-ch'ang, Chinese landscape painting was never the same again. However, it is intriguing that, as a high government official, he should have been thinking about placing himself in history as an important figure in art.

As we attempt to understand Tung Ch'i-ch'ang, and not to judge him according to either the traditional or modern standards, we free ourselves from many of the opinions expressed on him and realize that he was one of those who set standards and made rules. Once we begin to appreciate his problems and his solutions, as we reconstruct his life, we shall understand how he came to set these standards and rules. Each turn of his path will then seem more meaningful.

In 1555, the year Tung Ch'i-ch'ang was born, the event that stirred the nation and was to be remembered for generations was the martyrdom of Yang Chi-sheng (1516–55). Although Yang, executed while still in his prime, clearly failed to accomplish what he had set out to do, he succeeded brilliantly in making clear what he had wanted to express. His case demonstrated to a dramatic degree the faith a good Confucian official had in the traditional political system under the emperor. No matter how dark the time was, in the emperor there was light, if one only knew how to bring it out. No matter how powerful an evil official, a just emperor could always reduce him to a commoner, when the right time came, just as the sun would reduce an iceberg to water, from which it had been formed. Yang Chi-sheng was determined to bring justice back to the emperor's court. Three years before, he had prepared his famous memorial denouncing Yen Sung (1480–1568), the *ta-hsüeh-shih,* the most powerful official of the late Ming court, and his vicious son Yen Shih-fan. Knowing the gravity of the matter, and remembering well what had happened to the scores of others who had dared to incur the displeasure of the Yen father and son, Yang Chi-sheng carefully enumerated his charges against Yen Sung under five cardinal sins and ten great crimes. As suggested by these numerals, Yang Chi-sheng had also given his memorial a carefully styled composition. Before he presented it to the court, he fasted and chastened himself for three days.[19]

All these preparations and the literary style did not prevent Yen Sung from coming upon a weapon he could use against Yang. To the already offended emperor, Yen pointed out the irregularity of having the names of two princes among those mentioned to support the charges, probably secretly suggesting an alliance between officials and members of the royal household, a much dreaded relationship if not a taboo of the Ming court. At any rate, Yang Chi-sheng's case was as good as lost when the defendant named in his memorial was invited to study it. For this one crime, or sin, Emperor Shih-tsung had Yang Chi-sheng arrested.[20]

During the three years Yang Chi-sheng was in prison, his case pending, many intellectuals made rather emotional attempts to save him. Wang Shih-chen (1526–90), who later as a literary leader of his time had important influence on Tung Ch'i-ch'ang, volunteered to write for Yang Chi-sheng's wife an appeal on her husband's behalf. The writing of this appeal led to the execution of Wang Shih-chen's father, Wang Shu, a few years later when there was a chance for Yen Sung to take revenge.[21]

Yang Chi-sheng's martyrdom, compared with the death of many other heroes, was certainly much more dramatic. His refusal of a sedative before his torture became a popular legend.[22] Later, in prison, he calmly used a piece of porcelain to carve off the flesh around an infected wound, his jailor fainting at the bloody sight. Yang Chi-sheng could not have died without a last didactic message to the nation and to eternity, and so composed a poem of four lines before his execution:

> My righteous soul will soon return to the Great Unknown,
> And the redness of my heart will glow in history.
> I shall repay the benevolence I still owe the throne,
> As a loyal ghost, with a heavy memory.

At once, "the poem was passed on from mouth to mouth throughout the country, and the people were in tears memorizing it."[23]

The two villains of our story, the Yen father and son, were nevertheless talented persons and men of taste. The father, a celebrated scholar and writer, owned a library of rare and excellent books. The son had a particular fondness for good works of art. It was well known that he had used all his political influence to build his dazzling collection.[24] After several more officials had risked their lives to attack them, the Yen family finally lost the emperor's favor. Their property was confiscated in 1565, and the son, Shih-fan, was executed in the same year. The father, after living in banishment for a few years, died, ironically, in poverty and probably of starvation.[25]

Following the confiscation, Wen Chia, son of the great painter Wen Cheng-ming, was appointed to help inventory the famous paintings and calligraphy in the Yen collection. It took Wen Chia three months to go over the art treasures, which had been kept at four or five separate estates of the Yen family. Wen Chia published his notes in 1568.[26] A larger record of Yen's confiscated property was published under the title *T'ien shui ping-shan lu* ("Heaven Reduces to Water the Iceberg").[27]

In a few short years everyone in the anecdote, the hero and the villains, had died. Yet, even at the height of political strife and in full awareness of the dangers of the emperor's court, waves of young men took the examinations and entered government service.

Of course, not all the subjects of the Ming empire wanted to be officials. But before choosing to stay away from these examinations, one would think twice. To live as a commoner, without a degree or an official title, one had more taxes to pay and fewer ways to pass them on to the less fortunate. Moreover, the commoner was expected to perform labor services for the government and its officials. Some of the assignments were not very pleasant, having in many cases been designed to humiliate the person whom the officials did not like.

The painter Chang Lu, for instance, was a commoner. An official once forced Chang to paint a picture after he had been tortured and had his left hand chained, leaving only his right hand free.[28] Chou Ch'en, the teacher of T'ang Yin, was a commoner and a painter who had experienced similar treatment, and his tormentor was none other than Yen Sung himself.[29] Both painters had tried to evade their ruling officials and thus enraged them. The great Shen Chou (1427–1509) was once ordered to paint a mural, which he quietly did even though this had been someone's scheme to embarrass him. Judging from the tone in which this anecdote is narrated, Shen Chou might have called influential friends to his rescue and thus have avoided a demeaning task. But he considered it his duty to answer the summons, the wicked design behind it notwithstanding.[30] These commoner artists, unable to protect themselves without help from others, were in a class quite different from that of the scholar-official-artists.

"The youth of late Ming times would face many difficult decisions in the course of his life. But none was more difficult or more portentous than the decision whether or not to take the examinations which offered the only route to official status. In making his decisions with their often predictable consequences, the person placed in high relief for us the important elements of his own character. Into a world like this Tung Ch'i-ch'ang was born in the year Yang Chi-sheng died. In his life we shall see a microcosm of the experiences here described.

The small town of Shanghai, originally an eastern suburb of Hua-t'ing *hsien,* became a *hsien* itself in the year 1292 and by 1504, when its local history was compiled, could already boast some important persons. The Tung family of Shanghai established itself in 1459 when one of its members, Tung Lun, became a *Chü-jen,* and later, in 1464, a *chin-shih.* One after another, the descendants of Tung Lun passed the examinations and became prominent.[31]

Tung Ch'i-ch'ang, born on the nineteenth day of the first moon,[32] in the year 1555, was not a direct descendant of Tung Lun, but a poor relative of that distinguished family. His father, grandfather, and great-grandfather, the last a brother of Tung Lun's, had never won fame or fortune. The life of a fourth-generation commoner had its worries, and there was not much help coming from his rich cousins. When Tung Ch'i-ch'ang was old enough for school, his father, Han-ju, recited some passages from the classics for him to learn, and the boy quickly memorized them.

Tung Ch'i-ch'ang did not remain in his native Shanghai long. Some "twenty *mou* of poor farmland" (about three-odd acres) were listed in his name, and Tung as owner found himself subject to corvée for the

local government as a form of land tax. Having exhausted all methods
for avoiding the corvée, he finally had to run away from home—a drastic
step for an "earth-bound" commoner. According to the family records
quoted in the local history, Tung Ch'i-ch'ang by his flight became the
first member of the Tung family to live away from Shanghai, and with
his failure to return, the record of his own family in the local history
ended.[33]

Arriving in the bigger city of Hua-t'ing, the seat of Sungkiang fu, in
Kiangsu, Tung Ch'i-ch'ang became at seventeen a student in the prefectural school, receiving part of his support from the government. The
prefect, Chung Chen-chi, thought highly of the youth and, as Tung was
to recall in later years, figured in an important decision in his life. Tung
was taking an examination under Chung's supervision, possibly for the
hsiu-ts'ai degree, and was confident of first place. Chung placed him
second instead, giving as the reason Tung's poor calligraphy. Cha-
grined, Tung set about to perfect his calligraphy, beginning according
to his own account with the imitation of the style of Yen Chen-ch'ing
(708–84) of the T'ang dynasty. Another, earlier, T'ang master, Yü
Shih-nan (558–638), soon captured his attention, but Tung was becoming convinced that neither equaled the great calligraphers of the even
older Wei and Chin times. The youthful Tung may have been unaware of the effect his enthusiastic study of calligraphy would have on
his later life. An interesting immediate by-product of his pursuit of a
better model, however, was his conclusion that his search had brought
him closer than the celebrated calligraphers of his own dynasty, Wen
Pi (1470–1559) and Chu Yün-ming (1460–1526), to the secret of this
age-honored art. But as a student of limited means he had only the
reproductions of these past masters' work for his use and did not understand the importance of working with originals. Tung could imitate the
appearance of these famous examples but the subtlety and life-force of
the master's brush would continue to elude him. Only later, after seeing in Kashing many originals in the collection of Hsiang Yüan-pien
(1525–90), and still later in Nanking the original by Wang Hsi-chih
(321–79), greatest master of all time, did he realize how groundless
his conceit had been. Utterly discouraged by this sudden revelation of
the impossibility for him of reaching the pinnacle, he wanted to burn
his ink slab and brush then and there and put an end to his career as
a calligrapher.[34]

This great moment of despair was recalled by Tung Ch'i-ch'ang some
thirty years later as the beginning for his subsequent success in this art
and for his new appreciation of the creative process. His retrospective
account of this experience had a pronounced Ch'an Buddhist flavor.

Tung Ch'i-ch'ang compared his distress at the time with the experience of the T'ang-dynasty monk "Hsiang-yen upon meeting Tung-shan."[35] When Hsiang-yen could not comprehend the significance of a question the master had asked him, and for days could not find a suitable answer, he realized how hopelessly remote he still was from understanding the marvels of Ch'an. Sorrowfully, he decided to end his serious study of Ch'an and become instead a "purée and rice monk" (*chou-fan-seng*)— in other words, to eat instead of think.

Actually, in citing the humiliating experience of Hsiang-yen, Tung Ch'i-ch'ang betrayed his conceit even more forcibly, for it is well known that, in the career of the Ch'an monk, that moment of discouragement marked the beginning of his long journey to enlightenment. It would also be superfluous to point out that Tung Ch'i-ch'ang's recollection had a post-enlightenment character. His little story would have been quite pointless had he really burned his brush and ink slab.

Tung Ch'i-ch'ang took up painting in a much more relaxed atmosphere than the one in which he had started his serious study of calligraphy. Employed as a family tutor in Hua-t'ing by Lu Shu-sheng (1509–1605), Tung Ch'i-ch'ang tells us, he tried his hand on a landscape one evening in 1577 by candlelight and from then on liked to paint.[36] Obviously, to have had such profound effect on his life the incident had to be preceded by at least unconscious preparation. This can be found in his experiences during these formative days in Hua-t'ing among his literary and artistic friends there.

As a *hsiu-ts'ai* still in his teens, Tung Ch'i-ch'ang was already very well known for his natural gifts and literary talents. Because of this, he became rather popular among established Hua-t'ing families of literary and artistic standing. The elders took it upon themselves to educate him as if he had been their own; the younger set were eager to have him as a friend. Exciting and momentous changes in the history of Chinese painting and art criticism were to be sparked by the meeting of these youths.

When Tung Ch'i-ch'ang in his early twenties was invited to teach and to live in the prominent family of Lu Shu-sheng, he had ample opportunity to observe and to learn the ways of life in that sophisticated society. He could not but be impressed by his new friends' enthusiasm for the pursuit of excellence in art on the one hand, and their aloofness from political affairs on the other. Of these two realms of activity, creative work in the arts was safe while government service brought one daily into danger. To take no action was a good way to avoid criticism, but to criticize others and to follow this with a withdrawal from government in protest was a preferred formula—much safer than proposing a program of action and accepting the charge to carry it out. In retirement one was much more secure, less suspected by one's enemies, and free to enjoy the full privileges of the official class. While eagerly preoccupied with the arts, one was not deaf to the murmurs from Peking, and would welcome the news of the next more attractive appointment. Tung Ch'i-ch'ang's employer, Lu Shu-sheng, was one who played the game well. He survived many political storms, enjoyed from time to time an honorable retired life at home, and held the high-ranking office of President of the Board of Rites at the end of his career.[37] Lu Shu-sheng lived to be ninety-six, an accomplishment in those eventful years that amounted to a personal victory—indeed almost presupposed saintly virtue.[38]

Contributing significantly to Tung Ch'i-ch'ang's later career as a painter were three other friends, all his seniors. The first, Ku Cheng-i, a local gentleman-collector-painter who opened his collection of Yüan painting for Tung Ch'i-ch'ang to study, probably was also responsible for Tung's early painting lessons.[39] Ku's collection could, however, in no way be compared with that of Hsiang Yüan-pien, a rich merchant of Kashing who at one time employed Tung Ch'i-ch'ang to tutor his son. Hsiang must have given Tung solid training as a connoisseur, for the two often spent days on end examining and discussing pieces in that fabulous collection.[40]

While respecting Ku and Hsiang as his masters in his art training, Tung Ch'i-ch'ang had great affection for a third friend, Mo Shih-lung. At one time, Tung Ch'i-ch'ang studied with Mo at the latter's house and came to regard Mo's father as teacher and Mo Shih-lung himself as an elder brother.[41] Mo Shih-lung, perhaps the most brilliant of the younger group, appears to have been a handsome man, possessing both a great personal charm and, as befits an artist, a swift temper. Most of his contemporaries noticed his flair, but a few closer friends must have sensed that his unusual qualities had much deeper meaning. Looking back at the third quarter of the sixteenth century, Mo Shih-lung indeed looked in every way the leader of a new art movement.[42]

Around Mo Shih-lung gathered a small group of young artists and literary men who often met for discussions or pleasure. At times senior literary figures like Wang Shih-chen, whom we mentioned earlier, Wang Hsi-chüeh (1534–1610), and Mo's father, Mo Ju-chung (1508–88), would either be hosts, offer learned counsel, or make encouraging comments on their performances.[43] Once when only a few young friends were present, Mo Shih-lung painted in front of them a landscape that was immediately acclaimed as worthy of the great Yüan master, Huang

Kung-wang (1269–1354). All the excited guests wanted to keep it, and they had to draw lots to settle the matter. The lucky winner snatched the picture and happily left with it.[44]

Two characteristics of the new trend in art are suggested by this anecdote. First, clearly evident was the self-confidence and narcissism of Mo Shih-lung and his admiring friends. Second, there was a strong in-group feeling among them. Although Mo Shih-lung, Ku Cheng-i, Hsiang Yüan-pien, and Mo's other friends never formed a club or a cult for Yüan-dynasty masters, they all preferred painters of that era—a taste not shared by their elders, whose predilections covered a wide range of styles, with perhaps special admiration for the Southern Sung.[45] The group feeling of Mo and his friends seems even more important as a factor if we remind ourselves of the bustling activities of the *she*—clubs and fraternities for special purposes—of the late Ming period. Perhaps this artists' circle was even more exclusive than clubs with formal membership requirements.

In his provocative little pamphlet of sixteen short paragraphs on painting, *Hua shuo*, Mo Shih-lung made it very clear that there was a "we-group" and a "they-group." Occasionally, the spokesman of the "we-group" would condescendingly hint that everything of the "we-group" was superior, should the reader be so slow as not to see this for himself. Since the "we" never felt the need of talking to the "they," the second person "you" did not appear in the work.[46]

Convinced of the timeless validity of his theories, Mo Shih-lung referred to history, citing a long list of painters of the past as practicing what the "we-group" now stood for, and presenting a blacklist of those artists whose fame was great, but who were nonetheless on the wrong path. To the late Ming intelligentsia, many of whom were Ch'an enthusiasts after a fashion, he said that in painting, just as in Ch'an Buddhism, there had been a Southern and a Northern school since T'ang times. The "we-group" were to be identified with the Southern school.[47]

Mo Shih-lung always impressed one as having a way with words.[48] But when the important issue of Southern and Northern schools came up, he was more than just a superb word juggler. He performed the magic of bringing to condensation the humid air that had filled the late Ming atmosphere for some twenty-five years. Using Ch'an as a catalyst, he produced raindrops for everyone to see.[49] Mo Shih-lung never bothered to explain how the two schools in painting separated themselves, if there had been such a separation, so as to justify his comparison with the well-known event in Ch'an Buddhism, but simply asserted it as if it had been a historical fact. Nor did he make any reference to the Ch'an Buddhism around 1575, which, known as *K'uang-ch'an* ("Mad

Ch'an"), was a unique development and a far cry from the Ch'an of the Sixth Patriarch.[50] Yet Mo Shih-lung, with the power of suggestion, was able to make the issue absolutely clear and real to his audience.

When he made his reference to history, his position was not one of a historian and he was not even narrating a historical fact. He stated a point of view. When the view was made clear, the historical events became rearranged and were given their new meaning. His view was emotionally satisfying to his followers. It meant advocating a change from conventional ways of doing things, a turning inward to one's self for guidance. It was not a break with tradition, but, with a familiar ring of Ch'an, a claim to be truer to it than anyone else.

Today we could very well be writing about Mo Shih-lung instead of Tung Ch'i-ch'ang, had the former not suffered two serious disadvantages. Mo Shih-lung enjoyed an easy and early success, almost too glamorous for the good of his career. Living in a protected environment and hearing high praise from his elders, young Mo Shih-lung appears to have taken the struggle against the "they-group" too casually. He impresses us as a young, godlike knight about to slay an evil dragon that destiny has assigned to him, as if the inherent virtues represented by him assured the inevitable victory, and the dramatic revelation of his identity, or here the identity of his "school," alone were enough to shatter all resistance. Tung Ch'i-ch'ang had come from a different background. He knew what a struggle for survival meant, and knew there was never an end to it. Throughout his life, particularly in art, he was full of courage and curiosity, finding one new plateau above another until he died. Mo Shih-lung's second disadvantage was that he had no idea that he was to die young. He probably died in his thirties, unsuccessful in his civil service examinations and unhappy.[51] History was cruel to him and recorded little of his life. Both he and his father were given notices in the Ming History as appendixes to the biography of Tung Ch'i-ch'ang, who had survived to carry the standard for the new art movement handed him by Mo Shih-lung.

Mo Shih-lung and Tung Ch'i-ch'ang as a composite image somewhat resembled the spokesman-painter team of the mid-nineteenth-century French scene, Baudelaire (1821–67) and Delacroix (1799–1863). Unlike their French counterparts, however, here each played both roles. They appeared tandem in history, with Mo Shih-lung declaring the principles and Tung Ch'i-ch'ang amplifying them engagingly, systematically, and with great clarity and force. The resultant new style aimed at clarifying the elegant but suffocatingly crowded landscape painting of the late sixteenth century, which Mo Shih-lung had described as having been "built up with trifling details."[52] Trifling as they were, perfection of any one of these details demanded a long period of training. To those who looked upon painting as a medium of expression, this must have been considered a waste of time—overemphasis on the means at the expense of the ends. The painters of the Southern school had no patience with trifling details. Their goal was the sudden realization of excellence in art like the sudden enlightenment in Ch'an, bypassing the rituals.[53] What an exciting new freedom they now had! How different Chinese history might have been if the same iconoclastic changes had taken place in the bureaucratic system!

The new landscape style strove to be an end in itself. Not a vehicle for a narrative scene or a mood, indeed the new landscape sometimes even reversed the situation and employed a suggestion of a scene or a mood as integrated parts of its formal design. Figures rarely appeared and, if they did, were usually quite simple, with no more important a role than that of a tree or a rock. The titles for the new landscapes tended to be rather abstract, if not just "Landscape." To be sure, this mode in painting, as interpreted by various so-called Southern masters, was not entirely new, but the conscious singling out of this one mode to the exclusion of others was. Aside from any high-sounding philosophical meaning or even magic power claimed for it,[54] this type of landscape did have the virtue of fully respecting painting as a medium of visual expression. Representation and narration were renounced in favor of interpretation and personal statement. When an artist painted in this new autobiographical manner, he was also identifying himself with the long line of great masters of the past listed by Mo Shih-lung and subsequently revised by Tung Ch'i-ch'ang and a host of later critics. Considering this as the only approach worthy of the medium, the autobiographical painter thus claimed to be heir and interpreter of a great tradition.[55] (See Plates I–IV, following p. 278.)

The great masters' works were enthusiastically studied, but a new landscape in the style of one of the past masters was never a copy but a new rendition, often quite farfetched. Still, all was supposedly in good tradition—if not in form, then in spirit. Everyone was entitled to his view. The refined manner of representing details was a thing of the past. Bold, direct, and primitive approaches created a new elegance in crude and awkward forms. This was a time of changing standards.[56] In execution, it required a total involvement of the artist; mastery of technique and traditional idioms remained essential, but the new art also demanded the assertion of his own individuality, forged from his experiences in deliberately freeing himself from the traditions of his discipline. His habits of kinesthetic movements and rhythm joined his conscious effort in the re-creation of his personality traits and aspirations in the vehicle of landscape. The landscape in this sense was a self-portrait. To have a prominent figure in the landscape, perhaps walking beneath a magnificently shaped pine with a page boy following, as in the scenes of the Southern Sung or the early Ming, would mean a double image. This kinesthetic dexterity in doing semi-abstract images came close to resembling calligraphy. In this, again and again, one is reminded of tradition, but Tung Ch'i-ch'ang tells us: "No successful artist could possibly study the ancients without producing change!"[57] In this drive for self-expression and self-identification, his voice was the clearest and most eloquent, leaving Mo Shih-lung and the sixteenth century far behind. He taught the importance of self-identification via *un*learning, which in a most peculiar way reminds one of Descartes. He said, obviously drawing directly from his study of Ch'an and Buddhism in general: "When there is nothing left that you could still return, you have yourself left."[58] Only when the process of unlearning is completed can one have a glimpse of this self as an untarnished reality. It is this self that has been doing all the unlearning.

This art that was centered around the self, which in turn was in an exclusive group of kindred souls, necessarily produced its special artist-audience relationship and, with it, an aesthetics that could also be traced back in history. The artist, whose main concern was self-expression, could not go to his audience; his audience must come to him and, upon conversion, become one of the group. The Southern movement in the art of painting was characteristically rich in verbal expressions. The artist must have liked his own voice as much as his own painting. But he had a doctrine that denied preaching. Theoretically, support from the uninitiated should be shunned, not sought. Art still communicates, but it first serves to select its audience and, in doing so, screens most people out. This traditional ideal was dramatically described by the poet of the Warring Kingdoms period, Sung Yü, in his analogy of the singer who, moving from popular and contemporary tunes to lofty and classical compositions, steadily lost his audience along the way. Toward the end, of those several thousand who earlier were able to join in and to appreciate, only a handful remained. Sung Yü then explained: "Not only among the birds is there the *feng* [phoenix], among the fishes is there the *k'un* [leviathan], but also among *shih* [intellectuals] there is the *sheng-jen* [sage], whose ideals and actions are unique and who is alone above all others. How can a common person be expected to understand my behavior?"[59]

Applied to the creative artist, this obviously means that the more profound his message, the smaller will be his appreciative audience. But what is of great importance to us is the appearance of a value judgment without any justification. We may translate the general idea and say that the more personal one's message, the fewer will be those who have had common experiences. But this is to leave out the nature of these experiences. Simply because "so few people seemed to praise him," Sung Yü still might not be likened to a *sheng-jen*.[60] With this in mind, we may appreciate how the in-group feeling worked, and how those of the "we-group" could be so confident of themselves. When they made judgments, they also made their own rules.

It was in this artist-audience relationship that one looked back in history or forward into the future for kindred souls. Tung Ch'i-ch'ang said: "Not only do I regret that I cannot meet with the great masters of the past, but also I regret that they did not have the opportunity of meeting me!"[61]

This deliberate separation of the artistic elite from the masses resembles the separation of the social classes of late Ming China. Though far from new, both separations were definitely very pronounced at this time. However, the pinnacle of the pyramid was not really a castle in the air. It was obvious that Tung Ch'i-ch'ang communicated with more than just ancient masters. As we have mentioned earlier, he had admirers even outside of China, so the base of his pedestal reached rather far and wide. Indeed, popular taste soon caught on. It became common to have that elegant feeling of being alone in a crowd of philistines, and fashionable to write colophons for posterity to appreciate.

Painters of the Southern school are often referred to as the amateurs; and the Northern school, professionals.[62] But by the seventeenth century, when the Southern school became decisively predominant, there were probably just as many professional amateurs as real amateurs. The amateur had his distinction during the early period of the Southern movement, but when the revolt was victorious and the rebels enthroned, an amateur of the mid-seventeenth century was most likely just a bad artist.

The amateur Southern school painter, who cared only to communicate with his fellow literati, was the professional's artist. The professional painter, who, on the other hand, had the uninitiated masses to please and to awe, painted for the amateur. In what seems to be a riddle, we have here another clue to a special characteristic of Southern school painting. The professional employed refined details, significant subject matter, beautiful colors, and his well-trained hands, for the purpose of making pictures that would impress his audience. But, because of his concern for this approval, he had made his audience his judge. One does not need to know the first thing about handling a brush to criticize the drawing of a figure or to assert that a famous historical scene has not been faithfully represented. In other words, the painter, because of his attitude, submitted his work to be judged by standards that existed in other realms of interest such as anatomy or history. On a painting with an elaborate design the professional artist's signature would be small, if not also hidden, secondary in importance to the picture itself.

In contrast to the professional or the artisan, the Southern school painter took up his brush to express himself. Because of his different attitude, his painting was an expression and therefore an end in itself. If he could not draw, he would frankly—if not condescendingly—admit it. In the Sung *wen-jen* tradition, Su Shih had said: "To judge a painting by its faithfulness to nature only betrays one's own childlike judgment."[63] When it came to judgment, only those who also handled a brush, either in calligraphy or in painting, had a right to discuss the *pi* (brush work) and the *mo* (ink technique). And the knowledge of *pi-mo* became an avenue to connoisseurship. Frequently done in ink alone and without any narrative theme, paintings of this genre were more often referred to by the name of the artist than by the title of the scene depicted. His signature and autobiographical colophons, in prose or in verse, would loom large in the format. The artist overshadowed his painting. His quick execution, evolving a shorthand version of the details, would not cloud his message.

The seeds of all these important characteristics of the Southern school movement were in Mo Shih-lung's work. After Mo Shih-lung's death, Tung Ch'i-ch'ang often thought about his friend, dreamed about him, and credited him with the separation of the Northern and the Southern schools.[64] He lived to see the victory of Mo Shih-lung's campaign, and carried it on to a new phase where excellent professionals were able to explore fully the possibilities of the amateurs' exciting departure.

It would be the biographer's expediency at the expense of truth to say that Tung Ch'i-ch'ang found himself in the new movement in painting and went on to become the most influential artist in three hundred years. The art of painting was but one of many fashionable things he had learned to appreciate in elegant society. But a whole sequence of events were to convince him that his art and not his office would eventually give him a place in history. Even Mo Shih-lung sought success in the examinations. Tung Ch'i-ch'ang also was to seek a career in government service.

"For a proper life in the mountains, one should observe four basic principles. Trees should not be in neat rows; stones should not be consciously positioned; one's house should not be haughtily spacious; and one's chest should not house crafty schemes."[65] The author of this charming passage of four negative admonitions was Ch'en Chi-ju (1558–1639), Tung Ch'i-ch'ang's closest friend throughout his life.

Ch'en, a native of Hua-t'ing, was three years younger than Tung. The two went to the prefectural school together, each studying for the examinations. From the beginning, they held different views about life. Ch'en had his *hsiu-ts'ai* degree when he was twenty-one, but a few years later lost all desire to pursue the higher degrees. As a very sensitive young man who had gained early recognition among the literati, he renounced further political ambitions by a rather violent gesture: he burned his student's cap and gown, and started a long and pleasurable life as a country gentleman.[66] Freed from the government school system, Ch'en thereafter read and wrote for his own enjoyment. He built up a fine library and ventured into publishing as a business. He was the first to publish Mo Shih-lung's *Hua shuo*. His writings were in great demand, and he earned his living partly by writing for fees. He delegated many of the requests for his writings to his less popular and poorer writer friends when he had more than he could handle, or when a friend needed the job. Tutoring private students provided him another source of income and he also found time for many gentlemanly pursuits.

Among his many activities, a few stand out as significant self-expressions. Most important of all was his construction of a private temple to enshrine two Sung-dynasty philosophers, Lu Chiu-ling (1132–80) and his brother Chiu-yüan (1138–92), the founders of the so-called *hsin* school of Neo-Confucianism.[67] Ch'en Chi-ju's singling out of this branch of philosophy, which emphasized the self and advocated the returning to one's mind for truth and values, parallels Mo Shih-lung's appeal to the Southern school in Ch'an. Both men demonstrated forcibly their impatience to free themselves from the trifling refinements in every aspect of life which served no purpose but to trip well-meaning men on technicalities. These young men wanted to bypass, and if necessary to destroy, these meaningless obstacles so that meaningfulness might be achieved, be it enlightenment in philosophy, communication in art, or efficiency in government. But the fiber of their make-up lacked the strength for such ambitious actions. They were nevertheless confident that they saw the light. Ch'en Chi-ju was content just "to sit in his straw hut with incense burning."[68]

In the good tradition of Lu Chiu-yüan and Wang Shou-jen (1472–1528), our man in the mountains was not a hermit, even though the Ming History classified him as one. Ch'en was active in his community, looking after the poor, using his influence to bring about justice, and even seeking tax relief for the helpless villagers. Asked to edit the local history, he did a commendable job. This last item of course was in the Confucian tradition of didactic historian. Although he never served a day in the government, and indeed never answered any of the many calls from Peking, received because the emperors had heard about him, he was referred to as "a Prime Minister in the Mountains."[69]

Ch'en's heart must have been stirred a little when Ku Hsien-ch'eng (1550–1612) established his Tung-lin Academy and urged him to lecture there. But that was not enough to lure him out of his mountains. He declined the invitation, and when the scholars of that group later became violently involved in government strife, he said to a friend: "I do not want to celebrate their victories [now], because I do not want to mourn their dead later."[70] However, in those tortured years troubles often involved even the most cautious bystander. The victorious eunuch Wei Chung-hsien (1568–1627), after having bloodily subdued the scholars, noticed with pleasure the numerous temples then being built in his honor by sycophantic local officials. When such a temple was proposed for his home town, Ch'en Chi-ju, as a celebrated local writer, was requested to write a commemorative essay. He wanted no part of it. How he avoided that infamous chore is still something of a mystery. He is reported to have replied that not only was he, a commoner with no titles, too insignificant an author for such an important piece of literature, "but also Tung Ch'i-ch'ang should not be considered

---

PLATES

   I. Tung Ch'i-ch'ang, "Landscape with Straw Hut," 1597, painted for Ch'en Chi-ju while visiting with the latter. Three inscriptions by the artist, others by Emperor Ch'ien-lung of the Ch'ing dynasty. H. H. Wang Collection, Whitestone, New York.

  II. Tung Ch'i-ch'ang, "Landscape," before 1599, based upon a composition by Kuo Chung-shu (late tenth century), sections of a handscroll. Courtesy National Museum, Stockholm.

 III. Tung Ch'i-ch'ang, "Calling the Hermit at Ching-hsi," 1611. H. C. Weng Collection, New York.

 IV. Tung Ch'i-ch'ang, "The Ch'ing-pien Mountains," 1617. H. C. Weng Collection, New York.

  V. Tung Ch'i-ch'ang, "Poems," referring to his 1622 appointment to study the government documents on Shen-tsung's reign (1573–1619), preserved in Nanking. Private collection.

 VI. Tung Ch'i-ch'ang, "Landscape," 1623, album leaf, in the style of the Yüan master Wang Meng (1309–85). Formerly private collection, Shanghai.

I

II

III

青年圖像此荒蕪

丁巳夏五晦日寄

張恂其世文 董玄宰

積溝千年互紫雲

雲端稜尖見郡墟

秋光日雲塊清日

流沼亭中把卷出

　　昌玆

IV

繁霜書匆起石室陰秋例

更新 命 時有備史之 六代江山燒灰

陰稿文恐不到前朝

駈車宛蔡遊泛蓬麥出秋

悄似雁臣閱道晚来蒼茫

我論才少且不如人石渠書

搖轡回黃金屋恩須問收

新入洛愧吾先達夢初衣

似返會稽薪

萊亭董其昌稿

VI

qualified. Indeed, Tung Ch'i-ch'ang is one of the most famous writers and has occupied high offices, but he is now retired and living in the woods. To Lord Wei, he is but another man in the mountains, except that he has been qualified to wear the official hat and belt." He then suggested: "One should seek among those who are in government and favorably looked upon by his Lordship [to pen this composition]," and thus saved both his best friend and himself from disgrace, a deed much appreciated by Tung.[71] It was a close call, for only shortly before this Tung Ch'i-ch'ang had resigned from his post as President of the Board of Rites in Nanking and hurried home at the insistence of his friend.[72] Quietly active, Ch'en Chi-ju did not renounce his Confucian responsibility. To look after everything under heaven (*t'ien-hsia*), or under the emperor, was too much for him; he carefully carved out a small sphere of responsibility and conscientiously worked within it.

Tung Ch'i-ch'ang deeply admired his younger friend's wisdom and early decision to stay away from a hopeless situation. He also must have seen in Ch'en Chi-ju his own image as a man in the mountains. However, he could not keep himself entirely away from the city. He dedicated a building (*lou*; in this case it was probably a two-story wooden structure with a continuous open porch on all four sides around the upper floor), "Lai Chung Lou," in which to entertain Ch'en Chi-ju. Acknowledging this honor Ch'en Chi-ju wrote: "Wang Yüan-mei *hsiensheng* [Wang Shih-chen] used to have a Lai Yü Lou named after Wang Po-yü [Wang Tao-k'un]. Tung Hsüan-tsai [Tung Ch'i-ch'ang] has named Lai Chung Lou after me. When the two of us are on the upper floor of this building, we concern ourselves with nothing but masterpieces of calligraphy and painting."[73] Tung Ch'i-ch'ang confided to Ch'en Chi-ju, and rarely to anyone else, more of his problems—even doing so by correspondence when away from home.[74]

His expressed admiration for his younger friend's serene life notwithstanding, Tung Ch'i-ch'ang considered Ch'en's well-defined capsule of a world too small for himself. He was to move forward in a wider sphere.

K'uang Ch'an, the "mad" development in Chinese philosophy, which Chi Wen-fu called "seemingly Confucian [*ju*] but not really Confucian, and seemingly Ch'an but [again] not really Ch'an,"[75] was a movement that may be compared with the Southern school movement in painting. Both were iconoclastic, and both had been the result of long periods of suffocating refinement. Toward the end of the sixteenth century, when the movement was at its height, Li Chih became the central figure. Once Liu Yüan-ch'ing asked Tsou Shan: "Why nowadays are there so

many people following Li Chih?" Tsou answered: "Who does not want
to be a sage [*sheng*] or be called virtuous [*hsien*], but it was always
so inconvenient to become one. Now [according to Li Chih] nothing
seems to obstruct the path to enlightenment [Buddhahood]—not even
wine, women, wealth, and lack of self-control. This is quite a bargain,
and who does not like a bargain?"[76]

What appeared to Tsou Shan, and indeed to many others, a bargain,
a short cut to sagehood or to Buddhahood, was actually a difficult path
to follow. Later, when its ideals became popularized, the Southern
school was also accused of misleading the artist with this so-called bargain.[77]

It was easy even for the confused and unsympathetic audience of
the Southern school painter or of the Mad Ch'an philosopher to see what
the movements were trying to destroy. Their iconoclasm was patent.
It was, however, a more difficult task to discern the basically constructive ideals that had generated the movements. The glory that was to
come to the movement in painting never materialized in its counterpart
in philosophy. The Mad Ch'an philosophers, like Li Chih and his predecessor Ho Hsin-yin, were zealous reformers. They did not reach back
into history, passing beyond Wang Shou-jen, to honor Lu Chiu-yüan
with a private temple. They developed further the Lu-Wang trend of
thought, and ardently preached its practice. Both held to their uncompromising attitudes and met violent deaths in the government's persecution.[78]

One need not feel sad about the martyrdom of these Mad Ch'an
high priests. Their point having been made clear, martyrdom became
in a religious sense a triumphant conclusion to their lives. Yet the effect
of their stand had been clouded by unsympathetic and satirical anecdotes. Their madness (*k'uang*), like the awkwardness (*cho*) of the
wen-jen painter, was a proud quality that served to screen off the kind
of audience that told jokes about them. It is, therefore, easy to understand Li Chih's intuitive response to Tung Ch'i-ch'ang, the future high
priest of the Southern school movement. They first met in the spring
of 1598, in a temple outside of Peking. According to Tung Ch'i-ch'ang,
hardly had a few words been exchanged when Li abruptly declared that
he wanted Tung to be his bosom friend and that Tung had a better
understanding of (what to both of them was) truth than "so-and-so,
and so-and-so."[79] Tung Ch'i-ch'ang was then a young *chin-shih* who for
years had been interested in Ch'an. He and his friend Ch'en Chi-ju
often discussed Ch'an with various monks and were particularly interested in Chen-k'o (1543–1603). Both Chen-k'o and Li Chih, the two
leaders of the time in Ch'an and Mad Ch'an, praised Tung Ch'i-ch'ang

as a most promising student.[80] Tung Ch'i-ch'ang was happy and proud to receive such encouragement from these masters and to make their acquaintance, but he could not leave his course to follow them. As a matter of fact, Tung wrote to warn his beloved master, Chen-k'o, not to linger in Peking; shortly thereafter Chen-k'o became involved in a political complication and died in prison. One year later Li Chih committed suicide, also in prison.[81] Tung Ch'i-ch'ang could not see himself driven from city to city and getting in and out of prison preaching the reformer's doctrine. Nevertheless, Mad Ch'an had perhaps the most important influence upon him and his career in the Southern school movement. He was to do his preaching with his painting and calligraphy.

For fifteen years after he became a *hsiu-ts'ai* under prefect Chung Chen-chi, Tung Ch'i-ch'ang wandered from one interest to another, unable to concentrate on preparation for the examinations.[82] During this time he married, and his obedient wife, née Kung, spun, wove, and sewed to help support the family.[83] She stood the hardship of a poor student's wife well, never complaining, moreover, about Tung Ch'i-ch'ang's extravagance in spending on art the money he made tutoring students.[84]

Tung Ch'i-ch'ang knew he was a gifted person and wanted success to come to him effortlessly. Things did not, of course, happen that way. He failed the *chü-jen* examinations several times. In the end, according to his own account, it was the study of Ch'an that helped him to gain depth and to mature, and he succeeded in a spectacular way. He passed the *chü-jen* examinations in 1588, and took his *chin-shih* degree the next year.[85] When he left for Peking to take the last examinations, he was still a poor student and had to accept financial help from friends to make the three-month journey by boat up the Canal.[86] But soon he was to become rich and nationally known for his beautiful examination essays. Tung Ch'i-ch'ang was certainly reminded of his early examinations, when his calligraphy prevented his heading the list. This time, even before the results were out, Wang Hsi-chüeh, whom we mentioned earlier as one of the sponsors of the younger talents, wrote from Peking to a friend back home expressing his confidence in Tung Ch'i-ch'ang. And Wang congratulated him personally on his beautiful calligraphy.[87]

Tung Ch'i-ch'ang, with his privilege as a *chin-shih*, requested honorary titles for his commoner ancestors. The emperor granted the request and honored his father, grandfather, and great-grandfather. His wife now became a lady, sharing her husband's good fortune. By the strength of his success through the conventional channels, he was able to glorify his own ancestors to the generation as far back as the family founder, Tung Lun, of the richer Tungs of Shanghai.[88]

The year 1589—the year Tung Ch'i-ch'ang became a *chin-shih* and began his government career at the age of thirty-five—had a strange distinction in Chinese history. On New Year's Day, when it was customary for the emperor to receive greetings from his officials, there was an eclipse of the sun. At this omen, Emperor Shen-tsung canceled the New Year's Day ceremony, which he never resumed the rest of his reign. He was also to establish the notorious record of ignoring his court, administrative, and ceremonial duties for more than thirty years.[89]

Peking in 1589 was just reverting to normal after the death of the able and stern First Minister Chang Chü-cheng (1525–82) and the prompt reversal of Chang's major policies and persecution of his friends and appointees. The memory of the ten years of national prosperity and security under Chang's administration (1573–82) was still fresh, but was blended with memories of Chang's bloody repressions and of the revenge on Chang after his death. Many veteran statesmen from Chang's era were still in Peking, to become Tung's close associates.[90]

When more and more criticism of Chang Chü-cheng poured in after his death, the emperor gave orders to strip Chang of all titles and to confiscate his home in Chiang-ling. Inside the locked-up estate, waiting for the commissioners from Peking to come and take over the property, many starved to death. Prolonged torture of the members of his family followed, as the officials pressed for more money to be turned over. One of Chang's sons committed suicide in protest. Unbelievable as it all was, Chang Chü-cheng escaped a posthumous execution only because a number of selfless and righteous officials risked their lives to protest such punishment. Throughout Shen-tsung's reign, Chang's achievement could not be mentioned. The emperor, who as a young prince had had Chang as his tutor, now completely destroyed his teacher's image and sank low into all kinds of pleasure making and self-indulgence. He never again took an interest in his government.[91]

When Tung Ch'i-ch'ang came to Peking in 1589, the capital was a sorry sight for a newcomer. The government had just found its new but pathetic equilibrium after swinging the full course from Chang Chü-cheng's efficient government to Shen-tsung's equally efficient destruction. Now, apathy ruled.

The dilemma of action versus self-preservation had been forced on officials everywhere. Both in Peking and back home in Sungkiang, Tung Ch'i-ch'ang could read from the wrinkled faces of his seniors their conservative criticism of the comet-like personality of Chang Chü-cheng. His old employer Lu Shu-sheng, now eighty years old, had been home ever since the beginning of Chang's administration seventeen years before.[92] Two younger critics of Chang, friends of Tung, were now in high offices. Wang Hsi-chüeh, who, we will remember, had congratulated Tung in Peking, was now President of the Board of Rites and a member of the cabinet. Another of the righteous scholar type was T'ien I-chün, a *chin-shih* of 1568, now serving simultaneously as Vice President of the Board of Rites and as a Director of the Han-lin Academy. T'ien, nationally renowned for braving Chang Chü-cheng's anger, had joined a group headed by Wang which sought pardon from Chang himself for those who had memorialized against the First Minister's unorthodox decision to ignore the mourning period after his father's death. In this famous group protest, T'ien used the strongest language. Only his timely departure from Peking on leave saved him from Chang's reprisal. After Chang's death, he was called back, and promoted to his new positions.[93]

Tung Ch'i-ch'ang was elected a member of the Han-lin Academy the year he became a *chin-shih* and soon began studying under T'ien. The newcomer's calligraphy, painting, wit, and knowledge in Ch'an all contributed to his popularity. Unlike another *han-lin,* a certain Feng Shao-hsü, whom the others jokingly referred to as "someone aspiring to a piece of raw pork from the offerings in the Confucian Temple," Tung Ch'i-ch'ang was gay and enjoying his new environment.[94] Shortly after his arrival, however, T'ien I-chün became critically ill. The students got together to discuss the problem of escorting T'ien back to his native Ta-t'ien in faraway Fukien. Tung Ch'i-ch'ang volunteered to accompany the dying teacher, but before they could leave Peking, T'ien died. Keeping his word, Tung Ch'i-ch'ang asked for leave from the Academy and traveled with the coffin the several thousand *li* to T'ien's home. This long journey, which took several months, was unusually conducive to sober reflection on the career of his teacher and to the contemplation of his own future in government. Returning to the Academy next year, Tung was made a Compiler of History.[95]

The Han-lin Academy, training place for future high officials, was a difficult institution to enter. Beginning in the middle of the fifteenth century, the training program suffered sad degeneration. Once when a few young *chin-shih* demanded government positions and were refused by their superior on the ground of insufficient training, one of the group argued: "How can you talk about our training? Can one compare the kind of training we receive today [in 1464] with that of the reign of Yung-lo [1403–24]? Moreover, have you, sir, ever received any decent training?" At one time in 1493, the entire Academy went on "sick leave."⁹⁶

Tung Ch'i-ch'ang asked for leave in 1591 and returned home. There, with his new status, he devoted himself to collecting masterpieces of art.⁹⁷ Had it not been for an important development in Peking, it would be extremely difficult to say how long he would have remained in this early retirement.

For years Emperor Shen-tsung had been battling his court over the question of succession. He wanted to pass over his eldest son, Chu Ch'ang-lo, whom the ministers favored, and name another by his new favorite consort as the heir apparent. In 1594, the officials, under the first ministership of Wang Hsi-chüeh, finally won a partial victory, persuading the emperor at least to begin the education of the fourteen-year-old Chu Ch'ang-lo. The nation sighed with relief when the boy appeared in this solemn ceremony with the insignia traditionally associated with the crown prince, though the emperor waited seven years before making him heir apparent. Tung Ch'i-ch'ang, having been appointed one of the tutors, returned to Peking to assume his new duties.⁹⁸

Chu Ch'ang-lo was regarded as an intelligent and serious youth, and while his hopeless father must be deplored, one still had to consider the opportunity that tutoring the prince presented as a direct avenue to saving the country from ruin. Tung Ch'i-ch'ang was a devoted and enthusiastic tutor, earning in return the prince's special attentiveness.⁹⁹ In his selection of material from the classics for teaching, Tung Ch'i-ch'ang had in mind the current corruption in government and was bold in pointing out the meaning of the lessons in the ancient texts. In 1598, when the nation was hard pressed by the many new and heavy taxes, Tung Ch'i-ch'ang in his lessons asked the future emperor the meaning of *"lao-erh-pu-yüan"* ("[to lay] tasks on the people without their repining"), in the *Analects*.¹⁰⁰ The young prince answered in a clear tone and without hesitation: "It means that one must not exhaust the people." Quickly the anecdote was passed on and became welcome tidings to all who heard it.¹⁰¹

It was because of either the prince's special affection for his teacher or this particular lesson that Tung Ch'i-ch'ang was regarded as politically dangerous by some unknown but powerful official who was jealous of him. Almost immediately he received his next appointment at a somewhat higher rank, but far away from the court. Refusing this provincial position, he went home on "sick leave" instead.¹⁰² By this time, Tung Ch'i-ch'ang had been in office several years and in addition to tutoring the prince had performed such other official duties as representing the court at a provincial ceremony and supervising a provincial examination. It was another provincial examination that deepened his disillusionment with government. One year after coming out of retirement, Tung was conducting an examination in the province of Hu-kuang, and refused to give special favor to an influential family. The offended local power incited a riot, during which several hundred students attacked Tung's official residence and demolished his office. He himself escaped by climbing over the back wall, to discover later that an attempt on his life had thereby been frustrated. Tung Ch'i-ch'ang immediately submitted his resignation, but the court kept him on and ordered the local authorities to punish the rioters. Nevertheless, Tung went into retirement again and refused to accept any of the positions offered him by Emperor Shen-tsung's court.[103]

To educate the nation's youth was always considered in the Confucian tradition an important and pleasant duty of the scholar. Ch'en Chi-ju, even as a man in the mountains, was known for his interest in and generous assistance to the younger generation. This may be interpreted as a refusal to admit defeat, or an active preparation for the future. Tung Ch'i-ch'ang had long been dissatisfied with the education system. In 1597 he discussed the discouraging situation facing the nation's youth in a lengthy essay which was not without references to his own experience. Nine-tenths of the nation's available talent was blocked from serving the government by vicious obstacles created by special interests, Tung complained, and between those who were willing to serve and the government which needed them were an impenetrable wall of noncommunication and the threat of political purge. To the conscientious, appointment to office represented not an opportunity but a dilemma. If the aspiring official aimed at action, he would be prevented from achieving anything at all; and if he did not, he would become a parasite living off the government. Besides, the evil forces might find it necessary to destroy those that they could not recruit in order to safeguard their own interests. Tung went on to say: "The talented ones here in question would be doing the nation a great service if they would hide from such unfavorable exposures and preserve themselves."[104] Eight years later, in 1605, he finally learned his lesson and began at the age of fifty the preservation of himself.

Li Jih-hua (1565–1635), a friend ten years his junior, regarded Tung Ch'i-ch'ang as a rising political figure and regretted that he did not persist in a life of action. In 1609, four years after the incident at the provincial examinations, Li commented on a poem by Tung expressing his discouragement with political life and his disgust at the gossipers in the emperor's court. Li noted Tung's "overscrupulousness," saying:

"This old man has had some unhappy experiences in politics and is now
sensitive and worried. He can no longer take vilification and is afraid
of involvement. It is true that the currents along the political journey
are treacherous, but how about charging into it with a high tide?
History will be brightened by such daring spectacles!"[105] We may add
that indeed it would be a beautiful and bold tide that would glow as red
as blood in history! Li was in every way a delicate, refined, and genial
soul. He knew that he could not have done it himself but, as a person
of such disposition, he would have admired breathlessly any such performance. Time was now against Tung Ch'i-ch'ang. He had been in
retirement since 1605, and there was no sign of hope in Peking. Emperor Shen-tsung, who ascended the throne at the age of ten, reigned,
if we insist upon using this word, for forty-eight years. By that time,
Tung Ch'i-ch'ang had remained at home for fifteen years and was well
past sixty.

There was a difference between his retirement of 1598 and this one.
When he spurned the provincial position and stormed out of Peking as
the favorite tutor of the prince, he was a potential political threat. Now,
moving into the second decade of the seventeenth century, his prince,
although named heir apparent in 1601, was still a prince and not the
emperor; and he himself, showing the signs of age, no longer seemed
so threatening to his political foes. Tung summed up his new sense of
leisureliness in describing his boating life with Ch'en Chi-ju in 1599:
"We go wherever the winds chance to send us, and we meet with morning and evening clouds, gathering friends that need no formal invita-
tions, and riding in a boat that uses no anchor. . . . "[106] Now, in his
sixties, he might have only leisure left.

As Tung Ch'i-ch'ang advanced in age, he began to look after his own
comforts a little more. His household now ranked among the most
prominent in Hua-t'ing, and his estates, art collections, and pleasure
villas spread over a large area. Living as he had learned to live in the
high society to which he had come as a poor boy half a century before,
he forgot the lesson he gave to his prince—"*lao-erh-pu-yüan*"—and got
himself into trouble.

It started in a quiet and gentlemanly way, according to late Ming
and lower-Yangtze standards. Tung Ch'i-chang had a taste for beautiful women and, as a man of position and means, by 1616 had collected several concubines. Now, he expressed his admiration for a
young girl in the household of a Lu family who had once visited the
Tung household. Instead of going through the usual procedures, a
son of his, knowing that Lu himself had an interest in the servant's
daughter and was reluctant to let Tung have her, led a number of

servants in a raid on the Lu estate and made away with the beauty. The loser, nicknamed Lu the Black because of his well-built physique and dark complexion, declared that he would take revenge. To prevent further incident, the local dignitaries intervened, settling the gentlemen's dispute by giving Tung the girl.

Someone in town, as the second phase of the incident unfolded, decided that the story was good enough for a book. The work, an immediate sensation, was known as "The Tale of the Black and the White," and it had, as such tales usually did, two coupling sentences as subtitles to each chapter. The first chapter began: "The White Prince Raids by Night the Lu Homestead, / The Black *hsiu-ts'ai* Riots in Dragon Gate Lane." The book is now lost, but what happened later can be pieced together from several sources.[107] Soon after the book became popular, the story found its way into the repertoire of the wandering minstrels. Tung Ch'i-ch'ang was much enraged by the whole development and eager to identify the author so he could punish him. Following the testimony of a minstrel, the Tungs harassed a Fan family named by the singer. As an indirect result, the accused author, much humiliated, died of anger and frustration. From then on, a son of Tung Ch'i-ch'ang, led on by a particularly vicious servant, took over. When a group of Fan women, among them relatives of the Tungs, came crying and protesting to the Tung house, they were badly insulted. The townspeople became greatly provoked.

Since one of the Fans was a student in the local school, and therefore a member of the gentry, he appealed to the students. Soon there appeared on the streets many beautifully penned proclamations as well as unsigned posters attacking the Tung family and enumerating their crimes against the people. Tung's artistic style was also denounced. Later, these were joined by vulgar handbills spreading the word that the time to take revenge on the Tungs was near.

For years aggressive servants of the family and some of the unruly Tung sons had been intensely hated by the people. In the process of accumulating the family wealth, the Tungs had unscrupulously done much injustice to others in the town. These people had received little help from the authorities, many of whom had sided with Tung Ch'i-ch'ang.[108] Now their pent-up fury was to be translated into action.

Only as the many estates and buildings of the Tung family began to burn did the people grasp their full extent and number. The rest of the story was a fiery finish of the Tung dynasty—almost a prefiguring of the end of the Ming rule; the action came from outside of the small world lit by literary documents. We see masses of nameless and faceless people move into the picture and hands reach out from the darkness around the island of luxury to set it on fire. And in the great confusion we hear the people shout: "Want firewood for your stoves and rice for your families? Kill Tung Ch'i-ch'ang and we all shall live well!"[109]

The Tungs, aware that a riot against them was imminent, retreated to their estates and began to defend themselves with hired hands. Judging from the action of the mobs, the people had particular hatred for two of his sons and a servant named Ch'en Ming. Their houses were attacked first and destroyed.

As the riot went on into another day, people from as far as Shanghai, Ch'ing-pu, and Chin-shan began to arrive and join the townspeople, soldiers, and students already at the scene. "Two spirited youths, quick as monkeys, climbed onto the roof and, using two rolls of oil-soaked mats, started a fire on the front buildings."[110] Many from the crowd joined in and threw the Tungs' furniture into the fire. A northwesterly breeze spread the flames. The neighbors all put up lantern signs saying, "This is the property of the Yangs," or "T'angs," or "Wangs," to the east and the west of the Tungs' so that the crowd would come to their rescue when the flames came licking too close. The fire brightened the night, and the Tung houses were all destroyed except the one belonging to Tung Tsu-ho, the eldest son of Tung Ch'i-ch'ang, whose behavior toward the people had been better than his brothers'.[111]

Tung Ch'i-ch'ang, as the head of the family, was identified with all its evil doings, if not with all those of the upper classes. The rioters took down a tablet from the main hall of Tso-hua-an, a Buddhist temple, that had Tung's calligraphy inscribed on it. Slashing the tablet with knives, they cried: "Tung Ch'i-ch'ang is cut to pieces!"[112]

Although Tung Ch'i-ch'ang had escaped physical injury in the riots, the attack on his name hurt him deeply. Tung felt the attack undeserved but public forgiveness took a long time. For four years after the incident, the name of Tung Ch'i-ch'ang—most popular calligrapher for decades—was glaringly missing from local records of inscriptions written for the numerous memorial stones and public monuments. His name first reappeared on the list in 1620, when his former student, Chu Ch'ang-lo, became emperor. Tung Ch'i-ch'ang was acceptable again to his people.[113]

In the dark years between 1616 and 1620, Tung Ch'i-ch'ang, already in his sixties, had to admit that his life in the city, or symbolically in the world of men, had not been smooth, and that his friend in the mountains, Ch'en Chi-ju, had made a better choice in staying away from this restless world of unpredictables. Tung lost most of his accumulated wealth in the riots, including much of his treasured art collection. Of those pieces that escaped the burning and looting, many had to be sold to raise funds. Without a home, Tung moved his family to a gentry friend's estate to live, repaying the hospitality by painting many pictures and writing numerous pieces of calligraphy for his hosts.[114]

In these sobering years, it must have occurred to him that eventually he had to decide whether his art or his career in government was to give him a place in history. We are reminded of his comment on another period of chaos: "The people of the Wei-Chin time had a philosophy of preferring a cup of wine in lifetime to fame after death. This might be very wisely adopted for a career in government [in this time of ours], but it should not be the maxim for an artist."[115] His political frustration made his choice of career even easier: he should have left the city long ago and cultivated his acre of art in the mountains.

In his government career, he never broke through the stone wall of noncommunication. When a politician had no machine of his own and no intelligence network to tell him who his enemies were, he was not truly in politics. Tung Ch'i-ch'ang's political career was altogether outside of the wall.

In art, which to him was a language for dhyana and a means of communication,[116] he scaled wall after wall, each time discovering a new plateau. He envisioned clearly an image of perfection at each turn of the artistic movement, made brilliant judgments, and was bold, resourceful, and imaginative in his drive toward that goal. One may wonder why the lessons in one area of his life failed to help him in another.

Strange is the ideal of perfection in art! Once in sight, comprehended, or, as rarely is the case, achieved, it loses all its alluring mystery. The creative artist becomes as indifferent to it as a smoker to exhaled smoke. Moreover, with the first taste of success, a new image of perfection looms on the horizon.

When Tung Ch'i-ch'ang began his career as an artist, as we have seen, he held the old masters perfect, and he copied. He wanted nothing else but to be like the master he had selected to study, until he discovered another, whose quality he had come to appreciate only after having worked hard on the first.[117] But before he could paint or write as "well" as the old masters, or before he achieved perfection, he exclaimed: "No successful artist could possibly study the ancients without producing change!" And the ancient masters ceased to be perfect to him.

With the emphasis on change came a new self-identification: perfection now meant the completely *un*learned self. All the lessons in perfection that one could learn from the artistic tradition were identifiable as the glory of one ancient master or another, and thus "returnable" to them. The search for new expressions, however, awakened the self, which was identified as that which was not returnable to anyone else. Deep into this ancient soil of self the Southern school movement sank its taproot.

Tung Ch'i-ch'ang, the "overscrupulous" political figure in the emperor's court, if we may borrow the description from Li Jih-hua, was a spirited contender in the field of arts, bidding openly for fame. This is in the Confucian tradition and we may cite the *Analects* in Tung's support: "The student of virtue has no contentions. If it be said he cannot avoid them, shall this be in archery?" Tung Ch'i-ch'ang's archery was his art, and he was so doggedly after the champion in his mind, Chao Meng-fu—having disposed of Wen Pi and Chu Yün-ming, of course—that he was very much criticized by later writers as having been too aggressive and thus behaving in a manner unbecoming to a scholar.[118] The new Tung Ch'i-ch'ang, having discovered the excitement of *un*learning the orthodoxy, repeatedly criticized the Yüan master. "Having studied the art of calligraphy for thirty years," he wrote, " . . . I now realize that what seems unorthodox and dangerous practice is actually the direct, sound, and classical path to excellence. It is no use to tell this to the uninitiated." He continued: "The ancient masters never took the prosaic and static approach, because they used the surprising and the dynamic to achieve equilibrium. This is why Chao Meng-fu was a long way from the secrets of the Chin and T'ang masters!"[119]

What he was not aware of in the thirtieth year of his career was to embarrass him twenty years later. "Now I have been a student in this Tao of calligraphy for fifty years," he wrote in his late sixties, " . . . and I have been rather critical of Chao Meng-fu. Recently someone brought from Canton this masterpiece in the *hsiao-k'ai* manner by him to show me. How I regret that I have not encountered this until so late in my life! As a T'ang-dynasty poem put it so well: 'Beautiful is the twilight, but why has it to be so close to dusk?' "[120] Tung Ch'i-ch'ang had good reason to be humble. For a third image of perfection had revealed itself before this to the aging artist: it was the image of the dynamic equilibrium. He had thought that he alone had the secret of it, and considered Chao's well-balanced and comfortable style lacking in the excitement of change and of self. But instead he realized that he was admitted to the company of enlightened old masters only now. He had arrived on a new plateau and now saw what in his ignorance he had missed. He had been reconciled with the tradition, but it was a reconciliation made possible by hard-won self-knowledge and a creative step forward. (Plate VI.)

Such a sequence of three images of perfection reaffirms a universal and simple truth to be found in any tradition. The Southern school favored a Ch'an idiom to promote the first breakthrough, from the first perfection to the second, from tradition to change, and from study to enlightenment. Tung Ch'i-ch'ang, crediting the breakthrough to his deserving friend, said: "With the appearance of Mo Shih-lung on the scene came the separation of the Southern school of sudden realization of enlightenment and the Northern school of a gradual process of learning."[121] The same process of earning one's second freedom through the baptism of discipline is also in Confucianism, all the while known to Mo and Tung. Describing his maturity as a septuagenarian, Confucius said: "At seventy, I could follow what my heart desired, without transgressing what was right [disciplined correctness]." This is indeed the third perfection and the very essence of the serenity of the beautiful twilight, but it only comes near dusk, and after one has learned so well about what is right that it has become second nature. That such a maturity, as it is achieved first through learning and then through unlearning, cannot be the monopoly of any one school of philosophy is witnessed by a Christian example: "One has to taste the fruit of knowledge again in order to fall back into innocence."[122] The campaigner for a cause can always find a slogan somewhere, but it is more important that he use one his audience understands.

Late Ming scholars noticed the free three-way borrowing of ideas and idioms between Confucianism, Buddhism, and Taoism. It was a restless and changing time, and they needed a rich vocabulary.[123] What Tung Ch'i-ch'ang did not know, and we think we do, was that he had survived to see a new era. Iconoclastic activity was giving way to a period of reconstruction. With his unimpaired artistic sensitivity, he was able to prefigure what he otherwise could not appreciate: the reconstruction with a new accent, thanks to the Mad Ch'an, the Lu-Wang philosophy, and the artists' contribution, the Southern movement. The new ideal was to flower in the eighteenth century when reconstructed painting such as that of the Four Wangs and Shih-t'ao was new but once again built up with difficult-to-learn details.[124] Faith in knowledge and learning was restored, and handbooks, dictionaries, and encyclopedias enjoyed a popularity made possible when the separation of the "we-group" and the "they-group" ended in everyone's admission to the "we-group." The *Mustard Seed Garden Manual of Painting*, beginning publication in 1701, gained immediate popular support, and was frankly a tool to make art easy.[125] Tung Ch'i-ch'ang could not be held responsible for all these, but as the Southern movement had suggested the possibility of the iconoclastic approach and Tung had prefigured the reconstruction, he was apotheosized in the eighteenth century. The Four Wangs and their group claimed to be his descendants, and the "eccentrics" sought inspiration in his work.[126]

Emperor Kuang-tsung, the good student of Tung Ch'i-ch'ang, asked at his enthronement in 1620: "Where is my teacher Tung now?" And Tung Ch'i-ch'ang resumed his political life.[127] But what could a man of sixty-six still do? How could he be sure that he was to live to be eighty-two?

The young emperor started a sweeping new program and abolished many of the much-hated taxes, but in one month's reign one could not accomplish much. Kuang-tsung died a month later, in the famous "Red Pills Case," probably poisoned.[128] Tung Ch'i-ch'ang was still home preparing to leave for the capital when his former student died.

There were nevertheless to be many more trips to Peking.[129] Tung Ch'i-ch'ang accepted appointment as Director of the Court of Sacrificial Worship, and went up to the court of the next emperor, Hsi-tsung, in 1622.[130] He was ordered to study the government documents preserved in Nanking in connection with the compilation of the Veritable Records of Shen-tsung's rein (1573–1619). (Plate V.) Tung began his new assignment with great gusto and enthusiasm, but before a third of the documents—which literally filled many buildings—had been examined, the funds provided by the government for the job had been exhausted. Organizing a task force of readers and scribes of his own, Tung continued the work with his personal funds, eventually compiling a work of three hundred manuscript volumes. From this study he came to understand well the problems facing the late Ming Empire, and felt his duty lay in presenting to the court also a forty-volume work of selected memorials that had to do with these problems, which he had edited with comments, in the ardent hope that the government might learn the lesson from the past and correct the wrong. But the new emperor's court was embroiled in political strife and had no interest in the advice of a harmless old man. He was commended and his work was forgotten.[131]

At the urging of Ch'en Chi-ju, Tung Ch'i-ch'ang did not remain long in Peking. The bloody purging of the Tung-lin scholars by the eunuch Wei Chung-hsien made the capital in 1624 no place for serious political reconstruction. Both Tung and Ch'en were indeed lucky to have escaped with their lives the chore of writing in praise of the eunuch when a temple was built in their home town in honor of Wei.[132]

Tung was to be called to Peking once more. In 1627, Emperor Ssu-tsung, the last Ming emperor, ascended the throne. In his effort to rid his court of dark forces, he had Wei executed. Tung Ch'i-ch'ang, as a relic from the past who at the age of seventy-six had lived to see his fifth emperor, was invited to serve again in 1631. As he waddled up the Grand Audience Hall in front of the emperor, he could hear murmurs among the officials: "This is a living good omen from the earlier days. Like the *feng* and the *lin,* he now appears among us. May he bring back to us the good days again!"[133]

Tung Ch'i-ch'ang knew there was nothing that he could still do and asked repeatedly to be allowed to go home. His request finally granted, he returned to Hua-t'ing in 1634 as an eighty-year-old retired President of the Board of Rites with many high-sounding titles, and left the emperor's world of men to join his friend in the mountains.[134]

One day in 1636, Tung Ch'i-ch'ang ordered his family to dress him in a Taoist's costume and said: "Although I have occupied some of the highest positions in the government, I never belonged there. I belong to the 'clouds and the waters,' as you can see from my appearance and my manner. When you prepare my body for the funeral, dress me in silk belt, jade ring, cotton clothes, and straw sandals. I do not want to forget for one moment my inborn nature. Besides, I certainly do not wish to disgrace the official regalia!" Then he added, "Please send word to Ch'en Chi-ju that I shall be waiting for him in a few years in the other world."[135] Ch'en wrote the memorial ode for him, and died three years later in his mountain retreat.[136]

The Confucian literati always feel free to adopt different names to go with their various careers and hobbies. Thus whatever formal name one may have for official functions, one can always paint one's landscape under the name of "The Big Fool," or "The Blind Arhat," and admire paintings as "An Old Man Listening to the Pines."[137] The literati also frequently change their clothes to announce the different roles they are playing. When Ch'en decided to be a man in the mountains fifty years before, he burned his scholar's robe. Tung changed his official costume to that of a Taoist as he actually left the world of men to take his place in history.

Richard C. Howard

K'ANG YU-WEI (1858–1927):
HIS INTELLECTUAL BACKGROUND
AND EARLY THOUGHT

The lifetime of K'ang Yu-wei comes close to coinciding with the transitional period in Chinese history that began with the Taiping Rebellion and the Second Opium War and ended with the establishment by Chiang Kai-shek of the Nationalist government in Nanking— a period that witnessed the gradual disintegration of China's age-old imperial system and, with it, the disappearance of the Confucian synthesis as the dominant philosophy among China's ruling classes. Through much of this period K'ang Yu-wei was a prominent if ambiguous figure in political and intellectual circles. In politics he is associated with the late nineteenth-century reform movements, particularly that of 1898, and with the futile attempts in the early years of the Republic to restore the Manchu dynasty. In the intellectual history of the period he is best known for his controversial books on revision of the Confucian classical tradition and for his vigorous lobbying for adoption of his own version of Confucianism as state religion in both the moribund empire and the young Republic.

The overriding fact of his generation was China's confrontation with the expansive and materially superior civilization of the West, and K'ang, to a greater extent than most of his Chinese contemporaries, concerned himself with finding an answer to the implicit challenge to China's national integrity and cultural traditions. In K'ang's view the defense of China's cultural heritage, in particular the Confucian tradition, demanded a restatement and some modification of Confucian philosophy. Thus many of his major writings, including the *Hsin-hsüeh wei-ching k'ao* ("Forged Classics of the Wang Mang Period") and the *K'ung-tzu kai-chih k'ao* ("Confucius as a Reformer"), were in part attempts to recast the entire Confucian tradition into a new mold, which, he believed, would transform Confucianism into a viable body of doctrine that could hold its own in a modern world of competing ideologies.

K'ang's revision of the Confucian tradition reached a culmination in his *Ta-t'ung shu* ("Book of the Grand Unity"). Borrowing from the Kung-yang school of classical interpretation the concept of the "three ages" of historical evolution, he described world civilization as advancing from a past "period of disorder" through an "era of approaching peace" to a future "age of universal peace." With this "age of universal peace" K'ang equated the utopian conditions of the "grand unity" as outlined in the "Li-yün" ("Evolution of Rites") chapter of the *Li-chi* ("Record of Rites"). Within this historical scheme, K'ang envisioned the gradual evolution of Chinese and all other cultures of the world into a single world civilization. In this historical process, the Confucian traditions that had evolved during the past two thousand years would be gradually enlarged and transformed into a universal ideal of absolute justice and harmony.[1]

In the *Ta-t'ung shu*, K'ang offered many details of the future utopian society of the "grand unity." Politically, this society would be a worldwide federation of small communities governed by a democratically elected world parliament, in which each community would be equally represented; economically, property, including the means of production, was to be communally owned, and all produce was to be equally distributed; socially, everyone was to have equal rights, regardless of birth, race, or occupation. Moreover, there was to be complete sexual equality and freedom of mating, with no responsibility on the part of parents to rear their offspring; the family system itself was to be abolished and children were to be raised at public expense in nurseries and schools.[2]

This utopia was the final and most extreme of his "revisions" of the Confucian tradition. Even though he claimed to have derived these ideals from Confucius himself, and sought justification for them in various elements of Confucian learning, in actuality they did violence to every Confucian social and moral value. Thus in revising Confucianism, K'ang not only transformed but transcended it: in his *Ta-t'ung shu* Confucianism as it had been practiced for the past two thousand years was no longer the doctrine dominating the intellectual and spiritual life of the only true civilization, but merely a basis for man's progress to a higher level of existence in the world of the "grand unity."

According to K'ang Yu-wei, his theory of the "grand unity" and the *Ta-t'ung shu* itself were first formulated in 1884, that is, before he compiled his books on the forged classics (1891) and on Confucius as a reformer (1897).[3] However, studies by contemporary Chinese scholars have convincingly demonstrated that K'ang's assertions regarding the date of the *Ta-t'ung shu* were at best misleading. These scholars argue that he probably did not evolve his theory of the "grand unity" until sometime in the 1890's, and the *Ta-t'ung shu* as it now exists was not written before 1902.[4] Nevertheless, in certain unpublished manuscripts of K'ang's early works there are indications that as early as the mid-1880's he had already begun to form some of his radical social and political views on such subjects as world government, political and social equality, sexual freedom, and the abolition of the family, that were to appear later in the *Ta-t'ung shu*.

How did a man steeped and trained in the orthodox Confucianism of his day come to develop such radical ideas? In the present paper we shall seek the answer by an examination of K'ang's background, his early life, and his earliest known writings. The period covered is the first thirty years of his life, from his birth in 1858 until early 1888, shortly before he went to Peking to submit the first of his many memorials to the Kuang-hsü emperor.

Biographical materials on K'ang Yu-wei are numerous, but the study of his life, especially his early life, is complicated by the fact that his own writings—his autobiographical *Nien-p'u* being the most important— are the only primary sources of information. All his biographers, including his pupils Liang Ch'i-ch'ao, Chang Po-chen, and Lu Nai-hsiang,[5] first met K'ang in 1890 or after and thus had no direct knowledge of the early years of his life, when his basic ideas were being formed. Furthermore, K'ang's own account in his *Nien-p'u* of his first thirty years was evidently written later and includes a more-than-usual degree of retrospective rationalization and inevitable distortions, conscious or unconscious. Thus a good deal of what he wrote about his early life was colored by his later image of himself as a Confucian sage. But except in a very few instances where contemporary evidence is available, K'ang's account has perforce been accepted.

K'ang Yu-wei was descended from a family that had lived in Nanhai *hsien* in Kwangtung since the last years of the Sung dynasty. For several generations its members had claimed to be *shih*, or members of the literate class, and had served as clerks or secretaries in local yamens. From this undistinguished but strategic position in the bureaucracy, the family had, by the middle decades of the nineteenth century, achieved local prominence.[6]

The rise of the family began about the turn of the nineteenth century with K'ang Hui, who at the age of almost eighty became the first member of the family to win the *chü-jen* degree. K'ang Hui, regarded by his descendants as the founder of the family's scholarly traditions, was moved by a strong sense of duty to his family and devoted his life to improving its status in the world. To this end he practiced the strictest economies with himself and the utmost severities with his children in instructing them in their obligations to their family and ancestors. During a lifetime of dogged self-improvement, he undertook to master the elements of Confucian learning and to establish himself as a teacher of children in his native district.[7]

In acquiring the rudiments of scholarship, K'ang Hui was guided by the teachings of a number of Cantonese scholars, the most influential of whom was Feng Ch'eng-hsiu (1702–96), a personal friend.[8] A *chin-shih* of 1739 and an educator-official of local note, Feng was a firm adherent of the official Neo-Confucianism and of "solid" or "practical" learning (*shih-hsüeh*) based on the writings of Confucius and Mencius as interpreted by the Ch'eng brothers and Chu Hsi. Feng was also a friend and admirer of one of the model scholar-officials of the Ch'ing dynasty, Ch'en Hung-mou, and his major interest, like Ch'en's, lay in the moral and educational, rather than the metaphysical, aspects of the Neo-Confucian philosophy.[9] The basic feature of Feng's teaching was summed up in the phrase *kung-hsing shih-chien,* which meant the personal acting-out of the Confucian virtues in one's everyday life. Thus Feng criticized the scholars of the currently fashionable Han learning for their preoccupation with learned trifles and attacked the followers of Wang Yang-ming for their concern with useless meditation; more worthy was the man who diligently performed his duties in public office and, by setting a personal example of virtuous conduct, sought to improve the morals of the common people.[10]

From Feng Ch'eng-hsiu, K'ang Hui absorbed the fundamentals of the Neo-Confucian moral philosophy and passed them on to his descendants as part of the family tradition in learning. Armed with the moral teachings and sense of family obligation instilled into them by K'ang Hui, his sons and grandsons continued the process of building up the position of the family. To do so they developed a degree of professional specialization within the family, a practice common in the Ch'ing dynasty among families seeking to improve their social and economic status. While one branch of the family specialized in mastering Confucian learning with a view to passing the civil service examinations and obtaining positions in the bureaucracy, another branch engaged in money-making enterprises to provide financial support for the entire family during the long and costly period of academic preparation. In this way K'ang Hui's sons and grandsons, by simultaneously exploiting these two avenues to social advancement, achieved a modest rise in the family's fortunes.[11]

With the outbreak of the Taiping Rebellion and related local uprisings in Kwangtung, a new road to advancement was opened to the K'ang family. Investing heavily of its manpower and financial resources in support of the embattled Manchu dynasty, the "entrepreneurial" branch of the family, led by two of K'ang Yu-wei's great-uncles, raised levies to fight the rebel forces. By the time these uprisings were finally suppressed by the imperial armies, the K'ang family had risen to a position of leadership within its locality; one member, who had become a military leader of note under Tso Tsung-t'ang, eventually rose (without benefit, it appears, of even the *hsiu-ts'ai* degree) to provincial treasurer, and for a brief period served as interim governor of Kwangsi province. Meanwhile, within the "scholarly" branch of the family, one member, K'ang Yu-wei's grandfather, had succeeded in passing the examinations for the *chü-jen* degree and in obtaining government posts as director of studies in various counties in Kwangtung province.[12]

Thus by actively identifying its interests with the political fortunes of the reigning dynasty and by espousing the officially sanctioned Neo-Confucian orthodoxy, the K'ang family had within three generations succeeded in rising from relative obscurity to prestige and prosperity in its native district. It was at this auspicious stage in the family history that K'ang Yu-wei was born.

K'ang Yu-wei was undoubtedly exposed at an early age to his family's traditions: the simple but practical moral teachings of the orthodox school of Neo-Confucianism and a strong sense of obligation to maintain, and where possible to advance, the family's position by active support of the existing political and social order. During the first seven years of his life, many adult members of the family, including his father, were away from home taking part in the government campaigns against the Taipings in the north or against the local bandits in Kwangtung. The young K'ang was left at the family homestead, where one of his uncles directed his earliest training. This began, conventionally enough, with recitations from T'ang poetry, the *Great Learning*, the *Doctrine of the Mean*, the *Analects* of Confucius, and the *Classic of Filial Piety*. With the return of his elders from the wars in 1866, the eight-year-old K'ang found himself to be a favorite of his soldier-kinsmen, who admired his precocity. But while the Taiping wars had brought honor and prestige to the family, the arduous campaigns had exacted a heavy toll upon its members: several had been killed or had died of disease, and K'ang Yu-wei's father returned home with a fatal ailment from which he died early in 1868, leaving his widow with three young daughters, an infant son (K'ang Kuang-jen, executed in 1898), and K'ang Yu-wei, then ten years old.[13]

During the next eight years, K'ang's upbringing was either directly or indirectly under the supervision of his grandfather, K'ang Tsan-hsiu. When K'ang Yu-wei joined his grandfather in mid-1868, the latter was serving as director of instruction and principal of an academy in Lien-chou, in the mountainous Hunan border-region of northern Kwangtung.[14] Then in his early sixties, K'ang Tsan-hsiu had spent the greater part of his public career in educational posts at the *hsien* or *chou* level, and had acquired a reputation as a man of forbearance and kindness, an administrator of honesty and competence. In his youth he had absorbed the strict Neo-Confucianism of his own father and grandfather with its emphasis on the personal practice of the Confucian virtues. As a young man, his training in the orthodox Neo-Confucian views of the time had been reinforced by a period of study under a Cantonese scholar whose teachings were similar to, and in part derived from, those of Feng Ch'eng-hsiu, the friend and adviser of K'ang Tsan-hsiu's grandfather, K'ang Hui.[15]

It was these moral precepts of the Sung Confucians that K'ang Tsan-hsiu sought to instill in his young grandson. To illustrate the moral lesson that righteousness (*i*) was the prime requisite of the Confucian scholar, he would recall exemplary tales about the great scholars of the past. K'ang Yu-wei appears to have been a diligent and receptive pupil and, stirred by his grandfather's frequent allusions to the wise men of old, often imagined himself to be a great Confucian scholar like Chang Shih or Su Shih of the Sung period. Under the spell of such boyhood fancies the young K'ang Yu-wei took to regarding himself as superior to the other boys of his acquaintance, whom he treated with condescension.[16]

When K'ang was twelve years old, his grandfather was recalled from Lien-chou and took K'ang Yu-wei back with him to Canton. Dissatisfied with his grandson's progress in composition, he placed him under a special teacher in Canton to learn the "eight-legged" essay style of writing that was obligatory in the examinations. For the next five years, a succession of tutors both at his home and in Canton subjected him to the grueling discipline of this dreary style. K'ang, however, had little inclination toward this aspect of his training and gave only token attention to the instruction of his teachers. Rather than submit to this discipline, he stubbornly followed his own literary inclinations, chief of which was to browse at random through the large family library that had been built up by his great-uncles. But his lack of progress in the "eight-legged" essay continued to be a cause of concern to his grandfather, who finally succeeded in persuading him to take his preparations for the civil service examinations more seriously. After several months of steady application, K'ang sat for the *chü-jen* examinations in 1876 in Canton, but without success.[17]

Following this disappointment, K'ang, then eighteen years old, asked permission to study under Chu Tz'u-ch'i, a Cantonese scholar and teacher who for many years had been a highly esteemed friend of

K'ang's grandfather. A *chin-shih* of 1847, Chu Tz'u-ch'i (1807–81), in twenty years of teaching in his native Nan-hai county, had become famous as one of the leading Confucian scholars of Kwangtung. He had grown to maturity at a time when the school of Han learning was being established by Juan Yüan, one of its most distinguished exponents, at the Hsüeh-hai-t'ang Academy in Canton. In time many important Cantonese scholars came to oppose the narrow partisanship that separated the rival schools of Sung Neo-Confucianism and Han learning, and tended to combine the moral philosophy emphasized by the former and the systematic methods of textual research that had been developed by the latter.[18]

Though Chu Tz'u-ch'i took a prominent part in this eclectic movement, he gave greater emphasis to the Sung learning than to the Han learning. An advocate of the active life of virtue, he severely criticized the philosophy of intuition and meditation as practiced by the followers of Wang Yang-ming. Of the scholars of the recent past, Chu favored Ku Yen-wu, because he believed that Ku was nonpartisan in his scholarship and because Ku had taught that men of learning should devote their attention to affairs of government and the welfare of the people. In teaching his students, Chu placed equal emphasis upon the cultivation of moral behavior and the development of methodical scholarship; and in addition he instructed his pupils in the Six Classics, the standard histories, government records of the current dynasty, the *Li-hsüeh* of the Sung Neo-Confucians, and the study of literary style.[19]

In 1876, K'ang Yu-wei began his studies under Chu Tz'u-ch'i and recorded his initial reaction to Chu's teaching as follows:

I received his teaching as a traveler who finds lodging for the night, or as a blind man who sees the light. I cleansed my mind and put aside my desires and, with a concentration of purpose, gave myself wholly to his teaching. I felt with certainty that I would be able to read all of the books before I was thirty years old. I had no doubt that I would be able to do something about the world. From this time I gave no more thought to writing in the "eight-legged" essay style and regarded with disdain all considerations of wealth and high office. I held myself to be above and beyond the rank and file, and took as my companions the sages and heroes of old.[20]

Here K'ang clearly indicated that his ambition to become a sage—an aspiration first aroused some years before by his grandfather—had been rekindled and strengthened by Chu Tz'u-ch'i.

In 1877 K'ang received word of his grandfather's death by drowning. For close to a decade his grandfather had taken the place of both parent and teacher to K'ang, and his death appears to have been a severe blow to the nineteen-year-old youth. Taking temporary leave from his studies, he returned home and observed the mourning rituals for his grandfather with unusual seriousness. He studied the funeral rites of antiquity in great detail and carried them out with such literal precision that his relatives and neighbors looked askance. But undeterred by their disapproval, K'ang persevered for several months in performing his own version of the funeral rites until the coffin was finally buried.[21]

Following his return to Chu's school in 1878, K'ang's attitude toward his teacher seems to have undergone a gradual change. A maturing confidence in his own abilities, coupled with a conviction that his ambition to become a sage was increasingly justified, led him to assume a growing sense of his own superiority and an attitude of condescension to others. This inclination toward intellectual arrogance had been detected by Chu, who had frequent occasion to reprove his pupil for it. Owing to these tendencies, however, K'ang approached the point where he felt that he had learned all that he needed from Chu.[22]

It was at this stage in his personal development, late in 1878, that K'ang underwent a profound emotional crisis. The death of his grandfather the year before appears to have left him in the grip of ambivalent sentiments: it imparted to him a feeling that he was his own master, which no doubt contributed to his growing independence of mind;[23] but it also must have left him with an unsettling sense of loss and insecurity. One other point: following his return to Chu Tz'u-ch'i after his grandfather's death, K'ang had thrown himself into renewed and intensive study, which appears to have led to growing mental fatigue and emotional exhaustion.

These tensions, combined with a restless desire for self-assertion, seem to have been the background of a sudden and complete revulsion against his past intellectual training:

Buried as I was every day amid piles of old papers, my mind became confused, and I gradually developed a revulsion for them. Then one day I had a new idea. I thought: "Scholars like Tai Chen, who engage in textual research, fill their homes with the works they have written, but in the end, what is the use of all this?" Thus I gave it up, and in my own heart I longed to seek a place where I might pacify my mind and determine what would be my destiny. I suddenly abandoned my studies, discarded my books, shut my door, withdrew from my friends and sat in contemplation, nurturing my mind. My schoolmates thought it very queer, for there had been no one who had done this before, inasmuch as the Master was in favor of the personally active performance of the Confucian virtues and detested the study of Ch'an Buddhism. While I was sitting in contemplation, all of a sudden I saw that Heaven, Earth, and all the myriad things were all of one substance with myself, and in a great release of enlightenment I beheld myself a sage and laughed for joy; then suddenly I thought of the sufferings and hardships of all living beings and wept in melancholy. Abruptly I thought: "Why should

I be studying here and neglecting my kin? I should pack up immediately and go back to the thatched hut over my grandfather's grave." The students, observing that I sang and wept for no apparent reason, believed that I had gone mad, or was mentally ill. When winter came, I took my leave of Master Chu, having decided to return home and sit in contemplation.[24]

Apart from the emotional aspects of this experience, K'ang's intellectual revolt against the scholarship of Chu Tz'u-ch'i was directed in particular against that aspect of Chu's teaching which stressed the necessity of training in textual research, as expounded by Tai Chen, one of the leaders of the school of Han learning. Intellectually restless and impatient, K'ang forsook this long and tedious path to knowledge for the short cut offered by the intuitive schools of Chinese thought.

K'ang's break with Chu Tz'u-ch'i marked a definite turning point in his life. Thereafter he began to explore new avenues of learning that were to lead him far from orthodox traditions. After returning from Chu's school, he left home early in 1879 to continue the practice of meditation at Hsi-ch'iao-shan, a nearby mountain retreat. Removed from the conventions of society, he lived the solitary, uninhibited life of a Taoist hermit, going about with his hair unkempt, whistling and singing. At times he studied the books of Taoism and the Buddhist canon; at other times he sat in contemplation. During his meditations, he claimed to have experienced the successive stages of mystic enlightenment—the heights of elation, the depths of depression, the torments of demonic visions, and the triumphant emergence of his spirit from its trials.[25]

After a few months at Hsi-ch'iao-shan, his spiritual exercises were abruptly terminated. One of his uncles, who had but limited patience with K'ang's unconventional behavior, demanded that he come down from his mountain retreat and take the provincial examinations. When K'ang refused, his uncle cut off his allowance and thus forced him to return. Nevertheless, he stubbornly persisted in his chosen course of mental and spiritual development by secluding himself as best he could in the library or the gardens of the family estate.[26]

Summing up his meditations at Hsi-ch'iao-shan, K'ang wrote late in 1879:

I reflected upon the perils and hardships in the life of the people and upon how I might save them with the powers of wisdom and ability granted to me by Heaven. Out of commiseration for all living beings, and in anguish over the state of the world, I took it as my purpose to set in order all under Heaven.[27]

Although the wording here reflects his studies of Buddhism earlier in the year, the underlying spirit is clearly revealed in the words "to set in order all under Heaven." This was not the passive world-view of the Buddhist teaching but the active life of virtuous works sanctioned by Confucian tradition.

K'ang's views of Confucianism, however, differed radically from those of his family, which held the conventional view that by attaining public office one might improve at the same time the interests of the family and the welfare of the common people to a modest degree. K'ang's purpose was much more ambitious: to achieve the status of a sage, whose powers of wisdom and moral suasion would in themselves be sufficient to "set in order all under Heaven."

Although K'ang was generally reticent about his relations with his family, it is clear that the family elders were not in sympathy with his grandiose aspirations. While the deaths of his father and grandfather had left him with some degree of freedom from the demands of filial piety, K'ang was by now an adult member of the family group and was expected by his elders to fulfill certain family responsibilities. Since he had from childhood shown a marked aptitude for learning, he was under an obvious obligation to prepare himself for the civil service examinations and, if successful, to seek advancement in public office. But K'ang, with his long-standing aversion for the "eight-legged" essay and his exalted notions of becoming a Confucian sage, rejected the examinations and office-seeking as personally distasteful and unworthy of his high purpose.[28]

In spite of these lofty sentiments, K'ang did yield on occasion to strong family pressure. Thus in 1882, on the pretext of taking the *chü-jen* examinations in Peking, he made his first journey to the national capital; and in 1885 he took the provincial examinations in Canton. But in general he refused to bother with preparations for the examinations, and as a result his elders curtailed the family funds at his disposal. Although his mother sometimes gave him money for books from her limited personal resources, K'ang apparently had no funds of his own and complained that at times he could not even afford to buy ink or writing brushes.[29]

There was an admirable single-mindedness about K'ang's approach to his self-conceived mission in the world, and from late in 1879 to 1884 he applied himself to a program of intensive study that included governmental organization and political geography, exegeses of the classics by scholars of the Han learning, the writings of the great Neo-Confucian scholars, the dynastic histories, and the documentary compilations of the Ch'ing dynasty, all of which were subjects that he had studied under Chu Tz'u-ch'i. Unlike his former teacher, K'ang also read extensively in the literature of Buddhism.

A significant development of this period was his discovery of "West-

ern learning."[30]   His recent academic rebellion had left him particularly receptive to new ideas, and his interest in the West was quickly
aroused by references to political administration in the nations of Europe and America. To satisfy his curiosity, K'ang made the short journey to Hong Kong and came away much impressed by the European-
style buildings, the clean, orderly streets, and the disciplined behavior
of the policemen. Only after viewing such manifestations of Western
civilization, he noted, did he realize that the men of the West were
governed by definite legal systems and were not to be compared with
the barbarian I and Ti of antiquity.[31]

K'ang acquired maps and books dealing with the West, and read
earlier Chinese studies of the West, such as the *Hai-kuo t'u-chih* and the
Ying-huan chih-lüeh.[32] However, during the next three years K'ang was
obliged to remain close to the family settlement, where his energies
were almost entirely absorbed in his studies of Chinese learning. Not
until 1882 did he begin the study of the West in earnest. In that year
he went to Peking, ostensibly to take the examinations, and on his return passed through Shanghai. Observing the orderly administration
which the Westerners maintained in the foreign settlement, he deduced
that the governments in the Western nations themselves must be even
more advanced than in their dependent territories and that they must
possess a high level of public morality and learning. With a renewed
determination to study Western government, he purchased in Shanghai
large numbers of books in the "Western learning," which he began to
study intensively after his return to Kwangtung.[33]

By the 1880's, a considerable number of Western works were available in Chinese translation. The publications of the mission presses
included, in addition to Biblical texts and Christian tracts, books on
Western history, geography, technology, and science.[34] The translation
offices, recently established by the Chinese government, had by 1880
published translations of Western treatises on international law, history,
mathematics, and natural sciences.[35] The translation bureau of the
Kiangnan Arsenal in Shanghai had published some ninety-eight translations of Western works on mathematics, physics, chemistry, medicine,
military and naval science, geology, and geography.[36]

All these were, we know, available at the time of K'ang's visit to
Shanghai, along with many other sources of knowledge concerning the
West, but we do not know how much K'ang actually read. Two of his
biographers state that he bought all the translations of the Western
religious societies, the T'ung-wen-kuan in Peking, and the Kiangnan
Arsenal, as well as the translations that had been published by the
arsenals in Tientsin, Foochow, and Canton.[37] K'ang himself mentioned

only two publications by name: the *Hsi-kuo chin-shih hui-pien,* a periodical digest of world news published by the Kiangnan Arsenal; and the *Wan-kuo kung-pao,* a magazine edited in Shanghai by the American missionary Young J. Allen, which included articles on Christianity and other doctrines, Western history, political science, and technology, and brief periodic summaries of world news.[38]

From information supplied by his biographers and by K'ang himself, it appears that a large part of the translations studied by K'ang in the early 1880's were concerned with such subjects as science, technology, and mathematics. While K'ang conceded that in such works he found a source of great mental stimulation,[39] his major interest lay in the study of Western forms of government, a subject he felt to be inadequately covered by the translations available at the time. His dissatisfaction with the scope of existing translations was reflected in a statement he made subsequently (1886) to Chang Chih-tung, then viceroy in Canton:

There are too few Western books in China, and the Western works translated by Fryer all deal with such unimportant studies as military science and medicine. Of greater importance are the books on government, for in the Western learning there are a great many new principles, none of which exist in China. It is a matter of great importance to found a bureau to translate them.[40]

K'ang was, however, able to get a considerable amount of information about contemporary events in Europe and America, as well as in India, Southeast Asia, and Meiji Japan.

K'ang's intense interest in Western ideas on political administration seems to have been closely related to his sense of personal mission to "set in order all under Heaven." Though intellectually stimulating, "Western learning" had a more practical purpose for him, to supply additional knowledge that might be used in his life mission; yet the pursuit of this knowledge was never allowed to interfere with the studies of Chinese learning in which he has been engaged since 1879.

Toward the end of 1884, K'ang concluded his survey of Chinese learning and turned to the task of bringing together the conclusions he had drawn from his consideration of Confucian and Buddhist as well as Western thought. Earlier in the year, he had resided for a while in Canton, where he had applied himself to the study of the Buddhist canon and Neo-Confucian philosophy. But as tension mounted during the Sino-French dispute over Annam, the Chinese authorities placed the city under martial law; and in the autumn of 1884 rumors of an imminent French attack on Canton were followed by waves of antiforeign (largely anti-Christian) rioting that swept through Kwangtung province. Finding such unsettled conditions distracting, K'ang retired to the family settlement in Nan-hai, where, in the relative seclusion of the family library, he again devoted himself to reading and reflection.[41]

As the year drew to an end, K'ang entered into a state of profound mental abstraction, during which he experienced something of a mystic vision. According to K'ang, his vision began with a realization that both space and time were relative. This perception, while probably inspired by Taoist concepts, was couched in terms reflecting his studies of Western science:

A microscope magnifies many thousands of times, so that one sees a louse as a steamboat, and an ant as an elephant. From this I apprehend the principle that the big and the small are the same in size. A beam of light from an electrical apparatus travels many tens of thousands of *li* in a single instant. From this I grasped the principle that a moment and an eon are of the same duration. I learned that outside the biggest things are things still bigger, and that within the tiniest things are contained things still smaller.[42]

It was under the stimulus of such metaphysical insights that K'ang began to envision the possibility of a new intellectual synthesis. As later described in his autobiographical *Nien-p'u,* his vision encompassed a number of disparate concepts arbitrarily brought together to form what he referred to as his "system of the grand unity." For the cosmology of this "system," K'ang drew heavily from Neo-Confucian and Buddhist metaphysics, and to a much lesser extent from Western sciences. As part of the synthesis, K'ang also envisioned an ideal world of the future, "unified by a federation of nations, a blending of races, an amalgamation of religions," a unified world of social and economic equality in which all living beings would exist in a state of utter happiness.[43] Several elements in K'ang's account of this experience must be discounted as interpolations of his later ideas.[44] Nevertheless, it is clear that in the winter of 1884–85 K'ang made his first serious attempt to systematize a wide variety of ideas: Confucian, Buddhist, and Western.

Following this composite vision K'ang experienced what he described as a feeling of complete serenity—a feeling of spiritual self-sufficiency that left him unaffected by such worldly considerations as wealth, power, or fame. It was in this mood of spiritual elevation that he conceived his role in the world of men:

My appearance in this world is solely for the purpose of saving all living beings. It is for this reason that I do not dwell in Heaven, but enter into Hell; that I do not go to the Pure Land, but come to the world of corruption; that I do not exist as an emperor or king, but as one of the people. Unwilling to be pure by myself, to enjoy bliss in solitude, or to raise myself above others, I consider it easier in my task of helping and saving to be in intimate contact with all living beings. Thus every day I take the salvation of the world to be my intention, every instant I hold the salvation of the world to be my business, which I perform without regard for my person or my life. Since all the heavens are without limit, and there is no difference between the large and the small, I begin with the land that gave me birth, with the people I chance to meet, the many for whom I have close affection. In pity and commiseration, I succor and rescue them, ever crying out to the multitude and hoping that the multitude will follow me. This I hold to be the art of the "Way" and the manner in which to conduct myself.[45]

Apart from revealing his amazing egotism—the almost sublime condescension by which he set himself apart from and above his fellow men—this passage indicates how deeply K'ang's thinking at this time was influenced by Mahayana Buddhism. His conception of himself as a savior of the world closely resembles the Buddhist picture of the merciful Bodhisattva, who, after achieving enlightenment, voluntarily renounces a life of bliss in order to deliver the rest of mankind from its suffering.[46]

Soon after this vision of his role in a unification of the world, K'ang began to feel what may have been the effects of intensive study and emotional strain: he complained of severe headaches, so painful that he could hardly see, and although Western medicines brought gradual improvement in his condition he was unable to leave his room for several months. It was during this period of illness that K'ang, believing he was about to die, began to write down for posterity the ideas that he had recently envisioned.[47]

During the next two years he produced a number of books, two of which are of considerable importance. The first, written between 1885 and 1887, was inspired in part by K'ang's studies of Western geometry, as is indicated by its title, *Jen-lei kung-li* ("The Axioms [or Universal Principles] of Mankind"). The second notable work of this period, the *K'ang-tzu nei-wai p'ien* ("The Inner and Outer Books of the Philosopher K'ang"), was written during 1886–87.[48] These books were never published, at least in their original forms. However, among a collection of K'ang's personal papers there exist manuscripts of two short works, one of which is apparently a copy of the *K'ang-tzu nei-wai p'ien* written during the 1880's. The other, entitled *Shih-li kung-fa* ("Principles of Truth and Universal Laws"), has been identified as a somewhat later revision of the *Jen-lei kung-li* that K'ang wrote between 1885 and 1887.[49] These two manuscript works constitute what is probably the most reliable evidence available regarding the nature of K'ang's thinking during these years.

Of these two youthful works, the *K'ang-tzu nei-wai p'ien* appears from its intellectual content to be the earlier and is possibly the earliest of K'ang's writings still in existence. The fifteen sections (*p'ien*) of this book contain a curious miscellany of essays expressing points of view that are often inconsistent and even mutually contradictory. Several sections show the effects of his studies of Buddhism and "Western learning," but the book as a whole reveals that at the time it was written the influence of Confucianism, and particularly Neo-Confucian philosophy, was still predominant.

Among the more traditionally Confucian of K'ang's views were those regarding government. In the first section of the *Nei-wai p'ien* K'ang revealed his firm adherence to the traditional imperial system. Although admitting that China was only one among the nations of the world, even conceding the peculiarity of the institution of the emperor as the "son of heaven," he affirmed the validity of this form of government for China. Further, he avowed the *mystique* surrounding the "son of heaven" by extolling the almost magical powers of the emperor, who commanded the reverence of his officials and his people by virtue of the age-long accretion of moral and cultural force attached to his position. Thus, "with one or two men to advise him, the whole empire follows after him, for the civil order and strength of China are brought about by a turn of his palm."[50]

Intellectual conservatism was apparent not only in his views on China's political institutions but also in his attitudes toward China's cultural traditions. In another section of the *Nei-wai p'ien,* he argued that in the history of the world's societies customs and conventions had arisen that restrained and channeled men's impulses. In China these social institutions were derived from the teachings of Confucius; in India, from the Buddha; in Europe, from Jesus; and in the Moslem areas, from Mohammed. In comparing these major doctrines, K'ang left no doubt about which he considered to be the best: those that existed in China. The teachings of Confucius, embodying the ancient wisdom of China, were the most comprehensive and beneficial in the world. China's social customs and institutions grew from the sage's perceptions of the just relationships between sovereign and subject, father and son, man and wife. The harmonious society was seen as founded on virtuous individual patterns within an occupational hierarchy of scholar, farmer, artisan, and merchant. Traditional values transmitted by Confucius and his successors were the lifestream of China's superior culture. Although K'ang conceded that Buddhism might be a necessary complement to Confucianism, particularly in times of crisis, he dismissed Christianity and Islam as inferior and unnecessary. Confucianism, complemented by Buddhism, was the perfect formula, not just for men the world over, but for all other worlds, for life on all the stars and in all the heavens of the universe.[51]

While the *Nei-wai p'ien* reveals a strong attachment to China's political and cultural traditions, certain sections suggest an ambivalent attitude toward the society in which K'ang lived. In one section, where he contrasted the Confucian virtues of righteousness (*i*) and humaneness (*jen*), K'ang ascribed to the former many of the social evils then existing in China:

China's customs that exalt the ruler and bemean his subjects, that favor the male over the female, and that honor the "worthy" while repressing the "worthless"—these are what we mean by "righteousness." . . . Once popular practices and customs become fixed, they are held to be the epitome of "righteous" principles. Down to the present day, subjects prostrate themselves in awe of the ruler's majesty and dare not speak out; wives are held down as inferiors and, being uneducated, are kept in ignorance. These are most oppressive ways to treat subjects or wives. I fear that they are not really the epitome of "righteous" principles, but have only become so through popular custom. . . . I say that in another hundred years they will certainly change: as to these three customs, the ruler will not be exalted nor his subjects bemeaned; women will be treated with the same respect as men; and the "worthy" and the "worthless" will be deemed alike. Alas! This is the Buddha's teaching of equality![52]

This critical attitude toward his own society was clearly in conflict with his assertions elsewhere in the *Nei-wai p'ien* that the teachings of China's sages were superior to all other doctrines. In the passage above, K'ang explicitly condemned two of the traditions he had in another context glowingly ascribed to these sages: the relations established between the ruler and his subjects, and between man and wife. K'ang had conceded, with obvious reluctance, that the solution to these political and social inequalities was not to be found in Confucianism at all, but in the teachings of Buddhism.

K'ang identified the virtue of "righteousness" in the Confucianism of his day with oppression, self-interest, and conformity. In contrast was the virtue of humaneness, implying generosity, magnanimity, and universal, all-inclusive love, which K'ang viewed as a moral force counteracting the restrictive effects of "righteousness." This was particularly the case with regard to human understanding. K'ang believed that understanding was closely related to love, which was an aspect of humaneness. Commenting in another section of the *Nei-wai p'ien* on the selfish and parochial interests of contemporary Chinese scholarship, he stated that the breadth of one's understanding was in direct proportion to the scope of one's love. Thus for one who loves only himself or his own kin, understanding is limited to his own person or to the circle of his family; but for one whose love has expanded to encompass larger social units—his native locality, his province, and his country—his understanding is enlarged correspondingly. The ultimate point in this process was attained when a person's love, and hence his understanding, was such that he held the whole world to be one family in which China was but a single member.[53]

Although K'ang attributed this ideal to the legendary culture-heroes of Confucian tradition as well as to Confucius himself, it was actually much closer to the rival philosophy of Mo Ti. And it was the Mohist concept of universal love that K'ang regarded as the ultimate extension of the Confucian virtue of humaneness. Thus in the *Nei-wai p'ien*, K'ang had already found Confucian thought too narrow in scope, and even while seeking to remain within the Confucian tradition he had sought support for his own views in sources outside it—in Buddhism for his social ideals and in the Mohist philosophy for his moral views.

Several passages, such as the one below, are instructive as to the extent of the influence on K'ang's thinking of still another factor—the Western sources K'ang had studied so assiduously:

From the time that Buddhism first arose, there has been complete ignorance as to the ancient history of Indian civilization. Recently I saw the Westerner Alexander Wylie, who stated that both Euclid and Archimedes had lived during the Chou period, and that at that time mathematics had already become very profound. Yet he himself said that they had no understanding of decimal numbers, and that this theory had come from India. As to India's theory of decimals, it indicates a high level of development in all fields. Generally, when mathematics is highly developed, it is sure to be a period when government affairs are well regulated and civilization is flourishing. From this we can say that at one time civilization flourished greatly in India . . . and its wealth and prosperity almost equaled that of Europe of today.

K'ang then went on to deduce that India was probably the most ancient seat of civilization, older than that of Persia, Palestine, or Rome—older even than that of China.[54]

A developing tendency toward scientistic explanations was even more evident in his conjectures regarding man and the universe:

The extent to which human beings flourish on the Earth depends upon how closely the Earth revolves around the sun. When, in the very beginning, it was very close to the sun, the heat was so tremendous that man could not have endured it; only great plants and trees were able to flourish. Westerners have examined geological strata and say that the coal under the earth was transformed from such huge trees as these. As the Earth revolved about the sun at gradually increasing distances, there appeared huge beasts and birds. The bones of such gigantic beasts have been found in the region of Siberia. Now the creation of mankind also depends upon the inclination of the Earth to the sun. In the past, when Mongolia as well as Siberia lay in the path of the Equator and the Temperate Zone [*sic*], government, religion, and civilization at one time must have flourished. It is also said that formerly Venus and Mercury were close to the sun. They must have had plants and trees, birds and beasts, but could not have had human beings.[55]

The presence of such passages in the *Nei-wai p'ien* confirms K'ang's assertion in his *Nien-p'u* that he had written this work "while browsing through Western learning."[56] He had evidently obtained a considerable amount of information relating to mathematics, astronomy, geology, and world geography—facts accessible through Chinese translation in the 1880's. His reading gave him facts rather than values, information about the physical nature of the world rather than the political, social, or moral philosophies of the West. The fragmentary and superficial knowledge that K'ang abstracted from these translations does not appear to have had any profound effect upon his basic moral and political views; it was, rather, put to the service of a powerful and enterprising imagination to embellish a world-view that drew its major components from the politico-moral philosophy of Neo-Confucianism and the speculative metaphysics of Mahayana Buddhism.

Compared with the *Nei-wai p'ien*, the *Shih-li kung-fa* was a consistent and systematically organized work, remarkable both for a strange methodology and for the moral and social ideals outlined by K'ang. The *Shih-li kung-fa*, as the title suggests, was concerned with "principles of truth" and "universal laws." K'ang had set out to ascertain those human values that all nations of the world held to be valid ("principles of truth") and those human laws that men the world over could be expected to recognize as true ("universal laws").

To do this, K'ang proposed using the method of Euclidean geometry, by which the theorems were proved from the axioms. The precise logic of the mathematical reasoning that produced these immutable laws of geometry suggested to K'ang a method for deriving from the truths of human nature and society the immutable laws governing human morality and institutions. K'ang went even further, attempting a direct relation between the theorems of geometry and "eternal truths":

If these universal laws proceed from the axioms of geometry, their principles are relatively true; if they proceed from the laws that have been established by man, their principles are relatively false. Again, the laws that proceed from the axioms of geometry are termed "necessary truths" or "eternal truths"; laws established by man are termed "equivocal truths."[57]

Aware, however, of the practical difficulties of applying mathematical reasoning to human affairs and of the areas in human affairs beyond the scope of geometrical axioms, K'ang introduced another source of "universal laws," those values "most beneficial to human morality":

The fixed laws derived from geometrical axioms are but one part of the "universal laws." There are very few laws proceeding from the axioms of geometry that are applicable to human affairs, and this is why we must have man-made laws. . . . There are many institutions in the world to which the axioms of geometry do not apply; and not having laws that proceed from the axioms of geometry, we must rely on laws that are established by man. Laws established by man are fundamentally lacking in certainty, and so we can only deduce those that are most beneficial to human morality and regard them as "universal laws." But these must be deduced in common by all mankind. We may say, then, that they are universally deduced.[58]

Although the "universal laws" derived from geometry were immediately acceptable to all men, the "universal laws" derived from the criterion of what was "most beneficial to human morality," lacking the general validity of mathematical reasoning, could only be agreed upon after extensive discussion and deliberation by an assembly of experts on the subject.[59] Although K'ang made no explicit reference to a world parliament in the *Shih-li kung-fa,* such an organization was at least implied in his reference to an assembly that would be convened to determine which laws were to be regarded as "universal laws." He further intimated that he regarded the entire work as a collection of tentative "universal laws" to be presented to an assembly for discussion and possible adoption.[60] K'ang may well have had such an assembly in mind when he mentioned in his *Nien-p'u,* in 1884, "a federation of nations, a blending of races, and an amalgamation of religions" to unify the globe.[61]

The *Shih-li kung-fa* reflected this preoccupation with methodology. There were twelve topical sections, presented in accordance with a strictly formalized scheme that K'ang believed to be geometrical in nature, but several of these sections were almost devoid of content, as if K'ang had been satisfied for his immediate purposes merely to sketch their framework as an outline for further study. The internal organization of the sections was uniform and consisted of two parts: the first being "principles of truth" (*shih-li*), general statements regarding man and nature whose truth K'ang held to be obvious to everyone; the second being "universal laws" (*kung-fa*), specific social or individual rights derived from statements in the first part.

The first section of the *Shih-li kung-fa,* entitled "General Discussion of Mankind," will illustrate K'ang's procedure. Among his "principles of truth" were four statements:

1. that every man is part of the primordial stuff of heaven and earth;
2. that every man has a soul and an intelligence, but that each man's intelligence differs from all others;
3. that man is born with a disposition both to love and to hate, but that in his relations with others, love is the more beneficial; and
4. that man is born with good faith, while deceit is acquired through his contact with evil customs.[62]

In the second part, K'ang listed a number of "universal laws," including the following:

1. that man has the right to be his own master (here K'ang noted, without further explanation, that this was a law derived from geometrical axioms, that it was wholly in accord with the first two "principles of truth" listed above, and that it was also most beneficial to human morality);

2. that man-made laws should be applied in accordance with the idea of equality (K'ang noted that the equality of mankind was a "human axiom of geometry," and that while complete equality could never be employed in man-made laws, these man-made laws should still seek to approach the idea of equality);

3. that every social and political institution should be determined by all people after public discussion, and that for a law to become a "universal law" it must apply to everyone without exception (K'ang noted that this not only was derived from geometry, but was also most beneficial to human morality).[63]

It was, then, in the part dealing with "universal laws" that K'ang revealed his moral and social ideals. Succeeding sections contained proposals for "universal laws" that would provide for the establishment of a single parliament, which would carry out the business of government, and for public elections by which officials would be chosen for office.[64]

But of the "universal laws" appearing in the *Shih-li kung-fa*, perhaps the most startling were those that propounded K'ang's social ideals: that there should be complete equality between the sexes and complete freedom of either sex to choose and to change mates;[65] that children should all be raised in public institutions both to free the parents from the responsibilities of bringing up their offspring and to liberate the children from all obligations of filial piety;[66] and that students should have no obligation to adhere to the teachings of the sages or the instructions of their teachers unless the truth of these teachings could be adequately demonstrated.[67] K'ang claimed to have derived these ideals from the two basic principles, set forth in the first section, that all persons are equal and that everyone has the right to be his own master.

These concepts reappeared in much greater detail in his *Ta-t'ung shu*, and, in fact, K'ang was subsequently to refer to the *Shih-li kung-fa* as an early version of the *Ta-t'ung shu*.[68] It should be noted, however, that in the *Shih-li kung-fa* there is not a single reference to the theory of the "grand unity" (*ta-t'ung*) that became a central point in the *Ta-t'ung shu*. Furthermore, by the time he wrote the *Ta-t'ung shu*, K'ang had discarded all attempts to organize his ideas according to his pseudo-mathematical scheme. For these reasons, it is assumed that the ideas in the *Shih-li kung-fa* were elements in K'ang's thinking during the period in which he was still under the spell of Western mathematics (between 1883 and 1887),[69] but before he discovered the concept of the "grand unity" (about 1888 or 1889).[70]

Significant changes were taking place in K'ang's thinking during the 1880's, and the *K'ang-tzu nei-wai p'ien* and the *Shih-li kung-fa* form a kind of history of his intellectual development in those crucial years. The direction of K'ang Yu-wei's political career could perhaps have been predicted from these early writings, but even more pertinent to our purpose is the light these somewhat immature books throw on the sources of his radicalism.

The Sung Neo-Confucianism of his family training dominated his earliest extant work, the *Nei-wai p'ien,* but side by side with his affirmation of the superiority of the Confucian tradition was criticism of political and social inequities sanctioned by Confucian practice. From childhood K'ang had been imbued with the traditional Chinese concept of a Sinocentric world, unified by the subtle force of a superior civilization. Shattering this view was the picture K'ang got from Western literature of a pluralistic world, a dynamic and turbulent society of competing civilizations in which China, far from occupying the central position, was in many ways a backward member.

K'ang had set for himself the task of reconciling these two incompatible views of the world, choosing as the logical course the definition of those values valid for the entire world. His assumption that this could be accomplished by restating and enlarging the scope of the traditional Confucian values foundered as his investigations led to consciousness of inequities within the living Confucian tradition and of the innate narrowness of the Confucian world outlook. This intellectual quandary prompted him to suggest that the Confucian values of universal applicability were not those that were to be observed in the China of his time but those that would be observed in the future.

The shape of the future K'ang envisioned was first outlined in his *Shih-li kung-fa,* and his statement in it of his social and moral ideals offered graphic proof that his search for values of universal validity had already carried him well beyond the bounds of traditional Confucianism.

The radical nature of these ideals raises the most perplexing questions of intellectual origins. According to modern Chinese scholarship, K'ang found a basis for these ideas in his studies of Mahayana Buddhism and translations of Western books, as well as in the philosophy of Mo Ti.[71] That K'ang obtained many of his notions from these sources is undoubtedly true: his universalist concepts may well have been inspired by Buddhist and Mohist philosophy, and, as he himself indicated in the *Nei-wai p'ien*, his ideas of human equality were derived from Buddhism;[72] also, his concept of a parliament or assembly and of a federation of states probably came from his reading of translations from Western histories or news summaries.[73]

However, the source of K'ang's other notions, such as sexual freedom and abolition of the family, is more difficult to explain. Even though he may have found some justification for his ideas in Buddhist monasticism and in the accounts of the relative frequency of divorce in Western Europe,[74] there was little either in Buddhist literature or in available translations of Western books to account for the extreme views expressed in the *Shih-li kung-fa*. In the absence of other probable sources of inspiration, it is possible that his radical ideals reflected to some extent the development of his own personality and his reactions to his family and local environment.

As he emerged from adolescence to adulthood, K'ang became an independent, willful, even stubborn personality with boundless ambition and unshakable confidence in his own intellectual superiority. These strong traits of character, and his soaring aspirations to become a world savior, may well have caused him to chafe under the conventional obligations demanded by his elders. Because he refused to fulfill his duties to the family by concerning himself with the examinations, K'ang was obliged, for financial reasons, to pass much of his time between 1879 and 1887 in the midst of the numerous members of his clan. There he was in a position to observe at first hand the day-to-day realities of life within a large family group; and living in a state of continued tension with the family elders he may conceivably have begun to experience the first stirrings of antagonism toward his family environment, and even to feel that the family, with its innumerable obligations and duties, was an obstacle to the attainment of individual freedom and personal aspirations.

Detached by a series of mystical experiences from the orthodox Confucian training of his youth, enlightened by new perspectives gained from Buddhism and Western concepts, and personally dissatisfied with life inside the family group, K'ang may have begun to observe his surroundings with a critical eye and to question some of the family values sanctioned by Confucian tradition. Such conditions could in his case explain his notion that the family as an institution might better be abolished, leaving parent and child free to pursue their independent aspirations unencumbered by irksome obligations such as parental care or filial piety.

K'ang had ample opportunity in these years to observe the life of

Chinese women. From boyhood he had been keenly aware of the hardships endured by women—in particular the agonies of his sisters when
their feet were being bound and the tribulations of his mother, and
later his sisters, who were left as widows to support their children.[75]
K'ang was deeply affected by their plight and as he grew to maturity
became conscious of the unfairness of social conventions that required
widows to remain true to the memory of their dead husbands while
permitting men to remarry and have a number of concubines.[76] This
deeply rooted sympathy for his mother and sisters may well have been
a major reason underlying his insistence that women be recognized as
the social equals of men and be allowed the same sexual freedom.

It was such personal motivations, arising from little-known aspects
of K'ang's character and background, that may have been the determining factors in the development of a set of ideals antithetical to the
values basic to the Confucian tradition. But even though K'ang found
the conventional Confucian values inadequate for his own intellectual
and emotional requirements, he was loth to renounce the traditions in
which he had been trained since childhood. This reluctance was in
conflict with his vision of higher and more universal human ideals.
K'ang was partly aware of this inner contradiction and sought to resolve
it in his own mind. From his *Nei-wai p'ien* it would appear that he
viewed his radical ideals not as imperatives to immediate action but as
goals to be attained at some unspecified time in the future. Such a
position implied a belief in gradual change rather than an abrupt and
painful break with the past; and until these ideals were realized, K'ang
felt morally justified in adhering to the traditional values he still
cherished.

However, K'ang was not wholly content to relegate his new ideals
to an imagined future world. Committed to his self-image as a Confucian sage and a Buddhist savior, he believed it to be his duty to work
toward the realization of these ideals. Furthermore, his radical notions,
while partly inspired by mystical insights gained from Buddhism and
by new concepts from the West, also reflected a discontent with conditions in his own environment and a strong desire to change them. It
was probably a combination of these aspects of his character and of his
thought that lay behind his decision of 1888 to embark upon the career
of political reformer.

Joseph R. Levenson

LIAO P'ING AND THE CONFUCIAN
DEPARTURE FROM HISTORY

This is a very little paper, appropriately, about a small man. The sterile public career of Liao P'ing (1852–1932) seems merely to confirm the emptiness of his thought. His works are full of that old Confucian abomination, empty words. Why then write about this too-late Confucianist, this manikin and his myths? The answer begins in his dullness. Personal insignificance can be historically significant, and if Liao P'ing was an unpersuasive Confucianist, largely inactive in public life, this combination of negatives has its own interest.

What made his intellectual system fantastic, by any orthodox Confucian standard, was precisely its irrelevance to any conceivable action. Confucian thought had long preserved its vitality through a strong bureaucratic tie, an intimate relationship with politics—i.e., with the Confucian kind of history, the kind Confucianists made and wrote. A close interaction of action and thought was intrinsic to Confucianism. But by the time Liao died in 1932 the Confucian life was available to no one. There was nothing Confucian about politics now—though Confucianism could be a political issue—and Liao, the last thinker of the last Confucian school, unwittingly echoed the Confucian banishment from history with the banishment of history from his Confucian intellectual concerns.

Instead of history, Liao made prophecy the stuff of Confucianism: Confucius was a prophet, and Liao as well. Confucius, of course, had to be seen as a mighty force, if a quiet one, in his own day, but in Liao, at the end of the Confucian line, we have the seer without the doer. Certainly he was a prophet without excessive honor in his own county: the gazetteer for his birthplace (Ching-yen, in Szechwan), published in 1900 when Liao was in full maturity, records under the Liao surname simply: "P'ing of the present dynasty is a *chin-shih* [graduate of the third degree] and a teacher."[1]

This pale schoolmasterly image is most of the visible Liao. Born in

1852 in a relatively poor family (with a mildly prominent bureaucratic lineage on his mother's side), he devoted himself to study, though his father was a dealer in medicines and his brothers followed the lead into business. Later, Liao adopted the studio style, "San-yü T'ang" (Three Fish Hall), to commemorate his scholarly beginnings: one day, as a little boy, he offered his modest catch to the teacher in the village school and won admittance.

Books possessed him and in time Liao became the student of teachers like Wang K'ai-yün (1833–1916), a *Kung-yang* Classical scholar who taught Liao in the Tsun-ching (Revere the Classics) Shu-yüan in Chengtu, but who never cared to claim discipleship. In later days, Liao himself taught in this school for a time.

In the 1880's, while Liao was moving through the conventional series of civil service examinations, Chang Chih-tung, then the Canton governor-general, made him one of his secretaries, treating him with great informality and inviting him to teach in a branch of the academy Chang founded in 1887, the Kuang-ya Shu-yüan. It was in this period that he met K'ang Yu-wei (1858–1927) and influenced him (or was plagiarized by him) in the preparation of the *Hsin-hsüeh wei-ching k'ao* ("On the False Classics of the Hsin Learning"), one of the seminal documents of the Reform Movement of 1898.

After becoming a *chin-shih*, Liao was appointed an archivist, but he soon requested and received a transfer to teaching duties. In 1898 he was an instructor at Sui-ting-fu in his home province of Szechwan, totally out of active politics, when the Reform Movement, which had such affinities with his Confucian scholarship, flourished briefly and was suppressed. The official supervisor of studies in Szechwan, knowing that K'ang Yu-wei, object of the counterreformist Empress Dowager's most ferocious hostility, had taken his lead in Confucian matters from Liao, impeached the latter for outrageous opinions on the Classics, cashiered him, and committed him to surveillance by local officials. But Liao was so obviously harmless that the new governor of Chekiang, who admired his talents, was willing and able to appoint him a master in a school under his jurisdiction.

After the revolution of 1911–12, Liao for several years directed the Kuo-hsüeh Yüan, a school in Chengtu. His growing reputation as a recluse led the eminent Japanese historian Naitō, lecturing at Kyōtō University in 1915, to observe that Liao was in the mountains of Szechwan and did not want to come out. There had been an exception—Liao's trip in 1913 to speak to Confucian societies in Peking—but the commitment to withdrawal was confirmed in 1919, when Liao suffered a stroke that paralyzed his right side. Liao continued to write, with his left hand, depending on his eldest daughter to reduce the drafts to order. On October 6, 1932, he died during an outing in the country.[2]

Is there anything to chew on in this thin gruel? The Liao-K'ang relationship has some substance to it.

K'ang, claiming "coincidence," never faced up to the accusation, but Liao brought in the indictment; K'ang's sometimes dissident but always respectful disciple, Liang Ch'i-ch'ao (1873–1929), admitted the grounds; and Chinese and Japanese scholars have concurred in the verdict: K'ang's *Hsin-hsüeh wei-ching k'ao* (1891), his first great *succès d'estime* and *de scandale,* was lifted consciously and in considerable detail from the *P'i Liu p'ien* ("Treatise Refuting Liu Hsin"), and K'ang's *K'ung-tzu kai-chih k'ao* ("On Confucius as a Reformer") of 1897 similarly stole the thesis and the thunder from the *Chih-sheng p'ien* ("Treatise on Knowing the Sage"). Together, these treatises made up Liao's manuscript of 1886, *Chin ku hsüeh k'ao* ("On the 'Modern Text' and 'Ancient Text' Learning"). According to the charge, K'ang saw Liao's work at the home of one Shen Tseng-chih (1853–1922), sought an introduction to Liao in Canton, professed to be unimpressed by the latter's esoteric conclusions, and warned him against publishing these ideas, which would stain him with guilt as a teacher of unlawful doctrine. The next year, K'ang published his *Wei-ching k'ao,* "dashing it off [literally, leaning on a horse]," said Liao, "writing his book, truly breaking the tie of ethics."[3]

This lament, from a Confucianist, about the rape of his originality has a dying fall. Originality *per se* had never been a Confucian virtue, and a touchy insistence that you yourself, not your opponent, had made the startling new departure was the reverse of the rule of old Confucian controversy. Liao was consistent in his jealous claim to priority; his personal intellectual history, with its carefully delineated "six stages," recapitulated his credo of movement and freshness. Anyone who studies, he laid down, should have a "great change" in his theories every ten years, and a "small change" every three. One who fails of the small change may be termed a "mediocre talent," while one who misses the large change is an "abdicated talent."[4]

This call to make it new and this claim that K'ang had pilfered the prestige Liao deserved for making a new pronouncement were merely words. It was K'ang, plagiarist or not, who assumed the risks and made history. K'ang took these claims for Confucius as a reformer and made them relate to an actual modern reform, clothing them in action and reeling out for modern China the last thread of authentic Confucian commitment. But Liao, the verbalizer about originality, was just a conventional examination-passer, circumspect enough to move smoothly through the time-worn channels and to earn in 1889 easy traditional accolades from unreconstructed, and obviously untroubled, official examiners: "He creates splendid phrases . . . cites many Classics . . . is penetrating and clear in ancient teachings . . . selects refined vocabulary . . . is familiar with others' discussions and is not one of those who restrict themselves to their own confirmations or destructive critiques."[5] K'ang almost paid with his life in 1898 for what he made of Liao's hypotheses. But Liao in 1898 (earning Liang Ch'i-ch'ao's contempt even while Liang acknowledged him as intellectually the first comer) still shrank from implication, declaring that it was no intention of his to expound a battle position.[6]

Once Liao had proclaimed himself above the battle, there was nothing to keep him from soaring higher and higher, away from the ground of action and history where Confucius belonged. As a colleague commented in 1916, Liao, then in his self-styled fourth phase, dealing with "heaven" and "man," ascribed light and purity to heaven, heaviness and dross to earth.[7] Heaven had been Liao's destination ever since the K'ang coincidence, when the issue was still posed in historical terms, the Liao-K'ang *chin-wen* tradition's Confucius being taken to rival the orthodox *ku-wen's* Duke of Chou as the original fountain of wisdom. Shuffling off the dross and the heaviness, Liao had ended with a fantasy of levitation (literally) for all men at the end of days, when the earthly needs of food and clothing would have dropped away.[8]

Not surprisingly, possible disciples kept falling off Liao's ladder to the stars. As Liao moved from "revering Confucius" to "worshiping Confucius,"[9] his questioning followers turned increasingly to the antireligious anti-Confucianists—Wu Yü (1871–1949), for example, Liao's student in Szechwan, who turned to Ch'en Tu-hsiu at Peking University[10]—and Liao's little clan rapidly dwindled.

When Confucius was revered he was a political man, a figure in history, who invited men (the state's ministers of the Confucian ideal type) to learn from him how history should be made—what principles should apply and what judgments should be leveled, in the farthest tomorrow as in the Classical yesterday. The Classics (*transmitted* by the Confucius who was revered) exposed the paradigms of history, the eternal patterns of action. Process was unimportant, no passage of time could relativize the truth. But when Confucius was worshiped, he was a saint and an oracle, a transcendent, suprahistorical figure who foretold to men the end to which time was passing. The Confucius of the Liao P'ing image put all things to come in world history into the *I-ching* ("Book of Changes"), and all rules for posterity into the *Shih-*

ching ("Book of Poetry"), where the religion he founded was set forth in detail.[11] The Classics (*created* by the Confucius who was worshiped) enshrined the prophecies of history, intimations of actions yet unseen. The Classics were *new* with Confucius and, as Liao put it in 1894, new Classics were not old history.[12] Paradigmatic Classics—the Classics of *ku-wen* traditionalists, for whom knowledge and action were one—were history, accounts of visible events which made essentials manifest. But prophetic Classics of *chin-wen* provenance were the keys to history, not history themselves.

Liao's early attack on the accepted *ku-wen* Classics had committed him unequivocally to a religious rather than a historical view of Confucius. Liao meant to expose the "false Classics of the Hsin learning" —to borrow K'ang's version of Liao's indictment—to the end of establishing the "true" Classics (the *chin-wen* Classics) as creations of Confucius. But this amounted to admitting that the *chin-wen* Classics were forgeries by Confucius; that is, Confucius himself might seem like Liu Hsin, the alleged forger of the *ku-wen*, writing texts and pretending they were old. Of course, Liao had no intention of making this equation, and Confucius, therefore, had to be truly superhuman; if he were only human, he would be only an ideologue like Liu Hsin, who was bought and paid for, in Liao's opinion, by the usurper Wang Mang. How could one "forger," one concealer of his own authorship, be distinguished from the other unless Liu Hsin and Confucius were simply incommensurable, the first a dishonest historian, the second a pure and divinely inspired prophet? If the Six Classics were not history, it was because in the *ku-wen* version they were fiction and in the *chin-wen* version a miraculous rending of the veil of future time.

The Classics' passage from paradigm to prophecy can be seen in the space of one generation, from the usages of the practicing official Hsüeh Fu-ch'eng (1838–94), for example, to the fancies of the non-practicing Liao P'ing. Hsüeh, in a memorial of 1875, cited an ancient model as a lesson for contemporaries, in the approved traditional fashion of a Confucianist on duty, engaged in political action. "In ancient times," he wrote, "when Yüeh I attacked Ch'i, his first essential was alliance with Chao, and when Chu-ko Liang defended Shu, he first proceeded to unite with Wu. In general, preparedness demands the possession of allies. This is the way things are." (History, that is, is the record of reality, not process.) And the conclusion: "The overseas people have come to our China. Our sole recourse is diplomatic combination" (*ho-tsung lien-heng*, a phrase drawn from the pre-Ch'in *Chankuo ts'e*, referring to conflicting "Warring States" diplomatic plans in face of the Ch'in menace). And Hsüeh continued with a discussion of the "five strongest treaty nations, England, the implacable foe, France, Russia, the United States, and Germany." He saw the United States in particular as a possible ally, since America, he said, wanted a counterweight to European powers, and China's weakness added to Europe's strength.[13]

Again, in 1879, Hsüeh called attention to Japan's accession to power through her adoption of Western material techniques. He commended the same to China as a warning to Japan. "When Japan hears that China is becoming prepared, she must know the difficulties and retire. Who knows but that she will yield even while China is not yet equipped? This would be the subtle practice of the ancients, *hsien sheng hou shih*" ("first, voice; later, fact," i.e., to begin with deceptive propaganda claims of power so as ultimately to achieve one's objectives).[14] The phrase, considered here so applicable to contemporary circumstances, is a *Ch'ien Han shu* variant (biography of Han Hsin), via the *Shih-chi* biography of Marquis Huai-yin, of a *Tso-chuan* (Chao Kung, twenty-first year) Classical original.

Hsüeh, then, proceeding rationalistically, searched the ancient texts for parallels. Liao, on the other hand, mystically found metaphor in his researches. There is all the difference in the world (the difference between fullness of significance for practical action, and emptiness) between formulating a suggestion historically, e.g., "The situation of ancient Cheng in the Empire was *like* that of modern China in the larger world," and suggesting, with implications of precognition, that "the 'situation of ancient Cheng' *was* that of modern China."[15] A responsible Confucianist, even such a late and flexible one as Hsüeh Fuch'eng, had his antiquity for use. A dreaming Confucianist like Liao P'ing—intellectually irresponsible and appropriately not responsible for the political action a sound Confucianism entailed—had his antiquity for oracular conviction; future events *must* come, for the Classical sources provided, not prescriptions for freely chosen action, but a deterministic revelation of what actions must amount to.

Thus, Liao saw China's modern plight in the international jungle *prefigured* in Confucius' (alleged) *po-luan* words about the "age of chaos" in the *Kung-yang chuan*.[16] Confucius saw it coming and conveyed his vision esoterically. For Confucius' *Ch'un-ch'iu* ("Spring and Autumn Annals"), to which the *Kung-yang* was key, itself unlocked the future, when the ancient vision of the Great Harmony (*ta-t'ung*) would be realized, and the great course would be finally run from dissimilarity (*pu t'ung*) to sameness—all men the same as one another, then men the same as the *kuei* and *shen*, or spirits.[17] In order to see world prophecies in Classics which orthodox Confucianists deemed Chou-period histories,

Liao brought the *Chou-li* ("Rites of Chou") back to his canon (from which he had earlier banished it: see note 8); but the "chou" now was not an ancient dynastic name, but a futuristic "over-all" or "comprehensive."[18] It was another diffusion of historical particularity into a universal prophetic haze.

Hsüeh Fu-ch'eng, like any Confucianist with a public life, asked of the Classics, "What are we to do?" Liao P'ing, a Confucianist expelled from the world of doers, chopped the question down, in effect, to "What (or where) are we?" That which the older order of Confucianists had always meant as a stigma—"empty words" (*k'ung-yen*), the antithesis of action or the basic stuff of history—Liao explicitly, admiringly attributed to Confucius.

Liao's Confucius, in his stories about his idol, Wen Wang, for example, had an esoteric message to convey, wrapped within the spurious, metaphorical, outside "historical" surface. For Confucius, as a *su-wang* ("throneless king"), was confined to the inner realm of knowledge, barred from the outer realm of executive action, and he expressed his knowledge in specifically "empty words," words, that is, which did not record what they seemed to record—past and open politics—but future, hidden prospects. The *su-wang* idea, for Liao, was the informing idea of the Six Classics.[19]

Liao, with his claim to originality, boasted to K'ang Yu-wei that in his own work "there was not a single expression that was not new" (i.e., Liao was the first to reveal the esoterica), but, by the same token, "there was not a single meaning that was not old."[20] Thus Liao, in effect, paradoxically modeled himself on the *transmitting* Confucius of the orthodox conception. But in transmitting, proudly, the "empty words" of his "creative" Confucius, Liao carried the curse of the orthodox meaning of "empty words" into his own day. He himself was the speaker of empty words, empty of any relevance to the history of his times. Liao was transmitting to no one.

One might say (Liao certainly did) that he seemed to have transmitted to K'ang Yu-wei. And K'ang, to be sure, had not intended to be out of action; he led the Reform Movement of 1898. Was not this, after all, an example of Liao's Confucianism in action? Was a Confucian departure from history (from influence on the course of events) necessarily implied in the Confucian departure from history as locus of wisdom? Or, to put it another way, was Liao's empty life really the counterpart of his empty words, not simply coincidental?

To place Liao in Chinese history, it is important to see what happened to "prophetic" Confucianism in K'ang's hands. Liao was dissociated from public affairs, and it was only with this inward bent that he could make more and more fanciful departures from the *chin-wen* or *Kung-yang* Confucianism he once had shared with K'ang and Liang Ch'i-ch'ao. These three went three ways. Liang went beyond the *chin-wen* to post-Confucian (non-Confucian) considerations. K'ang retained his affirmations, but he ceased to develop them internally—that is, having failed to Confucianize politics (according to his lights), he avoided the Liao alternative of intensified cerebration and chose instead to keep a political commitment; but it was a commitment now to politicalize Confucianism, to make the preservation of Confucianism a political issue, in tacit recognition of the fact that Confucianism no longer governed political issues. K'ang, a radical in a Confucian Chinese world, was an antiradical in the post-Confucian nation, the Chinese part of the world, where Confucianism's chances lay with the Chinese "national essence." And K'ang, who had failed in 1898 to establish a Confucian case for radicalism against the traditional Confucian arguments for conservatism, finally, when the Republic came, with its iconoclastic aura, turned to making conservative arguments for Confucianism. Significantly, where once he had deemed it the most important thing in the world to separate "false" Classics from "true," now he defended the Classics indiscriminately. K'ang, in his Liao P'ing phase, had tried to make novelty Chinese, *per* Confucius. But when the monarchy fell, when the new was nakedly foreign, its sponsors rather dismissing Confucius than invoking his authority, K'ang joined those who adhered to the old in a new way; he advanced essentially romantic (relativist) arguments from "national essence" rather than rationalistic arguments from universal validity.

Other arguments for other causes deafened the twentieth century, and Confucianism was relegated to the past. In Liao, the vestiges of Confucianism and the biography of the Confucianist corresponded. Liao's "levitating" utopian creed bespoke the politically impoverished fantast, living into a time when bureaucracy and Confucianism no longer went together. One might say, as Chu Hsi had long ago said about Buddhist speculation, that such a Confucianism, *any* modern Confucianism, was *t'i* without *yung*, the essence without the operation, the work. And when, as was the case with modern problems, Confucian solutions ceased to work and Confucian wisdom ceased to compel, committed Confucianists were not the operators who made their way in public life. So much for Liao; and K'ang, after his reformist failure to give his ideas political life, passed into a political limbo himself. The Confucianism he cherished to the last was not strained to Liao's pitch of action-denying fantasy—K'ang never became as politically invisible as Liao—but it was a passive, no longer an action-enhancing Confucianism, a candidate for protection as a sort of historical monument, not a dominant molder of history in the making.

Liao, surpassing K'ang in utopianism, writing after him as he had written before him, was the last one to work on Confucianism as the primary matter of his mind. In so doing, he contrived cipher-biography and aery Confucianism in their purest form. Out of the main line of history himself, he deprived history of its old Confucian significance. And there lay his life's representative character, as a mirror image of the times.

NOTES

NOTES TO VALUES, ROLES, AND PERSONALITIES

1. The following references are to chapter and section of the *Analects*. I make no distinction between the more and the less authentic parts of the book, since all parts had equal authority in the period covered by our biographies.

(1) I.2, 7, 11; II.5, 6, 7, 8, 20; IV.18–21; IX.15, 24; XI.4, 21; XII.11; XIII.20.
(2) X; XII.1; XII.5.
(3) I.15; II.11, 23; III.14; VII.1–3, 19; XI.19.
(4) V.14, 27; VI.2; VII.1–3, 19, 27, 33; VIII.17; XI.1.
(5) II.19, 20; IV.17, 25; VII.21; VIII.2; XII.17–19, 22; XII.4.
(6) I.6; II.12; IV.5–7, 11.
(7) I.2; II.1, 3, 20; VI.6.
(8) I.6, 14; II.18; III.4, 20; V.19; VI.25, 27; VII.10; VIII.2; XI.15; XII.3, 23; XIII.21.
(9) III.7; VIII.5.
(10) VIII.7; IX.5.
(11) I.1, 16; II.21; III.24; VII.13, 15; IX.8.
(12) I.6, 8, 14; III.1; VI.19; IX.24; XII.24.
(13) V.16; IX.3, 9, 15; X.

2. The first reference is found in the *Yen-shih chia-hsün* by Yen Chih-t'ui, whose biography appears in this volume. Cf. Kuo-hsüeh chi-pen ts'ung-shu edition (Shanghai, 1937), ch. 2, p. 38. While modern practice gives the child a wide choice, the only objects placed before the child in Yen's account were those symbolic of a military or civil-official career. Yen describes it as a South China custom in his time.

3. Shu-sun T'ung—a "Confucian" with a large following of dependent scholars—addressing the Han founder. Cf. *Shih-chi* (T'ung-wen edition of 1884), ch. 99, p. 6*b*.

NOTES TO PROBLEMS OF CHINESE BIOGRAPHY

1. The term *lieh-chuan* in the *Shih-chi* and in the later histories covers not only biographies but also accounts of foreign peoples.
2. Personal communication.
3. Maspero, *Melanges posthumes*, III, 53–62.
4. Liu Chih-chi, *Shih-t'ung t'ung-shih*, II, *lieh-chuan* 6 (Ssu-pu pei-yao ed.), p. 13*b*.
5. On the detailed process of compilation, see the papers by Yang Lien-

sheng and myself in Beasley and Pulleyblank, eds., *Historians of China and Japan* (London, Oxford University Press, 1961).

6. See my article in *Historians of China and Japan* (note 5), and also P. Olbricht, "Die Biographie in China," *Saeculum*, VIII (1957), 224–35.

7. H. Franke, "Some Remarks on the Interpretation of Chinese Dynastic Histories," *Oriens*, III (1950), 113–22.

8. On such "commemorative biographies," see Olbricht, *op. cit.*, and, more especially, D. Nivison, "Aspects of Traditional Chinese Biography," a paper read at the seventy-sixth annual meeting of the American Historical Association, December 28, 1961 (to appear in the *Journal of Asian Studies*).

9. Nivison, *op. cit.*

10. H. Frankel, "Objektivität und Parteilichkeit in der Offiziellen Chinesischen Geschichtsschreibung vom 3 bis 11. Jahrhundert," *Oriens Extremus*, V (1958), 133–44.

11. Nivison, *op cit.*

12. R. C. Howard, "Biographical Writing in Modern China," a paper read at the seventy-sixth annual meeting of the American Historical Association, December 28, 1961 (to appear in the *Journal of Asian Studies*).

13. Chen Shih-hsiang, "An Innovation in Chinese Biographical Writing," *Far Eastern Quarterly*, XIII, No. 1 (1953), 49–51.

14. Ku Yen-wu, *Jih-chih lu* 19.

NOTES TO YEN CHIH-T'UI

1. Yen Chih-t'ui has biographies in the *Pei Ch'i shu*, I-wen yin-shu kuan reprint of the T'ung-wen, ch. 45, pp. 17a–26a, and *Pei shih*, ch. 83, pp. 18a–19b.

2. For a general survey of Buddhism in this period, see Arthur F. Wright, *Buddhism in Chinese History* (Stanford, Calif., 1959), pp. 42–64.

3. Yen's ancestor of eight generations before, Yen Han, has a biography in *Chin shu*, ch. 88, pp. 13a–15b.

4. The sack of Chiang-ling, the capital of Liang, is mentioned by William Acker, *Some T'ang and Pre-T'ang Texts on Chinese Painting*, pp. 122–23. Some lines by Yen describing the event are quoted there.

5. *Sui shu*, ch. 14, p. 33b, tells of a petition he made in 582 suggesting that the music of Liang be adopted as the state music of Sui, but this proposal was rejected. In the preface to the *Ch'ieh-yün*, dated 601, he is given the title of *Wai-shih* (Outside Scribe), which would indicate that he held no office under the Sui, although he did join the staff of Yang Yung as Literary Gentle (*Hsüeh shih*) before the prince was deposed in 600.

6. Takahashi Kunpei, "A Biography of Yen Chih-t'ui," *Kindai*, X (1955), 64, points out that this is one of the three literary pieces included in the standard histories with a commentary by the writer himself. This poem was recently treated by Chou Fa-kao, "A Comparison of Yen Chih-t'ui's 'Prose-Poem on Looking at My Life' and Yü Hsin's 'Prose-Poem on Sorrowing for Chiang-nan,'" *Ta-lu tsa-chih*, XX (1960), 1 ff., in which Chou attempted, not successfully, to trace the derivation of Yen's piece from that of Yü.

7. *Lun-yü*, ch. 16, p. 9b (Juan Yüan's edition of the *Shih-san ching chu-su*); Legge, *Confucian Analects*, p. 179.

8. Wang I-t'ung has collected many such passages from the histories in his *Wu-ch'ao men-ti*, Part B, pp. 35–44. A more comprehensive collection is in the Sung work *Chieh-tzu t'ung-lu* by Liu Ch'ing-chih, included in the *Ssu-k'u ch'uan-shu chen-pen* series. More recent examples of this genre were analyzed by Hui-chen Wang Liu, "An Analysis of Chinese Clan Rules: Confucian Theories in Action," in David S. Nivison and Arthur F. Wright, eds., *Confucianism in Action* (Stanford, Calif., 1959). Wang I-t'ung, p. 38, relates the development of the *chia-hsün* at this time to the concurrent emergence of the clans as an important social and political factor.

9. Etienne Balazs, *Le Traité économique du "Souei chou"* (Leiden, 1953), p. 211, n. 110, describes the *Instructions* as an "ouvrage précieux pour ses nombreux renseignements sur les moeurs et la civilisation du VIᵉ siècle." The *Instructions* has been cited in modern studies chiefly as a source of information on social customs; e.g., Moriya Mitsuo, "Nanjin to Hoku-jin," *Tōa-ronsō*, VI (1948), 36–60; Lü Ssu-mien, *Liang-chin nan-pei-ch'ao shih, passim.* The *Instructions* has also been quoted frequently for the linguistic and philological information it contains; e.g., G. Kennedy, "A Study of the Particle 'yen,'" *Journal of the American Oriental Society*, LX (1940), 194–95; A. C. Graham, "The Relation Between the Final Particles Yu and Yee," *Bulletin of the School of Oriental and African Studies*, XIX, No. 1 (1957), 120. A new edition entitled *Yen-shih chia-hsün hui-chu* has been prepared by Chou Fa-kao and published as Special Publication No. 41 of the Institute of History and Philology, Academia Sinica (Taipei, 1960). It contains various commentaries, ancillary materials, and index.

10. *Instructions*, ch. 1, pp. 2a–b (Pao-ching t'ang ed.). Literally, "I did not take care of my hems," a phrase still used in referring to carelessness of personal appearance.

11. *Pei Ch'i shu*, ch. 45, p. 18a.

12. *Instructions*, ch. 1, p. 2b. Some editions say "twenty years of age."

13. *Instructions*, ch. 1, p. 3b.

14. *Ibid.*, ch. 1, p. 13b. This passage is included in a quotation from the *Instructions* in Arthur Wright's Introduction to *The Confucian Persuasion* (Stanford, Calif., 1960), pp. 6–7.

15. *Instructions*, ch. 1, p. 4a.

16. *Ibid.*, ch. 1, p. 3b.

17. *Ibid.*, ch. 1, pp. 5b–6b.

18. *Pei Ch'i shu*, ch. 12, pp. 6b–10b; *Tzu-chih t'ung-chien*, ch. 170, pp. 5293–96 (Ku-chi ch'u-pan she ed.).

19. See, for example, *Lun-yü*, ch. 1, p. 8b; Legge, p. 144.

20. *Instructions*, ch. 1, p. 2b.

21. *Ibid.*, ch. 3, p. 4a.

22. *Ibid.*, p. 21b.

23. *Ibid.*, p. 7a.

24. *Sung shu*, ch. 73, p. 8b.

25. *Instructions*, ch. 3, pp. 1b–2a.

26. *Ibid.*, p. 9a.

27. *Ibid.*, ch. 1, pp. 7b–8a.

28. *Ibid.*, ch. 3, pp. 20b–21b. Ssu-lu served as a secretary on the staff of Li Shih-min at the beginning of the T'ang; *Chiu T'ang shu*, ch. 73, p. 7b, and *Hsin T'ang shu*, ch. 198, pp. 6a–b.

29. *Instructions,* ch. 3, p. 1a.
30. *Nan Ch'i shu,* ch. 33, p. 9b.
31. *Instructions,* ch. 3, p. 3a.
32. *Ibid.*
33. *Ibid.,* p. 3b.
34. *Ibid.,* p. 10b.
35. *Ibid.,* p. 9a.
36. Peter Laslett, "A One-class Society," *The Listener,* LXIII, No. 1620 (1960), p. 657.
37. *Wang I-t'ung, op. cit.,* pp. 58–61.
38. *Instructions,* ch. 7, p. 18b. For a discussion of this rite, see Ensho Ashikaga, "Notes on Urabon," *Journal of the American Oriental Society,* LXXI, No. 1 (1951), 71–74.
39. This chapter of the *Instructions* is included in the *Kuang hung-ming chi* by Tao-hsüan, 664 A.D. (*Taisho daizōkyō,* LII, Nos. 107–8). It is discussed by Leon Hurvitz in his translation of Tsukumoto Zenryū, "Wei Shou: Treatise on Buddhism and Taoism," *Yun-kang,* XVI, 33, n. 2, where it is stated that identifications of elements of Confucianism and Buddhism were quite common at this period.
40. Alfred Forke, *Geschichte der mittel-alterlichen chinesischen Philosophie* (Hamburg, 1934), pp. 238–43.
41. *Fa-yen,* ch. 2, pp. 1a–b (Ssu-pu ts'ung-k'an ed.); *Instructions,* ch. 4, p. 9a. According to Fung Yu-lan, Yang held that "anyone who expresses himself in writing should aim at spontaneity. To the extent that he succeeds or fails in so doing, the ideas he expresses are correspondingly significant or insignificant. To make one's ideas the embodiment of spontaneity, this is of the essence. As for the words in which these ideas are clothed, they are merely 'supplementary and decorative,' and cannot in themselves add to or subtract from the central essence of spontaneity." (*History of Chinese Philosophy,* II, 139.)

In answer to a letter of Ts'ao Chih (192–232) which cited Yang Hsiung's statement that the poetry of youth could not be surpassed, *Wen-hsüan,* ch. 42, p. 17b (Ssu-pu ts'ung-k'an ed.), Yang Hsiu (173–217) answered that this would imply that poetry in the *Shih ching* by the mature Chung-shan-fu and the Duke of Chou had imperfections (*Wen-hsüan,* ch. 40, p. 18a), which no one would care to admit. Yen here expands on this point.
42. *Instructions,* ch. 4, pp. 9a–b.
43. Fung, *op. cit.,* II, 139–46; A. Forke, *op. cit.,* pp. 84–89; R. P. Kramers, *K'ung Tzu Chia Yü,* pp. 78–79; W. Liebenthal, translator, "Wang Pi's New Interpretation of the *I Ching* and *Lun-yü,*" *Harvard Journal of Asiatic Studies,* X, No. 2 (1947), 130–33.
44. *Pei Ch'i shu,* ch. 45, p. 23b. The pairing of hexagrams as in this text is found, for example, in the *I-lin,* a Han work, but the phrases which Yen quotes are from the *I-ching,* ch. 2, p. 20a, and ch. 3, pp. 33a–b (Shih-san ching chu-su ed.).
45. *Han shu,* ch. 87B, p. 22b.
46. *Instructions,* ch. 4, p. 10a.
47. For example, a man who cut off the hands of thieves has a child born without hands. These stories are also included in the collection *Yuan-hun chih* ("Essay on Spirits with Grievances") written by Yen, a large part of

which is preserved, some in various collectanea, the rest in the *T'ai-p'ing kuang-chi,* under the title *Huan-yüan chi* ("Record of Returning Grievances"). The change of title seems to have occurred during the Sung. The *Ssu-k'u* editors recommended the work, despite its Buddhist theme of retribution, for its style and examples of good conduct. Modern writers, such as Cheng Chen-to, *Chung-kuo wen-hsüeh shih,* p. 226, and Lu Hsün, *Chung-kuo hsiao-shuo shih-lüeh,* p. 64, listed the work among those of the period that propagated Buddhist ideas. Others have gone even further in thus characterizing the stories. Actually, they have little in common with such avowedly Buddhist collections as the *Ming-hsiang chi, Hsüan-yen chi,* and *Ching-i chi.* Buddhism appears overtly no more than one would expect in stories from a period as permeated with Buddhism as was the time of Yen Chih-t'ui. The theme of retribution by wronged spirits had become identified with the Buddhists, although it appears in *Tso chuan,* but it was no longer a burning issue; cf. W. Liebenthal, "Chinese Buddhism During the Fourth and Fifth Centuries," *Monumenta Nipponica,* XI (1955), 77–78. Thus it does not appear accurate to say this was written with propagandist purposes in mind.

48. *Instructions,* ch. 5, p. 22b. Abhirati is the Eastern Paradise of the Aksobhya Buddha, and Sankha is the name of the future saintly king on earth. Both figure in the Pure-land sect; cf. Mochizuki, *Bukkyōdaijiten,* pp. 58a–b and 2596b–c. Satō Ichirō, "A Brief Account of *Yen-shih chia-hsün,*" *Tokyo-shinagakuhō,* I (1955), 205, also calls attention to the importance of this reference to the *cakravartin* king, but he develops a different line of thought.

49. See, for example, the fragments of the commentary on the *Odes* by Liu Fang of the Wei, collected in the *Yü-han shan-fang chi-i shu,* ch. 17, p. 28b.

50. *Shih-shuo hsin-yü* (Ssu-pu ts'ung-k'an ed.), ch. 1B, p. 17a.

51. *Pei shih,* ch. 81, p. 7b. For discussion of these regional differences, see also P'i Hsi-jui, *Ching-hsüeh li-shih* (Han-fen lou ed.), pp. 37a ff.; T'ang Ch'ang-ju, *Wei Chin nan-pei-ch'ao shih lun-ts'ung* (Peiping, 1955, 2d ed., 1957), pp. 361 ff.

52. *Instructions,* ch. 3, p. 13a. The phrase is the opening one in the *Classic of Filial Piety,* Satō, *op. cit.,* p. 201, punctuating differently, has the phrase, "Why necessarily Chung-ni?" which he takes to mean that learning should not be restricted to the Confucian texts, but I cannot agree with this.

53. This is suggested by T'ang, *op. cit.,* pp. 363–64. For the *hsüan-hsüeh,* see also W. Liebenthal, "Wang Pi's New Interpretation," pp. 124–61, and Arthur Wright, review of A. A. Petrov, *Wang Pi: His Place in the History of Chinese Philosophy,* in *Harvard Journal of Asiatic Studies,* X, No. 1 (1947), 75–88, and the literature cited there.

54. For example, see *Instructions,* ch. 5, pp. 6a–7b, where Yen declines to take part in resolving the conflict between the classics and more modern astronomical knowledge.

55. This work by Wang Ts'an (177–217) is no longer extant. See R. P. Kramers, "Conservatism and the Transmission of the Confucian Canon," *Journal of Oriental Studies,* II, No. 1 (1955), p. 128.

56. *Instructions,* ch. 3, pp. 13b–14a. Wei Shou, the author of the *Wei shu,* has biographies in the *Pei Ch'i shu,* ch. 37, pp. 1a–14b, and *Pei shih,* ch. 56, pp. 1a–18a. Wei Hsüan-ch'eng's biography is in *Han shu,* ch. 73, pp. 5a–20b.

57. A summary of the ideas on the origin and styles of script and of important lexical writings current during Yen's time is to be found in a petition of 514 by Chiang Shih, in *Wei shu*, ch. 91, pp. 18a–22a. Chiang derived the material for the first part of his document from Hsü Shen's preface to the *Shuo-wen*.

58. *Instructions*, ch. 3, pp. 25b–26a. For the *Ch'ieh-yün*, see Ch'en Yüan, "The Ch'ieh-Yün and Its Hsien-pei Authorship," *Monumenta Serica*, I, No. 2 (1935), 245–52; Ch'en Yin-k'o, "The Ch'ieh Yün: A Historical Study," *Lingnan Journal*, IX, No. 2 (1949), 1–18.

59. *Instructions*, ch. 6, pp. 25a–b. The "host" and "guest" were technical terms of the debates; see Arthur Wright, *Harvard Journal of Asiatic Studies*, X (1947), 81.

60. *Instructions*, ch. 5, pp. 2a–b. For the "ardent and yet cautious," that is, those who fall short of following the mean, see *Analects*, ch. 13, p. 8b; Legge, p. 136. The Excellent Scribe *lang-shih* appears in *Tso chuan*, ch. 45, pp. 36b–37a; Legge, p. 641; but more interesting is the same passage in *K'ung-tzu chia-yü* (Ssu-pu ts'ung-k'an ed.), ch. 9, pp. 18a–b, with the interpolation that his duty is "to record his master's excesses and make known his master's good points." Yen evidently does not agree. We take Excellent Scribe to refer to Pan Ku, since the preceding lines refer to four men whose biographies are found in *Han shu*, ch. 64.

61. *Shih-t'ung* (Ssu-pu ts'ung-k'an ed.), ch. 12, p. 18a, says that during the Sui, Yen and Hsin Te-yüan had a share in writing a *Wei shu* attributed to Wei Tan. The biographies of the former two men in the standard histories do not mention this joint venture, but it is interesting to note that Hsin and Wei were also members of the Wen-lin Academy during the Northern Ch'i (see note 87 below). This *Wei shu* is no longer extant, but *chuan* 3 of the standard *Wei shu* is said to have derived from it; see Chou I-liang, "Wei Shou's Historiography," *Yen-ching hsüeh-pao*, XVIII (1935), 113 and 144. Wei Tan's biography in *Sui shu*, ch. 58, pp. 2a–5b, preserves the principles of his history, which are concerned for the most part with the formal features of historical writing. Among them he pledged to include only those biographies significant for didactic purposes.

62. *Instructions*, ch. 3, p. 5a. Yen Shih-ku took the phrase "to be instructed by the traces of the past" (*shih-ku*) as his cognomen.

63. Yen Yen-chih (384–456) has biographies in *Sung shu*, ch. 73, pp. 1a–14a, and *Nan shih*, ch. 34, pp. 1a–5b. An abbreviated version of the *Kao t'ing* was included in the *Sung shu*, ch. 73, pp. 3b–11b, and additional fragments are to be found in the *Chin-lou-tzu*, *T'ai-p'ing yü-lan*, and elsewhere.

64. *Sung shu*, ch. 3, pp. 4a–b.

65. *Instructions*, ch. 4, p. 24b.

66. Frederick W. Mote, "Confucian Eremitism in the Yüan Period," in Arthur Wright, ed., *The Confucian Persuasion*, pp. 203–12.

67. *Instructions*, ch. 5, p. 8a.

68. *Ibid.*, ch. 4, p. 25a.

69. *Ibid.*, p. 26a; ch. 2, pp. 2a–b.

70. *Ibid.*, ch. 5, p. 3b.

71. *Ibid.*, ch. 3, p. 4a.

72. *Ibid.*, p. 7b.

73. *Ibid.*, ch. 4, p. 24b.

74. *Ibid.,* ch. 5, p. 2a.

75. *Ibid.,* p. 10b.

76. *Ibid.,* p. 12a.

77. *Ibid.,* p. 8a.

78. *Ibid.,* ch. 4, p. 8b. This is not to imply that loyalty to the house one serves is not in the baggage of the good official, as we shall see below in an example of Yen's loyalty. The career of his brother, Yen Chih-i (523–91), who probably raised Yen Chih-t'ui after the death of their father, also offers an example of what Yen meant. While serving the Northern Chou, Yen Chih-i refused to turn over to Yang Chien the imperial seal, which was in his care, despite all indications that the Chou dynasty was drawing to an end and that such a refusal might cost him his life. After the Sui was established, he continued to serve, transferring his loyalties to the new house. *Chou shu,* ch. 40, p. 12b.

79. *Instructions,* ch. 5, pp. 3a–b. *Li chi* (Shih-san-ching chu-su ed.), ch. 54, p. 21a; Legge, *Li Ki,* Part II, p. 345; *Analects,* ch. 19, p. 3a; Legge, p. 206.

80. *Sung shu,* ch. 73, p. 52.

81. *Pei Ch'i shu,* ch. 45, p. 24a.

82. *Han-fei-tzu* (Ssu-pu ts'ung-k'an ed.), ch. 10, p. 2b.

83. For the strategic importance of this city, see Hsü I-t'ang, "The Position of Hsiang-yang and Shou-ch'un in the Wars between North and South," *Chung-kuo wen-hua yen-chiu hui-k'an,* VIII (1948), 58–63.

84. *Tzu-chih t'ung-chien,* ch. 171, pp. 5327–28. For the secondary capitals of the northern dynasties, see Miyakawa Hisayuki, *Rikuchoshi kenkyu.* Han Feng has biographies in *Pei Ch'i shu,* ch. 50, pp. 8b–9b, and *Pei shih,* ch. 92, pp. 35b–37b.

85. Tsu T'ing has biographies in *Pei Ch'i shu,* ch. 39, pp. 3b–13a, and *Pei shih,* ch. 47, pp. 25b–35a.

86. Ts'ui Chi-shu, the instigator of the remonstration, had been a close associate of Tsu, while Feng Hsiao-yen and Chang Tiao-hu had much looser ties. P'ei Tse and Kuo Tsun are known only by name. The last of the six, Liu T'i, had betrayed Tsu's confidence in 567, causing Tsu's exile at that time and subsequent blindness. Liu had returned to office only after Tsu's fall from power in the early part of 573.

87. In 572 and part of 573, with the encouragement of Tsu T'ing, Yen was active in organizing and putting into operation the Forest of Literature Academy (*Wen-lin kuan*) at the court. The most notable scholars of the state were called to it, and an immense anthology was compiled as a subsidiary activity. In the main, the academy was given the literary responsibilities of the state, including the drafting of imperial decrees, of which Yen seems to have been in charge. The four persons among the six executed of whom we know something were all members of this academy. It is possible that bringing these eminent literati together gave them the feeling of group solidarity that encouraged some to make their almost unprecedented remonstration. Possibly also Han Feng saw in this company some threat to his power, or, as a goodly number were from the south, even a danger to the state. This group execution, in its inexplicability, resembles the massacre of Ts'ui Hao and those related to him in 450; see Wang I-t'ung, "A Note on the Real Cause of Ts'ui Hao's Execution in A.D. 450," *Ching-hua hsüeh-pao,* New Series, I, No. 2 (1957), 84–101.

88. *Pei Ch'i shu,* ch. 45, pp. 18a–b.

89. Wang Ch'ang said that as additional clothing is protection against cold, so self-cultivation is defense against criticism; *San-kuo chih*: Wei, ch. 2, p. 8b. The second is from *Hou Han shu,* ch. 72, p. 3b, where Tung Cho suggests that jealousy of him might cease if no further special favors were paid him.

90. *Pei Ch'i shu,* ch. 45, p. 24a.

91. Yen vividly described in the *Instructions,* ch. 5, pp. 4a–b and 8a, the dangers of holding office during the Ch'i. Given a more tolerant situation, he might have advocated more responsibility for the official. But in the time in which he lived, and which he foresaw for his descendants, to have done so would have been foolhardy.

92. *Pei Ch'i shu,* ch. 45, pp. 18a and 24a.

93. When asked what was the purpose of attempting to emulate the ancients, Yen answered that thus one may serve as an example to others. But, he adds, characteristically, in this way one acts so as to strengthen the position of the family and thus benefits one's descendants by bringing them office and good reputation; *Instructions,* ch. 4, pp. 23b–24a.

NOTES TO T'ANG LITERATI

1. *Chiu T'ang-shu (CTS),* ch. 190. The biographies can be counted in more than one way. My figure 101 takes in all those, including "attached" biographies, that give information beyond the man's name and his relationship to the person to whose biography he is attached, but I have excluded those "attached" biographies that do not mention literary achievements.

2. See Hans H. Frankel, "The K'ung Family of Shan-yin," *Tsing Hua Journal of Chinese Studies,* N.S., II, No. 2 (1961), pp. 303–4.

3. *CTS* (Po-na ed.), ch. 190A, p. 2a.

4. *Ibid.,* ch. 190C, p. 1b. The very title of the *fu,* "Felling Cherry Trees," is perhaps a jab at Li Lin-fu, whose surname means "plum tree." But the full significance of this episode escapes me. Does it reflect the conflict between the northwestern aristocrats, headed by Li Lin-fu, and the literati, represented here by Hsiao Ying-shih? On the other hand, Li in this story and elsewhere appears anxious to draw the literati to his side. The T'ang historiographers, strongly biased against Li, are ever ready to include material that tends to discredit him. See E. G. Pulleyblank, *The Background of the Rebellion of An Lu-shan* (London, 1955), p. 55.

5. *CTS,* ch. 190C, p. 20a.

6. *Ibid.,* ch. 190A, p. 3a.

7. *Ibid.,* ch. 190B, p. 11a.

8. *Ibid.,* pp. 10b–11a.

9. *Ibid.,* pp. 2a–b.

10. *Ibid.,* p. 3b.

11. *Ibid.,* pp. 14b–15b.

12. *Ibid.,* ch. 190C, pp. 1a–3a.

13. *Ibid.,* ch. 190B, p. 13b.

14. *Ibid.,* p. 1b.

15. *Ibid.*, ch. 190A, p. 8a.
16. See Hans Bielenstein, *The Restoration of the Han Dynasty* (Stockholm, 1953), pp. 73–74.
17. *CTS*, ch. 190A, p. 7a.
18. *Ibid.*, ch. 190C, pp. 1b–2a.
19. *Ibid.*, ch. 190A, p. 5a.
20. Stephen Spender, "The Making of a Poem," in Brewster Ghiselin (ed.), *The Creative Process* (New York, Mentor Books, 1959), pp. 122–23.
21. Malcolm Cowley, "Remembering Hart Crane," in *The Creative Process*, pp. 145–46.
22. *CTS*, ch. 190B, p. 2b.
23. Ho Chih-chang, *CTS*, ch. 190B, p. 15a; Li Po, ch. 190C, pp. 4a–b; Tu Fu, ch. 190C, p. 5a; Ts'ui Hsien, ch. 190C, p. 8a.
24. See Wang Yao, *Chung-ku wen-hsüeh shih lun chi* (Shanghai, 1956), pp. 28–48.
25. *CTS*, ch. 190C, p. 8a.
26. *Ibid.*, p. 2a.
27. *Chen-kuan cheng-yao* (Ssu-pu ts'ung-k'an ed.), ch. 7, pp. 8a–b.
28. *CTS*, ch. 190B, p. 5a.
29. *Ibid.*, pp. 11b–12a.
30. *Ibid.*, pp. 14b–15a.
31. *Ibid.*, ch. 190A, pp. 11b–12b.
32. *Ibid.*, ch. 190B, pp. 5b–7b.
33. *Ibid.*, pp. 13b–14a.
34. *Ibid.*, p. 20b.
35. *Ibid.*, ch. 190A, p. 10a.
36. *Ibid.*, ch. 190C, pp. 11a–18b.
37. *Ibid.*, ch. 190B, pp. 1b–2a.
38. *Ibid.*, ch. 190C, pp. 22b–23a.
39. *Ibid.*, ch. 190B, p. 3b.
40. Nagasawa Kikuya and Eugen Feifel, *Geschichte der chinesischen Literatur*, 2d ed. (Darmstadt, 1959), p. 202.
41. *CTS*, ch. 190C, p. 19b. Ling-hu Ch'u compiled a small anthology of recent T'ang poetry (Li Shang-yin is not included) for the emperor's perusal; see *T'ang-jen hsüan T'ang-shih* (Shanghai, 1958), pp. 191–255.
42. *CTS*, ch. 190B, p. 10b.
43. *Ibid.*, ch. 190C, p. 19a.
44. *Ibid.*, ch. 190B, p. 20a.
45. *Ibid.*, p. 2a; *Tzu chih t'ung-chien,* Ch'ien-feng second year, ninth month.
46. *CTS*, ch. 190B, p. 2a; *Tzu chih t'ung-chien,* Ch'ien-feng second year, ninth month.
47. *CTS*, ch. 190A, p. 14a.
48. *Ibid.*, ch. 190C, pp. 21a–b.
49. *Ibid.*, ch. 190B, pp. 9b, 10a.
50. *Ibid.*, ch. 190A, p. 6b.
51. *Ibid.*, p. 11a; ch. 190C, p. 6b. I am proud to point out that my own son has learned to recognize more than 1,500 Chinese characters before reaching the age of four (five *sui*).
52. *Ibid.*, ch. 190C, p. 2b.

53. *Ibid.*, p. 7a.
54. *Ibid.*, ch. 190B, p. 17b.
55. *Ibid.*, ch. 190C, p. 9b.
56. *Ibid.*, ch. 190B, pp.16a–17b.
57. *Ibid.*, ch. 190C, p. 2a.
58. *Ibid.*, ch. 190B, pp. 18a–20a.
59. *Ibid.*, ch. 190A, pp. 14a–b.

NOTES TO LU CHIH

The basic sources for this study are the surviving *Collected Works* of Lu Chih himself. These present a complex bibliographical muddle. Ch'üan Te-yü's preface to the original collection, which was entitled *Han-yüan chi*, says that there were ten chapters of edicts, seven of private memorials (*tsou-tsao*), and seven of official memorials (*chung-shu tsou-i*), making twenty-four chapters in all. Another version of this preface, cited in *Wen-hsien t'ung-k'ao*, ch. 232, pp. 1850c–51a, gives thirteen chapters of edicts. Modern editions almost all have twenty-two chapters (ten of edicts, six of each category of memorial), an arrangement that goes back at least to the Sung print reproduced in *Ssu-pu ts'ung-k'an*. There are two twenty-four-chapter editions known to me, one a late Ming edition edited by T'ang P'in-yin and Ma Yüan, the other an excellent critical edition with extensive commentary published in 1768 by Chang P'ei-fang. But the contents of these are identical with those of the Sung edition, and are said merely to have been rearranged to follow Ch'üan's preface. Chang P'ei-fang's edition is probably the best available, but as it is rare, I have given references to the *Works* in the *Ssu-pu ts'ung-k'an*.

Besides the complete works, there are also several editions of the memorials alone. These date from Sung times, when Lu Chih's work enjoyed a great vogue. The first of these, *Chu Lu Hsüan-kung tsou-i* (in fifteen chapters, with a commentary), was presented to the throne in 1132 by Lang Hua. This edition, which is reprinted in the *Shih-wan-chüan lou ts'ung-shu*, has a better text for the memorials than the *Ssu-pu ts'ung-k'an Works*. I accordingly cite the memorials from this edition, given in the notes as *Memorials*. Two editions of the memorials with commentaries similar to Lang Hua's were produced: one by Hsieh Fang-te, at the very end of the Sung, and one by P'an Jen in 1340. Neither is particularly helpful.

Abbreviations:

CTS   *Chiu T'ang shu* (Po-na ed.).
HTS   *Hsin T'ang shu* (Po-na ed.).
SL   *Shun-tsung shih-lu* (Kuo-hsüeh chi-pen ts'ung-shu ed. of *Han Ch'ang-li chi*, wai-chi).
TCTC *Tzu-chih t'ung-chien* (Ku-chi ch'u-pan she ed.; Peking, 1956).
TFYK *Ts'e-fu yüan-kuei* (Chung-hua shu-chü 1960 reprint of 1642 ed.).
THY   *T'ang hui-yao* (Kuo-hsüeh chi-pen ts'ung-shu ed.).
TT   *T'ung-tien* (Shih-t'ung ed., 1935).

1. J. B. Du Halde, *Description de la Chine* (1735), pp. 616 ff.
2. S. Balázs, "Beiträge zur Wirtschaftsgeschichte der T'ang-Zeit, Part 3,"

Mitteilungen des Seminars für Orientalische Sprachen zu Berlin, XXXVI (1933), 1–41.

3. E. G. Pulleyblank, "Neo-Confucianism and Neo-Legalism in T'ang Intellectual Life, 755–805," in Arthur F. Wright, ed., *The Confucian Persuasion* (Stanford, Calif., 1960), pp. 77–114, especially pp. 93–95.

4. Pulleyblank, *op. cit.*

5. See Su Shih, *Chin-ch'eng T'ang Lu Chih tsou-i cha-tzu,* included with most editions of Lu Chih's *Works.*

6. *SL,* ch. 4, pp. 6–9 (*Han Ch'ang-li chi,* wai-chi, ch. 8). Translation in Bernard S. Solomon, *The Veritable Record of the T'ang Emperor Shun-tsung* (Cambridge, Mass., 1955), pp. 37–41.

7. *CTS,* ch. 139, pp. 1a–18a.

8. Ch'üan Te-yü, *Lu Hsüan-kung Han-yüan chi hsü,* prefaced to all editions of *Works.*

9. *HTS,* ch. 157, pp. 1a–14b. In addition to these early biographies there are a number of recent *nien-p'u* of Lu Chih. I have employed the excellent *Lu Hsüan-kung nien-p'u* of the nineteenth-century scholar Ting Yen, which dates all the memorials accurately, though not, unfortunately, the edicts. There is also a useful *Nien-p'u chi-lüeh* appended to the 1818 edition of *Works* edited by Chou Yu and Wu Shao-juan, and to the Nien Keng-yao edition of *Works* reprinted in the *Ssu-pu pei-yao.* The latter also reprints a careful conflation of the *Chiu T'ang shu* and *Hsin T'ang shu* biographies entitled "T'ang ming-ch'en Lu Hsüan-kung chuan," which originally formed part of the collection *Li-tai ming-ch'en chuan,* compiled in 1728–30 by Chu Kao-an and Ts'ai Shih-yüan.

10. The I-wen chih of *HTS* (see T'ang-shu ching-chi i-wen ho-chih ed., Commercial Press, 1956), p. 363, lists Lu Chih, *I-lun piao-shu chi* in twelve chs., also *Han-yüan chi,* ten chs., compiler Wei Chu-hou.

11. Wei Chu-hou compiled the first draft of the *Shun-tsung Shih-lu,* in which Lu Chih's biography was included (see Han Ch'ang-li chi, ch. 38, p. 25, "Chin *Shun-tsung Huang-ti Shih-lu* piao-chuang"), and also edited the *Te-tsung shih-lu* together with Ling-hu Yü (see *TFYK,* ch. 554, p. 19a).

12. According to Ch'üan Te-yü's preface, he compiled a *Chi-chien fang* of fifty chapters. This is given in *HTS* I-wen chih, p. 284, and is listed in the *Ming Kuo-shih ching-chi chih* (*Ming-shih I-wen chih,* Commercial Press, 1957), ch. 4B, p. 1074.

13. See *HTS* I-wen chih, p. 268, which classes it with *T'ung-tien* and the various *Hui-yao* and says it had twenty chapters. The I-wen chih of *Sung shih* (Commercial Press, 1957), p. 161, classes it with *T'ung-tien* and *Po-shih liu-t'ieh* and gives it as having thirty chapters. It was still quite frequently mentioned in Sung times, and *Wen-hsien t'ung-k'ao,* ch. 228, p. 1828a, says that it comprised 450 sections and was very similar to the *Po-shih liu-t'ieh,* but more elegantly written. Besides this administrative encyclopedia, *Sung shih* (*loc. cit.,* p. 163) attributes to Lu Chih the authorship of a *Ch'ing-nang shu* in ten chapters, apparently a collection of literary quotations.

14. *Sung shih* I-wen chih (*loc. cit.,* pp. 54, 56) attributes to Lu Chih an *I-shih lu* in one chapter (also mentioned in *HTS* I-wen chih, p. 126), and a *Hsüan-tsung pien-i lu* in two chapters.

15. See *Teng-k'o chi-k'ao,* ch. 10, p. 31b (Nan-ching ko ts'ung-shu ed.).

16. See Ch'üan's preface, p. 2b.

17. According to the genealogy, *HTS*, ch. 73B, pp. 17a–b; *CTS*, ch. 139, p. 1a. But *Yüan-ho hsing-ts'uan* (Chin-ling shu-chü ed.), ch. 10, p. 2b, says that the father's name was Lu K'an-ju.

18. See *HTS*, ch. 73B, p. 17a.

19. See the list of notable clans discovered at Tun-huang and reprinted by Hsü Kuo-lin in *Tun-huang tsa-lu* (1937), pp. 153a–54b.

20. *T'ai-p'ing huan-yü chi*, ch. 91, p. 6a.

21. *HTS* I-wen chih, p. 154, lists the *Wu-chün Lu-shih tsung-hsi p'u* in one chapter.

22. Preserved in the modern clan genealogies. I have no access to a copy in London.

23. *Ta-T'ang chuan-tsai* (Chung-kuo wen-hsüeh ts'an-k'ao tzu-liao hsiao ts'ung-shu ed., 1957), p. 3.

24. *Wu-chün chih.*

25. *HTS*, ch. 73B, pp. 17a–b; *CTS*, ch. 139, p. 1a.

26. See biographies in *CTS*, *SL*, *HTS*. His paternal grandmother also came from a powerful noble family, the Cheng. Her epitaph, now, unfortunately, lost, is listed in *Pao-k'o ts'ung-pien*, ch. 7, p. 7a.

27. See p. 121 for the result of his relationship with Wei Kao.

28. There is some confusion over the date of his *chin-shih*. The various biographies say that he took it at the age of eighteen, which would have been in 771. But a note to *SL*, ch. 4, p. 6, says that he took it in 773, at which time he would have been twenty. This is accepted by *Teng-k'o chi-k'ao*, ch. 10, p. 31a, which also quotes Lu Chih's placing from an unspecified *Su-chou fu-chih* cited in *Yung-lo ta-tien*. The year was not a distinguished one. Of Lu's fellow candidates, only one, Yen Shou, became tolerably well known. The Chief Examiner was Chang Wei, who examined from 771 to 774. *Teng-k'o chi-k'ao* quotes a *fu* and a poem written by Lu Chih at the examination.

29. According to the class listed in *Teng-k'o chi-k'ao*, there was no strict rule as to when these examinations were taken. Lu Chih is assumed by the author to have taken his examination in 773.

30. *SL*, ch. 4, p. 6; *CTS*, ch. 139, p. 1a.

31. On his clan, see *HTS*, ch. 72C, pp. 17a–b.

32. He became Chief Minister for a short while in 782–83.

33. *SL*, ch. 4, p. 6; *CTS*, ch. 139, p. 1a; Ch'üan's preface.

34. *Ibid.*

35. *Ibid.*, *HTS*, ch. 157, p. 1a. He was shortly afterward given a nominal post as Under-Secretary of a subsection of the Board of Rites, but this was a sinecure.

36. See Sun Kuo-tung, "T'ang-tai san-sheng-chih chih fa-chan yen-chiu," *Hsin-ya hsüeh-pao*, III (1957), 108–12.

37. *CTS*, *loc. cit.*

38. This memorial is only preserved in *HTS*, ch. 157, pp. 1a–b, which gives a brief résumé.

39. See *THY*, ch. 78, pp. 1419–20.

40. Certainly he supported him in his factional struggle with Lu Ch'i, on which see *TCTC*, p. 227; *K'ao-i*, p. 7304.

41. See pp. 115–18.

42. For a genealogy, see *HTS*, ch. 71A, p. 13b. Biographies, *CTS*, ch. 135, pp. 5a–10b; *HTS*, ch. 167, pp. 1b–3a.

43. *CTS, loc. cit.* On this movement see Pulleyblank, *op. cit.*, pp. 83 ff.

44. *CTS,* ch. 135, p. 5a. He was so proud of this work that he adopted the *hao* "Lesser P'ei." Historical scholarship had a great vogue among his fellow refugees (see Pulleyblank, *op. cit.*, pp. 88–91), especially the study of early history, which had obvious lessons for the writers' own times.

45. *CTS,* ch. 135, p. 5a.

46. *Ibid.* The commissioner to this area, P'ei Po-yen, may have been a member of Yen-ling's clan.

47. *CTS,* ch. 135, p. 5a. *HTS,* ch. 167, p. 1a, ascribes this appointment to Lu Ch'i.

48. See Robert des Rotours, *Le Traité des fonctionnaires et traité de l'armée* (Leiden, 1947), I, 19, 194–95. Yet another such academy, the Hung-wen kuan, depended upon the imperial Chancellery (*Men-hsia sheng*).

49. See *TCTC,* ch. 226.

50. See *TCTC,* ch. 227, p. 7304; *CTS,* ch. 12, p. 7b.

51. See *TCTC,* ch. 227, p. 7329; *CTS,* ch. 125, p. 2a; *CTS,* ch. 12, p. 9b.

52. *CTS,* ch. 125, p. 7b, states categorically that Lu Ch'i engineered Chang's appointment to remove him from the capital. There was, however, more to this appointment. The previous governor of Feng-hsiang and Lung-yu was Chu Tz'u, close relative of the rebel Chu T'ao, and a part of his garrison force consisted of troops from Chu T'ao's province, Yu-chou. Chu Tz'u was therefore an obvious security risk in such a vital appointment, and was retired enfiefed with a splendid estate and fertile lands. It was imperative that his successor should be a man of great authority who could control Chu Tz'u's army. See *TCTC,* ch. 227, p. 7329; *CTS,* ch. 12, p. 9b.

53. See E. G. Pulleyblank, *The Background of the Rebellion of An Lu-shan* (London, 1955), pp. 75–81; Arthur Waley, *The Life and Times of Po Chü-i* (London, 1949), pp. 50 ff.

54. The best general account of the military governors of this period, though slightly out of date in some matters of detail, is Hino Kaisaburō, *Shina chūsei no gumbatsu* (Tokyo, 1941).

55. The power and autonomous authority of these four provinces is described in *TCTC,* ch. 225, pp. 7249–50. On the agreement, see also *TCTC,* ch. 226, pp. 7292–93. This agreement merely formalized the links between the four provinces. In addition, the families of their governors were closely linked by marriage alliances (see *HTS,* ch. 211, pp. 1a–b). Li Cheng-i, governor of the most important and powerful province of all, was a Korean mercenary by origin, which throws a new light on the influence of his countrymen in that area in the early ninth century, as described by Edwin O. Reischauer in *Ennin's Travels in T'ang China* (see *HTS,* ch. 213, p. 1a).

56. *TCTC,* ch. 225, p. 7255; *TCTC,* ch. 226, p. 7292; *HTS,* ch. 210, pp. 4a–b.

57. See *CTS,* ch. 48; *HTS,* ch. 51, p. 5b; *TCTC,* ch. 226, p. 7280.

58. This danger was intensified after 777, when the governor Li Cheng-i had taken the opportunity, in helping suppress the Li Ling-yao rebellion, to occupy five large and rich prefectures on the west and southwest, which brought him almost onto the canal along a long front. See *TCTC,* ch. 225, p. 7249; *HTS,* ch. 213, p. 1a; *CTS,* ch. 11, p. 25b; *CTS,* ch. 124, p. 7a. The vulnerability of the canal route in the face of any disorder in the southern Hopei–Honan region is clear from Chüan Han-sheng, *T'ang-Sung ti-kuo yü*

yün-ho (Chungking, 1944), pp. 42–92. For a penetrating analysis of the strategic situation in this area in the late T'ang, which is very relevant to the earlier period, see the study by Wang Gung-wu, *The Structure of Power in North China During the Five Dynasties* (University of Malaya Press, 1962).

59. See *TCTC*, ch. 226, p. 7277.

60. See *TFYK*, ch. 493, p. 22a; *HTS*, ch. 54, p. 2b; *T'ang ta-chao-ling chi* (Commercial Press, 1959), ch. 112, p. 584.

61. See *TCTC*, ch. 226, p. 7280; *CTS*, ch. 12, p. 5a.

62. See *TCTC*, ch. 226, pp. 7291 ff; *CTS*, ch. 12, pp. 6a–7a; *HTS*, ch. 211, p. 2b.

63. The best account of the military operations in the whole period 781–86, which were extremely complicated, is to be found in *TCTC*, chs. 226–32. Most important of the early campaigns was that of Li Hsi-lieh against Liang Ch'ung-i. See *CTS*, ch. 121, pp. 9a–b; *CTS*, ch. 145, p. 8a; *HTS*, ch. 225B, p. 1a, etc.; *TCTC*, ch. 227, pp. 7302 ff.

64. *TCTC*, ch. 227, pp. 7319 ff.

65. See *HTS*, ch. 211, pp. 4b–5b; *TCTC*, ch. 227, pp. 7307, 7316 ff.

66. *HTS*, ch. 211, p. 5a; *TCTC*, ch. 227, pp. 7322 ff.

67. *TCTC*, ch. 277, p. 7336.

68. *CTS*, ch. 121, pp. 9a–b; *HTS*, ch. 225B, p. 1a; *TCTC*, ch. 227, pp. 7316 ff.

69. *TCTC*, ch. 227, pp. 7336–37; *HTS*, ch. 225B, pp. 1a–b; *CTS*, ch. 145, pp. 8a–b.

70. *TCTC*, ch. 228, pp. 7345 ff.

71. *TCTC*, ch. 228, p. 7343, and *k'ao-i*; *CTS*, ch. 12, pp. 11a–b; *THY*, ch. 97, p. 1734. According to the latter, the negotiations were conducted by Chang I, and his appointment to the Feng-hsiang province (see note 52 above) may have been made with these negotiations in mind.

72. See *TCTC*, ch. 228, p. 7346, which gives a vivid picture of the wide region from which troops had been mobilized, and of the expense involved; and *HTS*, ch. 52, p. 2a.

73. *HTS*, ch. 52, p. 1b.

74. *CTS*, ch. 49, pp. 8a–b; *THY*, ch. 84, pp. 1545–46; *TFYK*, ch. 494, p. 26b; ch. 501, p. 12b; ch. 502, pp. 26a–27a; ch. 504, pp. 22b–23a; ch. 510, pp. 7a–8a.

75. *CTS*, ch. 48, p. 6a; *THY*, ch. 83, p. 1537; *TFYK*, ch. 488, p. 2b; *TFYK*, ch. 510, p. 7a.

76. *Works*, ch. 11, pp. 1a–9a; *Memorials*, ch. 1, pp. 6b–13b.

77. *Works*, ch. 11, pp. 9a–15b; *Memorials*, ch. 1, pp. 1a–6b.

78. *Memorials*, ch. 1, pp. 7b–9b.

79. *Ibid.*, pp. 10b–11b.

80. *Ibid.*, pp. 5b–6b.

81. See *Works*, ch. 10, pp. 5a–11b, for one letter to the Tibetan general and three to the Tibetan Chief Minister.

82. *Memorials*, ch. 1, pp. 5a–b.

83. *TCTC*, ch. 228, pp. 7344–45. Li Sheng's biography, *CTS*, ch. 133, p. 2a, attributes his withdrawal to sickness.

84. See *TCTC*, ch. 228, pp. 7350 ff.

85. *Ibid.*, pp. 7351–52.

86. Chu Tz'u was a former governor of Ching-yüan, who had been put

into retirement when Chu T'ao, his younger brother, rebelled. He was acclaimed as leader by the troops among the mutineers who had formerly been under his command. For his rebellion and the emperor's flight, see *TCTC,* ch. 228, pp. 7351 ff.; *CTS,* ch. 12, p. 12a; *CTS,* ch. 200B, pp. 1b–2b.

87. *CTS,* ch. 139, p. 1a; *SL,* ch. 4, pp. 6–7; Ch'üan's preface; *THY,* ch. 57, p. 978. These all derive from a common source, presumably the full version of Te-tsung's *SL,* or of Lu Chih's biography in the original Shun-tsung *SL.* These parallel passages throw some new light on the nature of the present *SL.* But this matter is too complicated to argue here.

88. See *Works,* chs. 1–10. There are eighty-five documents in all.

89. It is remarkable how closely the edicts issued by Te-tsung in 784–85 follow the spirit, and often the letter, of suggestions in Lu Chih's memorials. The extreme personal reliance placed on Lu by the emperor is graphically illustrated by an anecdote quoted in Ch'üan's preface, p. 2b. On the march to Liang-chou in 784, the emperor's entourage was split up, and the emperor, lodging in a post house in the mountains, called for Lu Chih. When the latter did not come, the emperor burst into a fit of weeping and offered a thousand pieces of gold to anyone in his retinue who could find Lu Chih. The same passage also shows that Lu was already on good terms with the Heir Apparent, the future Shun-tsung. The latter played a part later in saving Lu's life. See below, note 213.

90. *TCTC,* ch. 228, pp. 7359–60.

91. *Ibid.,* pp. 7362 ff.

92. *TCTC,* ch. 229, pp. 7386–87.

93. *TCTC, loc. cit.* The Uighurs had originally been called in by Wang Wu-chün as allies in his squabble with Chu T'ao, and had penetrated deep into northern Hopei following the withdrawal of the imperial army. See *TCTC,* ch. 228, p. 7365.

94. *TCTC,* ch. 228, p. 737; *CTS,* ch. 12, pp. 12b–13a.

95. *Works,* ch. 12, pp. 1a–7a; *Memorials,* ch. 2, pp. 1a–5a.

96. *Works,* ch. 12, pp. 7b–10a, especially pp. 9b–10a; *Memorials,* ch. 2, pp. 5a–7a, especially pp. 6b–7a.

97. See *CTS,* ch. 128, pp. 7a–8a; *Yen Lu-kung wen-chi,* ch. 1, pp. 5b–7b.

98. See *CTS,* ch. 12, p. 13a.

99. *TCTC,* ch. 229, pp. 7385–86.

100. *THY,* ch. 57, p. 979.

101. *Works,* ch. 12, pp. 7b–10a, 10a–18a; *Memorials,* ch. 2, pp. 5a–7a, 7a–12b.

102. *Works,* ch. 13, pp. 14a–b, 14b–16a; *Memorials,* ch. 3, pp. 1a–2b.

103. *Works,* ch. 13, pp. 16a–18a; *Memorials,* ch. 3, pp. 2b–4a.

104. *Works,* ch. 1, pp. 1a–6b; *T'ang ta-chao-ling chi,* ch. 5, pp. 27–28; *TFYK,* ch. 89, pp. 4a–7a.

105. A translation by P. Hervieu is included in Du Halde (note 1 above). This was taken from a Ch'ing collection of model documents compiled by imperial order.

106. See note 79 above.

107. *Memorials,* ch. 1, pp. 7b–9b.

108. Chu Tz'u had also shown that he too understood the economic causes of the popular discontent in the capital, and had meticulously continued the payment of salaries and honored official debts.

109. *TCTC,* ch. 229, pp. 7392–93.

110. See *THY*, ch. 57, pp. 978–79; *SL*, ch. 4, p. 7; *TCTC*, ch. 229, p. 7392.

111. See *THY*, ch. 59, pp. 1015–16.

112. *Works*, ch. 14, pp. 2b–6b; *Memorials*, ch. 4, pp. 1a–3b.

113. *TCTC*, ch. 229, pp. 7397–98; *CTS*, ch. 125, pp. 4b–5a.

114. *TCTC*, ch. 229, p. 7398; *CTS*, ch. 125, p. 5a; *CTS*, ch. 12, p. 14a.

115. As Vice-President of the Board.

116. *Works*, ch. 14, pp. 6b–8b; *Memorials*, ch. 4, pp. 3b–5a.

117. *TCTC*, ch. 230, pp. 7401–4.

118. *TCTC*, ch. 230, pp. 7404 ff.

119. See *TCTC*, chs. 230–31, and the biographies of Chu Tz'u (*CTS*, ch. 200B), Li Huai-kuang (*CTS*, ch. 121), Li Sheng (*CTS*, ch. 133), Ma Sui (*CTS*, ch. 134).

120. *CTS*, ch. 12, p. 16a.

121. *TCTC*, chs. 230–31.

122. *CTS*, ch. 145, pp. 9a–b; *TCTC*, chs. 231–32.

123. *Works*, ch. 15, pp. 11a–16b; *Memorials*, ch. 5, pp. 4b–8a.

124. *Works*, ch. 16, pp. 1a–5a; *Memorials*, ch. 5, pp. 8a–11a.

125. *Works*, chs. 3–5, 6–9.

126. *SL*, ch. 4, p. 7; *Works*, Preface, p. 2a.

127. *CTS*, ch. 139, p. 6a; *SL*, ch. 4, p. 7; *Works*, Preface, pp. 2a–b.

128. There is, as I mention above, some doubt whether in fact Lu himself collected his works or whether this was done by Wei Ch'u-hou.

129. These Acts of Grace are included in (*a*) *Works*, ch. 1, pp. 6b–13a, *TFYK*, ch. 89, pp. 7a–9a; (*b*) *Works*, ch. 2, pp. 1a–5a, *TFYK*, ch. 89, pp. 9a–11a, and a short résumé in *T'ang ta-chao-ling chi*, ch. 5, pp. 28–29; and (*c*) *Works*, ch. 2, pp. 5a–13b, *T'ang ta-chao-ling chi*, ch. 69, pp. 386–88.

130. See *TCTC*, ch. 231, pp. 7434–36; *ibid.*, p. 7453; *CTS*, ch. 143, p. 3b. See also *HTS*, ch. 212, p. 4b.

131. *CTS*, ch. 141, p. 6a; *HTS*, ch. 210, pp. 7b–8a.

132. *CTS*, ch. 141, p. 6b; *HTS*, ch. 210, p. 8a.

133. *Works*, ch. 7, pp. 7a–8a.

134. See *CTS*, ch. 52, p. 7b.

135. See *CTS*, ch. 139, p. 6b; *SL*, ch. 4, p. 7. *Works*, Preface, p. 2b, gives the impression that she had been escorted to the capital earlier, when Lu was first employed in the "inner office" (*Nei-shu*, i.e., the Han-lin Academy).

136. *CTS*, ch. 139, p. 6b; *Works*, Preface, p. 2b.

137. *CTS*, ch. 139, p. 6b; *Works*, Preface, pp. 2b–3a. For Wei Kao's biography, see *CTS*, ch. 140.

138. *CTS*, ch. 139, p. 6b; *SL*, ch. 4, p. 7; *Works*, Preface, p. 3a.

139. *CTS*, ch. 139, p. 6b; *SL*, ch. 4, p. 7.

140. *CTS*, ch. 139, pp. 6b–7a; *SL*, ch. 4, p. 7; *Works*, Preface, p. 3a.

141. On Lu Chih's conduct of the examinations, see Pulleyblank, *op. cit.* (note 3 above), pp. 94–95. The material concerning these examinations is collected in *Teng-k'o chi-k'ao*, ch. 1.

142. See *HTS*, ch. 139, p. 7a; Pulleyblank, *loc. cit.*

143. Te-tsung had moreover been a pupil of Li Pi during the An Lu-shan rising, and continued to visit him during Tai-tsung's reign when he was Heir Apparent and Li Pi was living in retirement at his private school, the P'eng-lai shu-yüan. *TCTC*, ch. 231, p. 7441.

144. See note 141 above.

145. *Teng-k'o chi-k'ao, loc. cit.*

146. For a vivid description of what such canvassing involved, see Waley, *The Life and Times of Po Chü-i*, pp. 17–20.

147. See Wu Hsüan-t'ung's biography, *CTS*, ch. 190C, pp. 6a–7a, especially p. 7a.

148. *CTS*, ch. 13, p. 7a; ch. 139, p. 6b.

149. *SL*, ch. 4, p. 7; *CTS*, ch. 139, p. 8b.

150. *Works*, ch. 17, pp. 1a–11a; *Memorials*, ch. 7, pp. 1a–7b.

151. *Works*, ch. 3, pp. 1a–5b, especially p. 4a. See also *T'ang ta-chao-ling chi*, ch. 70, pp. 390–91.

152. *THY*, ch. 57, p. 979.

153. The date is given as [*Hsing-yüan*] 4. There was no such date, and presumably *THY* has omitted the *nien-hao, Chen-yüan*. But in the fourth year Lu Chih was in retirement.

154. For a general discussion of this problem see Twitchett, "Lands under State Cultivation during the T'ang Dynasty," *Journal of Economic and Social History of the Orient*, II, No. 2 (1959), 90 ff.

155. *TCTC*, ch. 232, pp. 7494–95.

156. *THY*, ch. 89, p. 1619; *TFYK*, ch. 503, p. 22b; *HTS*, ch. 145, pp. 9a–b.

157. *CTS*, ch. 144, p. 5a; *TFYK*, ch. 503, pp. 23b–24a; *Yü-hai*, ch. 177, p. 26b; *HTS*, ch. 170, pp. 7b–8a.

158. *Works*, ch. 18, pp. 4b–17a; *Memorials*, ch. 9, pp. 1a–9a.

159. *Works*, ch. 19, pp. 1a–18a; *Memorials*, ch. 10, pp. 1a–13a.

160. *Ibid.*, especially *Memorials*, ch. 10, pp. 11b–12a.

161. *TCTC*, ch. 234, p. 7547.

162. See Pulleyblank, *loc. cit.* (note 3), p. 100 ff.

163. See *Liu Meng-te wen-chi*, wai-chi 9, pp. 1b–3a, "Wei Huai-nan Tu Hsiang-kung lun hsi-jung," and *HTS*, ch. 215a, p. 2a.

164. *Memorials*, ch. 9, pp. 2b–3b.

165. On the development of the Shen-ts'e armies see Hino Kaisaburō, *Shina chūsei no gumbatsu.*

166. See *TCTC*, ch. 229, p. 7397.

167. There is no adequate study of the Shu-mi yüan under the T'ang. A rather sketchy account is given by Sun Kuo-tung, "T'ang-tai san-sheng-chih chih fa-chan yen-chiu," *Hsin-ya hsüeh-pao*, III (1957), 112–16.

168. See *THY*, ch. 98, p. 1747; *TCTC*, ch. 233, pp. 7520 ff. The alliance with the Uighurs was brought about largely through the efforts of Li Pi, who wished also to bring the Arabs and Indians into an alliance to crush the Tibetans. See *TCTC*, ch. 232, pp. 7494–95; ch. 233, pp. 7501 ff.

169. See *THY*, ch. 97, pp. 1735–36; ch. 99, p. 1764; *HTS*, ch. 222A, pp. 4a–b; *CTS*, ch. 140, pp. 2a–b.

170. For a general discussion of finance in this period, see Twitchett, *The Financial Administration of the T'ang Dynasty* (Cambridge, 1962), especially chapters 2 and 6, and Chü Ch'ing-yüan, *T'ang-tai tsai-cheng shih* (Ch'angsha, 1944). Since I have dealt with the situation in great detail in this forthcoming volume, the following section is not fully annotated.

171. See *THY*, ch. 59, p. 1020; *T'ung tien*, ch. 23, p. 136c.

172. For examples of this, see the memorials from Yüan Chieh collected in *Yüan Tz'u-shan wen-chi*, ch. 10, pp. 4b ff., and especially pp. 9a–11a.

173. See Twitchett, "The Salt Commissioners after An Lu-Shan's Rebellion," *Asia Major*, IV, No. 1 (1954), 64 ff., and Chü Ch'ing-yüan, *Liu Yen p'ing-chuan* (1937).

174. They did not exercise any control over the important centers of production on the coast of Hopei and northern Shantung, which had been very important in the early part of the dynasty and continued to be a major source of smuggled salt.

175. See *TFYK*, ch. 496, p. 16b.

176. See Twitchett, *op. cit.* (note 173).

177. See *THY*, ch. 59, pp. 1015–16.

178. See Twitchett, *op. cit.* (note 170), and the extensive secondary material by Chinese and Japanese scholars there cited. Most recently Koga Noboru has suggested (*Tōyōshi kenkyū*, XIX, No. 3, 53–76) that the two-installment system was designed to bring policy into line with the economic situation in southern China, with its more diversified agriculture.

179. It has been widely assumed, on a misreading of the memorials of the late eighth century, that all taxation under the *liang-shui* system was money-based. This is erroneous. The Commissioners are specifically stated to have assessed the quotas in terms of "money and grain," and this is conclusively borne out by the very numerous acts of remission from the reigns of Te-tsung and Hsien-tsung.

180. See the memorials of Yüan Chieh cited in note 172. A distinction was however maintained with regard to labor services.

181. See the series of articles published in the late 1950's by Hino Kaisaburō and cited in Twitchett, *op. cit.* (note 170).

182. See *Memorials*, ch. 14, pp. 3b–4a.

183. See *TFYK*, ch. 488, pp. 1b–2a; *HTS*, ch. 52, p. 1a–b.

184. See Twitchett, *op. cit.* (note 173).

185. *THY*, ch. 83, p. 1537; *TFYK*, ch. 488, p. 2a; *CTS*, ch. 48, p. 6a.

186. See Twitchett, *op. cit.* (note 173).

187. For a comprehensive collection of price data (though not very imaginatively interpreted) see Ch'üan Han-sheng, "T'ang-tai wu-chia ti pien-tung," *Academia Sinica Journal*, XI (1947), 101–48.

188. See the materials presented by Hino Kaisaburō in "Ryōzeihō to bukka," *Tōyō shigaku*, XII (1955), 1–54; XIII (1955), 1–60.

189. *Works*, ch. 2, pp. 3b–4a.

190. The most likely date of this edict would appear to be 785 or 786. It is undated in *Works*, and none of the *Nien-p'u* ascribe a date to it.

191. *Works*, ch. 4, pp. 6a–7a; *T'ang ta-chao-ling chi*, ch. 112, p. 584.

192. See Twitchett, *op. cit.* (note 173).

193. See *TCTC*, ch. 234, p. 7530.

194. Chang P'ang fell together with Lu Chih in 794. See *SL*, ch. 4, p. 8; *TCTC*, ch. 235, pp. 7563, 7566.

195. Twitchett, *op. cit.* (note 173).

196. *TCTC*, ch. 234, pp. 7533–34; *CTS*, ch. 13, p. 7b; *CTS*, ch. 37, p. 9b. These floods came just before the harvest and devastated the whole plain from the area of Peking to the Yangtze valley, the crops being completely washed out.

197. *TCTC*, ch. 234, pp. 7359–60; *CTS*, ch. 49, p. 10a; *TT*, ch. 11, p. 10a; *TFYK*, ch. 493, p. 17a; *THY*, ch. 84, p. 1546.

198. See Balázs, "Beiträge zur Wirtschaftsgeschichte der T'ang-Zeit,"

Mitteilungen des Seminars für Orientalische Sprachen zu Berlin, XXXVI (1933), 1–41. This is very much to be preferred to the extract given in W. Theodore de Bary, *Sources of Chinese Tradition* (Columbia, 1959), pp. 416– 23. Not only is the latter translated from a badly cut text, but also the introductory remark of the editor is inaccurate and misleading, with its apparent assumption that the memorial was written against Yang Yen's original measure in 780.

199. See Pulleyblank, *op. cit.* (note 3), p. 100.

200. See *TCTC*, ch. 234, p. 7542. On the Nei Chuang-chai shih, see Katō Shigeshi, *Shina keizaishi kōshō,* pp. 261–82.

201. *Works,* ch. 19, pp. 18a–19a; *Memorials,* ch. 8, pp. 10b–11a.

202. *TCTC*, ch. 234, p. 7542.

203. *Works,* ch. 18, pp. 1a–2a; *Memorials,* ch. 7, pp. 12a–b. On the background of this incident, see Wang Gung-wu, "The Nanhai Trade," *Journal of the Malayan Branch of the Royal Asiatic Society,* XXXI, No. 2 (1958), 82–83.

204. See *CTS*, ch. 135, pp. 5a–b.

205. See Twitchett, *op. cit.* (note 173).

206. *Works,* ch. 18, pp. 2a–3b; *Memorials,* ch. 7, pp. 10b–12a.

207. See *CTS*, ch. 135, pp. 5b–9b.

208. See *Works,* ch. 20, pp. 2b–3a and 8b–12a; *Memorials,* ch. 11, pp. 1a–4a. See also *CTS*, ch. 135, pp. 5b–9b.

209. *TCTC*, ch. 235, p. 7562.

210. *SL,* ch. 4, p. 8; *CTS*, ch. 190C, p. 7a.

211. *SL,* ch. 4, p. 8; *CTS*, ch. 138, p. 3a.

212. *Works,* ch. 21, pp. 1a–20a; *Memorials,* ch. 12, pp. 1a–13b. On Lu Chih's subsequent dismissal, see *CTS*, ch. 13, p. 11a; *TCTC*, ch. 235, p. 7565.

213. *CTS*, ch. 13, p. 11a; *TCTC*, ch. 235, p. 7565. There may be more behind this appointment than is immediately apparent. The future Shuntsung had known Lu Chih since the days of exile, and moreover was the center of a group of progressives among whom was Liang Su, who had been closely associated with Lu Chih. According to *SL,* ch. 1, p. 86 (Solomon, p. 2), it was through the intercession of the Heir Apparent that P'ei Yen-ling was not made Chief Minister, and it may be that he also influenced Te-tsung to attach Lu Chih to his household.

214. See *SL,* ch. 4, p. 8; CTS, ch. 139, p. 17a; *TCTC*, ch. 235, p. 7566.

215. See *CTS*, ch. 139, p. 17a; *SL,* ch. 4, pp. 9–10; *TCTC*, ch. 235, p. 7566. According to *SL,* ch. 1, p. 86, the Heir Apparent preserved Yang Ch'eng from punishment over this incident.

216. *CTS*, ch. 139, p. 17b. This constituted a veiled threat of rebellion if Lu Chih were injured.

217. *CTS*, ch. 139, p. 17b; *SL,* ch. 4, p. 8. This story is repeated in many collections of anecdotes of late-T'ang date. However, during his retirement Lu Chih does seem to have had some connection with Li Chi-fu (see *CTS*, ch. 148, p. 3a; ch. 139, p. 17b), who later became an influential figure at Hsien-tsung's court, and eventually Chief Minister.

218. See *Ming kuo-shih ching-chi chih* (reprinted in *Ming-shih i-wenchih,* Commercial Press, 1957), ch. 4B, p. 1074.

219. See *HTS* I-wen chih (Commercial Press, 1956), p. 284. The work was entitled *Chen-yüan chi-yao-kuang li-fang,* in five chapters.

NOTES TO FENG TAO

Most of the material on Feng Tao is to be found in the *Chiu wu-tai shih* (hereafter *CWTS*) and the *Ts'e-fu yüan-kuei* (hereafter *TFYK*), both of which were based on official records, notably, the Veritable Records of the Five Dynasties. Supplementary material has been found scattered in miscellaneous works of the early Sung period, for example, the *Wu-tai shih pu* and the *Wu-tai shih ch'üeh-wen*. Background material is largely from the well-known sources, the old and new versions of the *Wu-tai shih* (the *CWTS* and the *HWTS*) and *T'ang shu* (the *CTS* and the *HTS*) and the *Tzu-chih t'ung-chien* (hereafter *TCTC*). In cases where this material has been discussed fully in my study *The Structure of Power in North China during the Five Dynasties* (University of Malaya Press, 1962) detailed references have not been attempted here.

All quotations from the twenty-four histories are from the Po-na-pen edition. For the *TCTC*, I have used the Ku-chi ch'u-pan she edition (ten vols., 1956), and for the *TFYK*, the edition with colophon dated 1672.

1. *Hsü T'ung-chih* (Wan-yu wen-k'u ed.), ch. 607, p. 6609. This opinion was so harsh that, soon afterward, Chao I (1727–1814) tried to explain why Feng Tao was respected by his own contemporaries; *Nien-erh-shih cha-chi* (Shih-chieh shu-chü ed., 1958), ch. 22, II, 302.

2. On the circumstances of Ch'ien-lung's reign (1736–95), see David S. Nivison, "Ho-shen and His Accusers: Ideology and Political Behavior in the Eighteenth Century," in *Confucianism in Action*, ed. David S. Nivison and Arthur F. Wright (Stanford, Calif., 1959), pp. 218–32. Also L. Carrington Goodrich, *The Literary Inquisition of Ch'ien-lung* (Baltimore, 1935), pp. 30–36, 44–53.

3. *Sung shih*, ch. 254, pp. 1a–4b; *TFYK*, ch. 52, pp. 16a–b.

4. *HWTS*, ch. 54, pp. 1a–2a.

5. *TCTC*, ch. 291, p. 9512.

6. Fan Chih was the author of *Wu-tai t'ung-lu* in 65 chuan, *Sung shih*, ch. 249, p. 4b. Ssu-ma Kuang quotes him on Feng Tao in *TCTC*, ch. 291, p. 9511. According to Hung Mai, *Jung-chai san-pi* (Wan-yu wen-k'u ed.), ch. 9, p. 7b, it was Fan Chih who preserved admiringly Feng Tao's notorious autobiography, the *Ch'ang-lo lao tzu-hsü*.

7. *CWTS*, ch. 126, p. 12a. The historians' comment on Feng Tao had reservations about his loyalty, but the biography (pp. 1a–11b) was flattering to him. On Hsüeh Chü-cheng and the other compilers, see Wang Gung-wu, "The *Chiu wu-tai shih* and History-Writing during the Five Dynasties," *Asia Major*, IV (1956), 4–6.

8. Wu Ch'u-hou, *Ch'ing-hsiang tsa-chi* (Pei-hai ed.), ch. 2, pp. 4b–5b.

9. Professors Y. Sudō, K. Hino, and their students have followed some of the suggestions of Professor T. Naito and investigated some of the economic and political problems, and we now have a much better understanding of the main changes during the ninth and tenth centuries.

10. For want of more accurate and convenient terms to represent *chieh-tu shih* and the territories they controlled, I have used here the general names "military governors" and "provinces," respectively. The material on these "provinces" has been briefly summed up in the *HTS*, chs. 210–12. See Wu T'ing-hsieh, "T'ang fang-chen nien-piao," *Erh-shih-wu shih pu-pien* (K'ai-ming ed.), VI, 7382–93.

11. *CWTS,* ch. 126, pp. 1a, 7a. Ying-chou was in Wei-po province, 763–75, and in Lu-lung province, 775–900, with a short break of a few months in 822. In 763–75 it bordered Lu-lung and Ch'eng-te provinces and in 775–900 it bordered Ch'eng-te and Ts'ang-ching provinces and was not far from the Wei-po provincial frontier; *HTS,* ch. 66, pp. 5a–14a.

12. *HTS,* chs. 210–12; Wu T'ing-hsieh, VI, 7385–87.

13. *CWTS,* ch. 135, pp. 1a–b; father of Liu Shou-kuang (ch. 135, pp. 4b–8a).

14. *CWTS,* ch. 126, p. 7a. This would mean that he was a descendant of the family of Feng Pa (d. 430), the founder of the Northern Yen dynasty, 409–36 (*Chin shu,* ch. 125, pp. 9b–14b), and Feng Hsi (fl. 450–65), the brother of an empress dowager and the father of two empresses of the Toba Wei dynasty, 386–534 (*Wei shu,* ch. 83A, pp. 9b–17a); and also of Feng Tzu-tsung (d. 571), a relative by marriage of the imperial house of Northern Ch'i, 550–77 (*Pei Ch'i shu,* ch. 40, pp. 2a–4a). This aristocratic family lost eminence in the early years of the T'ang dynasty and could only boast of two "good officials" (*liang-li*) who found a place in the *CTS* (ch. 185A, pp. 11a–b; also in *HTS,* ch. 112, pp. 11b–12a). Both these men, the cousins of Feng Yüan-ch'ang (fl. 680–705) and Feng Yüan-shu (fl. 684–710), had their homes at An-yang, nearly two hundred miles southwest of their ancestral home, and it is possible that the family dispersed during the seventh century and that Feng Tao's ancestors went about a hundred miles northeast to Ching-ch'eng.

15. *TFYK,* ch. 331, p. 27a; Hung Mai, *Jung-chai,* III, 77. Feng Tao said this soon after 942, when he was about sixty years old. It is, however, on record that his father died in late 923 or early 924, when he was already forty-one, hardly "young."

16. Denis Twitchett, "Chinese Biographical Writing," in W. G. Beasley and E. G. Pulleyblank, eds., *Historians of China and Japan* (London, 1961), pp. 85–114; also Wang, *Asia Major,* p. 6.

17. *CWTS,* ch. 126, p. 1a.

18. *CTS,* ch. 20A, p. 11a; *TCTC,* ch. 259, p. 8459; *TFYK,* ch. 7, p. 19a.

19. *CTS,* ch. 20A, p. 21a; *CWTS,* ch. 2, pp. 3a–b, and ch. 135, p. 12b; *TCTC,* ch. 262, p. 8535.

20. *CWTS,* ch. 72, p. 2a, and ch. 126, p. 1a; *TCTC,* ch. 268, p. 8747. It is possible that Feng Tao had joined Liu Jen-kung before 907 (that is, before Liu Shou-kuang seized power from his father), if we are to believe the biography of Han Yen-hui in *Liao shih,* ch. 74, p. 2a.

It is interesting to note that Feng Tao's service with Chang Ch'eng-yeh is recorded in detail in Chang's biography (*CWTS,* ch. 72, p. 2a). This either suggests that Feng Tao had a hand in Chang's Account of Conduct (see note 16) or in the collection of biographies compiled in 934 (Wang, *Asia Major,* p. 11) and wanted to show his gratitude to the old eunuch, or shows that the compilers of the *Chiu wu-tai shih* thought so highly of Feng Tao that they thought it to Chang's credit to have recognized Feng Tao's merits so early.

21. *CWTS,* ch. 67, pp. 4a–5a, and ch. 93, p. 1b. Feng Tao was supported by both Chang Ch'eng-yeh and Lu Chih (867–942), the Chief Administrator (*chieh-tu p'an-kuan*) at the time. They had both defended Feng Tao against the opposition of the expert in physiognomy, Chou Hsüan-pao (fl. 900–927). Chou's opposition to him was probably the result of Feng Tao's skepticism of

anything non-Confucian. The art of physiognomy based on the writings of Yüan T'ien-kang (fl. 605–34) and Hsü Chen-chün (fl. 320–74) had always been associated with Taoists, while Chou himself had started life as a Buddhist priest. *TFYK*, ch. 843, pp. 27a–b, and ch. 929, pp. 5a–b; Chou's biography, *CWTS*, ch. 71, pp. 8a–9a; Yüan's biography, *CTS*, ch. 191, pp. 3b–5a; Hsü's biography in Chao Tao-i, *Li-shih chen-hsien t'i-tao t'ung-chien* (Tao Ts'ang ed. 1923), *ts'e* 143, ch. 26, pp. 1a–20b.

22. *CWTS*, ch. 126, pp. 1b–2a; *TCTC*, ch. 270, p. 8848.

23. I examine this question of intimacy in the provincial organization and the Wu-tai courts in my study *The Structure of Power in North China*. For the events of Chuang-tsung's reign, see *CWTS*, chs. 30–34, and *TCTC*, chs. 272–74.

24. *TCTC*, chs. 256–66.

25. *TFYK*, ch. 337, pp. 31a–32a; *CWTS*, ch. 58, p. 6a; *TCTC*, ch. 275, p. 8999.

26. *TFYK*, ch. 551, pp. 20b–21a; *CWTS*, ch. 92, p. 7b; *TCTC*, ch. 279, pp. 9112–13, 9115.

27. *CWTS*, ch. 47, pp. 12a–b.

28. *CWTS*, ch. 92, pp. 7a–8a; *HWTS*, ch. 54, pp. 14b–15a.

29. "The sixteen prefectures of Yen and Yün" were offered to the Khitans by Shih Ching-t'ang in 936 as the price for their help in putting him on the throne. They were formally handed over in 938 and were a definite part of enemy country after 947. The Jurchens inherited them in 1124 and the Mongols after that in 1234. It was not until 1368, under the Ming dynasty, that a Chinese emperor ruled over the area again.

30. *CWTS*, ch. 126, p. 5b. The reference to a Ch'an priest and falconry was an idiom of the T'ang and Sung periods; see *Yüan-chien lei-han* (Tung-wen shu-chü ed., 1926), ch. 317, p. 8b, and *P'ei-wen yün-fu* (Wan-yu wen-k'u ed., 1937), ch. 25, p. 1265/3.

31. *CWTS*, ch. 126, pp. 5b–6a; *HWTS*, ch. 54, pp. 4a–b; *TFYK*, ch. 864, p. 7a.

32. *TFYK*, ch. 608, pp. 29b–31a. See T. F. Carter, *The Invention of Printing in China and Its Spread Westward* (New York, 1925), pp. 47–54.

33. *CWTS*, ch. 88, p. 1b; *Ch'i-tan kuo-chih* (Wan-yu wen-k'u ed.), ch. 2, p. 17. On Feng Tao's mission to the Khitans, *CWTS*, ch. 126, pp. 4a–b; *TFYK*, ch. 329, p. 19b, and ch. 654, pp. 13a–b; *Liao shih*, ch. 4b, pp. 1b–3a; *TCTC*, ch. 281, pp. 9188–89. On Ying-chou being given to the Khitans and its recovery in 959 (*TCTC*, ch. 294, p. 9897), the clearest analysis on this very controversial subject is Chang Ting-i's in *Hsien-hsien chih* (1925), ch. 2, pp. 4a–b. This is an improvement on *Ch'ien-lung Ho-chien-fu chih* (1760), ch. 1, pp. 26a–b, and certainly superior to the garbled versions in *Ch'ien-lung Hsien-hsien chih* (1761), ch. 1, p. 11b, and *K'ang-hsi Ho-chien-fu chih* (1678), ch. 2, pp. 12b–13a. See also *T'ai-p'ing huan-yü chi* (Chin-ling shu-chü ed., 1882), ch. 66, pp. 1b–2a, and *Tu-shih fang-yü chi-yao* (Chung-hua shu-chü ed., six vols., 1955), ch. 13, I, 573.

34. Wang Yü-ch'eng, *Wu-tai shih ch'üeh-wen* (Ch'ien-hua-an ts'ung-shu ed.), pp. 9b–10b. T'ao Yüeh, *Wu-tai shih pu* (Ch'ien-hua-an ts'ung-shu ed.), ch. 5, pp. 10a–b. Briefly summarized in *CWTS*, ch. 126, p. 10b.

35. *CWTS*, ch. 114, p. 3a, and ch. 126, p. 11a; *TFYK*, ch. 57, pp. 17a–b; *TCTC*, ch. 291, pp. 9502–3.

36. *T'ao yüeh,* ch. 5, p. 10b.

37. *T'ao yüeh,* ch. 3, p. 6b. Also *Ku-chin shih-hua,* quoted in *Ch'ien-lung Hsien-hsien chih,* ch. 19, pp. 23b–24a. Cf. a similar story about Li Ku (903–60) in *T'ao yüeh,* ch. 5, p. 11a. The "liquor households" (*chiu-hu*) were lowly families licensed to manufacture liquor.

38. *TFYK,* ch. 52, pp. 13a–17b, and ch. 54, pp. 23a–25b. Chou Shih-tsung (954–59) was very severe to some of the rich Buddhist temples but also paid his respects to the faith. In any case, Feng Tao served him for less than three months before his death.

39. *TFYK,* ch. 54, pp. 24b–25b.

40. Chao Feng, *CWTS,* ch. 67, pp. 6b–7b; Liu Hsü, *TFYK,* ch. 865, p. 21b; Ma Yin-sun, *TFYK,* ch. 821, p. 24b.

41. *CWTS,* ch. 126, p. 2b; *TFYK,* ch. 320, p. 17b. Examples of Feng Tao's help, *CWTS,* ch. 108, p. 1b; *TFYK,* ch. 955, pp. 4b–5a.

42. Sun Kuang-hsien, *Pei-meng so-yen* (Pei-hai ed.), ch. 19, pp. 5b–6a; *TFYK,* ch. 337, p. 23b; *CWTS,* ch. 126, p. 2b. The *T'u-yüan ts'e* in thirty *chuan* by Tu Ssu-hsien (c. 634–74) was lost during the Southern Sung dynasty. Four T'ang ms. fragments have been recovered from Tun-huang. The three of the Stein collection at the British Museum (S.614, S.1086, and S.1722) show that the work was presented in the form of "question and answer." The fragment S.1086 includes numerous quotations from philosophical and historical works extending from the *I Ching* to the history of the Liu Sung dynasty (A.D. 420–79). The fourth fragment in Paris (no. 2573) I have not seen.

Opinion on the *T'u-yüan ts'e* has varied considerably. Sun Kuang-hsien says it was well done in the style of Hsü Ling (507–83) and Yü Hsin (513–81); Ou-yang Hsiu held the work in contempt (*HWTS,* ch. 55, p. 8b); while Wu Lan-t'ing considered Ou-yang Hsiu to have been too harsh (*Wu-tai shih-chi chuan-wu pu* [Chih-pu-tsu chai ed.], ch. 4, pp. 5a–b). Also, Wang Ying-lin (1223–96) described the author as a minor follower of the T'ang Prince of Chiang (d. 674); *K'un-hsüeh chi-wen* (Wan-yu wen-k'u ed.), ch. 14, p. 1174; while Chao Kung-wu (fl. 1150–64) attributed the work to the famous scholar Yü Shih-nan (558–638) and might have confused the work with the *Pei-t'ang shu-ch'ao; Chün-chai tu-shu chi* (1884 ed.), ch. 14, pp. 16b–17a.

43. Feng Tao's three collected works were his *Ho-chien chi* in five *chuan;* a *Chi* in six *chuan* and a *Shih-chi* in ten *chuan; Sung shih,* ch. 208, pp. 10a–b. They were probably seen by Sung historians like Ou-yang Hsiu and his contemporaries and do not seem to have impressed them in any way. Nor perhaps did the works help the historians determine which of the official memorials were drafted by Feng Tao.

44. *CWTS,* ch. 67, pp. 8a–11b; *TFYK,* ch. 841, p. 9a. See Carter, *op. cit.,* pp. 47–54, where Feng Tao is described as a man of great power and ability. Anonymous, *Ai-jih chai ts'ung-ch'ao* (Shou-shan ko ts'ung-shu ed.), ch. 1, pp. 2a–3b.

45. *Wu-tai hui-yao* (Wan-yu wen-k'u ed.), ch. 8, p. 96; *TFYK,* ch. 608, pp. 29b–31a; *Sung shih,* ch. 431, pp. 27b–29a.

46. *TFYK,* ch. 37, pp. 24b–25a, and ch. 314, pp. 14b–16a.

47. *TFYK,* ch. 108, pp. 17b–18b. *Wu-tai hui-yao,* ch. 6, p. 76.

48. *TFYK,* ch. 314, pp. 15b–16a. The quotation from the *Book of His-*

tory comes from the Chün-ya section; *Shih-san ching chu-su* (Taipei, 1955), vol. 2, ch. 19, p. 11a.

49. Twitchett, "Chinese Biographical Writing," *loc. cit.* (n. 16); Wang, *Asia Major*, pp. 6–7.

50. Wang, *Asia Major*, Table I, p. 8.

51. See notes 26 and 28; Wang, *Asia Major*, pp. 13–14.

52. *HWTS*, ch. 54, p. 6a.

53. *CWTS*, ch. 126, pp. 5a–b.

54. *TFYK*, ch. 314, p. 14b.

55. *TFYK*, ch. 792, pp. 19a–20a.

56. *CWTS*, ch. 106, p. 4a, says Liu Shen-chiao died in the spring of 949, while *CWTS*, ch. 103, p. 1b, says he died in the second month of 950. Feng Tao's autobiography was dated the *chu-ming* month (that is, the fourth month) of 950; *CWTS*, ch. 126, p. 10b.

57. *CWTS*, ch. 126, p. 9b; *TFYK*, ch. 770, p. 27b. The *TFYK* text is corrupt.

58. I am grateful to Professor D. C. Twitchett for pointing out the latent Buddhism in Feng Tao's attitude to sacrifices. There is no evidence that Feng Tao was ever consciously Buddhist. His specific request here, I feel, reflects clearly how deeply Buddhist notions had penetrated into the Chinese mind, to the extent that they could even modify the oldest ideas of Confucian ritual.

59. *CWTS*, ch. 126, pp. 9b–10a; *TFYK*, ch. 770, p. 28a. Both texts omit the word *wu* before the remark on the sacrifice of male goats. The sentence does not make sense, however, except in the negative.

60. *Ch'ing-hsiang tsa-chi*, ch. 2, pp. 4b–5b.

61. *TCTC*, ch. 291, p. 9512.

62. *Ch'ing-hsiang tsa-chi*, ch. 2, p. 5b; *Neng-kai chai man-lu* (Shou-shan ko ts'ung-shu ed.), ch. 10, pp. 21b–22a.

63. For summaries of the main views on Feng Tao, see *Ch'ien-lung Ho-chien-fu chih*, ch. 17, pp. 38a–39b, and *Hsien-hsien chih*, ch. 11B, pp. 24a–27b. For Chao I's views, cf. *Nien-erh shih cha-chi*, ch. 22, p. 302.

64. Ou-yang Hsiu's famous essay "Cheng-t'ung-lun" ("Essay on the Orthodox Succession") and Su Shih's essay with the same title bring out the main argument of Sung historians; *Ou-yang wen-chung kung chi* (Wan-yu wen-k'u ed.), ch. 21, pp. 5–9.

The question of the Five Dynasties had been debated for a century before Ou-yang Hsiu. The problem was whether the Liang dynasty was orthodox or not and whether there were in fact only *four* rather than five dynasties. The issue was not resolved even after the term *wu-tai* had come into common usage early in the Sung, and the *TFYK* relegates the Liang dynasty to the section on dynasties not in direct line of succession (*jun-wei*).

65. Prince of Sung, Han Yin-ti, and Prince of Liang were sons; Prince of Lu and Chou Shih-tsung were adopted sons; Chin Shao-ti was a nephew and Chin Kao-tsu was the son-in-law of Ming-tsung.

66. On the traditions of the Ho-pei provinces, see note 12. The four were Ming-tsung, Han Kao-tsu, and Chou T'ai-tsu (see following note), and Sung T'ai-tsu in 960.

67. Ming-tsung, *TCTC*, ch. 274, X, pp. 8965–76; Han Kao-tsu, ch. 286, X, pp. 9335–66; Chou T'ai-tsu, ch. 289, X, pp. 9429–50.

68. Sung T'ai-tsu, Chao K'uang-yin, was a native of Cho-chou in Lu-lung province and descended from three generations of officials in the province. His own father then joined the service of the governor of Ch'eng-te province, also in Hopei, before joining the Sha-t'o leader Chuang-tsung. Chao K'uang-yin himself was born in the barracks of Ming-tsung's imperial army at Lo-yang; *Sung shih*, ch. 1, pp. 1a–2a. And Sung T'ai-tsu retained as his most senior minister Fan Chih, the great admirer of Feng Tao (see note 6); ch. 1, pp. 4a–b.

69. See note 33; *CWTS*, ch. 137, pp. 8a–b.

70. *Liao shih*, ch. 1, p. 2a; *CWTS*, ch. 137, p. 2a (the date is wrongly given here as 907) and pp. 8a–b; K. A. Wittfogel and Feng Chia-sheng, *History of Chinese Society: Liao* (Transactions of the American Philosophical Society, 1948), pp. 239, 573.

71. *CWTS*, ch. 137, pp. 8b–9a; Yang Lien-sheng, "A 'Posthumous Letter' from the Chin Emperor to the Khitan Emperor in 942," *Harvard Journal of Asiatic Studies*, X (1947), 424–28.

72. *HWTS*, ch. 54, pp. 4a–b; *CWTS*, ch. 126, p. 5b; *Liao shih*, ch. 4, pp. 14b–15a; *TCTC*, ch. 286, X, p. 9330.

73. *HWTS*, ch. 35, pp. 1a–2a and 7b–9b. This is clear in Ou-yang Hsiu's comments on the six men. The irony is that they were so obviously disloyal that no one argued about them afterward, whereas Feng Tao's case was fought over in the eleventh century and thus had special attention drawn to it.

74. *Han shu*, ch. 87B, pp. 6a–14a, and ch. 100A, pp. 18b–23b; *Chin-shu*, ch. 51, pp. 1a–b, and ch. 94, pp. 19b–20a; *Liang shu*, ch. 50, pp. 9b–10a.

There are several more examples, like Chang Heng's (78–139) *Ying-wen* (*Hou Han shu*, ch. 89, pp. 2a–12a), Ts'ai Yung's (131–92) *Shih-hui* (*Hou Han shu*, ch. 90B, pp. 2a–11a), and Shu Hsi's (fl. 280–300) *Hsuan-chü shih* (*Chin shu*, ch. 51, pp. 13a–14b).

75. *Shih chi*, ch. 126, pp. 8a–9a, and *Han shu*, ch. 65, pp. 15b–18b.

76. *CTS*, ch. 166, pp. 7a–8a.

77. Wang Ch'ung, *Lun-heng chi-chieh* (Ku-chi ch'u-pan she ed.), ch. 30, pp. 579–92. Alfred Forke, *Lun-heng: Philosophical Essays of Wang Ch'ung* (Leipzig, 1907), pp. 64–82.

78. *CWTS*, ch. 126, p. 10a; *TFYK*, ch. 770, p. 28a.

79. *CWTS*, ch. 126, p. 10a; *TFYK*, ch. 770, p. 28b.

NOTES TO FROM MYTH TO MYTH

1. *Shuo-Yüeh ch'üan chuan.* For earlier versions see Sun K'ai-ti, *Jih-pen Tung-ching so chien Chung-kuo hsiao-shuo shu-mu* (Shanghai, 1953), pp. 50–52. A wide collection of popular lore of Yüeh Fei is found in *Yüeh Fei ku-shih hsi-ch'ü shuo-ch'ang chi* (Tu Ying-t'ao ed.) (Shanghai: Ku-tien wen-hsüeh, 1957). See also Robert Ruhlmann, "Traditional Heroes in Chinese Popular Fiction," in Arthur F. Wright, ed., *The Confucian Persuasion* (Stanford, 1960), p. 154 and note 52. The latest literary treatments of Yüeh Fei's life are the dramas *Yüeh Fei* by Ku I-chiao (Commercial Press, 1940) and Cheng Lieh's *Ching-chung po shih-chü*, 4 vols. (Nanking, 1948).

2. See L. C. Arlington and William Lewinsohn, *In Search of Old Peking* (Peking, 1935), pp. 231–32.

3. By Chang Ying (*Sung shih*, ch. 404), a historiographer who wanted in this way to rid Yüeh K'o's (1183–?) compilation of the odium of private bias. Chang finished his rewrite only three years after Yüeh K'o had finished his biography, and incorporated it into his book *Nan-tu ssu chiang chuan*, which also contains biographies of three other generals of the time. His version is contained in the *Chin-t'o hsü-pien*, ch. 17. See Teng Kuang-ming, *Yüeh Fei chuan* (Peking, 1955), pp. 284–85.

4. *O-wang hsing-shih pien-nien*, incorporated in the *Chin-t'o ts'ui-pien*. The *Chin-t'o ts'ui-pien* and the *Chin-t'o hsü pien* have been used in the Che-chiang shu-chü edition of 1883.

5. One of them has been pointed out by Ichimura Sanjirō, Chinese translation by Ch'en Yü-ch'ing in *Shih-hsüeh tsa-chih*, I (1929), and by Teng, *op. cit.*, pp. 282–83; others by Teng, *op. cit.*, pp. 281–82 and 289–303.

6. After all this has been said, it must be stated that in face of these handicaps Yüeh K'o worked with a remarkable degree of integrity. The *Ssu-k'u t'i-yao* authors are full of praise for his reliability. Cf. Wan-yu wen-k'u edition, II, 1959.

7. Hsiung K'o's biography is in *Sung shih*, ch. 445. The *Kuang-ya ts'ung-shu* contains a reprint of the *Yung-lo ta-tien* version of his *Chung-hsing hsiao-li*. See *Ssu-k'u t'i-yao*, I, 1035.

8. 1129–1206. His compilation is entitled *Chung-hsing liang ch'ao sheng-cheng*.

9. 1166–1243. His *Chien-yen i-lai hsi-nien yao-lu* is also contained in the *Kuang-ya ts'ung-shu*. On his book, see *Ssu-k'u t'i-yao*, I, 1041.

10. See Otto Franke, *Geschichte des chinesischen Reiches*, IV (Berlin, 1948), 4–5, following the *Ssu-k'u t'i-yao*.

11. On this point see Liang Yüan-tung, "Yüeh Fei Ch'in Kuei chiu an," in *Jen-wen Yüeh-k'an*, VIII, No. 5 (June 15, 1937).

12. *Sung Yüeh chung-wu-wang chi* (Pan-mou-yüan ed., 1865). A handy annotated selection is contained in *Wu chung chi*, Hu huai-shen ed. Cheng-chung wen-k'u, XXXI (Taipei, 1954).

13. See *Nien-erh-shih cha-chi* (Ts'ung-shu chi-ch'eng ed.), ch. 25, pp. 514–16; *Ssu-k'u t'i-yao*, III, 3312.

14. Most of what remained at that time was compiled by Yüeh K'o in the section "Po shih chao-chung lu" of his *Chin-t'o hsü-pien* and by Hsü Meng-hsin in his *San-ch'ao pei-meng hui-pien* (various editions: Hsü's dates are 1124–1204; on his book, see *Ssu-k'u t'i-yao*, II, 1070). Hsü's work also contains an anonymous, apparently independent, but not entirely reliable biography of Yüeh Fei. The Pan-mou-yüan edition of Yüeh Fei's collected works has appended a collection of episodical material, drawn from a variety of private sources.

15. Two *nien-p'u* have been helpful, the one by Ch'ien Ju-wen, *Sung Yüeh O-wang nien-p'u*, 6 ts'e, preface dated 1924 (a careful edition of Yüeh's works is appended), and the one by Li Han-hun, *Yüeh Wu-mu nien-p'u*, 2 vols. (Shanghai: Commercial Press, 1948). Of recent biographies the one by Teng Kuang-ming, mentioned in note 4, seems to be the most critical. The first edition of this was published by Sheng-li in 1945. Wilfrid Allan, *Makers of Cathay* (Shanghai, 1938), pp. 144–52, contains a short biographical sketch. As far as a critical compilation of the dates of his life goes, Teng Kuang-ming's recent book appears to exhaust almost all the possibilities our sources offer.

16. My exposition is based on the sources mentioned above unless otherwise indicated.

17. The collection *Yüeh Chung-wu-wang wen-chi* (prefaces by Ts'ao K'un and Wu P'ei-fu, dated 1921) contains some specimens of his calligraphy. Most famous is his calligraphy of the two *Ch'u-shih-piao* by Chu-ko Liang, which have been carved in stone. See *Yüeh Wu-mu shu ch'u-shih-piao* (Tachung ed.) (Shanghai, n.d.).

18. Biography in *Sung shih*, ch. 363.

19. His biography puts this incident only into the period after his first term of military activity.

20. T'ung Kuan, together with Ts'ai Yu, pursued at that time the make-believe war of Sung against the crumbling Liao.

21. See Mary Clabaugh Wright, *The Last Stand of Chinese Conservatism* (Stanford, 1957), chap. iv.

22. 1057–1128. Biography in *Sung shih*, ch. 360.

23. Biography in *Sung shih*, ch. 475.

24. Chang Hsien was one of the main commanders of the Yüeh-chia-chün and was executed with Yüeh Fei's son.

25. Died 1154. Biography in *Sung shih*, ch. 369. He was one of the four great field commanders of the time.

26. Died 1142. Biography in *Sung shih*, ch. 369.

27. 1089–1151. Biography in *Sung shih*, ch. 364.

28. Ho Fu (Sung) states in his *Chung-hsing kuei-chien* that Yüeh Fei himself started his military career as a *hsiao-yung*.

29. See Ruhlmann, *op. cit.*, pp. 173–75, for a description of Kuan's personality in popular fiction.

30. There are slight variations in the tradition of this phrase.

31. On this trait see Ruhlmann, *op. cit.*, p. 168.

32. Adapted from the translation by Wang Sheng-chih found in Robert Payne, ed., *The White Pony* (New York, 1947), p. 359. The one given in Wong Man, *Poems from China* (Hongkong, 1950), p. 108, is another song to the same tune.

33. The way this incident is recorded leaves doubtful how and when Yüeh Fei voiced his displeasure. There is reason to believe that the sources have been manipulated here in Yüeh's disfavor. There is enough evidence, however, to show that Yüeh Fei felt grave concern about this matter, and there is no reason to dismiss the entire incident as fictitious.

34. See Jung-pang Lo, "China's Paddle-Wheel Boats," *Tsing-hua Journal*, New Series, II, No. 1 (May 1960), 195–97.

35. Why the myth has added Chu-hsien-chen as a final point of this campaign is a riddle to me. Chu-hsien-chen would have brought him somewhat closer to the old capital, K'ai-feng, but not near enough to make an issue out of it. Color symbolism is the only explanation that comes to mind.

36. Joseph Campbell, *The Hero with a Thousand Faces* (New York, 1956), p. 391.

NOTES TO CHU HSI'S POLITICAL CAREER

I want to thank Professors Arthur F. Wright and David S. Nivison for many valuable suggestions and corrections. I am also grateful to the Committee on East Asian Studies of Stanford University for financial support while writing this paper.

1. Yeh Shih's writings are contained in the *Yung-chia ts'ung-shu,* and a selection of his works is also found in the Ssu-pu ts'ung-k'an and Ssu-pu pei-yao. For a summary of his thought, see Hsiao Kung-ch'üan, *Chung-kuo cheng-chih ssu-hsiang-shih* ("A History of Chinese Political Thought") (Taipei, 1954; 1st ed., 1945–46), pp. 465–69. Herbert Franke in "Die Agrarreformen des Chia Ssu-tao," *Saeculum,* IX (1958), 345–69, discusses Yeh Shih's scheme for government estates.

2. Cf. the bibliographical notice on *Chih-chai Hsien-sheng wen-chi* by Etienne Balazs and Yves Hervouet (Sung Project, Paris, 1957).

3. For a biographical sketch of Ch'en Liang, see Lin Mousheng, *Men and Ideas* (New York, 1942), pp. 174–85.

4. Chu Sung, "Hsien-chün hsing-chuang" ("Biographical Account of My Late Father"), in *Wei-chai chi* ("The Collected Works of Chu Sung") (Ssu-pu ts'ung-k'an, Hsü pien ed.), ch. 12, p. 1a.

5. Official titles in this paper are rendered in accordance with E. A. Kracke, Jr., *Translation of Sung Civil Service Titles* (Sung Project, Paris, 1957).

6. For Chu Sung, see Chu Hsi's biographical notice in *Hui-an hsien-sheng Chu wen-kung wen-chi* ("The Collected Works of Chu Hsi"), hereafter cited as *Wen-chi* (Ssu-pu ts'ung-k'an ed.), ch. 97, pp. 18b–28b. Cf. Chu Hsi's epitaph on his father, *Wen-chi,* ch. 94, pp. 24b–25b. I have been unable to consult the *Wei-chai-kung nien-p'u* by the Ch'ing scholar Chu Yü listed by Minnie C. van der Loon in "Nien-p'u List" (Sung Project, Paris, 1955), p. 12.

7. Feng Ch'i (1558–1603), *Sung shih chi-shih-pen-mo* ("Comprehensive Account of Sung History"), hereafter cited as *SSCSPM* (Peking, 1955), III, 651.

8. The most valuable source for Chu Hsi's life is the *Chu-tzu nien-p'u* ("Chronological Record of Master Chu's Life"), compiled by Wang Mou-hung (1668–1741). This work has been reprinted by the Commercial Press, Shanghai, in the Ts'ung-shu chi-ch'eng series, which is the edition used in this study. Following the chronological arrangement called for by a *nien-p'u* (chronological record of a man's life), Wang Mou-hung quotes two earlier *Nien-p'u* based on the *Nien-p'u* by Chu Hsi's disciple Li Fang-tzu. He also quotes the *Chu-tzu hsing-chuang* ("Biographical Account of Master Chu") by Huang Kan, another pupil of Chu Hsi, the official biography of Chu Hsi in the *Sung shih* (ch. 429), as well as pertinent letters, memorials, prefaces, conversations, etc. In a critical appendix ("*k'ao-i-fu*") Wang discusses disparities among the various sources. (Hereafter Wang Mou-hung's *Nien-p'u* is cited as "*Nien-p'u*"; unless indicated otherwise, he is himself citing one of the earlier *Nien-p'u.*) I have been unable to consult other *Nien-p'u* listed in Minnie C. van der Loon, "Nien-p'u List," pp. 10–12. A useful chronological table of events in Chu Hsi's life is contained in the appendix to Chou Yü-t'ung's *Chu Hsi* (Shanghai, 1933). In Western languages, the most extensive biographical treatment of Chu Hsi is in J. Percy Bruce, *Chu Hsi and His Masters* (London, 1923), pp. 55–96, which, however, should be used with care. A useful summary of Chu Hsi's life is also contained in Carson Chang, *The Development of Neo-Confucian Thought* (New York, 1957),

pp. 243–53. Very useful for the study of Chu Hsi's political career is Li Hsin-ch'uan, "Hui-an hsien-sheng fei su-yin" ("The Master Hui-an Did Not Spend His Life in Retirement"), in *Chien-yen i-lai ch'ao-yeh tsa-chi* ("Miscellaneous Memoranda Concerning the Court and the Country Since the Chien-yen Period (1127–1130)"), hereafter cited as *CYTC* (Ts'ung-shu chi-ch'eng ed.), IV, 444–48. Also see the modern study by Po Shou-i, *Ts'ung-cheng chi chiang-hsüeh chung-te Chu Hsi* ("Chu Hsi as an Official and Educator") (Peking, 1931).

9. *Nien-p'u*, p. 2, quoted from Huang Kan, *Chu-tzu hsing-chuang* (hereafter cited as *Hsing-chuang*).

10. *Wen-chi*, ch. 98, p. 27a.

11. *Nien-p'u*, p. 2, quoted from *Hsing-chuang*.

12. *Ibid.*, p. 2, quoted from Chu Hsi's Discourses.

13. *Ibid.*, pp. 3–4, which quotes from the earlier *Nien-p'u* and from Chu Hsi's epitaphs on these men.

14. The average age of successful candidates in 1148 was 35.64 years. For a study of the list of successful candidates in this year, see E. A. Kracke, Jr., "Family vs. Merit in Chinese Civil Service Examinations under the Empire," *Harvard Journal of Asiatic Studies*, X (1947), 103–23.

15. *Nien-p'u*, pp. 9–12.

16. Yeh Shih wrote a memorandum on this shrine. See *Shui-hsin chi* ("Collected Works of Yeh Shih") (Ssu-pu pei-yao ed.), ch. 10, pp. 4b–5b.

17. Huang K'an's description is found in *Nien-p'u*, pp. 232–33. It is quoted by Carson Chang, *Development*, pp. 252–53.

18. *Nien-p'u*, p. 228.

19. *Mencius*, VII A, XXI, 4. The poem is found in *Lung-chuan wen-chi* ("Collected Works of Ch'en Liang") (Ssu-pu ts'ung-k'an ed.), ch. 10, p. 6a. It has been translated by Carson Chang, *Development*, pp. 312–13.

20. *CYTC*, IV, 444; *Nien-p'u*, pp. 15, 248–49; *Wen-chi*, ch. 22, pp. 1a–b.

21. *CYTC*, IV, 444.

22. *Wen-chi*, ch. 11, pp. 1a–11a, and ch. 13, pp. 1a–3b, 3b–5a, 5a–6a.

23. *Ibid.*, ch. 13, p. 4a and *passim*.

24. *Nien-p'u*, p. 20. Ts'eng Ti's biography, which also provides some information on Lung Ta-yüan, is found in *Sung shih* (Po-na ed.), ch. 470, pp. 12a–16b. In a later memorial Chu Hsi cites Ts'eng and Lung as typical of palace favorites who exercised improper influence. Cf. *Wen-chi*, ch. 11, p. 22a.

25. *Nien-p'u*, p. 20; *Wen-chi*, ch. 24, pp. 10b–11a.

26. "Wu-hsüeh po-shih tai-tzu." The Military Academy was first established under Emperor Shen-tsung (r. 1067–85) and was one of six specialized national schools. See Ch'en Ch'ing-chih, *Chung-kuo chiao-yü shih* ("History of Education in China") (Shanghai, 1936), p. 223.

27. *Nien-p'u*, p. 30; *CYTC*, IV, 445. Chu Hsi's record of Ch'en's life is contained in *Wen-chi*, ch. 96, pp. 1a–36a.

28. In the tenth month of 1168 Ch'en was appointed Right Executive of the Department of Ministries, Executive of Grave Matters in the Secretariat-Chancellery, and concurrently Commissioner of Military Affairs. In the eighth month of 1169 he became Left Executive in the Department of Ministries. He was dismissed in the fifth month of 1170. *Sung shih*, ch. 34, pp. 8a–b, 10b; ch. 142, p. 6b.

29. *Nien-p'u*, p. 34; *Wen-chi*, ch. 22, pp. 1b–2a.

30. *Wen-chi*, ch. 24, p. 28a. This passage is also quoted in *Nien-p'u*, p. 35.

31. *Sung shih*, ch. 34, p. 8a.

32. *Nien-p'u*, p. 43; *CYTC*, IV, 445.

33. For Chu Hsi's declination, see *Wen-chi*, ch. 22, pp. 2b–3a. It is quoted in *Nien-p'u*, p. 45.

34. *CYTC*, IV, 445.

35. These declinations are found in *Wen-chi*, ch. 22, pp. 3a–5a. Wang Mou-hung did not consider these declinations worth quoting in his *Nien-p'u*.

36. *CYTC*, IV, 445.

37. For these declinations, see *Wen-chi*, ch. 22, pp. 5a–10a. Cf. *Nien-p'u*, pp. 54–55.

38. *Nien-p'u*, pp. 62–63, quoted from the earlier *Nien-p'u*, the *Hsing-chuang*, and one of Chu Hsi's declinations. For these two declinations, see *Wen-chi*, ch. 22, pp. 10b–12a. Cf. *CYTC*, IV, 445.

39. This letter is contained in *Wen-chi*, ch. 25, pp. 17b–19b. It is quoted in its entirety in *Nien-p'u*, pp. 63–65.

40. *Wen-chi*, ch. 25, p. 18b.

41. *Ibid.*, p. 19a.

42. *SSCSPM*, III, 679.

43. *CYTC*, IV, 445.

44. *Nien-p'u*, pp. 74–75.

45. *Analects*, IV, 16. Cf. *Nien-p'u*, p. 96. Other material on Lu Chiu-yüan's visit is quoted in *Nien-p'u*, pp. 96–101.

46. *Nien-p'u*, pp. 29, 31, 44–45.

47. *Ibid.*, pp. 80, 85, 91, 94–95. During the drought Chu Hsi submitted no fewer than twenty-three official requests for relief.

48. These requests are listed in *Nien-p'u*, pp. 79, 80, 85, 90, 93.

49. *Wen-chi*, ch. 11, pp. 16b–17a.

50. *Sung shih*, ch. 429, p. 4b; *SSCSPM*, III, 648. For a critical discussion of this incident, see *Nien-p'u*, p. 291. Cf. *CYTC*, IV, 446.

51. *Nien-p'u*, p. 101.

52. For these declinations, see *Wen-chi*, ch. 22, pp. 17b–21a; also *Nien-p'u*, p. 102. Chu Hsi had been awarded the new post in recognition of his services in combating famine in Nan-k'ang.

53. *Nien-p'u*, p. 105.

54. Chu Hsi discussed loan granaries in the fourth memorial, *Wen-chi*, ch. 13, pp. 17b–18a. For additional material on his promotion of granaries see his six memoranda on this subject, *Wen-chi*, ch. 77, pp. 25a–27b; ch. 79, pp. 17a–18b, 18b–20a, 20a–21a; ch. 80, pp. 17a–18a, 22a–23b; and two proclamations, *Wen-chi*, ch. 99, pp. 15a–22a, 22a–b. Chu Hsi's scheme is discussed by Yang Lien-sheng, *Money and Credit in China* (Cambridge, Mass., 1952), p. 76. Cf. H. R. Williamson, *Wang An Shih* (London, 1935–37), II, 174–76. Chu Hsi's scheme called for cooperation between the government and village leaders.

55. *Nien-p'u*, pp. 109–11, 113, 114; *Wen-chi*, ch. 16, pp. 26a–27a, 28b–29b; ch. 17, pp. 1a–2a, 3a–4a, 14b–15a; ch. 21, pp. 9b–10b.

56. The texts of these indictments are contained in *Wen-chi*, ch. 18, pp. 17a–32a; ch. 19, pp. 1a–27a. Some of Chu Hsi's charges are summarized by Chü Ch'ing-yüan in "Nan-Sung kuan-li yü kung-shang-yeh" ("Southern Sung Officials and Commerce"), in *Shih-huo*, II, No. 8 (September 16, 1935), 37–39. Aspects of the indictments are also discussed by Yang Lien-sheng in

"The Form of the Paper Note Hui-tzu," *Harvard Journal of Asiatic Studies,* XVI (1953), 365–73. Page 366, note 3, of this article contains a useful discussion of the bibliography on the merits of the case.

57. Hsiao Kung-ch'üan lists T'ang Chung-yu together with Lü Tsu-ch'ien, Hsüeh Chi-hsüan (of Yung-chia), Ch'en Fu-liang, Ch'en Liang, and Yeh Shih. According to Hsiao, T'ang emphasized utility (*yung*). Cf. Hsiao Kung-ch'üan, *Chung-kuo cheng-shih ssu-hsiang shih,* IV, 461, and 477, n. 98. For a list of T'ang's writings, see Hsiao Kung-ch'üan, *op. cit.,* IV, 477, n. 98; or Yang Lien-sheng, *op. cit.,* p. 365, n. 3. According to Yeh Shao-weng, a follower of Yeh Shih and a friend of Chu Hsi's disciple Chen Te-hsiu, T'ang Chung-yu belonged to the philosophical school of the Su family (Su Hsun, Su Tung-po). See Yeh Shao-weng, *Ssu-ch'ao wen-chien lu* ("Record of Things Heard and Seen at Four Courts") (Ts'ung-shu chi-ch'eng ed.), p. 39.

58. Chu Hsi's relationship with the other philosophers listed by Hsiao Kung-ch'üan as exemplifying the same tendency as T'ang Chung-yu was cordial, and in the case of Lü Tsu-ch'ien very friendly. For the possibility that Chu Hsi was unconsciously influenced by T'ang's enemies, see his exchange of letters with Ch'en Liang. Cf. *Lung-chuan wen-chi* (Ts'ung-shu chi-ch'eng ed.), pp. 234–35. *Wen-chi,* ch. 36, pp. 19a–b.

59. Chou Mi, *Ch'i-tung yeh-yü* (Ts'ung-shu chi-ch'eng ed.), ch. 17, p. 226. The title of this work signifies "the Sayings of an Uncultivated Person of the East of Ch'i." It is from the *Shu ching,* II, i. 13, and was quoted by *Mencius,* V A, iv, 1. This story is still used to discredit Chu Hsi. Cf. Fan Wen-lan, *Chung-kuo t'ung-shih chien-pien,* pp. 600–601.

60. According to Yeh Shao-weng, the emperor held the Su school in high esteem and was not yet familiar with the doctrines of the Ch'eng school. He was therefore inclined to be lenient toward T'ang Chung-yu. See Yeh Shao-weng, *Ssu-ch'ao wen-chien lu,* p. 39. Cf. Chou Mi, *Ch'i-tung yeh-yü,* p. 226. On Wang's support of T'ang, see also *Nien-p'u,* p. 115.

61. Fung Yu-lan, *History of Chinese Philosophy,* trans. by Derk Bodde (Princeton, 1953), II, 412.

62. *SSCSPM,* III, 679–80.

63. *Ibid.,* p. 680.

64. *Wen-chi,* ch. 22, pp. 26a–b. Partially quoted in *Nien-p'u,* p. 120.

65. For Yang's political views cf. his memorial of 1185 in *SSCSPM,* III, 625–55. Also in 1185 Yang had placed Chu Hsi at the head of a list of men he recommended to the government, observing that although Chu was by nature inclined to be timid, he was firm and ardent in a crisis. Cf. Yang Wan-li, *Ch'un-hsi chien-shih lu* ("Record of Men Recommended during the Ch'un-hsi Period") (Ts'ung-shu chi-ch'eng ed.), p. 1.

66. *Nien-p'u,* p. 139.

67. *Wen-chi,* ch. 22, p. 29a. Chu Hsi's declinations are contained in *Wen-chi,* ch. 22, pp. 28b–30a.

68. Cf. Chu Hsi's fourth declination, *Wen-chi,* ch. 22, pp. 29b–30a. See also *Nien-p'u,* p. 141.

69. *Nien-p'u,* p. 142, quoting from *Hsing-chuang.* The phrase "rectify the mind and make the thoughts sincere" comes from *The Great Learning,* I, 4, James Legge, *The Chinese Classics,* I (Oxford, 1893), 357–58.

70. *Nien-p'u,* p. 141.

71. Literally "several tens."

72. *SSCSPM*, III, 680.

73. *Ibid.* Cf. *Nien-p'u*, p. 143, which quotes from Chu Hsi's biography in the *Sung shih*.

74. *SSCSPM*, III, 680–81; *Sung shih*, ch. 394, pp. 10a–b; *CYTC*, IV, 432–34.

75. *Wen-chi*, ch. 11, pp. 18b–40a. *Nien-p'u*, pp. 145–64.

76. *Mencius*, IV A, xx. *The Great Learning*, "The Text of Confucius," p. 4. *Tung tzu-wen chi* ("Collected Works of Tung Chung-shu") (Ts'ung-shu chi-ch'eng ed.), pp. 4–5. For the Ch'eng brothers, see Chu Hsi and Lü Tsu-ch'ien, compilers, *Chin-ssu lu* (Ts'ung-shu chi-ch'eng ed.), pp. 236–37.

77. Cf. James T. C. Liu, "An Early Sung Reformer: Fan Chung-yen," in John K. Fairbank, ed., *Chinese Thought and Institutions* (Chicago, 1957), pp. 126, 128.

78. *Wen-chi*, ch. 11, p. 25b.

79. *SSCSPM*, III, 659. *Nien-p'u*, p. 164, quoting from *Hsing-chuang*.

80. Cf. *Nien-p'u*, Critical Appendix, p. 318.

81. For Chu Hsi's proposals for a land survey, see *Wen-chi*, ch. 19, pp. 33a–39a; ch. 21, pp. 15a–22b, 24a–26a; and ch. 100, pp. 8a–10a.

82. *Wen-chi*, ch. 19, p. 33b.

83. The text does not clearly indicate whether Chu Hsi saw a causative relationship between these two events, but strongly suggests that there is a connection.

84. *Wen-chi*, ch. 23, pp. 5a–b.

85. *Nien-p'u*, Critical Appendix, pp. 312–13.

86. *Nien-p'u*, p. 180. Liu Cheng was himself from one of the prefectures covered by the proposal for a land survey.

87. *Wen-chi*, ch. 28, pp. 19b–23a, especially pp. 21a–22b. The pertinent part of the letter is quoted in *Nien-p'u*, pp. 183–84.

88. *Wen-chi*, ch. 28, p. 22a.

89. Among the positions Chu Hsi declined were those of Collator of the Imperial Library, Fiscal Intendant for Hunan West, and a post as Pacification Official. It is not quite clear whether Liu Cheng recommended him for the first two positions. Liu did recommend him for the post as Pacification Official. See *Nien-p'u*, Critical Appendix, p. 325.

90. Cf. *Nien-p'u*, p. 189, and the Critical Appendix, p. 325.

91. *Ibid.*, p. 191. Liu Cheng had recommended Chu Hsi for the position in T'an-chou. Cf. *Nien-p'u*, Critical Appendix, p. 325.

92. *Ibid.*, p. 193, which quotes the earlier *Nien-p'u* as well as the *Hsing-chuang*.

93. The five memorials are contained in Wen-chi, ch. 14, pp. 9b–16b.

94. Cf. *Nien-p'u*, pp. 201–12.

95. *Nien-p'u*, p. 213.

96. *SSCSPM*, III, 682.

97. *Sung shih*, ch. 394, pp. 1a–1b. Cf. *Nien-p'u*, p. 218, where this is quoted, and *SSCSPM*, III, 684.

98. Yeh Shao-weng, *Ssu-ch'ao wen-chien lu*, pp. 115–18. Cf. *SSCSPM*, III, 684. According to the *Sung shih*, ch. 429, p. 17b, Shen Chi-tsu accused Chu Hsi of ten crimes, but the *Sung shih* does not list these crimes. The number ten may here have only symbolic meaning, as such accusations were often made in groups of ten, twenty, thirty.

99. *SSCSPM*, III, 682–83.

100. For the list of these men see *SSCSPM*, III, 684–85; *CYTC*, I, 80–81; or Ch'iao-ch'uan Ch'iao-sou (pseud.), *Ch'ing-yüan tang-chin* ("The Prohibition of the Faction during the Ch'ing-yüan Period (1195–1200)") (Ts'ung-shu chi-ch'eng ed.), pp. 1–5. This work also includes a list of thirty-six men who made the charges and an account of the entire affair. The lists of men on both sides of the controversy are also incorporated in Huang Tsung-hsi (1610–95) and Ch'üan Tsu-wang (1705–55), *Sung-Yüan hsüeh-an* ("Writings of Sung and Yüan Philosophers"), ch. 97.

101. *Nien-p'u*, p. 197.

102. The thought of thirty-five of the fifty-nine men is discussed in greater or lesser detail in the *Sung-Yüan hsüeh-an*. This work has also been followed in ascertaining intellectual affiliations.

103. In the *Sung-Yüan hsüeh-an* no intellectual affiliation is given for any of the men who attacked "the clique of false learning," and their thought is not discussed. Biographical information on the supporters of Han T'o-chou is less adequate than that on his opponents. Forty-two of the fifty-nine men attacked for "false learning" have biographies in the *Sung shih*, while of the thirty-six men listed as their opponents only ten have biographies. These ten biographies do not disclose any common affiliation with a school of thought.

104. Chou Mi, *Chi-tung yeh-yü*, p. 139. Although Chou Mi criticized Chu Hsi in regard to the T'ang Chung-yu case and had a low opinion of many of the followers of Tao-hsüeh, he held Chu Hsi in high esteem. It is worth noting that Chou Pi-ta, himself one of the men attacked for "false learning," was also highly critical of followers of Tao-hsüeh. Cf. the quotation from Chou Pi-ta in T'ao Hsi-sheng, *Chung-kuo cheng-chih ssu-hsiang-shih* ("History of Chinese Political Thought") (Taipei, 1954; 1st ed., 1942), IV, 112, 113.

105. *Nien-p'u*, p. 216.

106. *Sung shih*, ch. 429, p. 19a.

107. *Ibid.*, p. 20a.

108. Recounted by the Ming scholar Chu Kuo-chen in his *Yung-ch'uang hsiao-p'in* and quoted by Ting Ch'uan-ching, *Sung-jen i-shih hui-pien* ("Collection of Anecdotes Concerning Men of the Sung") (Shanghai, 1958; 1st ed., 1935), II, 859. For legendary material concerning Chu Hsi's birth, see *Nien-p'u*, Critical Appendix, pp. 242–43.

109. A good example is Chu Hsi's treatment of the *Analects*. Cf. Arthur Waley, *The Analects of Confucius* (London, 1938), pp. 73–74.

110. Li Kuang-ti (1642–1718), comp., *Chu-tzu ch'üan-shu* ("Complete Works of Chu Hsi") (Wen-yuan tang shu-fang ed., n.d.; 1st ed., 1713), ch. 64, pp. 26b–27b.

111. *CYTC*, IV, 444.

NOTES TO YEH-LÜ CH'U-TS'AI

Bibliographical Note

The main sources used in the present article are:

(1) The funerary inscription written for Yeh-lü Ch'u-ts'ai by Sung Tzu-chen (1187–1267) in 1267. Its full title is *Chung-shu-ling Yeh-lü Kung shen-tao-pei* ("Spirit-Way Stele of His Excellency Yeh-lü, Chief of the Secretariat").

It is found in the *Kuo-ch'ao wen-lei*, ch. 57, pp. 9b–24a. Sung was a contemporary of Yeh-lü Ch'u-ts'ai and knew him quite well. It is likely, therefore, that he had direct knowledge of many of the events he relates. In composing the inscription (hereafter cited as *Stele*), Sung also made use of the biographical information contained in the obituary for Yeh-lü Ch'u-ts'ai by Chao Yen and in the tomb inscription composed by Li Wei. As both these earlier sources are now lost, we cannot say to what extent Sung drew upon them.

(2) The biography of Yeh-lü Ch'u-ts'ai in *Yüan shih*, ch. 146, pp. 1a–11a. Although based on the *Stele*, this biography (hereafter cited as *Biography*), contains some additional information which must have been obtained from the no longer extant *Tobciyan* ("History") or *Shih-lu* ("Veritable Records").

(3) The *Chan-jan chü-shih wen-chi* ("Collected Works of Chan-jan chü-shih") in 14 *chüan*, which contains 505 "pieces" (mostly poems) written by Yeh-lü Ch'u-ts'ai between 1216 and 1236. This is an important source on Yeh-lü Ch'u-ts'ai's life, and Wang Kuo-wei made extensive use of it for his *Nien-p'u* of the statesman. The first edition of Yeh-lü Ch'u-ts'ai's collected works was published in P'ing-yang in 1234. It comprised only 9 *chüan*. The edition in 14 *chüan* published after 1236 is the one reproduced in the Ssu-pu ts'ung-k'an edition on the basis of a Yüan manuscript copy. This edition is hereafter cited as *Works*.

(4) The *Hsi-yu lu* ("Record of a Journey to the West") by Yeh-lü Ch'u-ts'ai. Written in 1228 and published in 1229, the *Hsi-yu lu* contains a sketchy description of the places seen (sometimes only heard of) by Yeh-lü Ch'u-ts'ai during his years in Central Asia (1219–26), followed by a sharp attack on Ch'ang-ch'un and the Ch'üan-chen sect. The geographical section occupies only one-fourth of the whole. By the end of the thirteenth century this work already was very rare. Professor Ch'en Yüan has suggested that Yeh-lü Ch'u-ts'ai's son Chu, who had strong Taoist leanings, may have destroyed the printing blocks after his father's death (*Yenching Hsüeh-pao*, No. 6 (1929), p. 1010). A considerable portion of the polemical part of the *Hsi-yu lu*, about a thousand words, was incorporated by Hsiang-mai in the *Pien-wei lu* (Taishō ed., No. 2116) of 1291. A few years later, Sheng Ju-tzu made an abstract of the geographical section and included it in the first chapter of his *Shu-chai lao-hsüeh ts'ung-t'an* (Chih-pu-tsu chai ts'ung-shu ed., *chi* 23). Subsequently, the *Hsi-yu lu* disappeared from circulation. Toward the end of the last century Li Wen-t'ien edited Sheng Ju-tzu's text, to which he appended a useful commentary, under the title of *Hsi-yu lu chu* (Ling-chien-ko ts'ung-shu ed., 4th ser.). The text collated by Sheng was translated into English by E. Bretschneider in *Mediaeval Researches from East Asiatic Sources* (London, 1888; rep. 1910), I, 13–24. In 1927, Professor Kanda Kiichirō found a manuscript copy of the complete *Hsi-yu lu* in the Kunaishō Toshoryō and edited it in the same year. The complete *Hsi-yu lu* was published in China immediately after by Lo Chen-yü on the basis of the Kanda edition. In the following notes, all references to the *Hsi-yu lu* are to the Kanda edition.

Unless otherwise specified, references to literary texts are to the Ssu-pu ts'ung-k'an edition, and references to the dynastic histories are to the Po-na-pen edition.

Notes

1. Jean-Pierre Abel-Rémusat, "Yeliu-thsou-thsai, Ministre tartare," *Nouveaux mélanges asiatiques*, II (1829), 64–68. Abel-Rémusat's source for this study was the biography of Yeh-lü Ch'u-ts'ai in the *Yüan-shih lei-pien* (1759), ch. 11, pp. 1a–6b.

2. See the Bibliographical Note above.

3. H. Franke, *Geld und Wirtschaft in China unter der Mongolen-Herrschaft* (Leipzig, 1949), p. 36; H. F. Schurmann, *Economic Structure of the Yüan Dynasty* (Cambridge, Mass., 1956), pp. 66–67 and *passim*, and his "Mongolian Tributary Practices of the Thirteenth Century," *Harvard Journal of Asiatic Studies*, XIX (1956), 361 ff. See also R. P. Blake, "The Circulation of Silver in the Moslem East Down to the Mongol Epoch," *Harvard Journal of Asiatic Studies*, II (1937), 323–25.

4. Chang Hsiang-wen, *Chan-jan chü-shih nien-p'u* ("Chronological Biography of Chan-jan chü-shih"), Nan-yüan ts'ung-kao, 1st ser.; Takao Yoshitaka, "Yaritsu Sozai no bukkyō shinkō" ("The Buddhist Faith of Yeh-lü Ch'u-ts'ai"), *Rokujō-gakuhō*, CCXXIV (1920), 383–401; Ch'en Yüan, "Yeh-lü Ch'u ts'ai fu tzu hsin-yang chih i-ch'ü" ("The Belief of Yeh-lü Ch'u-ts'ai and His Son"), *Yenching Hsüeh-pao*, No. 6 (1929), 1007–13; Ch'en Yüan, "Yeh-lü Ch'u-ts'ai chih sheng tsu nien" ("The Dates of Birth and Death of Yeh-lü Ch'u-ts'ai"), *ibid.*, No. 8 (1930), 1469–72; Yen Tun-chieh, "Yeh-lü Ch'u-ts'ai chih li-suan hsüeh" ("Yeh-lü Ch'u-ts'ai's Knowledge of Calendrical Computation"), *I-shih pao*, "Wen-shih fu-k'an," No. 35 (June 17, 1943); Sun K'o-k'uan, "*Chan-jan chü-shih chi* chung ti Chung-yüan ju-shih ch'u-k'ao" ("Preliminary Study of the Confucian Scholars Mentioned in the *Chan-jan chü-shih chi*"), *Ta-lu, tsa-chih*, XII (1956), 182–86; Wang Kuo-wei, *Yeh-lü Wen-cheng Kung nien-p'u* ("Chronological Biography of His Excellency Yeh-lü Wen-cheng") (hereafter quoted as *Nien-p'u*), Hai-ning Wang Ching-an hsien-sheng i-shu ed., *ts'e* 32. For a brief review of the *Nien-p'u* see P. Pelliot, "L'Edition collective des œuvres de Wang Kouo-wei," *T'oung-pao*, XXVI (1929), 160–61. A biography of Yeh-lü Ch'u-ts'ai, based on the *Nien-p'u*, has been published by Iwamura Shinobu under the title *Yaritsu Sozai* ("Yeh-lü Ch'u-ts'ai") (Tokyo, 1942).

5. Abel-Rémusat, p. 86.

6. W. Barthold, *Zwölf Vorlesungen über die Geschichte der Türken Mittelasiens*, Deutsche Bearbeitung von Theodor Menzel (Beiband zu *Die Welt des Islams*, Bd. 14/17) (Berlin, 1935), p. 167.

7. E. Blochet, "Deux Résidents mongols en Chine et en Asie Centrale, de Tchinkkiz Khagan à Khoubilai," *Bulletin of the School of Oriental and African Studies*, IV (1926), 257–68. Blochet's identification of Yeh-lü Ch'u-ts'ai with Mahmūd Yalawac, untenable on both historical and linguistic grounds, has been curtly dismissed by Pelliot in *T'oung-pao*, XXVI (1929), 161.

8. See Sun K'o-k'uan, p. 186.

9. *Stele*, p. 10a.

10. See his biography in *Liao shih*, ch. 72, pp. 1a–3a; and K. A. Wittfogel and Feng Chia-sheng, *History of Chinese Society, Liao (907–1125)* (Philadelphia, 1949), *passim*.

11. See his biography in *Liao shih*, ch. 112, pp. 4b–5a; and Wittfogel, pp. 401, 402.

12. Yüan Hao-wen, *Ku Chin shang-shu yu-ch'eng Yeh-lü Kung shen-tao-pei* ("Spirit-Way Stele of His Excellency Yeh-lü, Late Assistant of the Right in the Presidential Council of Chin"), *Kuo-ch'ao wen-lei*, ch. 57, p. 2a.

13. See Yüan Hao-wen. This is also the main source for Yeh-lü Lü's biography in the *Chin shih*, ch. 95, pp. 1a–3a.

14. Yüan Hao-wen, pp. 3b–4a.

15. *Ibid.*, pp. 4a–b.

16. *Ibid.*, pp. 6b and 8b.

17. *Nien-p'u*, "yü-chi," p. 2a.

18. In his article "Yeh-lü Ch'u-ts'ai chih sheng tsu nien," mentioned above, Ch'en Yüan conclusively shows that the correct dates of Yeh-lü Ch'u-ts'ai's birth and death are 1189 and 1243.

19. *Stele*, p. 10b.

20. *Works*, ch. 12, p. 18a.

21. *Stele*, p. 10b.

22. *Nien-p'u*, p. 3a.

23. *Stele*, p. 10b.

24. This statement is found in Wan-sung's preface to the *Works*, p. 2a. On Wan-sung see below, n. 27.

25. *Works*, ch. 12, p. 2a.

26. *Ibid.*, ch. 8, pp. 21a–b.

27. According to Nogami Shunjō, Wan-sung was the leading Buddhist personality of the Chin dynasty. See *Ryō-Kin no bukkyō* (Kyoto, 1953), pp. 199–200. Wan-sung is the literary name of the monk Hsing-hsiu (1166–1246), a native of Ho-nei (modern Ch'in-yang *hsien*, Honan). He attained enlightenment under the Ts'ao-tung master Hsüeh-yen, who made him his spiritual successor. Held in high esteem by Chang-tsung, Wan-sung was appointed abbot of the important Wan-shou Temple and then of the Pao-en Temple in Peking. He is the author of several Buddhist works, some of which are extant. See his biography in the *Hsin-hsü kao-seng chuan* (Pei-yang yin-shua chü ed., 1923), ch. 17, pp. 3b–4b; Nogami, *passim*; Nukariya Kaiten, *Zengaku shisōshi* (Tokyo, 1923), II, 420 ff.

28. Wan-sung occupies the twenty-third place in the line of transmission of Ch'ing-yüan (Hsing-ssu).

29. *Works*, ch. 13, p. 23b, and n. 119 below.

30. See Wan-sung's preface to the *Works*, p. 1b, and *ibid.*, ch. 8, p. 21b.

31. *Hsi-yu lu*, p. 1a.

32. *Stele*, p. 11a; *Biography*, p. 1b. In his poem "Tzu-tsan" ("Self-eulogy") Yeh-lü Ch'u-ts'ai states that his beard and whiskers reached the waist (*Works*, ch. 8, p. 28a).

33. *Stele*, pp. 11a–b.

34. Yeh-lü Ch'u-ts'ai is also said to have greatly impressed Cinggis Qan with his accurate prediction of eclipses (*Stele*, p. 11b). However, the calendar he composed in Central Asia, called *Hsi-cheng keng-wu-yüan li* ("Western Campaign Calendar of the *Keng-wu* Year"), was never adopted officially by the Mongols (*Yüan shih*, ch. 52, p. 1b). On this calendar see Yen Tun-chieh's article quoted above, and Yabuuchi Kiyoshi, "Gen-Min rekishō-shi" ("History of the Calendrical Systems of the Yüan and Ming"), *Tōhō-gakuhō*, XIV (1944), 266–67.

35. L. Wieger, *Textes historiques* (Hien-hien, 1922), II, 1652.

36. *Stele,* pp. 11b–12a. According to B. Laufer, the expression *chüeh-tuan* is a counterpart of the word "monoceros." See his *Prolegomena on the History of Defensive Armor* (Chicago, 1914), p. 95.

37. After Sheng Ju-tzu, *Shu-chai lao-hsüeh ts'ung-t'an,* ch. 1, pp. 1a–b.

38. This has already been suggested by Hung Chün in the *Yüan-shih i-wen cheng-pu* (Kuo-hsüeh chi-pen ts'ung-shu ed.), p. 278.

39. E. Balfour, *The Cyclopaedia of India* . . . (London, 1885), III, 406.

40. "Shang-lin fu," *Liu-ch'en chu wen-hsüan,* ch. 8, p. 7a.

41. *Sung shu,* ch. 29, p. 47a.

42. W. Barthold, *Turkestan Down to the Mongol Invasion* (London, 2d ed., 1958), p. 453.

43. According to Rashīd al-Dīn, the reasons for his turning back were the difficulty of crossing the mountains, the bad climate and drinking water, and the report that the Tanguts had revolted. See O. I. Smirnova, tr., *Sbornik letopisei* (Moscow, 1952), 1/2, 225. This is partly confirmed by Juwainī. See J. A. Boyle, tr., *The History of the World-Conqueror* (Manchester, 1958), I, 137–38.

44. *Hsi-yu lu,* pp. 4b–5a. On Liu Wen see also A. Waley, *Travels of an Alchemist* (London, 1931), pp. 38–39.

45. *Hsi-yu lu,* p. 4b.

46. T'ao Tsung-i, *Nan-ts'un Cho-keng lu,* ch. 10, p. 4a; E. Chavannes, "Inscriptions et pièces de chancellerie chinoise de l'époque mongole," *T'oung-pao,* IX (1908), 302. This document is dated June 14, 1219.

47. T'ao Tsung-i, p. 4b; Chavannes, p. 304.

48. *Hsi-yu lu,* p. 5a.

49. Wang Kuo-wei, *Ch'ang-ch'un chen-jen Hsi-yu chi chu* (Hai-ning Wang Ching-an hsien-sheng i-shu ed., *ts'e* 39), "fu-lu," p. 1a; Chavannes, pp. 305–8.

50. In the *Works* there are forty-five pieces written "to the rhymes" of poems by Ch'ang-ch'un. They are listed in the *Nien-p'u,* "yü-chi," p. 3b. Ch'ang-ch'un's name, however, does not appear in any of them: instead we find the two characters *ho jen* (to the rhymes of someone else), or the name of a different person. The substitution has been purposely made by Yeh-lü Ch'u-ts'ai, who, though displeased later with Ch'ang-ch'un, did not feel like destroying the poems altogether. See Ch'en Yüan, "Yeh-lü Ch'u-ts'ai fu tzu hsin-yang chih i-ch'ü," p. 1009.

51. *Hsi-yu lu,* p. 5b.

52. *Ibid.,* p. 6a. Cf. also the *Hsüan-feng ch'ing-hui lu* (Tao-ts'ang ed., *ts'e* 76), p. 6a.

53. *Hsi-yu lu,* pp. 6a–b.

54. *Ibid.,* p. 5b.

55. *Ibid.,* p. 7b.

56. *Hsüan-feng ch'ing-hui lu,* p. 8a; Waley, pp. 24–25.

57. The text of the edict is found in Wang Kuo-wei, "fu-lu," p. 1b. Translated by Chavannes in *T'oung-pao,* V (1904), 368–71.

58. Wang Kuo-wei, *op. cit.,* B, p. 7b; Waley, p. 119. From this source we learn that the edict was issued on April 9, 1223.

59. *Hsi-yu lu,* pp. 7a and 8b.

60. See P. Demiéville, "La Situation religieuse en Chine au temps de Marco Polo," in *Oriente Poliano* (Rome, 1957), p. 200.

61. Hsiang-mai, *Pien-wei lu* (Taishō ed., No. 2116), p. 766c; *Hsi-yu lu*, pp. 7a–b.

62. Of the friendly relations between Ch'ang-ch'un and Shih-mo Hsien-te-pu there is ample evidence in the *Hsi-yu chi*. See Waley, pp. 133 ff.

63. *Hsi-yu lu*, p. 8a.

64. See Waley, pp. 132, 134–37, 146–47. Cf. also the edict that Cinggis Qan remitted verbally to Ch'ang-ch'un through his envoy A-li-hsien in October 1223 (Chavannes, 1904, p. 372).

65. *Works*, ch. 8, p. 18a.

66. *Hsi-yu lu*, Preface, p. 1b.

67. See Ch'en Yüan, *op. cit.*, pp. 1007–9.

68. *Nien-p'u*, p. 9b.

69. *Hsi-yu lu*, p. 9a.

70. Yeh-lü Ch'u-ts'ai criticizes the meek behavior of the Buddhist clergy in the *Hsi-yu lu*, p. 11a.

71. *Stele*, p. 12a.

72. *Hsi-yu lu*, pp. 10a–b.

73. *Stele*, p. 12a; *Biography*, pp. 2b–3a.

74. *Biography*, p. 3a; *Stele*, pp. 12a–b, gives a much shorter account. The Persian sources refer to some embarrassment felt by Ögödei at the time of his election, and of his repeated refusal of the imperial dignity. See J. A. Boyle, *op. cit.*, pp. 186–87; and E. Blochet, ed., *Djami el-Tévarikh* (London, 1912), p. 16. This was partly required by Mongol custom, but was also partly due to a situation not entirely in his favor.

75. Su T'ien-chüeh, *Yüan-ch'ao ming-ch'en shih-lüeh* (Ts'ung-shu chi-ch'eng ed., No. 3357), p. 59.

76. J. A. Boyle, *loc. cit.*, and E. Blochet, pp. 16–17.

77. Su T'ien-chüeh, p. 200.

78. Schurmann, *Economic Structure*, pp. 2 ff., 29.

79. *Stele*, pp. 12b–13a; *Yüan shih*, ch. 2, p. 1b.

80. *Biography*, p. 3b.

81. *Ibid.*, pp. 3b–4a.

82. *Yüan shih*, ch. 91, p. 1a; *Stele*, p. 12b.

83. *Stele*, p. 13a. In the *Stele* the tax collection bureaus are called *K'o-shui-so*, which is short for *Cheng-shou k'o-shui-so* (cf. *Yüan shih*, ch. 94, p. 21a). The names of the Chinese scholar-officials appointed as tax collectors are found in *Yüan shih*, ch. 2, p. 2a.

84. See Schurmann, "Mongolian Tributary Practices," pp. 312 ff., 362 ff.

85. *Stele*, pp. 12b–13a. Details of the various rates in effect in the year 1232–33 are found in the *Hei-Ta shih-lüeh chien-cheng* (Hai-ning Wang Ching-an hsien-sheng i-shu ed., *ts'e* 37), pp. 11a–b. See Schurmann, "Mongolian Tributary Practices," pp. 312–14, 362, and *Economic Structure*, pp. 89, 213, and 220, n. 1.

86. *T'ung-chih t'iao-ko* (Kuo-li Pei-p'ing t'u-shu-kuan ed., 1930), ch. 29, pp. 8a–9a.

87. *Stele*, p. 11a.

88. *Ibid.*, pp. 13a–b. When a few months later some people laid charges against Hsien-te-pu, Ögödei empowered Yeh-lü Ch'u-ts'ai to deal with the case, thus offering him an opportunity for revenge. Yeh-lü Ch'u-ts'ai refused (p. 13b). Hsien-te-pu was still in office in July 1235 (see *Eiin Eiraku-daiten zampon gosatsu*, Tōyō-bunko sōkan [Tokyo, 1930], ch. 19416, p. 8a).

89. *Stele,* pp. 13b–14a; *Biography,* p. 4b. On this occasion, Yeh-lü Ch'u-ts'ai's two assistants, the well-known "protonotarius" Cinqai and the Jurchen Nien-ho Chung-shan, were appointed Left and Right Prime Minister respectively. See the *Sheng-wu ch'in-cheng lu chiao-chu* (Hai-ning Wang Ching-an hsien-sheng i-shu ed., *ts'e* 38), p. 81a.

90. *Ibid.,* p. 81a.

91. *Stele,* pp. 13a and 19b.

92. *Ibid.,* p. 14b.

93. *Economic Structure,* p. 66; *Hei-Ta shih-lüeh chien-cheng,* p. 11a.

94. *Stele,* pp. 16a–b. This estimate is confirmed by Meng Ssu-ming in his *Yüan-tai she-hui chieh-chi chih-tu* ("Social Classes in China under the Yüan Dynasty"), *Yenching Hsüeh-pao,* Mon. Ser., No. 16 (1938), p. 177.

95. *Stele,* p. 16a.

96. *Stele,* p. 16b. It showed a total population for North China of 1,730,000 households, i.e., about eight and a half million people (see Schurmann, *Economic Structure,* p. 67). The last national census taken in 1207–8 by the Chin had shown, for their whole empire, a population of 7,684,438 households, equal to 45,816,079 individuals. See the *Hsü wen-hsien t'ung-k'ao* (Wan-yu wen-k'u ed.), p. 2885a.

97. *Stele,* pp. 16b–17a.

98. *Ibid.,* p. 17a; Schurmann, "Mongolian Tributary Practices," pp. 363 ff.

99. *Stele,* p. 15a; *Biography,* p. 5b. The text of Yüan Hao-wen's letter to Yeh-lü Ch'u-ts'ai (dated June 1, 1233) is found in *Kuo-ch'ao wen-lei,* ch. 37, pp. 1a–3a. Of the fifty-four people "recommended" by Yüan Hao-wen, over half are known to history, and several of them, such as Wang O, Li Yeh, Liu Ch'i, Yang Huan, Hsü Shih-lung, Yang Kuo, and Shang T'ing, rank among the great scholars of the thirteenth century. According to the *Fo-tsu li-tai t'ung-tsai* (Taishō ed., No. 2036), ch. 21, p. 704a, the credit for restoring K'ung Yüan-ts'u to his hereditary title and office goes to the Ch'an master Hai-yün, who apparently recommended him strongly to the Mongol judge Šigi-Qutuqu.

100. *Stele,* p. 15b; *Biography,* pp. 5b–6a. In 1266 the Bureau of Literature was moved from P'ing-yang to Peking, and in the following year it became the *Hung-wen-yüan* or Department for the Development of Literature (*Yüan shih,* ch. 6, pp. 8b and 10b). In 1273 the *Hung-wen-yüan* was absorbed into the newly established *Pi-shu-chien* or Board of Imperial Archives (*Hsü wen-hsien t'ung-k'ao,* p. 4056b).

101. *Biography,* pp. 5b–6a; *Yüan shih,* ch. 146, p. 14a (Biography of Yang Wei-chung); T'u Chi, *Meng-wu-erh shih-chi* (1934), ch. 61, p. 3a (Biography of Liu Min).

102. See Waley, *op. cit.,* pp. 17–18.

103. Miao Tao-i, the leader of the Ch'üan-chen sect at the beginning of the fourteenth century, had been Qaišan's tutor before he became emperor.

104. *Biography,* pp. 7b–8a; *Yüan shih,* ch. 81, pp. 2b–3a.

105. *Yüan shih,* ch. 2, p. 6b.

106. *Stele,* p. 18a.

107. *Fo-tsu li-tai t'ung-tsai,* ch. 21, pp. 703c–704a.

108. See P. Ratchnevsky, *Un Code des Yuan* (Paris, 1937), p. lxviii; and also his "Die mongolischen Grosskhane und die buddhistische Kirche," in *Festschrift F. Weller* (Leipzig, 1954), p. 501.

109. *Stele*, pp. 19a–20a. Cf. Schurmann, *Economic Structure*, pp. 89–90.

110. See the *Hei-Ta shih-lüeh chien-cheng*, p. 8b; a translation of the relevant passage by F. W. Cleaves is found in *Harvard Journal of Asiatic Studies*, XIV (1951), 503.

111. *Stele*, p. 20a, and *Nien-p'u*, p. 23a. On Cinqai's hostility toward the Muslims see R. Grousset, *L'Empire mongol* (Paris, 1941), pp. 542–43.

112. *Stele*, pp. 18b–19a.

113. *Yüan shih*, ch. 2, pp. 7a–b.

114. *Stele*, p. 21a.

115. *Ibid.*, p. 21b.

116. *Ibid.* Weng-shan is the present Wan-shou shan. Yeh-lü Ch'u-ts'ai's death occurred on June 2, 1243.

117. *Works*, ch. 8, pp. 15b–16a.

118. *Hei-Ta shih-lüeh chien-cheng*, p. 26b. In colloquial.

119. Hsing-hsiu, *Wan-sung lao-jen p'ing-ch'ang T'ien-t'ung Chüeh ho-shang sung-ku Ts'ung-yung-an lu* (Taishō ed., No. 2004), ch. 1, p. 228a. Cf. also Nogami, p. 220, n. 10.

120. On Li Ch'un-fu see Nogami, pp. 209–19, and Takao Yoshitaka, "Kindai ni okeru dōbutsu nikyō no tokuchō" ("Characteristics of Taoism and Buddhism in the Chin Period"), *Shina-gaku*, V (1929), 148–51.

121. *Works*, ch. 2, p. 15a. Cf. also *ibid.*, ch. 6, p. 20b.

122. *Ibid.*, ch. 8, p. 19b. Cf. also *Hsi-yu lu*, p. 11b.

123. *Hsi-yu lu*, p. 10b.

124. *Ibid.*, p. 4b.

125. *Works*, ch. 12, p. 18b.

126. *Ibid.*, ch. 6, pp. 15a–b.

127. *Ibid.*, ch. 8, pp. 27a–b.

128. *Stele*, p. 14b.

129. *Ibid.*, pp. 14b–15a. According to another contemporary source, the credit for sparing Pien-liang goes to Ögödei's personal physician Cheng Ching-hsien, who, incidentally, was one of Yeh-lü Ch'u-ts'ai's closest friends. See *Nien-p'u*, "yü-chi," p. 4b.

130. *Biography*, p. 7b; translation of the relevant passage by C. S. Gardner in *Harvard Journal of Asiatic Studies*, II (1937), 325.

131. *Stele*, p. 23a.

132. *Hsi-yu lu*, Preface, pp. 1a–b.

133. *Works*, ch. 8, p. 19b.

134. *Hsi-yu lu*, p. 10a.

135. *Ibid.*, Preface, p. 1a.

136. *Works*, ch. 13, pp. 22a–23a. Cf. "Yaritsu Sozai no bukkyō shinkō," p. 395.

137. Cf. the passages relating to the Small Tranquillity and the Great Peace (*ta-p'ing*) in the *Hsi-yu lu*, pp. 11b–12a. These clearly show that Yeh-lü Ch'u-ts'ai's realistic attitude was bitterly criticized at the time by scholars who advocated the precedence of moral over administrative reform.

138. *Yüan shih*, ch. 157, p. 4b (Biography of Liu Ping-chung). 'Abd ar-Rahmān was executed by order of Güyüg (Ting-tsung, r. 1246–48) during the "purges" following his election.

139. *Yüan shih*, ch. 2, p. 9b.

140. Abe Takeo, "Gen-jidai no hōginsei no kōkyū" ("Study of the Pao-

yin System of the Yüan Dynasty"), *Tōhō-gakuhō*, XXIV (1954), 270–74. See also Schurmann, "Mongolian Tributary Practices," pp. 369 ff.

141. *Yüan shih*, ch. 125, p. 11b (Biography of Kao Chih-yao). See also Demiéville, *op. cit.*, p. 217.

142. *Yüan shih*, ch. 157, p. 2a. For an interesting study of the influence of the Chinese advisers on Qubilai, see Yao Ts'ung-wu, "Hu-pi-lieh tui-yü Han-hua t'ai-tu ti fen-hsi" ("Analysis of Qubilai's Attitude toward Siniciza-tion"), *Ta-lu tsa-chih*, XI (1955), 22–32.

NOTES TO CHIA SSU-TAO

1. Otto Franke, *Geschichte des chinesischen Reiches*, IV (Berlin, 1948), 310; Harold Frisch, "Die letzten Jahre der Sung," *Mitteilungen des Seminars für Orientalische Sprachen zu Berlin*, XXIX (1926), 180. A convenient summary of the traditional Chinese views may be found in *Sung shih chi-shih pen-mo* (Chung-hua shu-chü ed., 1955), ch. 102, pp. 873–79; ch. 103, pp. 880–84; and ch. 105, pp. 888–91.

2. Wolfram Eberhard, *Chinas Geschichte* (Bern, 1948), p. 253; *A History of China* (Berkeley and Los Angeles, 1950), p. 236. Chia Ssu-tao is also called a "reformer" by E. S. Kirby, *Introduction to the Economic History of China* (London, 1954), p. 157.

3. See, e.g., P. Olbricht, "Die Biographie in China," *Saeculum*, VIII (Freiburg, 1957), 224–35; Denis Twitchett, "Chinese Biographical Writing," in W. G. Beasley and E. G. Pulleyblank, eds., *Historians of China and Japan* (London, 1961), pp. 85–114.

4. H. Franke, "Das Chien-teng yü-hua des Li Ch'ang ch'i," *Zeitschrift der deutschen morgenländischen Gesellschaft*, CIX (1959), 344.

5. Cf. Chiang Liang-fu, *Li-tai jen-wu nien-li pei-chuan tsung-piao*, rev. ed., 1959. The date of birth is found in the thirteenth-century work by Lü Wu, *Tso-shih chien-ts'ao* (Ssu-k'u ch'üan-shu chen-pen ed.).

6. H. Franke, *Geld und Wirtschaft in China unter der Mongolen-Herrschaft* (Leipzig, 1949), pp. 24, 61.

7. For this work see *Ssu-k'u ch'üan-shu tsung-mu t'i-yao* (Commercial Press ed.), ch. 47, p. 1046.

8. A good account of Chia Ssu-tao's career has been given by Miyazaki Ichisada, *Tōyōshi kenkyū*, VI (1941), 54–73. See also *Tōyō rekishi daijiten*, I, 495; *Ajia rekishi jiten*, II, 162.

9. From a passage in the biography (*Sung shih*, ch. 474, p. 13a) it may be assumed that Shih Yen-chih, Prefect of the Metropolitan District, thought highly of Chia's abilities.

10. *Sung shih* (Po-na ed.), ch. 403, pp. 7b–8a.

11. *Sung shih*, ch. 403, pp. 5a–8a.

12. *Ibid.*, ch. 44, p. 3a.

13. *Tso-shih chien-ts'ao, Chien-po Lü kung chia-chuan*, p. 1b; Huang Chen, *Ku-chin chi-yao i-pien* (Pi-chi hsiao-shuo ta-kuan ed.), p. 1b.

14. Chou Mi, *Ch'i-tung yeh-yü* (Shuo-k'u ed.), ch. 17, p. 2a.

15. *Sung shih*, ch. 41, p. 11b.

16. *Ibid.*, p. 14a.

17. *Ibid.*, ch. 43, p. 8b.

18. The list of offices held by Chia Ssu-tao, given below, is drawn chiefly from the corresponding entries in the Basic Annals of the *Sung shih*, with some additional data from his biography in the *Sung shih* (ch. 474).

Before 1231: Granary Intendant (*Ssu-ts'ang*) in Chia-hsing on account of his father's merits.

1234, third month: Supervisor of the Ritual Fields (*Chi-t'ien ling*).

1238, second month or earlier: Assistant of the High Office of Imperial Family Affairs (*Ta-tsung cheng-ch'eng*, grade 7b).

1240: Superintendent of Foundries in the Chiang-huai provinces (*Tu ta-k'ang-yeh kung-shih*).

1241, fourth month: Lesser Lord of the Imperial Treasury (*T'ai-fu shao-ch'ing*, grade 6a) and Tax Commissioner for Hu-kuang province (*Hu-kuang tsung-ling ts'ai-fu*).

1243: Vice-Minister of Finance (*Hu-pu shih-lang*, grade 3b).

1245: Assistant Regulator (*Chih-chih fu-shih*) of Yen-chiang; Prefect of Chiang-chou and Pacificator (*An-fu shih*) of Chiang-hsi; Academician of the Pao-chang ko.

1246, third month: Assistant Commissioner for the Military Colonies in Ch'i and Huang prefectures (*T'un-t'ien fu-shih*).

1246, ninth month: Prefect of Chiang-ling, Military Commissioner (*Ts'e-ying shih*) for K'uei province, and Regulator for Ching-hu province (*Chih-chih shih*); Academician of the Fu-wen ko.

1249, third month: Pacificator and Great Regulator (*An-fu chih-chih ta-shih*) for Ching-hu province; Academician of the Pao-wen ko.

1250, third month: Prefect of Yang-chou, Great Regulator (*Chih-chih ta-shih*) for the Huai provinces; Academician of the Tuan-ming tien.

1250, ninth month: Cumulatively Pacificator (*An-fu shih*) of Huai-hsi province.

1253, sixth month: Great Academician of the Tzu-cheng tien.

1254, sixth month: Cumulatively Coadministrator of the Bureau of Military Affairs (*T'ung-chih shu-mi-yüan shih*, grade 2a); Baron of Lin-hai.

1256: Assisting Civil Councillor of State (*Ts'an-chih cheng-shih*, grade 2a) and Great Commissioner for the two Huai provinces.

1257, first month: Commissioner of Military Affairs (*Chih shu-mi-yüan shih*, grade 1b).

1257, second month: Pacificator for the two Huai provinces.

1258, eleventh month: Special Commissioner (*Hsüan-fu shih*) for the two Huai provinces, cumulatively Commissioner of Military Affairs.

1259, first month: Commissioner of Military Affairs and Special Great Commissioner (*Hsüan-fu ta-shih*) for Ching-hsi, Hu-nan-pei, and Ssu-ch'uan provinces.

1259, ninth month: Commanding Officer (*Chieh-chih*) in Chiang-hsi and the two Kuang provinces.

1259, tenth month: Right and Grand Councillor (*Yu-ch'eng-hsiang*, grade 1a), Commissioner of Military Affairs; Duke of Mao.

1259, twelfth month: Duke of Su.

1260, fourth month: Lesser Preceptor (*Shao-shih*); Duke of Wei.

1261, fourth month: Grand Tutor (*T'ai-fu*).

1265, fourth month: Grand Preceptor (*T'ai-shih*); Duke of Wei.

1267, second month: Supreme Military Commander.

1273, third month: Head of the Emergency Bureau.
1274, twelfth month: All armies are put under Chia's command.
1275, March 26: Chia removed from office.
1275, October 9: Death.

19. *Ku-chin chi-yao i-pien,* p. 6a.

20. *Ibid.,* p. 7a.

21. *Sung shih,* ch. 42, p. 10.

22. See his biography in *Sung shih,* ch. 418; *Sung chi san-ch'ao cheng-yao* (Pi-chi hsiao-shuo ta-kuan ed.), ch. 3, p. 5a.

23. *Sung shih,* ch. 47, p. 9a.

24. *Ku-chin chi-yao i-pien,* pp. 8a–b. It must, however, be remembered that Chiang Wan-li, a *soi-disant* adversary of Chia, contributed a postface to the laudatory poems written by Chia's follower Liao Ying-chung. Chou Mi, *Kuei-hsin tsa-chih* (Chin-tai pi-shu ed.), *hou-chi,* pp. 29b–30a. And Ma, that "able man" who is said to have been put aside by Chia, memorialized in 1270 that Chia, who wanted to withdraw from office for health reasons, should stay in office. *Sung shih,* ch. 46, p. 15b.

25. *Sung chi san-ch'ao cheng-yao,* ch. 3, p. 7a.

26. *Ibid.,* p. 2b; see also Chia's *lieh-chuan.* The activities of the eunuch Tung Sung-ch'en are the subject of a separate chapter in the *Sung shih chi-shih pen-mo,* pp. 846–50.

27. *Ibid.* These letter boxes were, however, no invention of Chia's; they were used as early as the T'ang period (618–906).

28. *Sung chi san-ch'ao cheng-yao,* ch. 3, p. 7a.

29. *Sung shih,* ch. 46, pp. 15b–16a. A description of how these lists were kept can be found in the short story "Mu-mien an Cheng Hu-ch'en pao-yüan" in *Ku-chin hsiao-shuo* (Jen-min wen-hsüeh ch'u-pan she ed.), p. 340.

30. *Sung chi san-ch'ao cheng-yao,* ch. 4, pp. 2b–3a.

31. *Sung shih,* ch. 42, p. 10a.

32. *Ibid.,* ch. 44, p. 5a.

33. *Ibid.,* p. 13a.

34. *Ibid.,* ch. 474, pp. 14b–15a; ch. 45, pp. 1a–2a.

35. *Ku-chin chi-yao i-pien,* p. 8a.

36. *Ibid.; Sung shih,* ch. 45, pp. 8b, and ch. 474; *Sung chi san-ch'ao cheng-yao,* ch. 3, pp. 2a–b.

37. *Sung shih,* ch. 43, p. 13a. The biography of that officer, Wang Teng (*Sung shih,* ch. 412, pp. 18a–19b), does not mention this incident. It is recorded (*ibid.,* p. 18b) that Wang Teng had drawn the plans for the fortification of Chiang-ling, which had been ordered by Chia.

38. *Yüan shih,* ch. 9, p. 7a.

39. O. Franke, *Geschichte,* IV, 325.

40. *Sung chi san-ch'ao cheng-yao,* ch. 4, p. 3a.

41. *Sung shih,* ch. 46, p. 16b.

42. *Sung shih,* ch. 45, p. 9a. This passage gives the impression of being a later interpolation. See also *Sung chi san-ch'ao cheng-yao,* ch. 3, p. 2a, and Chia's *lieh-chuan.*

43. *Yüan shih,* ch. 4, pp. 5b–6a.

44. *Ibid.,* ch. 159, pp. 14b–15a.

45. *Ibid.,* ch. 4, p. 5b.

46. *Ibid.,* p. 5a.

47. *Yüan shih,* ch. 157, pp. 20a–23a.

48. *Yüan shih,* ch. 4, pp. 7b–8a.

49. Wang Yün, *Ch'iu-chien hsien-sheng ta-ch'üan wen-chi* (Ssu-pu ts'ung-kan ed.), ch. 96 ("Yü-t'ang chia-hua"), pp. 6b–7b.

50. *Ibid.,* ch. 81, pp. 8b–9b.

51. It should be noted that Hao's confinement did not amount to real imprisonment. He found time to write no fewer than seven books, among these a voluminous "Continuation of the History of the Later Han Dynasty" (*Hsü Hou-Han shu*) in ninety chapters. See *Ssu-k'u ch'üan-shu tsung-mu t'i-yao,* p. 1100.

52. *Yüan shih,* ch. 157, p. 23b.

53. *Sung shih,* ch. 45, p. 5a.

54. The long memorial that Hao Ching presented to the Mongol leaders is preserved in *Yüan shih,* ch. 157, pp. 13b–20a.

55. *Ku-chin chi-yao i-pien,* p. 7b.

56. *Sung chi san-ch'ao cheng-yao,* ch. 3, p. 3a.

57. *Sung shih,* ch. 47, p. 5a.

58. Sudō Yoshiyuki, "Nansō-matsu no kōtempō," *Tōyō Gakuhō,* 1953, nos. 3–4, pp. 31–63; no. 1, pp. 45–65. See also H. Franke, "Die Agrarreformen des Chia Ssu-tao," *Saeculum,* IX (1958), 345–69.

59. *Ch'i-tung yeh-yü,* ch. 17, p. 9a.

60. *Ibid.,* p. 13b.

61. Recent works by historians in Mainland China deal with Chia Ssu-tao in the same way as traditional Chinese historiography. See, e.g., Fan Wen-lan, *Chung-kuo t'ung-shih chien-pien* (Shanghai, n.d.), pp. 423, 447; Lü Chen-yü, *Chien-ming Chung-kuo t'ung-shih* (Peking, 1955), p. 448. The same is true for non-Communist historians; see, e.g., Lo Hsiang-lin, *Chung-kuo t'ung-shih* (Hong Kong, 1956), I, 304; Miu Feng-lin, *Chung-kuo t'ung-shih yao-lüeh* (Taipei, 1954), p. 113.

62. *Ch'i-tung yeh-yü,* ch. 17, pp. 2a–b.

63. *Kuei-hsin tsa-chih, hou-chi,* pp. 12b–13a.

64. A good example is a satirical poem on Chia by Liu Hsün (1240–1319), *Yüan shih chi-shih* (Basic Sinological Series), p. 76. This poem expresses the opinion that Chia has done so much for the reunification of the empire under the Yüan dynasty that he should be honored for his achievement in the new capital. Many such poems have been included in *Ku-chin hsiao-shuo,* ch. 22; see note 66.

65. *Sung shih,* ch. 474, p. 21a.

66. *Ku-chin hsiao-shuo,* ch. XXII ("Mu-mien an Cheng Hu-ch'en pao-yüan"). See Cyril Birch, "Feng Meng-lung and the *Ku-chin hsiao-shuo,*" *Bulletin of the School of Oriental and African Studies,* XVIII (1956), 71, n. 2; Robert Ruhlmann, in Arthur F. Wright, ed., *The Confucian Persuasion* (Stanford, Calif., 1960), p. 147.

67. Chao Pi, *Hsiao-p'in chi* (Shanghai, 1957), pp. 95–99.

68. *Ibid.,* p. 61.

69. Shen Ch'i-feng, *Hsieh-to* (preface dated 1791; Pi-chi hsiao-shuo ta-kuan ed.), ch. 9, p. 6a.

70. Chu Mei-shu, *Mai-yu chi* (preface dated 1874; Pi-chi hsiao-shuo ta-kuan ed.), ch. 5, pp. 9b–10b.

71. Ch'ü Yu, *Chien-teng hsin-hua,* story number 20; see H. Franke in *Zeitschrift der deutschen morgenländischen Gesellschaft,* CVIII (1958), 377.

72. A detailed account of Chia's literary and editorial activities is to be found in *Kuei-hsin tsa-chih, hou-chi,* pp. 29b–30a. On Chia as an art collector see Toyama Gunji, "Ka Shidō ni tsuite," *Shodō Zenshū,* XVI (1955), 25–27.

73. *Tōhō bunka kenkyūsho kanseki bunrui mokuroku* (Kyoto, 1945), pp. 560–61.

74. The title is *Chiang-hsing tsa-lu* (editions in Shuo-fu, Ku-chin shuo-hai, etc.)

75. Liao's editions have the imprint of his studio Shih-ts'ai t'ang. See also K. K. Flug, *Istoriya kitaiskoi pechatnoi knigi sunskoi epokhi X-XIII vv.* (Moscow-Leningrad, 1959), pp. 34–45.

76. *Kuei-hsin tsa-shih, hou-chi,* p. 30b; T'ao Tsung-i, *Cho-keng lu* (Ts'ung-shu chi-ch'eng ed.), ch. 6, p. 89; P. Pelliot, *Les Débuts de l'imprimerie en Chine* (Paris, 1953), p. 98; J. J. L. Duyvendak, *T'oung-pao,* XLII (1953), 392–93.

77. See note 23.

78. The moving story of his death is told in *Kuei-hsin tsa-chih, hou-chi,* pp. 21b–22b.

79. It has been reprinted in the Ming collection *I-men kuang-tu* (1567–73). See also B. Laufer, *Insect Musicians and Cricket Champions* (Field Museum Leaflet No. 22) (Chicago, 1927), p. 6.

80. Several reprints, e.g., *Ch'ung-chiao shuo-fu,* ch. 20, pp. 1a–8a.

81. Ch'u Chia-hsüan, *Chien-hu chi* (preface dated 1695), *shou-chi* (Pi-chi hsiao-shuo ta-kuan ed.), ch. 1, p. 10.

82. A clear picture of his pragmatic attitude in matters of government is given by a memorial of 1264 during the controversy on the "public field laws." This memorial, incidentally, is one of the very few surviving documents from his pen. The opening sentences are significant: "Recently, in answer to an imperial decree, a general discussion was held where mutual accusations were raised. But everything said on that occasion seemed to me a conversation in the empty air or words motivated by private rancor. Right and wrong, however, cannot be obscured thereby." *Ch'i-tung yeh-yü,* ch. 17, p. 7a.

83. An episode in a collection of anecdotes compiled about 1340 praises Chia's energy and common sense. A fire had broken out in the palace area, but Chia was not unduly alarmed and showed considerable skill in taking appropriate measures, which finally resulted in checking the fire before it reached the Imperial Ancestral Temple. See Cheng Yüan-yu (1292–1364), *Sui-ch'ang tsa-lu* (Shuo-k'u ed.), pp. 2b–3a. Chia is described as a brilliant boy even in the highly tendentious *Mu-mien an Cheng Hu-ch'en pao-yüan* (Ku-chin hsiao-shuo ed.), p. 333: at the age of seven he was more intelligent than others and "knew books by heart after having read them once."

84. Toyama Gunji (*op. cit.,* p. 25) compares Chia to Ts'ai Ching (d. 1126), who was at the same time a "bad last minister" and a great patron of the arts.

NOTES TO KAO CH'I

1. Many editions of the various collections of Kao Ch'i's works exist. Throughout this essay, references are to the excellent comprehensive edition in six *ts'e* in the *Ssu-pu pei-yao*, which is a reprinting of the annotated edition of the eighteenth-century scholar Chin T'an. Chin's fine chronological record (*nien-p'u*) of Kao and other supplementary materials relevant to his biography are also included there. The chief compilation of the poetry (*Ch'ing-ch'iu shih-chi*) is here abbreviated *CCSC*.

2. Chin T'an's *nien-p'u*, referred to in note 1, makes a valuable beginning toward this goal.

3. *The Poet Kao Ch'i, 1336–1374*, written in 1959 and 1960 (Princeton University Press, 1962). The reader is referred to that book for documentation and fuller discussion of many of the points dealt with in this essay. That biography, it might be noted, makes only selective use of the biographical details found in Kao Ch'i's poetry; it could be greatly expanded.

The present essay, written independently, is not a digest of the book, but it draws on it to the extent of including translations of four poems, together with some accompanying comments as these appear in the book. Otherwise, however, this essay has its own focus.

4. "The South" referred to is the "historical South," not the true geographical south of modern China; it is the Yangtze valley, especially the lower or eastern portion of it, and sometimes more limited still, meaning the area south of the Yangtze in Kiangsu and Chekiang.

5. *CCSC*, ch. 11, p. 1a.

6. Some poems of most of the members of the circle are to be found in such standard general anthologies as the *Yuan shih hsüan*, the *Yüan-shih chi-shih*, and the *Ming-shih chi-shih*. See *The Poet Kao Ch'i, 1336–1374*, for names and further identification of the members of Kao Ch'i's circle.

7. Hsü Pen, whose collection is called *Pei kuo chi;* Chang Yü, whose collection is called *Ching chü chi;* Yang Chi, whose collection is called *Mei an chi*. All three collections are to be found in the *SPTK*, series III.

8. Wang Ch'ung-wu is the only modern scholar who, to my knowledge, has written significantly about Kao Ch'i; see his "Tu Kao Ch'ing-ch'iu 'Wei Ai Lun,' " written in 1942 (in *CYYY*, XII (1947), 273–82). Wang suggests the interpretation of Kao Ch'i's life and death sketched in this essay and further developed in *The Poet Kao Ch'i, 1336–1374*. Yoshikawa Kōjirō has written an interesting brief comment on an aspect of Kao Ch'i's poetry; see "Kō Sei-kyū," No. 86 in his series "Ningen shiwa," in *Tosho*, No. 123, 1959.

9. That is, more and fuller literary collections, plus gazetteers, informal histories, and fuller auxiliary sources. The possibilities for documenting the events of Ming and Ch'ing history are virtually inexhaustible when the historian broadens his view to include all such ancillary materials.

10. That is, Hsü Pen and Chang Yü.

11. Sung K'o, one of the group, is regarded as an important calligrapher of the time. Several other members of the circle had a serious interest in calligraphy and some achievement in this art.

12. Wang Ch'ung-wu, *op. cit.*, first tentatively explored this idea, which further research fully corroborates.

13. *Ch'ing-ch'iu i-shih*, p. 1a.

14. This poem, found in *CCSC*, ch. 7, pp. 12b–13a, is called "In Imitation of Lo-t'ien." Lo-t'ien is the cognomen of the famous T'ang poet Po Chü-i, whose simple and direct style Kao Ch'i here skillfully imitates.

15. *CCSC*, ch. 3, p. 23b.

NOTES TO TUNG CH'I-CH'ANG

During my study of Tung Ch'i-ch'ang, begun over ten years ago, I have enjoyed warm encouragement and continued help from Professor Yang Lien-sheng and Dr. Ch'iu K'ai-ming of Harvard University, Professor and Mrs. J. LeRoy Davidson, now of the University of California, Los Angeles, and Mr. and Mrs. Fang Chao-ying, now of Canberra, Australia. Professor Arthur F. Wright, Yale University, has given me many valuable suggestions during my preparation of this article, and has been generous with his time in going over the manuscript.

I am grateful to Yale University for a Morse Fellowship and to the American Council of Learned Societies for its fellowship grant during the year 1958–59. These enabled me to do research in Taiwan, Hong Kong, and Japan on problems concerning late Ming thought.

Abbreviations:

Ch'an	Tung Ch'i-ch'ang, *Hua-ch'an-shih sui-pi* (1720).
Ch'en-mei-kung	Ch'en Chi-ju, *Ch'en-mei-kung hsien-sheng chi* (1641, The National Central Library Collection, Taichung, Taiwan).
Chi (9-4-4)	Tung Ch'i-ch'ang, *Jung-t'ai chi* (1630), *wen-chi* 9 chüan, *shih-chi* 4 chüan, *pieh-chi* 4 chüan.
Chi (4-6)	———, *Jung-t'ai chi* (1635), *shih-chi* 4 chüan, *pieh-chi* 6 chüan.
Chi, *Wan-Ming*	Chi Wen-fu, *Wan-Ming ssu-hsiang shih lun* (Chung-king, 1944).
Ch'i-chen	Tsou I, *Ch'i-chen yeh-ch'eng* (Palace Museum, Peking, 1936).
Ch'ien, *Shih*	Ch'ien Mu, *Kuo-shih ta-kang* (Taipei, 1958).
Chou, "Kuan-ts'ang"	Chou K'o, "Kuan-ts'ang Ch'ing-tai chin-shu shu-lüeh" ("A Study of the Ch'ing Dynasty Banned Books now in the Kuo-hsüeh Library"), *Kuo-hsüeh Library Bulletin*, 4th year.
Chu, *Chang*	Chu Tung-jun, *Chang Chü-cheng ta-chuan* (Shanghai, 1947).
CNWLT	*Chung-kuo nei-luan wai-huo li-shih ts'ung-shu* ("A Collection of Historical Documents on China's Internal Strife and Foreign Invasions") (Shanghai, 1947), 3d ed., 17 vols.
Hua-t'ing	*Hua-t'ing hsien-chih* (1878).
KKCK	*Ku-kung chou-k'an* ("Palace Museum Weekly").
KKSHC	*Ku-kung shu-hua-chi* ("Calligraphy and Paintings in the Palace Museum") (Peiping, 1929–35), 45 vols.

KK 300	*Ku-kung ming-hua san-pai-chung* (Taichung, 1959).
Li, *Min-pien*	Li Wen-chih, *Wan-Ming min-pien* (Shanghai, 1948).
Li, *Nan-Wu*	Li Yen-hsia, *Nan-Wu chiu-hua-lu* ("Old Yarns from Southern Wu") (1915).
Li, *Yün-chien*	Li Shao-wen, *Yün-chien tsa-shih* (Shanghai, 1935).
Mei-ts'ung	*Mei-shu ts'ung-shu* (Shen-chou kuo-kuang-she ed., 1947), 20 vols.
Meng, *Ming*	Meng Shen, *Ming-tai shih* (Taipei, 1957).
Min-ch'ao	Anonymous, *Min-ch'ao Tung-huan shih-shih*, *CNWLT*, VII, 219–56.
Mo, *Hua shuo*	Mo Shih-lung, *Hua shuo* in *Mei-ts'ung*, XVI.
Pao-yen-t'ang	Ch'en Chi-ju, *Pao-yen-t'ang cheng-hsü-kuang-p'u-hui-pi-chi* (1616).
Po-shih-ch'iao	——, *Po-shih-ch'iao chen-kao* (Shanghai, 1935).
Shanghai (1504)	*Shang-hai hsien chih* (1504).
Shanghai (1871)	—— (1871).
Ssu-k'u	*Ssu-k'u ch'üan-shu tsung-mu t'i-yao.*
Sung-chiang (1818)	*Sung-chiang fu-chih* (1818).
Ting, *Dictionary*	Ting Fu-pao, *Fo-hsüeh ta tzu-tien.*
Ts'ao, *Shuo-meng*	Ts'ao Chia-chü, *Shuo-meng* in *Ch'ing-jen shuo-k'uai.*
Tung, *Liu-chung*	Tung Ch'i-ch'ang, *Chen-miao liu-chung tsou-shu hui-yao* (Yenching University, 1937).
Wan-hsiang	Ch'en Chi-ju, *Wan-hsiang-t'ang hsiao-p'in* (Shanghai, 1936).
Wei-shui	Li Jih-hua, *Wei-shui-hsüan jih-chi* (Chia-yeh-t'ang).
Wu, *Nien-p'u*	Wu Jung-kuang, *Li-tai ming-jen nien-p'u* (Wan-yu wen-k'u ed., 1939).
Wu-tsa-tsu	Hsieh Chao-chih, *Wu-tsa-tsu* (Kyoto, 1822).

1. Ch'in Tsu-yung, *T'ung-yin lun-hua* (1882), *shou*, p. 6a.

2. Chang Tai, *Lang-hsüan wen-chi* (Shanghai, 1935), pp. 8–9; see also pp. 13–14, 91, 94–95, 138–40.

3. Meng, *Ming*, pp. 368–73.

4. Li, *Yün-chien*, II, 14a–15a. Chang Tai, *T'ao-an meng-i* (Shanghai, 1936), has numerous short articles on the manners and tastes of the time. Epicures will delight in reading his "Fang-wu," pp. 41–42, which is a learned catalogue of delicacies from all parts of China.

5. Li, *Min-pien*, pp. 120–21.

6. Chang Chü-cheng (1525–82) is a good example, since he was on both ends of such measures.

7. Among them, Matteo Ricci (Li, *Yün-chien*, II, 19b); Tung Ch'i-ch'ang knew him; see *Chi* (9-4-4), *pieh* III, pp. 7a–9b. Princes Fu and Lu (Meng, *Ming*, p. 368).

8. *CNWLT*, II, 5; Li, *Min-pien*, pp. 1–3, 25–34.

9. The ten years of Chang Chü-cheng's administration (1573–82) are the best example.

10. Tung Ch'i-ch'ang died when he was eighty-two (Chinese count). Modern scholars agree on Tung Ch'i-ch'ang's dates as 1555–1636. *Ming shih*, saying that he lived to be eighty-three (ch. 288, *lieh-chuan* 176), was

responsible for the confusion that once existed. *Sung-chiang* (1818) quoted *Ming shih* with a correction to this effect (ch. 54, p. 28a). *Shanghai* (1871) followed this with additional details (ch. 19, pp. 24a–25b).

11. *Chi* (9-4-4), *pieh* IV, p. 28b.

12. *Ch'en-mei-kung*, ch. 15, pp. 29b–30a.

13. He made a compilation of three hundred manuscript volumes of important government documents of the Wan-li (1573–1619) period. From this experience he completed a critical study of the problems of late Ming, which was published in 1937 by Yenching University with the title *Shen-miao liu-chung tsou-shu hui-yao*, 40 chüan. Cf. *Ch'en-mei-kung*, ch. 36, p. 3a.

14. *Ming shih*, ch. 288, *lieh-chuan* 176. The study of Tung Ch'i-ch'ang is complicated by the peculiar situation that developed during the Ch'ing dynasty. His main work, *Chi* (9-4-4), and some writings by Ch'en Chi-ju were among the books banned by the Ch'ing court. But his paintings and calligraphy were the favorites of the Ch'ing emperors. I suspect that these developments had much to do with Tung Ch'i-ch'ang's being classified as one of the "literary figures" in *Ming shih*. For the banning of Tung Ch'i-ch'ang's books, see Chou, "Kuan-ts'ang," pp. 1–12. Teng Chih-ch'eng recognizes Tung's talent as a statesman and historian in his preface to Tung, *Liu-chung*.

15. *Ch'an*, ch. 1, pp. 3b–4a, 7b–8a, 23b–24a; *Chi* (4–6), *pieh* IV, pp. 29b–30a. One wonders what Tung Ch'i-ch'ang would have thought if told that, later, Chang Chao (1691–1745), a much inferior Ch'ing calligrapher, was also given the same posthumous name, *Wen-min*.

16. He ran away from Shanghai and later took his examinations in Hua-t'ing. This was a serious offense under the law; see Wu Yin-ming, "Tung Ch'i-ch'ang yen-chiu," in *Hsin-ya shu-yüan hsüeh-shu nien-k'an* (Hong Kong, 1959), I, 13. However, this was probably a quite commonplace happening; see Li, *Nan-Wu*, ch. 18, pp. 10a–b.

17. *Chi* (4–6), *pieh* IV, pp. 29b–30a; V, p. 33b. In 1295, Chao Meng-fu painted the well-known "Autumn Colors of Mts. Ch'üeh and Hua" (*KK 300*, ch. 4, Pl. 146). Tung Ch'i-ch'ang began to evolve his own style in the last decade of the sixteenth century.

18. As a result of the Southern school movement, Chinese painting developed along two lines. We may call the one followed by the Four Wangs the right-hand development, which reconstructed the landscape after the iconoclastic movement; and the one followed by the eccentrics, including the famous Pa-ta-shan-jen and Shih-t'ao, the left-hand line, which continued to explore the possibilities of self-expression suggested by the Southern doctrines. However, soon after the successful experiments on both paths, and as they contributed from the left and from the right to the development of Chinese painting, they joined forces again in the main current and both became classics in the painting tradition. On the well-known indebtedness of both sides to Tung Ch'i-ch'ang see the brilliant discussion by Wu Yin-ming, *op. cit.* For important new light on the problem of Pa-ta and Shih-t'ao, see Wen Fong, "A Letter from Shih-t'ao to Pa-ta-shan-jen and the Problem of Shih-t'ao's Chronology," *Archives of the Chinese Art Society of America*, XIII (1959), 22–53.

19. *Ming shih*, ch. 209, *lieh-chuan* 97.

20. Yen Sung played an important role in both the rise and death of Yang Chi-sheng. He first tried to buy the younger man with political favors, and later, having realized that Yang had always despised him and continued openly to be his arch accuser, secretly maligned him to the emperor (*mi-kou-yü-ti*), *Ming shih*, ch. 209, *lieh-chuan* 97. Technical errors in a memorial, such as a miswritten word, could cause clubbing; see *Ming shih*, ch. 95, *chih* 71. For the two princes mentioned by Yang to support his charges, see the lives of Princes Yü and Ching in *Ming shih*, ch. 120, *lieh-chuan* 8.

21. *Ming shih*, ch. 204, *lieh-chuan* 92, under Wang Shu (Shu also pronounced Yü); and ch. 287, *lieh-chuan* 175, under Wang Shih-chen.

22. After his arrest, as he was being led away to be clubbed (*chang*), Yang Chi-sheng was offered a kind of python's bile believed to have pain-killing effects. Refusing, he said, in a play on the word *tan* (bile), which also means "courage": "I have my own bile! Why should I need anything from the python!" *Ming shih*, ch. 209, *lieh-chuan* 97.

23. *Ibid.*, Yang did not specify to whom or to what he owed the "benevolence" (*en*). We may be sure, however, he meant *kuo-en*, the benevolence one receives from one's emperor, who symbolizes the nation and the dynasty. Earlier in this biography of Yang in *Ming shih* we read: "Having been promoted four times in one year, Yang was determined to repay the *kuo-en* he owed. Thus he drafted his memorial to accuse Yen Sung within a month after he had taken office."

24. *CNWLT*, VII, 37.

25. *Ming shih*, ch. 308, *lieh-chuan* 196. And comments in Meng, *Ming*, pp. 244–49.

26. *CNWLT*, VII, 203.

27. *Ibid.*, pp. 33–179.

28. *KKCK*, IV, No. 78, 3.

29. *Ibid.*; cf. the case of Tai Chin (*Wu-tsa-tsu*, ch. 7, pp. 32a–b).

30. *Ming shih*, ch. 298, *lieh-chuan* 186.

31. *Shanghai* (1871), ch. 19, pp. 24a–25b, and ch. 32, pp. 40b–41b; *Shanghai* (1504), ch. 1, p. 1b.

32. *Ibid.* Tung wrote on his birthday, "the nineteenth day of the first moon," in 1632, saying that he was "seventy-eight *sui*" (*Tung-hua-ting shu-hua lu*, p. 17). Ch'en Chi-ju, in 1614, celebrating Tung's sixty-*sui* birthday, gave the same day as birthday (*Wan-hsiang*, ch. 2, p. 259).

33. *Shanghai* (1871), ch. 19, pp. 25a–b.

34. *Ch'an*, ch. 1, pp. 8a–9a. He probably studied earlier the style of Mi Fei (1051–1107) and step by step began his long process of finding out about earlier and earlier masters. *Shanghai* (1871), ch. 19, p. 25a; also *Chi* (4–6), *pieh*, ch. 5, pp. 8b–9a.

35. In citing the anecdote of the T'ang dynasty monks, Tung Ch'i-ch'ang actually referred to the wrong monk. Tung-shan in the story should really be Wei-shan of the Wei-yang sect. The names of these monks are: Chih-hsien for Hsiang-yen, Liang-chieh for Tung-shan, and Ling-yu for Wei-shan. See *Ch'an*, ch. 1, p. 9a; *Sung kao-shen chuan*, ch. 13, pp. 3b–4a; and Ting, *Dictionary*, pp. 1618, 1665, and 2068. Tung Ch'i-ch'ang's point, however, is perfectly clear: incorrect identification of the monk does not affect the expressiveness of his statement. This slip is interesting, as it is characteristically Tung and also common among late Ming writers. A casual attitude,

as we shall see later, features in a significant way in the ideology of the Southern school movement.

36. Tung Ch'i-ch'ang was not consistent concerning this date. See *Chi* (4–6), *pieh*, ch. 2, p. 20b, and ch. 4, p. 25b; *Chi* (9-4-4), *pieh*, ch. 2, p. 3b. Cf. *KKSHC*, ch. 2, Pl. 1. The problem is further complicated by the question of the authenticity of the painting here involved.

37. *Ming shih*, ch. 216, *lieh-chuan* 104.

38. *Ch'en-mei-kung*, ch. 15, pp. 29b–30a; also ch. 36, pp. 3b–4a.

39. *KKSHC*, ch. 2, Pl. 1; cf. Chiang Shao-shu, *Wu-sheng-shih shih*, ch. 4, p. 4b; and *KKSHC*, ch. 44, Pl. 13.

40. *Wu-tsa-tsu*, ch. 7, pp. 28a–b; *Chi* (9-4-4), *wen*, ch. 8, pp. 30a–31b; *Ch'an*, ch. 1, pp. 8b–9a.

41. *Chi* (9-4-4), *wen*, ch. 2, p. 11a; ch. 3, p. 42a. *Ch'en-mei-kung*, ch. 36, p. 1b.

42. For a general understanding of Mo Shih-lung's talent, personal charm, and life, read his *Shih-hsiu-chai chi*, *passim*. Also Li, *Nan-Wu*, ch. 13, pp. 4a–b; ch. 14, p. 6b; ch. 17, p. 12b.

43. Li, *Nan-Wu*, ch. 19, pp. 7a–b; Lu Shih-hua, *Wu-yüeh so-chien shu-hua-lu*, ch. 4, pp. 60b–61a; *Wang Shih-chen nien-p'u*, Wan-li 5.

44. This anecdote appears in several places, for example, Li, *Yün-chien*, ch. 1, p. 12b; Li, *Nan-Wu*, ch. 16, pp. 10a–b.

45. *KKCK*, III, No. 74, 2 ff.

46. For a textual discussion of this work, see Yü Shao-sung, *Shu-hua shu-lu chieh-t'i*, ch. 3, pp. 21b–23a. Mo used the term "we-group" (*wo-tang*), Li, *Nan-Wu*, *pu-i*, p. 1a.

47. Mo, *Hua shuo*, p. 307.

48. Li, *Nan-Wu*, ch. 14, p. 6b; also, for his defeat in a game of words, *ibid.*, ch. 15, p. 3a.

49. This is a very involved problem. Other terms had been in use, but the borrowed term from Ch'an finally communicated the idea. See Ho Liang-chün, *Ssu-yu-chai hua-lun*, in Mei-ts'ung, XII, 43–45; see also Yang Lien-sheng, "A Study of the Grammar and Vocabulary as Found in *Lao Ch'i-ta* and *P'u-t'ung-shih*, Two Old Korean Textbooks on Colloquial Chinese," *Bulletin of the Institute of History and Philology, Academia Sinica*, XXIX, 197–208.

50. Chi, *Wan-Ming*, pp. 33–47.

51. Mo Shih-lung, *Pi-chu*, in *Ch'i-chin-chai ts'ung-shu*. He died between 1582 and 1588. *Ch'en-mei-kung*, ch. 6, pp. 10a–11b.

52. Mo, *Hua shuo*, p. 304 and also p. 306.

53. *Ch'an*, ch. 2, pp. 21a–b.

54. Mo, *Hua shuo*, p. 306. According to him, if the practice of landscape painting is followed correctly, one can achieve longevity. By the same token, perversity would be destructive of one's life force. See also *Ch'an*, ch. 4, p. 3a.

55. For lists of the so-called Northern and Southern school masters see Mo, *Hua shuo*, p. 307; *Ch'an*, ch. 2, pp. 15a–b and 21a–b. Space does not permit a detailed discussion on Tung's stylistic development in this short biography. For the changing landscape style see Nelson Wu, "Tung Ch'i-ch'ang: The Man, His Time, and His Landscape Painting," unpublished doctoral dissertation, Yale University, 1954.

56. *Ch'an*, ch. 2, pp. 44b–45a.

57. Here he refers specifically to calligraphers. *Ch'an,* ch. 1, p. 6b.

58. *Ch'an,* ch. 1, pp. 13a–b.

59. Sung Yü, "Tui Ch'u-wang wen," *Wen-hsüan,* ch. 45, pp. 1b–2a.

60. For an example without the added value judgment we may cite from Fowler, *Modern English Usage* (1926), p. 212: "An allusion that strikes a light in one company will only darken counsel in another; most audiences are acquainted with the qualities of *a Samson,* fewer with those of *a Dominie Sampson,* fewer still with those of *the Laputans,* and yet fewer again with those of *Ithuriel's spear.*"

61. Tung Ch'i-ch'ang did not claim that he was the first man to regret this. *Ch'an,* ch. 1, pp. 23b–24a.

62. This matter has been twice discussed in this series of publications. See Joseph R. Levenson, "The Amateur Ideal in Ming and Early Ch'ing Society: Evidence from Painting," in John K. Fairbank, ed., *Chinese Thought and Institutions* (Chicago, 1957), pp. 320–41; and James F. Cahill, "Confucian Elements in the Theory of Painting," in Arthur F. Wright, ed., *The Confucian Persuasion* (Stanford, Calif., 1960), p. 116.

63. "*Lun hua i hsing ssu / Chien yü erh t'ung lin.*" Su Shih, *Su-Tung-p'o chi, Kuo-hsüeh-chi-pen ts'ung-shu,* 3d ed. (Shanghai, 1934), ch. 16, p. 63.

64. *Ch'an,* ch. 2, pp. 34a–b, 43b–44a. *Chi* (9-4-4), *wen.* ch. 3, p. 42b.

65. Li, *Nan-Wu,* ch. 14, p. 12a.

66. *Sung-chiang,* ch. 54, pp. 28a–b.

67. *Ibid.*

68. *Ibid.*

69. Ts'ao, *Shuo-meng,* ch. 2, pp. 3a–b, comparing him with T'ao Hung-ching of the Six Dynasties. See also Li, *Nan-Wu,* ch. 7, pp. 11a–b; ch. 21, p. 7a.

70. *Sung-chiang,* ch. 54, p. 28b; Li, *Nan-Wu,* ch. 11, p. 26b.

71. *Sung-chiang,* ch. 81, p. 9b. Ch'en, describing the horrifying reign of terror, said: "We survived by pretending to be deaf and dumb" (*Po-shih-ch'iao,* p. 8).

72. *Ch'en-mei-kung,* ch. 15, p. 30a; ch. 36, pp. 3b, 5a.

73. *Po-shih-ch'iao,* p. 11.

74. *Ch'an,* ch. 2, p. 13b; *Ch'en-mei-kung,* "Lai-chung-lou sui-pi hsü," ch. 5, pp. 20a–b.

75. Chi, *Wan-Ming,* p. 33.

76. Tsou Shan (*hao,* Ying-ch'üan). See *Ming shih,* ch. 283, *lieh-chuan* 171, under Tsou Shou-i; Chi, *Wan-Ming,* p. 46.

77. *Wu-tsa-tsu,* ch. 7, pp. 21a–b and 22a–b. But Wang Yüan-ch'i, a student of Tung's style, thought differently. He gave Tung credit for "having cleaned the cobweb [from landscape painting] in one sweep" (from colophon of *Wang-ch'üan* Scroll, C. C. Wang Collection, New York).

78. Chi, *Wan-Ming,* p. 40; *Chi* (9-4-4), ch. 1, pp. 12b–13a.

79. *Ch'an,* ch. 4, p. 18b.

80. *Ch'an,* ch. 4, pp. 18b, 19b–20a.

81. Li cut his own throat with a razor on the fifteenth day of the third moon and died that night. Chi, *Wan-Ming,* p. 40; cf. Jung Chao-tsu, *Li Cho-wu p'ing-chuan* (Shanghai, 1937), p. 56. Tung urged Chen-k'o to leave Peking, but to no avail (*Ch'an,* ch. 4, pp. 19b–20a). Even when Tung was

studying Ch'an with Chen-k'o, he still had his eye on the examinations and a government career. He asked the monk: "Would my preparations for the examinations be in the way of my Tao?" The master replied: "It is like the man who is obsessed by his fondness for women. Still, as he thinks about sex all day long, he eats, puts on his clothes, and meets his social obligations. But should he try not to think about sex, his obsession would become worse. Li Po once wrote in a poem: 'I pull out my sword and cut the water in the stream, yet the stream flows on!' " (*Chi* (9-4-4), *pieh*, ch. 1, pp. 12b–13a.) In Tung's case, both his government career and his Tao were his obsessions.

82. Li, *Nan-Wu*, ch. 4, p. 8a.

83. *Ch'en-mei-kung*, ch. 19, pp. 15a–16a, 20a–21b; ch. 36, pp. 5a–b.

84. Li, *Nan-Wu*, ch. 19, p. 14a.

85. Tung credited his success to his study of Ch'an. *Ch'an*, ch. 4, pp. 17a–b. *Ch'en-mei-kung*, ch. 6, pp. 7a–b.

86. *Ibid.*, ch. 8, pp. 11a–b.

87. *Ibid.*

88. *Chi* (9-4-4), *wen*, ch. 8, p. 7a; *Shanghai* (1871), ch. 17, pp. 14 ff.

89. Meng, *Ming*, p. 283; *Ming shih*, ch. 20, *pen-chi* 20, Wan-li seventeenth year.

90. Among Tung's close acquaintances, those directly involved in the Chang Chü-cheng case were Wang Hsi-chüeh, T'ien I-chün, and his old employer Lu Shu-sheng, who resigned and went home at the beginning of Chang's era and remained critical of Chang. *Ming shih*, ch. 216, *lieh-chuan* 104; ch. 218, *lieh-chuan* 106. Li, *Nan-Wu*, ch. 11, pp. 13b–14a.

91. For Chang Chü-cheng's career, see the excellent biography, Chu, *Chang*, pp. 139, 147–50, 154–72, 175–78, 186–87, 261–304, 345–49, 370, 382–94; and Yang To, *Chang Chiang-ling nien-p'u* (Changsha, 1938). Tung Ch'i-ch'ang began his government career in a similarly promising manner. Like Chang Chü-cheng, he was appointed a Han-lin and made a Compiler of History after becoming a *chin-shih*. They both had the opportunity of teaching the heir apparent in their respective periods and were known for their enthusiasm and intelligence as teachers. Over the same path many had gone on to be influential in government. *Ming shih* (ch. 72, *chih* 48) comments: "Beginning around 1425 or 1426, those who held the position of *Ta-hsüeh-shih*, because of their tutor-student relationship with the emperor, were often given the high ranks of the Three *Ku*, the three dukes [the Junior Proctor, Tutor, and Guardian to the Heir Apparent]." As a young *chin-shih* and tutor to the heir apparent, Chu Ch'ang-lo, Tung had reason to be enthusiastic and ambitious. But Chang Chü-cheng's sad ending—confiscation of his property, torture of his descendants, stripping of his titles, and his own narrow escape from a posthumous execution—must have been disheartening to ambitious Ming officials. Tung, on the other hand, apathetic toward his government career after many discouraging experiences, managed to keep his title of Grand Tutor of the Heir Apparent.

92. *Ming shih*, ch. 216, *lieh-chuan* 104.

93. *Ibid.*, also ch. 288, *lieh-chuan* 176.

94. *Chi* (9-4-4), *wen*, ch. 1, p. 13b; also *hsü* by Ch'en Chi-ju.

95. *Ming shih*, ch. 288, *lieh-chuan* 176.

96. Ch'ien, *Shih*, pp. 497–98.

97. Tung Ch'i-ch'ang had been collecting art even when he was making

a meager living as a family tutor (Li, *Nan-Wu*, ch. 19, p. 14a). Now as a *chin-shih*, he should have little difficulty in obtaining what he wanted. There would be gifts given him in exchange for friendly relationship, property given him to use and thus be protected by him, and quite frequently poor people would come with their families to become his servants and to live with him. An exaggerated picture of this may be found in Wu Ching-tzu, *Ju-lin wai-shih*, ch. 3.

98. *Ming shih*, ch. 218, *lieh-chuan* 106; ch. 288, *lieh-chuan* 176.

99. *Ibid.*

100. Legge, XX, 2; *CNWLT*, I, *San-ch'ao yeh-chi*, p. 6.

101. *Ch'en-mei-kung*, ch. 36, p. 4a.

102. Li, *Nan-Wu*, ch. 21, p. 3a. Cf. *Ming shih*, ch. 288, *lieh-chuan* 176.

103. *Ch'an*, ch. 3, pp. 3b, 8b–9a; Ts'ao, *Shuo-meng*, ch. 2, pp. 2b–3a.

104. *Chi* (9-4-4), *wen*, ch. 5, pp. 1a–7a.

105. Li Jih-hua, *Wei-shui-hsüan jih-chi* (Chia-yeh-t'ang ed.), Wan-li 37th year, 5th moon, 22d day.

106. *Ch'an*, ch. 3, pp. 2a–b.

107. Ts'ao, *Shuo-meng*, ch. 2, pp. 2b–3a, 7b–8a. *CNWLT*, ch. 7, *Min-ch'ao Tung-huan shih-shih*, pp. 219–56. Lu Hsin-yüan, *Jang-li-kuan kuo-yen lu* (1892), ch. 24, pp. 7b–8a. Chang Ta-jung, *Tzu-i-yüeh-chai shu-hua lu* (1892), ch. 12, pp. 12b–13a. Shen Ping-hsün, *Ch'üan-chai-lao-jen pi-chi* (Chia-yeh-t'ang ed.), ch. 3, pp. 11a–11b. Wen Ping, *Ting-ling chu-lüeh* (manuscript copy), ch. 7; I wish to thank Mr. T. Yuneyama of the Seikadō-bunko, Tokyo, for the privilege of using this. *Ch'en-mei-kung*, ch. 18, pp. 31a–b; ch. 19, p. 15b.

108. Ts'ao, *Shuo-meng*, ch. 2, p. 8a. *Ch'en-mei-kung*, ch. 15, pp. 27b–28a.

109. *Min-ch'ao*, p. 220.

110. *Ibid.*, p. 221.

111. *Ibid.*, pp. 221–22. What an illuminating detail this is! The eldest, brought up probably when the family was poor, was the least spoiled. Cf. the sons of Fan Li (T'ao-chu-kung) of the Warring Kingdoms period.

112. *Ibid.*, p. 222.

113. *Ibid.*, p. 225. *Sung-chiang*, ch. 73, p. 20b, from 1615 through 1620.

114. Tung Ch'i-ch'ang wrote about his "broken home" and said that he had practically nothing left. He was eager to sell some Sung dynasty calligraphy which had escaped the fire because at that time it had not been in the house. See Chang Ta-jung, *Tzu-i-yüeh-chai shu-hua lu* (1892), ch. 12, pp. 12b–13a. He went to live with a Shen family. Shen Ping-hsün, the author of *Ch'üan-chai-lao-jen pi-chi*, was then still young. Shen recalled in his book how his family enjoyed Tung's stay with them and how members of his family would frequently request Tung to write colophons for their collections and to paint and to write for them (ch. 3, pp. 11a–b). This may account for the relatively large number of his works dated to this period. Apparently, his art was privately sought after, at least by fellow gentry, although publicly denounced. Plate IV bears the date 1617. See *Ch'en-mei-kung*, ch. 19, pp. 15a–16a.

115. Tung Ch'i-ch'ang, *Tung Ssu-po hsien-sheng hsiao-p'in*, ch. 1, p. 11a, in *Huang-Ming shih-liu ming-chia hsiao-p'in*.

116. The name "Hua-ch'an Shih" (the Painting-dhyana Studio of Tung Ch'i-ch'ang) frequently referred to is the result of his having a seal carved with the characters *"Hua Ch'an."* (*Ch'an*, ch. 2, p. 27b.)

117. *"Chüeh-hsiao,"* "to be exactly alike" (*Ch'an*, ch. 1, pp. 21b–22a), vs. *"Wu-chia-fa,"* "my own method" (pp. 23b–24a).

118. Tung Ch'i-ch'ang repeatedly revealed his rivalry with Chao Meng-fu. Examples in *Ch'an* alone are numerous: ch. 1, pp. 3b–4a, 7b–8a, 12b, 31a, 39b–40b, 43a–b, and many other places. For *Analects*, see Legge, III, 7.

119. *Ibid.*, ch. 1, pp. 3b–4a.

120. *Chi* (9-4-4), *wen*, ch. 5, pp. 32a–b.

121. *Ch'an*, ch. 2, p. 34a. Cf. "But when Mo Shih-lung came out [as a painter and writer], the South and North *gradually* separated into schools" (Osvald Siren, *The Chinese on the Art of Painting*, Peiping, 1936, p. 133) and Victoria Contag's remark: "Seit der Zeit Mo Shih-lung's verfolgt man *allmählich* eine Trennung in zwei Schulen, eine südliche und eine nördliche" ("Tung Ch'i-ch'ang's Hua Ch'an Shih Sui Pi und das Hua Shuo des Mo Shih-lung," *Ostasiatische Zeitschrift*, IX, 85).

122. I paraphrase Heinrich von Kleist. "Therefore," I said somewhat confused, "we would have to eat again of the tree of knowledge to fall back into the state of innocence?" "To be sure," he replied. "That's the last chapter of the history of the world." From his "Essay on the Puppet Theater" (Eugene Jolas, tr.), *Partisan Review*, XIV (Jan.–Feb., 1947), 72. For *Analects*, see Legge, II, 4.

123. Chi, *Wan-Ming*, pp. 46–47; also according to Ch'ien Ch'ien-i, see Li, *Nan-Wu*, ch. 4, p. 8a.

124. Wang Shih-min (1592–1680), Wang Chien (1598–1677), Wang Yüan-ch'i (1642–1715), and Wang Hui (1632–1717). See works in *KK 300*.

125. *Ta-Ch'ing hui-tien* completed 1690, *P'ei-wen-chai shu-hua-p'u* ordered to be compiled 1705, *P'ei-wen yün-fu* completed 1711, *Mustard Seed Garden Manual of Painting*, over twenty editions since 1701. These are quite different from the casual compilations that typified late Ming encyclopedias. I discussed some aspects of the different attitudes of these two periods in my review of Mai-mai Sze, *The Tao of Painting*, in the *Journal of Aesthetics and Art Criticism*, December 1957, pp. 279–81; and in "The Ch'ing Dynasty," in *The Art of the Manchus* (Syracuse, N.Y.: Everson Museum of Art, 1959), pp. 4–5.

126. See note 18. Pa-ta Shan-jen was a Tung enthusiast.

127. *Ming shih*, ch. 21, *pen-chi* 21, ch. 288, *lieh-chuan* 176; *CNWLT*, I, *San-ch'ao yeh-chi*, pp. 5–18.

128. For Tung Ch'i-ch'ang's comment on his former student, see *CNWLT*, I, *San-ch'ao yeh-chi*, p. 18.

129. On these last trips between his home in the south and Peking, Tung Ch'i-ch'ang had the opportunity to see for himself the tumultuous world outside the "dumbbell" area of relative orderliness. He had to abandon his usual route, the comfortable boat trip along the Grand Canal, and took an inland route to avoid Shantung, where the White Lotus bandits had been active; see *Chi* (9-4-4), *wen*, ch. 8, p. 63, *Ming shih*, ch. 22, *pen-chi* 22.

130. *Ibid.*

131. *Ch'en-mei-kung*, ch. 36, pp. 2b–3a. See also note 13.

132. See note 71 about their "pretending to be deaf and dumb." *Sung-chiang*, ch. 81, p. 9b, *Po-shih-ch'iao*, p. 8. The expression "Instead of playing the role of Wen-ch'ang, we would rather be T'ien-lung and Ti-ya" comes from the iconography of the god of literary talent, Wen-ch'ang, and his two attendants, the Heavenly Deaf and the Earthly Dumb. *Ming shih*, ch. 50, *chih* 26.

133. *Ch'en-mei-kung*, ch. 36, p. 3b.

134. Li, *Nan-Wu*, ch. 6, pp. 29b–30a. *Ming shih*, ch. 288, *lieh-chuan* 176. Even the Ch'ing emperor Sheng-tsu (K'ang-hsi) honored him with a tablet; see *Hua-t'ing*, ch. 22, p. 25a. For the notion of the "City of Man," and of the mountain outside, see my *Chinese and Indian Architecture* (New York: Braziller, 1962).

135. Li, *Nan-Wu*, ch. 19, p. 13b. *Ch'en-mei-kung*, ch. 36, pp. 5b–6a.

136. *Ch'i-chen*, ch. 14, pp. 1b–2a. For a discussion of the attitudes and manners involved, see my article, "The Toleration of Eccentrics," *Art News*, May 1957, pp. 26–29, 52–54.

137. These are the pen-names, or art-names, of Huang Kung-wang, Shih T'ao, and Lu Shih-hua, all Taoist in flavor. To identify one's role by putting on special attire and going under a special name is a long tradition. See my "Eccentric" article, *op. cit.* Tung's self-identification notwithstanding, his critics have called him everything from the best painter and calligrapher in three hundred years to a bad artist who could not draw; or from a talented statesman and historian, a great Confucian scholar, to a corrupt landlord, indulging in comfort and alchemy.

NOTES TO K'ANG YU-WEI

1. For general discussions of the *Ta-t'ung shu*, see Fung Yu-lan, *A History of Chinese Philosophy*, translated by Derk Bodde (Princeton, 1953), II, 684–91; and Laurence Thompson, *Ta T'ung Shu: The One-World Philosophy of K'ang Yu-wei* (London, 1958), pp. 37–57.

2. A translation or paraphrase of K'ang's description of this utopia appears in Thompson, *op. cit.*, parts II, V–VIII.

3. K'ang Yu-wei, *Li-yün chu* (Yen-k'ung ts'ung-shu), preface, p. 3a; K'ang, *Ta-t'ung shu* (Shanghai, 1935), preface, pp. 8–9; and K'ang, *K'ang Nan-hai tzu-pien nien-p'u*, in Chien Po-tsan and others (compilers), *Wu-hsü pien-fa* (Shanghai, 1953), IV, 117–18. Hereafter, the latter work will be cited as *Nien-p'u*.

4. See Hsiao Kung-ch'üan, "K'ang Yu-wei and Confucianism," *Monumenta Serica*, XVIII (1959), 105–9; and Ch'ien Mu, *Chung-kuo chin san-pai-nien hsüeh-shu shih* (Commercial Press, 1937), pp. 698–701. Ch'ien noted (p. 700) that K'ang probably began to use the term *ta-t'ung* about 1894–95.

5. See Liang Ch'i-ch'ao, *Nan-hai K'ang hsien-sheng chuan*, in *Yin-ping-shih ho-chi, wen-chi*, III; Chang Po-chen, *Nan-hai K'ang hsien-sheng chuan* (Ts'ang-shu ts'ung-shu ed.), n.p., n.d.; and Lu Nai-hsiang and others, *Hsin-chien K'ang Nan-hai hsien-sheng chuan* (Wan-mu ts'ao-t'ang ed.), n.p., 1929. Two other important biographical works have been based largely on the

biographies noted above, and on K'ang's autobiographical *Nien-p'u*: Chao Feng-t'ien, "K'ang Ch'ang-su hsien-sheng nien-p'u kao," *Shih-hsüeh nien-pao*, II (September 1934), 173–240; and Yang Fu-li, "K'ang-Liang nien-p'u kao" (Tientsin, 1938), mimeographed.

6. For a résumé of K'ang's family history, see his *Sung-fen-chi hsü*, in *Pu-jen tsa-chih*, II (1913), *fu-lu*, 1–4.

7. K'ang Hui was the first of several members of the family to have his name included in the local gazetteer of his native *hsien*. He obtained the *chü-jen* in 1804 by special dispensation often granted to aging candidates. See Cheng Meng-yü and others (compilers), *Hsü-hsiu Nan-hai hsien-chih* (1872), ch. 15, pp. 7a–8a; and K'ang Yu-wei, *Liu-fen-chi hsü*, in *Pu-jen tsa-chih*, II (1913), *fu-lu*, 5–6.

8. K'ang, *Liu-fen-chi hsü*.

9. For Ch'en Hung-mou, see Arthur W. Hummel, *Eminent Chinese of the Ch'ing Period*, I, 86–87.

10. For Feng's biography, see Lao T'ung, *Feng Ch'ien-chai hsien-sheng nien-p'u* (Hsüeh-ku-t'ang ed., 1910); and P'an Shang-chi and others (compilers), *Nan-hai hsien-chih* (1835; reprinted 1869), ch. 39, pp. 19a–25a. K'ang Hui also studied under another prominent Kwangtung scholar, Feng Min-ch'ang, noted in Hummel, *op. cit.*, II, 858.

11. K'ang, *Liu-fen-chi hsü*, pp. 5–6. For a genealogical chart of the K'ang family, see Chao Feng-t'ien, *op. cit.*, p. 175; and K'ang, *Nien-p'u*, p. 108. For occupational specialization within families, see Ho Ping-ti, "Aspects of Social Mobility in China 1368–1911," *Comparative Studies in Society and History*, I, 4 (June 1959), 338, and *passim*.

12. For K'ang's great-uncles, see biographies of K'ang Kuo-hsi in *Po-tsu Chung-chih kung liu-t'ai-chü-shih i-kao hsü*, in *Pu-jen tsa-chih*, VIII (1913), *fu-lu*, 1–2; and in *Hsü-hsiu Nan-hai hsien-chih*, ch. 17, pp. 10a–12b; for his younger brother, K'ang Kuo-ch'i, in *Ch'ing-shih kao*, ch. 433, pp. 3b–4b, and Ch'en Jung and others (compilers), *Ch'ung-hsiu Nan-hai hsien-chih* (1910), ch. 16, pp. 6b–15a; for K'ang Yu-wei's grandfather, K'ang Tsan-hsiu, see *ibid.*, ch. 15, pp. 10a–10b, and K'ang Yu-wei, *Lien-chou i-chi hsü*, in *Pu-jen tsa-chih*, VII (1913), *fu-lu*, 1–2.

13. K'ang, *Nien-p'u*, pp. 107–10; and Chao Feng-t'ien, *op. cit.*, p. 174.

14. K'ang, *Nien-p'u*, p. 110.

15. *Ch'ung-hsiu Nan-hai hsien-chih*, ch. 15, pp. 10a–10b; and K'ang Yu-wei, *Lien-chou i-chi hsü*, p. 1. For K'ang's grandfather's teacher, Ho Wen-chi, see *Hsü-hsiu Nan-hai hsien-chih*, ch. 13, pp. 40a–41b.

16. K'ang, *Nien-p'u*, pp. 110–11. K'ang mentioned that he also emulated the famous Taoist patriarch Ch'iu Ch'u-chi (Ch'ang-ch'un) of the Yüan period and the Buddhist sixth patriarch, Hui-neng.

17. *Ibid.*, pp. 111–12.

18. *Ibid.*, p. 112. For Chu Tz'u-ch'i, see *Ch'ing-shih kao*, ch. 480, pp. 36a–37a; *Ch'ung-hsiu Nan-hai hsien-chih*, ch. 14, pp. 4b–12b; *Chu Chiu-chiang hsien-sheng nien-p'u*, in Chien Chao-liang (ed.), *Chu Chiu-chiang hsien-sheng chi, chüan shou*, ch. 2, pp. 1a–42a; and K'ang, *Chu Chiu-chiang hsien-sheng i-wen hsü*, in *Pu-jen tsa-chih*, IV (1913), *fu-lu*, 9–12. See also Jung Chao-tsu, "Hsüeh-hai-t'ang k'ao," in *Ling-nan hsüeh-pao*, III: 4 (June 1934), 13–15, 23–47.

19. For Chu's scholarship, see especially his *Nien-p'u*, in Chien Chao-liang, *op. cit., chüan shou*, ch. 2, pp. 24b–36b. See also K'ang, *Chu Chiu-chiang hsien-sheng i-wen hsü*, pp. 9–10; and K'ang *Nien-p'u*, p. 112.

20. K'ang, *Nien-p'u*, pp. 112–13.

21. *Ibid.*, p. 113.

22. *Ibid.*, pp. 113–14.

23. *Ibid.*, p. 114.

24. *Ibid.*, pp. 113–14.

25. *Ibid.*, p. 114.

26. *Loc. cit.* K'ang's uncle appears to have been a younger brother of K'ang's father. That he highly disapproved of K'ang's ideals can be seen from K'ang, *Lo I-jen mu-chih*, in *Ai-lieh-lu* (Canton, 1914?), p. 20.

27. K'ang, *Nien-p'u*, p. 115.

28. *Ibid.*, p. 114. K'ang himself noted that after his grandfather died he was largely his own master.

29. *Ibid.*, pp. 115–16, 118. For the fact that his mother gave him financial and moral support during this period, see K'ang, *Hsien-pi Lao t'ai-fu-jen hsing-chuang*, in *Ai-lieh-lu*, p. 6.

30. K'ang, *Nien-p'u*, pp. 115–18.

31. *Ibid.*, p. 115.

32. *Loc. cit.* For brief notes on the *Hai-kuo t'u-chih* and the *Ying-huan chih-lüeh*, see the biographies of their compilers, Wei Yüan and Hsü Chi-yu, in Hummel, *op. cit.*, I, 310, and II, 851. For the latter work see also Dorothy Ann Rockwell, "The Compilation of Governor Hsü's *Ying-huan chih-lüeh*," in *Papers on China*, XI (1957), 1–28 (Harvard University Center for East Asian Studies).

33. K'ang, *Nien-p'u*, p. 116.

34. For translations into Chinese by the mission press, see Alexander Wylie, *Memorials of Protestant Missionaries to the Chinese* (Shanghai, 1861), *passim*; and Chang Hsi-t'ung, "The Earliest Phase of the Introduction of Western Political Science into China," *Yenching Journal of Social Studies*, V (July 1950), 1–29.

35. W. A. P. Martin, *A Cycle of Cathay* (New York, 1897), pp. 235, 293 ff.; and Knight Biggerstaff, "The T'ung Wen Kuan," *Chinese Social and Political Science Review*, XVIII (1934–35), 307–40.

36. John Fryer, "An Account of the Department for the Translation of Foreign Books at the Kiangnan Arsenal, Shanghai," *North China Herald*, XXIV, 661 (January 29, 1880), 77–81. For a general survey of these translations, see Tsuen-Hsuin Tsien, "Western Impact on China through Translation," *Far Eastern Quarterly*, XIII (May 1954), 305–27.

37. Liang Ch'i-ch'ao, *op. cit.*, p. 61; and Lu Nai-hsiang, *op. cit.*, p. 4b.

38. The *Hsi-kuo chin-shih hui-pien* was begun at the Kiangnan Arsenal in 1873 under the editorship of Carl T. Kreyer, an American ex-missionary. In 1878, Young J. Allen became editor for a brief period. The *Wan-kuo kung-pao* ("A Review of the Time") was begun as a monthly by Young J. Allen in 1868, and was published until 1883. It was later (1889) revived under the editorship of Timothy Richard. At the end of each issue was a summary of world news, entitled "Ko-kuo chin-shih." See *Wan-kuo kung-pao*, XI–XV (1878–83), *passim*. K'ang noted that he began to read the former publication in 1879, and the latter in 1883. See *Nien-p'u*, pp. 115, 116.

39. K'ang, *Nien-p'u,* p. 116.
40. *Ibid.,* p. 119.
41. *Ibid.,* p. 117. See also Lloyd Eastman, "The Kwangtung Anti-foreign Disturbances during the Sino-French War," *Papers on China,* XIII (December 1959), 1–31.
42. K'ang, *Nien-p'u,* p. 117.
43. *Ibid.,* pp. 117–18.
44. For instance, K'ang's references to the "three sequences" (*san-t'ung*) and to the "three ages" (*san-shih*), both taken from the writings of the Kung-yang school, as well as to the "grand unity" (*ta-t'ung*), have been shown to have been first used by K'ang at a date considerably later than 1884–85. See Ch'ien Mu, *op. cit.,* pp. 666, 698–700; and Hsiao Kung-ch'üan, *op. cit.,* pp. 107–9.
45. K'ang, *Nien-p'u,* p. 118.
46. See the definition of "Bodhisattva" in William Soothill and Lewis Hodous, *A Dictionary of Chinese Buddhist Terms,* p. 389.
47. K'ang, *Nien-p'u,* p. 118.
48. *Ibid.,* pp. 118–20.
49. See Hsiao Kung-chüan, *op. cit.,* pp. 108 (note 38) and 110–12, for a discussion of these works. Both books are included in a microfilm copy of K'ang's manuscript works made in 1947 by Dr. Mary C. Wright in Peking for the Hoover Library.
50. *K'ang-tzu nei-wai p'ien* (hereafter cited as *Nei-wai p'ien*), pp. 1a–1b (*Ho-p'i p'ien*).
51. *Ibid.,* pp. 8a–9a (*Hsing-hsüeh p'ien*).
52. *Ibid.,* p. 16a (*Jen-wo p'ien*).
53. *Ibid.,* p. 13a (*Chüeh-shih p'ien*).
54. *Ibid.,* p. 22a (*Chao-yü p'ien*).
55. *Ibid.,* p. 23a (*Chao-yü p'ien*).
56. K'ang, *Nien-p'u,* p. 119.
57. *Shih-li kung-fa, fan-lieh,* p. 2a.
58. *Ibid.,* p. 2b.
59. *Ibid.,* p. 1a.
60. *Ibid.,* p. 1b.
61. See note 43.
62. *Shih-li kung-fa,* p. 3a.
63. *Ibid.,* pp. 3a–4a.
64. *Ibid.,* pp. 12, 21a.
65. *Ibid.,* pp. 5a–b.
66. *Ibid.,* pp. 8a–b.
67. *Ibid.,* pp. 10b–11a.
68. K'ang T'ung-pi, ed., *Pu K'ang Nan-hai hsien-sheng tzu-pien nien-p'u* (microfilm of manuscript copy obtained by the author through the courtesy of Dr. Lo Jung-pang), p. 6b; translated in Hsiao Kung-ch'üan, *op. cit.,* p. 110.
69. K'ang, *Nien-p'u,* pp. 116–19. K'ang stated that after writing down the *Jen-lei kung-li,* in 1885, he gave up the study of mathematics (p. 118).
70. Hsiao Kung-ch'üan, *op. cit.,* pp. 113–15.
71. *Ibid.,* pp. 113–14; and Ch'ien Mu, *op. cit.,* p. 665.
72. See note 52.
73. The term *i-yüan* (parliament) occurred, for instance, in the news

reports from France and Germany appearing in the *Hsi-kuo chin-shih hui-pien,* I (1873), 11b; the phrase *ho-chung-kuo* (confederation of states) was used in reference to the unified kingdom of Italy; *ibid.,* I, 18a.

74. In the *Shih-li kung-fa,* for example, K'ang appended a long note on French statistics on marriage and divorce to buttress his arguments for sexual freedom. These statistics were for the year 1891, indicating that parts of the *Shih-li kung-fa* date from that year or later, even though the principal ideas in the book appear to date from the mid-1880's (see pp. 6a–b).

75. K'ang's youthful reactions to foot-binding are mentioned in his *Ta-t'ung shu,* p. 214; and in his *Nien-p'u,* p. 116. In 1882–83, over the protests of the family elders, he forbade the binding of his own daughters' feet and tried, without success, to organize an anti-foot-binding society in his native district. For his feelings regarding his mother and sisters as widows, see his *Hsien-pi Lao t'ai-fu-jen hsing-chuang,* and his *Lo I-jen mu-chih,* both in the *Ai-lieh-lu,* pp. 5–6, 19–21.

76. *Nei-wai p'ien,* p. 16a (*Jen-wo p'ien*).

NOTES TO LIAO P'ING

1. Wu Chia-mou, *Ching-yen chih* ("Gazetteer of Ching-yen") (n.p., 1900), ch. 23, p. 7a.

2. These biographical data come from Liao P'ing, "Lü li" ("Personal Chronicle"), *Ssu-i-kuan ching hsüeh ts'ung-shu* (a collection of classical studies published by Liao P'ing) (Chengtu, 1886), ts'e 14, pp. 1a–2b; Yang Chia-lo, *Min-kuo ming-jen t'u-chien* ("Biographical Dictionary of Eminent Men of the Chinese Republic") (Nanking, 1937), I, ch. 1, pp. 12–13; Yang Yin-shen, *Chung-kuo hsüeh-shu chia lieh-chuan* ("Biographies of Chinese Scholars") (Shanghai, 1939), p. 482; Morimoto Chikujō, *Shinchō Jugaku shi gaisetsu* ("A General Survey of the History of Confucian Learning in the Ch'ing Dynasty") (Tokyo, 1931), pp. 322–23; Ojima Sukema, "Ryō Hei no gaku" ("Liao P'ing's Learning"), *Geibun,* VIII, No. 5 (May 1917), 426; Shimizu Nobuyoshi, *Kinsei Chūgoku shisō shi* ("History of Modern Chinese Thought") (Tokyo, 1950), p. 422; Fukui Kōjun, *Gendai Chūgoku shisō* ("Recent Chinese Thought") (Tokyo, 1955), p. 24; Naitō Torajirō, *Shinchō shi tsūron* ("Outline of Ch'ing History") (Tokyo, 1944), pp. 162–63; Liao P'ing, "Chung-wai pi-chiao kai-liang pien-hsü" ("Preface to a Comparative Listing of Chinese and Foreign Reforms"), *Liu-i-kuan ts'ung-shu* (Chengtu, 1921), ts'e 8, p. 25a.

3. Ojima, pp. 435–36; Fukui, p. 23; Liang Ch'i-ch'ao (Immanuel C. Y. Hsü, tr.), *Intellectual Trends of the Ch'ing Period* (Cambridge, Mass., 1959), p. 92; Yang Chia-lo, ch. 1, p. 13; Yang Yin-shen, p. 482; Naitō, pp. 162–63; Shimizu, p. 442; Hashikawa Tokio, *Chūgoku bunkakai jimbutsu sōkan* ("General Directory of Intellectuals of the Chinese Republic") (Peking, 1940), pp. 661–62; Morimoto, pp. 323, 332; Fung Yu-lan (Derk Bodde, tr.), *A History of Chinese Philosophy* (Princeton, 1953), II, 709; Kung-ch'üan Hsiao, "K'ang Yu-wei and Confucianism," *Monumenta Serica,* XVIII (1959), 126–31; Ch'ien Mu, *Chung-kuo chin san-pai nien hsüeh-shu shih* ("History of Chinese Scholarship in the Last Three Hundred Years") (Taipei, 1957), II, 642–46.

The invidious reflection on K'ang is rejected by Chang Hsi-t'ang, editor of Liao P'ing, *Ku-hsüeh k'ao* ("On the 'Ancient Text' Learning" [first published 1894]) (Peiping, 1935), on the inconclusive grounds that Liao's work was published after K'ang's and seems in two places to refer to K'ang's opinions as independently relevant. See preface, p. 1; pp. 19, 29; colophon, p. 2.

4. Ojima, p. 444.

5. "Hui-shih chu-chüan" (essays, copied out in red, of successful candidates at the metropolitan examinations), *Ssu-i-kuan ching-hsüeh ts'ung-shu*, ts'e 14, pp. 1a–b.

6. Liang, p. 92; Ch'ien, II, 651.

7. Liu Shih-p'ei, "Chih Liao Chi-p'ing lun T'ien jen shu" ("Letter to Liao P'ing on Heaven and Man"), *Chung-kuo hsüeh-pao*, No. 2 (February 1916), p. 1a.

8. Detailed accounts of the changes in Liao's thought may be found in Fung, pp. 705–19, and in two articles by Ojima, the one already cited, in *Geibun*, VIII, No. 5 (May 1917), 426–46, and "Rokuhen seru Ryō Hei no gakusetsu" ("Six Stages in the Development of Liao P'ing's Theories"), *Shinagaku*, II, No. 9 (May 1922), 707–14. For the early Liao (of the *Chin ku hsüeh-k'ao* exploited by K'ang), with his *chin-wen, ku-wen* distinction between emphases, respectively, on Confucius and the Duke of Chou, the elder Confucius and the younger Confucius, the *Wang-chih* (section of *Li-chi*) and the *Chou-li*, the *Ch'un-ch'iu* and the *Chou-li*, prescription for change and for following Chou tradition, Confucian authorship of Classics and Confucian transmission of older histories, see Uno Tetsujin (tr. Ma Fu-ch'en), *Chung-kuo chin-shih Ju-hsüeh shih* ("History of Chinese Confucian Learning in Modern Times") (Taipei, 1957), II, 431–34.

9. Fukui, pp. 29, 116.

10. *Ibid.*, p. 9.

11. Liao P'ing, "Lun Shih hsü" ("On the Preface to the *Shih-ching*"), *Chung-kuo hsüeh-pao*, No. 4 (April 1916), pp. 1a–2b. In "Fu Liu Shen-shu shu" ("Reply to Liu Shih-p'ei"), *Chung-kuo hsüeh-pao*, No. 2 (February 1916), p. 1a, Liao wrote: "The *Shih-ching* is related to the *I-ching* as *t'i* to *yung*."

12. Ch'ien, II, 644.

13. Hsüeh Fu-ch'eng, "Yung-an wen-pien" ("Collection of Hsüeh Fu-ch'eng's Writings"), *Yung-an ch'üan-chi* ("Collected Works of Hsüeh Fu-ch'eng") (1884–98), ts'e 1, pp. 20a–b.

14. Hsüeh Fu-ch'eng, "Ch'ou yang ch'u-i" ("Rough Discussion on the Management of Foreign Affairs"), *Yung-an ch'üan-chi*, ts'e 15, pp. 13a–16a, esp. 15a.

15. And Ch'in Britain, and Lu Japan, etc. See Ojima, "Ryō Hei no gaku," pp. 437–38.

16. Liao P'ing, "Yü K'ang Ch'ang-su shu" ("Letter to K'ang Yu-wei"), *Chung-kuo hsüeh-pao*, No. 8 (June 1913), p. 19.

17. Liao P'ing, "Ta-t'ung hsüeh-shuo" ("The Theory of the Great Harmony"), *ibid.*, pp. 1–2, 10–11; Ojima, "Ryō Hei no gaku," p. 438.

18. Ojima, "Ryō Hei no gaku," pp. 436–37.

19. For "empty words" as the proper medium of the providentially "throneless king," see *ibid.*, p. 434.

20. Liao, "Yü K'ang Ch'ang-su shu," p. 19.

Index